The Musical Classroom

Fifth Edition

The Musical Classroom

Backgrounds, Models, and Skills for Elementary Teaching

Patricia Hackett

Carolynn A. Lindeman
San Francisco State University

Prentice Hall

Upper Saddle River, New Jersey 07458

Library of Congress Cataloging-in-Publication Data

Hackett, Patricia
The musical classroom : backgrounds, models, and skills for elementary teaching / Patricia Hackett, Carolynn A. Lindeman.—5th ed.
p. cm.
Includes bibliographical references and indexes.
ISBN 0–13–026262–5
1. School music—Instruction and study. 2. Elementary school teaching. I. Lindeman, Carolynn A. II. Title.

MT1 .H12 2001
372.87'044—dc21 00-041678

Acquisitions editor: Christopher T. Johnson
Production editor: Laura A. Lawrie
Copy editor: Laura A. Lawrie
Manufacturing and prepress buyer: Benjamin D. Smith
Image permission coordinator: Michelina Viscusi
Editorial assistant: Evette Dickerson
Cover design: Bruce Kenselaar

This book was set in 10.5/12 Times Roman by Stratford Publishing Services, Inc. and was printed and bound by Courier Companies, Inc.
The cover was printed by Courier Companies, Inc.

Acknowledgments appear on page xvii, which constitutes a continuation of the copyright page.

Prentice Hall

A Division of Pearson Education
Upper Saddle River, New Jersey 07458

Printed in the United States of America

10 9 8 7 6 5 4 3 2 1

ISBN 0-13-026262-5

Prentice-Hall International (UK) Limited, *London*
Prentice-Hall of Australia Pty. Limited, *Sydney*
Prentice-Hall Canada Inc., *Toronto*
Prentice-Hall Hispanoamericana, S.A., *Mexico*
Prentice-Hall of India Private Limited, *New Delhi*
Prentice-Hall of Japan, Inc., *Tokyo*
Pearson Education Asia Pte. Ltd., *Singapore*
Editora Prentice-Hall do Brasil, Ltda., *Rio de Janeiro*

Dedicated to our friend and coauthor,
the late James M. Harris

Contents

To Instructors

The Musical Classroom: Backgrounds, Models, and Skills for Elementary Teaching, Fifth Edition, is designed primarily for use in a one-semester music course for the elementary education major and can also serve as a resource for music education majors and in-service teachers. The book is available by itself or as a book/CD package. *The Musical Classroom* helps students develop skills in music teaching while at the same time providing introductory experiences in playing and reading music.

WHAT'S IN *THE MUSICAL CLASSROOM*?

The text is divided into four sections and six appendixes.

Section One, Backgrounds for Teaching Music is an introduction to teaching music in the elementary classroom. The section begins with an introduction, "Music in the Elementary School," followed by a description of the elements of music and the music-making experiences that are the basis for the model experiences in Section Two. A chapter on "The World of Music" introduces students to the many styles of music and identifies their importance in the curriculum. The current approaches to elementary curriculum are concisely described, including the Kodály and Orff approaches and the Gordon Learning Theory. The "Curricular Developments" chapter presents material for special learners and up-to-date information on music technology in the classroom. Also in this edition are discussions of cooperative learning, integrating music, the arts, and other subjects into the curriculum, and the prekindergarten child and music. The National Standards for Music Education, Grades K–4, are presented and integrated throughout Section One. Section One concludes with an introduction to "Planning and Assessing Music Learning." Practical applications of the curricular approaches and developments presented in this section are highlighted throughout the model experiences of Section Two.

Section Two, Model Experiences for Teaching Music is a concrete expression of Section One, "Backgrounds for Teaching Music." Section Two consists of 48 model experiences, sequentially organized and based on the elements of music: melody, rhythm, harmony, form, and expressive qualities (tempo, dynamics, timbre). The 59 musical selections for the 48 model experiences are included on an accompanying CD (see p. 441). The model experiences may be taught in the college classroom by instructors or by students, with large or small groups. They may also be used in elementary classrooms. The model experiences move from simple to complex through three levels: I (Kindergarten and Grade 1), II (Grades 2 and 3), and III (Grades 4 and 5). Each model focuses on a single music concept and provides for assessing student learning through stated objectives and indicators for success. Key terms are identified. Learning may be expanded by using the Follow-Ups and the Projects for College Students that follow each model. A listing of "Related Literature and Media for Children" is included for many model experiences. Practical applications of the curricular approaches and developments presented in Section One are highlighted throughout the model experiences of this section.

Musical examples in the model experiences are from *all* styles: standard orchestral literature from Bach to Stravinsky, world music, American jazz, and folk and school songs that have proved their appeal to generations of students and teachers. Songs used in the model experiences are within the singing ranges specified for each of Levels I–III.

Section Three, Instruments provides introductory information about playing Autoharp, guitar, baritone ukulele, piano, and soprano recorder as well as information about the singing voice. There are descriptions of hand and body positions, fingerings, and strums, including keyboard drawings, chord frames, tuning instructions, and fingering charts. Lists of specific songs that may be used in a sequential music-reading and skills curriculum are presented for each instrument. These sequential lists identify songs by key, by number of chords/pitches, and by strumming patterns. All songs may be found in Section Four of the text.

Section Four, Songs features 135 songs from a variety of styles for use in the model experiences and instrumental work. Nearly all the favorite songs of the earlier editions are retained. and there are several songs new to this fifth edition.

Six **Appendixes** are presented, including (A) Reference Material for Music Fundamentals; (B) Evaluation Forms; (C) Descriptions of the Elementary Music Series; (D) A Collection of Chants, Proverbs, and Poems; (E) Timeline of Music and History; and (F) Resources. The text concludes with a **Glossary,** a list of the CD contents, and two **Indexes.**

HOW TO USE *THE MUSICAL CLASSROOM* IN YOUR COLLEGE CLASSROOM

The Musical Classroom, Fifth Edition, is designed primarily for the elementary education major with no music background. The authors suggest integrating Sections One to Four simultaneously. Descriptions of ways that instructors can use the various components follow.

Many instructors begin a course for the nonmusic major with a concise review, a presentation of the fundamentals of music, or both. Because college students often "teach as they have been taught," the authors recommend introducing model experiences (Level I) simultaneously with the fundamentals study. In this way, fundamentals work can continue while appropriate experiences for elementary school children are introduced. These Level I model experiences may be taught by the college instructor or by college students with music background, and at the conclusion of each model, students can review music fundamentals (in the Projects for College Students) in connection with the concept in the model experience.

To apply fundamentals to music making, the authors recommend simultaneously starting instrumental study (keyboard, soprano recorder, guitar, baritone ukulele) with the Level I model experiences. Some instructors may wish to have all students in a class study the same instrument; in that case, a particular instrumental focus of Section Three could be used. Guitar, soprano recorder, baritone ukulele, and keyboard are introduced, and lists of melodies in order of difficulty are presented. All specified melodies are in the text. For example, "The Keyboard" identifies many songs in the five-finger position, and "The Recorder" includes a list of nearly 50 songs.

Section Three's information about instruments can be used with an entire class, by small groups, or by individuals. If a class meets in a room with multiple keyboards, an instructor can use "The Keyboard" portion of Section Three. Other instructors may prefer to have students choose an instrument to learn and then study the instrument in small groups. For example, a recorder group could be utilizing "The Recorder" portion while a guitar group works with "The Guitar" portion. All instrumental groups could be working simultaneously or individual students could use a specific instrumental portion of Section Three and work on their own, with instructor guidance. A student who already plays one instrument can independently use this material to review previous skills (or to learn a new instrument) and can refer to the sequential lists of songs to locate material in the text.

The semester work might continue with the instrumental and music fundamentals study in combination with presentations of model experiences from Levels II–III given by students. Section One, "Backgrounds for Teaching Music," could be used at any point in the course, but introducing some of the material before students begin presenting model experiences may make music learning more meaningful.

Model experiences are designed to provide for maximum flexibility and usefulness. Additional music is listed at the end of each model experience under Other Music, and any of these selections may substitute for the musical example presented by the authors. Level I model experiences are designed for use with Kindergarten and Grade 1 students, but they may also serve older students as a review or an assessment of basic concepts, skills, and vocabulary. (When using Level I model experiences with older students, it would be appropriate to substitute musical examples that are age-appropriate for the older students.) Although statements to pupils are suggested (in capital letters in the text), these experiences are intended as models and should be modified to reflect varying learning objectives and styles. Indeed, college students are challenged to design their own model experiences using assignments that are included at the end of each level. These assignments suggest possible songs and orchestral selections to use and become more challenging at each successive level.

Instructors can assess student learning by using the numerous Projects for College Students. At the conclusion of each level I–III is an Evaluation for College Students, as well as assignments that provide guidelines for creating original lessons and evaluating elementary music series textbooks.

When instructors integrate the instrumental and music fundamentals study (Section Three, Appendix A, and Level I), conceptual music experiences for elementary school children (Section Two), and backgrounds on music in the elementary school (Section One), college students simultaneously develop their musical and teaching skills. Although this integration is advocated by the authors, college professors should obviously use the components of the text in any sequence or combination that will work for them.

To Students

The Musical Classroom, Fifth Edition, is designed for you, the prospective elementary school teacher. It assumes no background in music, but it does assume that you have a genuine interest in bringing music and children together.

You might think "How can I teach music? I cannot play the piano or even sing very well." One does not need to be an accomplished performer to teach music in the elementary classroom. You do need a fundamental understanding of how music "works," and you do need to know how to convey that understanding to others.

To help you prepare to teach tomorrow's children, *The Musical Classroom* includes model lessons in music that may be understood (and taught) with little or no musical background. In fact, it is possible to develop an understanding about music while teaching others. And this active involvement in teaching nearly always leads to a desire to develop performance skills. We believe it is possible to do all of these simultaneously: to develop an understanding about music, to share that understanding while teaching others, and to learn to play a musical instrument.

This text succeeds only when those who use it say, "We did it ourselves." As every journey begins with a single step, the use of this text represents that first step. Its music and models should be used to develop a philosophy and style so meaningful and so personal that the model will hardly be remembered. Only *you,* the learner, can plan the lifetime journey that will expand *your* musical literacy, refine *your* performance skills, and perfect *your* teaching skills. Those who love music and children with equal passion will always be able to develop their own ingenious means for bringing children into intimate touch with all the excitement of the *world of music.*

Acknowledgments

Developing *The Musical Classroom* required the help and support of a number of people.

We wish to thank our students in Music for Children classes at San Francisco State University. Working with students from such rich and varied cultural backgrounds has been an exciting experience. It is truly the authors who have been educated.

We acknowledge the help of family, friends, and colleagues who have provided thoughtful and critical comments and suggestions in the preparation of this fifth edition. We particularly wish to note the valuable contributions of:

- Dorothy Burgess, Special Education Teacher, Soo Hill School, Escanaba, MI, for assistance with Teaching Music to Special Learners

- Rachel Nardo, Assistant Professor of Music, San Francisco State University, for assistance with Music Technology

The skills and experience of our production editor, Laura Lawrie, have contributed immeasurably to this fifth edition.

And finally, we must thank our wonderfully supportive husbands and partners, Jim and Al, for their love and understanding.

Permission to use the following materials is gratefully acknowledged.

"The Clam" by Shel Silverstein, from *The Birds and the Beasts Were There,* William Rossa Cole, editor.

Curwen Hand Signs drawn by Florence Holub, San Francisco, CA.

"Don Gato" and "My Father's House" used by permission of Silver Burdett & Ginn.

"It's Raining" ("¡Que Ilueva!") from *Hispanic Music for Arizona Children* (1993). Barbara Andress (Ed.). The Arizona Early Childhood Music Collaborative Project. Used with permission.

"The Mango." Tagalog song collected and notated by Miriam B. Factora. Used by permission.

"Music Touches Children Most of All" and "Put Your Hand in My Hand" by Teresa Jennings. Copyright © 1991 by Plank Road Publishing, P.O. Box 26627, Wauwatosa, WI. International copyright secured. All rights reserved. Used by permission.

"Pipe Dance Song, " "Rock-Passing Song," "Sakura," "Song for the Sabbath," and "Yokuts Grinding Song" from Patricia Hackett, *The Melody Book: 300 Selections from the World of Music for Piano, Guitar, Autoharp, Recorder, and Voice.* 3rd ed. (1998), Prentice Hall.

"Song of the Dragon" from *Fun, Food and Festivals,* by Kathryn G. Obenshain, Alice D. Waller, and Joyce Merman. Copyright © 1978 by Shawnee Press, Inc. (ASCAP) International Copyright Secured. All Rights Reserved. Reprinted by Permission.

The Musical Classroom

Section One
Backgrounds for Teaching Music

Courtesy of MENC: The National Association for Music Education

I
Music in the Elementary School

Since music and children seem naturally to go together, it is no wonder that music has long been an important part of the elementary school curriculum. In fact, music has been part of the school curriculum since 1838, when Lowell Mason, considered the father of American music education, introduced vocal music into the Boston public schools (Brand, 1992). In Mason's day, and for many decades after, elementary music instruction focused mainly on singing and music reading. Gradually the classroom music curriculum expanded to include listening, playing informal instruments, and creative and movement activities. Since the 1960s, it has also focused on helping children develop concepts about music. Today's curriculum is a rich and varied program that allows children the opportunity to explore and learn about the world's music through a variety of means.

Almost every elementary school district today includes some form of music instruction—some districts have elementary music specialists, and others rely solely on classroom teachers to teach all subjects. Most educators believe that the best instructional format is one in which music specialists have the primary responsibility for teaching music but work in close collaboration with classroom teachers, who have the unique opportunity to make music a part of the daily life of the students and integrate music with the total curriculum. Certainly, whoever is responsible for teaching music to children should be well trained in the subject, understand the developmental characteristics of elementary school children, and through a personal love of music and children be able to ignite the spark to turn children on to the exciting world of music.

THE CLASSROOM MUSIC PROGRAM

Before children ever walk through the doors of an elementary school, they have had multiple exposures to music and have experienced music in many different ways. As infants, they naturally "babble"; as two- and three-year-olds, they invent little "singsongs" or tunes and twirl and rock to music; as four- and five-year-olds, they make up songs to accompany their play, learn to sing familiar songs, and move to music in all kinds of interesting ways. In prekindergarten programs, children play many kinds of classroom instruments; explore sounds; create dramatizations to songs; play singing games; and respond to music of various types, times, and cultures. Certainly, children in their preschool years experience music joyfully and playfully—music and life seem to go together!

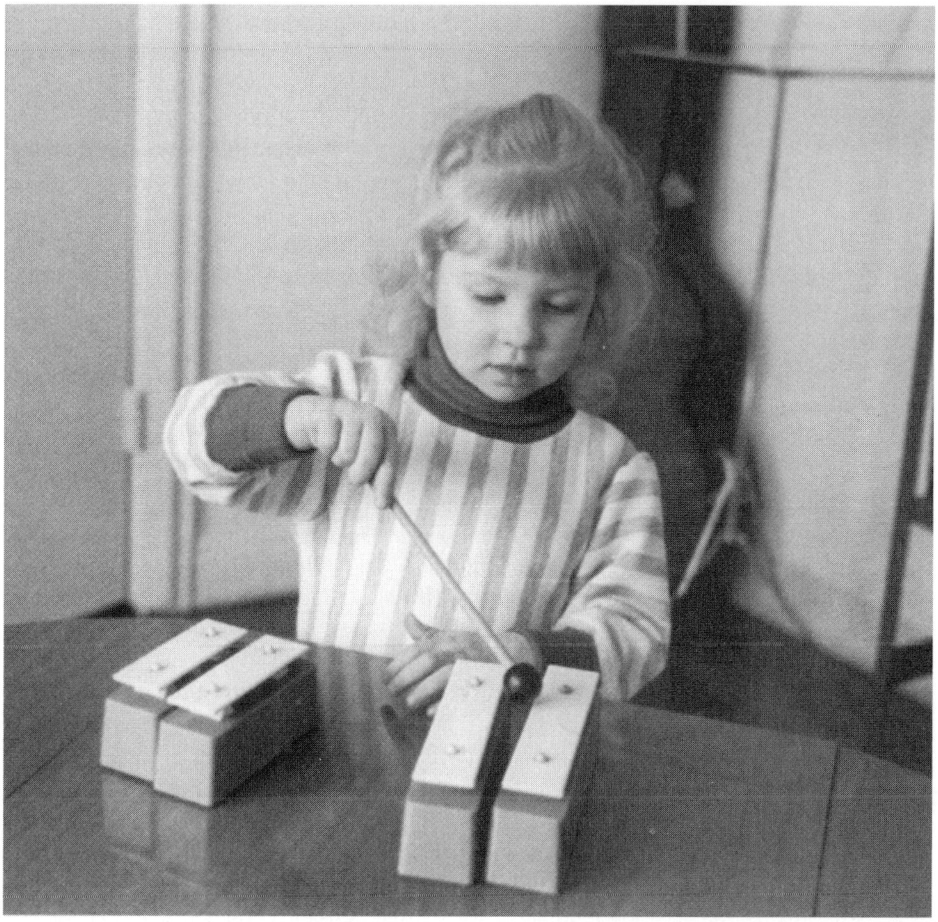

Courtesy of Barbara Andress

Once children enter elementary school, they are ready to embark on an exciting journey that will help them expand their musical understanding and participate fully in America's musical culture. This journey must be well planned and carefully sequenced. It must include music-learning experiences that will lead to clearly defined skills and knowledge but at the same time offer the joy and personal satisfaction that are inherent in music. Music instruction must be offered and available to all children. Music for Every Child—Every Child for Music must be the motto for music at the elementary school level.

Such a program for all elementary school children is referred to as the "classroom music program" or the "general music program." Its emphasis is on providing a sequential music-learning curriculum for all children. In addition, children in the upper grades should be able to elect to study formally a wind or string instrument as well as have the opportunity to sing in choral ensembles. These instrumental and choral experiences should augment the classroom music program—a curricular program intended for all children.

WHY MUSIC IN THE ELEMENTARY SCHOOL

> Music is worth knowing. It is a field of study with its own body of knowledge, skills, and ways of thinking. The ability to perform, create, and listen to music with understanding is desirable for every member of society. Studying music transmits cultural heritage, develops each person's musical potential, provides an opportunity for creativity and self-expression, helps

> students understand the nature of humankind, enables students to become sensitive listeners, cultivates a unique symbol system, and enhances the quality of life. (*Teaching General Music,* 1991:1)

The foregoing rationale articulates clearly and forcefully why music must be at the core of the elementary school curriculum. The study of music contributes significantly to a child's complete education. It helps students understand their own culture and the cultures of others. It enables them to develop creativity, learn self-discipline and teamwork, increase their sense of self-worth, develop listening skills, and engage in creative problem solving and abstract thinking. It allows them to explore and develop their musical intelligence as well as their linguistic, logical-mathematical, spatial, bodily-kinesthetic, interpersonal, and intrapersonal intelligences. The study of music prepares a child for a lifetime of aesthetic pleasure (*Why Music: The Critical Curriculum for America's Children,* 1998).

In addition to the musical reasons that music is part of the core curriculum in the elementary school, substantial information documents the value that music study offers to other subject areas. This information is included in "Integrating Music, the Arts, and Other Subjects" in Chapter VI.

Although there is no conclusive evidence that participation in music leads to improved academic performance in other subjects, statistics show that there may be such a connection. For example, in 1999, students taking music courses scored 53 points higher on the verbal portion of the SATs and 39 points higher on the math portion than students who took no arts courses (The College Board, Profile of College-Bound Seniors National Report for 1999). The College Board also reported a correlation between the length of time spent studying six academic subjects, including arts and music, and improved SAT scores. Students who took more than four years of music and the other arts scored 51 points higher on the verbal SATs and 38 points higher on the math SATs in 1999 than those who took no course work in the arts.

The study of music can make an extraordinary contribution to a child's education. Not only is music shown to have a positive influence on students' academic achievement, it also offers them unique experiences not possible in any other curricular area. Music is a powerful art form, and as students are involved in meaningful musical experiences, their sensitivity to music and their aesthetic response in general increase by leaps and bounds. And to increase students' enjoyment of and sensitivity to music is the goal of music in the elementary school.

WHAT ELEMENTARY SCHOOL CHILDREN SHOULD LEARN ABOUT MUSIC

Music-learning experiences should help children grow in three areas, or, using the more formal term, the three domains of learning: the cognitive, the psychomotor, and the affective. The cognitive domain encompasses intellectual learning: knowing, understanding, and thinking. The psychomotor domain focuses on the manipulative or physical skills: singing, playing, moving, and performing music. The affective domain emphasizes feeling and emotion: interests, attitudes, values, and appreciation.

In music learning, as in other learning, the three domains do not exist in isolation but are related to one another. For example, when students are asked to identify the steady beat of a piece of music, the cognitive area is implied. If the students are to enjoy and to value that piece, however, the affective domain is involved. When students are asked to create body movements in association with that steady beat, the psychomotor domain is specified. All three domains are present if a student verbally labels the steady beat and then moves to the music with sensitivity.

WHAT CHILDREN NEED TO KNOW AND BE ABLE TO DO IN MUSIC

Is there broad consensus within the education community about what knowledge, skills, and concepts all children should learn in music and all the other school subjects? How do we know whether the children of the United States measure up in music? These questions are being wrestled with in a broad new educational reform movement under way that many say may be the most significant development in music education since Lowell Mason introduced music into the schools in 1838.

In 1994 the U.S. Congress approved the Goals 2000: Educate America Act. This legislation established the arts as one of the core subject areas in which students should be able to demonstrate competence. Therefore, national voluntary content and achievement standards were defined for dance, music, theatre, and the visual arts. The content standards specify what students should know and be able to do, and the achievement standards specify the desired levels of attainment. These standards reflect a national consensus about what skills and knowledge students should have when they exit grades 4, 8, and 12 and apply to every student through grade 8 and to every student enrolled in music beyond grade 8.

In 1997, the National Center for Education Statistics, for the first time in almost twenty years, assessed students' knowledge in music. This 1997 assessment was limited to eighth-grade students only, but it is expected in 2007 that students at the elementary, middle and high school levels will be assessed.

National Standards for Music Education

Nine content standards for grades kindergarten through 12 have been established in the subject area of music:

National Standards in Music

1. Singing, alone and with others, a varied repertoire of music
2. Performing on instruments, alone and with others, a varied repertoire of music
3. Improvising melodies, variations, and accompaniments
4. Composing and arranging music within specified guidelines
5. Reading and notating music
6. Listening to, analyzing, and describing music
7. Evaluating music and music performances
8. Understanding relationships between music, the other arts, and disciplines outside the arts
9. Understanding music in relation to history and culture

(From *National Standards for Arts Education.* Copyright © 1994 by Music Educators National Conference. Used by permission. The complete National Arts Standards and additional materials relating to the Standards are available from Music Educators National Conference, 1806 Robert Fulton Drive, Reston, VA 20191-4348, 800–336–3768.)

Achievement standards are specified for each of the content standards and are organized by levels: K through 4, 5 through 8, 9 through 12. In *The Musical Classroom,* only the achievement standards for grades K through 4 are included, and they are integrated throughout the text. For example, the chapter on music-making activities (Chapter III) includes the six achievement standards for the second content standard—performing on instruments, alone and with others, a varied repertoire of music.

Teachers should use these voluntary national standards as guidelines for instruction. They represent what teachers and curriculum leaders nationwide believe *all* students should be able to learn and achieve in music.

THE AMOUNT OF TIME THAT SHOULD BE ALLOCATED FOR MUSIC

To bring music and children together, sufficient time in the school day must be allocated for music instruction. At the elementary school level, students should have music on a daily basis. In kindergarten, music should be integrated into the curriculum throughout the day, with at least 12 percent of contact time devoted to musical experiences. Students in grades 1 and 2 should have music in 20- to 30-minute periods, and students in grades 3 through 5 should have music in 25- to 45-minute slots. The recommended amount of classroom music instruction per week in grades 1 through 5 (excluding time devoted to elective instrumental or choral instruction) is not less than 90 minutes (*Opportunity-to-Learn Standards for Music Instruction,* 1994).

MATERIALS AND EQUIPMENT NEEDED TO TEACH MUSIC

To offer a viable elementary classroom music program, it is necessary to have basic instructional materials and equipment. First, a set of music textbooks with accompanying recordings should be available for each grade level in a school building. These textbooks should be not more than six years old. (See descriptions of elementary music series in Appendix C.) Second, a variety of classroom instruments such as rhythmic (drums), melodic (xylophones), and harmonic (Autoharps and Chromaharps) should be accessible for classroom use. (Section Three includes specific examples of the large array of instruments available.) Third, a quality sound reproduction system (CD player, audio player, phonograph) is vital for helping students hear music at its best. Fourth, technological equipment such as a computer, music software, CD-ROM-compatible computers, and music-related CD-ROMs should be available for music-learning experiences.

CHAPTER SUMMARY

All elementary school children must have access to a quality classroom music program taught by qualified teachers. Music contributes significantly to a child's total growth and must be studied for its own sake as well as for its extramusical values. For students to grow musically and prepare for a lifetime encounter with music, the study of music must begin in the early grades and continue throughout the students' school years.

PROJECTS FOR COLLEGE STUDENTS

1. Write a rationale for the importance of music in a child's total development. Include the musical reasons as well as the extramusical ones. (Also review the information presented in Chapter VI.)
2. Review the nine content standards in music presented in this chapter. In small groups, discuss your elementary school music experiences and how well they "measure up" to the national standards in music.

CHAPTER REFERENCES

BRAND, MANNY, ed. (Fall 1992). "Lowell Mason: A Realistic Portrayal." *Quarterly Journal of Music Teaching and Learning* 3(3):3–75.

CAMPBELL, PATRICIA SHEHAN. (March 2000). "What Music Really Means to Children." *Music Educators Journal* 86(5):32–36.

CUTIETTA, ROBERT, DONALD L. HAMANN, and LINDA MILLER WALKER. (1995). *Spin-offs: The Extra-Musical Advantages of a Musical Education.* Elkhart, IN: United Musical Instruments U.S.A., Inc.

DAVIDSON, JENNIFER. (1994). *TIPS: Thinking Skills in the Music Classroom.* Reston, VA: Music Educators National Conference.

Eloquent Evidence: Arts at the Core of Learning. (1996). President's Committee on the Arts and Humanities and the National Assembly of State Arts Agencies.

FISK, EDWARD B. (1999). *Champions of Change: The Impact of the Arts on Learning.* President's Committee on the Arts and Humanities.

GARDNER, HOWARD. (1992). *Multiple Intelligences: The Theory in Practice.* New York: Basic Books.

Growing Up Complete: The Imperative for Music Education. (1991). Report of the National Commission on Music Education. Reston, VA: Music Educators National Conference.

LEHMAN, PAUL R. (March/April 1993). "Why Your School Needs Music." *Arts Education Policy Review* 94(4):30–34.

LINDEMAN, CAROLYNN A. (September 1997). "Advocacy 101," FrontLines Column, *Music Educators Journal* 84(2):6–7.

LINDEMAN, CAROLYNN A. (May 1998). "At the Core," FrontLines Column, *Music Educators Journal* 84(6):6–7.

LINDEMAN, CAROLYNN A. (1998). *Why Music: The Critical Curriculum for America's Children.* The Music Leadership Letter. Silver Burdett Ginn.

Music Makes the Difference: Music, Brain Development and Learning. (2000). Reston, VA: MENC: The National Association for Music Education.

National Standards for Arts Education. (1994). Reston, VA: Music Educators National Conference.

Opportunity-to-Learn Standards for Music Instruction. (1994). Reston, VA: Music Educators National Conference.

PALMER, MARY, comp. (1988). *TIPS: Getting Started with Elementary School Music.* Reston, VA: Music Educators National Conference.

The School Music Program: A New Vision, (1994). Reston, VA: Music Educators National Conference.

SMITH, JANICE. (Fall 1995). "Using Portfolio Assessment in General Music." *General Music Today* 9(1):8–12.

STAUFFER, SANDRA L., and JENNIFER DAVIDSON, eds. (1995). *Strategies for Teaching K–4 General Music.* Reston, VA: Music Educators National Conference.

"Student Musical Activities and Achievement in Music: NAEP 1997 Arts Assessment." (December 1999). NAEP FACTS, 4 (1).

Teaching General Music: A Course of Study. (1991). Reston, VA: Music Educators National Conference.

WEINBERGER, N. M., comp. (Winter 2000). " 'The Mozart Effect': A Small Part of the Big Picture." *MuSICA Research Notes* VII(1). www.musica.uci.edu/.

II
An Introduction to the Elements of Music and Music Concepts

Elementary school children need to be involved in musical experiences that help them develop musical skills and formulate concepts or understandings about music. Children naturally develop music concepts as they explore music through singing, listening, moving, creating, reading, and playing instruments. Understanding the process of how concepts develop, which music concepts may serve as the basis for instruction, and how this fits in with the whole child's development is important for teachers of children in grades K through 5.

Concepts may be described as understandings that remain in the mind following learning experiences. Concepts are generalized ideas that are formed after learners make connections and determine relationships among ideas. Concepts cannot be taught—they are formed through meaningful experiences. For a concept to be truly understood, it must be transferred to another setting. For example, if children have had a number of experiences with the music concept that songs can have parts that are contrasting or the same, they can apply this knowledge to a new song or listening selection. For this concept to become part of a deeper understanding, it must continually be experienced in a variety of contexts. In other words, conceptual learning is a spiralling or cyclical process and teachers need to plan instruction to facilitate that process.

In *The Musical Classroom,* music concepts provide the foundation for learning about music and are categorized by the elements of music: melody, rhythm, form, harmony, timbre, dynamics, and tempo. These elements, or common properties, may serve as a "cognitive map" for the teacher in planning conceptual experiences for elementary school students. Each model experience in Section Two focuses on a single concept illustrating one of these elements and is designed to lead to a fundamental understanding about that concept. However, melody, rhythm, harmony, form, dynamics, timbre, and tempo never occur singly in music; rather, they are combined and interrelated. Because music is a temporal art, each model experience facilitates—simultaneously—perception and conceptualization. Great care has been taken to suggest how this may be accomplished without diminishing the aesthetic impact of the art.

In the following section, each element of music is introduced, music concepts within each element are described, and in some cases information is given that

Courtesy of MENC: The National Association for Music Education

suggests how and when each element or concept might be introduced to children. At the conclusion of the section, a complete chart of all the music concepts and their related elements introduced in the model experiences of *The Musical Classroom* is presented.

THE ELEMENTS OF MUSIC

The following definitions of the elements of music are used throughout the text:

- **Melody** is a linear succession of sounds (pitches) and silences moving through time; the horizontal structure of music.
- **Rhythm** refers to all the durations of sounds and silences that occur in music as well as to the organization of these sounds and silences in time.
- **Harmony** is the simultaneous sounding of two or more pitches; the vertical structure of music moving through time and supporting the melody.
- **Form** is the overall structural organization of a musical composition and the interrelationships of musical events within the overall structure.
- **Expressive qualities** are those qualities (dynamics, tempo, timbre) that, combined with other musical elements (melody, rhythm, harmony, and form), give a composition its unique musical identity.

Expressive Qualities

Tempo, dynamics, and timbre are the musical elements that often communicate most directly and forcefully. Even young children readily perceive and respond to these expressive qualities.

Tempo refers to the speed of the musical sounds and silences. Children demonstrate their perceptions and understandings of tempo through movement and action-oriented experiences. For example, young children can move fast and slow to contrasting tempos heard in a piece of music, and older students can remember and compare a graduated series of tempos from slow to fast.

The louds and softs in music, the *dynamics,* are easy to hear and identify. Children, however, sometimes mistakenly associate down or lower with soft dynamics and up or higher with loud dynamics. This may be in part because they often hear "Turn the television up!" Therefore, it is important to provide experiences that will help students apply the terms loud and soft correctly.

Timbre ("TAM-br"), the characteristic sound (tone color or quality) of a voice or an instrument, often stands out as the most distinctive part of the music. A prekindergartener who hears a melody played on a violin and then on a tuba may think the melody itself has been changed (Pflederer and Sechrest, 1968:19–36). Students should have many opportunities to hear live and recorded performances on traditional orchestral instruments. Vocal and instrumental timbres of world cultures also fascinate many children. Music of twentieth-century composers explores timbre using an array of electronic, instrumental, and (sometimes) environmental sounds. Experiences that focus on timbre can also help students become familiar with a variety of musical styles.

Melody

Melodies consist of a linear succession of sounds (pitches) and silences moving through time. Each melody is a unique combination of pitches, which together create a discernible contour or sense of unity.

Musical pitches are produced by a vibrating medium. The rapidity of vibration creates the quality referred to as "high" or "low" *pitch.* A high pitch vibrates more rapidly than a low pitch. Children need to use the terms *high* and *low* accurately, and not mistake *higher* for louder and *lower* for softer (Zimmerman, 1971:7). Teachers can clarify this concept by playing step bells with the highest-pitched bar at the top and the lowest-pitched bar at the bottom. Students can then associate what they hear with what they see.

Pitches in a melody move up or down or remain the same. Students can experience various pitch directions through xylophone playing, movement, singing, and visual experiences. The direction of the melody may be by *step* (pitches that are close together) or by *skip* (pitches that are farther apart). In fact, a melody can have a distinct *contour* as it moves up and down, and repeats. Look at the song "Sally, Go 'Round the Sun" and notice how the melody moves (see next page). Connect the pitches on the score to discover the contour (shape of the melody), and then move your hand (in the air) to show the ups, downs, and repeats as the melody is performed.

Pitches in a melody are notated on a *staff* (five parallel lines). Pitches at the top of the staff are higher than those at the bottom. Steps are located next to each other, whereas skips are created by jumping over at least one line or space.

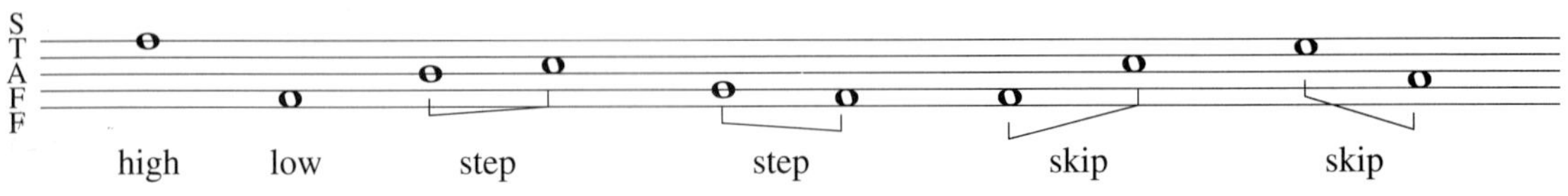

SALLY, GO 'ROUND THE SUN

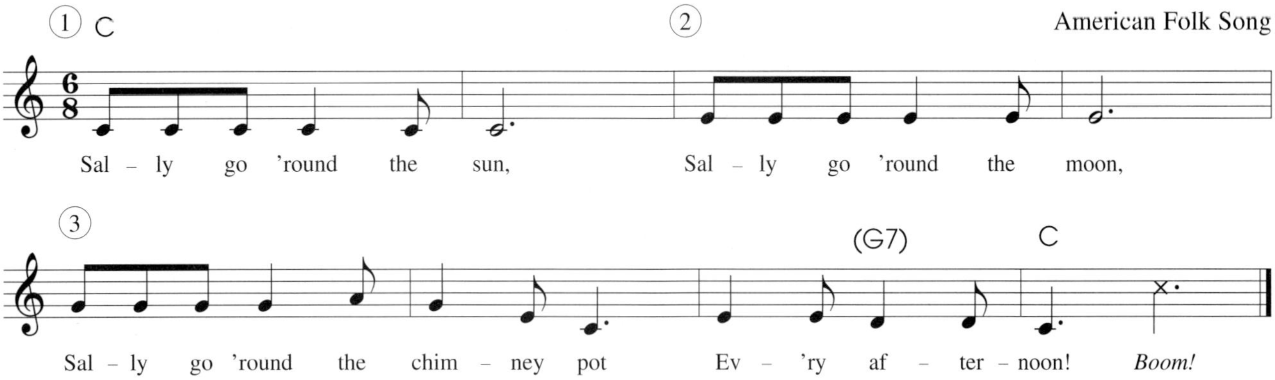
American Folk Song
1 C
2
3
(G7)
C
Sal - ly go 'round the sun, Sal - ly go 'round the moon,
Sal - ly go 'round the chim - ney pot Ev - 'ry af - ter - noon! Boom!

High/low and up/down/same pitches are all governed by a kind of musical grammar called *scales* (*scala,* Latin meaning "ladder"). Music that is based on a scale and centered on a particular pitch (the tonic or tonal center) is considered *tonal.* The two scale forms most familiar to us are the *major* and *minor* scales, but the pentatonic, blues, and many other scales and modes also serve as the framework for much of the world's music.

To speak a language, it is not necessary to have a conscious understanding of its rules. So it is with musical scales. Knowing that a song uses a minor scale is probably of greater use to the teacher than it is to the student. Students might, of course, learn how to construct a minor scale. But until a child is ready to use such facts creatively and expressively, this kind of knowledge is premature (Taebel, 1974:170). An experienced teacher can judge this readiness and recognize when children have the background that makes scales meaningful.

Much contemporary classical music uses pitch organizations and techniques other than scales, such as the twelve-tone row and octave displacement. Music that is not based on a scale or centered on a particular pitch is considered *atonal.*

Rhythm

Music is an art of motion, of continuous flow. Rhythm refers to all the durations of the sounds (and silences) in the musical flow. Rhythm also refers to the organization of these sounds and silences in time. All rhythms in music may be translated into physical responses. Because movement is one of the best ways to experience rhythm, elementary classroom music programs always include such experiences.

A recurrent pulsation is called a *beat.* Beat governs all the other sounds and silences in a composition. Even young children can perform steady beats, but they may have difficulty adjusting their beat to the music or coordinating their beats with others. With appropriate experiences, this skill gradually develops (Petzold, 1966:257). Tap a steady beat while the song "Sally, Go 'Round the Sun" is performed.

Meter refers to the grouping of beats into sets of two or three. In some music the beat groupings are obvious to the ear; in other music they are not. For example, the oom-pah-pah of "Amazing Grace" is easy to identify as a beat grouping of three (or triple meter).

At the age of nine or ten, children must clap, tap, or sing to identify meters they hear in music. Eventually students can identify meter by internalized means instead of by overt actions. At this point they are ready to be introduced to meter signatures (the visual symbols used to show meter). For example:

2 = two beats per measure (beat groupings of two)
4 = quarter note (♩) gets one beat

A piece of music always contains tones that are longer or shorter than the beat. Movement experiences that focus on *long and short durations* help youngsters physically feel and express their rhythmic understandings. After a variety of experiences with long and short durations, students are ready to use informal and formal notation to represent duration. Reading rhythms is easier for most children when verbal cues are associated with specific notes, such as "ta" for a longer duration and "ti" for a shorter one (Atterbury, 1992).

A *rhythm pattern* is a specific combination of long and short sounds. For example:

Rhythm patterns can be expressed through movement, singing, or playing instruments. Ultimately rhythm patterns are combined into the longer rhythm of a melody. Tapping the rhythm of the words of "Sally, Go 'Round the Sun" sounds the *melodic rhythm.*

Form

Musical form is often compared to architecture because it refers to the overall structure of a musical composition. In architecture, music, and the other arts, unity and variety are achieved through repetition and contrast. The *phrase* is an important building block in musical form. A phrase may be compared to a simple sentence or a clause in speech, because it is a musical segment with a clear beginning and a clear ending. "Sally, Go 'Round the Sun," for example, has four phrases.

The phrases in a song may be grouped into distinct *sections.* "Yankee Doodle" is an example of a song with two sections: a verse and a refrain. The sections of "Yankee Doodle" contrast with each other, and its form is referred to as AB (also called *binary form*). "Shoo, Fly" is an example of a song with three sections: the first and the third are the same, with the second contrasting. This musical design is referred to as ABA (*ternary form*). Songs are an ideal starting point for understanding longer compositions that contain many sections.

Longer compositions are more challenging for children to listen to and understand. Teachers need to focus students' attention on the musical elements that will be meaningful to them. This will help them learn to hear what is the same and what is different. Students can listen for instrumental (and vocal) timbre and also for melodies and rhythms.

Through overt behavior, students can demonstrate what they hear and understand about musical form. Techniques frequently used include body movements or playing instruments along with the music. Another technique is to provide shapes or letters for students to manipulate while they are listening. For example, a square might represent the opening section of the music, and a circle, the contrasting section. Experiences of this kind are important because ultimately teachers do not "teach"; instead, they help students identify (and understand) what the students themselves perceive through their senses.

Harmony

Harmony results when two or more pitches are sounded simultaneously. Harmony gives an added dimension to melody and is sometimes compared to perspective in the visual arts. Children constantly hear melodies performed with harmony, but prekindergarteners seem to focus mainly on the melody. In the elementary classroom, harmony can be introduced by adding pitches to a familiar melody. For example, the "ev'ry afternoon" pitches may be repeated over and over while singing the melody of "Sally, Go 'Round the Sun." One (or more) of these ostinatos may be sung or played along with a melody.

Multiple sounds also result when "Sally, Go 'Round the Sun" is sung as a two- or three-voice round. A *round* is a melody that is performed by two or more groups entering at different times.

Various textures can be created when melodies and harmonies are combined. Combinations of separate, distinct melodies are a special kind of harmony and texture called *polyphony.*

Chords are the main building blocks of harmony and include at least three pitches sounded simultaneously. When a single melody is supported by a series of chords, a *homophonic* texture results.

The above "melody with chords" results when classroom singing is accompanied by an Autoharp or a Chromaharp, a piano, or a guitar. (In many of the elementary music series textbooks, chords for a song are shown by uppercase letters above the staff.)

Children can play chordal accompaniments on an Autoharp or on resonator bars. Accompaniments that use only two or three different chords are easiest to play. Play the C Major chord on an Autoharp while singing "Sally, Go 'Round the Sun."

Chords relate to melody, and the adult listener nearly always knows when the chords "fit" (are consonant) with the melody. Prekindergarteners show little discrimination one way or the other, but by the age of nine they seem to develop a preference for consonant harmony (Valentine, 1962:217–218).

CHAPTER SUMMARY

The elements of music that provide a framework for conceptual learning are melody, rhythm, harmony, form, and the expressive qualities of tempo, dynamics, and timbre. Although in the previous section each element has been described separately, they never occur one at a time. Instead, the elements are woven together into a "moving tapestry" of music.

Teachers must help students focus their perception on and increase their understanding of the elements of music. Each learning experience succeeds when it helps children respond to the emotional and aesthetic aspects of music.

SCOPE AND SEQUENCE CHART OF MUSIC CONCEPTS

ELEMENTS OF MUSIC	LEVEL I CONCEPTS	LEVEL II CONCEPTS
Melody	• Pitches can be high or low • Pitches can move up • Pitches can move down • Pitches in a melody can stay the same	• Music can be performed in a connected or disconnected style • Pitches can be high or low • Pitches in a melody can move by step • A song usually ends on the home tone • Melodies can include skips of an octave
Rhythm	• Chants can move with a steady beat • Music can move with a steady beat • The rhythm of a melody includes long and short sounds	• The rhythm of a melody includes long and short sounds • Rhythm patterns can include sounds of long and short duration • Beats can be grouped in twos • Beats can be grouped in threes
Harmony	• A melody can be performed alone or with an accompaniment	• Drones and ostinatos can add harmony to a melody
Form	• Songs may have a clear ending • Repeating patterns can create unity • Melodies can be made up of sections that are different	• Melodies are divided into smaller parts called phrases • Phrases often end on a long tone
Expressive Qualities	• Music can be soft and loud or become gradually softer or louder (dynamics) • Music can move in a fast and slow tempo • Sound is produced by a vibrating object • Each voice has its own special sound (timbre)	• Each instrument has its own special sound • Each instrumental family has its own distinctive sound

LEVEL III CONCEPTS		ELEMENTS OF MUSIC
• Pitches can move by stepping up or down • A melody can exhibit a distinctive contour as it moves up or down or repeats • Music can be based on major or minor tonality		**Melody**
• Beat groupings of twos and threes can be combined to create asymmetric meter		**Rhythm**
• Chords consist of three or four pitches stacked in thirds	• Chord tones can be played one after another as a song accompaniment	**Harmony**
• Phrases in a melody can be the same or different • Sections of a composition can contrast with one another and sections can be repeated (ABA) • The initial section of a composition alternates with contrasting sections in rondo form	• In call-and-response form, responses can be identical to the call, or contrasting • Each of the three phrases in "twelve-bar" blues consists of four "bars" • Sections of a composition can contrast with one another and sections can be repeated (rag)	**Form**
• Each instrument has a characteristic timbre that when combined with others can create a sound piece • Instruments can be identified and grouped by their timbres and materials	• Sounds are produced by vibrations and amplified on both acoustic and electronic instruments • The elements of music can be identified and compared in music of different historical periods	**Expressive Qualities**

PROJECTS FOR COLLEGE STUDENTS

1. Name the five elements of music used as the framework for conceptual learning in this text. Briefly describe each.
2. Write a summary of an article from the references that follow.
3. In small groups, develop a list of TV programs for children. Discuss how music is used in each. Are music concepts taught, or is music used to teach other subjects?

CHAPTER REFERENCES

ALVAREZ, BARBARA J. (1993). "Developing Music Concepts." In *Music in PreKindergarten: Planning and Teaching,* Barbara Andress, ed., 29–32. Reston, VA: Music Educators National Conference.

ATTERBURY, BETTY W. (1992). "Research on the Teaching of Elementary General Music." In *Handbook of Research on Music Teaching and Learning,* Richard Colwell, ed., 595. New York: Schirmer Books.

BURNSED, VERNON. (Fall 1998). "The Effects of Expressive Variation in Dynamics on the Musical Preferences of Elementary School Students." *Journal of Research in Music Education* 46(3): 402.

FEIERABEND, T. CLARK SAUNDERS, JOHN M. HOLAHAN, and PAMELA E. GETNICK. (Fall 1998). "Song Recognition among Preschool-Age Children: An Investigation of Words and Music." *Journal of Research in Music Education* 46(3):358.

FLOWERS, PATRICIA J. (April 1985). "How Children Communicate about Music." *Music Educators Journal* 71(8): 44.

FLOWERS, PATRICIA J. (Spring 1998). "Music Vocabulary of First-Grade Children: Words Listed for Instruction and Their Actual Use." *Journal of Research in Music Education* 46(1): 10.

FLOWERS, PATRICIA J., JOEL WAPNICK, and LASHELL RAMSEY. (Fall 1997). "Structured and Unstructured Musical Contexts and Children's Ability to Demonstrate Tempo and Dynamic Contrasts." *Journal of Research in Music Education* 45(3): 352.

JAMES, LORINDA. (1998). "Action Research: Conducting Activities for Third Graders." *Teaching Music* 5(5):43.

MEHR, NORMAN. (April 1985). "Helping Children Perceive Melody." *Music Educators Journal* 71(8):29.

MOOREHEAD, GLADYS, and DONALD POND. (1978). *Music of Young Children.* Santa Barbara, CA: Pillsbury Foundation for the Advancement of Music Education. Four volumes.

PETZOLD, ROBERT G. (1966). *The Development of Auditory Perception of Musical Sounds by Children in the First Six Grades.* Madison: University of Wisconsin.

PFLEDERER, MARILYN, and LEE SECHREST. (Spring 1968). "Conservation-type Responses of Children to Musical Stimuli." *Council for Research in Music Education* 13,19.

TAEBEL, DONALD K. (Fall 1974). "The Effect of Various Instructional Modes on Children's Performance of Music Concept Tasks." *Journal of Research in Music Education* 11(3):170.

VALENTINE, C. W. (1962). *The Experimental Psychology of Beauty.* London: Methuen.

ZIMMERMAN, MARILYN P. (1971). *Musical Characteristics of Children.* Washington, DC: Music Educators National Conference.

III
Music-Making Activities

Children learn by doing. Active, hands-on music experiences enable children to demonstrate through behavior their conceptual understandings. Learning seems to be most effective when a concept is experienced through several modes: aural, motor, visual, tactile, and verbal. Music learning can be demonstrated through several kinds of behaviors: singing, playing instruments, moving to music, reading and notating music, creating music, and describing music. In the conceptual model experiences of *The Musical Classroom,* music-making activities are not ends in themselves but are designed to lead to enjoyment, aesthetic sensitivity—and conceptual learning.

Courtesy of MENC: The National Association for Music Education

The following describes music-making activities that are important in the elementary classroom and offers guidelines for teachers to consider as they engage students in active music making.

MUSIC-MAKING ACTIVITIES: LISTENING

Listening, or the aural mode, is central to every aspect of music making. In addition to the aural skills required in music-making activities such as playing instruments, singing songs, and creating accompaniments, "pure" listening or listening for its own sake should be the focus of many music-learning experiences. Students hear music all around them every day, but pure listening to music is an active skill, and one that needs to be developed and nurtured. Through numerous and diverse listening opportunities, students can expand their musical understanding and increase their enjoyment of music. Children need to develop specific listening skills to become perceptive, critical, and successful music learners.

Learning to listen attentively to music is a big challenge for children. To help focus their attention, teachers need to plan music-listening experiences that involve the children as active participants. This can be accomplished through an activity such as movement or with the use of visual aids. Movement and visual aids, however, should be used only to elicit responses to particular events in the music. For example, kindergarten and first-grade children can respond with fast and slow walking to demonstrate changing tempos in music such as Brahms's Hungarian Dance no. 5, model experience, p. 124. Or they can use puppets as props to show the long and short sounds in an orchestral piece such as "Kangaroos" from the *Carnival of the Animals* (Saint-Saëns) (see p. 164). These experiences are effective ways for students to demonstrate their perceptual understanding.

In addition to planning listening experiences that actively engage the students, teachers can encourage students to listen attentively by maintaining eye contact with them and giving full attention to the music throughout the listening activity. (Students are more likely to stay "on task" when they see their teachers concentrating on the music.) Teachers should not be tempted to review lesson plans or read the jacket notes of a CD while asking students to listen attentively to the music. Teachers should model attentive listening behaviors as well as show enthusiasm for the music through appropriate facial expressions. It is very important that teachers not talk (or allow the children to talk) while the music is playing but rather give good oral directions before the listening and only visual cues during the listening experience. Both teachers and students should be good models of correct concert etiquette (Wilcox and Crum, 1995:5–6).

Teaching students to listen to music involves gradually increasing their attention span. Listening experiences should initially feature short pieces and gradually increase to longer ones. For example, the listening selections used in kindergarten and first-grade model experiences in this text are generally one to one-and-a-half minutes in length. By the end of Level III experiences, students are listening to compositions several minutes long. No matter what the length or complexity of a particular selection, students need to hear it many times. As they engage in repeated listenings, their understanding of the music will deepen, and as a result, their enjoyment of the music will be greater.

Guidelines for Listening

1. *Plan well-organized listening experiences that will, through movement, visual aids, and the like, engage students as active participants.*
2. *Guide students to listen to musical selections with focused attention.*
3. *Maintain eye contact with students, show interest and excitement about the music through facial expressions, and give full attention to the music to encourage student attention when music is being played.*
4. *Refrain from talking while the class listens to selected music—insist that students do the same.*
5. *Select music of appropriate length and complexity for the age of the students.*
6. *Direct students to listen for something specific in the music each time the piece is heard.*
7. *Engage students in repeated listenings to specific pieces of music to enable them to perceive the music more fully and become "old friends" with the pieces.*
8. *Use quality sound equipment to play recorded selections so that students experience the very best performances.*

Listening Maps and Call Charts

To facilitate music learning, numerous techniques and teaching aids are used to help structure and organize listening experiences. Both listening maps and call charts have proven to be successful tools for focusing student attention on specific events in a piece of music.

A listening map is simply a clear, visual representation of the important features in a particular composition. The map might include pictures, graphic designs, geometric forms, or brief excerpts of music notation. Whatever is included in the map is presented for the sole purpose of helping children better understand the inner workings of the musical selection. Maps can be either teacher-designed or student-designed (with teacher guidance!). They can be presented on a board, large tablet, or transparency to be used in front of the class, or can be prepared on paper and duplicated for each individual student.

A *listening map* is featured in the Level I Model Experience "Ballet of the Unhatched Chicks" from *Pictures at an Exhibition* (Mussorgsky), p. 128. Since Mussorgsky based his composition on a drawing (by Victor Hartmann) suggesting chicks in their shells, this map depicts in sequence the musical events with pictures of a chick in various stages breaking out of its shell. The teacher points to the pictures as the piece unfolds.

A *call chart,* a written or visual guide to the important events in a musical selection, differs from a listening map in that it identifies the particular musical events by number. The teacher announces the number, or "call," that coincides with each musical event as it occurs.

A call chart is included in a model experience that uses "Piffle Rag" (Yelvington) as its focus (p. 222). This call chart guides students to discover the structural form of the selection by involving them in completing the chart. The teacher "calls out" the eight different sections as they occur. Students write down on their individual worksheets the correct letters for the repeated and contrasting sections and words to describe the various sections.

Listening maps and call charts are just two instructional tools that have been effectively used to guide the listener through a piece of music. Nearly all the elementary music series textbooks (see Appendix C) include some examples of maps and charts. Teachers should be creative in designing similar tools to facilitate focused listening.

National Standards for Music Education

Standard 6. Listening to, Analyzing, and Describing Music

Standard 6, one of the nine National Standards for Music Education for grades K through 12, specifies what students should know and be able to do in listening to, analyzing, and describing music. For this content standard, there are five achievement standards.

By the end of grade 4, students will need to

a. identify simple music forms when presented aurally;
b. demonstrate perceptual skills by moving, by answering questions about, and by describing aural examples of music of various styles representing diverse cultures;
c. use appropriate terminology in explaining music, music notation, music instruments and voices, and music performances;
d. identify the sounds of a variety of instruments, including many orchestral and band instruments, and instruments from various cultures, as well as children's voices and male and female adult voices;
e. respond through purposeful movement to selected prominent musical characteristics or to specific musical events while listening to music. (From *National Standards for Arts Education.* Copyright © 1994 by Music Educators National Conference. Used by permission.)

Summary

Children hear music all around them every day. They need to develop aural skills that will enable them to listen attentively and perceptively to music so that their own personal understanding and enjoyment of music will increase. Our goal as teachers should be to "grow" intelligent and appreciative music listeners—ones who will be able to make informed judgments concerning music and the role it can play in their lives.

PROJECTS FOR COLLEGE STUDENTS

1. Plan an original music-listening experience for students in second/third grade or fourth/fifth grade. Follow the guidelines in the model experience assignments Level II (pp. 189 and 190) or Level III (pp. 233–235).
2. Create a listening map for second/third-grade students to follow as they listen to "Chinese Dance" from the *Nutcracker* Suite (Tchaikovsky) (see p. 161).

REFERENCES

BLETSTEIN, BEVERLY. (September 1987). "Call Charts: Tools from the Past for Today's Classroom." *Music Educators Journal* 74(1):53–56.

BYRNES, SUZANNE RITA. (Winter 1997). "Different-Age and Mentally Handicapped Listeners' Response to Western Art Music Selections." *Journal of Research in Music Education* 45(4):568–579).

FLOWERS, PATRICIA J. (December 1990). "Listening: The Key to Describing Music." *Music Educators Journal* 77(4):21.

PAXCIA-BIBBINS, NANCY. (Spring 1998). "Listening with a Whole Mind: Holistic Learning in the Music Classroom." *Teaching Music* 11(3):11–13.

MILLER, SAMUEL D. (October 1986). "Listening Maps for Musical Tours." *Music Educators Journal* 73(2):28–31.

SIMS, WENDY L. (December 1990). "Sound Approaches to Elementary Music Listening." *Music Educators Journal* 77(4):38–42.

WILCOX, ELLA, and GAIL CRUM, comp. (June 1995). "No Bubblegum During Beethoven." *Teaching Music* 2(6):30–31.

See also Resources, Appendix F: "Listening," "Prekindergarten: Listening," "Western Art Music," "World Music," "Jazz," "Women in Music," "Popular Music."

MUSIC-MAKING ACTIVITIES: PLAYING INSTRUMENTS

Musical instruments are an exciting and colorful aspect of elementary classroom music. Children develop concepts about music as they play melodies, create and play rhythmic accompaniments to songs, add harmony to melodies, and create sound effects for movement, stories, and poems. Instruments can be used singly and in combination. Teachers need to be sure that the instruments introduced are appropriate for the level of the student's musical and motor development, and that each child has opportunities to play. Students should learn how to handle the instruments properly and also develop correct playing techniques. Teachers need to establish routine procedures for distributing, collecting, and caring for instruments.

Instruments that are used in elementary classrooms include rhythm instruments, small wind instruments, barred instruments such as xylophones, Autoharps/Chromaharps, Omnichords (an electronic Autoharp) and QChords (a digital guitar), acoustic and electronic keyboards, stringed instruments, and handbells and chime bars.

Rhythm Instruments

Small percussion instruments playable with a minimum of instruction are usually called "rhythm instruments." A variety of durable instruments with a good musical tone should be available in every classroom or school. Sets of instruments often include several types of drums, tambourines, sleigh bells, rhythm sticks, sand blocks, wood blocks, finger cymbals, and triangles (see illustrations, p. 23). Latin percussion instruments are often included, such as maracas (shakers), guiro (scrapers), castanets, and claves (a pair of rhythm sticks), as are large cymbals and gongs.

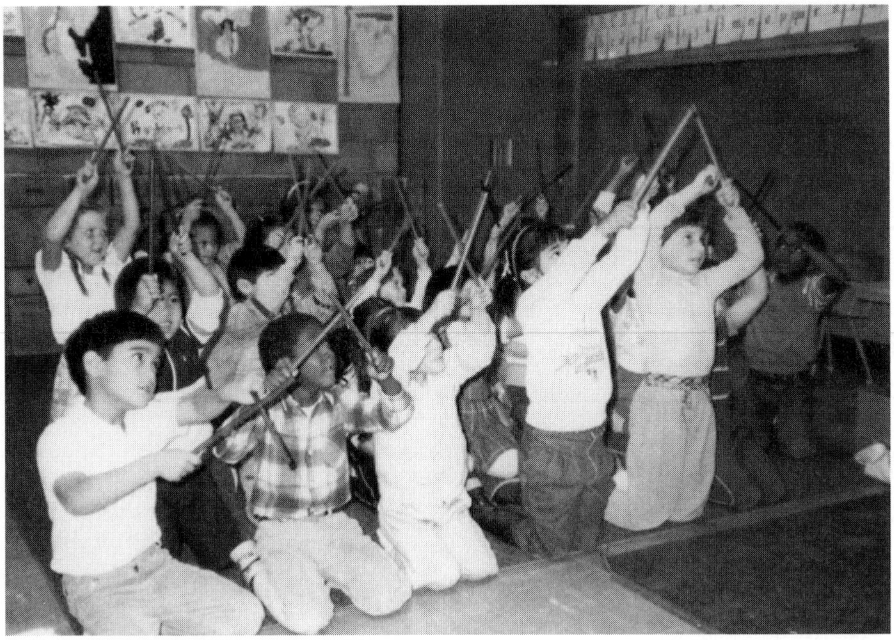

Photo by Patricia Hackett

Rhythm Instruments in the Classroom

Youngsters learn much about their world through experiences with objects, texture, and shape. As soon as children can bang, stroke, or tap instruments should be available to them. Young children of almost any age can use rhythm instruments for sound effects with songs and stories. Kindergarteners can create sound effects for "The Three Bears," using higher-pitched and lower-pitched instruments to fit the bears' voices (see model experience, p. 133).

Five- and six-year olds love to play an instrument along with their own walking and marching; at this age they can maintain a steady beat, and play soft/loud, or slow/fast, to show the quality of their movements. In Model Experiences "Golden Gate" (p. 116), and "Riding in the Buggy" (p. 118) kindergarten children play rhythm instruments along with the steady beat of a chant and a song.

SELECTED CLASSROOM INSTRUMENTS

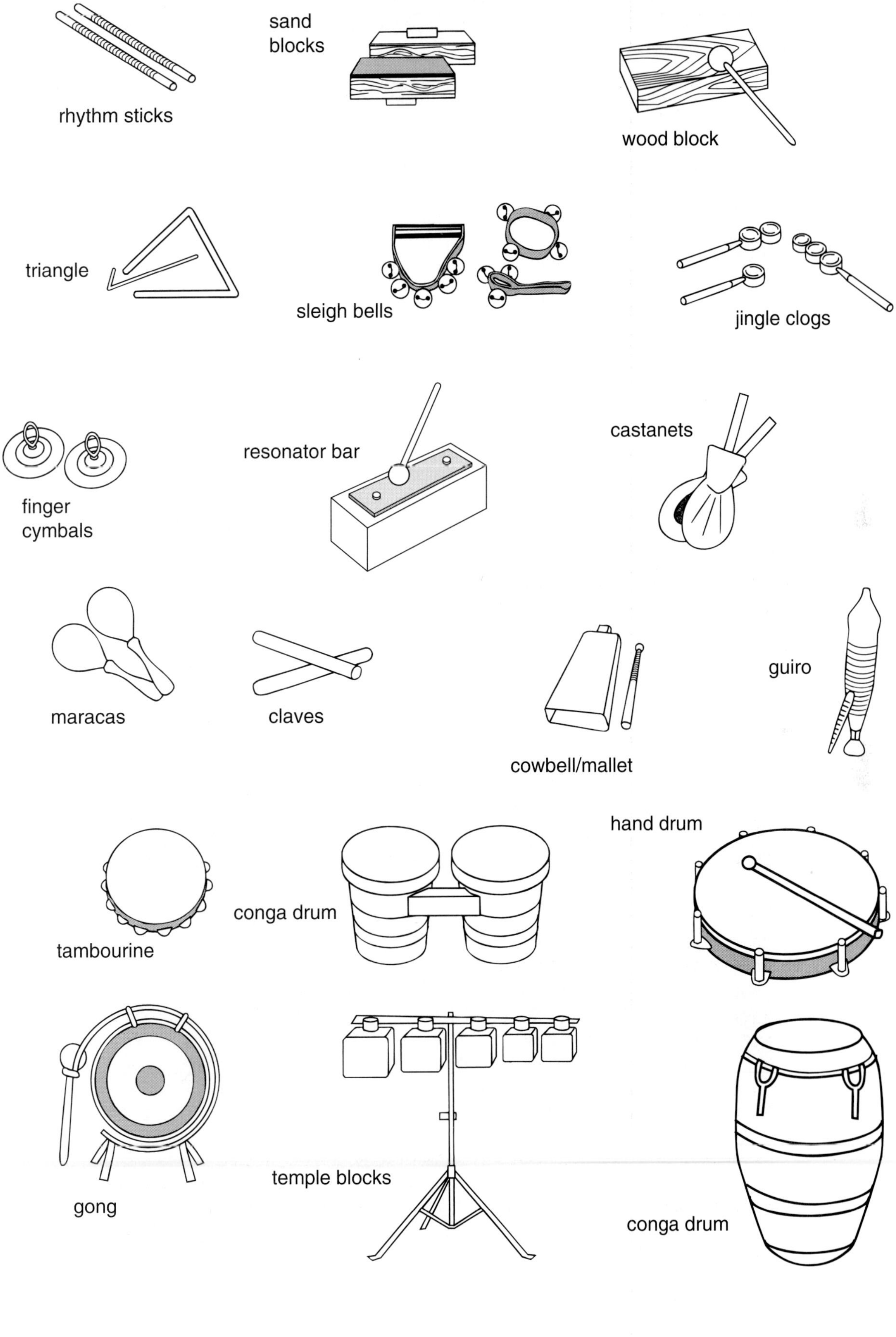

In grades 2 and 3, children continue many of the activities suggested above. They can also add instrumental rhythm patterns to songs because their eye-hand coordination is improving. For example, students might play drums, cymbals, and gongs to create a Chinese-style percussion ensemble for the "Song of the Dragon" (p. 185).

Fourth graders can make and play their own replicas of rhythm instruments, such as rattles, tambourines, and drums. The instruments should be durable and produce a quality sound. Replicas of selected Latin American, African, or Hawaiian instruments are also possibilities. For example, students can use two smooth pebbles to serve as *ili ili* (stone castanets) to accompany the song "Hawaiian Rainbows" (p. 203). They also might like to construct instruments such as Hawaiian-style gourd shakers and drums.

Creating a percussion composition is a familiar challenge for fifth graders if they have used rhythm instruments in previous grades. The special sound of different instruments is explored along with a haiku poem (p. 204), as students decide when to use each instrument as an accompaniment for a nature poem. At this age they can use percussion instruments to improvise rhythm patterns along with "Jamaica Farewell" (p. 228) because their eye-hand coordination is much improved.

Wind Instruments

Small wind instruments—song flute, Tonette, and soprano recorder—are included in many classroom music programs. The best of the inexpensive winds is the recorder, because it has a wider range of pitches and offers (potentially) the best tone quality. Grade four is a suitable time to begin small winds, when most students are able to coordinate finger placement with breathing. However, playing two or three pitches, involving short phrases and simple rhythms, can begin as early as grade 3. Elementary music series textbooks introduce the soprano recorder in grade 3 or 4, and there are short lessons and easy parts to play through subsequent grade levels.

The recorder comes in five sizes (see "The Recorder," Section Three). The soprano recorder is usually chosen for elementary music programs because it is small enough for children's hands. Learning often begins with the pitches G, A, and B, as does the instruction in Section Three. Songs for soprano recorder contained in this text

Courtesy of MENC: The National Association for Music Education

are listed in "The Recorder," Section Three, along with eight songs (p. 270–272) for beginning recorder. See also Appendix F, "Recorder Books."

Barred Instruments

Xylophones, resonator bars, metallophones, glockenspiels, song bells, and step bells are used for both melody and harmony. Barred instruments come in many sizes and have either wooden or metal bars that are played using mallets. Small barred instruments are placed on tabletops or desks, and large instruments, built with legs, are played while standing. Many are constructed so that bars can be removed when not needed. Resonator bars (metal bars sitting above a resonator box) are separate bars that are arranged in a set like a xylophone. Each resonator bar can be removed from the case and placed in front of a student. Song bells are made of metal; the metal bars are attached to a small wooden frame that can be set upon a tabletop. Step bells are similar to song bells but are built on a vertical frame resembling stair steps.

Barred instruments can be played by students of all ages, according to their level of physical development. To coordinate their playing with a song's steady beat, children need to be approximately age five or six. Playing a single bar along with a song is a great beginning, as in Model Experience, "Wake Me!" (p. 142). Second and third graders can play simple melodic fragments or drone harmony using two pitches, as they do for "Chatter with the Angels" (p. 182). Full chords can be handled by fourth graders, as in "Hey, Lidee" (p. 210), where each child plays three notes in a chord. Complex mallet work should be delayed until students are older and have greater eye-hand facility, as in the song with steel-drum-style accompaniment, "Jamaica Farewell" (p. 228).

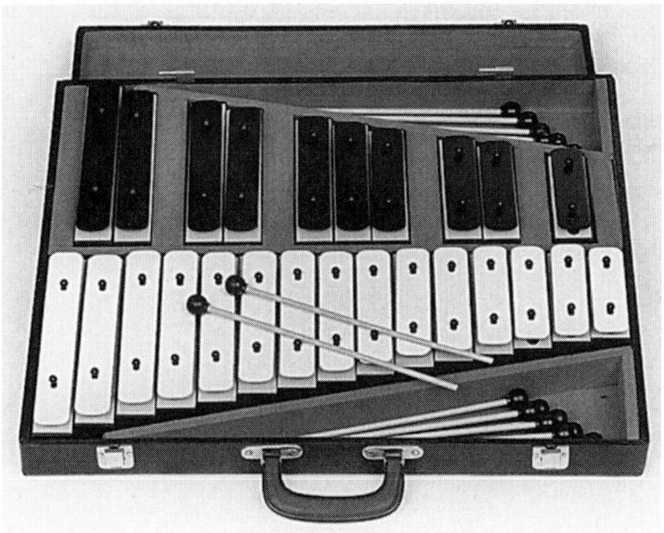

Resonator bars (left) and step bells. Courtesy of Rhythm Band, Inc.

Autoharp, Chromaharp, Omnichord, and QChord

The Autoharp, the Chromaharp, the Omnichord, and the QChord are instruments used mainly for accompanying songs (see "Autoharp and Chromaharp," p. 244). Strumming techniques used on the acoustic Autoharp and Chromaharp can be transferred to the Omnichord or the QChord, electronic instruments that are easy to play.

Chromaharp

Both the Autoharp and the Chromaharp consist of strings, chord bars, and a resonator box. Chordal harmony results when a chord bar is pressed while the strings are strummed. Kindergarteners are thrilled to strum as the teacher presses the chord buttons. Youngsters in first and second grade can share these roles, one pushing the chord buttons and another strumming. Fourth and fifth graders can play the instrument by themselves, but they need practice time before they can keep a steady rhythmic accompaniment as they finger different chord buttons.

The Omnichord and the QChord are electronic instruments that are used in ways similar to the Autoharp—mostly for accompanying singing. They are both small and portable, with a built-in amplifier. However, the Omnichord (shaped like an Autoharp or Chromaharp) is no longer in production, having been replaced by the QChord. The QChord is less expensive than the Omnichord and is similar in many ways; however, the QChord offers many additional features—and never needs tuning. The QChord is an electronic instrument shaped to suggest an electric guitar (see photo). Batteries provide power, although an AC adapter is available. The QChord is played on a table top, or in guitar position when a guitar strap is added. (The instrument weighs four pounds

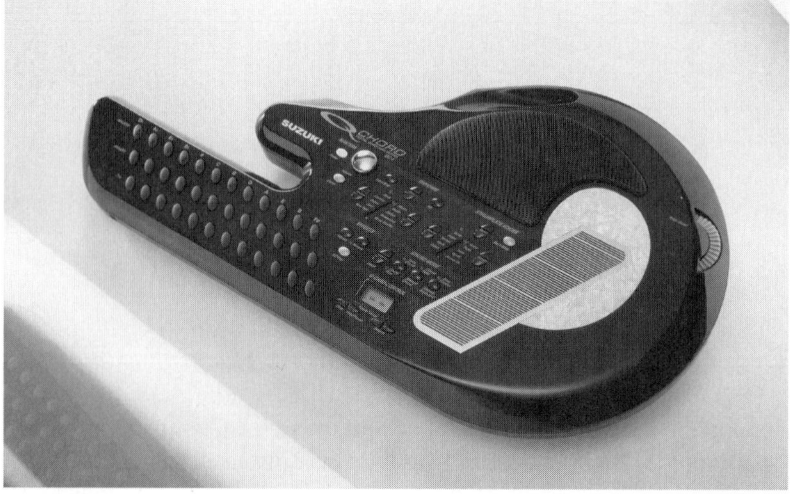

QChord. Courtesy of Suzuki Corporation.

and uses eight "C" batteries.) It will simultaneously produce chords having an instrumental timbre, in a choice of rhythms and styles.

The QChord comes with 84 preprogrammed chords, and can be programmed to play a repeating series of chords for the song of your choice, such as in "Frère Jacques!" (p. 299) or "Jamaica Farewell" (p. 323). With just the touch of a button, the QChord can also provide an automatic bass line for a song, or program an introduction and ending, or add a "drum fill."

When a player strums the plate, ten different timbres are readily available. However, rather than strum, the player can choose from ten preset rhythms, such as waltz, rock, and country. For example, a player might choose a "banjo strum" to accompany Model Experience "Looby Loo" (p. 127).

Students can explore and compare the timbres of Autoharp, Chromaharp, or QChord in the Model Experience, "Wabash Cannon Ball" (p. 218).

Keyboards

Both an acoustic piano and an electronic keyboard can produce melody and harmony. Playing a keyboard instrument offers students of all ages concrete experiences with music concepts and notation, and helps develop spatial reasoning skills (see "The Keyboard," Section Three).

The Piano

The piano can be used to play chord tones, song fragments, drones, ostinatos, and full chords. For example, in the "Chatter with the Angels" model experience (p. 182), students can play the drone on piano instead of on the (recommended) xylophone. The same instrumental change can be made in other lessons, such as "Hey, Lidee" (p. 210).

Electronic Keyboards

Two types of electronic keyboards are used in elementary classrooms: the basic keyboard and the synthesizer. Basic keyboards are the least expensive and have the convenience of portability, battery operation, and self-contained speakers. These basic keyboards have preset rhythms and automatic chord accompaniments. In contrast, synthesizers are keyboards that contain computers and are programmable (they don't have preset rhythms and chords), and they need additional components, such as speakers—resulting in greater cost. They usually have MIDI capability. (See Chapter Five for MIDI information.)

The preset rhythms (percussion only—no pitched sounds) of basic electronic keyboards encompass different styles and meters, such as waltz time. These keyboards can produce an array of timbres, for example, clarinet and honky-tonk piano. Basic keyboards also provide chord accompaniments that are automatic or manual, and each manufacturer has a different system for accessing them.

The special features of electronic keyboards can be exploited—for example, to produce sound effects for children's stories or plays. Since basic keyboards can produce many rhythms and timbres, they are ideal for exploring rhythm and style. For example, students can choose a preset rhythm "backup" in a suitable style (such as banjo or rock) for a song. (See "Wabash Cannonball," p. 218.) Drones, ostinatos, and song fragments for piano or xylophone can be transferred to any electronic keyboard. Programmable synthesizer keyboards offer special opportunities for original composition because the results can be saved by recording them in the synthesizer's memory.

Elementary music series include keyboard experiences for all grade levels, usually in ways similar to those for barred instruments and resonator bars. Electronic keyboards are found at every grade level in a surprising number of situations. They are

Courtesy of MENC: The National Association for Music Education

found in Japan's elementary schools, for example, and the state of Oregon has a general music curriculum using electronic keyboards. Children in a Long Island elementary school use synthesizers in many creative ways (Wiggins, 1993), as do students in Connecticut (Bissell, 1995).

Stringed Instruments

The Guitar

The guitar is introduced in fifth or sixth grade or when students' small-muscle coordination is adequately developed. Introductory guitar work begins with chord roots, simplified chords (using only four strings), or chords that use only one or two fingers (see

"The Guitar," Section Three). Elementary music series present guitar in grade 5 or 6 and have short lessons and easy parts to play—usually as song accompaniments. Guitar instruction is more manageable when small groups or pairs of students work together.

The Ukulele

The ukulele is a four-stringed instrument similar to the guitar (that is used in similar ways). It comes in two sizes: soprano and baritone. Learning the baritone ukulele sometimes precedes guitar study, because the baritone's strings are the same as the highest four strings of the guitar, making it easy to transfer skills to the guitar. Both the guitar and the ukulele need to be tuned before each use.

Handbells and Chime Bars

Handbells and chime bars are high-quality, expensive instruments used in some elementary music programs. In grades 4 or 5 most children have developed the motor skills to be successful with this activity. A handbell is a bell with handle; a chime bar is a metal tube with an attached mallet on the top. Each handbell and chime bar is portable and is held in the hand. Both types of instruments are made of metal and come in sets of graduated sizes (pitches). A player is assigned to a specific handbell (or chime bar) and plays only that pitch when it is needed. Each type of instrument has a particular playing technique. Handbells and chime bars can be played in harmony, but they are often used for melody, as in the follow-up to "Ebeneezer Sneezer," in which each player plays one handbell or chime bar in an eight-note scale (p. 178). (Available chime bars are called Choirchimes and ToneChimes, each name being the trademark of a particular manufacturer.)

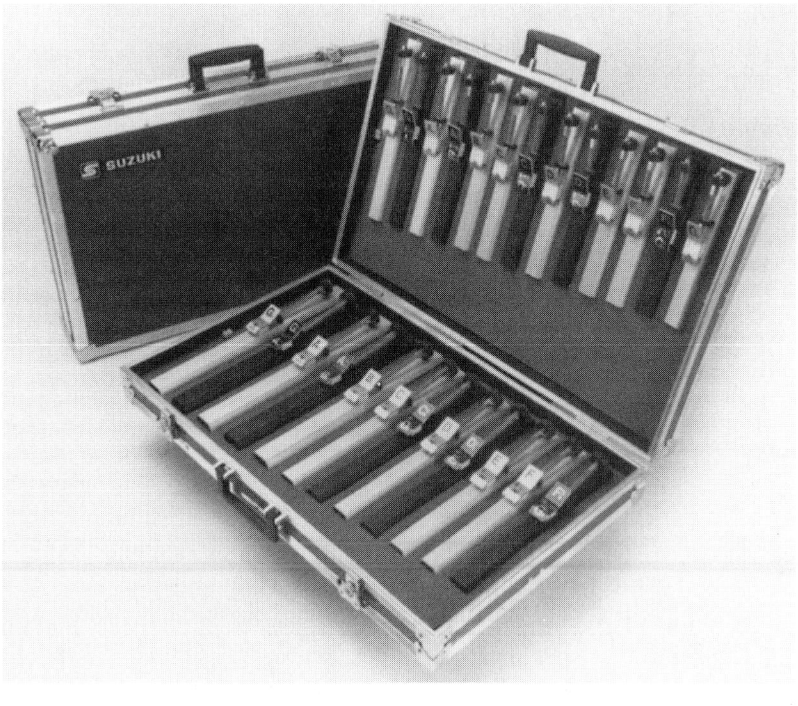

ToneChimes. Courtesy of Suzuki Corporation.

Guidelines for Using Instruments

1. *Purchase good-quality instruments, and insist that students use them properly.*
2. *Rotate the use of instruments, and have a way to keep track of individual use.*
3. *Devise a simple distribution and collection system.*
4. *Have a secure place to store the instruments, one that is not too hot or too cold.*
5. *Regularly check instruments that need to be tuned and maintain all instruments in good working order.*

National Standards for Music Education

Standard 2. Performing on Instruments, Alone and with Others, a Varied Repertoire of Music

Standard 2, one of the nine National Standards for Music Education for grades K through 12, specifies what students should know and be able to do in playing instruments. For this content standard, there are six achievement standards.

By the end of grade 4, students will need to

a. perform on pitch, in rhythm, with appropriate dynamics and timbre, and maintain a steady tempo;
b. perform easy rhythmic, melodic, and chordal patterns accurately and independently on rhythmic, melodic, and harmonic classroom instruments;
c. perform expressively a varied repertoire of music representing diverse genres and styles;
d. echo short rhythms and melodic patterns;
e. perform in groups, blending instrumental timbres, matching dynamic levels, and responding to the cues of a conductor;
f. perform independent instrumental parts[1] while other students sing or play contrasting parts. (From *National Standards for Arts Education.* Copyright © 1994 by Music Educators National Conference. Used by permission.)

Summary

Instrumental experience gives a concrete basis for conceptual learning about music, and also leads to expanded sensorimotor skills and spatial reasoning. Rhythm instruments, barred instruments, Autoharps, Chromaharps, electronic Autoharp or digital guitar, winds, strings, and keyboard instruments offer melody and harmony experience

[1]For example; simple rhythmic or melodic ostinatos, contrasting rhythmic lines, harmonic progressions, and chords.

and should be played by students at every grade level. Students need to learn correct playing and handling techniques, and teachers need skills in teaching instruments, tuning instruments, and distributing and collecting instruments and equipment. Playing instruments is important when music reading is a primary objective, but performance also gives the experiential basis for understanding melody, rhythm, harmony, form, and especially the expressive qualities of music.

PROJECTS FOR COLLEGE STUDENTS

1. In small groups, review a selected elementary music series and note how particular instruments are used in different grades. One group could review keyboards, another group barred instruments. Groups should compare their reviews with each other and then share with the class.
2. Review "Leading a Song" (p. 37), and then prepare song accompaniments for Autoharp, QChord, or guitar. To select songs for your chosen instrument, refer to the Section Three lists of one-, two-, and three-chord songs. Learn one piece in each category, and prepare to accompany a group of singers. Review and evaluate your success in playing and leading the song(s).
3. Visit a store or Web site that sells a variety of electronic musical instruments or visit a campus computer/music lab with keyboards. (For resources, see Appendix F, "General Music Retailers," and "Addresses.") Evaluate the musical potential of each electronic instrument and list ways it could be used in the elementary classroom.

REFERENCES

BISSELL, PATRICIA M. (July 1995). "Keyboards Launch Students into Music." *Music Educators Journal* 82(1):29–31.

BOODY, CHARLES G., comp. (1990). *TIPS: Technology for Music Educators.* Reston, VA: Music Educators National Conference.

GREENBERG, MARVIN. (November 1992). "The Ukulele in Your Classroom." *Music Educators Journal* 79(3):43–48.

LINDEMAN, CAROLYNN A. (2000). *PianoLab: An Introduction to Class Piano.* 4th ed. Belmont, CA: Wadsworth.

MCANALLY, ELIZABETH ANN. (June 1998). "Reward Time Can Be Learning Time." *Teaching Music* 5(6):34–35.

MCBRIDE, MICHAEL B., and MARVA BALDWIN. (2000). *Meeting the National Standards with Handbells and Hand Chimes.* Joint publication of Schulmerich Bells, Scarecrow Press, and MENC. Available from MENC.

OLSON, LYNN FREEMAN. (Winter 1987). "Inviting Keyboards into the Magic Circle of Music, Part II: A Song Experience Moves to the Black Keys." *General Music Today* 2(3):3–4.

OLSON, LYNN FREEMAN. (Fall 1987). "Inviting Keyboards into the Magic Circle of Music, Part I." *General Music Today* 1(1):7–9.

WALCZYK, EUGENIA BULAWA. (October 1991). "Kids on Keyboards Learning Music Concepts." *Music Educators Journal* 79(2):40–43.

WALKER, DAVID S. (Fall 1989). "Using Instruments in Today's General Music Classroom: A 'Primer' for the New Teacher; A Review of the Fundamentals for the Experienced Teacher." *General Music Today* 3(1):14–17.

WIGGINS, JACKIE. (May 1993). "Elementary Music with Synthesizers." *Music Educators Journal* 79(9):25–30.

WIGGINS, JACKIE. (1991). *Synthesizers in the Elementary Music Classroom: An Integrated Approach.* Reston, VA: Music Educators National Conference.

See also Resources, Appendix F: "General Music Retailers," "Recorder Books," "Orff-Schulwerk," "Prekindergarten: Moving and Playing Instruments."

MUSIC-MAKING ACTIVITIES: SINGING

Since colonial times, singing has been popular in the United States. Fine choral singing for the church was the main purpose of private "singing schools" in the eighteenth century. Music first became a regular part of the public-school curriculum in 1838, when music educator Lowell Mason persuaded the Boston School Committee that vocal music met their curriculum criteria because it was intellectually, morally, and physically of benefit to students. During the nineteenth and early twentieth centuries, music programs in elementary school consisted mainly of singing, and there were many opportunities to sing in church, home, and community.

Today, it often seems that listening to others sing on TV and recordings may be more common than singing oneself or singing with others in group settings. Partly in response to this situation, MENC: The National Association for Music Education, in cooperation with other music organizations, launched a campaign to help Americans of all ages renew their love of singing. The campaign establishes a song repertoire for singers of all ages to share. Two song books are a result of this effort: *Get America Singing . . . Again!* (43 songs) and *Get America Singing . . . Again!* Volume II (45 songs). Both song books are available from Hal Leonard Corporation, and from general music retailers (see Appendix F).

Photo by Patricia Hackett

Although curricular emphases may change over the years, singing should be an important part of the elementary music curriculum. Along with other music-making activities, such as listening, playing instruments, moving, creating, and reading music, singing can be a means to help children develop music concepts. The material that follows presents information for preservice teachers about children's voices; singing in kindergarten through grade 5; leading and teaching songs; the role of the classroom teacher; and the National Standards in singing for grades K–4.

Children's Voices

A child's singing voice should be clear, open, and light, not heavy, pinched, or forced. Youngsters may need help in distinguishing among their many voices and to find that special voice just for singing. They may not understand how their playground voices are different from their singing voices, or how their speech range voice is different from their higher singing voice—but they soon learn. Youngsters can be amazing imitators, and in fact sometimes misuse their voices by copying the sound of their favorite popular singers. Children also listen to one another, and those who are better singers can be excellent models. Of course, a teacher with a fine singing voice is the best model, but youngsters can also benefit from hearing children sing on the elementary music series recordings that contain many excellent examples (see Appendix C). Most importantly, children should be encouraged to sing solos, as well as to sing with others.

A clear, open, and light voice requires good singing posture for breath control. Breath control is dependent upon a flow of air that is constant and unrestricted. Every child should understand that his/her voice is a special instrument and to use it properly, correct singing posture is important. (See "The Voice," p. 273.) Young singers can vary the dynamics and tempo of a song when they have more control of their breathing and tone (as early as age six or seven) and they enjoy adding all kinds of expression to their songs!

Children often sing a wide range of pitches when making up stories and sing-songs, but their "song range" at ages five and six is about five or six pitches. As their voices develop and their bodies mature, they increase their singing range to 12 or more pitches at age 10.

At every stage of development, children learn that all kinds of music-making involves careful *listening* and in singing, they need to listen to their own and others' voices. Listening carefully helps youngsters improve their vocal quality, their musical expression, and signals they are ready to sing in harmony.

As early as age eight or nine, youngsters can sing simple kinds of harmony, such as ostinatos, partner songs, or an easy round. They will be better able to handle harmony involving two different melodies by the age of 9 or 10. They also learn to follow a conductor, blend their voices with others, and sing with clear diction. By this stage, boy's voices have developed added richness (*resonance*), and some boys' voices may begin to change.

Good singing involves the total child, physically, mentally, and emotionally and is a complex developmental skill. The joy of singing—once established—can remain throughout a lifetime.

Singing in the Elementary Classroom

The stages outlined below describe student singing skills that teachers of particular grade levels may expect to find from kindergarten through grade 5.

It is important for students to hear a model of the desired voice quality: another student's, the teacher, or a carefully selected recording. The elementary school music series contain many suitable examples (see Appendix C). Commercial recordings for children are available, but teachers need to use judgement in choosing performances. The recording's singer and his/her vocal range need to be appropriate for children to use as a model. Over-amplified and "pop" recordings are not recommended.

Because the development of singing is dependent upon maturation and experience, individual variation can be tremendous. Keep in mind that *at each developmental level, most children will need help with in-tune singing and maintaining a light, unforced vocal quality.*

Kindergarten and Grade 1 (Level I model experiences)

The fortunate child enters kindergarten with a rich musical background provided by parents, caregivers and preschool teachers during these critical early years. This lucky child is usually able to sing short songs or song fragments pretty much in tune, and has had many additional music experiences. However, many children will need to learn that singing is different from speaking, shouting, and other vocal expressions. Teachers need to assess what their students can understand and do, and then plan singing experiences accordingly.

For example, dramatizing a story such as "The Three Bears" will focus attention on register by using higher- or lower-pitched voices to depict the different characters. This shows the teacher whether a child can differentiate pitch levels.

To find out if a student can vocally match pitches, the teacher can create short questions using the teasing chant of childhood.

Teacher:

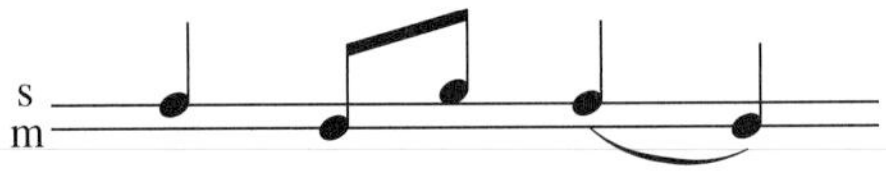

"What is your name?"__

Child:

"My name is Deb - by."

Uncertain singers may use a speaking register (around middle C) or a "head" register (up to about high C), or some combination of the two. If a child cannot match the pitch because it is too high or too low, the teacher can shift to a different range. Often the shift will be to a higher register.

At this age, songs should be short: eight (or 16) measures in length, as in "Riding in the Buggy." (See model experience, p. 118.) Singers need to breathe at the ends of phrases, and at this stage, their lung capacity and breath control are limited.

Songs are easier to learn when they have repeated words or pitches, such as "Matarile" (see p. 144). Kindergarteners and first-graders enjoy simple singing games (see "Sally, Go 'Round the Sun," p. 122). They can also play rhythm instruments such as drums and sticks with their songs, as in "John, the Rabbit" (see p. 130).

The words of the chosen songs need to be age-appropriate. These students enjoy songs, games, and chants about their world of animals, friends, family, neighbors, make-believe, and special occasions. Many suitable materials are found in this text. See "Chants" (Appendix D), and Section Four, "Songs."

Grades 2 and 3 (Level II model experiences)

The majority of Grade 2 children can sing familiar, simple songs in tune, and their voices remain light and fairly thin. (Again, their singing skills and music experiences may differ markedly.) Their singing range expands, extending approximately from B (below middle C) to D or E (above high C). They can sing with more expression because their physical control has improved and they are able to vary the dynamics and hold pitches longer. For example, students hold four-beat notes while using sign language with Model Experience "My Father's House" (p. 170).

Second-graders can manage more complex singing games. (See "Willowbee," p. 162.) They are able to sing or play simple ostinatos (repeated patterns) on barred instruments. This adds harmony parts to a song (as in "Chatter with the Angels," p. 182).

In grade 3, short songs with repetition are still easier to learn and memorize, but phrases can be longer. However, uncertain singers will need more individual help, and need opportunities to sing limited-range songs (four to six pitches). They can also "chime in" when easy song parts repeat. (Choose songs that are not "childish.") Consider the following from Section Four: "Trampin'," "Hey, Lidee!," "Over My Head," "Circle Right," "Old House," and "When the Saints Go Marchin' In."

Some grade 3 students are ready to sing in parts (harmony) if they can sing unison songs accurately and confidently. Teachers can begin with ostinatos, a type of harmony that is either improvised, or derived from part of the song. For example, the "din, din, don" phrase of "Frère Jacques!" becomes an ostinato when sung continuously with the melody. Ostinatos can be created from many rounds, such as "Hey, Ho! Nobody Home" and "Scotland's Burning" (see Section Four).

At this age, children enjoy harmonizing with a *round* (a melody performed by two or more groups entering at different times). Choose a limited-range song the students can sing accurately, such as "Lady, Come," p. 329, or "Sally, Go 'Round the Sun," p. 357. Divide the class into two sections. Decide in advance when each group should start and stop.

Partner songs are different songs that share a similar meter and sequence of chords (see below), and may be sung simultaneously when they are in the same key and tempo. Each of two groups sings a different melody, which makes it easier to "hold on" to one's own part. (Listed songs in this text are indicated by page numbers.)

Partner Songs: "Sandy Land," p. 358, "Bow, Belinda," p. 283, and "Skip to My Lou," p. 366.
Partner Songs: "Old Brass Wagon," p. 345, "Paw-Paw Patch," and "Skip to My Lou," p. 366.
Partner Songs: "The Farmer in the Dell," "Sally, Go 'Round the Sun," p. 357, and "Looby Loo," p. 334.

The world of grade 2 and 3 students expands and they enjoy songs about early America, great adventures, transportation, fantastic and media characters, geography, and songs of other peoples (including easy foreign-language songs).

Grades 4 and 5 (Level III model experiences)

Upper elementary school students may differ greatly in their singing experience and therefore, in their willingness to sing. Girls' voices remain fairly light, and boys' voices gain added richness (*resonance).* Some try to imitate the style and voice quality of favorite singers and need reminders to produce a clear, unforced tone quality. Because of greater physical control, they can handle songs with more challenging rhythms, dynamics, articulation (*legato* and *staccato*), and sustained pitches. This means they can sing with considerable expression and modify dynamics, phrasing, and diction—producing an artistic interpretation. Their range expands from approximately A (below middle C) to F above high C, but teachers will once again find tremendous variation.

Grade 4 and 5 children continue to sing ostinatos, rounds, and partner songs that are more challenging than previously. They may also sing along with a chord-root harmony part as another student plays a barred instrument. See Model Experiences "Hey, Lidee," p. 210, and "Joe Turner Blues," p. 221.

Courtesy of MENC: The National Association for Music Education

Partner songs continue to interest children at this stage, particularly if they are more challenging. The singers will need to *listen* carefully to one another, and work on balancing the two parts and following a conductor. Divide the class into groups based on their part. Place insecure singers close to secure ones—without singling out either type of singer for attention. (Boys are often the most hesitant singers, and are not automatically grouped together.) Because harmony is difficult for many youngsters, it may prove helpful to divide the class into groups of *unequal* size and have the larger group sing harmony. (Listed songs found in this text are indicated by page numbers.)

Partner song: "It's a Small World," p. 321 (combine verse and refrain)
Partner Songs: "Circle Right," p. 288 and "Scotland's Burning," p. 360.
Partner Songs: "Frère Jacques!" p. 299, "Three Blind Mice," and "Row, Row, Row Your Boat."

Uncertain singers need limited-range songs to develop their vocal skills. (*All* students would participate!) Teachers should choose songs with fairly sophisticated texts, since at this age students can be very particular in their song preferences. Following are some suggestions; all are found in this text: "Kum Ba Yah," "Michael, Row the Boat Ashore," "Hey, Lidee," "He's Got the Whole World in His Hands," and "When the Saints Go Marchin' In."

Uncertain singers are frequently successful with the limited-range response parts of African American songs such as "Grizzely Bear," "Sing Hallelu," and "Mary Had a Baby" (see Section Four, "Songs"). Have the students sing (and/or play) ostinatos, as described in Level II, above. Secure singers should sing the limited-range parts, too, so that targeted students are not embarrassed.

The National Standards for Music Education specify that by the end of grade 4 students should be able to sing from memory a varied repertoire of songs representing genres and styles from diverse cultures. This standard corresponds well with children's interests at this level, because they like to sing about history, adventures, other cultures and countries, and to sing selected popular songs. (Teachers will need to preview each song to ensure its suitability.)

Leading and Teaching Songs

Leading a Song

Singing familiar songs can be a great way to start a school year—and each school day! This will allow the teacher to assess the level and quality of students' singing. Begin by selecting a song both teacher and students can sing, and be sure the words are age-appropriate for the grade level—not too "childish," or too "mushy!" A teacher needs to know at least one verse from memory, and the correct pitches and rhythms. When leading songs teachers need to consider some basic techniques, to make the process move quickly and keep the singers on task.

> *Guidelines for Leading a Song*
>
> 1. *Think the first few words of the song to yourself (and the rhythm and pitches, too!).*
> 2. *Sing the starting pitch aloud, using the first word of the song (or a neutral syllable), and have the class sing it.*
> 3. *In the tempo of the song, sing "One, two, ready, sing" and give a clear signal for the singers to start. (Use a hand gesture or nod of the head.)*
> 4. *Keep the singers together by using conducting (or any gesture) that would indicate a steady beat and give them a sense of the timing.*
> 5. *Maintain eye contact with the students at all times; show your enjoyment of the song!*
> 6. *On the song's last note, signal the singers to hold until you give a cutoff gesture.*

Teaching a Song

After selecting an appropriate new song (see "Children's Voices," p. 33), the teacher needs to introduce it—using techniques that will "grab" the students' interest and attention. Some ways to motivate singers include giving background information about the song or telling its story. Physical, more active motivation allows the teacher to actually observe what the students perceive as they listen to the song, and do one of the following:

1. Tap the song's steady beats.
2. Clap hands on the very last word or note.
3. Close eyes and tell what they hear on a song recording (for example, a child singing, a trumpet playing).

4. Watch the teacher's hand and "do as I do." (Teacher uses hand/arm to show pitch levels, rhythms, or both.)
5. Listen for the name of the song's person, place, animal, and so on.
6. Sing (or clap) the repeated parts.
7. Pantomime recurring words of the song as they hear them.
8. Tell (or show with hand levels) how the pitches move on particular song words, such as from a high pitch to a low one.

This "introduction" to the song can be repeated, with students doing the same activity or a different one. Discuss with students what they have discovered.

When children teach songs to one another, they teach by rote: aurally, without music notation. Very often the song is repeated over and over again, until the whole song is learned "by heart." In the classroom, songs can be taught either by rote or by note—and taught as a "whole," or in "parts" (phrases). Each method has a long history. However, many teachers use a combination of all these ideas.

An example of the whole song approach is found in the Model Experience "Hop Up, My Ladies" (p. 186). As students listen to the whole song, they are asked to discover when the melody skips from a lower to a higher pitch. (See the "Focus" question of "Step One," p. 186.) Students use body movements to show these high and low pitches. Note reading is incorporated when students play the middle C to high C skips on a xylophone or resonator bars (see p. 186).

Very often, locating the easy and difficult parts of a song helps in planning a teaching method. Short songs and those with repeated words are obviously easiest to learn. The song's first and last phrases are in prominent positions, and are readily learned. Repeats of words or melodies, or a song's *refrain* (such as "Glory, glory, hallelujah!") make for relatively smooth sailing. However, parts with tricky rhythms, or tongue-twisting words need to be isolated and practiced until they are correct.

The "Wake Me!" model experience (p. 142) involves a song with different words in every phrase. Therefore the strategy is to divide the song into parts (or phrases) and consecutively sing each, having students echo, as shown below. (The teacher has first introduced the song in its entirety.)

Teacher: "Wake me! Shake me!"
Students: "Wake me! Shake me!"
Teacher: "Don't let me sleep too late."
Students: "Don't let me sleep too late."
Teacher: "Gonna get up bright and early in the mornin',"
Students: "Gonna get up bright and early in the mornin',"
Teacher: "Gonna swing on the Golden Gate."
Students: "Gonna swing on the Golden Gate."

Next, the teacher sings two parts, and the students echo:

Teacher: "Wake me! Shake me! Don't let me sleep too late."
Students: "Wake me! Shake me! Don't let me sleep too late."
Teacher: "Gonna get up bright and early in the mornin',
Gonna swing on the Golden Gate."
Students: "Gonna get up bright and early in the mornin',
Gonna swing on the Golden Gate."

Finally, the teacher sings the whole song, and the students echo it. Note reading may be incorporated later.

As soon as they are able, children should sing independently and unaccompanied, without the help of the teacher's voice or recordings. Keys to independent singing include knowing a song well—probably from memory. At that point, singers can concentrate on achieving high levels of accuracy in pitch, rhythm, diction, dynamics, and the other elements that are necessary for an artistic performance. (See National Standards, below.)

The Role of the Classroom Teacher

Some school districts have an elementary music specialist for classroom music instruction and some do not. When a specialist is available, the classroom teacher helps implement the music curriculum and reinforces learning between the specialist's once- or twice-weekly visits. A teacher who sings confidently and accurately can be very effective—and teachers who are vocally insecure can use song recordings. An understanding of children's voices and age-appropriate songs is necessary.

A knowledgeable classroom teacher can make important contributions to a child's singing. For example, correct posture is essential for good singing. A teacher can help youngsters to keep the crown of the head high, as if it were being pulled up by a puppeteer's string. Arms hang easily at their sides, with neck and jaw relaxed. When inhaling, the shoulders should not rise. These guidelines apply whether singers are standing, sitting on the floor, or on a chair (sitting away from the back of the chair). (For more information, see "The Voice," p. 273.)

The classroom teacher is in a perfect position to integrate music across the curriculum and into children's lives. Preschool teachers often provide their own music curriculum, as do some who work with special learners. *The Musical Classroom* provides information about music for prekindergarten children, (p. 97), music for special learners (p. 90), multicultural music (p. 53), and integrating the arts into the curriculum (p. 84). These chapters offer ideas and materials to the classroom teacher who believes that *all children deserve opportunities to learn about music and the other arts.*

Most important, every teacher needs to maintain an encouraging, positive attitude toward the singing efforts of each and every student. Often the nonsinging adult was "turned off" in childhood by the negative attitude or careless remark of a teacher or a parent. Keep in mind that every child with normal hearing and vocal physiology can learn to sing. Singing is a developmental skill that improves with practice, so children must have many opportunities to sing. A sensitive teacher will nurture children's inherent love of song.

National Standards for Music Education

Standard 1. Singing, Alone and with Others, a Varied Repertoire of Music

Standard 1, one of the nine National Standards for Music Education for grades K through 12, specifies what students should know and be able to do in singing. For this content standard, there are five achievement standards.

By the end of grade 4, students will need to

a. sing independently, on pitch and in rhythm, and with appropriate timbre, diction, and posture, and maintain a steady tempo;
b. sing expressively with appropriate dynamics, phrasing, and interpretation;
c. sing from memory a varied repertoire of songs, representing genres and styles from diverse cultures;
d. sing ostinatos, partner songs, and rounds;
e. sing in groups, blending vocal timbres, matching dynamic levels, and responding to the cues of a conductor. (From *National Standards for Arts Education.* Copyright © 1994 by Music Educators National Conference. Used by permission.)

Summary

Singing is a long-established tradition in American schools. It is important because it is a direct and satisfying human expression. Classroom teachers and music specialists are responsible for vocal music instruction for kindergarten through grade 5 students. Teachers need to be knowledgeable about children's voices, implementing a singing program in elementary grades, leading and teaching songs, the role of the classroom teacher in music learning, and the "Singing" standards of the National Standards for Music Education.

Singing is one of the most natural ways for children to make music. The voice is their own personal musical instrument, and most youngsters babble and sing expressively from infancy. Children must have frequent opportunities to continue their singing during school years as they mature physically, emotionally, and socially.

Every day, students need opportunities to sing. Along with other music-making activities, vocal music is important because it aids in the perceptual, cognitive, emotional, and musical development of each child. The voice is a gift that includes the gift of song.

PROJECTS FOR COLLEGE STUDENTS

1. Practice your song leading techniques and lead your class in a song of your choice. Or prepare and teach a song by rote.
2. In small groups, review songs that kindergarten and first-grade children might sing. Each group could select one of these sources: elementary music series; song collections in the materials list that follows; music used in the Kodály method; or songs published by Hap Palmer, Walt Disney, Sesame Street, or the Muppets. Evaluate factors such as vocal range, phrase lengths, and words. Compare your findings and share them the class.
3. In a small group, discuss some of the following issues. Did you sing in school or elsewhere? Do you have a favorite artist or song? Any enthusiasms or fears about singing? If you haven't much interest in singing, why do you think this is so? What implications do your answers have for your work with children? Based on your own experiences and on information in this chapter, make a list of some key things you could (realistically) do to develop children's singing; specify a particular grade level. Compare your ideas and share them with the class.
4. Assess your own singing skills. What areas need improvement? Identify some situations where you can sing, such as university or church groups. Summarize what you know about adult vocal development and singing. (See "The Voice," p. 273.)

REFERENCES

APFELSTADT, HILARY. (Winter 1988). "Setting the Stage for Good Singing." *General Music Today* 2(2):7–8.

GOETZE, MARY, and YOSHIYUKI HORII. (Winter 1989). "A Comparison of the Pitch Accuracy of Group and Individual Singing in Young Children." *Bulletin of the Council for Research in Music Education* 7(1):42–49.

KAZEZ, DANIEL. (April 1985). "The Myth of Tone Deafness." *Music Educators Journal* 71(8):46–47.

KLINGER, RITA, PATRICIA SHEHAN CAMPBELL, and THOMAS GOOLSBY. (Spring 1998). "Approaches to Children's Song Acquisition: Immersion and Phrase-by-Phrase." *Journal of Research in Music Education* 45(1):24–34.

LYON, JOHN T. (September 1993). "Teaching All Students to Sing on Pitch." *Music Educators Journal* 80(2):20–22.

MCGRAW, GWENDOLYN. (1997). *Young Children's Poor Pitch Singing: The Relationship Between Cognitive Processes and Habitual Use of Chest Voice for Singing.* DAI 57A (09) 3866. (University of Georgia, Athens).

MOORHEAD, GLADYS, and DONALD POND. (1978). "Chant." In *Music of Young Children,* vol. 1. Santa Barbara, CA: Pillsbury Foundation for the Advancement of Music Education.

NOLAN, EVONNE, comp. (August 1994). "Sing for Your Skills." *Teaching Music* 2(1):32–33.

MUSIC EDUCATORS NATIONAL CONFERENCE, comp. (1996) *Get America Singing . . . Again!* (2000) and *Get America Singing . . . Again! Volume II.* Milwaukee, WI: Hal Leonard Corporation.

PHILLIPS, KENNETH H. (Spring 1993). "Back to Basics: Teaching Children to Sing." *General Music Today* 6(3):30–32.

PHILLIPS, KENNETH H. (1992). "Research on the Teaching of Singing." In *Handbook of Research on Music Teaching and Learning,* Richard Colwell, ed., 568–576. New York: Schirmer Books.

PHILLIPS, KENNETH H. (1992). *Teaching Kids to Sing.* New York: Schirmer Books.

PHILLIPS, KENNETH H. (Spring 1989). "The Problem Singer: What Does Research Suggest? Part II." *General Music Today* 2(3):24–29.

PHILLIPS, KENNETH H. (Winter 1988). "The Problem Singer: What Does Research Suggest? Part I." *General Music Today* 2(2):19–23, 32.

RUTKOWSKI, JOANNE, and MARIA RUNFOLA, comp. (1997) *TIPS: The Child Voice.* Reston, VA: Music Educators National Conference.

SMITH, JANICE. (Fall 1995). "Using Portfolio Assessment in General Music." *General Music Today* 9(1):8–12.

SZABO, MOIRA (Winter 1999). "Why Don't Boys Sing?" *General Music Today* 12(2):11–14.

WEINBERGER, N. M., comp. (Fall 1996). "Sing, Sing, Sing!" *MuSICA Research Notes* Vol. III(2). www.musica.uci.edu

See also Resources, Appendix F: "Singing," World Music," "Kodály Approach," "Prekindergarten: Singing."

MUSIC-MAKING ACTIVITIES: MOVEMENT

Children are naturally physically active. Because they use their bodies and minds to help them understand their world, movement seems an ideal way for children to explore music. Musicians and music educators have long recognized the importance of movement; for example, two European curricular approaches make extensive use of movement with music: Dalcroze eurhythmics and Orff-Schulwerk (see Chapter V for both). Both approaches demonstrate the close association between movement and playing instruments. All the elements of music can be expressed through movement: melody, rhythm, harmony, form, and expressive qualities. As a result:

- Movement to music aids in understanding music concepts.
- Movement to music contributes to physical development.
- Movement to music develops creativity and imagination through interpretation of music.

Types of Movement

Movement can be categorized into four types: fundamental movements, creative movement, singing games and dances, and patterned rhythms.

Fundamental movements are either locomotor, such as walking and running, or nonlocomotor, such as clapping and finger snapping. Marching is explored in Model Experience "Parade," p. 120, and nonlocomotor movements in "Riding in the Buggy," p. 118. *Creative movements* are interpretive, sometimes rhythmic, sometimes not (see "Elephant" and "Aviary," p. 132). Singing games and dances include children's singing games such as "Sally, Go 'Round the Sun" (see p. 122), and dances such as "Shoo, Fly," p. 158. Patterned rhythms include "Head–Shoulders Baby" Follow-Up 2 (p. 139) with its rhythmic hand movements. All these types of movement need to be frequent experiences, at every grade level.

Guidelines for Movement Activities

1. Provide enough space for free, safe movement.
2. Devise procedures and techniques to help move students from one area to another (such as playing beats on a tambourine or repeating a part of the music that was just heard).
3. Before the whole class dances, demonstrate dance movements with one or two students. This modeling helps because most children learn movements by imitation.
4. Use props such as hats or scarves if students are self-conscious.
5. Balance opportunities for structured and spontaneous responses.
6. Use a variety of music.

Stages in Movement Activities

Practical application of movement and dance is highlighted and integrated into the model experiences for kindergarten through grade 5 classrooms found in Section Two of this text.

Kindergarten and Grade 1 (Level I)

Most children enter kindergarten with locomotor movements well developed; they can slide, jump, sway, and hop. The kindergarten child is ready for simple circle or follow-the-leader dances and games such as "Looby Loo" model experience, p. 126. (Children will benefit by having a pre-marked circle in the dance area, and by having a rest between activities that involve holding hands!) Their small-muscle control needs more refinement through patterned rhythms (such as echo clapping) and through playing rhythm instruments with their own movements. Kindergarteners can creatively move to show high and low pitches for "Elephant" and "Aviary" (Saint-Saëns) (p. 132). First-grade children (try to) adjust their movements to fit the music, but their fast and slow movements may or may not coincide with the fast and slow tempos of Hungarian Dance (Brahms) (p. 124). First graders enjoy structure, as in the circle and partner-swinging dance of "Wishy Washy Wee" (p. 136).

Grades 2 and 3 (Level II)

Grade 2 students can perform an easy folk dance to show the refrain of "Shoo, Fly" (p. 158). The "Willowbee" game (p. 162) involves a line with an arch that dancers pass

Courtesy of MENC: The National Association for Music Education

under—a type appropriate for kindergarten through grade 2 students. Second and third graders continue patterned movements such as clapping and patsching (slapping thighs) to show beat groupings (see "Stars and Stripes Forever" by Sousa, p. 170). Third-grade children devise a creative "dragon dance" for "Song of the Dragon" (p. 184).

Grades 4 and 5 (Level III)

Fourth and fifth graders are interested in playing instruments such as keyboards and resonator bars, especially when the topic is twelve-bar-blues (see "Joe Turner Blues," p. 220). Older students are somewhat hesitant to move with music if they have had few previous experiences, so fairly structured and "adult" activities may be in order.

Fourth graders can show groups of five beats with body rhythms in "Take Five" (p. 226). Movement with "Viennese Musical Clock" (Kodály) (p. 209) involves creating actions of (mechanical) clock figures to fit the music's rondo form. Fifth graders enjoy patterned rhythms such as a creating a snapping and clapping "hand jive" for the "Piffle Rag" (p. 222), in Follow-Up 2. These children are ready to perform more sophisticated Latin American or Native American dances. (See Resources, Appendix F: "Movement," "World Music.")

Summary

Music and movement are important in the total development of the child and aid in developing musical concepts, physical skills, and creativity. Movement develops sequentially, using fundamental and creative movement, singing games and dances, and patterned rhythms employed as students develop. Because movement involves overt physical action, teachers can immediately assess a student's response. Movement-to-music experiences correlate with those in theatre, dance, and physical education, and they all provide for personality development, individual achievement, and physical control. All these extramusical objectives can be met, since they also refine the child's perception and understanding of music.

PROJECTS FOR COLLEGE STUDENTS

1. Learn and teach a singing game or an easy folk dance (with singing).
2. In small groups, discuss your own movement experiences. Did you play singing or rope-skipping games? What movement activities were you introduced to in school? Did you study ballet? Dance to popular music? How are your experiences the same as (or different from) those of today's children? How will this affect your teaching?
3. List one singing game or dance for each grade level (K, 1st, 2nd). Put the songs in sequential order according to the motor and social development necessary for children to successfully learn and enjoy them. Be prepared to justify your sequence.

REFERENCES

FARBER, ANNE. (December 1991). "Speaking the Musical Language." *Music Educators Journal* 78(4):30–34. (improvisation)

HALL, MARIANNE. (August 1999). "Dance in the Music Classroom." *Teaching Music* 6(1):30–1, 46. (list of selected recordings and videos)

HSU, GRACE OON BEE. (May 1981). "Movement and Dance Are Child's Play." *Music Educators Journal* 67(9):42–43.

NEILL, JACK. (January 1990). "Elementary Music Con Moto." *Music Educators Journal* 76(5):29–31.

O'HAGIN, ISABEL B. (Fall 1998). "A Discovery Approach to Movement." *General Music Today* 12(1):16–20.

See also Resources, Appendix F: "Movement," "Dalcroze Eurhythmics," "Prekindergarten: Moving and Playing Instruments."

MUSIC-MAKING ACTIVITIES: CREATING MUSIC

Opportunities to create music should be a part of every classroom music experience, at every grade level. Children are innately creative, and their creativity should be cherished, nurtured, and expanded through quality music experiences. Creative music experiences encourage self-expression (and bolster self-esteem) and place students in the role of composer. Through such experiences, students become more intimately and actively involved with the raw materials of creative work—melody, rhythm, harmony, form, and as a result, they begin to understand how the musical elements interact and interrelate.

Young children often begin their creative expression in music by exploring the world of sound—body and vocal sounds, the special and distinctive sounds of class-

Courtesy of MENC: The National Association for Music Education

room instruments, and the unique sounds created by countless objects of nature and from manufactured articles. Sound stories or instrumental accompaniments to stories and songs are just two ways they can express their creative ideas through sound exploration. For example, students can create a sound story for *Where the Wild Things Are* using classroom instruments to highlight the contrasting parts (p. 157). Such experiences help heighten aural perception and sensitivity.

Children can also experiment with their own variations on familiar songs. They can make up new verses to favorite songs such as "Riding in the Buggy." Composition is involved when they compose and arrange ostinatos to accompany the melody of "Chatter with the Angels" in Model Experience Follow-Up 1 (see p. 183).

Students will better understand musical form if they create or compose their own compositions in two sections (AB), three sections (ABA), or rondo form (ABACADA). Suggestions for such composing experiences are provided in model experiences such as "Carillon" (p. 207).

Children can make up or improvise "answers" to "questions" using clapping or other body sounds. Older students can improvise a steel-drum-type accompaniment to a song such as "Jamaica Farewell" (p. 228) or create an instrumental accompaniment to a haiku poem (p. 204).

Creative experiences of all kinds need to be more widely used in the elementary classroom, because they help children understand how melody, rhythm, harmony, form, and the expressive qualities of music work together. Most of the model experiences in *The Musical Classroom* include opportunities for students to compose and improvise and be "creators," and numerous music software programs encourage and enable students to doodle and invent.

National Standards for Music Education

Standards 3 and 4, two of the nine National Standards for Music Education for grades K through 12, specify what students should know and be able to do in improvising, composing, and arranging music.

Standard 3. Improvising Melodies, Variations, and Accompaniments

For this content standard, there are four achievement standards.

By the end of grade 4, students will need to

a. improvise "answers" in the same style to given rhythmic and melodic phrases;
b. improvise simple rhythmic and melodic ostinato accompaniments;
c. improvise simple rhythmic variations and simple melodic embellishments on familiar melodies;
d. improvise short songs and instrumental pieces using a variety of sound sources, including traditional sounds, nontraditional sounds available in the classroom, body sounds, and sounds produced by electronic means.[2]

Standard 4. Composing and Arranging Music within Specified Guidelines

For this content standard, there are three achievement standards.

By the end of grade 4, students will need to

a. create and arrange music to accompany readings or dramatizations;
b. create and arrange short songs and instrumental pieces within specified guidelines;[3]
c. use a wide variety of sound sources when composing. (From *National Standards for Arts Education.* Copyright © 1994 by Music Educators National Conference. Used by permission.)

Summary

As students create their own compositions and perform them (or help others do so), they experience the roles of conductor, composer, and performer. They become aware of the need to notate their musical sounds so that those sounds can be remembered and can be played by others. Students who manipulate a wide spectrum of sounds may become more accepting of unfamiliar music they encounter. Most of all, they can begin to understand the principles of interaction of all the elements of music: melody, rhythm, harmony, form, and expressive qualities.

PROJECTS FOR COLLEGE STUDENTS

1. In small groups, discuss your own school experiences with creative music activities. How are your experiences the same as (or different from) those of today's children? Prepare a rationale for why creative experiences in music are important to children and share with the rest of your class.
2. Review one of the music software programs to discover how children can create compositions electronically. Check out *Music Ace*'s doodle pad, *Making Music,* or *Juilliard Music Adventure.* (For specifics see Appendix F, "Selected Music Software.")

[2]Traditional sounds include voices, instruments. Nontraditional sounds include paper tearing, pencil tapping. Body sounds include hands clapping, fingers snapping. Sounds produced by electronic means include personal computers and basic MIDI devices, including keyboards, sequencers, synthesizers, and drum machines.

[3]For example, a particular style, form, instrumentation, or compositional technique.

REFERENCES

Balkin, Al. (January 1985). "The Creative Music Classroom." *Music Educators Journal* 71(5):43–46.

"Creative Thinking in Music." (May 1990). Special issue of *Music Educators Journal* 76(9).

"Creativity and Improvisatory Experiences in General Music." (Spring 1995). Special issue of *General Music Today* 8(3). Six articles with teaching strategies for elementary students (as well as special learners); includes one way to use the digital sequencer for composition projects.

"Focus on Composition." (December 1994). Special issue of *Teaching Music* 2(3).

"Focus on Improvisation." (April 1995). Special issue of *Teaching Music* 2(5).

Hamann, Donald L., ed. (1991). *Creativity in the Music Classroom: The Best of MEJ.* Reston, VA: Music Educators National Conference.

"Improvisation." (December 1991). Special issue of *Music Educators Journal* 78(4).

O'Hagin, Isabel B. (1998). "A Discovery Approach to Movement." *General Music Today* 12(1):16–20.

Tait, Malcolm J. (1992). "Whispers, Growls, Screams and Puffs . . . Lead to Composition." In *Elementary General Music: The Best of MEJ,* edited by Betty W. Atterbury. Reston, VA: Music Educators National Conference.

Wiggins, Jackie. (1990). *Composition in the Classroom: A Tool for Teaching.* Reston, VA: Music Educators National Conference.

Wiggins, Jackie. (April 1989). "Composition as a Teaching Tool." *Music Educators Journal* 75(8):36–38.

Wiggins, Jackie. (March 1999). "Teacher Control and Creativity." *Music Educators Journal* 85(5): 30–35, 44.

See also Resources, Appendix F: "World Music," "Orff-*Schulwerk,*" "Selected Music Software," "Integrating Music."

MUSIC-MAKING ACTIVITIES: READING AND NOTATING MUSIC

Learning to read and notate music enables students to be musically literate and independent music learners. Once students acquire basic music-reading skills, they can explore music more fully while in school and carry this knowledge into adult life. Music notation (a visual representation of pitch and duration) has little meaning for children unless it is associated with sound. The aural and visual connection is crucial for understanding that what you see is what you hear.

Children learn to speak a language before they read it. The same process should also guide the teaching of music notation. Children need many opportunities to experience musical sounds, and only when their sensorimotor and perceptual skills are appropriately developed should they be introduced to the visual means for representing those sounds. For example, in the Model Experience "Golden Gate" (p. 116), children first chant and clap steady beats before being introduced to beat lines associated with those sounds. In later follow-up to this experience, they are shown how the beat lines can be transformed into traditional music notation.

Informal notation such as the lines for steady beats or graphic notation for pitch levels is often used for introductory experiences. These informal reading or notating experiences are followed by more formal notation as in the Model Experience "Willowbee" (p. 162). In this Level II strategy, students read from staff notation and play pitches that move by step. Throughout *The Musical Classroom,* notation is presented only when students have an immediate musical need to use it and when it is considered to be developmentally appropriate.

Many teachers have discovered that syllables or related mnemonic devices are most effective in teaching rhythm-reading skills (Shehan, 1987). A number of such systems or approaches exist. For example, in the Kodály approach, syllables such as "ta" for quarter notes and "ta-a" for half notes are spoken as a means to read and perform rhythms accurately. (See p. 72 for a complete listing of the Kodály syllables.) Rhythm syllables used by Edwin E. Gordon (see p. 76) are devised so that the syllable "du" always falls on a downbeat. An example of the Gordon system follows:

Rhythm Syllables used in the Theory of Music Learning

Similarly, sol-fa syllables (*do, re, mi*) or numbers are often used as a tool for pitch reading. For example, a Level III model experience (p. 201) introduces three melodic themes from the selection "Pianists" (*Carnival of the Animals*), using a pegboard and golf tees to "notate" the themes. Students then notate the melodies in staff notation and learn to sing the melodies with syllables, pitch names, and numbers.

As of this writing, the Kodály approach may be the (vocal) reading program found most often in elementary general music classes (see p. 70). The National Standards for Music Education describe standards for music reading that, to be achieved, will require a music curriculum that is considerably more intense and structured than those found in most elementary schools. As with reading language, reading music is a complex skill that is developmental, and that requires regular instruction and continuous reinforcement.

National Standards for Music Education

Standard 5. Reading and Notating Music

Standard 5, one of the nine National Standards for Music Education for grades K through 12, specifies what students should know and be able to do in reading and notating music. For this content standard, there are four achievement standards.

By the end of grade 4, students will need to

a. read whole, half, dotted half, quarter, and eighth notes and rests in 2/4, 3/4, and 4/4 time signatures;
b. use a system (that is, syllables, numbers, or letters) to read simple pitch notation in the treble clef in major keys;
c. identify symbols and traditional terms referring to dynamics, tempo, and articulation and interpret them correctly when performing;
d. use standard symbols to notate meter, rhythm, pitch, and dynamics in simple patterns presented by the teacher. (From *National Standards for Arts Education.* Copyright © 1994 by Music Educators National Conference. Used by permission.)

Summary

The ability to read music is a desirable skill that should be neither neglected nor overemphasized. Certainly, reading and notating music should be incorporated into the school music curriculum when students have acquired a background of music experiences to make meaningful use of such notation. Once students have acquired music literacy skills, students will be able to be independent music learners throughout their lives.

PROJECTS FOR COLLEGE STUDENTS

1. In small groups, examine an elementary music textbook series to learn how and when music-reading skills are introduced; notice if music reading takes place while playing instruments. Discuss and summarize your findings.
2. For the following songs write the rhythmic syllables used in the Kodály approach (p. 73) below the pitches. (Songs are found in Section Four.) "Down Came a Lady," "Lady, Come," "Pease Porridge Hot," "Who's That Yonder?"

REFERENCES

Gordon, Edwin E. (September 1999). "All About Audiation and Music Aptitudes." *Music Educators Journal* 86(2):41–44.

Hodges, Donald A. (1992). "The Acquisition of Music Reading Skills." In *Handbook of Research on Music Teaching and Learning,* edited by Richard Colwell, 466. New York: Schirmer Books.

Jordon-DeCarbo, Joyce. (September 1997). "A Sound-to-Symbol Approach to Learning Music." *Music Educators Journal* 84(2):34–37, 54.

Junda, Mary Ellen. (September 1994). "Developing Readiness for Music Reading." *Music Educators Journal* 81(2):37–41.

O'Brien, James P. (May 1974). "Teach the Principles of Notation, Not Just the Symbols." *Music Educators Journal* 60(9):38.

Shehan, Patricia K. (Spring 1987). "Effects of Rote Versus Note Presentations on Rhythm Learning and Retention." *Journal of Research in Music Education* 35:117–126.

See also Resources, Appendix F: "Kodály Approach," "Recorder Books," "Selected Music Software."

CHAPTER SUMMARY

Elementary school children learn about music as they become actively engaged in music making. Music-making activities such as listening, playing instruments, singing, movement, creating music, and reading music provide the modes for students to express themselves musically. These activities should never be ends in themselves but should serve as the means for students to demonstrate their conceptual understandings about music and to express their own musicality.

IV
The World of Music

Some profound changes in American society have taken place in recent decades. These include social and educational reform movements, and rapid developments in technology and electronic media. As early as the 1960s, music educators reexamined their long-held beliefs and practices in response to the findings of several important music conferences. Among these, the Yale Seminar (1962) and the Tanglewood Symposium (1967) shared a common concern: music used in school programs was limited in scope and poor in quality. The great classics of Western music were seldom included (e.g., music of Bach, Mozart) and certain styles were almost totally neglected (Palisca, 1964). The Tanglewood Symposium recommended that "music of all periods, styles, forms, and cultures belongs in the curriculum" (Choate, 1968:139). Some additional recent developments that have influenced music education are described in Chapter Five, "Approaches to Curriculum." The recent Vision 2020 declaration of MENC: The National Association for Music Education has reaffirmed the goal of music education to make a place for all music in the curriculum, "to insure that the best of the Western art tradition and other musical traditions are transmitted to future generations" (in Hinckley, 2000:23).

In recent years, the music curriculum has greatly expanded in scope and become more comprehensive, especially in elementary and middle school general music. Less emphasis is placed on rote learning, and more on composition and improvisation. (This is in addition to singing, playing instruments, listening, movement, and reading music.) The music curriculum of the twenty-first century should be eclectic, and include Western art music, world music, jazz, popular music, and music by both men and women composers. These inclusions correspond to curriculum trends apparent in ethnic studies and integrative education, and are directly reflected in the National Standards for Music Education, Standard 9 "Understanding Music in Relation to History and Culture," and Standard 7, "Evaluating Music and Music Performances" (see pp. 62–63).

Teachers of music (and the other arts) need to consider artistic and cultural equity when making choices for an already crowded curriculum.

Specific information about Western art music, world music, jazz, women in music, and popular music; their place in the curriculum; instructional approaches; and references follows.

WESTERN ART MUSIC

"Classical music" is a popular term for art music of Western civilization, usually created by a trained composer. Western art music is the music of Mozart and Vivaldi, or of Richard Strauss and Philip Glass, and certainly should be an important part of the school curriculum.

Most children enter the elementary classroom with a strong preference for familiar music—and either a neutral or a negative attitude about Western art music. Students with a background of music at home and school show less influence of peers and media in their musical preferences (O'Brien, 1986:28). One study found that preference levels for classical music "assume a gentle U-shaped curve corresponding to grade level, with higher preferences in the lowest grades and again at college level" (LeBlanc et al., 1996:55–56).

Teachers and musicians throughout the United States are working together to bring more children (and adults) in touch with Western art music. Orchestras in major cities offer events and/or a music education Web site, as does New York City's famous Carnegie Hall. Cable channel VH1 features a variety of special music programs in support of music education that may be videotaped for use in classrooms. (See Resources, Appendix F, "Addresses.") The regular inclusion of Western art music in the elementary school curriculum, along with activities such as those described, will help students get in touch with the beauty and excitement of classical music.

Positive attitudes that lead to the enjoyment of Western art music can be systematically developed. Teachers need to use techniques based on the research about listening, student attitudes, and behavior that is presented below. It helps tremendously when knowledgeable teachers are enthusiastic and show their own enjoyment of the music!

Approaches to Teaching Western Art Music

A number of specific, research-based techniques and strategies to develop positive attitudes toward classical music are summarized by O'Brien (1986) and follow. Teachers need to repeat the music (three to eight times) at spaced intervals—although too many repetitions can have a negative effect on preference (Merrion, 1989:25). They should also match the complexity of the piece to the students' musical development; for example, shorter, livelier music is better for inexperienced listeners. Most students need directed experiences so that their listening is focused, especially if they are musically inexperienced.

Teachers should (initially), avoid introducing music with a very high intensity level, a "jumpy" melody, or dissonant harmonies, because such music may produce a negative response. In beginning experiences, students respond positively to music with a quick tempo, a variety of dynamic levels, driving rhythm, and melodic repeats. (Examples would be Grieg's "In the Hall of the Mountain King" and Ravel's *Bolero.*) Students prefer orchestral music to vocal art music, and when vocal music is played, it should have minimal vibrato (Hedden, 1990). A curriculum could begin with "liked elements" first and then progress to music with "disliked elements." A sequence might be fast instrumentals, slow instrumentals, fast vocals, and then slow vocals.

Many model experiences in this text make use of Western art music. In general, the Level I lessons use shorter, "brighter" pieces with a quick tempo, such as "Ballet of the Unhatched Chicks" (Mussorgsky) (p. 128). "Chinese Dance," a short selection from Tchaikovsky's *Nutcracker Suite,* is used in a Level II model experience (p. 160), as is the longer "Jesu, Joy of Man's Desiring" (J. S. Bach) (p. 176). More complex compositions are included in Level III, such as Beethoven's "Archduke" Piano Trio (p. 230). Each model experience focuses on the elements of music, and the students' attention is specifically directed to a music element, for example, melody, timbre, or form. Elementary music series also include lessons using classical pieces, and their approach, choice of music, and sequence are similar to those of *The Musical Classroom.*

Teacher Behaviors That Establish Positive Attitudes toward Western Art Music

1. *Maintain a high energy level while presenting the music.*
2. *Verbalize own liking for the music ("It's so exciting the way the drums . . .").*
3. *Show approval and enthusiasm for students' efforts ("You were really listening to that trumpet!").*
4. *Give full attention to the music and maintain eye contact with students.*

Other approaches introduce Western art music by playing recordings (without specific conceptual goals) during snack or nap time, artwork, or movement, or have students create mental images while listening (Giles, Hayes, and Grant, 1993). Some music educators suggest using classical music with a familiar melody, such as Rossini's William Tell Overture, with its "Lone Ranger" theme, the "Elvira Madigan" movie theme (Mozart), and Vaughan Williams's Fantasia on Greensleeves.

Summary

A truly comprehensive curriculum needs to include Western art music to bring students in touch with one of the highest artistic expressions of Western civilization. A teacher's enthusiasm—and carefully chosen music—can sometimes work miracles!

PROJECTS FOR COLLEGE STUDENTS

1. In small groups, discuss and report your answers to the following questions. Did you hear Western art music in school or elsewhere? Do you have a favorite classical composer or piece, and how often have you listened to it? If you don't respond to Western art music, why do you think this is so? What implications do your answers have for your work with children?
2. Based on your own experience and on information in this chapter, make a short list of some key things you could do to develop positive attitudes toward classical music in children of different ages. Share your lists with others.

REFERENCES

BURNS, KIMBERLY. (Spring 1995). "Teaching Music Listening Skills." *General Music Today* 8(3):31–32.

GILES, MARTHA M., NANCY HAYES, and LAURA GRANT. (Spring 1993). "The Effects of Imagery on Listening Skills." *General Music Today* 6(3):15–18.

HEDDEN, STEVEN K. (December 1990). "What Have We Learned about Building Student Interest?" *Music Educators Journal* 77(4):33–37.

HINCKLEY, JUNE. (March 2000). "Why Vision 2020?" *Music Educators Journal* 86(5):21–24, 66.

LeBlanc, A., W. L. Sims, C. Siivola, and M. Obert. (Spring 1996). "Music Style Preferences of Different Age Listeners." *Journal of Research in Music Education,* 44:49–59.

Merrion, Margaret, ed. (1989). *What Works: Instructional Strategies for Music Education.* Reston, VA: Music Educators National Conference. Teaching strategies based on specific research findings.

O'Brien, Wanda. (March 1986). "Opening Doors: Forming Positive Attitudes Toward Classical Music." *Music Educators Journal* 72(7):25–31.

Paxcia-Bibbins, Nancy. (Spring 1998). "Listening with a Whole Mind: Holistic Learning in the Music Classroom." *General Music Today* 11(3):11–13.

Refer to "Listening," Chapter Three. Also see Resources, Appendix F, "Western Art Music," "Listening," "Prekindergarten: Listening."

WORLD MUSIC

Music is a vital part of every human society. Those who study world music and its place in culture (ethnomusicologists) have found an astonishing variety of music in every part of the globe. Ethnomusicology has shown us that there is no universal language of music but a multiplicity of musical languages—and each expresses the aesthetic and social principles of its culture. World music must be included in the school curriculum so that students understand that music of Western civilization is just one of the musical languages in our global village.

The many styles of world music include music of America's ethnic groups (e.g., Slavic, Native American, Irish) and of regions such as the Middle East, Japan, and India. Each type of music has a history and a repertoire of pieces; each has its own special approach to composition, performance, and use of instruments; and each preserves its tradition for future generations—even though styles are changing and mixing continuously (acculturation).

Steel drums of Trinidad

In general, the music of each region has a distinctive sound. For example, the music of Sub-Saharan Africa sounds different from that of Southeast Asia. Regions can include several different cultures and types of music, just as in the United States there is music of many cultures. Each culture's music is varied, too, so that Native Americans have several types of music (e.g., Navajo and Sioux). American musicians who perform their own traditional music (such as Greek) may also enjoy many other styles of music—from Country and Western to Top 40 to Western art music. Because of technology, an incredible variety of musical styles is known and enjoyed worldwide.

Over the past century, some music educators introduced world folk song and instruments of world music into the elementary general music curriculum. But before the social revolution of the 1960s, folk songs of English-speaking peoples were the main ingredients of general music. The conferences at Yale University (1962), Tanglewood (1967), and the Vision 2020 symposium (2000) spurred music educators to include world music in the curriculum, as did the Civil Rights Act of 1964 and Public Law 92-318 of 1972. In the introduction to the National Standards for Arts Education (1994) the following point is made about cultural diversity and the arts:

> The cultural diversity of America is a vast resource for arts education and should be used to help students understand themselves and others. The visual, traditional, and performing arts provide a variety of lenses for examining the cultures and artistic contributions of our nation and others around the world. Students should learn that each art form has its own characteristics and makes its distinctive contributions, that each has its own history and heroes. . . . Subject matter from diverse historical periods, styles, forms, and cultures should be used to develop basic knowledge and skills in the various art disciplines. (CNAEA: 1994:13–14)

The elementary curriculum of the twenty-first century includes many types of world music. Teachers can present and compare music from different ethnic groups, resulting in a multicultural music curriculum.

The practical use of world music in the elementary classroom raises many questions for teachers, such as:

1. How can teachers learn about world music?
2. What is the American ethnic mix?
3. Which style(s) of world music should be introduced?
4. What are the goals and benefits of a multicultural music curriculum?
5. Which teaching approaches are possible?
6. What resources for culturally authentic music are available?

How Can Teachers Learn about World Music?

Music specialists and classroom teachers are equally important in a multicultural music curriculum, and both need to learn about the cultural context of world music—how it is interrelated with dance, drama, ritual, and visual elements (Jordan, 1992:739). The music specialist understands the structure and concepts of music and can help develop objectives, create singing and playing activities, and locate appropriate materials. The classroom teacher plays an important role because he or she knows the curriculum and the students and how each child can benefit from a multicultural music program. The classroom teacher also may be more connected to the community of students, school, and parents.

Both classroom teachers and music specialists need to learn more about the different styles of world music. Through parents, teachers might locate ethnic musicians in the community who are willing to share their culture, perform, and even give music lessons. Many universities offer courses or summer workshops in world music that are planned especially for teachers. Song books with cultural information (often with re-

Student (left) with her veena teacher in Madras, India. Courtesy of James W. Hackett.

cordings) are available from general music retailers, and many professional materials such as those from MENC: The National Association for Music Education, offer substantive information. What's important is for all teachers to take the first step!

What Is the American Ethnic Mix?

Every American is "ethnic"—including European Americans. The ethnic character of the United States is continually altered by immigration. Remarkable changes occurred after the Immigration Reform Act of 1965, and the United States census of 1990 shows that people of color make up about 20 percent of the general population.

1990 POPULATION AND PERCENT DISTRIBUTION FOR THE UNITED STATES BY RACE AND HISPANIC ORIGIN

	NUMBER	PERCENTAGE
White	199,686,070	80.3
African American	29,986,060	12.1
Hispanic origin	22,354,059	9.0
Other race	9,804,847	3.9
Asian or Pacific Islander	7,273,662	2.9
American Indian, Eskimo, Aleut	1,959,234	0.8
Total:	248,709,873	

Almost 50 percent of Asian and Hispanic-origin immigrants live in Illinois, New York, Florida, Texas, and California, often within particular metropolitan areas. In those regions, children of color make up a large percentage of the student population. California's population of students of color exceeded that of white students in 1989. By the year 2020, children of color will make up about 46 percent of the nation's student population (Banks, 1997:5), and percentages in some regions may be far larger. These demographics make the multicultural curriculum an imperative, since nearly all teachers will work with students from diverse ethnic, cultural, and racial backgrounds

Boy with Indonesian drums (Kendhang). © Copyright by William M. Anderson, Center for the Study of World Musics, Kent State University. Used by permission of the author.

sometime during their career. Teachers will need new knowledge, skills, and attitudes for the multicultural curriculum, and for the multicultural music curriculum.

Which Style(s) of World Music Should Be Introduced?

The cultures represented in your classroom and in your community can be the basis for choosing the particular world music(s) to emphasize in the curriculum. In a classroom with many Vietnamese and Mexican American children, the music of those two cultures could be studied—as found in the United States and, if possible, in the country of origin. For example, a teacher might introduce a Mexican American song during Hispanic Heritage Month in September. A next step could be to explore music and its place in culture, both in the United States and in Mexico. Students will discover that the music of Mexican Americans is similar to that of Mexico but also different from it. And Mexico's music has roots in both Mexican Indian and Spanish music. Vietnamese music could be similarly examined. Studying the two cultures in depth would add perspective to the total program, which would include other music topics and activities.

What Are the Goals and Benefits of a Multicultural Curriculum?

The multicultural music curriculum can have both musical and nonmusical goals. The nonmusical goals of a music curriculum are similar to social science goals. Both share humanistic goals to promote self-awareness and self-esteem, build empathy for others, and encourage respect for the dignity of all human beings. In exploring world music,

Musical Goals for a Multicultural Curriculum

1. *Students experience a wide palette of musical sounds.*
2. *Students understand that there are many different but equally logical (and valid) ways of making music.*
3. *Students learn that many cultures have music as sophisticated as the student's own.*
4. *Students become polymusical, by performing, creating, and composing music in different styles. (Anderson and Campbell, 1996:2–4)*

children also (ideally) explore a people's customs, history, geography, and beliefs; combining music with social studies enriches both subjects. Such experiences align with social and global rationales for including world music in the schools (Fung, 1995).

Teachers observe many benefits from a multicultural music curriculum. Anecdotal reports indicate that multicultural music instruction *raises self-esteem*; *expands cultural awareness* of students from different backgrounds; *builds sensitivity toward classmates;* and helps children with a different primary language *learn the patterns of English, build vocabulary,* and *aids in memorization and sequencing* (Sousa, 1992:26). More research, however, is needed to confirm these findings, because studies of multicultural music programs have so far validated mostly musical outcomes, not extramusical ones (Campbell, 1992:27).

Instructional goals and objectives need to be established for both music and integrated subjects in a multicultural curriculum. The musical goals of such a curriculum are to help children learn about the language of music.

Musical goals are the basis for the model experiences for kindergarten through grade 5 classrooms, found in Section Two of this text. Practical applications of integrated learning (e.g., social studies, dance) are presented and highlighted in activities that follow the model experiences. Integrated learning is also presented in Chapter IV (pp. 84–90), along with practical applications from model experiences.

Which Teaching Approaches Are Possible?

Teachers can implement musical goals by focusing on music concepts, performance, listening, integrated learning, or a combination of these (Anderson and Campbell, 1989:5–6). In this text, music concepts serve as the focus for all music-learning experiences, and the multicultural model experiences make use of performance and focused listening as well.

For example, a music concept is explored in "Corn Grinding Song" (p. 214), when students focus on a Navajo melody that moves high and low, and repeats. This is expanded to concepts about vocal timbre and rhythm, suggested in a follow-up activity, and students notice details such as pulsation in the singer's voice. Greater understanding results when the same (and different) music concepts are discovered in other music, such as a Navajo "Yei Be Chai" song (see "Other Music," p. 238). Through the music of Native Americans, students can learn that there are different but equally logical (and valid) ways of making music.

Performance involves music-making activities such as singing, playing, and movement. Singing the "Song of the Dragon" is an example, and as a follow-up activity, the students play percussion instruments, creating a Chinese-style folk ensemble (see p. 185). These are first steps in becoming polymusical.

Focused listening is necessary when students explore vibrating objects and identify two different African instruments in the Model Experience "Anaguta Drums" (p. 140). This helps youngsters discover a wider palette of musical sounds. Focused listening to world music instruments is also important as students listen to and compare the music of North Africa, Vietnam, and Bali (p. 216). In this cross-cultural experience, they discover music as sophisticated as their own.

What Resources for Culturally Authentic Music Are Available?

Ethnic musicians in the community are a valuable resource, and they are often delighted to perform for students and introduce their culture. Culturally authentic recordings suitable for the classroom are becoming more readily available than ever before—and may even be previewed through some online vendors.

The elementary music series provide a comprehensive basis for a general music curriculum, although teachers may wish to add supplementary world music materials. Kindergarten through grade 5 series contain many folk song recordings, but only a few use indigenous language and instruments. Teachers can also explore publications and sound recordings from MENC: The National Association for Music Education, World Music Press, Smithsonian Folkways Records, and general music retailers. Instruments of world music, such as African bells and Mexican maracas, are available from a number of sources (see Appendix F: "General Music Retailers").

Summary

There are many musical languages in our global village. America's ethnic mix makes a multicultural music curriculum a necessity, and teachers need new knowledge and skills to implement such a curriculum. Through world music, children can benefit in many musical and nonmusical ways as they explore their own and others' cultural heritage. The musical goals of a multicultural curriculum are to help students understand the language of music through exploring music concepts, performance, playing instruments, and integrated learning. Music is the perfect medium to build a cultural bridge in American classrooms.

PROJECTS FOR COLLEGE STUDENTS

1. Write a rationale for the importance of world music in the curriculum. Include the musical reasons as well as the nonmusical ones.
2. Observe (either individually or in pairs) an elementary school music class that includes students from a variety of backgrounds. How are the children exploring the four musical goals described in this chapter? Suggest two ways in which these goals might be more effectively implemented with these children.

REFERENCES

ANDERSON, WILLIAM M., and PATRICIA SHEHAN CAMPBELL, eds. (1996). *Multicultural Perspectives in Music Education.* 2d ed. Reston, VA: Music Educators National Conference. Book; two audio CDs available.

ANDERSON, WILLIAM M., and MARVELENE MOORE, eds. (1997). *Making Connections: Multicultural Music and the National Standards.* Reston, VA: Music Educators National Conference. Book; audio CD available.

BANKS, JAMES A. (1997). *Teaching Strategies for Ethnic Studies.* 6th ed. Boston: Allyn & Bacon.

CAMPBELL, PATRICIA SHEHAN. (1996). *Music in Cultural Context: Eight Views on World Music Education.* Reston, VA: Music Educators National Conference. Book.

CAMPBELL, PATRICIA SHEHAN. (Spring 1992). "Research for Teaching Music from a Multicultural Perspective." *General Music Today* 5(3):26–28.

CONSORTIUM OF NATIONAL ARTS EDUCATION ASSOCIATIONS. (1994). *National Standards for Arts Education.* Reston, VA: Music Educators National Conference, 13–14.

FUNG, C. VICTOR. (July 1995). "Rationales for Teaching World Musics." *Music Educators Journal* 82(2):36–40.

GOODKIN, DOUG. (July 1994). "Diverse Approaches to Multicultural Music." *Music Educators Journal* 81(1):39–43.

JORDAN, JOYCE. (1992). "Multicultural Music in a Pluralistic Society." In *Handbook of Research on Music Teaching and Learning,* Richard Cowell, ed. New York: Schirmer Books.

MCCULLOUGH-BRABSON, ELLEN. (November 1990). "Instruments from Around the World: Hands-on Experiences." *Music Educators Journal* 77(3):46–50.

SARRAZIN, NATALIE. (January 1995). "Exploring Aesthetics: Focus on Native Americans." *Music Educators Journal* 81(4):33–36.

SOUSA, MARILYN. (Fall 1992). "What Music Makes the Difference: Multicultural Music." *Journal of Music Teacher Education* 2(1):24–28.

TITON, J. T., L. FUJIE, D.P. MCALLESTER, M. SLOBIN, and D. LOCKE, contributors. (1996). *Worlds of Music.* 3rd ed. New York: Simon & Schuster; ISBN 002872612X. Book; audio CD or cassette available.

VOLK, TERESA M. (1997). *Music, Education, and Multiculturalism: Foundations and Principles.* Oxford University Press.

WILCOX, ELLA, comp. (February 1995). "Open a New Door in Preschool Music." *Teaching Music* 2(4):38–39.

Also see Resources, Appendix F: "World Music," "Integrating Music," "General Music Retailers."

JAZZ

One of America's original art forms, jazz was developed by African Americans at the beginning of the twentieth century. Spirituals, blues, and ragtime were followed by Dixieland jazz, which became the popular music of the 1920s. This evolved into the (white) big-band swing that dominated the pop scene in the 1930s and 1940s. After World War II, Dizzy Gillespie and Charlie Parker were leaders in developing a new jazz style called bebop. Since the 1950s, jazz has become more complex and technically challenging for the listener. The many modern jazz styles include bebop, cool, free, and fusion. Even though it is not a commercially popular style, modern jazz is widely appreciated, as are the singable tunes and lively "four-beat" rhythms of early jazz and swing. Ironically, jazz is little known to some African American students.

Most elementary music programs do not include jazz as part of the curriculum. Current elementary music books contain a few jazz lessons or recordings and few opportunities for improvisation. However, jazz can and should be introduced into the elementary classroom. Jazz can be explored within the framework of music elements (such as melody, rhythm, and form) and music-making activities. For example, the twelve-bar blues is presented in the Model Experience "Joe Turner Blues" (p. 220), along with a young people's bibliography of African American musicians such as Duke Ellington and Louis Armstrong. Also included are guidelines for improvising melodic phrases in the blues scale and creating original blues lyrics. Different jazz styles are found in "Diga Diga Doo" (popularized by the Duke Ellington band) (p. 224), "Piffle Rag" (p. 222), and "Take Five," the Dave Brubeck Quartet's modern jazz composition (p. 226). These four model experiences can serve as the basis for a jazz unit for fourth and fifth graders. In addition, jazz pieces are listed throughout the "Other Music" suggestions of the model experiences. All of the above activities explore the main characteristics of jazz—syncopated rhythms and improvisation—so that students can get in touch with this exciting and distinctive American creation.

REFERENCES

BUTTRAM, JOE B. (Winter 1993). "The Blues: Roots of a Musical Legacy." *General Music Today* 6(2):5–10.

LUMM, GEORGE. (Fall 1994). "Introducing Jazz Improvisation in General Music." *General Music Today* 8(1):13–17.

MILLER, SAMUEL D. (February 1984). "Lessons in the Blues." *Music Educators Journal* 70(6):39–40.

SALES, GROVER. (1992). *Jazz: America's Classical Music.* New York: DaCapo Press.

THOMAS, WILLIE. (Winter 1993). "Jazz Everyone?" *General Music Today* 6(2):39–41.

ZENDT, LAURIE. (Winter 1993). "Jazzin' Up General Music." *General Music Today* 6(2):19–22.

See also Resources, Appendix F: "Jazz."

WOMEN IN MUSIC

Women have been active as musicians from earliest times. Many gained considerable recognition during their lifetimes: French composer-harpsichordist Elisabeth Claude Jacquet de la Guerre (1666 or 1667–1729), German composer-pianist Clara Wieck Schumann (1819–1896), French conductor-composer Nadia Boulanger (1887–1979), and American singer Marian Anderson (1902–1993). Others were probably better known for their nonmusical achievements. For example, Hildegard von Bingen, a nun of the Middle Ages, was well known for her mysticism and writings on religious visions, medicine, and physics, but not for her extraordinary chants (lyrical poems set to music). Hildegard would undoubtedly be shocked to learn that her chants are being listened to today by thousands and many record stores have a sizable collection of her recorded chants.

Until recently, the history of women in music was not included in the school curriculum, let alone the college curriculum. A curriculum change is needed, beginning as early as the elementary grades. The story of women in music must be shared. Students should be introduced to music by women just as they are introduced to music of various historical periods, styles, mediums, and cultures. And this introduction, at the elementary school level, should be presented in the same way other music is presented—through an integrative approach in the regular classroom lessons (Lindeman, 1992:57).

Finding materials to help in this integration may be challenging. Fortunately, after decades of ignoring historical women musicians, elementary music series are finally featuring some: See *Share the Music* (2000, Macmillan/McGraw-Hill) and *The Music Connection* (2000, Silver Burdett Ginn-Scott Foresman) series. However, teachers will need to locate books, photographs, recordings, and other materials to tell the complete story.

In *The Musical Classroom,* a composition by Gladys Yelvington (American, 1891–1950) is used to teach sectional form in the Model Experience "Piffle Rag" (p. 222). Libby Larsen's "Four on the Floor" is one of the selections featured in the model experience on p. 230. Music by women composers is also included in the lists of other music found in the model experiences. Teachers should also include other activities about women musicians in their classrooms. For example, a composer-of-the-month project (or conductor- or musician-of-the-month) could be initiated or bulletin

Peanuts reprinted by permission of United Features Syndicate, Inc.

board displays created (especially during March, Women's History Month). With a combination of classroom activities and guest visits by women musicians, the complete story of women in music can be shared with students.

REFERENCES

JEZIC, DIANE. (1988). *Women Composers: The Lost Tradition Found,* 2d ed. Book and two audio cassettes available from Leonarda Productions, Inc. (P.O. Box 1736, New York, NY 10025-1559).

KENDALL, CATHERINE W. (1993). *Stories of Women Composers for Young Musicians.* Shar Products Co.; ISBN 096108782X.

KOZA, JULIA EKLUND. (March 1992). "Picture This: Sex Equity in Textbook Illustrations." *Music Educators Journal* 78(7):28–33.

LINDEMAN, CAROLYNN A. (March 1997). "Hildegard Who?" in FrontLines Column. *Music Educators Journal* 83 (5): 4–5, 46.

LINDEMAN, CAROLYNN A. (1992). "Teaching about Women Musicians: Elementary Classroom Strategies." *Music Educators Journal* 78(7):56–59.

LINDEMAN, CAROLYNN A., ed. (1985). *Women Composers of Ragtime.* Bryn Mawr, PA: Theodore Presser. Biographies and music.

The Norton/Grove Dictionary of Women Composers. (1995). New York: W. W. Norton.

NELSON, PAULA D. (August 1999). "A Woman's Place Is in Music History." *Teaching Music* 7(1):36–38.

PENDLE, KARIN, ed. (1991). *Women and Music: A History.* Bloomington: Indiana University Press.

See also Resources, Appendix F: "Women in Music."

POPULAR MUSIC

Popular music includes Broadway musicals, soul, rock, country, rap, hip-hop, and others. Until the 1940s and 1950s, music educators considered popular music of little worth and actually "dangerous" (Mark, 1996:204). Although educators continue to argue about its merits, popular music has become the main choice of students as early as third or fourth grade (Merrion, 1989:23). Recent research shows that fifth graders prefer "easy listening" and popular music. The same research shows students also enjoy (equally) rock, Dixieland, ragtime, band march music, country/bluegrass, and electronic music (Merrion, 1989:23). Most of these styles are nominally represented in elementary music series, especially older pop songs and Broadway show tunes, but there are few rock or Top 40 songs. This is because copyright fees are expensive, lyrics are inappropriate, or the music won't "sound like the record" (meaning it is not in its original form). In fact, these are the same reasons that pop music is not included in this text.

When suitable materials are available, popular music should be presented in a way that has musical integrity—and not just as a social or psychological support for students (Cutietta, 1991:27). This means a focus on the elements of music (e.g., harmony and rhythm) and on the special sound (timbre) of pop instruments (Pembrook, 1991:31). From this perspective, popular music can fit into the curriculum on the same basis as Western art music, world music, and jazz.

REFERENCES

CUTIETTA, ROBERT A. (April 1991). "Popular Music: An Ongoing Challenge." *Music Educators Journal* 77(8):26–29.

CUTIETTA, ROBERT A. (April 1985). "Using Rock Videos to Your Advantage." *Music Educators Journal* 77(6):47–49.

MARK, MICHAEL L. (1996). *Contemporary Music Education.* 3rd ed. New York: Schirmer Books.

MERRION, MARGARET, ed. (1989). *What Works: Instructional Strategies for Music Education.* Reston, VA: Music Educators National Conference. Teaching strategies based on specific research findings.

PEMBROOK, RANDALL G. (April 1991). "Exploring the Musical Side of Pop." *Music Educators Journal* 77(8):30–34.

Popular Music Resources

Pop Hits Listening Guides. Five issues during the school year. Teacher-only pages, student worksheets (reproducible), recording (of a current pop hit). Grades 5–12. Available from Pop Hits Publishing, 4745 Poplar Ave., Ste. 212, Memphis, TN 38227; (888)844-7454; fax (901)820-0027; www.pophitspublishing.com/.

Music . . . Alive. Selections from classical to jazz to current pop and rock. Grades 6–12; 5 issues during the school year; student magazines, one teacher's guide, one audio CD or cassette; printed music of at least one hit song in each issue. Cherry Lane Magazines, P.O. Box 430, Port Chester, NY 10573.

National Standards for Music Education

Standard 9. Understanding Music in Relation to History and Culture

Standard 9, one of the nine National Standards for Music Education for grades K through 12, specifies what students should know and be able to do in understanding music in relation to history and culture. For this content standard, there are five achievement standards.

By the end of grade 4, students will need to

a. identify by genre or style aural examples of music from various historical periods and cultures;
b. describe in simple terms how elements of music are used in music examples from various cultures of the world;
c. identify various uses of music in their daily experiences and describe characteristics that make certain music suitable for each use;
d. identify and describe roles of musicians[1] in various music settings and cultures;
e. demonstrate audience behavior appropriate for the context and style of music performed.

[1]For example, orchestra conductor, folk singer, church organist.

Standard 7. Evaluating Music and Music Performances

Standard 7, one of the nine National Standards for Music Education for grades K through 12, specifies what students should know and be able to do in evaluating music and music performances. For this content standard, there are two achievement standards.

By the end of grade 4, students will need to

a. devise criteria for evaluating performances and compositions;

b. explain, using appropriate music terminology, their personal preferences for specific musical works and styles. (From *National Standards for Arts Education.* Copyright © 1994 by Music Educators National Conference. Used by permission.)

CHAPTER SUMMARY

Elementary music programs should include music of all styles and periods—Western art music, world music, jazz, music of women composers, and popular music. Both students and teachers need to expand their knowledge of the many styles of music. A teaching approach based on conceptual music learning develops musical goals as well as nonmusical ones. Using what we know about conceptual learning and about listening to music, teachers can help students discover that which is the most enduring and powerful within our entire world of music.

PROJECT FOR COLLEGE STUDENTS

Review an elementary music textbook (and recordings) for a selected grade level to learn which styles of music are introduced. Make a list summarizing your findings.

CHAPTER REFERENCES

Choate, Robert A., ed. (1968). *Documentary Report of the Tanglewood Symposium.* Washington, DC: Music Educators National Conference.

Hinckley, June. (March 2000). "Why Vision 2020?" *Music Educators Journal* 86(5):21–24, 66.

Palisca, Claude V. (1964). *Music in Our Schools: A Search for Improvement.* Report of the Yale Seminar on Music Education. Washington, DC: U.S. Department of Health, Education and Welfare, Office of Education. OE-33033, Bulletin 1964, no. 28.

V
Approaches to Curriculum

Various curricular approaches, pedagogical techniques, methodologies, philosophies, and learning theories abound for teaching music to children. Several European curricular approaches to music education have been imported and adapted for American classrooms. The most popular ones are Orff-*Schulwerk,* developed by German Carl Orff, and the Kodály approach, developed by Hungarian Zoltán Kodály. In addition, some teachers incorporate movement elements of Dalcroze eurhythmics, an approach formulated by Swiss Émile Jaques-Dalcroze, in their elementary curriculum. The influence of American approaches such as the Comprehensive Musicianship Program (CMP), the Manhattanville Music Curriculum Program (MMCP), and the music-learning theory developed by Edwin Gordon is also apparent in the elementary music curriculum. While some teachers may focus their teaching on a single approach, most use an eclectic one.

The main components of Orff-*Schulwerk,* the Kodály approach, Dalcroze eurhythmics, Gordon's music learning theory, Comprehensive Musicianship and the eclectic approach are presented in this chapter. Practical applications of the Orff-*Schulwerk* and Kodály approaches are highlighted and integrated into the model experiences for kindergarten through grade 5 classrooms found in Section Two of this text. However, the primary approach of the model experiences in *The Musical Classroom* is an eclectic one.

THE COMPREHENSIVE MUSICIANSHIP APPROACH

Comprehensive musicianship (CM), as an educational approach and philosophy, is designed to help students become comprehensive musicians—to gain insight into the nature and structure of music, to learn how to relate and synthesize the various facets and areas of musical experience, and to develop an awareness of the world's music. Three broad categories (common elements, musical functions, and educational strategies) are at the heart of the CM approach.

The common elements aspect refers to the idea that certain elements of music (such melody and rhythm) are common to any culture, tradition, or style. These elements are experienced through performance, analysis, and composition (musical functions). The educational strategies include a "hands-on" approach to music learning, a study of music of numerous cultures and historical periods, and an in-depth study of music concepts.

Two music education projects of the 1960s and 1970s led to the comprehensive musicianship approach: the Contemporary Music Project and the Manhattanville Music Curriculum Program. Both emphasize contemporary and avant-garde (new, experimental) music, and they have similar goals and curricula.

History of Comprehensive Musicianship

The beginnings of the concept of comprehensive musicianship can be traced back to 1959, with the Young Composers Project (YCP) supported by the Ford Foundation. American composer Norman Dello Joio (b. 1913) observed school music programs and discovered that the music of classical contemporary composers was seldom included and that students knew little about the process of music composition. The Ford Foundation supported Dello Joio's recommendations, and the YCP placed young (collegiate) composers in the public schools, where they could have experience composing for school music groups and at the same time give students the unusual opportunity to witness the creative process "at work."

Through the YCP program, it became clear that music teachers lacked the skills and knowledge to teach contemporary music. In 1962 the Music Educators National Conference (now MENC: The National Association for Music Education) received funding from the Ford Foundation to expand the YCP by offering seminars and workshops to help teachers better understand and use contemporary music. In addition, pilot projects were set up in elementary schools to develop models for teaching contemporary music and for developing experiences to stimulate creativity and composition. This expanded YCP project came to be known as the Contemporary Music Project (CMP). In 1968 a five-year extension followed, and the project was officially completed in 1973, after more than ten years of significant research in music teaching and learning.

History of the Manhattanville Music Curriculum Program

The Manhattanville Music Curriculum Program (MMCP) was a U.S. Office of Education research project (6-1999) developed between 1967 and 1970. Under the direction of Ronald B. Thomas, the program, named after the Manhattanville College of the Sacred Heart (Purchase, New York), was designed as an alternative curriculum for music educators dissatisfied with traditional approaches. MMCP is a sequential music-learning program for primary grades through high school with an emphasis on contemporary music and on discovery as a teaching/learning technique. Two of the project's curricular results are the books *MMCP Interaction* (an early-childhood curriculum) and *MMCP Synthesis* (a comprehensive curriculum for grades 3 to 12).

The music-learning sequence in MMCP is organized according to these elements of music: timbre, dynamics, pitch, form, and rhythm. These elements are first presented at lower levels, then repeated at higher levels in a spiralling approach. In MMCP, the teacher acts as a facilitator, not a lecturer, as students explore and discover the elements of music. Student activities center on composition, though many activities add to musical growth:

1. Composing, performing, conducting, evaluating
2. Listening to recordings
3. Singing for joy and pleasure
4. Research and oral reports

5. Skill development
6. Student performance
7. Guest performance

Music-reading skills are developed in composition projects throughout MMCP Synthesis.

Comprehensive Musicianship in the Elementary Classroom

The strengths of CMP and MMCP include their emphasis on creativity through composition and their inclusion of new, experimental music. Although CMP was originally intended for college students, its main application has been in the elementary music curriculum. Elementary students must be able to work independently and cooperatively to benefit from the CM approach. The validity and the success of individual and small-group activities hinge on the quality of planning and evaluation by teachers (and students).

The CM approach continued to influence music education through the 1970s and 1980s and still seems remarkably up-to-date, with its emphasis on discovery, creativity, cooperative learning, and individualized instruction. The term comprehensive musicianship expresses the goals of the CM approach: to understand music "aurally, structurally, historically, and culturally" so that learners can "understand and enjoy music to its fullest potential" (Campbell, 1991:20).

PROJECT FOR COLLEGE STUDENTS

Select a particular grade-level textbook of an elementary music series and review how the curriculum is organized (by concepts, by topic, or by skills). Is it a spiral curriculum? Notice the opportunities for creative and composition projects. Also notice what styles of music are included. Summarize and report on your findings.

REFERENCES

CAMPBELL, PATRICIA SHEHAN. (1991). *Lessons from the World: A Cross-Cultural Guide to Music Teaching and Learning.* New York: Schirmer Books.

COLWELL, RICHARD, ed. (Fall 1990). "The Contemporary Music Project." *Quarterly Journal of Music Teaching and Learning* 1(3):2–78.

THOMAS, RONALD B. (June 1991). "Musical Fluency: MMCP and Today's Curriculum." *Music Educators Journal* 78(4):26–29.

THOMAS, RONALD B. (March 1990). "Designing a Curriculum for the Gifted and Talented." *Music Educators Journal* 76(7):54–58.

THOMAS, RONALD B. (August 1970). *Manhattanville Music Curriculum Program: Final Report.* Washington, DC: United States Office of Education, Bureau of Research. ERIC document ED 045 865.

COMPREHENSIVE MUSICIANSHIP RESOURCES

JUILLIARD SCHOOL OF MUSIC. (1970). *Juilliard Repertory Library.* Cincinnati, OH: Canyon Press.

THOMAS, RONALD B. (1971). *MMCP Interaction: Early Childhood Music Curriculum.* Clifton Park, NY: Media Materials.

THOMAS, RONALD B. (1971). *MMCP Synthesis: A Structure for Music Education.* Clifton Park, NY: Media Materials.

THE ORFF-*SCHULWERK* APPROACH

Carl Orff (1895–1982) was a German composer and man of wide-ranging interests. He not only distinguished himself as a noted composer of works such as *Carmina Burana* but also developed a child-centered approach to music education. Orff's music education approach became known as *Schulwerk* (German, meaning "schoolwork").

History and Background

The origins of Orff-*Schulwerk* can be traced back to the 1920s. Inspired and enthused by "the New Dance Wave" and by Jaques-Dalcroze's eurhythmics, Orff established a school in Munich with dancer Dorothee Gunther. The *Guntherschule,* which opened in 1924, was a professional school for training physical-education teachers, dancers, and gymnasts. Unlike the other European gymnastics and dance schools, it combined the study of movement with music.

The *Guntherschule*'s curriculum was based on what Orff called the "elemental" style (derived from the Latin word *elementarius,* meaning "pertaining to the elements, primeval, basic"). To Orff, elemental music meant "never music alone, but music

Courtesy of MENC: The National Association for Music Education

connected with movement, dance and speech—not to be listened to, meaningful only in active participation" (Carder, 1990:142). In elemental music, Orff suggested a parallel between the historical development of music and the musical growth of an individual.

Orff composed the music to be used in the *Guntherschule* curriculum and designed special instruments that were in keeping with the elemental style. The instruments were similar to those of an Indonesian gamelan ensemble in tonal quality and construction. They included barred instruments: xylophones with a wood timbre, metallophones with a metal timbre, and glockenspiels with a bell-like timbre, as well as recorders, small percussion instruments, and drums.

The *Guntherschule* flourished until World War II, when the school was bombed. All the special instruments and materials were destroyed, and Orff's educational activities were curtailed until 1948.

Early in 1948, Orff was invited to give a series of educational broadcasts on Bavarian radio. He was challenged to adapt his *Guntherschule* ideas and music to the needs and abilities of children. Over the next few years, Orff, assisted by his former student Gunild Keetman, developed and refined his *Schulwerk* through programs that involved children actively in experiencing and making music (with singing becoming a more important component of the program). The curricular results of this development were the five volumes of *Music for Children* (Orff and Keetman, 1973) (see Appendix F).

Gradually Orff's approach to music education was introduced and tried in settings other than the radio broadcasts. Experimental courses with children were initiated by Gunild Keetman in the early 1950s at the Mozarteum Academy of Music in Salzburg, Austria. Orff-*Schulwerk* became a part of the Mozarteum's curriculum, and Salzburg became its headquarters.

Through interested educators and publications, the *Schulwerk* approach has spread to many countries throughout the world. In particular, the Orff approach is incorporated in some elementary schools in the United States and is used with many adaptations, including those for special learners.

The Orff Approach

Although the Orff approach does not follow a prescribed method or course of study, several components are basic to the approach. Perhaps the most fundamental components are exploration and experience. Children are encouraged to explore and experience music through movement, singing, playing instruments, and improvisation. They explore and experience first by imitation, then by creation; they proceed from the part to the whole, from the simple to the complex, and from individual to ensemble experiences.

The exploration and experiencing of the musical elements begins with rhythm, followed by melody, and finally harmony. Form is introduced almost from the beginning of rhythmic study.

Rhythm grows out of speech and movement patterns. Children rhythmically speak chants, rhymes, and sayings and through these experiences explore accent and meter as well as phrasing and simple sectional forms. Speech experiences are accompanied by body rhythms: clapping, patschen (slapping thighs), finger snapping, and foot tapping.

Melody follows rhythm, with singing and playing experiences. The falling third, *sol-mi,* is the first interval introduced, followed by the syllables *la, re,* and finally *do* to complete the entire pentatonic (five-tone) scale. After children have had considerable experience with the pentatonic scale, major and minor scales and modes are added. Reading music notation is a peripheral goal.

Drones (open fifths) and ostinatos (repeated rhythmic/melodic patterns) are used for instrumental accompaniments, thus introducing harmony. Harmony is also experienced through the singing and playing of rounds and canons.

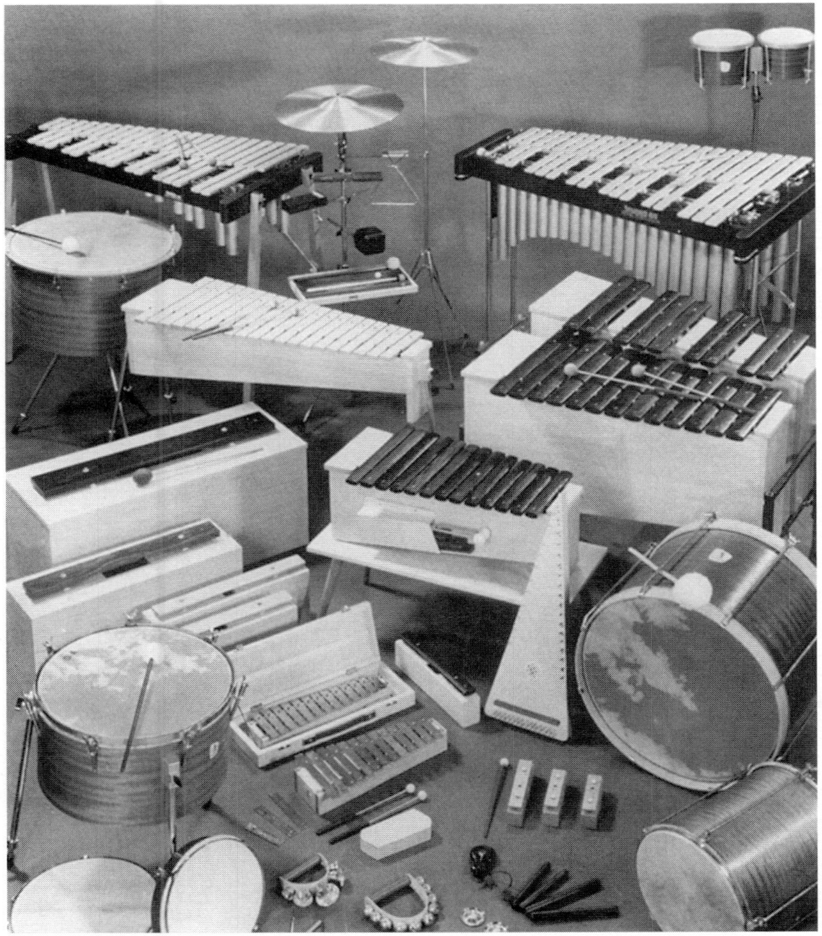

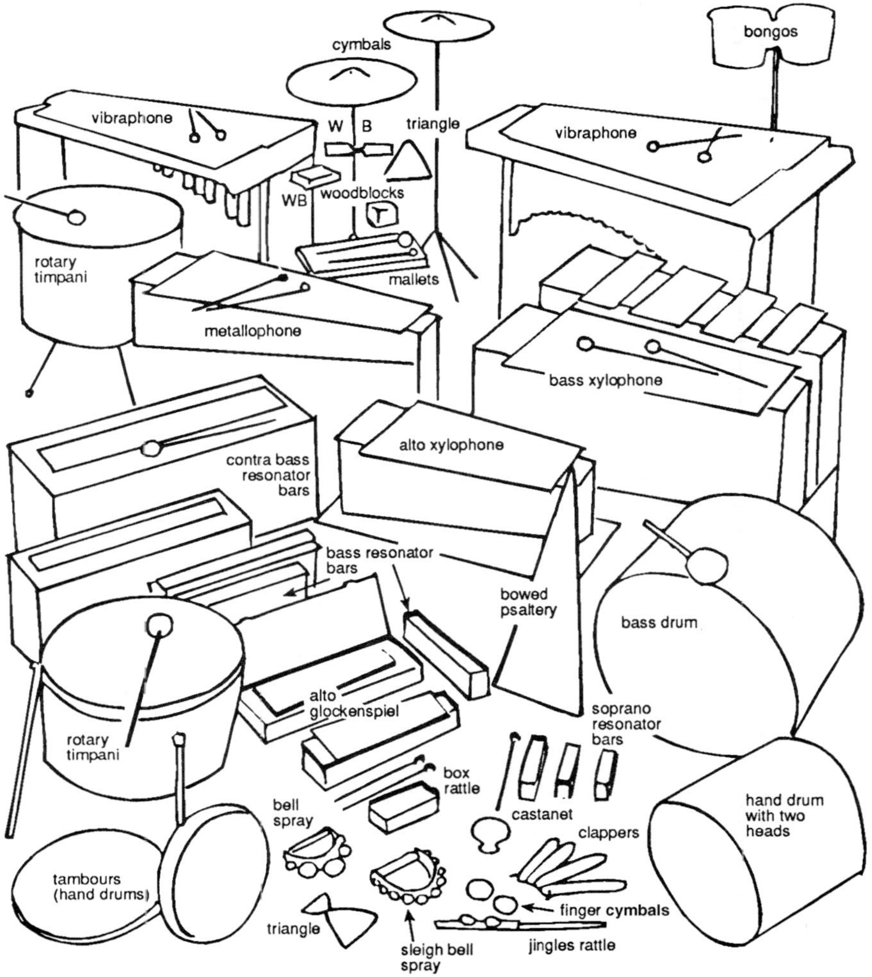

Studio 49 Instruments for Orff-*Schulwerk*. Courtesy of MMB Music, Inc.

Improvisation is an important part of all experiences: speech, movement, singing, and playing instruments. Improvisation begins with brief rhythmic/melodic patterns and gradually expands to longer, more complex patterns—to introductions, codas, accompaniments, and entire melodies.

Playing instruments is also a vital part of every Orff-*Schulwerk* experience. The instrument collection is a "must" in the approach and includes those instruments noted earlier: tuned drums; barred instruments such as xylophones, metallophones, and glockenspiels in various sizes; and baroque recorders. These instruments, collectively called the instrumentarium (pictured on p. 69), are of high quality and, therefore, fairly expensive.

Orff-*Schulwerk* has great appeal to teachers and students, for it involves active music making and many creative activities. American adaptations of the approach must include a wide assortment of music to replace much of the European material.

PROJECTS FOR COLLEGE STUDENTS

1. In small groups, prepare a list of model experiences (in the text) that incorporate the use of Orff instruments. Some groups may locate only Level I experiences; others, Level II; and still others, Level III. Finally, each group should select one example and prepare an instrumental accompaniment for performance.
2. Examine how Orff-*Schulwerk* adaptations are accomplished in the elementary music series. Choose a particular grade level to review and write a brief report of your findings.

REFERENCES

BEVANS, JUDITH. (March 1969). "The Exceptional Child and Orff." *Music Educators Journal* 55(7):41. Also in *Education of the Visually Handicapped* 1(4) (December 1969):116.

CARDER, POLLY. (1990). "Part Three: Carl Orff." In *The Eclectic Curriculum in American Music Education: Contributions of Dalcroze, Kodály, and Orff.* 2d ed., Polly Carder, ed., 107–160. Reston, VA: Music Educators National Conference.

SHAMROCK, MARY. (February 1986). "Orff-Schulwerk: An Integrated Foundation." *Music Educators Journal* 72(6):51–55.

STRINGHAM, MARY, comp. *Bibliography of Materials in English Concerning Orff-Schulwerk.* (1977). Cleveland, OH: American Orff-Schulwerk Association.

American Orff-*Schulwerk* Association (AOSA): see Appendix F, "Addresses."

Also see Resources, Appendix F: "Orff-*Schulwerk*," "General Music Retailers."

THE KODÁLY APPROACH

The Kodály approach is a vocal approach to music literacy: the ability to read, hear, and think music. Based on Hungarian folk music, this program began in Hungary in the 1930s under the guidance of the composer and musicologist Zoltán Kodály

("KOH-dye") (1882–1967). As a young man, Kodály began field studies (with composer Béla Bartók) to collect, record, and notate native Hungarian (Magyar) folk music. Finding very little music literacy, Kodály saw the need to make music education available to everyone—and not just the talented few. Using musical ideas he discovered in Magyar music, he began to compose for children's voices, and to put together the curriculum that is known and used throughout the world as the Kodály approach.

Singing (*a cappella*) is the foundation of the approach. Kodály believed that everyone could be musically literate if instruction began early and used the musical "mother tongue" (folk song) and other music of the "highest" quality. Singing, listening, movement, ear training, and creating are developed at every grade level; each lesson also includes work with expressive qualities and the other elements of music. As students work with rhythm and pitch, they are introduced to notation through syllables for speaking rhythms, and tonic *sol–fa* syllables with the Curwen hand signs.

The curriculum that Kodály and his colleagues developed eventually gained state support and became compulsory. His curriculum recommends that music education begin in nursery school and continue through primary and secondary school, and that special (public) music schools be provided for gifted students.

Rhythm Syllables

Rhythm syllables adapted from Emile-Joseph Chevé (French, 1804–1864) are used from the outset (p. 73). At first, notation is presented without note heads, and syllables approximating the rhythms are chanted. Shorter durations (eighth and quarter notes) are presented before longer durations (half and whole notes). The specific order depends on the music used. For example, American folk music uses rhythms (and pitches) in different ways than Hungarian folk music does, so American teachers modify the order of presentation.

Tonic *Sol–Fa* and Curwen Hand Signs

In the tonic *sol–fa* system, syllables are used for pitches of the scale and are movable from one scale to another. As a result, *do–re–mi* in C Major always sounds similar to *do–re–mi* in F Major. In the Kodály approach, the tonic (or tonal center) in major scales is *do* and in minor scales, *la*. The syllables were developed by Sarah Glover (English, 1786–1867) but have generally been attributed to her countryman John Curwen.

The physical hand signs used by Curwen (see p. 72) to accompany the tonic *sol–fa* were adapted by Kodály for Hungarian schools and were further revised for American schools. Both the syllables and the hand signs help students develop inner hearing—the ability to hear the melody in one's head while looking at music notation. (The hand signs are performed by positioning one's hands to show high and low. For example, low *do* is performed at about waist level, *sol* in front of the face, and high *do* just above the head.)

Music Reading

Folk songs that use a pentatonic scale (*do–re–mi–sol–la*) are taught first, and form the basis for beginning music-reading experiences. The syllables for *fa* and *ti* are introduced later because they create half-step intervals that may be difficult to sing in tune. The letter names for notes are also learned. After children have had considerable experience with this pentatonic scale, the complete major scale is introduced, as are minor scales and modes. Although the exact order of *sol–fa* syllables depends on the music used, one possible sequence follows: *sol, mi, la, re, do,* low *la,* low *sol,* high *do,* high *re, fa, ti, si.*

This sequence is cumulative. Students sing many different combinations of syllables, learning tones in relation to each other (not single tones). For example, the first three syllables learned (*sol, mi, la*) are sung in many combinations: *sol–mi–la, sol–la–mi, mi–sol–la, mi–la–sol, la–sol–mi,* and *la–mi–sol,* and in many songs.

CURWEN HAND SIGNS

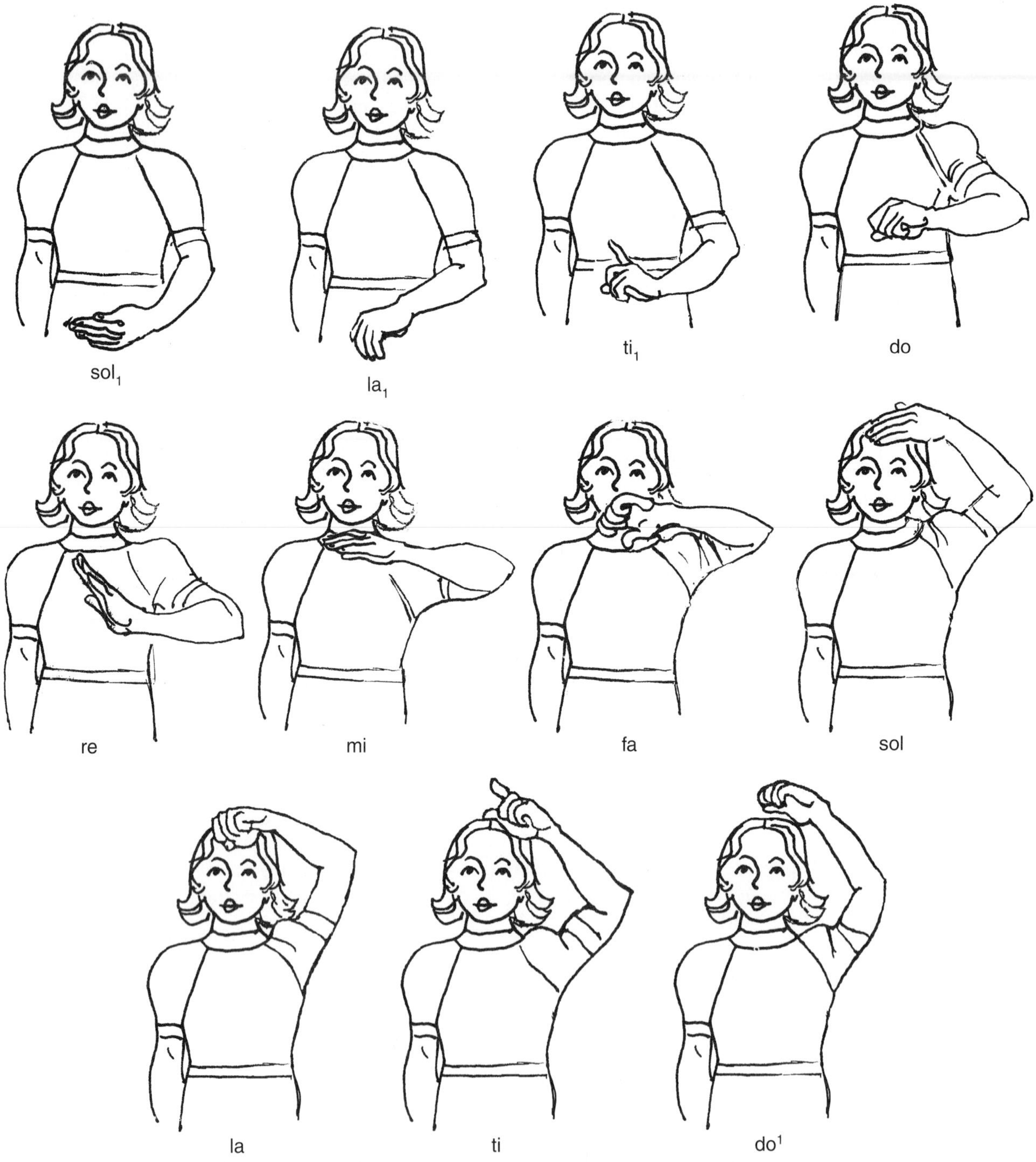

RHYTHM DURATIONS AND SYLLABLES

Complete Notation / *Rhythm Notation*

Rhythm Syllables (Hungary)	*Rhythm Syllables* (by Pierre Perron, Canada)*
ta	ta
ti - ti	ti - ti
ti - ri - ti - ri	tika - tika
ti - ta - ti	syn - co - pa
tai - ti	tum - ti
ti - ri - ti ta	tika - ti ta
ti - ti - ri ta	ti - tika ta
trip - le - ti ta	tri - o - la ta
tim - ri / ti - rim	ti - ka / tikum
ti - tai	ti- tum
ta - a *(hold for 2 beats)*	too
ta -a - a *(hold for 3 beats)*	toe
ta - a - a - a *(hold for 4 beats)*	tay

EXAMPLE OF RHYTHM SYLLABLES IN NOTATION

ta ta ti - ti ta ti - ri - ti - ri ti - ti - ri ta shh (Hungary)
ta ta ti - ti ta ti - ka - ti - ka ti - ti - ka ta (sh) (Pierre Perron)*

*The Canadian rhythm syllables are used in some America Kodály programs.

Adapting Kodály for American Schools

Kodály practice in America varies somewhat. For example, instead of Hungarian folk music, teachers in different regions use folk music that reflects their students' multicultural heritage. Some American teachers incorporate Kodály ideas into an eclectic curriculum similar to that found in the elementary music series (and in *The Musical Classroom*). In fact, Kodály's approach is eclectic, because he uses tools and ideas from music educators in England, France, and Germany. After developing his basic philosophy, Kodály incorporated tonic *sol–fa* (Curwen), rhythm syllables (Chevé), and the basic teaching process of Pestalozzi (Carder, 1990:56).

Optimum conditions for using the Kodály approach include a relatively stable school population and time in the curriculum for two to five lessons per week over the course of several years. With the guidance of capable teachers, students taught according to Kodály principles will read music as fluently as they read language and will be able to transfer their music reading from voice to instruments.

PROJECTS FOR COLLEGE STUDENTS

1. In Level II model experiences, find an example of the use of rhythm syllables to speak and perform rhythms and an example of the use of Curwen hand signs to accompany tonal patterns.
2. Read and report on an article or a book from the resources list found in Appendix F, "Kodály Approach."
3. In small groups, develop three lists of songs that include only the pitches *la–sol–mi, mi–re–do,* and *la–sol–mi–(re)–do.* Use Section Four as your source.

REFERENCES

BOSHKOFF, RUTH. (October 1991). "Lesson Planning the Kodály Way." *Music Educators Journal* 79(2):30–34.

CARDER, POLLY. (1990). "Zoltán Kodály." In *The Eclectic Curriculum in American Music Education: Contributions of Dalcroze, Kodály, and Orff.* 2d ed., Polly Carder, ed., 53–106. Reston, VA: Music Educators National Conference.

CHOKSY, LOIS. (1998). *The Kodály Method I: Comprehensive Music Education.* 3rd ed. Upper Saddle River, NJ: Prentice Hall.

FORRAI, KATALIN, and JEAN SINOR, transl. (1988). *Music in Preschool.* Budapest: Corvina Press. (Available at Boosey and Hawkes)

ZEMKE, SISTER LORNA. (1977). *The Kodály Concept: Its History, Philosophy and Development.* Champaign, IL: Mark Foster Music; www.i5ive.com/

Organization of American Kodály Educators (OAKE): see Appendix F, "Addresses and Web Sites."

See also Resources, Appendix F: "Kodály Approach," "General Music Retailers," "World Music."

DALCROZE EURHYTHMICS

Musician/educator Émile Jaques-Dalcroze (Swiss, 1865–1950) was a pioneer of music and movement education. Jaques–Dalcroze established a school and theatre in Hellerau, Germany, that attracted many leading artists. Some of the educators who visited Hellerau were Carl Orff and Maria Montessori. Jaques-Dalcroze also founded the Institut Jaques-Dalcroze in Geneva, which continues to function today.

Jaques-Dalcroze formulated a comprehensive philosophy of music teaching for learners of any age. His curriculum uses body and mind integration in developing musicianship and includes the following three components: eurhythmics (Greek, "good rhythm or flow"), experiencing elements of music through body movement; solfège, singing with *sol–fa* syllables; and improvisation, creating music extemporaneously. All three components plus intensive listening are included in Dalcroze instruction, but the eurhythmic portion seems to receive more attention in current application.

Eurhythmics should begin at an early age—four or five is considered ideal. The purpose is to encourage free body movement in response to music. For example, walking movements may be the natural response to music in a moderate tempo, whereas running movements would be more appropriate for faster tempos. These beginning experiences (ages four to five) lead to more complex responses involving dual coordination, such as walking to the music's steady beat while clapping the rhythm of the melody (ages nine to ten).

Dalcroze teachers develop piano improvisation skills so they can adjust their tempo to that of the learner. However, teachers may also use short recorded musical selections or patterns played on rhythm instruments to stimulate movement. Movements are to show the constantly changing flow of motion and express physically what one hears and feels in the music (e.g., dynamics, phrasing, form, and style). In eurhythmics experiences, students use their bodies as musical instruments; they show their musical understanding through movement.

Jaques-Dalcroze's theories are explained in his two books, *Rhythm, Music and Education* and *Eurhythmics, Art and Education,* but a teacher needs direct instruction to thoroughly understand and use the approach. A number of institutes, colleges, and universities offer courses, with several accredited to award Jaques-Dalcroze certificates. Workshop demonstrations are often presented at regional, national, and international music and arts conferences.

PROJECTS FOR COLLEGE STUDENTS

1. Write a report based on one of the articles or books presented in the "References" or "Resources," below.
2. In small groups, review selected grade-level books from an elementary music series and note the activities that show the influence of Dalcroze Eurhythmics. Discuss and summarize your findings.

REFERENCES

ABRAMSON, ROBERT M. (1998). *Feel It: Rhythm Games for All.* Miami, FL: Warner Brothers Publications. Book and two audio CDs. Available at Musik Innovations. See Resources, Appendix F, "General Music Retailers."

ABRAMSON, ROBERT M. (1992). *Dalcroze Eurhythmics with Robert M. Abramson.* Video; demonstration lessons and games with Juilliard School of Music students and faculty. Available at Musik Innovations. See Resources, Appendix F, "General Music Retailers."

ABRAMSON, ROBERT M. (1973). *Rhythm Games for Perception and Cognition.* Hialeah, FL: Columbia Pictures. Audio cassettes.

BACHMANN, MARIE-LAURE. (1991). *Dalcroze Today: An Education Through and Into Music.* Oxford: Clarendon Press.

BLACK-SCHNEBLY, JULIA, and STEPHEN MOORE. (1997). *The Rhythm Inside: Connecting Body, Mind and Spirit Through Music.* Portland, OR: Rudra Press.

CALDWELL, TIMOTHY. (March 1993). "A Dalcroze Perspective on Skills for Learning." *Music Educators Journal* 79(7):27–28.

CAMPBELL, PATRICIA SHEHAN. (Spring 1991). "Rhythmic Movement and Public School Education: Progressive Views in the Formative Years." *Journal of Research in Music Education* 39(1):12–22.

FARBER, ANNE. (December 1991). "Speaking the Musical Language." *Music Educators Journal* 78(4):30–34.

FARBER, ANNE, and LISA PARKER. (November 1987). "Discovering Music Through Dalcroze Eurhythmics." *Music Educators Journal* 74(3):43–45.

JAQUES-DALCROZE, ÉMILE, CYNTHIA COX, ed., and FREDERICK ROTHWELL, transl. (1972/1930). *Eurhythmics, Art and Education.* New York: Benjamin Blom.

JAQUES-DALCROZE, ÉMILE, and HAROLD F. RUBINSTEIN, transl. (1967). *Rhythm, Music and Education.* Abridged reprint edition. London & Whitstable: The Riverside Press. Available at Dalcroze International School of Music.

JOHNSON, MONICA DALE. (April 1993). "Dalcroze Skills for All Teachers." *Music Educators Journal* 79(8):42–45.

LANDIS, BETH, and POLLY CARDER. (1990). "The Dalcroze Approach." In *The Eclectic Curriculum in American Music Education: Contributions of Dalcroze, Kodály, and Orff.* 2d ed., Polly Carder, ed., 5–51. Reston, VA: Music Educators National Conference.

MEAD, VIRGINIA HOGE. (1994). *Dalcroze Eurhythmics in Today's Music Classroom.* New York: Schott Music Corporation.

MEAD, VIRGINIA HOGE. (January 1996). "More Than Movement: Dalcroze Eurhythmics." *Music Educators Journal* 82(4):38–41.

VANDERSPAR, ELIZABETH. (1998). *Dalcroze Handbook: Principles and Guidelines for Teaching Eurhythmics.* Dalcroze Society of America. Available at Musik Innovations. See Resources, Appendix F: "General Music Retailers."

DALCROZE EURHYTHMICS RESOURCES

ABRAMSON, ROBERT M. *Feel It.* Miami, FL: Warner Brothers Publications. Book and two audio CDs; sequenced rhythm games.

ABRAMSON, ROBERT M. (1978). *Rhythm Games for Perception and Cognition.* Hialeah, FL: Columbia Pictures. Book with audio cassettes.

THEORY OF MUSIC LEARNING: EDWIN E. GORDON

A recent development in music teaching and learning is the theory of music learning of Edwin E. Gordon. Gordon, a contemporary American music researcher who is probably best known for his tests to measure music aptitude, developed a skill-learning hierarchy specific to music. Central to his theory is audiation—the ability to "hear" music in the mind.

Gordon's skill-learning hierarchy is divided into two categories—discrimination learning and inference learning. Discrimination learning, or learning by imitation or rote, precedes inference learning. To learn by inference is to think for oneself or to perform tasks that have not been learned by rote. There are five levels of discrimination learning and three levels of inference learning.

Discrimination Learning

The following list identifies the discrimination-learning levels in sequence and briefly interprets each.

Level	*Interpretation*
Aural/Oral	Children listen to and repeat tonal rhythm patterns performed by the teacher. These patterns are to music what words are to language. When students can sing in tune a variety of tonal patterns and can chant rhythmic patterns keeping a steady beat, they are ready to work with verbal association.
Verbal association	Children sing the previously learned tonal patterns with syllables (do, re, mi, etc.) and chant the previously learned rhythmic patterns with speech syllables such as "du," "da," "di," and so on. They learn to associate "proper" terms with these patterns.
Partial synthesis	Students discriminate among groups of previously learned tonal and rhythmic patterns and interpret them as being in meters, major or minor, and so on. This is similar

	to hearing groups of words in language and being able to interpret them as being sentences.
Symbolic association	Students read written symbols or music notation of familiar patterns and perform them. They associate these symbols with what they have already audiated ("heard" in the mind) and are thus able to notate these tonal and rhythmic patterns.
Composite synthesis	Students comprehend and notate previously learned tonal and rhythmic phrases (a grouping of patterns in a series). This is similar to the aural discrimination of patterns at the partial synthesis level, but now students can read and write them as well.

Inference Learning

Unfamiliar tonal and rhythmic patterns are integrated into the learning process in inference learning. The three levels of inference learning are identified and described as follows:

Level	*Description*
Generalization	Students compare sets of tonal or rhythmic patterns, some familiar and some not, and decide aurally which are the same and which are different. In addition, they identify names or labels for the patterns and read or write unfamiliar tonal or rhythmic patterns.
Creativity/Improvisation	Students create or improvise different but related tonal and rhythmic patterns in response to patterns performed by the teacher. They can also read or write these patterns.
Theoretical understanding	After students have developed the knowledge and skills outlined in the previous levels, they are ready to discern why music is what it is. Just as one would not teach children how to diagram a sentence before they can speak the language fluently, children need not learn the rules and technical aspects of how music "works" and how it is put together until they know how to audiate, synthesize, read, write, create, and improvise.

Although inference learning is dependent on discrimination learning, it is possible to approach these higher-order learning stages spirally when readiness dictates. "By combining discrimination and inference learning in a sequential learning process, students can learn about all music skills in an orderly fashion" (Mark, 1996:158).

Implications for Music Learning

It is important to remember several points about Gordon's theory of music learning. First, it is not a method for teaching music. Second, it appears to promote a part approach to learning, an approach that differs from the whole approach that many researchers advocate. Third, it does provide some important guidelines for teachers to use to involve students in meaningful music learning. Following are some of those guidelines.

1. Begin with sound and move to symbol—hear, label, symbolize.
2. Plan music-learning experiences for children in a sequential manner so that learning is not fragmented.
3. Adjust the music-learning sequence to the child's readiness.

4. Follow the same steps in music learning that children follow in their language development. Learn words (or tonal/rhythmic patterns) first to acquire a vocabulary and then combine those words (or tonal/rhythmic patterns) into sentences (or phrases).

Edwin E. Gordon is author of *Jump Right In!* and *Music Play;* see "Theory of Music Learning Resources," below.

PROJECTS FOR COLLEGE STUDENTS

1. If one were following the Gordon theory of music learning, what levels of discrimination learning would be missing if a teacher started beginning recorder instruction for fourth-graders by teaching them to read notation? Describe.
2. Read more about the Gordon theory using materials listed in "References" (below); then review *Music Play* (Valerio et al.) (below) or *Jump Right In! The Music Curriculum* (Gordon et al.) described in Appendix C. Report on your readings.

REFERENCES

Brand, Manny, ed. (Spring/Summer 1991). "The Work of Edwin Gordon." *Quarterly Journal of Music Teaching and Learning* 2(1–2):3–47.

Gordon, Edwin E. (September 1999). "All About Audiation and Music Aptitudes." *Music Educators Journal* 86(2):41–44.

Gordon, Edwin E. (1997). *An Introduction to Research and the Psychology of Children.* Chicago: G.I.A. Publications.

Gordon, Edwin E. (1997). *Learning Sequences in Music: Skill, Content, and Patterns: A Music Learning Theory.* Chicago: G.I.A. Publications.

Gordon, Edwin E. (1997). *A Music Learning Theory for Newborn and Young Children.* Chicago: G.I.A. Publications.

"The Music Learning Theory of Edwin E. Gordon." (Winter 1995). Special issue of *General Music Today* 8(2).

Gordon, Edwin E. (1979). *Primary Measures of Audiation.* Chicago: G.I.A. Publications.

Gordon, Edwin E. (1997). *Study Guide for Learning Sequences in Music.* Chicago: G.I.A. Publications.

Jordan-DeCarbo, Joyce. (September 1997). "A Sound-To-Symbol Approach to Music Learning." *Music Educators Journal* 84(2):34–37, 54.

Walters, Darrel L. (1992). "Sequencing for Efficient Learning." In *Handbook of Research on Music Teaching and Learning,* Richard Colwell, ed., 535. New York: Schirmer Books.

THEORY OF MUSIC LEARNING RESOURCES

Gordon, Edwin E., et al. *Jump Right In!* Music curriculum grades K–8; Chicago: G.I.A. Publications, Inc., 7404 S. Mason Ave., Chicago, IL 60638; (800)-442-1358; www.giamusic.com. For a description of *Jump Right In!,* see Appendix C.

Valerio, Wendy H., Alison M. Reynolds, Beth M. Bolton, Cynthia C. Taggart, and Edwin E. Gordon. *Music Play.* Early childhood music curriculum. Book with audio CD; 57 songs and chants.

THE ECLECTIC APPROACH

Although some teachers may use just one of the aforementioned approaches in their curriculum, most teachers incorporate and integrate ideas and techniques from many different sources in their teaching. Since each group of students is different, teachers must select appropriate methods and materials for their particular teaching situation and teaching style. The individualizing of one's curricular approach offers students an eclectic music curriculum. This is the approach used in *The Musical Classroom.* The model experiences in this text focus on engaging children in conceptual music learning, creating, while utilizing, and adapting a variety of curricular approaches and teaching techniques to do so. The ultimate goal is to help students deepen their understanding of music through conceptual experiences, to bring them in touch with a variety of ways to experience music, and as a result, to increase their enjoyment of and sensitivity to music as an art.

CHAPTER SUMMARY

Elementary music programs in the United States incorporate many different curricular approaches. Three have been imported from Europe and adapted for American classroom music programs—Orff-*Schulwerk* (an approach focusing on improvisation, movement, and instrument playing), the Kodály approach (an approach that stresses singing and music reading), and Dalcroze eurhythmics (an approach offering ideas in integrating music and movement). In addition to the European approaches, the music-learning theory of American Edwin E. Gordon has influenced the music curriculum at the elementary level, as has the comprehensive musicianship approach (an approach that emphasizes common elements, musical functions, and educational strategies). Many teachers draw from the ideas offered in these approaches as they develop their own special eclectic approach to teaching music to children.

PROJECT FOR COLLEGE STUDENTS

Review selected grade-level books from an elementary series (see Appendix C) to determine whether the books reflect a particular approach (Orff, Kodály, Dalcroze, Gordon) or an eclectic approach. Prepare a report describing and documenting your decision.

RESOURCES

CAMPBELL, PATRICIA SHEHAN, and CAROL SCOTT-KASNER. (1995). "Methods of Teaching Music to Children." Chapter 3 in *Music in Childhood,* 47. New York: Schirmer Books.

COSTANZA, PETER, and TIMOTHY RUSSELL. (1992). "Methodologies in Music Education." Sec. E in *Handbook of Research on Music Teaching and Learning,* Richard Colwell, ed., 498. New York: Schirmer Books.

MARK, MICHAEL L. (1996). "Teaching Methods." In *Contemporary Music Education.* 3rd ed. New York: Schirmer Books.

STAUFFER, SANDRA L., and JENNIFER DAVIDSON. (1996). *Strategies for Teaching K–4 General Music.* Reston, VA: Music Educators National Conference.

VI
Curricular Developments

The curriculum in America's elementary schools is always expanding and changing. Technological advances dictate change. New research suggests different ways to approach learning. Changing demographics and the school population necessitate varying learning and teaching strategies (Madsen, 2000). Some important curricular developments that affect the elementary school music curriculum are addressed in this chapter: music technology, the integration of music with other subjects, teaching music to special learners, cooperative learning, and the renewed emphasis on education in early childhood.

MUSIC TECHNOLOGY IN THE ELEMENTARY CLASSROOM

Technological innovations over the past several decades have important implications for elementary school music programs. The computer, MIDI technology, electronic instruments, and interactive multimedia have changed the way music is performed, conceived, and even learned. Many of these latest innovations, even the World Wide Web, have made their way into the elementary classroom and into the lives of children. Teachers must learn about this new technology and use it as one would use any new music educational tool—to enhance music learning and increase students' fascination with music.

Information about computers (and MIDI) and interactive multimedia as related to elementary classroom application follows. Specific information about electronic keyboards, Omnichords (electronic Autoharps) and QChords (digital songcard guitars), however, is included on pp. 25–27. A wide variety of music software is available and appropriate for use in the elementary music classroom. Since teachers must use good judgement in choosing software appropriate for their students, a set of guidelines for evaluating music software follows. A resource list of "Selected Music Software" is included in Appendix F.

Computers (and MIDI)

Computers are an important educational tool in schools across the country. These incredible machines have graphic and sound capabilities to assist in music teaching and learning. They can display music notation and sound specific pitches simultaneously and when connected to electronic keyboards (with MIDI capability), they can become "instruments."

Computers are especially good at providing individualized instruction, creative music activities, and collaborative learning opportunities. Teachers can introduce music concepts and skills in the classroom and then let students practice and expand on them through carefully selected software. It may be effective to have a movable music workstation so that the teacher can demonstrate and introduce new software to the entire class, and then the workstation (complete with headphones) can be moved to a place in the room where students can work individually or in small groups with the various programs.

To allow a computer and a variety of electronic instruments to "speak" to each other and communicate music in a common language, a special connecting link (a wired cable) is needed. This special link is called MIDI (Musical Instrument Digital Interface) and is pronounced "MID-ee." MIDI is able to connect or interface an electronic keyboard with other electronic keyboards or a keyboard with a computer. This interface translates software commands and parameters and standardizes the electronic details of the signals sent. For example, an electronic keyboard with MIDI capability may have three ports: MIDI IN, MIDI OUT, and MIDI THRU. These connections transfer MIDI information into, from, or through the keyboard or computer to which the five-prong cable is attached. When MIDI interfaces an electronic keyboard and a computer, it allows a student to play on the electronic keyboard and look at the music on the computer screen. Depending on the software, it is possible to compose music, store the music in the computer's memory, notate the music, play it back, and even edit it.

Courtesy of MENC: The National Association for Music Education

A variety of music software is available for the computer. Some programs call for an electronic keyboard with MIDI capability. A listing of "Selected Music Software" is included in Appendix F.

Interactive Multimedia

The broad term interactive multimedia refers to the integration and combination of many different media (film, video, books, photography, music) into a single flexible medium. This medium allows students to interact with the various learning media by means of a personal computer.

The most common medium is a specially designed compact disc known as CD-ROM. CD-ROM (compact disc read-only memory) is a compact disc loaded with data (memory) that can be played (read) into a computer. It combines high-quality sound with text, photographs, and animation in an informative presentation. Students interact with these programs using a personal computer equipped with a CD-ROM player and some kind of selection device such as a mouse, a joystick, or a touch screen. Many music CD-ROM programs are currently available and appropriate for the elementary classroom. (See "Selected Music Software" for elementary classroom music in Appendix F.)

Music CD-ROMs can be used with both individual students and groups of students. Because there is so much information contained in a CD-ROM program, it is important that teachers provide guidance on how to use the program so that students will not become frustrated or overwhelmed.

DVD (digital versatile disc) technology has paralleled the development of CD audio technology. It is considered even more advantageous because it offers all the pluses of interactive CDs yet includes full-motion video. DVD players are now included with many computers. The instructive possibilities of all interactive multimedia seem unlimited, and the potential for providing students with one-on-one instruction using a variety of different learning media (by means of a personal computer) is very exciting.

Choosing Music Software for the Classroom

Since so much music software is available and more is being created each day, it is essential that teachers carefully preview, evaluate, and select only the highest quality for use in the classroom. Quality software not only offers sequenced individualized instruction, but also provides opportunities for creative activities and a tracking method for the teacher to use in keeping tabs on student learning. Some guidelines to use in evaluating music software follow.

An evaluation form to assess software is found in Appendix B; a list of software that may be particularly useful in elementary classroom music programs is included in Appendix F. Consider how the software can, with a teacher, improve instruction and bring about more meaningful music learning.

World Wide Web

The Internet has literally opened up a new door in technology. Its potential as a teaching/learning tool is unlimited. Students and teachers alike can access a wide variety of information that can assist in the study of music. Teachers may wish to assign Internet research projects or refer students to *Internet Practice-and-Drill Sites for Music Learning or Virtual Learning Centers* (Thompson, 1999). Without question, students are intrigued with the World Wide Web and with the increasing availability of Internet

Guidelines for Evaluating Music Software

1. *Documentation* Does the written information (paper-based) provided include adequate documentation about the hardware requirements, program goals, and software features?
2. *Presentation Techniques* Is the information presented visually and aurally accurate and in an interesting and engaging way? Are the instructions clear whether spoken or written? Is the format easy to follow?
3. *Visual/Audio Effects* Is the screen design appealing and appropriate? Are the graphics and audio helpful and effective in presenting the information?
4. *Content* Is the music content appropriate for the age level and factually accurate? Is there consistent feedback to help students learn the content? Are there opportunities for students to be creative or "play" with musical ideas?
5. *Instructional Strategies* Are the strategies effective and creative in presenting the music content? Will students be actively engaged in the music-learning process and challenged to learn about music?
6. *Technical Considerations* Is the program technically easy to use? Are there clear instructions for using buttons, keys, etc.? Is it crashproof? Is a tracking method available for collecting and monitoring student work?

resources, this valuable tool should be used to engage students in music learning experiences (both in and out of the classroom). Web sites are included throughout the Resources, Appendix F, especially in "Selected Computer Software," and "Addresses and Web Sites."

Summary

Teachers must keep current on the latest developments in instructional technology. This medium offers extraordinary opportunities for individualized instruction in music and creative music learning activities. Teachers must take full advantage of these exciting teaching and learning tools.

PROJECTS FOR COLLEGE STUDENTS

1. Using the evaluation form in Appendix B, review and evaluate (with a classmate) a music software program from the "Selected Music Software" list in Appendix F.
2. Take an informal survey of the available technology in several elementary schools in your area. Try to determine how and in what subject areas the technology is used. Report your findings and compare them with those of other class members.
3. Compare the Level II model experiences (and music concepts) with the "Selected Music Software" in Appendix F. Identify one or more software programs that could be used to enhance a particular model experience.
4. Review the Opportunity-to-Learn Standards for Music Technology (www.menc.org) to see what the recommendations are for equipping and staffing K–5 classrooms with music technology.

REFERENCES

BERZ, WILLIAM L., and JUDITH BOWMAN. (1994). *Applications of Research in Music Technology.* Reston, VA: Music Educators National Conference.

"Computer-Assisted Instruction in Music." (June 1994). *Teaching Music* 1(6):34–35.

FOREST, JOYCE. (March 1995). "Music Technology Helps Students Succeed." *Music Educators Journal* 81(5):35–38, 48.

FOWLER, CHARLES. (September 1990). "Recognizing the Role of Artistic Intelligences." *Music Educators Journal* 90(77):1, 24–27.

GRISWOLD, HAROLD E. (November 1994). "Multiculturalism, Music, and Information Highways." *Music Educators Journal* 81(3):41–46.

HIGGINS, WILLIAM R. (1992). *A Resource Guide to Computer Applications in Music Education.* Updated yearly. Order from Messiah College, Grantham, PA 17027; (717) 766–2511.

KASSNER, KIRK. (May 2000). "One Computer *Can* Deliver Whole-Class Instruction." *Music Educators Journal* 86(6):34–40.

MARANS, MICHAEL. (August 1993). "CD-ROM Explosion." *Keyboard* 19(8):35–44, 94.

MEUTH, LARRY. (April 1993). "MIDI Technology for the Scared to Death." *Music Educators Journal* 79(8):49–53.

The MTNA Guide to Music Instruction Software. 2d ed. (1993). Cincinnati, OH: Music Teachers National Association.

PETERS, G. DAVID. (November 1992). "Music Software and Emerging Technology." *Music Educators Journal* 79(3):22–25, 63.

RUDOLPH, THOMAS E. (1996). *Teaching Music with Technology.* Chicago: G.I.A. Publishing.

THOMPSON, KEITH P. (November 1999). "Internet Resources for General Music." *Music Educators Journal* 86(3):30–36.

VENNEMEYER, JIM. (June 1999). "Orff + Technology = Composition for Kids." *General Music Today* 6 (6): 36–38

WIRT, RONALD. (February 1998). "Suppose We Compose." *General Music Today* 5 (4): 38–39, 53.

INTEGRATING MUSIC, THE ARTS, AND OTHER SUBJECTS

Music and the other arts stimulate and enhance learning in every subject. Students can explore their feelings, their creativity, and their cultural heritage in an integrated curriculum. Such a curriculum helps students understand the relationships between subjects—to make sense out of fragmented skills and knowledge so they can see the "big picture."

Arts educators throughout the nation have recognized the importance and value of an integrated curriculum, and have developed standards to guide teaching and learning. The standard(s) for understanding music, arts, and other disciplines is found on p. 88.

Before integrating music and the arts, it is helpful to review the commonalities among the arts and the importance of arts education. Teachers need to learn the approaches and topics that are useful in making connections across the curriculum.

Comparing the Arts

Each of the arts has unique media and symbolic systems. Each has formal elements that are expressed in different ways but with commonalities that can be compared and contrasted. This means that music and the other arts can be connected in the curriculum. For example:

- Music composers use elements such as melody, rhythm, form, and timbre to organize sounds.
- Visual artists explore color, line, volume, and so forth, in media such as wood and watercolor.
- Dancers explore space, time, and force, as in folk or modern dance.
- Actors in theatre focus on language in acting, improvisation, and playmaking; elements of acting parallel some elements of the other arts, such as tempo, timbre, time, and space.

The Arts and Intelligence

Music, dance, visual arts, and theatre are special languages of both ideas and feeling. Do artists such as dance pioneer Martha Graham, composer Igor Stravinsky, and visual artist Pablo Picasso have a special type of intelligence? Psychologist Howard Gardner believes that all individuals have at least seven intelligences but that no single intelligence is inherently artistic (Fowler, 1990). In his theory of multiple intelligences, Gardner describes seven intelligences as spatial, bodily/kinesthetic, musical, verbal/linguistic, logical/mathematical, interpersonal, and intrapersonal. Gardner suggests that

> in dance . . . bodily kinesthetic intelligence is important, but so is musical intelligence, spatial intelligence, and probably other intelligences as well. (in Fowler, 1990:25)

Visual artists probably represent spatial intelligence, and musicians, musical intelligence. But schools do little to develop these different intelligences. Linguistic and logical skills are often the only measure for success in school, and the other intelligences are ignored (Fowler, 1990: 25). Arts educator Elliot W. Eisner suggests that we organize the curriculum "to optimize whatever potential intelligences individuals possess" (Fowler, 1990: 26). Arts education is critical if the arts intelligences of every child are to be developed.

Arts Education Stimulates All Learning

When a school has a rich arts curriculum, students excel in all subjects. For example, the Learning to Read Through the Arts program (originally developed in New York City) uses arts as the main stimulus for all learning. In this program, praised by the

U.S. Department of Education, students make "substantial gains in achievement" that are retained over several years, and they have an improved attitude toward learning in general (Collett, 1991:43). Similarly, the Ashley River Creative Arts Elementary Magnet School (Charleston County, South Carolina) places the arts at the core of the curriculum for its ethnically diverse population. As a result:

> Students at the [arts] school consistently earn the highest scores in their county on standardized tests of achievement in reading and other traditional academic subjects, and also far outpace the norms for their state. (Shuler, 1991:26)

The elementary school in Aiken, South Carolina, is well known for its arts-integrated curriculum; the school wins state and national awards, and students consistently post high marks on the Stanford Achievement Test and the California Test of Basic Skills (Williams, 1991:11). And there are many other examples (Barry, 1992:12; Shuler, 1991:26). One of the most important features of this integration is that *every student participates in the arts,* and not just a talented few.

Integrating Music and Other Subjects

There are many reasons for integrating music and the other arts into the elementary curriculum. They can be an exciting stimulus for many other subjects because they provide for creative, "hands-on" experiences. Also, the arts have many features in common with other subjects.

- The arts are a means of expression and communication, as are the language arts and literature.
- The arts complement some elements of science, mathematics, and physical education.
- The arts are a dynamic part of culture and history and provide additional ways of understanding the world, blending readily with the social studies curriculum.

Finally, arts curricula share many educational goals with other subjects because they help develop

- critical and creative thinking;
- interpersonal skills;
- democratic and human values;
- meaningful social participation.

The arts can therefore play a central role in educating the whole child.

When music is integrated with other subjects, instructional goals need to be established for both music and the other subjects. For example, a start at integrating social studies and music might be to sing "Yankee Doodle" during Revolutionary War study. But singing the song is just a beginning, because if students are to learn something about music they must also explore the song's elements (e.g., melody, rhythm, tempo) and the song's use and importance during the war. *Music should be more than a tool for learning other subjects.* A valid integrative experience should deepen the understanding of music as well as that of the other discipline(s) involved.

Ways music can be linked to the other arts and other subjects are described below. Practical applications of interdisciplinary learning are highlighted and integrated into the model experiences for kindergarten through grade 5 classrooms, found in Section Two of this text. Subjects integrated include dance/movement, language arts, literature, science, social studies, theatre, and visual art.

Integrated learning in the elementary classroom can be organized in a number of ways. The thematic approach and the parallel concepts approach are two such organizations.

The Thematic Approach to Integrated Learning

The thematic approach focuses on a theme or topic, adding material to the existing curriculum without greatly reorganizing it. The thematic approach is illustrated in the Model Experience "Ballet of the Unhatched Chicks" (p. 128), a lesson using the topic of chicks to help children explore long and short musical sounds. Students also compare living things and discover their own uniqueness as humans by classifying animals. As a result, students have integrated experiences with music, social studies, science, and visual art.

Science and social studies are integrated in the model experience "Anaguta Drums" (p. 140), as students discover how sound is produced by the vibrating parts of two African instruments and then learn about the African American Kwanzaa celebration. Students may experience the home and family life of Japan after creating an accompaniment to a haiku poem (p. 204).

In addition, throughout *The Musical Classroom* are model experiences that focus on African American, Navajo Indian, Mexican American, Chinese New Year, and Jewish Hanukkah topics. During these lessons, students explore music elements and also examine the arts of the particular culture:

- How are the arts expressed in that culture?
- How are they used and valued?
- What are the roles of individuals and groups?
- How has that culture contributed to and blended with American culture?

Lessons can also explore the lifestyles, celebrations, and history of various cultures.

The elementary music series often include suggestions for interdisciplinary learning (see Appendix C). See classified or special indexes under categories such as "Social Studies," "Poems," "Fine Art Reproductions," and "Holidays."

Other possible themes for integrated learning follow. Page numbers identify related songs found in Section Four.

Holidays: Chinese New Year p. 368; Christmas pp. 303, 327, 363, 365, 372, 387, 390, 395; Fourth of July pp. 279, 280, 374, 393; Halloween pp. 301, 373; Hanukkah pp. 284, 306, 307, 340; Martin Luther King Day pp. 364, 386; Thanksgiving pp. 298, 349, 385.

History: Civil War p. 281; cowboys p. 347; transportation pp. 295, 300, 354, 383; Revolutionary War p. 392; Earth Day/Ecology pp. 320, 374.

Themes depicted in different arts can be compared, using topics and music such as *animals* (Carnival of the Animals by Saint-Saëns); *nature* (Nuages [clouds] by Debussy); *places* (Grand Canyon Suite by Grofè); and *transportation* (Little Train of the Caipira by Villa-Lobos).

The Parallel Concepts Approach to Integrated Learning

The parallel concepts approach is especially appropriate for the arts. This approach focuses on common concepts found in dance, music, theatre, and the visual arts. Common concepts include color, repetition, contrast, and balance.

A curriculum for this approach is usually organized so that students can examine the common elements or concepts from several perspectives. Each discipline is distinct, with unique skills and symbolic systems, so commonalities should not be forced. For example, even though the word *line* is used in both music and the visual arts, the concept has a technically different meaning in each art.

Contrasts in visual art and dance are integrated in a model experience that begins with students creating abstract drawings for connected and disconnected musical pitches (see "Barcarolle," p. 156). As a follow-up, students create contrasting body movements for "Barcarolle" and "Devil's Dance."

Forms that balance and repeat are the basis for two different model experiences. Students create original blues lyrics (p. 221) using the three-line form of blues, as well as its repetitions and rhyme scheme. In the Model Experience "Carillon" (p. 206) that embodies ABA form, students examine balance in cathedral architecture.

Density, color, and use of space in visual art are explored in the Model Experience "Wake Me!" (p. 143). After performing a melody alone and with accompaniment, students compare two paintings of a cowboy: one with a colorful background, the other without. Repetition is the focus of the "John the Rabbit" lesson (p. 131). Students sing repeated parts of a song and then explore repetition in poems and paintings.

Many elements can be compared and contrasted across subjects, including

- texture (arts, science),
- form (arts, architecture, literature, science),
- repetition (arts, architecture, literature),
- space (arts), style (arts and architecture), and
- color (arts, science).

Some broader perspectives could be *culture and ethnicity* (how our culture is shaped by various ethnic groups), *migration and immigration* (conflicts, effects on resident populations, homesickness), *ecology* (how societies perceive and value the environment), and *technology* (how it changes arts and culture).

The Role of the Classroom Teacher

The classroom teacher is in a perfect position to integrate music and the other arts with other subjects. Classroom teachers know their students and the curriculum and are connected to the community of students, school, and parents. Classroom teachers can choose the best time to relate music and the other arts to the social studies, language arts, or science curriculum. They are familiar with the cultural background of each student, and they can observe how children benefit from the self-esteem that a successful arts experience provides. Working individually, with a team, or with specialists, the classroom teacher is in an ideal position to relate the arts to each child's experience.

National Standards for Arts Education

The National Standards for Arts Education specify content and achievement standards in music, dance, drama/theatre, and the visual arts for grades K through 12. These standards offer a framework for developing a curriculum and articulate what all students should know and be able to do in the arts. Each art is presented as a discrete discipline, but standards are included that recognize connections between music, the other arts, and subjects outside the arts.

National Standards for Music Education

Standard 8. Understanding Relationships between Music, the Other Arts, and Disciplines Outside the Arts

Standard 8, one of the nine National Standards for Music Education for grades K through 12, specifies what students should know and be able to do in understanding relationships between music, the other arts, and disciplines outside the arts. For this content standard, there are two achievement standards.

By the end of grade 4, students will need to

a. identify similarities and differences in the meanings of common terms[1] used in the various arts;
b. identify ways in which the principles and subject matter of other disciplines taught in the school are interrelated with those of music.[2] (From *National Standards for Arts Education.* Copyright © 1994 by Music Educators National Conference. Used by permission.)

Summary

When subjects are integrated in the elementary classroom, curricular goals need to be established for subjects individually and collectively. An arts-integrated curriculum contributes to excellence in all subjects and reinforces the idea that the arts are serious subjects with high standards. Music and the other arts are valuable in and of themselves, as well as for their associated educational value. The arts use symbolic systems that represent many forms of intelligence. The classroom teacher is an ideal person to integrate music and the other arts and to provide arts experience for *all* students.

PROJECTS FOR COLLEGE STUDENTS

1. In small groups, review the follow-up activities for model experiences in Level I or Level II that integrate the arts. Then prepare two original correlations for a Level I or II model experience of your choice. Align these correlations with the achievement standards of the National Standards for Music Education presented in this section. One correlation should use the thematic approach, and the other the parallel concepts approach. Describe or present your ideas to the entire class.
2. Prepare an original model experience that integrates music with another arts area or with a discipline outside the arts. Use the parallel concepts approach and align your model experience with an achievement standard of the National Standards for Music Education. Describe or present your model experience.

REFERENCES

Barry, Nancy H. (Winter 1992). "Reaching At-Risk Children Through Music and the Arts." *General Music Today* 5(2):12–14.

Blecher, Sharon, and Kathy Jaffee. (1998). *Weaving In the Arts: Widening the Learning Circle.* Portsmouth, NH: Heinemann; ISBN 0325000328. The authors, elementary teachers, describe their integrated arts curriculum.

Campbell, Linda, Bruce Campbell, and Dee Dickinson. (1998). *Teaching and Learning Through Multiple Intelligences,* 2nd ed. Allyn & Bacon; ISBN 0205298484.

Collett, Mary Jane. (November 1991). "Read Between the Lines: Music as a Basis for Learning." *Music Educators Journal* 78(3):42–45.

Consortium of National Arts Education Associations. (1994). *The National Standards for Arts Education.* Reston, VA: Music Educators National Conference.

Fallin, Jana R. (March 1995). "Children's Literature As a Springboard for Music." *Music Educators Journal* 81(5):24–27.

[1]For example, form, line, contrast.

[2]For example, foreign languages: singing songs in various languages; language arts: using the expressive elements of music in interpretive readings; mathematics: mathematic basis of values of notes, rests, and time signatures; science: vibration of strings, drumheads, or air columns generating sounds used in music; geography: songs associated with various countries or regions.

Fowler, Charles. (September 1990). "Recognizing the Role of Artistic Intelligences." *Music Educators Journal* 90(77):1, 24–27.

Fowler, Charles. (1996). *Strong Arts, Strong Schools: The Promising Potential and Shortsighted Disregard of the Arts in American Schooling.* Oxford University Press; ISBN 0195100891.

Gardner, Howard. (1999). *Intelligence Reframed: Multiple Intelligences for the 21st Century.* New York: Basic Books.

Hoffman, Steve, and Linda Lanner, eds. (1989). *Learning from the Inside Out.* Wheaton, MD: Association for Early Childhood Education International; ISBN 0871731193. Integrating art, film, dance, drama, music, storytelling, puppetry, and writing.

Kite, Thomas S., Thomas Smucker, Stan Steiner, and Mina Bayne. (March 1994). "Using Program Music for Interdisciplinary Study." *Music Educators Journal* 80(5):33–36, 53.

McCoy, Claire W. (Spring 1994). "Music and Children's Literature: Natural Partners." *General Music Today* 7(3):15–19.

Miller, Beth Ann. (Fall 1994). "Whole Language? Whole Music!" *General Music Today* 8(1):3–8.

National Center for Education Statistics. (September 1998). "The NAEP 1997 Arts Education Assessment: An Overview." *Music Educators Journal* 85(2):1–6 (insert). Includes matrix for assessment across the arts.

Shuler, Scott C. (November 1991). "Music, At-Risk Students, and the Missing Piece." *Music Educators Journal* 78(3):21–29.

Visual and Performing Arts Framework for California Public Schools: Kindergarten Through Grade Twelve. 3d ed. (1996). Sacramento, CA: California State Department of Education.

Volkman, Roberta. (Fall 1994). "Music Through Language." *General Music Today* 8(1):18–19.

Walker, Pam Prince. (1993). *Bring in the Arts: Lessons in Dramatics, Arts, and Story Writing for Elementary and Middle School Classrooms.* Portsmouth, NH: Heinemann; ISBN 0453086111.

Williams, Harold M. (1991). *The Language of Civilization: The Vital Role of the Arts in Education.* Washington, DC: The President's Committee on the Arts and the Humanities.

Zap! Computer program covers the physics of sound, light, and electricity for a concert. Ages 8–12. For details see "Selected Music Software" in Appendix F.

See also Resources, Appendix F: "Integrating Music," "World Music."

TEACHING MUSIC TO SPECIAL LEARNERS

Every elementary classroom includes students with varying abilities and disabilities. Teachers must meet the challenge to help all students reach their full learning potential, including those who are considered exceptional or special learners.

Special learners are "those whose physical attributes and/or learning abilities differ from the norm, either above or below, to such an extent that an individualized program of special education is indicated" (Heward and Orlansky, 1992:27). Students who are mentally impaired, learning disabled, visually impaired, hearing impaired, physically challenged, and gifted and talented and those who may have behavior or communication (speech and language) disorders are often identified as special learners. In addition, there are some children who may be considered at risk for becoming special learners because of home conditions (abuse, economic deprivation) or birth conditions (premature birth, fetal drug or alcohol syndrome).

The Inclusive Classroom

Before 1975, special learners were generally isolated in special self-contained classes. With the passage in 1975 of PL 94-142, the Education for All Handicapped Children Act, students with disabilities were to be placed in the least restrictive environment (LRE), which, in many cases, became the regular elementary school classroom. Individualized education programs (IEPs) were also to be developed annually for each special learner.

In 1990, the Education of the Handicapped Act was renamed Individuals with Disabilities Education Act (IDEA) (PL 101-476) and with the passage of an amended version of IDEA (PL 105-17) in 1997 the IEP team (including classroom and music teachers) must try to educate and include all children in the least restrictive environment, which, in most cases, is the elementary classroom. As a result of these legislative changes, all teachers (classroom and music teachers) have been challenged to learn

Guidelines for Working with Special Learners

1. *Consult and work cooperatively with the school or district's special education facilitator to plan instruction.*
2. *Establish clear objectives and evaluate each child's readiness for the established objectives.*
3. *Plan concrete, action-oriented music experiences that allow students to explore music through a variety of multisensory modes (visual, tactile, kinesthetic, etc.).*
4. *Use several different music-making activities — singing, playing instruments, moving, creating, listening — with the child.*
5. *Match songs to the child's vocal register, lowering or raising the key of the song if necessary.*
6. *Match tempos to the child's tempo.*
7. *Be consistent in expectations and procedures.*
8. *Post classroom rules and procedures (with picture cues), signing charts and other visuals.*
9. *Be aware of keeping the noise level in your classroom at a manageable one for the auditory-sensitive student.*
10. *Allow for many opportunities to be "right" and give praise when it is earned.*

how to reach and teach students with special needs and to provide a learning environment in which all students can succeed and grow in an inclusive classroom.

Music must be an important part of the education of *all* students, and special learners are no exception. Students with special learning needs can participate in meaningful musical experiences, gaining skills, knowledge, and satisfaction. Those with disabilities can benefit from music instruction and will, through music, refine their auditory, language, visual, and motor skills. In fact, many students respond best to a music modality and many classroom and special education teachers use music to help teach the basic skills.

Teachers continuously need to adapt their methods and procedures for teaching music to meet the differing needs of special learners. The music concepts introduced may well be the same as those for the other students, but teaching strategies, equipment, or musical instruments will need modification. The single-concept approach of the model experiences in this text should limit distractions and help certain special learners focus on a specific learning task. Particular activities in the model experiences may be used to provide a challenge for those special learners who need to expand their learning. As with all students, it is important to repeat and reinforce music concepts learned. Learning objectives should be modified to allow students with special learning needs to participate according to their own capabilities and at their own pace.

Special Learners and the Music Classroom

Many model experiences in Section Two include suggestions for meeting the needs of special learners. The following includes some basic information and recommendations for teaching music to students who are mentally impaired, learning disabled, visually impaired, hearing impaired, physically challenged, gifted and talented, as well as those who may have behavior disorders. In addition to these categories, there are increasing numbers of students with other types of disabilities in today's classroom—these disabilities range from aphasia, Attention Deficit Disorder (ADD), autism to fetal alcohol syndrome, fragile X, and traumatic brain injury. Classroom and music teachers need to consult and work with the special education facilitator in their school to learn how best to maximize the music learning experience for students with any kind of disability.

Mentally Impaired

Students who are mentally impaired differ in their musical capacities, as do all other students. One task at a time is most comfortable, along with much repetition during a lesson. Students will succeed through imitation—for example, clapping and singing in response to the teacher (or other classmates). Songs with action and other concrete stimuli are helpful in their learning. For example, body parts can be identified along with a song's words, or the teacher can use puppets to depict the action of a musical story.

If students who are mentally impaired sing in a low voice, songs may be dropped by three or four pitches to help them begin matching tones. They need to explore and expand their voices by whispering, speaking, and singing throughout their range.

Like all students in the classroom, students who are mentally impaired need to feel successful. When they are not able to tell the answer, they may be able to show the answer. With a sensitive teacher's patience and encouragement, they will gain needed self-confidence and independence.

Learning Disabled

Processing aural and visual information is usually difficult for students with learning disabilities or perceptual handicaps. In this case, teachers should emphasize initially the music-learning mode for which a student shows preference: singing, playing, listening, creating, or reading music. The use of one mode at a time seems to work best. For example, students can sing the melody of a song until it is learned well and later add steady-beat clapping along with the melody.

Singing games and dances will need practice, since students who are learning disabled need extra concentration for spatial tasks and following directions.

Visual cues will help them (and their classmates) remember the lyrics of a song and the steps of a singing game or dance. If frustration occurs, "time-outs" provide the needed rest and quiet isolation.

Visually Impaired

Students who are visually impaired (blind or with low vision) need seating close to the front of the class, enlarged charts, and two- and three-dimensional study aids. In addition, teachers can use flannelboards and felt cutouts for notes and shapes or use the student's hand to show the five lines and four spaces of the staff. Autoharp, Chromaharp, and resonator bars can be labeled with Braille music signs or other tactile cues.

Teachers must constantly describe verbally what is happening in the classroom so the students who are visually impaired may hear what they cannot see.

Students, including those who are visually impaired, benefit from experiences that build their comprehension of space. Singing games and dances performed in an ordered, unchanging setting will help children build physical and social self-confidence, as well as concepts about physical space.

Hearing Impaired

Students with varying levels of hearing impairment are often mainstreamed for music learning. Musical vibrations are amplified through hearing aids. Each child's aid needs to be properly adjusted to hear the singing, playing of instruments, and recordings that are a part of music class. Students with hearing impairments can feel vibrations by using instruments such as drums, Autoharp, Chromaharp, and resonator bars. Instruments that can play sustained tones may work better than percussive instruments with short, dry sounds.

Low pitches are usually heard better than high pitches so students may initially sing in a lower range. However, they will need to explore and discover the difference between speaking and singing voices and work to expand their singing range. A singer who is hearing impaired may benefit from sitting next to a student with a strong, clear singing voice. Students who are hearing impaired seem to respond better to rhythmic aspects of music than to pitch and perform rhythmically more accurately when music is performed in the moderate tempo range (Darrow, 1985).

Language development is helped when teachers choose songs that reflect the natural rhythm and pitch of speech. Since many students use lip reading as an aid to understanding, charts and other materials should be held close to the teacher's face while the teacher describes them. Any supplemental tactile and vibrotactile devices will also greatly aid hearing-impaired students. Many students who are hearing impaired sign to communicate. Teachers should incorporate signing with singing activities whenever possible. All students in the music classroom can benefit from signing—those with normal hearing have the opportunity to learn another language while those who are hearing-impaired learn more about music.

Physically Challenged

Students with physical disabilities or health handicaps do not always need more time to complete their music activities but frequently need modified equipment. If necessary, instruments can be altered to have larger handles or straps, or they can be hung (with Velcro straps) from overhead supports.

Rhythm sticks, for example, can be made of one- or two-inch-diameter doweling. Mallets can be attached to hands or gloves with Velcro. Easy participation is possible by using electronic instruments that respond to a light touch (such as synthesizers or electronic pianos) or that include a pressure-sensitive board (such as an Omnichord). Lap tables should be provided for students in wheelchairs.

During movement activities, substitute motions will aid some learners: fingers can "walk" in the air, heads can bob, or wheelchairs can move in time to the music. Since students with physical disabilities will prefer to do the same activities as their peers, a sensitive teacher might involve half the class in motions that these special learners can perform while the other half participates in locomotor movements.

Gifted and Talented

Gifted and talented children are those who have the natural ability to excel—some may excel in only one thing; others may excel in several areas.

These children may be intellectually gifted or have advanced abilities in other areas, such as the visual or performing arts.

Teachers may recognize these students by their ability to pick up ideas quickly in the classroom and relate those ideas to other contexts. Or they may be identified by the depth of their thinking and questioning—even their solutions, perhaps unusual, to problems and questions. Students with special music talent may quickly learn to read music, show great skill and musicianship in learning to play an instrument, or demonstrate exceptional creativity in composing and arranging activities.

To help these students achieve their potential, teachers must offer numerous opportunities for them to be challenged. Often small-group and individualized projects may provide these types of experiences. Projects that involve conducting research, using computer and CD-ROM music programs, and playing and composing music at an electronic keyboard are some possibilities.

Children who are gifted and talented have special needs just as other special learners do. They should be offered every opportunity to be enriched and challenged in the elementary classroom.

Behavior Disorders

Students with significant behavior disorders are in our school classrooms too and are described by Sylvia Rockwell as "tough to reach, tough to teach." (Rockwell, 1993) These students exhibit extremely inappropriate behavior—behavior that inhibits their academic progress. These "troubling and troubled children" are a challenge for teachers as they work to meet the needs of these special learners and the other students in their class. Students with behavior disorders need teachers who will give them the needed love, attention, and discipline they require, but at the same time, not change or bend class rules especially for them. There are a variety of different strategies and interventions available to help teachers remain in control of the classroom and themselves as they work with students with behavior disorders.

Summary

Since 1975 many special learners are included in the regular elementary classroom and it appears that we are moving into an era where special education and general education will no longer be separate entities. Teachers must be prepared to meet the challenges of planning instruction for students with a wide range of abilities and disabilities so as to ensure that all students develop their potential. Certainly students who are classified as challenged or special should experience the joy of music, because music knows no limitations. Music can reach each and every learner.

PROJECTS FOR COLLEGE STUDENTS

1. Visit an elementary class that includes special learners. If possible, observe the class during music and notice how the students with disabilities respond and what kinds of activities are especially appropriate. Prepare a report (oral or written) to share with classmates.
2. Review the model experiences of *The Musical Classroom* and choose one example of a music activity for special learners in each category of disability. Summarize how each example would be appropriate for the special learners.
3. "Try on" a handicap to discover what the limitations are for different disabilities. For example, wear a blindfold during class. Describe your experience.

REFERENCES

ATTERBURY, BETTY W. (1990). *Mainstreaming Exceptional Learners in Music.* Englewood Cliffs, NJ: Prentice Hall.

BERNSTORF, ELAINE D., and BETTY T. WELSBACHER. (March 1996). "Helping Students in the Inclusive Classroom." *Music Educators Journal* 82(5):21–26.

BUCK, GLENN H. (November 1992). "Classroom Management and the Disruptive Child." *Music Educators Journal* 79(3):36–42.

CHADWICK, D. M., and C. A. CLARK. (November 1980). "Adapting Music Instruments for the Physically Handicapped." *Music Educators Journal* 67(3):56–59.

COATES, PATRICIA. (November 1985). "Make Music Mainstreaming Work." *Music Educators Journal* 72(3):31–32.

DARROW, ALICE-ANN. (September 1987). "Exploring the Arts of Sign and Song." *Music Educators Journal* 74(1):33–35.

DARROW, ALICE-ANN. (February 1985). "Music for the Deaf." *Music Educators Journal* 71(6):33–35.

FORREST, RENEE, DIANE MACLAY, and JANET MONTGOMERY. (December 1997). "In Step with Inclusion." *Teaching Music* 5 (3): 56–57, 74.

GFELLER, KATE. (1992). "Research Regarding Students with Disabilities." In *Handbook of Research on Music Teaching and Learning,* Richard Colwell, ed. New York: Schirmer Books.

GFELLER, KATE. (April 1989). "Behavior Disorders: Strategies for the Music Teacher." *Music Educators Journal* 75(8):27–30.

GILBERT, JANET PERKINS. (February 1977). "Mainstreaming in Your Classroom: What to Expect." *Music Educators Journal* 64(6):64–68.

GRAHAM, RICHARD M. (January 1988). "Barrier-free Music Education: Methods to Make Mainstreaming Work." *Music Educators Journal* 73(5):29–33.

HERLEIN, DORIS G. (1975). "Music Reading for the Sightless: Braille Notation." *Music Educators Journal* 62(1):42–45.

HEWARD, W., and M. ORLANSKY. (1992). *Exceptional Children.* New York: Macmillan.

HUMPAL, MARCIA EARL, and JACQUELYN A. DIMMICK. (March 1995). "Special Learners in the Music Classroom." *Music Educators Journal* 81(5):21–23.

LAM, RITA C., and CECILIA WANG. (April 1982). "Integrating Blind and Sighted Through Music." *Music Educators Journal* 68(8):44–45.

"Mainstreaming." (April 1990). Special issue of *Music Educators Journal,* 76(8).

ROCKWELL, SYLVIA. (1993). *Tough to Reach, Tough to Teach (Students with Behavior Problems).* Reston, VA: Council for Exceptional Children.

SCHABERG, GAIL, comp. (1989). *Tips: Teaching Music to Special Learners.* Reston, VA: Music Educators National Conference.

"Teaching Special Students." (April 1980). Special issue of *Music Educators Journal,* 68(8).

WALCZYK, EUGENIA BULAWA. (July 1993). "Music Instruction and the Hearing Impaired." *Music Educators Journal* 80(1):42–44.

COOPERATIVE LEARNING

Finding ways to meet individual needs or differentiate instruction is a goal of classroom teachers and music teachers. Each student is unique and finding ways to tailor instruction to meet individual needs is a challenge that teachers face every day. Teachers consistently use a wide variety and range of teaching strategies and techniques to differentiate instruction.

One teaching strategy that works effectively with many students is cooperative learning. Cooperative learning is an instructional strategy that involves students working together in small, interdependent teams of two to six students. The teams are usually grouped heterogeneously. Each member of the group actively participates in the assigned task and interacts with other group members. Generally, each group member is assigned a role, such as: facilitator, reader, timekeeper, checker, praiser. All team members share responsibility for group leadership, and teachers continually observe and assess group functioning and interaction.

Because cooperative-learning activities require students to explain their views and listen to others' views, evaluate and assess their own work, and support and help one another, students grow in many ways. The results are often increased achievement, cognitive development at higher levels, growth in self-esteem, and a more positive attitude toward school. Cooperative learning techniques also help to motivate the disinterested or reluctant student, teach team-building skills and offer opportunities to practice social skills. In addition, minority students have shown far greater academic gain in classrooms using cooperative learning as compared with classrooms using traditional learning strategies (Kagan, 1986:231–298).

Cooperative-learning strategies can be used for part of a lesson or for an entire lesson. Examples of such strategies are highlighted and integrated into the kindergarten through grade 5 model experiences in Section Two as well as in the "Projects for College Students" that are presented throughout the text. For example, in the Model Experience Haiku Sound Piece, p. 204, fourth- and fifth-grade students are asked (in small groups) to create a sound piece based on a haiku poem while college students as a follow-up to the Model Experience "Sally, Go 'Round the Sun" (p. 122) work in cooperative learning groups to determine which National Standards were addressed and which were not addressed in two lessons and then present their list to the larger group citing reasons for their decisions.

Guidelines for Cooperative Learning Strategies

1. *Arrange the classroom to maximize small group learning.*
2. *Assign students to groups—usually in random order.*
3. *Identify each team's task(s), assign and explain individual roles, note what social skills are expected, and explain the criteria for evaluation. Set a reasonable time limit.*
4. *Observe and assess all group interactions.*
5. *Conclude the strategy with students sharing and evaluating their achievements.*

As students learn to work in small groups cooperatively, they develop not only music skills but also social ones. Additionally, the musical classroom becomes a more exciting and interesting learning environment. What follows are some guidelines for planning cooperative learning strategies.

REFERENCES

BALOCHE, LYNDA, and LISA C. DELORENZO. (Fall 1994). "Cooperative Learning: Making Music Together." *General Music Today* 8(1):9–12.

FOOT, H. C., M. J. MORGAN, and R. H. SHUTE. (1990). *Children Helping Children.* New York: Wiley.

HAMILTON, HILREE J. (Winter 1998). "Improvisation, Composition, and Peer Interactions: Music Learning in a Cultural Context." *General Music Today* 11 (2): 4–13.

JOHNSON, D. W., and R. T. JOHNSON. (1984). *Circles of Learning: Cooperation in the Classroom.* Alexandria, VA: Association for Supervision and Curriculum Development.

JOHNSON, D. W., and R. T. JOHNSON. (1984). *Learning Together and Alone: Cooperative, Competitive, and Individualistic Learning.* Englewood Cliffs, NJ: Prentice Hall.

KAGAN, S. (1986). "Cooperative Learning and Sociocultural Factors in Schooling. In *Beyond Language: Social and Cultural Factors in Schooling Language Minority Students.* Los Angeles: California State University, Evaluation, Dissemination, and Assessment Center.

KAPLAN, PHYLLIS, and LENORE POGONOWKI. (1992). *Cooperative Learning in the Music Classroom.* Reston, VA: Music Educators National Conference. Video, 29 min. Music teachers with student demonstration groups explore cooperative learning.

KAPLAN, PHYLLIS, and SANDRA STAUFFER. (1994). *Cooperative Learning in Music.* Reston, VA: Music Educators National Conference.

SHARON, S. (1990). *Cooperative Learning: Theory and Research.* New York: Praeger.

SLAVIN, R. E. (1990). *Cooperative Learning: Theory, Research, and Practice.* Englewood Cliffs, NJ: Prentice Hall.

STATON, BARBARA, and MERRILL STATON. (1991). "Cooperative Learning." In the *Music and You* elementary music series. New York: Macmillan.

THE PREKINDERGARTEN CHILD AND MUSIC

There is hardly a baby who does not coo, sing, babble, or move to music, but musical responses begin even before the baby is born. At five months, the fetus can hear voices and music, move in rhythm to music, and react (by kicking) to loud noises—and even be disturbed by rock music (Whitwell and Riddell, 1991:1)! The newborn recognizes the rhythm, pitch, and expression of the mother's voice and distinguishes it from other female voices (Weinberger, 1999; Fox, 1991:43). In view of such findings, it is never too early to begin music experiences.

Many educators believe that musical aptitude is present at birth and flourishes in a nurturing environment (Gordon, 1993). In fact, psychologist Howard Gardner suggests that music is one of the first intelligences to manifest itself (Gardner, 1993). Teachers of prekindergarten children must learn how to nourish this musical potential.

Play is central to the young child's learning. This was recognized as early as the eighteenth century by Frederick Froebel, the founder of the Kindergarten. In the 1950s and 1960s, however, criticisms of American education led teachers and parents to

Courtesy of Susan Kenney

believe that greater success in later life would result from early "academic" training. As a result, some young children had long periods of "seat time" with workbooks and ditto sheets, perhaps threatening their interest in future learning. Today, prekindergarten educators recognize that learning should be developmentally appropriate and needs to "fit the young child, rather than making the child fit the now traditional pattern of formal schooling" (Palmer and Sims, 1993:3).

Prekindergarten children enjoy all kinds of music activities: moving, playing instruments, singing, listening, and exploring music concepts. Because music has been part of American kindergartens since the early 1900s, a great deal is known about what young children can do and learn in each of these areas. When the National Standards for Music Education were developed in 1994, music educators decided that it was critical not only to identify what K–12 students should know and be able to do, but also what prekindergarten children can learn and demonstrate. Therefore, four Prekindergarten Standards were developed. The National Standards for Music Education specify four content standards for prekindergarten:

- singing and playing instruments,
- creating music,
- responding to music,
- and understanding music.

(The achievement standards for each prekindergarten content standard are presented on page 101.)

Information on moving, playing instruments, singing, listening, and concept development is presented below, along with some developmental "markers" and a few (of many) possible ideas for activities.

Sources for listed music materials and instruments are found in Resources, Appendix F, "General Music Retailers."

Moving and Playing Instruments

Music is almost synonymous with movement, and the prekindergarten child especially discovers the world by physically acting upon it (Palmer and Sims, 1993:8). Rhythm and movement experiences should be age-appropriate and need to focus on process rather than product.

Playing rhythm instruments (see Chapter III) relates to motor development as well as to aural skills. Prekindergarteners can respond to timbre, duration, and dynamics. They need access to high-quality musical instruments so they can explore sound, group the instruments by type, and play instruments with songs and stories. (Teachers can use music from Resources, Appendix F: "Prekindergarten: Singing.")

Developmental stages and suggested activities in moving and playing instruments follow (summarized from McDonald and Simons, 1989:98–99; Scott-Kasner, 1992:8).

See Resources, Appendix F: "Prekindergarten: Moving," for songs, recordings, and videos.

Age	*Developmental Stage*	*Activities*
Infants	Visual, tactile, kinesthetic awareness expands	Adults interact by singing, chanting, imitating sounds, and by moving to music; provide exposure to selected music
2–3 yrs.	Walks, hops, jumps; claps to rhythm	Match drumbeat to child's movement
3–4 yrs.	Changes movement suddenly; gallops; eye–hand coordination developing	Learn easy singing games; clap patterns; play mallet and percussion instruments
4–5 yrs.	Improves control: slides, begins to skip	Continue age 3–4 activities; move to loud and soft music; classify and group instruments by type

Singing

Teachers need to sing to, with, and for the young child—and always be positive toward any and all efforts to sing. Singing interactions with infants should be frequent, playful, informal, and nonjudgmental. Several developmental stages and suggested activities in singing are presented below and on page 33. (Refer to Appendix F, "Singing," and "Prekindergarten: Singing" for song books and recordings.)

Age	*Developmental Stage*	*Activities*
3 mos.	Matches pitches	Sing to child; imitate sounds; lullabies
6–9 mos.	Babbles on a few pitches	Sing, move hands and feet, pat-a-cake
18 mos.	Develops speech	Sing fragments and child responds
2 yrs.	Sings more pitches	Encourage made-up child songs
2–3 yrs.	Sings familiar song parts	Sing songs and chants to and with child
3–4 yrs.	Sings whole songs, tonic may change; can begin small-group work	Songs within five or six pitches; provide small-group music activities
4–5 yrs.	Sings with more accurate pitch and rhythm	Build song repertoire; continue music in small groups

Listening

All parents observe that their young children are responsive to sounds. The infant responds by moving and singing and seems to prefer human sounds (McDonald and Simons, 1989:82). From birth, infants can notice timbre and dynamics and distinguish between two different timbres (Scott-Kasner, 1992:643). At five months of age, an infant can listen to singing or to a musical instrument for up to 30 minutes (McDonald and Simons, 1989:41).

Prekindergarten youngsters are open to all kinds of music and will benefit from a musically rich environment—with an adult who shows enjoyment of the music (McDonald and Simons, 1989:87). Children should dance, sing, move, and listen to a musical piece *many* times, not just once. Gordon (1993) strongly recommends playing "adult" recordings of music in all styles instead of "children's records" with a story-telling text. (Youngsters would focus on the music rather than on the story.) Pieces should be short and have a steady tempo, frequently changing dynamics, and "pleasing" but contrasting timbres (Brand, 1985:31).

See Resources, Appendix F: "Prekindergarten: Listening," for recordings. Also refer to Chapter III, "Listening."

Concept Development

Prekindergarten children often understand more than they can tell and comprehend many music concepts about timbre, dynamics, rhythm, melody, form, and texture. Sometimes questions about "comparatives" will bring out a response: "Does this (clapped) beat get slower or faster?" "Let's sing the song loudly, and then quietly." Prekindergarteners can demonstrate an understanding of the following music elements and concepts (McDonald and Simons, 1989:85).

Timbre: Identify (aurally) selected orchestral instruments and families.
Dynamics: Distinguish between loud and soft.
Rhythm: Identify steady beats, and fast and slow tempos.
Form: Identify same and different phrases.
Texture/harmony: Recognize accompanied and unaccompanied melody.

Several approaches to curriculum may be used with prekindergarteners. Young children can learn through any of the approaches described in Chapter V if the approaches are specially adapted: the eclectic, Orff-*Schulwerk,* Kodály, Dalcroze, and comprehensive musicianship. For resources based primarily on concept development, see Appendix F: "Prekindergarten: Curriculum."

Music Centers

The learning environment often determines what is learned, and how. Both space and equipment help music happen. Prekindergarten children need space for individual learning and, when they are ready, for small-group activities. Each type of area needs to be separate from, and look distinct from, the other areas. The large area should allow children to move freely, without bumping into each other—or the furniture.

The areas for learning might be organized as "music centers" where children can explore different music subjects. For example, a "listening center" might include instruments, a tape or CD player with individual headset, recordings, and picture books about music. Some music educators create additional, separate centers for playing, reading, and singing activities. A large "sound box" of cardboard or plywood can be outfitted on the inside with chimes, drums, and xylophones. (Idea by early childhood music specialist Barbara Andress.) This will give a private space for exploration. Other ideas are to have a soft (arm) chair for singing, and an area with a collection of hats or scarves that children can use in moving to music.

Standards for Music Education: Prekindergarten

These standards specify what children should know and be able to do by age 4. (From *The School Music Program: A New Vision.* 1994. Copyright © 1994 by Music Educators National Conference. Used by permission.)

1. **Content Standard: Singing and playing instruments**
   Achievement Standard:
   Children

a. use their voices expressively as they speak, chant, and sing
b. sing a variety of simple songs in various keys, meters, and genres,[3] alone and with a group, becoming increasingly accurate in rhythm and pitch
c. experiment with a variety of instruments and other sound sources
d. play simple melodies and accompaniments on instruments

2. **Content Standard: Creating music**
   Achievement Standard:
   Children

a. improvise songs to accompany their play activities
b. improvise instrumental accompaniments to songs, recorded selections, stories, and poems
c. create short pieces of music, using voices, instruments, and other sound sources
d. invent and use original graphic or symbolic systems to represent vocal and instrumental sounds and musical ideas

3. **Content Standard: Responding to music**
   Achievement Standard:
   Children

a. identify the sources of a wide variety of sounds[4]
b. respond through movement to music of various tempos, meters, dynamics, modes, genres, and styles to express what they hear and feel in works of music
c. participate freely in music activities

4. **Content Standard: Understanding music**
   Achievement Standard:
   Children

a. use their own vocabulary and standard music vocabulary to describe voices, instruments, music notation, and music of various genres, styles, and periods from diverse cultures

[3]For example, folk songs, ethnic songs, singing games.
[4]For example, crying baby, piano, guitar, car horn, bursting balloon.

b. sing, play instruments, move, or verbalize to demonstrate awareness of the elements of music and changes in their usage[5]
c. demonstrate an awareness of music as a part of daily life

Summary

It is never too early to bring children in touch with music. All children have musical potential, and prekindergarteners learn best through play: singing, playing instruments, and moving to the music they hear. Music activities need to happen every day, and throughout each day, because young children need repetition to learn—and to enjoy—music. If parents, caregivers, and teachers encourage developmentally appropriate musical experiences, prekindergarten children and music can become "the best of friends."

PROJECT FOR COLLEGE STUDENTS

Visit a preschool or day-care center and find out how music is integrated into the program. Briefly describe the situation, including the physical environment. Tell which music-making activities (e.g., singing, moving) are encouraged and what musical instruments and recordings are available. Explain how the program reflects a particular curricular development (Chapter VI) or approach to curriculum (Chapter V). Review the "Early Childhood Position Statement" of MENC (see www.menc.org/ or Whitlock, 1998) and describe how the program reflects this philosophy. Summarize your findings.

REFERENCES

ANDERSON, J. DIANNE. (Winter 1991). "Children's Song Acquisition: An Examination of Current Research and Theories." *Quarterly Journal of Music Teaching and Learning* 2:4.

ANDRESS, BARBARA. *Music in Early Childhood.* M & R Newsletters, P. O. Box 51064, New Berlin, WI 53151.

ANDRESS, BARBARA, ed. (1989). *Promising Practices: Prekindergarten Music Education.* Reston, VA: Music Educators National Conference.

ANDRESS, BARBARA. (Spring 1998). "Where's the Music in 'The Hundred Languages of Children?' " *General Music Today* 11(3):14–17. Discusses the Reggio Emilia approach.

ANDRESS, BARBARA L., and LINDA MILLER WALKER, eds., comps. (1992). *Readings in Early Childhood Music Education.* Reston, VA: Music Educators National Conference.

BRAND, MANNY. (1985). "Lullabies That Awaken Musicality in Infants." *Music Educators Journal* 71(7):28–31.

CAMPBELL, PATRICIA SHEHAN. (1998). *Songs in Their Heads: Music and Its Meaning in Children's Lives.* Oxford University Press; ISBN 019511101X.

Early Childhood Creative Arts. (1992). Reston, VA: Music Educators National Conference. Proceedings of the International Conference on Early Childhood Creative Arts.

FEIERABEND, JOHN M. (Summer 1995). "Music and Intelligence in the Early Years." *Early Childhood Connections: Journal of Music-and-Movement-Based Learning,* 1(3):5–13.

FEIERABEND, JOHN M. (1990). *TIPS: Music Activities in Early Childhood.* Reston, VA: Music Educators National Conference.

FLOHR, JOHN W., DANIEL C. MILLER, and DIANE C. PERSELLIN. (June 1999). "Recent Brain Research on Young Children." *Teaching Music* 6(6):41–43, 54.

FOX, DONNA BRINK. (1991). "Music, Development, and the Young Child." *Music Educators Journal* 77(5):42–46.

[5]For example, changes in rhythm, dynamics, tempo.

GARDNER, HOWARD. (1993/1983). *Frames of Mind: The Theory of Multiple Intelligences.* 10th ed. New York: Basic Books; ISBN 0465025102.

GORDON, EDWIN E. (1993). *Learning Sequences in Music.* Chicago: G.I.A. Publications.

LEVINOWITZ, LILI M. (Fall 1998). "The Importance of Music in Early Childhood." *General Music Today* 12(1):4–7.

LINDEMAN, CAROLYNN A. (August 1997). "Baby Talk" in FrontLines Column. *Teaching Music* (5(1)):6–7.

LITTLETON, DANETTE. (Fall 1998). "Music Learning and Child's Play." *General Music Today* 12(1):8–15.

MCDONALD, DOROTHY T., and GENE M. SIMONS. (1989). *Musical Growth and Development: Birth Through Six.* New York: Schirmer Books.

Music and Early Childhood. (July 1999). Special Issue of *Music Educators Journal* 86(1).

PALMER, MARY, and WENDY L. SIMS, eds. (1993). "Guidelines for Music Activities and Instructions." In *Music in Prekindergarten: Planning and Teaching,* 19–27. Reston, VA: Music Educators National Conference; ISBN 1565450175.

PONICK, F. S., comp. (October 1999). "What's Happening in Early Childhood Music Education?" *Teaching Music* 7(2):30–37.

SCOTT-KASNER, CAROL. (1992). "Research on Music in Early Childhood." In *Handbook of Research on Music Teaching and Learning,* Richard Colwell, ed. New York: Schirmer Books.

SIMS, WENDY L., ed. (1995). *Strategies for Teaching Prekindergarten Music.* Reston, VA: Music Educators National Conference.

Sing! Move! Listen! Music and Young Children. Reston, VA: Music Educators National Conference; ISBN 165450248. Video; 18 min.

SZABO, MOIRA. (Spring 1999). "Early Music Experience and Musical Development." *General Music Today* 12(3):17–19.

TURNER, MARK E. (July 1999). "Child-Centered Learning and Music Programs." *Music Educators Journal* 96(10):30–33, 51.

WEINBERGER, N. M., comp. (Winter 1999). "Lessons of the Music Womb." *MuSICA Research Notes* VI(1). Summary of research on music responses *in utero* and in newborns. See: www.musica.uci.edu/.

WHITLOCK, LINDA J., comp. (April 1998). "Sudden Assignment: Teach Prekindergarten Music." *Teaching Music* 5(5):40–41, 74.

WHITWELL, GISELLE, and CECILIA RIDDELL. (1991). *Orff Before Birth? Implications for the* Schulwerk. Paper presented at the National Conference, American Orff-*Schulwerk* Association, San Diego, California.

See Resources, Appendix F: "Addresses," for selected prekindergarten associations and publications.

CHAPTER SUMMARY

There are many up-to-date ways to stimulate music learning: through the use of music technology; by integrating music, the arts, and other subjects; and through cooperative learning. All these educational developments can be incorporated into the music curriculum, because with appropriate adaptation, they can serve special learners, prekindergarten children, and students of all types and ages.

CHAPTER REFERENCE

MADSEN, CLIFFORD K., ed. (2000). *Vision 2020: The Housewright Symposium on the Future of Music Education.* Reston, VA.: MENC: The National Association for Music Education. Historical overview by Mark, and essays by Reimer, Gates, Lehman, Jellison, Spearman, and Yarbrough.

VII
Planning and Assessing Music Learning

What should elementary school children learn about music? How can that learning be assessed? These are two important questions to be asked by any teacher working with children in a school setting. If elementary school children are to be sensitive to the power of music and to grow musically, then careful planning and meaningful assessment of music learning must be at the top of a teacher's instructional agenda.

Planning requires teachers to consider carefully *what* will be learned and *how.* Assessment necessitates examining *how well or to what degree* students have learned what was planned. These learning and evaluation plans are most often stated in the form of goals and objectives.

PLANNING: GOALS AND OBJECTIVES

Planning for music learning requires formulating goals and objectives. Goals are broad, general statements, usually few in number, that indicate long-range outcomes and reflect the philosophical basis for the curriculum and program. Such statements are central to curriculum planning and development. Goals are generally prepared for an entire school music program (K through 12) and may even be stated for the elementary school music program in particular. One of the goals of a K through 12 music program is to help students

Sample Goal

> To understand the role music has played and continues to play in the lives of human beings (*The School Music Program,* 1986).

Objectives, on the other hand, are more specific statements of what the students will learn as a result of music instruction and should be easily measurable. They are directly related to the long-term goals and are simply more-precise statements to make the goals operational. Objectives are stated for immediate music-learning experiences such as weekly or daily lessons as well as for monthly or yearly plans. Once objectives have been formulated, assessment can take place.

Numerous books, articles, learning kits, and other materials are available to assist in the writing of objectives. The approaches and terminology vary, but the common denominator in most sources is that an objective should specify how the learner will demonstrate learning (observable behavior).

The verb chosen to specify desired behavior must connote observable activity. Action verbs appropriate for formulating objectives in music include *sing, move, play,* and *clap.* A teacher can readily listen to or watch a student do these activities. These action verbs clearly indicate how students will demonstrate their music learning. Verbs such as *recognize, understand,* and *know* do not connote observable activity and should be avoided.

Each model experience in *The Musical Classroom* has a stated objective indicating what students should know and be able to do as a result of that particular musical experience. The stated objective for the Level II model experience on p. 164 is

Sample Objective

To identify aurally the long and short durations in the rhythm of a melody and to demonstrate that recognition by manipulating puppets.

Guidelines for Planning Music Learning

1. *Make a list of realistic goals for the school year. Review the school district's music curriculum guide and the scope and sequence charts in the elementary music series used in the school, the state's music curriculum framework, and the National Standards for Music Education for help in developing these goals.*
2. *Establish a list of short-term objectives for each grading period or each month.*
3. *Create lesson plans for immediate learning experiences that align with both the short-term objectives and the long-range goals. Remember that reviewing and reinforcing previous music learning must be included in this planning step.*
4. *Evaluate how well your short-term plans are "taking small steps" toward your long-range goals.*
5. *Revise and modify your plans as needed.*

LESSON PLANNING

To ensure that meaningful music learning takes place and that students are actively engaged, teachers need to plan exciting, interesting, and educationally sound lessons. Every lesson should begin with an activity that "grabs" the students' attention and motivates them to "stay tuned in." Throughout the lesson a variety of activities should be included to maintain students' interest and hold their attention. It is also important to plan how to move from one activity to another following a logical sequence and providing an appropriate transition (Small, 1992). The close of the lesson is just as important as the opening—it should "wrap up" what has taken place during the lesson (especially the music learning) and leave students with positive thoughts about the music experience.

SAMPLE LESSON PLAN

There are many different ways to commit a lesson plan to paper. The exact style is of little importance, but what is important is that the plans reflect the precise music-learning focus, a statement of what students should know and be able to do, the main points of the lesson, and the specifics regarding materials. The lesson-plan (or model-experience) format used in *The Musical Classroom* is one example of how to organize for music learning. This format, with descriptions of each category, follows.

MODEL EXPERIENCE FORMAT

MUSIC CONCEPT

This is the single understanding that will result from using the music and the process of the model experience.

Music

This is the musical selection upon which the model experience is based. Songs are notated in alphabetical order in Section Four. Musical selections are on the accompanying CD.

Objective

This is a statement that specifies what students will be able to *do* as a result of the musical experience. Teachers should note *how* the students will demonstrate their music learning: through singing, playing instruments, body movements, and so forth.

Materials

Recordings, books, and other equipment are specified. Worksheets for student use should be prepared in advance.

[Lesson begins here]

WHEN A SENTENCE IS WRITTEN IN CAPITAL LETTERS, IT SUGGESTS A PHRASE OR A QUESTION THAT MAY BE SPOKEN BY THE TEACHER EXACTLY AS IT APPEARS.

FOCUS

To capture the attention of your students, a focus statement or action is suggested for your use. (Create your own, to reflect *your* personality!) Although the focus statements in *The Musical Classroom* are brief and concise, some teachers are able to elaborate and expand on them without losing the interest of their class.

Key Terms

Key terms are noted in the margin. Consistent and repeated use of these terms facilitates learning.

Steps 1, 2, 3

Each operation is numbered, suggesting a logical sequence for development of music concepts and skills.

Special Learners
Orff Adaptation
Kodály Adaptation
Cooperative Learning

Margin notes recommend adaptations for special learners and special approaches to music teaching. These are described in Section One.

Indicator of Success

This identifies how and when students demonstrate understanding of the music concept. Most often, the teacher must watch and listen carefully as the class sings, plays, moves, and so forth.

SUMMARY

At the end of an experience, it is important to summarize the music concept. Rather than announcing this summary to the class, elicit it *from* them.

[Lesson ends here]

ASSESSMENT

This indicates how, in different music, students can show they perceive the studied concept.

Follow-Up

To be enjoyed, music usually must be heard until it becomes an old friend. Exciting music contains much that can be discovered on subsequent days. Music concepts also need exploration and refinement. This section includes activities that may serve as follow-ups to the model experience.

Relationships to other subjects are suggested by activities in related arts, language arts, literature, science, and social studies. Program ideas are also provided.

Projects for College Students

Music Fundamentals

These give instructors ideas for developing additional lessons and creative experiences for students, reading related research and articles of a professional nature, performing music, studying music fundamentals (often using technology) and discussing critical issues in elementary music education. There are opportunities for individual assignments and for small- and large-group activities.

Related Literature and Media for Children

Noted here are children's books, films/videos, and recordings for music and related subjects.

Other Music

Every model experience in *The Musical Classroom* includes a list of selections that exemplify the same music concept. Teachers may choose other selections that are more familiar, more available, or more appropriate for their particular classes.

[Now, turn to p. 132 and take a look at this format in a model experience.]

ASSESSING MUSIC LEARNING

Once goals and objectives have been prepared and stated and instruction has taken place, it is important to determine *if* and *how well* the objectives have been met. Teachers must assess student learning in a reliable, valid, systematic way. Therefore, assessment in music cannot be limited to multiple-choice or paper-and-pencil tests. Techniques must be used that require students to demonstrate a particular musical behavior or skill. This type of assessment—one that requires actual performance in an authentic setting—is known as *authentic assessment.* (See chart on next page.)

Sample Assessment Strategy

For each model experience in *The Musical Classroom,* an assessment strategy is specified. Each strategy relates to the stated objective for the lesson and assesses student learning through a demonstrable activity. For example, the objective and assessment strategy for the Level I model experience focusing on fast and slow tempo, p. 124, follows.

Objective: To identify aurally sounds and music that move fast and slow and to demonstrate that recognition in body movements.
Assessment: Students sing a familiar song once fast and once slow, demonstrating that they can differentiate between the two tempos and can describe the differences.

The National Assessment of Educational Progress (NAEP)

Just as teachers regularly assess student learning in their own classrooms, states offer measurements to assess student learning and gather data about student achievement at the state level. Nationally, the National Assessment of Educational Progress (NAEP) measures what U.S. students know and are able to do in various subject areas.

NAEP, a congressionally mandated project of the National Center for Education Statistics, U.S. Department of Education, gathers information from a nationally representative sample of students to provide results for the nation. Since 1969, assessments have been conducted to provide comprehensive information on student knowledge and skills at ages 9, 13, and 17 and more recently for students in grades 4, 8, and 12. Most frequently, students are assessed in mathematics, reading, writing, and science and less frequently in history, civics, music, and the visual arts. Music was assessed in 1972 and 1978 and was part of the NAEP Assessment of Arts Education in 1997. Only eighth-grade students were included in the 1997 music assessment, but it is expected that in 2007 students at all levels will be part of the NAEP music assessment.

The NAEP Arts Assessment 1997 was directly related to the *National Standards for Arts Education* released in 1994. In fact, the development of the framework for the arts assessment and for the national standards was a coordinated effort. The standards state what students should know and be able to do in music and the other arts (the "what"), and the National Arts Assessment addresses "how" the expected learning might be measured or appraised. Both the national standards and the arts assessment project offer a common vision and a national consensus of school arts education in general and music education in particular.

Methods or Techniques for Authentic Assessment

1. *Performance demonstrations or tests such as playing a chordal song accompaniment on Autoharp or Chromaharp or clapping a steady beat while singing a song*
2. *Checklists or anecdotal reports that describe verbal and nonverbal behavior*
3. *Audio or video recordings that document samples of students' musical behavior*
4. *Portfolios (collections of student work) that chronicle and monitor student learning over a period of time*
5. *Interviews or conferences with students to determine the depth of their understanding and give students a chance to reflect on their achievement*

PROJECTS FOR COLLEGE STUDENTS

1. Write an objective for a musical experience in which young children move their bodies to show upward/downward melodic direction. Make sure the statement includes observable behavior.
2. Create an original model experience following the assignment guidelines presented at the conclusion of Level I, Level II, and Level III model experiences. Design an assessment strategy for your original lesson.
3. Review the "Scope and Sequence Chart of Music Concepts" on pp. 114–115. Using this chart as a basis, draft an assessment form that may be used by a classroom teacher to keep a record of student learning for a school year.

REFERENCES

"Assessment." (Fall 1999). Special issue of *General Music Today*, 13(1):3–22.

"Assessment in Music Education." (September 1999). Special issue of *Music Educators Journal,* 86 (2).

Brophy, Timothy S. (2000). *Assessing the Developing Child Musician: A Guide for General Music Teachers.* Chicago: GIA Publications.

Brophy, Timothy S. (July 1997). "Reporting Progress with Developmental Profiles." *Music Educators Journal,* 84(1):24–27.

Brummett, Verna M., and Jennifer Haywood. (Fall 1997). "Authentic Assessment in School Music: Implementing a Framework." *General Music Today* 11(1):4–10.

Kassner, Kirk. (January 1998). "Would Better Questions Enhance Music Learning?" *Music Educators Journal,* 84(4):29–36.

Mager, Robert F. (1962). *Preparing Instructional Objectives.* Belmont, CA: Fearon.

National Standards for Arts Education. (1994). Reston, VA: Music Educators National Conference.

Performance Standards for Music: Strategies and Benchmarks for Assessing Progress Toward the National Standards, Grades Pre-K–12. (1996). Reston, VA: Music Educators National Conference.

Small, Ann. (1992). "Pacing: The Tempo of Teaching." In *Elementary General Music: The Best of MEJ.* Reston, VA: Music Educators National Conference.

Smith, Janice. (Fall 1995). "Using Portfolio Assessment in General Music." *General Music Today,* 9(1):8–12.

The School Music Program: A New Vision. (1994). Reston, VA: Music Educators National Conference.

The School Music Program: Description and Standards. 2d ed. (1986). Reston, VA: Music Educators National Conference, 14.

Sims, Wendy, et al. (February 2000). "Why Should Music Educators Care About NAEP?" *Teaching Music*, 7(4):40–45.

"Student Musical Activities and Achievement in Music: NAEP 1997 Arts Assessment." (December 1999). NAEP FACTS, 4 (1).

Whitcomb, Rachel. (May 1999). "Writing Rubrics for the Music Classroom." *Music Educators Journal,* 85(6):26–32.

Winner, E., L. Davidson, and L. Scripp, eds. (1992). *Arts PROPEL: A Handbook for Music.* Cambridge: Harvard Project Zero and Educational Testing Service.

CHAPTER SUMMARY

Quality music teaching involves careful planning for music learning as well as a systematic assessment of what students have learned. Learning and evaluating plans are often stated in the form of goals and objectives. Once goals and objectives have been prepared, instruction can then be planned, and the educational processes and products assessed. Student learning should be measured using methods that are reliable, valid, and performance-based, such as those used in authentic assessment.

Section Two

Model Experiences for Teaching Music

Photo by Patricia Hackett

The model experiences in this section are grouped according to three levels: Level I—kindergarten and first grade; Level II—second and third grades; and Level III—fourth and fifth grades. All musical selections for the forty-eight model experiences are included on an accompanying CD. See p. 114.

At the beginning of each level, the sequence of songs and listening selections are listed, the music concepts are identified and the developmental characteristics of children are introduced. At the end of each level are an evaluation of the college student's understanding of the level, an original model experience assignment, and an elementary music series textbook assignment.

Each Level III model experience includes the term ***Standards*** and a flag logo in the margin opposite "Assessment." These refer to the National Standards for Music Education, K–4. The particular content and achievement standards that are addressed in the model experience are indicated by a number and letter following the term ***Standards.*** Page numbers show where in this text the standard is described. Standards are similarly identified for "Follow-Up" and "Projects for College Students."

Guidelines for student presentations of model experiences follow.

TO STUDENTS

Presenting a Model Experience

"Try your wings" teaching music in a college or elementary classroom by using one of the model experiences in this text. Consider your own enthusiasms and strengths as you make your selection.

If your "best instrument" is the CD player, choose a model experience based on orchestral, jazz, or world music pieces. If singing is one of your strengths, select a song experience. (However, even an insecure singer can handle a lesson that has a song recording, and many model experiences are specially designed for this.) If you enjoy moving to music, choose a model experience involving movement. Or consider models that involve cooperative learning and integrating arts and other subjects. Music involves so much variety that there is sure to be an avenue that will lead you to successful music teaching.

After selecting a particular model experience, study its format, referring to the description on pp. 107–108.

Prepare your lesson so it fits within the time frame recommended by your instructor. If time allows, also prepare a follow-up activity to use on a different day.

Now review the following guidelines, which describe what to do before, during, and after presenting a model experience.

BEFORE PRESENTING A MODEL EXPERIENCE

1. Study the entire model experience carefully. Be sure the music concept and the procedures described are clear to you. See your instructor if you have any uncertainty.
2. Find out as much as possible about the background of your learners. If possible, visit the group before you start teaching. Learn what books, materials, and audiovisual equipment will be available to you.
3. If you will be using a recording, listen to it several times. Be sure to practice finding the specific band on the recording or CD so that you can find it quickly *during* the presentation.
4. Practice using any materials (recordings, instruments, pegboard, etc.). Make certain that premusic practice activities are conducted in the tempo of the music on the recording.
5. Study the objective stated for the experience. Be prepared to evaluate the learners' demonstration of their understanding.
6. Prepare yourself fully regarding the sequence of the lesson so that you know what comes next.
7. If possible, secure an audio- or videotape recorder for recording your presentation.

WHILE PRESENTING A MODEL EXPERIENCE

1. Grab the students' attention at the very beginning of the lesson. Use the suggested focus or a similar idea that reflects your own personality and strengths. Make the opener as brief and concise as possible, keeping in mind that you must capture the students' interest in the music to follow.
2. Involve students *actively* as soon as you can and as frequently as you can. The activities suggested in the model experience (clapping, singing, moving, playing instruments, etc.) will lead in this direction. Interact with students throughout the lesson to focus their learning. (Lecturing and dispensing information with little interaction

with the learners has not proved to be an effective teaching technique for elementary school students.)

3. Try to keep interest high and to maintain excitement by moving at an appropriate pace. Observe the students and let their degree of success dictate the tempo of the work. You must move quickly enough to keep students intrigued and involved but slowly enough to let ideas sink in, so students feel comfortable with the material.
4. Maintain eye contact with the class at all times to keep them "on task." Your enthusiasm can be contagious and help them stay "tuned in." Be expressive, dramatic, and humorous.
5. Ask clear, direct questions. With children it is important to direct and phrase questions in such a manner that you do *not* elicit a response from all twenty-five at the same time! Statements in capital letters within the model experience should provide ideas. And with young children, you may first want to ask "*Show* me . . ." before you ask "*Tell* me. . . ."

AFTER PRESENTING A MODEL EXPERIENCE

Evaluate the effectiveness of your presentation (use the Self-Evaluation Form in Appendix B). If you were able to record your presentation, replay the recording. Review the observations made by your instructor or by others present during your teaching. If you were peer teaching, ask your classmates to fill out the Evaluation Form for Model Experience Participants (Appendix B).

Level I: Model Experiences for Kindergarten and First Grade

SEQUENCE OF SONGS AND LISTENING SELECTIONS LEVEL I (GRADES K–1)

Music	*CD Track*	*Page*
"Golden Gate" (traditional chant)	0	p. 116
"Riding in the Buggy" (American folk song)	1	p. 118
"Parade," from *Divertissement,* by Ibert	2	p. 120
"Sally, Go 'Round the Sun" (American folk song)	3	p. 122
Hungarian Dance no. 5, by Brahms	4	p. 124
"Looby Loo" (American folk song)	5	p. 126
"Ballet of the Unhatched Chicks," from *Pictures at an Exhibition,* by Mussorgsky	6	p. 128
"John the Rabbit" (American folk-game song)	7	p. 130
"Elephant," from the *Carnival of the Animals,* by Saint-Saëns (Excerpt)	8	p. 132
"Aviary," from the *Carnival of the Animals,* by Saint-Saëns (Excerpt)	9	
"Five Angels" (German folk song)	10	p. 134
"Wishy Washy Wee" (American folk song)	11	p. 136
"Head–Shoulders, Baby" (African American game song)	12	p. 138
"Anaguta Drums" (Africa) (Excerpt)	13	p. 140
"Muno Muno" (Africa) (Excerpt)	14	
"Wake Me!" (African American folk song)	15	p. 142
"Matarile" (Mexican folk song)	16	p. 144
"Sing about Martin!" by "Miss Jackie" Weissman	17	p. 146

SEQUENCE OF MUSIC CONCEPTS—LEVEL I (GRADES K–1)

Elements of Music	*Music Concepts*
RHYTHM	Chants can move with a steady beat ("Golden Gate")
RHYTHM	Music can move with a steady beat ("Riding in the Buggy")
DYNAMICS	Music can be soft or loud or become gradually softer or louder ("Parade")
FORM	Songs may have a clear ending ("Sally, Go 'Round the Sun")
TEMPO	Music can move in a fast and slow tempo (Hungarian Dance no. 5)
FORM	Melodies can be made up of sections that are different ("Looby Loo")
RHYTHM	The rhythm of a melody includes long and short sounds ("Ballet of the Unhatched Chicks")
FORM	Repeating patterns can create unity ("John the Rabbit")

Elements of Music	*Music Concepts*
MELODY	Pitches can be high or low ("Elephant" and "Aviary")
MELODY	Pitches can move up ("Five Angels")
MELODY	Pitches can move down ("Wishy Washy Wee")
MELODY	Pitches in a melody can stay the same ("Head–Shoulders, Baby")
TIMBRE	Sound is produced by a vibrating object ("Anaguta Drums" and "Muno Muno")
HARMONY	A melody can be performed alone or with an accompaniment ("Wake Me!")
RHYTHM	The rhythm of a melody includes long and short sounds ("Matarile")
TIMBRE	Each voice has its own special sound ("Sing about Martin!")

DEVELOPMENTAL CHARACTERISTICS OF KINDERGARTEN AND FIRST-GRADE CHILDREN

In order to plan meaningful music learning and appropriate musical experiences, teachers need to understand the developmental characteristics of children at each stage of their growth. The following are important developmental characteristics of kindergarten and first-grade children. These address their physical, mental, cognitive, and musical growth as well as their development in terms of relationships with people and their surroundings. While many children exhibit these developmental characteristics, some may function at a younger level or even an older level. The needs of special learners are described on pp. 90–95.

LEARN BY DOING	Children learn primarily by doing—hands-on experiences work best. Learning results from the interaction of children's own thinking and their experiences.
SHOW BY DOING	Children show what they know and understand by doing—language and speech skills are limited but rapidly developing.
SHORT ATTENTION SPAN	Children have short attention spans and can concentrate only for relatively short periods of time. They tire easily.
LARGE-MUSCLE COORDINATION	Children have better large-muscle coordination than small-muscle coordination.
LIKE TO PLAY INSTRUMENTS	Children can play simple classroom instruments to accompany singing and creative movement activities.
LIKE TO MOVE	Children enjoy moving to music with locomotor, nonlocomotor, and creative movements. They can learn simple play-party games and folk dances.
LIKE TO SING	Children like to sing, especially their favorite songs, and may become so enthusiastic that they shout rather than sing. They should be encouraged to sing in tune and with a pleasant, light tone. Their singing range is generally limited to five or six pitches and gradually increases. They should have many opportunities to sing individually as well as with others.
LIMITED HARMONIC PERCEPTION	Children have difficulty perceiving multiple sounds, thus limiting their harmonic perception.
INTEREST IN IMMEDIATE SURROUNDINGS	Children are curious about and alert to everything around them.
NEED PRAISE	Children need lots of individualized attention, encouragement, and positive reinforcement.

PREMUSIC CONCEPT Chants can move with a steady beat (*Rhythm*)

Chant "Golden Gate" (traditional chant)

Objective To identify aurally a chant that moves in steady beats and to demonstrate that recognition through body movements

Your voice and body

Patsch means to pat tops of thighs.

FOCUS

Key Term: ***steady beat***

Step 1: Begin patsching steady beats and invite students to TRY SOME STEADY BEATS WITH ME. When steady beats are well established, suggest they KEEP THOSE STEADY BEATS GOING WHILE I ADD SOME WORDS.

Special Learners
Encourage any kind of movement for feeling the beat.

Two	Four	Six	Eight
I	I	I	I
Meet me	at the	Golden	Gate.
I	I	I	I
If you're	late,	I won't	wait
I	I	I	I
Two	Four	Six	Eight.
I	I	I	I

Step 2: Discuss the words of the chant—note the rhyming words. Teach each line of the chant in echo form while maintaining steady-beat patsching. When all the lines are learned, announce WE'RE READY TO DO THE WHOLE CHANT TOGETHER. I'LL KEEP THE STEADY BEATS GOING; YOU JUST CHANT THE WORDS. Repeat several times. Encourage expressive speaking. If students are able, have them patsch as they repeat the chant.

Indicator of Success

SUMMARY

Step 3: WHEN DO *YOU* LIKE TO SAY CHANTS? Elicit answers like "jumping rope, bouncing a ball," and so on. IT'S EASY TO KEEP BALL BOUNCING AND ROPE JUMPING STEADY WHEN WE USE A CHANT WITH A STEADY BEAT.

ASSESSMENT After students learn or review a different chant (e.g., "Engine, Engine," Appendix D), they are able to patsch or clap a steady beat with the words.

Follow-Up

1. Steady beats can be performed with other body rhythms. For example, students could tap fingertips together, forming a Golden Gate Bridge with their arms.

2. Students can mark the steady beats with their feet by moving about the room as they chant.

Kodály Adaptation

3. While the class chants, mark beat lines (|) on the board. Repeat the chant, pointing to the beat lines. (If students are able to read, the words of the chant could also be written on the board.) Have students take turns pointing to the beat lines as the class chants. The class could also speak "ta" for each beat.

Orff Adaptation

4. Accompany the chant with a steady-beat accompaniment on a rhythm instrument such as a small drum or a tambourine, or on a barred instrument (e.g., xylophone or resonator bars) using the pitches C (low) and G played simultaneously.

Projects for College Students

5. Choose a chant from Appendix D or from another source. Practice chanting/patsching the words with a steady beat. Mark the words on which the steady beats occur and draw quarter notes under those words. Remember when chanting rhymes that a beat is often felt (and performed) *after* the last word in a line:

"Pease, porridge hot," |			

Cooperative Learning

6. Teach your chant from #5 above to other members of a small group. Follow the lesson guidelines for the "Golden Gate" chant. After teaching, reflect on your experience as you complete the Self-Evaluation Form in Appendix B.

Visual Art

7. Locate works of a visual artist that could be related to steady beats because they show a regular series of similar objects. See the work of painter Wayne Thiebaud.

Other Chants

See collection in Appendix D.

MUSIC CONCEPT Music can move with a steady beat (*Rhythm*)

Music "Riding in the Buggy" (American folk song), p. 354

Objective To identify aurally a song that moves with a steady beat and to demonstrate that recognition in body rhythms

Materials CD, track 1

FOCUS

Key Term: ***beat***

Special Learners
Encourage any kind of movement for feeling the beat.

Step 1: Review steady-beat clapping with chants. Then, invite students to LISTEN TO A SONG AND CLAP THE STEADY BEATS. Sing the song or play the recording, with students clapping steady beats.

Step 2: Discuss the lyrics: what a buggy is and who is riding in it. Sing again, with students dramatizing how they hold the reins and bounce (gently) as to a steady beat of a horse's hooves. Encourage them to sing the "Riding in the buggy, Miss Mary Ann" parts. Repeat the singing and moving, also learning the "She's a long way from home" phrase.

Step 3: Create new verses about other vehicles, such as cars or buses and substitute student names for "Mary Ann." Have students show how they "drive" with hands on an imaginary steering wheel, "turning" from left to right on every other beat.

Indicator of Success

Step 4: While the class sings, mark beats (|) on the board. Repeat the song, pointing to the beats. Invite students to take turns pointing to the beats as the class sings and moves (or claps).

```
| | | |

| | | |

| | | |

| | | |
```

```
Riding in the buggy, Miss Mary Ann, Miss
|                |            |    |
Mary Ann, Miss Mary Ann.
|    |           |    |
Riding in the buggy, Miss Mary Ann, She's a
|                |            |    |
long way from home.
|         |       |         |
```

SUMMARY

Step 5: WHAT A GOOD JOB YOU DID SHOWING THE STEADY BEATS IN THE SONG!

ASSESSMENT Students keep a steady beat as they sing a different but familiar song and point to the beats with reasonable accuracy.

Follow-Up

1. Have students use the beat chart and point to steady beats of "Riding in the Buggy" as they sing.

Kodály Adaptation

2. Introduce traditional notation by converting the beat lines (|) to quarter notes (♩). Repeat singing and clapping while pointing to the quarter-note beats. Students could practice speaking the quarter-note beats with "ta."

Movement

3. Choose songs or listening selections from "Other Music," below, and involve students in steady-beat experiences. Use locomotor movements like marching or nonlocomotor movements like moving arms, swaying, and stepping in place. Students could also play rhythm instruments.

Orff Adaptation

4. Play C (low) and G alternately on a barred instrument along with the singing.

Creative Movement

5. Have students freely explore movements depicting vehicles such as cars, trucks, and buses. Use the "Riding in the Buggy" song or instrumental pieces from "Other Music."

Projects for College Students

6. Perform steady beats with a listening selection from "Other Music," or choose a familiar song and, with a partner, mark the words on which the beats occur.

Music Fundamentals
Technology

7. Review all notes that may be used to represent the beat: half, quarter, eighth and the common meter signatures (Appendix A). Use a software program such as *Music Ace* or *Essentials of Music Theory* to study and practice note reading (Appendix F).
8. Study the section on "Singing," pp. 32–41, paying close attention to the Children's Voices section and the expected singing skills of kindergarten and grade 1 students. Based on your reading, make a list of some key points to keep in mind about kindergarten and first-grade singers.

Other Music (Section Four unless indicated)

"Hickory, Dickory, Dock"
"Hokey Pokey"
"Ring Around the Rosy"
"Rock-Passing Song" ("Obwisana")
"Rocky Mountain," *The Music Connection* 2; *Share the Music* 3
"Sally, Go 'Round the Sun"
"Wake Me!"
"Wishy Washy Wee"
See "Marches," *Bowmar Orchestral Library*
"March, Little Soldier" (*Memories of Childhood*), by Pinto, *Bowmar Orchestral Library,* "Classroom Concert"
"March of the Toys" (*Babes in Toyland*), by Herbert, *Share the Music* K
"Semper Fidelis," by Sousa, *The Music Connection* 6
"South Rampart Street Parade," by Allen, Bauduc, Haggart, *Share the Music* K
"Spring" (*The Four Seasons*), by Vivaldi, *Share the Music* 1
"Viennese Musical Clock" (*Háry János Suite*), by Kodály, CD, track 42

MUSIC CONCEPT Music can be soft or loud or become gradually softer or louder (*Dynamics*)

Music "Parade," from *Divertissement,* by Jacques Ibert ("ee-BEAR") (French, 1890–1962)

Objective To identify aurally the parts of a musical composition that are soft and loud and to demonstrate that recognition by responding with appropriate body movements

Materials CD, track 2

FOCUS

Key Terms: ***loud, soft, steady beat***

Special Learners Students unable to do locomotor movements could "march" with hands on thighs.

Step 1: Review steady-beat clapping. Experiment with soft and loud steady-beat clapping. When students can demonstrate the two dynamic levels, tell them to LISTEN TO A PIECE OF MUSIC THAT BEGINS SOFTLY BUT HAS LOUD PARTS TOO. CLAP THE STEADY BEATS AND SHOW WHEN THE MUSIC IS LOUD OR SOFT.

Step 2: Discuss the dynamic changes in "Parade." HOW DID THE MUSIC BEGIN? (*soft*) WAS IT SOFT OR LOUD IN THE MIDDLE? (*loud*) WHAT HAPPENED AT THE END? (*became gradually softer*)

Indicator of Success

Step 3: Ask students to think of ways to show soft steps (tiptoe), loud steps (marching), and steps for in between loud and soft (walking). Choose a group to try those movements with the music. Repeat, giving all students an opportunity to move. (Students not moving could be clapping steady beats.)

SUMMARY

Step 4: Compliment students on their success in demonstrating dynamic changes. Elicit from students the order of dynamic changes in "Parade." Announce the title of the piece and ask students if they can decide where the parade was located (far away or up close) when the music was soft, when it was loud, when it was in between loud and soft.

ASSESSMENT Students sing a familiar song once soft and once loud and describe the differences.

Follow-Up

Literature

1. Read Gene Baer's story *Thump, Thump, Rat-a-Tat-Tat* (Harper Trophy, 1989) inviting children to join in on the repeated lines using the appropriate loud and soft inflections.

Movement Game

2. Play a loud/soft movement game. Using a drum, first explore moving to steady beats. Then suggest different movements if the drum sounds loud or soft—for example, jumping for loud, tiptoeing for soft.

Cooperative Learning

3. In groups of twos and threes, have students search in the classroom for objects that produce loud and soft sounds. Groups should find three and be prepared to share them with the class.

Visual Art

4. Study paintings such as *Winter Evening* by Millet and *Parade* by Jacob Lawrence for contrasts of color, line, shape, and subject. Students should decide what mood each painting creates for them—which painting suggests sound and activity and which suggests quiet—and explain the reasons for their choices.
5. Prepare cards with a variety of dynamic symbols, e.g., *f, p, mp* (see Appendix A for symbols and their meaning). Arrange the cards in any order. Then create a "sound piece" by playing instruments with dynamic contrasts in the order shown by the cards. A conductor may be needed to indicate the changes.

Projects for College Students

Music Fundamentals

6. Study the dynamic terms and signs in Appendix A.
7. Study the section on "Listening," pp. 18–21, paying particular attention to the part on listening maps. After reviewing this information and the sample map on p. 152, create a listening map of "Parade" for children to use.

Other Music

"Baris" (gamelan orchestra of Bali), *Music from the Morning of the World,* audio CD, Wea/Atlantic/Nonesuch

"Dream March" (*Red Pony* Suite), by Copland. *Copland: Orchestral Works,* audio CD, Sony Classics.

MUSIC CONCEPT Songs may have a clear ending (*Form*)

Music "Sally, Go 'Round the Sun" (American folk song), p. 357

Objective To identify aurally the ending in the song and to demonstrate that end by jumping and turning on the final pitch

Materials Large pictures of sun, moon, chimney (with a pipe at the top)
CD, track 3

FOCUS

Key Term: ***end***

Special Learners
Encourage students to sign the key words.

Step 1: Discuss what students do just before leaving home to come to school: put on jackets, backpacks, and so on. Ask WHAT IS THE LAST THING YOU DO WHEN YOU LEAVE HOME? (*close the door*) Note how closing the door suggests the end of being at home.

Step 2: SONGS CAN ALSO HAVE A CLEAR ENDING. Sing or play a recording of the song and ask students to LISTEN TO A SONG ABOUT A GIRL NAMED SALLY AND SEE IF YOU CAN DISCOVER WHAT THE LAST WORD IS. (*"Boom"*) Repeat with students standing, jumping, and speaking on the word *boom.*

Step 3: Question students about the lyrics: *sun, moon, chimney pot, ev-'ry afternoon.* Sing the entire song (with recording) using the pictures for visual cues. Repeat.

To give students a visual reference for a moving circular line, make a circle on the floor with duct or masking tape.

Arrange students in a circle with hands joined and have them "go 'round" (clockwise), stepping on the steady beats, as the song is sung. Remind them to jump on the ending word, *boom.* Repeat several times, encouraging students to join in singing and to jump and turn as *boom* is shouted. (On each repeat of song, students should change direction from clockwise to counterclockwise.)

Indicator of Success

SUMMARY

Step 4: WHAT A GOOD JOB YOU DID SHOWING WHEN THE SONG COMES TO AN END! WHAT WAS THE LAST WORD? (*"boom"*)

ASSESSMENT As students become familiar with different compositions (see "Other Music," next page), they identify each piece's ending.

Follow-Up

1. Teach a chant (Appendix D) or read a story and let students discover the final word(s).

Movement

2. Choose a selection from "Other Music" and create a movement experience to accompany it that will help children show the ending.

Science

3. Form a large circle with one child in the center to be the "sun." Have another child step just inside the circle to be the "earth" and to walk around the "sun." Accompany this by singing new words to fit this idea about the solar system. Repeat so that other children can be the "sun" and the "earth."

Visual Art

4. Have students include the earth, the sun, and themselves in a drawing or painting. When finished, discuss how their colors, proportions, and so forth, express their feelings about the earth and their place on it.

Projects for College Students

5. Sing the song as a round.

Cooperative Learning

6. In small groups, review all the songs in Level I model experiences. Circle the lowest and the highest pitches for each. How many pitches do most of the songs span? Also note the lyrics for each of the songs. Do they match the interest level of kindergarteners and first graders? Discuss and share your findings.

Cooperative Learning

7. Review the nine National Standards for Music Education, p. 5. In small groups, decide which content standards are addressed in "Sally, Go 'Round the Sun" and "Parade" (p. 120) model experiences. Refer to both the lesson sequence and the follow-ups. Present your list to the larger group and give reasons (and examples) for your decisions. Are any standards not addressed?

> *Note*
>
> *Cadence* is the musical term for the ending of a phrase, section, or piece.

Other Music (Section Four unless indicated)

"Hokey Pokey"
"London Bridge"
"Ring Around the Rosy"
"Wishy Washy Wee"
"Russian Dance" (*Nutcracker* Suite), by Tchaikovsky, *Bowmar Orchestral Library,* "Stories in Ballet and Opera," *Share the Music* 2

MUSIC CONCEPT Music can move in a fast and a slow tempo (*Tempo*)

Music Hungarian Dance no. 5, by Johannes Brahms (German, 1833–97)

Objective To identify aurally sounds and music that move fast and slow and to demonstrate that recognition in body movements

Materials

CD, track 4
Drum
Large pictures of objects moving fast and slow, e.g., speed boat, turtle

---

FOCUS

Key Terms: ***fast, slow***

Indicator of Success

Special Learners Students unable to do locomotor movements could move puppets or pass bean bags to show fast and slow.

Step 1: Hold up the pictures for students to see and ask WHICH PICTURES SHOW FAST AND WHICH SHOW SLOW. Encourage children to discuss the various objects and the fast and/or slow movements of each.

Step 2: Next, on a drum, play steady beats very slowly. WAS I PLAYING FAST OR SLOW? (*slow*) Have students stand and try slow, sliding steps to the drum beats. Next, play fast beats in the tempo of a quick walk. Have students try the quick-walk movements.

Step 3: Tell the students that music can move both fast and slow and that I WANT YOU TO SHOW ME WITH YOUR MOVEMENTS WHEN THIS MUSIC IS FAST AND WHEN IT IS SLOW. Before playing the recording, arrange students in a space that will allow them to move freely and safely— suggest that they walk very slowly to their "ready" position. Encourage the quick walk, moderate walk, and slow sliding steps for the frequent changes from fast to slow in the music.

SUMMARY

Step 4: After students have moved to the music, invite them to briefly discuss how their movements matched the slow and fast tempos. Conclude by noting that those tempo changes made the music more interesting.

ASSESSMENT Students sing a familiar song (see "Other Music," next page) once fast and once slow, demonstrating that they can differentiate between the two tempos and can describe the differences.

Follow-Up

Movement Game

1. Play the drum/moving game, but introduce gradually getting faster (*accelerando*) and gradually getting slower (*ritardando*).

Dramatization

2. Step the steady beats and chant "Engine, Engine" (Appendix D). Incorporate tempo changes with train movements. For example, children could chant and move faster as the train leaves the station and slow down when it arrives at the station.

Cooperative Learning Dramatization

3. In groups of twos and threes, students can find pictures of objects, animals, or people that move fast or slow. They should discuss and dramatize their finds with the class.

Projects for College Students

Music Fundamentals

4. Study the Italian names for tempo terms (Appendix A).
5. Study the "Movement" section on pp. 41–44, noting the four types of movements and those in which kindergarteners and first graders can appropriately be involved. Decide which types were used in the "Parade," "Sally, Go 'Round the Sun," and Hungarian Dance no. 5 model experiences.

Other Music

"Devil's Dance" (*A Soldier's Tale*), by Stravinsky (mostly fast), CD, track 19

"The Elephant" (Hap Palmer) (slow/fast/slow), *Learning Basic Skills Through Music, 1* (Hap Palmer Activity Record)

"In the Hall of the Mountain King" (*Peer Gynt* Suite no. 1), by Grieg (gradually faster), *Bowmar Orchestral Library,* "Legends in Music," *Bowmar's Adventures in Music Listening,* Level 2, *The Music Connection* K and 2, *Share the Music* 2

"The Little Train of Caipira" (*Bachianas Brasileiras* no. 2), by Villa-Lobos (slow/fast/gradually slower and faster), *Bowmar Orchestral Library,* "Miniatures in Music," *The Music Connection* K and 2, *Share the Music* K

"Russian Dance" (*Nutcracker* Suite), by Tchaikovsky (mostly fast), *Bowmar Orchestral Library,* "Stories in Ballet and Opera," *Share the Music* 2

"Sicilienne," by Maria Theresia von Paradis (slow)

"The Swan" (*Carnival of the Animals*), by Saint-Saëns (mostly slow), *Bowmar Orchestral Library,* "Animals and Circus," *Bowmar's Adventures in Music Listening,* Level 1, *The Music Connection* 2

MUSIC CONCEPT Melodies can be made up of sections that are different (*Form*)

Music "Looby Loo" (American folk song), p. 334

Objective To identify aurally the sections of the song that are different and to demonstrate that recognition by responding with contrasting movements

Materials CD, track 5

FOCUS

Step 1: Arrange students in a circle. Sing the first section ("Here we go . . .") or play the recording, asking them to PATSCH A STEADY BEAT ALONG WITH OUR SONG. Ask questions about the words and repeat several times with students joining in singing.

Special Learners Students unable to do locomotor movements could "walk" with their hands on thighs.

Step 2: When section is learned, have students sing and walk in a circle. Demonstrate first. Say, BEGIN WALKING WHEN I START TO SING. BE SURE TO STOP WHEN I STOP! Encourage a light, swinging walk.

Key Terms: ***sections/parts, different***

Special Learners Encourage students to sign the key words.

Step 3: Note that this is only part of the song. Tell them that ON THE OTHER PART WE WILL SIT DOWN IN THE CIRCLE TO HEAR ABOUT SOME DIFFERENT MOVEMENTS. Sing the second section ("I put my right hand . . .") or play the recording. Explain that this part is about taking a bath and how we might first put one hand into the water to check its temperature. Help students learn the new section by echoing your singing or with the recording.

Step 4: Ask students to stand in place in the circle, ready to sing and pantomime this section. Have them MOVE YOUR RIGHT ARM INSIDE OR OUTSIDE AS YOU SING. Review the first part of the song, singing and moving in a circle. Ask ARE THOSE MOVEMENTS DIFFERENT FROM PUTTING OUR ARM INTO THE WATER? (*yes*) Review the "I put my right arm . . ." section where they need to stand in place. As students become confident, have them sing both sections, changing movements for each.

Indicator of Success

SUMMARY

Step 5: Ask HOW MANY DIFFERENT SECTIONS WERE THERE IN OUR SONG? (*two*) Discuss what was different—the words, the melody, the movement.

ASSESSMENT As students become familiar with different songs (see "Other Music," next page), they perform different movements along with different sections of a song.

Follow-Up

1. Learn additional verses of the song. Create different body movements for each verse while keeping the "Here we go . . ." movements the same.
2. Using contrasting felt shapes (e.g., square and circle) to reinforce contrasting sections in music, have students place a shape on a flannelboard at the *beginning* of each section of the song.

Projects for College Students

3. Plan an evaluatory experience to assess students' perception of different sections of a piece of music.

Cooperative Learning

4. In small groups, analyze the following songs found in Section Four. Label the initial section A and the contrasting section B. Share and compare your group's findings with the rest of the class.

   "I'd Like to Teach the World to Sing"
   "It's a Small World"
   "Oh, Susanna"
   "This Land Is Your Land"
   "We Three Kings"
   "Yankee Doodle"

5. Prepare an Autoharp accompaniment for "Looby Loo." Create a different strum for each contrasting section. Identify and sing the starting pitch of the song and plan a strummed introduction. Review "Sally, Go 'Round the Sun" and "Riding in the Buggy" and add an Autoharp accompaniment.

Other Music (see Section Four)

"Hey, Lidee"
"Get on Board"
"Shoo, Fly"
"Wishy Washy Wee"

MUSIC CONCEPT The rhythm of a melody includes long and short sounds (*Rhythm*)

Music "Ballet of the Unhatched Chicks," from *Pictures at an Exhibition,* by Modest Mussorgsky ("moo-ZOR-skee") (Russian, 1839–81)

Objective To identify aurally the long and short durations in the rhythm of a melody and to demonstrate that recognition in body movements

Materials
CD, track 6
Baby chick puppet or toy
Listening Map for Children as shown on p. 152, copied onto a large chart

---

FOCUS

Key Terms: ***short sounds, long sounds***

Step 1: Show the baby chick puppet or toy and ask students to identify and describe. PRETEND YOU ARE A BABY CHICK, PECKING WITH ITS BEAK. SHOW WITH YOUR HAND WHAT KIND OF MOVEMENT YOU MIGHT MAKE. Help students form a "beak" with thumb and fingers to show their ideas. Comment on students' fast and slow movements and on how the chick uses its beak to hatch out of its shell.

Step 2: Tell students they are going to hear some music about a chick pecking and breaking out of its shell. Have them look at the Listening Map, first noticing the last two pictures. Then have them tell what is happening in each picture. Have students follow the pictures as they listen to the recording. Ask them to LISTEN FOR THE SOUND WHEN THE CHICK FINALLY BREAKS OUT OF THE SHELL (last two pictures).

Indicator of Success

Listening Map for Teachers, p. 151

Step 3: Repeat the listening map experience with students depicting the entire story with hand movements (short pecking followed by a long peck). Help them show the "resting" portion (for about fifteen seconds during number 5 at the beginning of the B section) by "putting their chick to rest" and holding the position. Help them understand that fast movements go with *short* musical sounds and slow movements with *long* sounds. Repeat the listening and movement until most students are successful.

SUMMARY THE LONG AND SHORT SOUNDS REALLY GAVE US AN IDEA HOW THE CHICK HATCHES OUT OF ITS SHELL.

ASSESSMENT After students become familiar with different compositions (see "Other Music," next page), they show short sounds by fast movements and long sounds by slow movements.

Follow-Up

Science

Cooperative Learning

1. Have the students classify animals into groups by asking each child to bring to school a picture of an animal. Prepare a bulletin board by dividing it into four sections with a picture of a different animal in each section. Have the students, in small groups, decide which category their animals go in and then thumbtack their pictures in the appropriate sections. Groups should explain why the other animals are like their own.

Social Studies

2. Help children appreciate their uniqueness as human beings as they discover how each living thing is a special, individual creature. Use poems and illustrations in Prelutsky's *The Beauty of the Beast* (see Appendix F, Integrating Arts, 2) to explore the several categories of animals featured (insects, reptiles, birds, mammals, and sea creatures) and compare characteristics such as their biological needs and sensory equipment with those of humans. Help students draw conclusions about the role of all creatures in our life on the planet.

3. Draw short and long horizontal lines on the board and while rhythmically pointing to each, have students clap or move hands in thc air. Try patterns such as – – – – —, — – – – –, – – — – – —, and – – – – — —.

Projects for College Students

Cooperative Learning
Dramatization

4. In small groups, plan a simple, but creative movement/dramatization for "Ballet of the Unhatched Chicks"—one that corresponds to the short and long sounds in the music. Suggest possible costumes and props too. Share your group's plan either by describing it or by demonstration.

Related Literature and Media for Children

Legg, Gerald. (1998). *From Egg to Chicken* (Lifecycles). Franklin Watts.

Shimizu, Kiyoshi and Sylvia A. Johnson. (1987). *Inside an Egg.* Lerner Publications.

Other Music

"Arrival of the Queen of Sheba" (*Solomon*), by Handel, *The Music Connection* K—excerpt only (short sounds)

"Ase's Death" (*Peer Gynt* Suite), by Grieg, *Bowmar Orchestral Library,* "Legends in Music," *The Music Connection* K—excerpt only (long sounds)

Pictures at an Exhibition, by Mussorgsky (complete), *Bowmar Orchestral Library,* "Musical Pictures: Mussorgsky"

"The Wild Horseman" (*Album for the Young*), by Schumann, *Share the Music* K (both long and short)

MUSIC CONCEPT Repeating patterns can create unity (*Form*)

Music "John the Rabbit" (American folk-game song), p. 326

Objective To identify aurally the repeated patterns in a rhythm game and in a song and to demonstrate that recognition by performing the repeated patterns

Materials
CD, track 7
Sticks or claves
D (low) resonator bar

FOCUS

Key Terms: ***repeat, pattern, unity***

Step 1: Challenge the students to play an echo game with you. I AM GOING TO CLAP A PATTERN. I WANT YOU TO ECHO ME EXACTLY. Clap some different patterns for students to repeat. Have individual students make up patterns for the class to echo, and note that the class *repeats* them.

Step 2: Ask the students to tell what animal you are describing, giving them clues such as *floppy ears, fluffy tail, hippety hop (rabbit).* Using the "teasing chant" of childhood (*sol–mi*) and the above words, create sung (and clapped) patterns for the class to repeat.

Step 3: I KNOW A SONG ABOUT A RABBIT NAMED JOHN. CAN YOU DISCOVER THE PART THAT IS REPEATED? After singing the song or playing the recording, discuss the "Oh, yes" repeats and encourage students to sing that part with you.

Indicator of Success

Special Learners Encourage children to show the repetitive parts in any way they can. Use signing for the key words.

Repeat the singing with body movements for "Oh, yes." For example, both hands as rabbit ears that bend twice on each response. Encourage students to discover what John is doing as they listen and sing. Discuss the lyrics and create visuals for key words (peas, etc.) to assist in learning the words of the song.

Step 4: Have a student play the "Oh, yes" part with rhythm sticks or claves as the class sings and pantomimes the stick playing. Introduce the D resonator bar for the "Oh, yes" part. Involve the entire class by holding the bar and moving quickly from student to student, inviting each to play during the song.

SUMMARY

Step 5: Conclude by noting how important the repeated part was in the echo game and in the song. Clap a few more patterns for them to repeat, and review the repeated tonal pattern in the song.

ASSESSMENT As students become familiar with different songs (see "Other Music," next page), they identify and perform the repeating pattern.

Follow-Up

Literature

1. Read a poem or story that has repeated lines and invite students to join in speaking those lines. Two good examples are Shel Silverstein's "The Clam" (see Appendix D) and Eric Carle's "The Very Clumsy Click Beetle" (New York: Philomel Books, 1999).

Visual Art

2. Study paintings for repetition, such as *The Pie Counter* or *Sugar Cones,* by Wayne Thiebaud; *The Equatorial Jungle,* by Rousseau; or *Little Girl in a Blue Chair,* by Mary Cassatt. Discuss what repeats in each and how these repetitions unify the artwork.

3. Play the echo game using children's names. Clap and chant names with the class repeating each.

Orff Adaptation

4. Add a steady-beat accompaniment by alternating D (low) and A on a barred instrument (xylophone, metallophone, resonator bars).

Projects for College Students

5. Listen to "Old Uncle Rabbit" in *Afro-American Blues and Game Songs,* Library of Congress AFS L4, edited by Alan Lomax. Describe how this version is different.

Visual Art

6. Plan a creative art project for students that illustrates repetition.

Music Fundamentals
Technology

7. Notate four-beat rhythm patterns as clapped by your instructor or a classmate. Use quarter, eighth, and half notes. Review and practice note reading using a software program such as *Music Ace* or *Essentials of Music Theory* (Appendix F).

Cooperative Learning

8. Study the "Playing Instruments" section, pp. 21–31. In small groups, list the instruments, by category (rhythm, wind, etc.), that are age appropriate for kindergarten and grade one students. Note which are used in the "John the Rabbit" lesson and follow-ups. What additional instruments might be used with the song?

Other Music (Section Four unless indicated)

"All Around the Kitchen"
"Gogo"
"Grizzely Bear"
"Old MacDonald," *The Music Connection* 2, *Share the Music* 1

MUSIC CONCEPT Pitches can be high or low (*Melody*)

Music "Elephant" and "Aviary" (Excerpts) from the *Carnival of the Animals,* by Camille Saint-Saëns ("sa[n] saw[n]s") (French, 1835–1921)

Objective To identify aurally pitches that are mostly high and mostly low and to demonstrate that recognition by choosing and playing high/low sounds on a barred instrument and by creating contrasting movements to high and low music

Materials

CD, tracks 8, 9

Large pictures of objects that illustrate high and low, for example, airplane high in the sky and airplane on the ground

Barred melody instrument (preferably in stepladder position)

Two cards labeled *high* and *low*

FOCUS

Step 1: Display the pictures and ask students WHICH PICTURES SHOW HIGH AND WHICH SHOW LOW. As the pictures are discussed, encourage students to demonstrate with their hands high and low concepts.

Key Terms: ***high/low***

Special Learners Students should show high vs. low in any way they can.

Step 2: Explore high and low sounds on the barred melody instrument (hold on end with the large bars down), associating hand movements with the pitch level. Use the cards to introduce the words for the differing pitch levels.

Step 3: WHO CAN SHOW US HOW TO USE OUR WHOLE BODY TO SHOW HIGH AND LOW? (Stand tall on tiptoe to show high and squat down close to the ground to show low.) Explain that the students will hear two different pieces of music and will show with body movements whether the music is *mostly* high or *mostly* low. Listen to an excerpt of each before trying the creative movements. (The cards could be held up to remind students which movement to try.)

Indicator of Success

SUMMARY

Step 4: Choose a group to try out their creative movements with the two pieces. Encourage contrasting movements (tiptoe vs. crouching low). Compliment/discuss student success with contrasting movements for the high and low music.

ASSESSMENT As students become familiar with similar compositions (see "Other Music," next page), they show the differences between the two pitch levels through body movements and by describing what they hear.

Follow-Up

Cooperative Learning

1. In small groups, students find objects in the room that produce high and low sounds and share their finds with the class.

2. To experience pitch levels with speaking voices, chant a rhyme from Appendix D all in high voices or all in low voices. Chant while walking the beat (use tiptoe steps for high-voice chanting and crouching low for low-voice chanting), or chant with body rhythms (clap hands high and low, etc.).

Dramatization

3. Tell or read the story of "The Three Bears," emphasizing the pitch level for the little wee bear (high), the mama bear (middle), and the papa bear (low). Invite students to repeat certain lines with you. Later, to develop a "sound story," use rhythm instruments (or synthesizer) to represent each character in the story.

Science

4. Experiment with filling two identical containers (glasses, jars) with differing amounts of water until one container sounds high and one sounds low. (Tune as closely as possible to the musical scale.) Strike container with a wooden or hard-rubber mallet. (Students should learn that *the length of the air column* determines the pitch—not the amount of water.)

Visual Art

5. Locate the high and low body positions in Degas's painting *The Dancers.*

Cooperative Learning

6. Using a variety of rhythm instruments, students in small groups should decide which ones produce high sounds (e.g., triangle) and which ones low sounds (e.g., large drum). Use the instruments for an accompaniment to a chant (see 2, above) or to accompany the movement experience with "Elephant" and "Aviary."

Projects for College Students

Music Fundamentals
Technology

7. Using the treble clef, write out, in staff notation, all pitches from A below middle C to high A, using quarter or half notes. Review stem placement and check your work with the staff in Appendix A. Practice pitch reading with music software programs such as *Music Ace* or *Essentials of Music Theory* (Appendix F).

8. In addition to "Elephant" and "Aviary," the *Carnival of the Animals* includes other parts. Review what the titles of these parts are and the background of this composition and its composer; view the video (see p. 165).

Other Music

"Ballet of the Unhatched Chicks" (*Pictures at an Exhibition*), by Mussorgsky (high), CD, track 6, *The Music Connection* K, 2, *Share the Music* K

"Bydlo" ("Ox-Cart") (*Pictures at an Exhibition),* by Mussorgsky (low), *Bowmar Orchestral Library,* "Musical Pictures: Mussorgsky," *Share the Music* K

"Dance of the Reed Pipes" (*Nutcracker* Suite), by Tchaikovsky (high), *Bowmar Orchestral Library,* "Stories in Ballet and Opera," *The Music Connection* 3

"Dance of the Sugarplum Fairy" (*Nutcracker* Suite), by Tchaikovsky (high), *Bowmar Orchestral Library,* "Stories in Ballet and Opera," *Bowmar's Adventures in Music Listening,* Level 1, *Share the Music* 2

"Ketjak" (monkey chant from Bali) (opening section), *Golden Rain,* audio CD, World Music Library

"Sounds and Songs of Humpback Whales," Special Music Company, CD or audiocassette

"Whales Alive" by Paul Winter, audio CD, BMG/Living Music

MUSIC CONCEPT Pitches can move up (*Melody*)

Music "Five Angels" (German folk song), p. 298

Objective To identify aurally and visually pitches moving up and to demonstrate that recognition by singing and using hand motions

Materials
CD, track 10
Flannelboard with felt letters: C, D, E, F, G
Resonator bars: C, D, E, F, G
Five mallets

Key Term: ***up***

FOCUS

Step 1: Distribute five resonator bars to five students and arrange in order at the front of the room left to right: C, D, E, F, G. Have students play bars in ascending order. DID THE PITCHES GO UP OR DOWN? Repeat several times, asking class to show with their hands the direction of the pitches.

G
F
E
D
C

Step 2: Display the flannelboard and felt letters. As players identify the letter written on their bar (then go back to their seats), place the five letters in ascending arrangement. Point to the letters as the class sings the letter names and moves hands in an upward motion.

Indicator of Success

Step 3: THESE PITCHES THAT MOVE UP ARE VERY IMPORTANT IN A SONG ABOUT SOME ANGELS. Sing the song or play the recording, asking the students to count the number of times they hear the upward pitches. (Pointing to the flannelboard will help!)

Special Learners Prepare five visuals (one for each angel) to help children remember the order and the words. Use signing for the key words.

Step 4: Discuss the five times the pattern is heard, and the five angels and their jobs. Invite class to sing parts of the song at first and then the entire song several times. Reinforce the concept "up" with hand motions, pointing to letters, and so on.

SUMMARY

Step 5: OUR SONG WAS ABOUT TRYING TO WAKE AN ANGEL *(up)*? Review how the pitches, voices, and bars all moved up on the part about the angels and their jobs.

ASSESSMENT As students sing a similar song that is familiar to them (see "Other Music," next page), they show the upward pitches with their hands.

Follow-Up

Dramatization

1. When students are familiar with the words, dramatize the song. In groups of six, let children take turns acting out the words while the class sings.

Special Learners Numbers (1, 2, 3, 4, 5) may be easier to understand.

2. Scramble the five resonator bars and challenge students to arrange them in sequential order *by listening* to the pitches. Help them to aurally identify the lowest bar and place first in line and then proceed in ascending order (left to right).
3. Make a 5-step tone ladder on chart board with "C D E F G." Use while singing the song.

Orff Adaptation

4. Add an accompaniment by playing C (low) and G alternately or at the same time on barred instruments. Create an instrumental introduction and a coda (brief ending) for the song performance.

Projects for College Students

Kodály Adaptation

Music Fundamentals

5. Sing the "Five Angels" pattern using *do, re, mi, fa, sol.* Use Curwen hand signs (p. 72) along with the *sol–fa* syllables. Learn to use the *sol–fa* syllables with these melodies:
   "Hot Cross Buns," p. 271
   "Pease Porridge Hot," see Section Four
   "Go Tell Aunt Rhody," see Section Four
   "When the Saints Go Marching In," see Section Four

Music Fundamentals Technology

6. Study the whole- and half-step distances between these first five pitches of the major scale. Transfer this exact whole–half-step sequence starting on a different pitch such as D, F, or G. (Each scale should sound like *do, re, mi, fa, sol.*) For practice with whole and half steps, use a software program such as *Music Ace* or *Essentials of Music Theory* (Appendix F).

Music Fundamentals Technology

7. Learn about major scales using *Music Ace* or *Essentials of Music Theory* software. Notate major scales beginning on C, G, and F. Play and sing each.

Other Music (see Section Four)

"Miss Mary Mack" (C, D, E, F)
"When the Saints Go Marching In" (C, E, F, G)

MUSIC CONCEPT — Pitches can move down (*Melody*)

Music — "Wishy Washy Wee" (American folk song), p. 391

Objective — To identify aurally and visually pitches moving down and to demonstrate that recognition by singing and moving arms in a downward direction at the end of the verse and refrain

Materials — CD, track 11

FOCUS

Key Terms: ***down, pitch, high to low***

Step 1. Teacher chooses a partner. Face each other and join both hands. Ask class to LISTEN TO A SONG AND FIND OUT WHO WE ARE. As you sing the song or play the recording, swing arms from right to left along with the music. (Wearing sailor hats would give an additional clue!)

Step 2: Discuss the words so as to discover WHO ARE WE? (*sailors*) and WHERE DO WE COME FROM? (*o'er the sea*). Direct attention to the part "Come along with me," and as you sing the song or play the recording again, ask students to DECIDE HOW YOU SHOULD MOVE YOUR HAND TO SHOW THE WAY THE MUSIC GOES: UP OR DOWN. (*down*)

Special Learners Encourage students to sign the key words.

Step 3: Discuss student responses and ask them to sing "Come along with me" and move one arm in a downward motion. Incorporate the gesturing of "coming along" with moving downward (use a large arc) as they sing the "Come along with me" phrase in the song.

Indicator of Success

Step 4: Review the words in the verse, writing key words such as *come from o'er, sea, go away,* and *me* on the board. Review the words phrase by phrase, gesturing downward on the last phrase. Sing the entire song, doing the motion on the last phrase of the verse and the last phrase of the refrain. Note how the pitches moved down on "Come along with me."

SUMMARY

Step 5: Invite students to learn a sailor dance. Form a circle with two "sailors" in the center. While the class sings the verse, the sailors swing in the center, elbows linked. On the "Come along with me" phrase at the end of the verse, each sailor selects one circle member to stand in front of. These two face each other with arms outstretched and hands joined. (Students in the circle should show the downward motion with their arms.) During the refrain, the partners shift weight from one leg to the other. (If students are able, move arms back and forth in the same direction as the feet, in a "sawing" motion.) On the final "Come along with me," the two dancers from the circle become the new "sailors" in the middle (the original "sailors" take their places in the circle) while the students in the circle once again show the downward motion with their arms. The song and dance begin again. As you conclude the dance, ask students to tell you again how the pitches moved on the "Come along with me" phrase.

ASSESSMENT — As students sing a similar song that is familiar to them (see "Other Music," next page), they show the downward pitches with their hands.

Follow-Up

1. Arrange the C, D, E, F, and G resonator bars stepwise using a step-bar frame, blocks of wood or books to raise the higher pitches and show the stepping from low to high. Help students decide which bar goes on the bottom (C), which on the next step, and so forth, so they can play the descending pattern "Come along with me" (G–F–E–D–C). Notice the size of the bars in relation to the pitch.
2. Using bars in 1, play descending (and ascending) patterns and have students show the pitch levels with their hand. Show patterns on the board with five short lines that descend (or ascend) and similarly have students move hands.

Pitches moving down	Pitches moving up
—	—
—	—
—	—
—	—
—	—

3. As the teacher blows up a balloon and releases it, have students watch its movement. As the air comes out, will the balloon go upward or downward, or both? (Idea demonstrated by Dr. David Woods.)

Project for College Students

4. Accompany a group of singers on Autoharp or some other instrument; select a Level I song. Review the section on leading songs in "Singing," p. 37. Have an observer evaluate your success.

Other Music (see Section Four)

"Hey, Lidee" (G, F, E, D, C)
"Looby Loo" (G, F, E, D, C)
"My Dreydl" (G, F, E, D, C)

MUSIC CONCEPT Pitches in a melody can stay the same (*Melody*)

Music "Head–Shoulders, Baby" (African American game song), p. 309

Objective To identify aurally repeated pitches in a melody and to demonstrate that recognition through singing, hand movements, and playing resonator bars

Materials CD, track 12
F resonator bar, plus two others of any pitch

FOCUS

Step 1: Ask students to hold up fingers to show various numbers, 1 through 10. LISTEN AND TELL ME WHAT NUMBERS ARE USED IN THIS SONG ("1, 2, 3"). Sing verse 1 or play the recording.

Step 2: While presenting the song, invite students to hold up fingers to show "one, two, three." Students should join in singing the "one, two, three" part when they are able.

Key Term: *same pitch*

Special Learners Students can sign the numbers and the body parts.

Step 3: Note that resonator bars may be added during "one, two, three," but first the class must decide whether one bar, two bars, or three bars should be chosen. As the class sings the song, draw these lines on the board for the "one, two, three" part.

___ ___ ___
(1) (2) (3)

Indicator of Success

Step 4: Ask class how the singing looks like these lines (*the line stays on the same level, just as the singing stays on the same pitch*). Have class sing the song and USE YOUR HAND TO SHOW THE LEVEL LINE, JUST AS IF YOU WERE DRAWING IT ON THE BOARD. After students have concluded that only one bar will be used, have students take turns playing the "one, two, three" part on the F resonator bar.

SUMMARY

Step 5: Conclude with the class singing the song, touching "head and shoulders," and a classmate playing the "one, two, three" part on the bar. Ask students HOW DID THE PITCHES MOVE ON OUR "ONE, TWO, THREE" PART? (*they stayed the same*) Note that parts of songs often stay on the same pitch.

ASSESSMENT As students sing a similar song (see "Other Music," next page), they identify and show with their hands pitches that stay on the same level.

Follow-Up

1. Learn all the verses of the song, and have students touch the various body parts as they sing.

Movement Game

2. Play the pat-a-cake game with a partner on the "one, two, three" part and touch the body parts on the rest of the song.

1	2	3
right, clap	left, clap	both hands

3. Play a tone-matching game to help young children develop control of their singing voices. The teacher might sing *on a single pitch:*

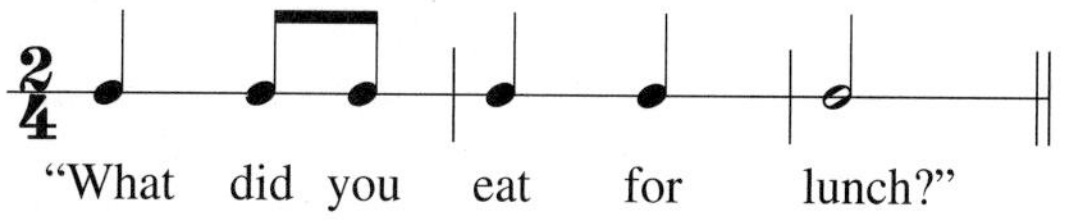

"What did you eat for lunch?"

Using the teacher's same pitch, a student might answer:

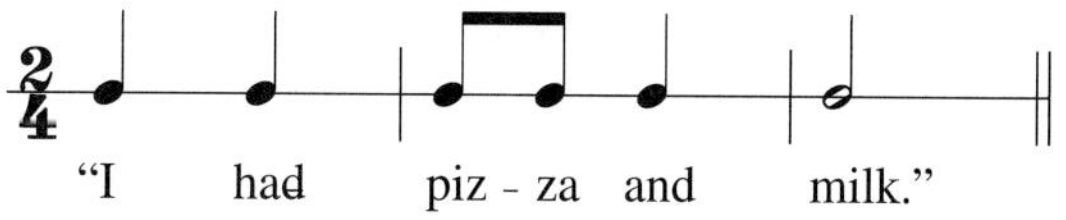

"I had piz - za and milk."

The teacher could roll or throw a ball to the student who is to answer the question; the student rolls or throws the ball back to the teacher when finished singing.

Project for College Students

4. Select a song from "Other Music." Draw a line to connect repeated pitches in the song. Sing the song or play it on an instrument.

Other Music (Section Four unless indicated)

"Hop, Old Squirrel"
"John the Rabbit"
"Long-Legged Sailor"
"Sally, Go 'Round the Sun"
"Sabre Dance," from *Gayane,* by Khachaturian, *Share the Music* 3

MUSIC CONCEPT Sound is produced by a vibrating object (*Timbre*)

Music "Anaguta Drums" (Africa) and "Muno Muno" (Africa) (Excerpts)

Objective To identify visually and aurally vibrating objects and instruments and to demonstrate that recognition by pantomiming appropriate movements along with a recording.

Materials
CD, tracks 13,14
Drum, coin
Thumb piano (see Note and drawing on next page or in *Musical Instruments of the World* [1997]. Diagram Group. ISBN: 0806998474). Optional CD available.

FOCUS

Key Terms: ***moving, vibrating, drum, thumb piano***

Step 1: Review an African song the class knows, such as the "Rock-Passing Song" ("Obwisana"). After singing, discuss where the song is from, and ask students to NAME AN IMPORTANT INSTRUMENT AFRICANS LIKE TO PLAY. (*the drum*)

Step 2: Holding a drum, invite a student to MAKE THE DRUM "TALK" by striking the drumhead with the palm of the hand. Move through the group, letting other students have a turn.

Place a coin on the drumhead and ask students WHAT WILL HAPPEN TO THE COIN WHEN THE DRUMHEAD IS HIT? (*the coin bounces*) WHY DOES THE COIN BOUNCE? (*the drumhead moves/vibrates*) Select different students to "bounce the coin." Emphasize that when the drumhead moves/vibrates, the coin bounces.

Step 3: Briefly discuss with students drumming and when drums are used in different cultures. (See Note, next page.) Challenge students to PLAY WITH THE AFRICAN DRUMMERS (*pantomime*) as they listen to the "Anaguta Drums" recording.

Indicator of Success

Step 4: Hold up a thumb piano and identify it as another African instrument. (See Note, next page). Demonstrate how it is cradled in two hands and the tips of the bars are plucked by alternating thumbs. Holding a thumb piano (but with bars pointing *away from* your body), move through the group so students can play the bars and feel the vibrations.

Step 5: Tell students that they're going to hear a thumb piano played in "Muno Muno," a song that tells an African boy "not to get too big for his britches." Ask what this means, and briefly discuss their ideas about ways children in America and Africa are similar. Play the recording and invite students to pantomime playing a pretend thumb piano.

Indicator of Success

SUMMARY

Conclude by noting YOU REALLY HELPED THOSE INSTRUMENTS MOVE (VIBRATE) AND MAKE THEIR SOUNDS! Briefly review the information on drums, thumb piano, and African music, and pantomime (in the air) playing the drum and thumb piano.

ASSESSMENT As students become familiar with different drum and thumb piano pieces, they identify each piece's instruments and vibrating parts.

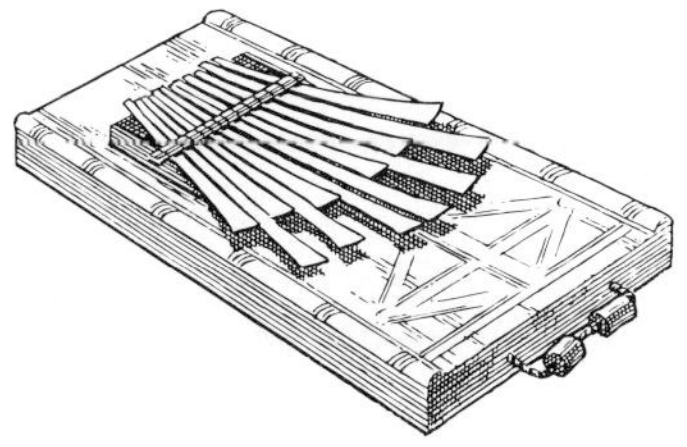

Thumb "piano"

> *Note*
>
> Drums are played around the world in many types of music, from rock to classical to world music. In Africa there is an incredible variety of drums. African music is functional, so drumming is usually for a specific purpose: dancing, sending messages, and working, and for religious rites such as funerals. In "Anaguta Drums," however, village elders of north central Nigeria are playing for their own enjoyment. The thumb "piano" has many names (*kalimba, mbira, sansa*), depending on the region of Africa. Different pitches are produced on metal bars of differing lengths. The thumb piano's box (or soundboard) reinforces the sound (as does a drum's body). In "Muno Muno" the thumb piano plays the introduction to a humorous song that tells a Ugandan boy that "it takes more than hair on your chest to be a man." (The complete song is found in *Pearl of Africa Reborn.* See "Other Music," below.)

Follow-Up

Cooperative Learning

1. Have students in small groups make and play a drum, using resources such as oatmeal boxes and coffee cans. Groups should share their construction plans with the class and demonstrate their drum. See Margaret McLean, *Make Your Own Musical Instruments* (Minneapolis: Lerner, 1988).

Social Studies/ Multicultural

2. Introduce the culture of African Americans by relating Nigerian drum music to the Kwanzaa celebration's Nigerian roots. Based on Nigerian harvest festivals, Kwanzaa lasts for seven days, beginning December 26, and includes gift giving, music, and storytelling. Kwanzaa was established in 1966 by Dr. Maulana Karenga as a rededication to greater achievement and more meaningful lives, and celebrates seven principles: unity, self-determination, collective work and responsibility, cooperative economics, purpose, creativity, and faith. Invite parents or community members to tell about Kwanzaa traditions. Have a classroom Kwanzaa observance (see "Related Literature," below).

Projects for College Students

Cooperative Learning

3. Review "Playing Instruments," pages 21–31. In small groups, have each group review a different grade level of an elementary music series to learn which instruments are introduced and whether world music instruments are included. List the instruments and share your findings with the class.

Related Literature and Media for Children

Music and the science of sound materials are listed on p. 193.

Ford, Juwanda G. (1997). *K is for Kwanzaa: A Kwanzaa Alphabet Book.* Cartwheel Books; ISBN: 0590922009.

Other Music

"Drum Duet" (Africa, Malenke people), *The Music Connection* 4

Pearl of Africa Reborn: Samite of Uganda, Shanachie 65008, audio CD, audiocassette

Pieces of Africa. (1992). Kronos Quartet. Audio CD, Wea/Atlantic/Nonesuch

"Senagalese Drumming" (Africa), *The Music Connection* 6

MUSIC CONCEPT A melody can be performed alone or with an accompaniment (*Harmony*)

Music "Wake Me!" (African American folk song), p. 384

Objective To identify melody and accompaniment and to demonstrate that recognition by singing a melody with and without accompaniment

Materials CD, track 15
Resonator bars: F, A, and C
Three mallets

FOCUS

Key Terms: ***melody, accompaniment***

Step 1: REST YOUR HEAD ON YOUR ARMS AND CLOSE YOUR EYES WHILE I SING A "WAKE UP" SONG. Establish pitch on the F resonator bar and sing the entire song. At end of song, have students raise their heads and open their eyes; ask them questions about the lyrics, such as: Where were we going to swing? (*Golden Gate*) Don't let me sleep too _____? (*late*)

Step 2: Teach the song phrase by phrase. Correct mistakes and repeat phrases sung incorrectly. Then teach two phrases at a time.

Special Learners Students can pantomime or sign the song's verses. Prepare visual cues to help with the order of the words.

Teacher: "Wake me! Shake me!"
Students: "Wake me! Shake me!"
Teacher: "Don't let me sleep too late."
Students: "Don't let me sleep too late."
Teacher: "Gonna get up bright and early in the morning,"
Students: "Gonna get up bright and early in the morning,"
Teacher: "Gonna swing on the Golden Gate."
Students: "Gonna swing on the Golden Gate."

Teacher: "Wake me! Shake me!
Don't let me sleep too late."
Students: "Wake me! Shake me!
Don't let me sleep too late."
Teacher: "Gonna get up bright and early in the morning,
Gonna swing on the Golden Gate."
Students: "Gonna get up bright and early in the morning.
Gonna swing on the Golden Gate."

Indicator of Success

Step 3: Have students sing entire song. Praise students by commenting on how well that *melody* was sung. Repeat, stressing they are singing the melody without accompaniment.

Step 4: Place the F, A, and C bars where everyone can see them. Ask HOW MANY BARS DO YOU SEE? (*three*) Tell students to watch and listen as they sing the song again. Play the F, A, and C bars simultaneously, as an accompaniment to the singing; use a steady-beat rhythm.

Step 5: Note how THOSE THREE BARS "WORKED TOGETHER" WITH OUR VOICES AND "DRESSED UP" THE MELODY. Discuss briefly other melodies they've heard accompanied by guitar, piano, organ, and other instruments.

Indicator of Success

Step 6: Select a student to join you by playing either the F or the C bar, using a steady beat. Give different students an opportunity to play the bars by singing other verses of the song and by creating new verses.

SUMMARY

HOW MANY BARS OR PITCHES DID WE PLAY FOR AN ACCOMPANIMENT? (*three*) WHAT DID WE ADD WHEN WE PLAYED THOSE THREE BARS ALL AT THE SAME TIME? (*accompaniment*) AND WHAT WERE OUR VOICES SINGING? (*melody*)

ASSESSMENT

Students sing (unaccompanied) a similar song that is familiar to them (see "Other Music," below), play appropriate bars as an accompaniment, and describe what they are doing.

Follow-Up

1. Transfer knowledge about accompaniments to the Autoharp. One student can press the chord button (firmly) while another strums steady beats. Accompany "Wake Me!" by strumming an F major chord throughout. Help students understand they are playing several different strings/pitches to create accompaniments.

Orff Adaptation

2. Two players can add a steady-beat accompaniment by (a) alternating low F and high F (octave) on a barred instrument or (b) playing low F and high C simultaneously (drone).

Visual Art

3. Compare two paintings, such as *The Cow Puncher* by Remington and *Night in Old Wyoming* by Johnson. Decide which painting has a colorful background and which does not. Review the "Wake Me!" song (with and without accompaniment) and have students decide how a particular painting reminds them of a particular song version, and why.

Projects for College Students

4. Read Orff-*Schulwerk,* pp. 67–70, and use the information to evaluate Orff adaptations for Grades K and 1 in elementary music series books (Appendix C.)

Music Fundamentals
Technology

5. Write and play the major triads: C, F, G, B♭, D, and A and the seventh chords: G7, C7, and A7. Use software programs such as *Music Ace* or *Essentials of Music Theory* to learn more about chords.

Other Music (see Section Four)

"Down Came a Lady" (C Major)
"Dulce" (D Minor)
"Pease Porridge Hot" (C Major)
"Sally, Go 'Round the Sun" (C Major)

MUSIC CONCEPT The rhythm of a melody includes long and short sounds (*Rhythm*)

Music "Matarile" (Mexican folk song), p. 338

Objective To identify aurally the long and short sounds in the rhythm of the melody and to demonstrate that recognition by singing and clapping the melody

Materials CD, track 16

FOCUS

Key Terms: ***beat, long/short, rhythm of melody***

Step 1: Sing or play the recording of "Matarile," asking students to PATSCH A STEADY BEAT WITH OUR SONG. Repeat, asking students to listen for the repeated word (*"Matarile"*). Practice saying *Matarile* and the "Ma-ta-ri-le, ri-le, ri-le (ron)" phrase, noting that these are Spanish words. (Pronunciation is found in Section Four.)

Step 2: Have students sing only the "Matarile" part when it comes in the song. As they repeat their singing, invite them to CLAP THE WAY THE WORDS GO for the entire song. Note how they were clapping lots of long and short sounds.

Step 3: Introduce the "What do you want?" and the "I want to jump" parts. Help students pronounce the words and chant/clap the rhythm of the words. Students should now be ready to sing all of the song and clap the way all the words go. Repeat until the clapping is secure.

Step 4: Arrange students in a circle and have them perform the song, alternating between a complete sing-through and stepping the beat followed by a sing-through and clapping the rhythm of the melody. Help students note the differences.

SUMMARY
Indicator of Success

Step 5: WHO CAN CLAP THE RHYTHM OF THE ENTIRE "MATARILE" SONG ALONE? Have individuals demonstrate with the class singing. Comment on the combination of long and short sounds in the song.

ASSESSMENT As students become familiar with different songs (see "Other Music," next page), they keep a steady beat as well as perform the long and short sounds in the melody.

Follow-Up

1. Have students play the rhythm of the melody on rhythm sticks as they sing.

Kodály Adaptation

2. Have the students clap the rhythm of the melody while thinking the words but not saying them aloud. This is important as an "inner-hearing" experience.

Kodály Adaptation

3. When both the beat and the rhythm of the melody are secure, students should walk the beat and clap or play the melody's rhythm at the same time.
4. Students should learn the Spanish verses of "Matarile."

Projects for College Students

Kodály Adaptation
Cooperative Learning

5. Use rhythm syllables to read the rhythm of "Matarile" (ta = ♩ ti-ti = ♫). In small groups, perform rhythm syllables with the songs in "Other Music."
6. Sing "Matarile" as you walk the beat and clap the rhythm of the melody. Try this with other familiar songs.

Multicultural

7. Review an elementary music series book (see Appendix C) to determine how many of the book's songs (and instrumental pieces) are of Mexican American, Mexican, and Latin American origin. Also review accompanying recordings and supplementary multicultural materials. Do the lessons include cultural information? Spanish-language texts? Pronunciation guides? Culturally authentic recordings? Could you use these materials in your area's schools? Why or why not?

Other Music (Section Four unless indicated)

"Bobby Shaftoe," p. 271
"Dulce"
"Hop, Old Squirrel"
"Hot Cross Buns," p. 271
"Pease Porridge Hot"
"Ring Around the Rosy"
"Rock-Passing Song" ("Obwisana")

MUSIC CONCEPT Each voice has its own special sound (*Timbre*)

Music "Sing about Martin!" by "Miss Jackie" Weissman, p. 364

Objective To identify aurally selected voices and to demonstrate that recognition by naming classmates after hearing their singing

Materials CD, track 17
Photograph of Dr. Martin Luther King, Jr.

FOCUS

Key Term: ***special voice/sound***

Special Learners Encourage students to sign the key words. Create a visual to help them remember the order of the words. (See below)

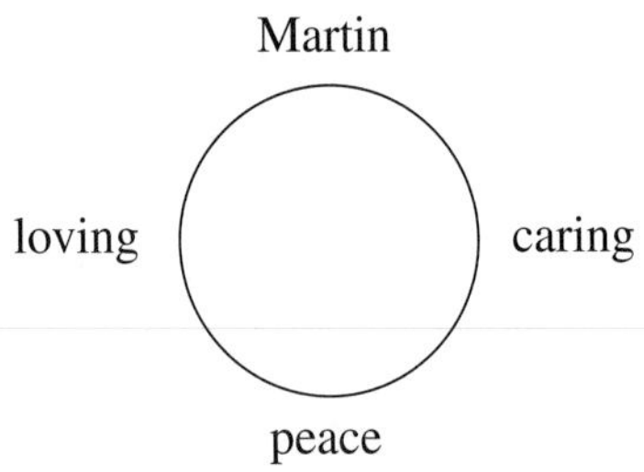

First graders are acquainted with the voices of classmates and are usually more willing to sing alone than are college students.

Step 1: Have students guess whom (Dr. Martin Luther King, Jr.) you are describing, by giving clues (see NOTE on next page). Show a picture of Dr. King and discuss with students some of Dr. King's achievements. Explain that they are going to learn a song about him.

Step 2: Sing the song or play the recording, asking students to DISCOVER WHAT THE WORDS TELL US ABOUT DR. KING (*caring, peace, loving*). Write each word on the board as students recall it. Then have them create a hand movement for key words such as *loving* (hands on heart) and *around the world* (draw a circle in air with arms).

Step 3: Teach the song by asking students to ECHO EACH PART YOU HEAR, AND USE HAND MOVEMENTS (step 2).

Step 4: Repeat the song several times, designating small groups to sing the echo. Finally, divide the class into two groups and have them take turns singing the responses (with hand movements). Compliment them on the special sound of each group.

Step 5: Challenge students to close their eyes and identify just one child by his or her voice. Have them play an identification game. Choose one person to be "It" (the guesser) and to sit away from the group, with eyes covered. Locate a student volunteer to sing the echo parts. Choose quietly, so that "It" cannot hear who is chosen. Sing the song, encouraging the class to sing the "call" part but to listen during the solo response. (Lower the recording's volume on the solo.) Continue until "It" can correctly name the solo singer. Praise "It," because YOU REALLY LISTENED CAREFULLY TO THE SPECIAL SOUND OF (*child's name*) VOICE! Continue the game with previous soloist becoming the new "It."

Indicator of Success

SUMMARY Conclude by briefly discussing how each of us is a special person—as Dr. King was—and EACH OF OUR VOICES HAS ITS OWN SPECIAL SOUND.

ASSESSMENT As students sing other songs that include echo or solo parts (see "Other Music," next page), they identify the voices of classmates.

Follow-Up

Social Studies

1. Help students learn about Dr. King and others who have helped make their world a better place; discuss their family members who have similar ideals or goals.

2. As a game, have students identify voices of familiar recording artists, such as Barney (the purple dinosaur), Big Bird, or current popular artists. Include a variety of timbres, such as a man's, a woman's, and a child's voice.

Social Studies

3. Have students learn more about the physical dimensions of self by exploring their singing voice and contrasting it with their other voices, such as talking, whispering, and calling. Use "Hello, There!" (see "Other Music"). Pantomime the different voices, such as holding a telephone for talking or cupping a hand beside the mouth for calling. Or use a pretend microphone or an "echo chamber" device.

Science

4. Help students learn that sound echoes from a surface. Take the class to the playground and then have one student move to the middle of the playground and blow a whistle. Ask the class to remember the sound. Have a second student stand about five feet from an *inside corner* of the building and blow a second whistle. Ask students to describe the difference in the two sounds (*the sound from the whistle close to the building was louder*). Ask them why this is so (*the sound bounced off the building and was reflected to our ears along with the original sound of the whistle*). A follow-up activity could be to examine the surface that the sound echoed from (hardness, brick, concrete) and compare it with resilient materials used in the classroom to prevent echoes (those that absorb sound, such as plaster walls, bulletin boards, and acoustical tile). (Idea by William K. Esler, Florida Technological University.)

Projects for College Students

5. Explore vibrations during talking, whispering, and singing. Place your fingers lightly on your larynx (Adam's apple) or on your cheekbones just below the eyes and close to the nose; feel the changes for each voice (sustained vibrations for singing, a broken vibration for talking, no vibrations for whispering).

6. Review the section on singing in the elementary classroom (pp. 32–41). Classify your own voice and vocal range as suggested in "The Voice" (p. 273).

> *Note*
>
> Dr. Martin Luther King, Jr. (1929–68) was an African American Baptist minister and civil rights leader. In the 1950s and 1960s he used peaceful, nonviolent methods to work for equality for African Americans in housing, jobs, and politics. Dr. King was awarded the Nobel Peace Prize in 1964. One of his most memorable speeches was "I have a dream . . .". Dr. King was assassinated on April 4, 1968. A federal holiday commemorates his birthday, January 15.

Related Literature and Media for Children

Marzalo, Jean. (1993). *Happy Birthday, Martin Luther King.* New York: Scholastic Trade; ISBN: 0590440659.

Other Music (echo songs or call/response songs)

"Charlie over the Ocean," see Section Four (sing an echo of each phrase)
"Gogo," see Section Four
"Hello, There!" see Section Four
"John the Rabbit," see Section Four
"Lemonade," *The Music Connection* 1 or *Share the Music* 2
"Rosie, Darling Rosie," *The Music Connection* 1

EVALUATION FOR COLLEGE STUDENTS

A. Identify those music concepts within melody, rhythm, form, harmony, and expressive qualities that children in kindergarten and grade 1 can perceive.
   1. melody concepts
   2. rhythm concepts
   3. form concepts
   4. harmony concepts
   5. expressive qualities concepts

B. Describe at least three developmental characteristics of children in kindergarten and grade 1. How will these characteristics suggest appropriate musical experiences?

C. Study the following songs. Circle those that are in the appropriate singing range of children in kindergarten and grade 1 and explain why. (Songs are found in Section Four.)

   "Do as I'm Doing"
   "Jim-Along, Josie"
   "Pele E"
   "Rig-a-Jig-Jig"
   "Sandy Land"

D. Describe these musical terms:
   1. steady beat
   2. dynamics
   3. timbre
   4. tempo
   5. rhythm of a melody

E. Notate four-beat rhythm patterns (♩ = one beat) using a variety of note durations and rests.

F. In small groups, review each model experience (and its follow-up) in Level I to determine which of the nine National Standards for Music Education (p. 5) are addressed in each. After your tally, discuss the results. Which received more attention and which received less? Why?

G. Discuss, in small groups, how special learners can and should be included in music learning experiences. Identify several types of special learners and reflect on how their needs were met in Level I model experiences.

ORIGINAL MODEL EXPERIENCE ASSIGNMENT—LEVEL I

Plan one to three original model experiences for children in kindergarten/first grade (Level I). Base each experience on *one* of the three specified concepts and songs. Each experience should be prepared in a step-by-step sequence using a similar format to the models in *The Musical Classroom* (see the sample outline that follows). Specific information about each component of the experience follows.

1. The *music concept and the song* are specified. (Songs are found in Section Four.) Plan how to present this concept and music to children.
2. State the *objective* for the experience, making sure that how and what students will do to demonstrate their understanding is included (see pp. 104–105).

3. *Model sequence.* Be sure to include key terms and age-appropriate music-making activities. Pay special attention to the opening ("Focus") and closing ("Summary") of the experience. Specify the exact part of the music that is the main focus of the experience. Identify by lyrics, rhythm, pitches, or placement in the song.

   Plan two *follow-up activities.* One activity should be a follow-up to the music concept presented in the model experience. Another follow-up activity should focus on a different subject area such as social studies, literature, or science.

	1.		2.		3.
MUSIC CONCEPT	Pitches can move up (*Melody*)	*or*	Pitches can move down (*Melody*)	*or*	The rhythm of a melody includes long and short sounds (*Rhythm*)
Music	"Miss Mary Mack," p. 340		"Looby Loo," p. 334, CD, track 5		"Hop, Old Squirrel," p. 316

Objective

Materials

FOCUS
Key Terms

Step 1.

Step 2.

Step 3.

Step 4.

Indicators of Success

SUMMARY

ASSESSMENT

Follow-Up

(One activity to reinforce music concept and one related to another curricular area)

Music

1.

2.

____

(other curricular area)

EVALUATING AN ELEMENTARY MUSIC SERIES TEXTBOOK ASSIGNMENT—LEVEL I

Evaluate the teacher's edition of an elementary music series textbook for kindergarten or grade one. (See descriptions of the three series in Appendix C and select one.) Prepare an evaluation of no more than three pages. The written report should demonstrate knowledge of music concepts and vocabulary.

Describe how well and to what extent the textbook and resources represent a comprehensive music curriculum. Refer to the chapter categories described in Section One of *The Musical Classroom.* Briefly describe the textbook's organization, visual presentation, directions for teachers, ease of use, and various resources (e.g., recordings, handbooks). Include discussion and supporting data on the following topics.

1. Elements of music and music concepts
2. Music-making activities
3. The world of music
4. Approaches to curriculum
5. Curricular developments
6. Planning and assessing music learning

Conclude by indicating if you can imagine yourself using this music textbook. Why or why not?

RESOURCE FILE—LEVEL I

Listening Map for Teachers ("Ballet of the Unhatched Chicks" Model Experience, p. 128)

The form of this piece is AABA. Mussorgsky's composition is based on a drawing by Victor Hartmann of chicks in their shells.

A section

1. Chick pecks and peeps inside shell (sec: 0–14)

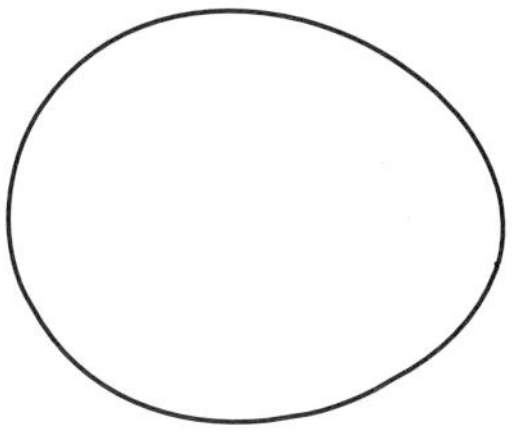

A chick can always be heard peeping inside air sack of its shell.

2. Tiny hole appears (sec: 15–16; one long sound)

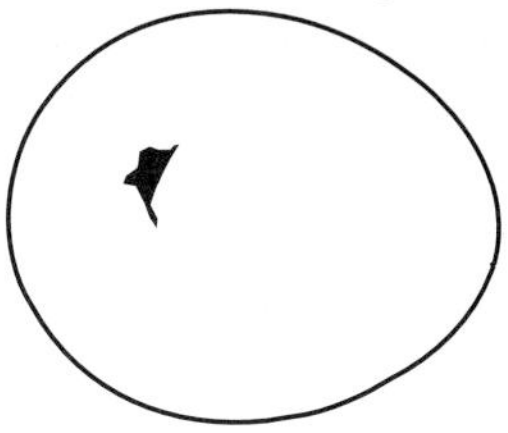

A section

3. Chick pecks and peeps again (sec: 17–28)

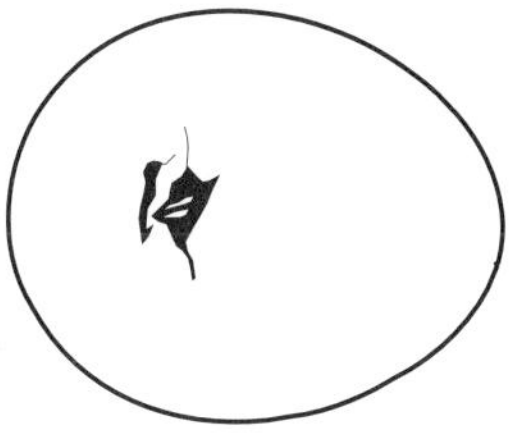

4. Hole is enlarged (sec: 29–31; one long sound)

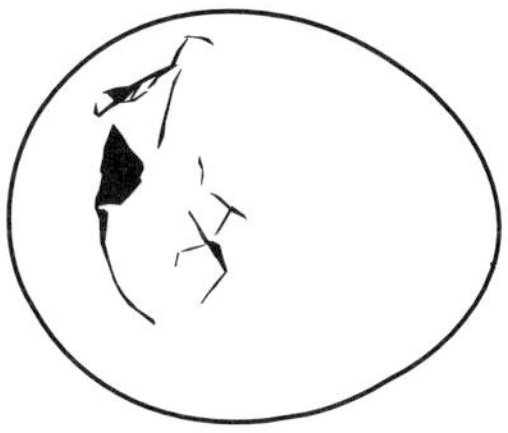

B section

5. Chick rests (sec: 32–44)

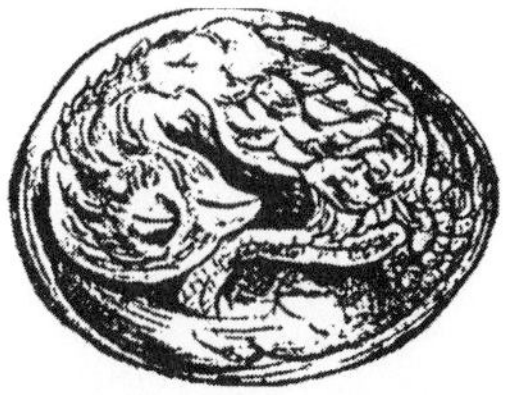

The chick always rests a few hours after making the first hole in the shell.

6. Chick gently resumes pecking (min: 45–53)

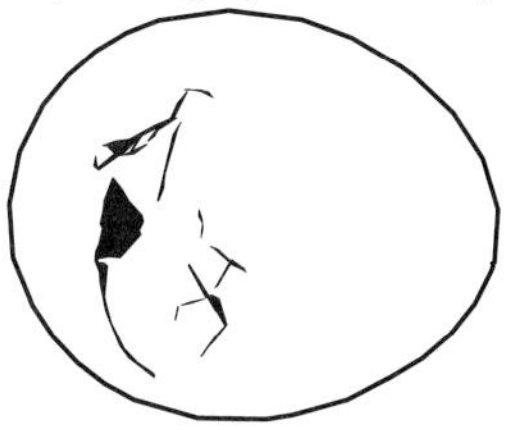

A section

7. Fast pecking and peeping, shell develops a large crack (min: 54–1:09)

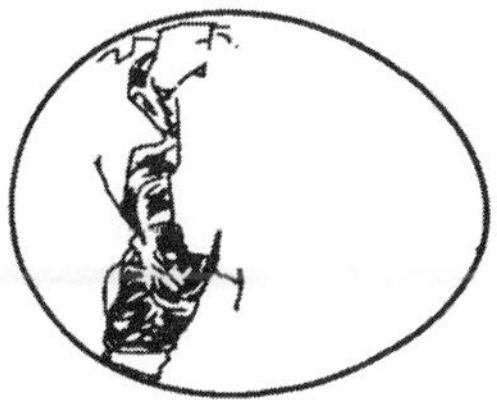

8. Two mighty kicks of the chick's feet push chick out of shell (min: 1:10, two long sounds)

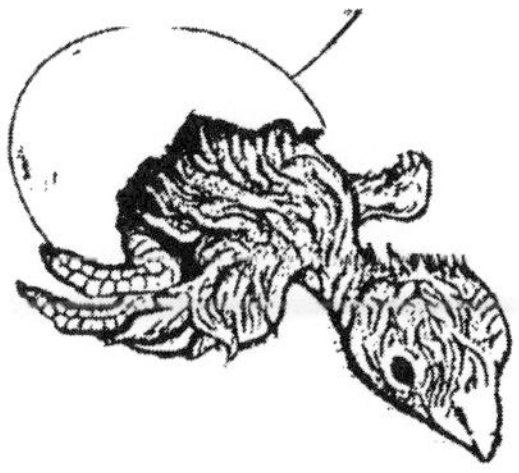

9. Chick staggers, then flops on stomach to rest (three seconds of soft, high sounds)

The chick is tired and wet; its feathers dry and fluff out in about two days. It is full grown in about 6 months.

Listening Map for Children (for "Ballet of the Unhatched Chicks," p. 128)

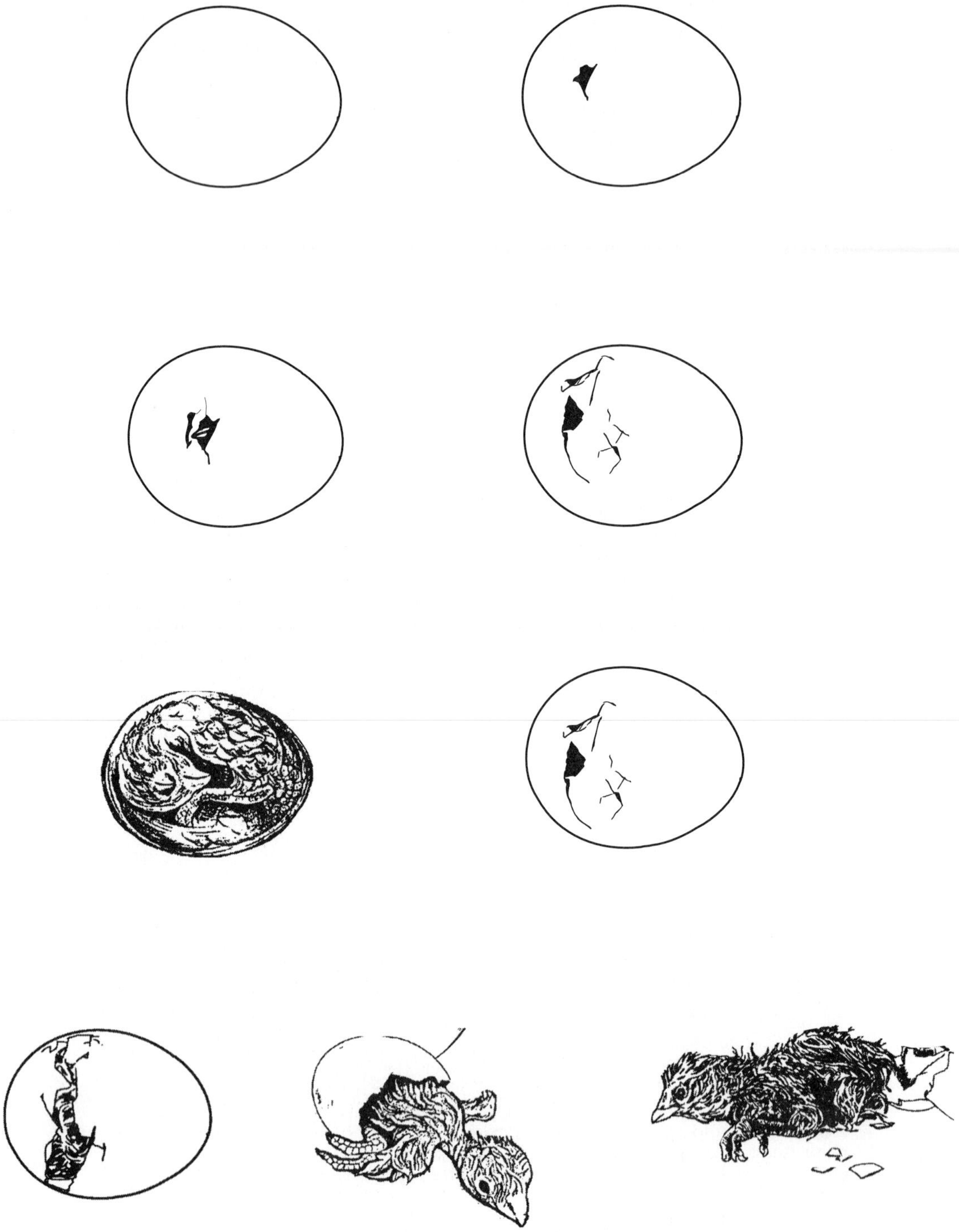

Level II: Model Experiences for Second and Third Grades

SEQUENCE OF SONGS AND LISTENING SELECTIONS LEVEL II (GRADES 2–3)

Music	*CD Track*	*Page*
"Barcarolle," from *Tales of Hoffman,* by Offenbach (Excerpt)	18	p. 156
"Devil's Dance," from *The Soldier's Tale,* by Stravinsky	19	
"Shoo, Fly" (music by Frank Campbell; text by Billy Reeves)	20	p. 158
"Chinese Dance," from *Nutcracker* Suite, by Tchaikovsky	21	p. 160
"Willowbee" (American folk song)	22	p. 162
"Kangaroos," from *Carnival of the Animals,* by Saint-Saëns	23	p. 164
"Bingo" (American folk song)	24	p. 166
"Cielito Lindo" (Mexico: trumpets) (Excerpt)	25	p. 168
"Cielito Lindo" (Mexico: guitar) (Excerpt)	26	
"The Stars and Stripes Forever," by Sousa (Excerpt)	27	p. 170
"My Father's House" (American song)	28	p. 172
Canzona, by Gabrieli (Excerpt)	29	p. 174
Trout Quintet, fourth movement, by Schubert (Excerpt)	30	
Serenade for Wind Instruments, Theme and Variations (K.361), by Mozart (Excerpt)	31	
Toccata, third movement, by Chávez (Excerpt)	32	
"Jesu, Joy of Man's Desiring," from Cantata No. 147, by Bach (Excerpt)	33	p. 176
"Ebeneezer Sneezer," by Olson	34	p. 178
"Hanukkah" (Hebrew folk song)	35	p. 180
"Chatter with the Angels" (African American song)	36	p. 182
"Song of the Dragon" (Chinese folk melody)	37	p. 184
"Hop Up, My Ladies" (American folk song)	38	p. 186

SEQUENCE OF MUSIC CONCEPTS—LEVEL II (GRADES 2–3)

Elements of Music	*Music Concepts*
MELODY	Music can be performed in a connected or disconnected style ("Barcarolle" and "Devil's Dance")
FORM	Melodies are divided into smaller parts called phrases ("Shoo, Fly")
MELODY	Pitches can be high or low ("Chinese Dance")
MELODY	Pitches in a melody can move by step ("Willowbee")
RHYTHM	The rhythm of a melody includes long and short sounds ("Kangaroos")
RHYTHM	Rhythm patterns can include sounds of long and short duration ("Bingo")
TIMBRE	Each instrument has its own special sound ("Cielito Lindo")
RHYTHM	Beats can be grouped in twos ("The Stars and Stripes Forever")
FORM	Phrases often end on a long tone ("My Father's House")
TIMBRE	Each instrumental family has its own distinctive sound (Canzona, Trout Quintet, Serenade for Wind Instruments, Toccata)
RHYTHM	Beats can be grouped in threes ("Jesu, Joy of Man's Desiring")
MELODY	Pitches in a melody can move by step ("Ebeneezer Sneezer")
RHYTHM	The rhythm of a melody includes short and long sounds ("Hanukkah")
HARMONY	Drones and ostinatos can add harmony to a melody ("Chatter with the Angels")
MELODY	A song usually ends on the home tone ("Song of the Dragon")
MELODY	Melodies can include skips of an octave ("Hop Up, My Ladies")

DEVELOPMENTAL CHARACTERISTICS OF SECOND- AND THIRD-GRADE CHILDREN

Teachers need to understand the developmental characteristics of children at each stage of their growth in order to plan meaningful music learning and appropriate musical experiences. What follows are some important developmental characteristics of second- and third-grade children. They address their physical, mental, cognitive, and musical growth as well as their development in terms of relationships with people and their surroundings. While many children exhibit these developmental characteristics, some may function at a younger level or even an older level. The needs of special learners are described on pp. 90–95.

CONCRETE EXPERIENCES	Children continue to learn through actively involving, hands-on experiences but are better able to internalize processes.
MOVE TO MUSIC	Children enjoy locomotor, nonlocomotor, and creative movements to music. In simple play-party games and folk dances, boys may not readily choose girls as partners, but, when assigned to a partner, they seem to participate willingly.
RAPID LANGUAGE DEVELOPMENT	Language and vocabulary develop rapidly, and children can apply correct labels to objects and activities.
READING SKILLS	Language reading skills are developing and children start learning to read and notate music.
INCREASED ATTENTION SPAN	Children can concentrate and focus their attention for longer periods of time, but they tend to alternate between very active and very quiet periods.
SMALL-MUSCLE COORDINATION	Small-muscle coordination and fine motor skills improve, enabling children to learn to play instruments such as the recorder.
SINGING VOICE	Children gain more control of their singing voices, and as a result, their singing becomes more accurate and their voices are distinguished by a clear, open, and unforced quality. They are able to sing accurately and expressively by themselves and with others. Their singing range increases from five or six pitches to as many as ten.
EXPANDED HARMONIC AWARENESS	Children are more aware of harmony through experiences with the Autoharp and with tuned and untuned instruments to accompany their singing. They also enjoy singing in harmony by performing partner songs, ostinati, and simple rounds.
GROUP WORK AND PEERS	Children like to work and play in groups; peers of the same sex are particularly important.
LOVE HUMOR AND FANTASY	Children are curious and interested in everything. They love songs with ridiculous humor and fantastic adventures.
NEED PRAISE	Children need positive reinforcement for their achievements.

MUSIC CONCEPT Music can be performed in a connected or disconnected style (*Melody*)

Music

"Barcarolle," from *Tales of Hoffman* (Excerpt), by Jacques Offenbach ("AWE-fuhn-bahk") (German, 1819–80)

"Devil's Dance," from *The Soldier's Tale,* by Igor Stravinsky ("strah-VIHN-skee") (Russian, 1882–1971)

Objective

To identify compositions that use mostly connected and mostly disconnected melodies and to demonstrate that recognition by drawing abstract figures on paper while listening to music

Materials

CD, tracks 18, 19

Two different-colored sheets of construction paper for each student: one light, bright color and one darker color, and two crayons of contrasting color for each

FOCUS

Key Terms: ***smooth/ connected, detached/ disconnected***

Barcarolle: A boatsong of Venetian gondoliers; always in 6/8 or 12/8 meter, and a moderate tempo.

Step 1: WHEN I CALL OUT A WORD, USE ONE HAND TO SHOW WHAT THE WORD SUGGESTS. FOR EXAMPLE, IF I SAY "POP-CORN POPPING," WHAT KIND OF LINE WILL YOU DRAW IN THE AIR? SHOW ME. Continue with several examples: airplane taking off, jackhammer, typing, waterfall, and so on. Discuss with students that SOME OF THOSE MOVEMENTS WERE SMOOTH AND CONNECTED, AND SOME WERE CHOPPY AND DISCONNECTED. MUSIC CAN BE LIKE THAT, TOO.

Step 2: Tell students they will listen to two pieces of music and draw something that will match each piece. Distribute paper, two different colors to each student. Play part of each composition, and after they have heard both, ask them to choose the color they want to use for each.

Step 3: Distribute crayons, two colors to each student. Caution class to avoid drawing pictures of recognizable objects. Encourage them to draw the same things they drew in the air. MAKE YOUR DRAWING LOOK EITHER SMOOTH OR DISCONNECTED. Play each composition for the drawing experience. Move through the group to observe students as they draw.

Indicator of Success

Step 4: Ask one half of class to hold up their drawings for "Barcarolle" for all to see. Ask how they look the same and why. (*smooth, connected lines*)

SUMMARY

Use the same process with the other half of the class for "Devil's Dance." Note the drawings that contain many separate dots or marks or zigzags that look like the choppy, disconnected melodies in the music. Elicit from students how the musical selections were contrasting and the drawings, too.

ASSESSMENT

Students perform a familiar song with some phrases smooth and connected, other phrases choppy and disconnected.

Follow-Up

Movement

1. Try movements to each piece. "Barcarolle" may inspire smooth ice skating or sliding while "Devil's Dance" will likely suggest jumpy or hoppy abstract movements.

Literature

2. Compose a "sound story" by expressively using a variety of classroom instruments along with a story having two contrasting sections, such as *Where the Wild Things Are,* by Maurice Sendak.

3. Using two flashlights, each covered with a different color cellophane, explore with students how they could create a "light show" (room lights off) for "Barcarolle" and "Devil's Dance." Some ideas might evolve such as "dancing" one of the flashlights on the ceiling and walls in smooth, long movements for "Barcarolle" and using the other for contrasting short, jumpy movements for "Devil's Dance."

Projects for College Students

4. Study "Integrating Music, the Arts, and Other Subjects" in Chapter VI. Then review an elementary music series book for grade 2 or 3 to learn how the textbook authors connect music and the other arts. Summarize your findings.

5. Review the "Creating Music" section on pp. 44–47 and specifically note the National Standards 3 and 4. Which achievement standard are students working toward in Follow-Up 2 above? How important are creative music activities for children? Why?

Other Music

"Dance Macabre," by Saint-Saëns (connected and disconnected), *Bowmar Orchestral Library,* "Legends in Music"; *The Music Connection* 5

"Dance of the Toy Flutes" (*Nutcracker* Suite), by Tchaikovsky (disconnected) *Bowmar Orchestral Library,* "Stories in Ballet and Opera"; *The Music Connection* 3

"March," by Prokofiev (disconnected), *Bowmar Orchestral Library,* "Marches"; or *The Music Connection* K

"March of the Dwarfs," by Grieg (disconnected), *Bowmar Orchestral Library,* "Nature and Make Believe"

"Kangaroos" (*Carnival of the Animals*), by Saint-Saëns (connected and disconnected), CD, track 23

"Sunrise" (*Grand Canyon Suite*), by Grofé (connected), *Bowmar Orchestral Library,* "American Scenes"

"The Swan" (*Carnival of the Animals*), by Saint-Saëns (connected), *Bowmar Orchestral Library,* "Animals and Circus"; *Bowmar's Adventures in Music Listening,* Level 1; *The Music Connection* 2

MUSIC CONCEPT Melodies are divided into smaller parts called phrases (*Form*)

Music "Shoo, Fly" (music by Frank Campbell, American; text by Billy Reeves, American), p. 362

Objective To identify aurally a musical phrase and to demonstrate that recognition by singing and by changing movement directions on each phrase

Materials CD, track 20
Tambourine

Key Term: ***phrase***

FOCUS

Special Learners Students can move a hand puppet or any other prop to show forward and backward stepping. Encourage students to sign the key words.

Step 1: Introduce the tambourine. Playing steady beats on the tambourine, have students move to a space in the room where they can do forward and backward movements. After students are in their places, tell them that THE TAMBOURINE WILL TELL US WHEN TO MOVE AND WHEN TO STOP. WHEN YOU HEAR THE TAMBOURINE, WALK FORWARD. BUT WHEN THE TAMBOURINE STOPS, YOU STOP, TOO. Before striking the tambourine, give preparatory counts such as ONE, TWO, READY, WALK. Play four steady beats; students should take four steps forward. Continue with students trying four steps backward. Then challenge them to take four steps forward, followed by four steps backward (without stopping in between). Teacher might shake the tambourine to signal the different directions (tapping vs. shaking).

Step 2: LET'S SEE HOW THAT FOUR-BEAT STEPPING FITS THE "SHOO, FLY" SONG. Sing *refrain* and play the tambourine as students repeat their stepping. "Shoo, Fly" has four phrases, with each phrase four beats (steps) long: forward four beats, backward four beats, forward four beats, backward four beats. Review the words and repeat until students can comfortably sing the refrain with their stepping.

Help students discover THE PHRASES IN THE "SHOO, FLY" PART REALLY HELPED DECIDE WHEN TO CHANGE DIRECTION. Remind them that they probably took a breath to sing each phrase, too!

Step 3: To try a folk dance for "Shoo Fly," arrange students in a circle facing center with hands joined. Students should raise arms as they move forward four beats and lower arms as they move backward four beats. Repeat, but add singing with the movements for the four phrases.

Step 4: Continue the dance with the verse part of "Shoo, Fly" ("I feel, I feel . . ."). Students can slide clockwise, facing center with hands joined, on the first half of the verse and counterclockwise on the second half of the verse. Finally, have them return to the forward/backward movements for the refrain. (Refrain/Verse/Refrain)

Indicator of Success

SUMMARY

Ask HOW MANY PHRASES ARE THERE IN THE "SHOO, FLY" PART OF OUR SONG? (*four*) Have them demonstrate their understanding by singing just the "Shoo, Fly" part and holding up fingers for each phrase (1, 2, 3, 4) as they sing. Play steady beats on the tambourine once again, until all students have moved back to their seats.

ASSESSMENT

As students sing a familiar but different song (see "Other Music"), they show the phrases by stepping in different directions and raising consecutive fingers as they sing.

Follow-Up

Phrase/Beat Chart

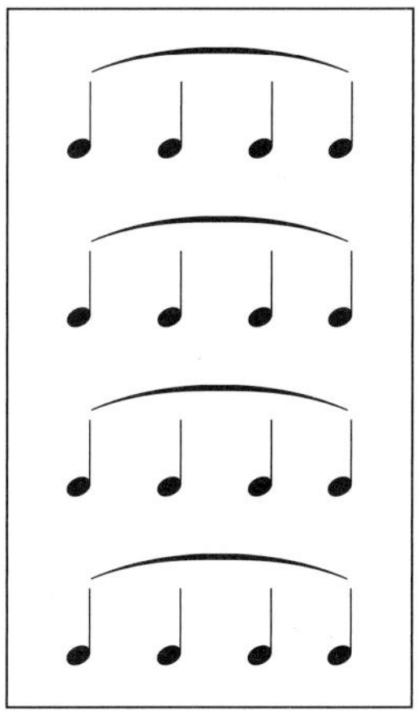

1. Learn to sing the other verse(s) of "Shoo, Fly."
2. Use the Phrase/Beat Chart while singing "Shoo, Fly." Students or teacher can point to each steady beat. This will fit the song's refrain but will need to be repeated during the verse.

Dance

3. Try a more challenging dance for the song's verses. Designate two students standing next to each other in the circle as the leaders, and two students opposite the leaders as "the arch." The two students who are "the arch" raise arms to form an arch. The two leaders walk across the circle with the others following them, pass under the arch, separate, and return to place. When all have passed under the arch, hands are joined, and the refrain begins. (For the refrain, use the movements presented in the model experience.)

Projects for College Students

Cooperative Learning

4. In small groups, determine the number and length of phrases of songs listed in "Other Music." Compare your findings with others.
5. Many children's songs consist of four-beat phrases, and many will "fit" the chart shown above. Locate several of these songs in your text and learn to sing or play them. Why might these short four-beat phrases be easier for young children to sing?
6. Read and be prepared to discuss the information about Leading and Teaching Songs in the "Singing" section in Chapter III. Consider your previous and current singing experiences and decide how initially you will feel most comfortable and successful leading and teaching songs to young children (e.g., recordings, direct teaching).

Other Music (see Section Four)

"Bow, Belinda"
"Jim-Along, Josie"
"Looby Loo"
"Old Brass Wagon"
"Sally, Go 'Round the Sun"
"Skip to My Lou"

MUSIC CONCEPT Pitches can be high or low (*Melody*)

Music "Chinese Dance," from *Nutcracker* Suite, by Pyotr Ilyich Tchaikovsky ("chy-KAWF-skee") (Russian, 1840–93)

Objective To identify aurally the high-pitched and low-pitched phrases that recur and to demonstrate that recognition by raising hands and cards during the phrases

Materials CD, track 21
Paper squares four inches by four inches for each student; one color for half the class and a different color for the other half

---

Step 1: Discuss and demonstrate the idea of a conversation. Elicit ideas of "taking turns talking," questions and answers, and so on.

FOCUS

Step 2: WE ARE GOING TO LISTEN TO A COMPOSITION THAT IS LIKE A MUSICAL CONVERSATION—ONE SHORT PHRASE IS ANSWERED BY ANOTHER.

Key Terms: ***high, low***

The class can be divided into two groups: one for raising hands when the first phrase is heard and the second for raising hands when the second is heard. Play the entire piece. (These paired phrases alternate six times throughout: Introduction abababababab Coda.) After the introduction, help the groups identify their parts and signal students not to raise hands during the ending (the coda).

Indictor of Success

Special Learners Two cards—one labeled high and one labeled low—could be prepared to help students remember the order and pitch level.

Step 3: Distribute cards of one color to the first-phrase group and the other color to the second. Ask students to raise and bounce their cards as they listen to the music again and to notice whether their phrase is mostly high or mostly low. Review meaning of high/low pitch levels. Which instruments played high? (*flute, piccolo*) Which instruments played low? (*violin, cello*)

Step 4: After listening, help students to verbalize that THE FIRST PHRASE IN EACH PAIR WAS HIGH-PITCHED AND THE SECOND WAS LOW-PITCHED. Then, tell students that the class is going to count how many high-pitched and how many low-pitched phrases are heard. Choose several "counters" in each phrase group to count silently as the groups listen and raise cards. After groups have determined that each has six phrases, select one student from each to collect six cards from his or her group to place on the board tray as class listens one more time. (The two students should place the cards—one at a time—on the board tray as the music is heard.)

SUMMARY

Using the card display as a visual, review with students how one phrase is answered by another throughout the piece. Ask them to tell you which phrases have high pitches, which have low, and how many phrases there are of each.

ASSESSMENT Students demonstrate or describe the differences between high and low parts in similar compositions (see "Other Music," next page).

Follow-Up

1. Use high and low rhythm instruments—for example, triangle and large drum—with the two melodies in the music. Students in each group could play as their group's melody is heard.

Dramatization

2. Read the question–answer poem "The Secret Song" (see Appendix D) to students, asking them to identify the creatures who answer the questions. Divide the class into groups and have the groups alternately read parts of the poem. Use high and low voices and creative characterization for each part.
3. Help students learn about the *Nutcracker* ballet and Tchaikovsky through stories, videos, and CDs (see below).

Projects for College Students

Creative Movement

4. Plan a movement interpretation for "Chinese Dance," emphasizing the contrast of high and low parts. Describe your plans or explore them with a small group of students.

Listening Map

5. Create a "picture map" of "Chinese Dance" for students to follow as they listen. Ideas could include alternating six flute "figures" (high part) with the six cello "figures" (low part). How could you picture the introduction and the coda?

Note

A suite is an instrumental work in several movements. In the seventeenth and eighteenth centuries, suites usually consisted of dance movements, as in the English Suites of J. S. Bach. In the nineteenth century, suites were often orchestral arrangements from operas and ballets. Tchaikovsky's *Nutcracker* Suite is an example of this type of suite. Twentieth-century composers also use the suite form.

Related Literature and Media for Children

Hautzig, Deborah. (1999). *Story of the Nutcracker Ballet.* Econo-Clad Books; ISBN: 080890065.

Hoffmann, E. T. (1991). *Nutcracker.* New York: Crown, illustrated by Maurice Sendak. Grade 3 up.

Nutcracker. (Tchaikovsky). Video by Jim Gamble Puppet Productions. Color, 30 min., ages 3 up. Friendship House; (800) 791-9876; www.friendshiphouse.com.

Tchaikovsky Discovers America. Classical Kid Series. Book and audio CD. Wea/Atlantic/Children's Group.

Other Music

"Kangaroos, " CD, track 23 or "Cuckoo in the Deep Woods" (*Carnival of the Animals*), by Saint-Saëns, *Bowmar Orchestral Library,* "Animals and Circus"

MUSIC CONCEPT Pitches in a melody can move by step (*Melody*)

Music "Willowbee" (American folk song), p. 390

Objective To identify aurally three pitches stepping down and to demonstrate that recognition by singing, playing, and doing hand motions when the pattern is heard

Materials CD, track 22
Resonator bars C to C^1, a mallet, and a stepbar frame (if available)

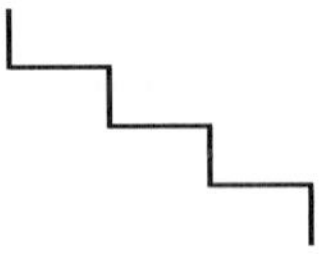

FOCUS
Key Terms: ***skip, step, up/down***

Step 1: Draw stairs on board (see margin). Elicit from students that one can go up/down on each step or skip. Display a set of resonator bars arranged on a stepbar frame. Play a series of pitches skipping at least two bars at a time and ask students ARE THE PITCHES SKIPPING OR STEPPING FROM ONE TO ANOTHER? Invite one or two students to demonstrate stepwise movement on the bars and note that stepping means that pitches are close together or "just next door."

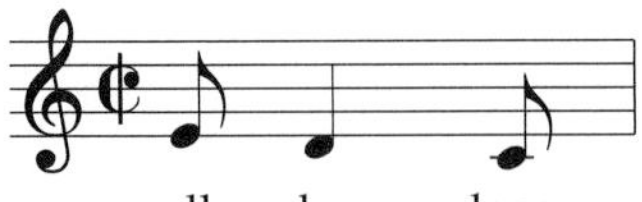

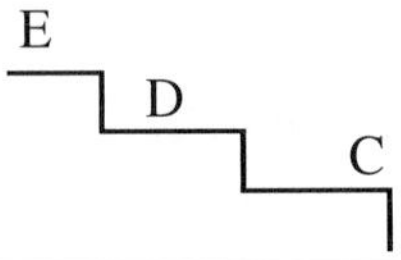

Step 2: Place the E, D, and C bars where all can see them, and play this descending pattern several times. Sing or play the recording and have students LISTEN TO A SONG THAT HAS THESE THREE PITCHES STEPPING DOWN. RAISE YOUR HAND WHENEVER YOU HEAR THE PATTERN. (*end of song*) Sing several times, allowing students to take turns playing the pattern while other class members sing and demonstrate with hand motions the "all day long" part. During this playing, encourage students to sing the entire song.

Indicator of Success

Step 3: To play a singing game with the song, have students form two lines facing each other. On "This' the way . . ." partners stand in place, swinging crossed hands joined from side to side but stopping *on the pattern.* For "Walkin' down . . . ," partners raise their joined hands, forming an arch under which the lead couple moves down the "alley"/line. The lead couple stops at the end of the line *on the pattern.*

Indicator of Success
SUMMARY

Step 4: Conclude with students singing as much of the song as they can, playing bars and doing hand motions. HOW DID THE PITCHES MOVE IN OUR PATTERN—BY STEP OR SKIP? (*step*) IN WHAT DIRECTION—UP OR DOWN? (*down*)

ASSESSMENT As students sing other songs with stepwise patterns (see "Other Music," next page), they show the stepwise movement with hand motions and in singing.

Follow-Up

Kodály Adaptation

1. Introduce hand signs (*mi, re, do*) and notation for "All day long." Refer to p. 72.

Movement

2. Learn additional verses of "Willowbee" and perform differing movements (dancing, skating, etc.) as each pair moves "down the alley."

Special Learners

3. Do an "Apple Twist" to the song. Standing or in wheelchairs, partners could hold an apple or a ball between their foreheads and sway to the music without losing the apple. (Idea suggested by Marcelle Vernazza in *Music Plus,* Pruett Publishing Co.)

Orff Adaptation

4. Create an accompaniment to the song, using xylophones, metallophones, and/or glockenspiels of differing pitch levels. Create an introduction and a conclusion. Some ideas follow.

Projects for College Students

Music Fundamentals

5. Study whole- and half-step distances on the keyboard.

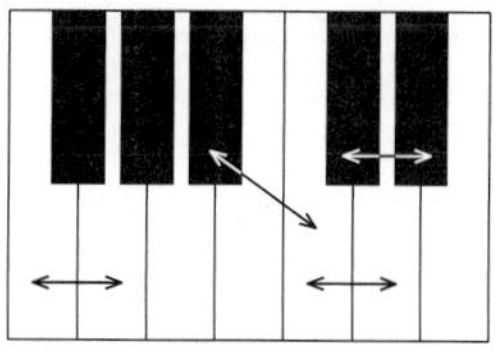

whole steps

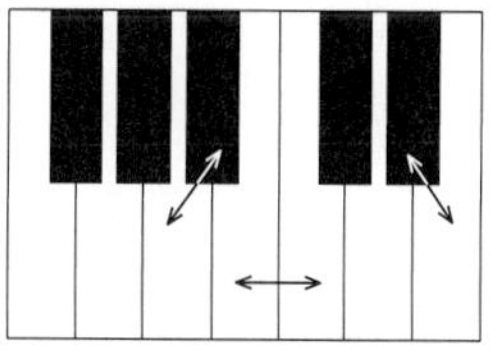

half steps

Music Fundamentals

6. Write whole steps and half steps in staff notation.

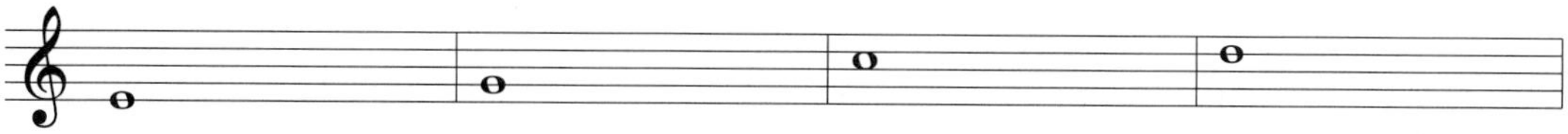

Write the pitch: a half step up a whole step up a half step down a whole step down

7. Review the songs in Level II Model Experiences to determine if they are in the appropriate singing range for second and third graders. Locate at least six other songs in the text that would be appropriate for this age level.

Other Music (Section Four unless indicated)

"Lady, Come"
"Li'l Liza Jane," *Share the Music* 1 and 4; *The Music Connection* 5
"Long-Legged Sailor"
"Miss Mary Mack"
"My Dreydl"
"Rocky Mountain," *The Music Connection* 3; *Share the Music* 2
"Tideo," *The Melody Book; Share the Music* 3

MUSIC CONCEPT The rhythm of a melody includes long and short sounds (*Rhythm*)

Music "Kangaroos," from *Carnival of the Animals,* by Camille Saint-Saëns ("sa[n] saw[n]s") (French, 1835–1921)

Objective To identify aurally the long and short durations in the rhythm of a melody and to demonstrate that recognition by manipulating puppets appropriately

Materials CD, track 23
A small branch of a tree (with leaves), about two feet tall
Two puppets:
1. a sock puppet resembling a cat
2. a small, artificial bird on a stiff wire or stick (wire/stick about fifteen inches long)

FOCUS

Step 1: PRETEND YOU ARE CATS LOOKING AROUND FOR A BIRD. SHOW WHAT TYPE OF MOVEMENT YOU MIGHT MAKE. Select a few students to describe or act out their ideas, which might include crouching and stalking.

Key Terms: ***short sounds, long sounds***

Continue with bird movements, selecting a different group to act out the short, quick movements of a tiny bird.

Step 2: Play the music and ask the class to LISTEN ESPECIALLY TO HEAR IF A BIRD AND CAT SEEM TO MOVE AT THE SAME TIME. (*no*)

Ask WHEN THE SHORT SOUNDS ARE HEARD, WHICH CREATURE IS MOVING? (Most students will say: *bird*) DURING THE LONGER SOUNDS, WHICH CREATURE MOVES? (*cat*) Students could imagine short movements being like a bird's "tweet" and long movements like a cat's lengthy "mee—ow."

Indicator of Success

Step 3: Have students depict the bird with one arm, the cat with the other, while they hear the music again. Ask them to think of a plot to go with the actions. (Observe students who are successful and who might be the first puppeteers.)

Discuss students' ideas for a plot or story. (These ideas should reflect the two musical ideas alternating throughout, concluding with a high-pitched chord.)

Indicator of Success

Step 4: Display the puppets and choose two students to act out the cat and bird story. Place puppeteers on either side of a third student holding the tree branch. Have them fit their story to the music. Repeat with several groups of students.

SUMMARY

Elicit from students what they learned about the music and conclude that THE LONG AND SHORT SOUNDS (AND THE HIGH AND LOW PITCHES) MADE THAT VERY GOOD MUSIC FOR OUR PUPPET SHOW.

ASSESSMENT As students become familiar with similar compositions (see "Other Music," next page), they show the differences between long and short sounds through body movements and by describing what they hear.

Follow-Up

Dramatization

1. Create a movement dramatization similar to the puppetry action. Make simple costumes such as bird wings, whiskers, and so on.

Visual Art

2. Construct a long–short collage using materials such as yarn cut into two different lengths. Notice how the differing colors, placement, and so forth, are unified by the similar lengths and texture.
3. Engage students in learning about the entire composition *Carnival of the Animals* by viewing the video listed below.

Projects for College Students

Creative Movement

4. Plan simple movement ideas for other parts of the *Carnival of the Animals* suite (see "Other Music"). Describe your plans, or explore them with a small group of students. Identify other parts of the suite and suggest ways they can be used in the classroom. (Description of the suite form is found on p. 161.)

> *Note*
>
> Saint-Saëns described *Carnival of the Animals* as "a zoological fantasy" and included many realistic and witty effects—such as including pianists in his musical zoo! (See model experience, p. 200.) *Carnival* was composed in 1866 but not publicly performed in Saint-Saëns's lifetime. (For the suite, Ogden Nash later wrote humorous verses that are usually incorporated into a performance.) Camille Saint-Saëns, French composer, pianist, and organist, is known for his keyboard, orchestral, and operatic works.

Related Literature and Media for Children

Saint-Saëns. *Carnival of the Animals.* Video by Jim Gamble of Puppet Productions. Color, 30 min., ages 3 up. Friendship House; (800)791–9876; www.friendshiphouse.com.

Other Music

"Ballet of the Unhatched Chicks" (*Pictures at an Exhibition*), by Mussorgsky, CD, track 6

"Long-Eared Persons" and "Hens and Roosters" (*Carnival of the Animals*), by Saint-Saëns, *Bowmar Orchestral Library,* "Animals and Circus"

"Tuileries" (*Pictures at an Exhibition*), by Mussorgsky, *Bowmar Orchestral Library,* "Musical Pictures: Mussorgsky"

"Yokuts Grinding Song," Section Four (short/long in accompaniment)

MUSIC CONCEPT Rhythm patterns can include sounds of long and short duration (*Rhythm*)

Music "Bingo" (American folk song), p. 282

Objective To identify aurally and visually the long and short sounds in the rhythm pattern of the word *Bingo* and to demonstrate that recognition in clapping and singing

Materials CD, track 24

FOCUS

Key Terms: ***rhythm pattern, long, short***

Special Learners Students can sign (finger spell) the letters of B-i-n-g-o.

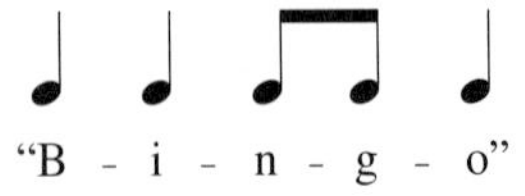

Step 1: Clap the following rhythm pattern and ask students to ECHO MY CLAPPING EXACTLY: 

After several repetitions, have students clap or speak the rhythm syllables ("ta ta ti-ti ta") for the pattern several times. Then notate the pattern on the board. Have them clap and read.

Sing the song or play the recording and let students know the PATTERN OF LONG AND SHORT SOUNDS IS VERY IMPORTANT IN A SONG. WHEN YOU HEAR THE PATTERN, CLAP OR SING WITH ME. (Pattern occurs three times, each time "B-i-n-g-o" is spelled in the song.) If the "Bingo" song is unfamiliar to students, teach each phrase separately, with class echoing.

Step 2: Review what was sung when the pattern was clapped and write those letters under the rhythm pattern. The class should sing the song again, clapping the pattern as the teacher points to the notation and identifying how many times it is heard.

Step 3: Sing six times, playing the traditional "game." The first time, sing song and clap the "Bingo" pattern. The second time, omit "B" and clap instead. The third time, omit "B" and "I" and clap. Continue until all letters are omitted and the entire pattern is clapped. (Five cards with the five letters will visually help children with the game.)

Indicator of Success

Step 4: WHO CAN SHOW OR TELL WHICH LETTERS SOUNDED SHORTER THAN THE OTHERS? (*"n" and "g"*) TOGETHER WITH THE OTHER LONGER LETTERS, THEY CREATED A RHYTHM PATTERN OF SHORT AND LONG SOUNDS. WHO CAN CLAP THE PATTERN AGAIN?

SUMMARY

ASSESSMENT

As students become familiar with rhythm patterns in different songs (see "Other Music," next page), they demonstrate or describe the differences between long and short sounds.

Follow-Up

1. Place strips of masking tape on the floor, showing the long and short durations: ___ ___ _ _ ___. Have students "walk the pattern" one after another while the class sings the song. Remind the walkers to take faster (and shorter) steps on the shorter lengths of tape.

Kodály Adaptation
Cooperative Learning

2. Using short (five-inch) lengths of doweling or Popsicle sticks, give a small group of students a bundle of eight or ten. Have students place the sticks vertically in front of themselves, creating the "B-I-N-G-O" pattern:

   . Invite them to create other four-beat patterns of long/short durations. Clap or use body rhythms to perform the patterns created.

Orff Adaptation

3. Play a name-clapping game. Chant and clap the rhythm of each student's name and have the class echo. For example:

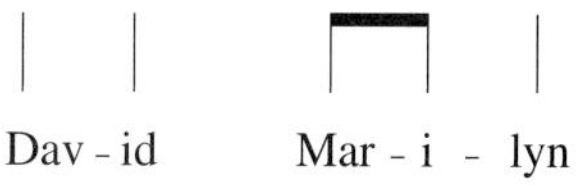

Visual Art

4. Study Mondrian's *Color Planes in Oval* and decide how the lines used in this geometric painting are of varying lengths.

Projects for College Students

Kodály Adaptation
Cooperative Learning

5. Create a number of four-beat rhythm patterns using quarter and eighth notes. Write out in traditional notation or "stick" notation on cards large enough for a class to see. Share the cards in a clapping/reading experience in small groups.

Kodály Adaptation

6. Write the rhythm syllables for all the notes in "Bingo." Review the "Reading and Notating Music" section on pp. 47–49.

Other Music (Section Four unless indicated)

"All Around the Kitchen" ("Doodle, doodle, doo")
"Gogo" ("Cham-ni-a-mo-go-go")
"John the Rabbit" ("Oh, yes")
"Love Somebody" ("Yes, I do")
"Old MacDonald" ("E-i-e-i-o"), *The Music Connection* 2, *Share the Music* 1

MUSIC CONCEPT Each instrument has its own special sound (*Timbre*)

Music "Cielito Lindo" (Excerpt) (Mexico)

Objective To identify visually and/or aurally two different instruments and to demonstrate that recognition by discussing, naming, and describing the instruments while listening to recordings

Materials CD, tracks 25, 26
Trumpet and guitar pictures (see p. 192)
Picture of mariachi group (see p. 192)
Map showing the U.S.A. and Mexico

FOCUS

Key Terms: ***mariachi, trumpet, guitar***

Step 1: Have students sing "Matarile," p. 338, or any Mexican American song that they have previously learned. Review what they know about music in Mexican American lives. (See Note, p. 191.) Using the map, have students locate the United States and Mexico.

Step 2: Show picture of mariachi group (see p. 192). Ask students HOW CAN YOU TELL WHAT COUNTRY THESE MEN COME FROM? (Mexico: *hats, special costumes*) Determine that they are holding musical instruments, and ask WHAT IS THE NAME OF THEIR GROUP? (*mariachi*) Help class identify the instruments (*trumpet, violin, Mexican guitars*), and discover when the mariachi plays. (See Note, next page, and drawings of different guitars p. 192.)

Indicator of Success Play the "Cielito Lindo" trumpet recording, and have class LISTEN AND DECIDE WHICH INSTRUMENT FROM THE MARIACHI YOU HEAR THE BEST AND IS PLAYING THE MELODY. (*trumpet*) Show the trumpet picture, and ask questions that help students notice its features, such as the material (*brass*) and the form (*tubing, mouthpiece, valves*). Introduce the Spanish word for trumpet (*trompeta*).

Replay the trumpet recording, inviting students to THINK OF A WORD THAT DESCRIBES THE SPECIAL SOUND OF THE TRUMPET. After listening, elicit terms such as *bright.*

Step 3: Display the guitar picture. Point out the guitar's features, such as the material (*strings, wood*), the rounded form, and the soundbox (*to amplify the sound*). Introduce the Spanish word for guitar (*guitarra*).

Indicator of Success Play the guitar version of "Cielito Lindo," and ask students to think of at least two words that describe the guitar's special sound (such as *warm*).

Step 4: Challenge students to a final listening game. Explain that they will hear the two instruments again.

Indicator of Success When they hear the trumpet and the guitar, have them pantomime the playing position of each to show recognition.

SUMMARY Conclude by briefly eliciting from students information about the mariachi and Mexican American music. Review the two instruments and their special sounds.

ASSESSMENT As students hear different trumpet and guitar music, they describe and aurally identify each instrument.

Follow-Up

Multicultural

1. Music (and mariachi) are often part of Mexican American celebrations. Read *Hello Amigos* (see p. 193) and learn how friends and family celebrate the birthday of Frankie Valdez. Is music a part of Frankie's party? What "happy birthday" songs do they sing?

Multicultural
Social Studies

2. Have a Mexican Heritage Day during Hispanic Heritage Month in September or in May during Cinco de Mayo. Involve members of the school and community.

Science
Cooperative Learning

3. Form small groups and give each group one thin and one thick rubber band. Have them find several things that cause the two rubber bands to sound different (thickness, length, and tension). They might pull and listen to it vibrate or pinch off about the same length from two different thicknesses. They can pull gently, then hard, to discover various playing techniques. Then have them help you list on the board all the things that cause the rubber bands to sound different (see Appendix F, "Integrating Music"). Look at a guitar to discover how its strings sound different because of varying thickness, tension, and length.

Projects for College Students

Multicultural

4. Develop a mariachi unit for a selected grade level. Devise strategies for listening to mariachi recordings, and a mariachi bulletin board. Also see *Los Mariachis! An Introduction to Mexican Mariachi Music* (World Music Press), a twenty-page booklet with audiocassette.

> *Note*
>
> The mariachi, a strolling folk orchestra, includes violins, trumpets, guitars and guitar variants, and sometimes a Mexican harp. Mariachi groups perform at weddings, birthdays, saints' days, mass, and other celebrations, dressed in ornamented and fitted jacket, pants, and riding boots. Mariachi is an old tradition, but its modern form probably began in the 1800s in the Mexican state of Jalisco. Until the 1930s mariachi was the music of country people, and musicians dressed in simple peasant clothes. Today, costumes, brilliant instrumental passages, and falsetto singing are typical of mariachi performances.

Related Literature and Media for Children (see p. 193)

Other Music

Mas Canciones, Linda Ronstadt, audio CD, Wea/Elektra Entertainment
"Cielito Lindo," *The Music Connection* 4

MUSIC CONCEPT Beats can be grouped in twos (*Rhythm*)

Music "The Stars and Stripes Forever" (Excerpt) by John Philip Sousa ("SOO-zuh") (American, 1854–1932)

Objective To visually and aurally identify beat groupings in two and to demonstrate that recognition through body rhythms and in a stick game

Materials CD, track 27
Rhythm sticks
Notation on board or chart (see below)

FOCUS

Key Terms: ***beat, downbeat, groups of twos***

Special Learners Encourage students who are hearing impaired to point to beats on a chart and help all students to feel the beats in twos in any way they can.

Step 1: Point to the two examples of beat groupings and ask WHICH EXAMPLE, NUMBER 1 OR NUMBER 2, SHOWS BEATS GROUPED INTO SETS OF TWO? (*number 1*)

1. 

2. 

Direct students' attention to the visual difference in the two examples. Demonstrate that difference by having the class perform steady beats in groups of two (*lap,* clap) and in groups of three (*lap,* clap, clap). Continue until students are comfortable with the twos and threes. Then have class try the twos motions (*lap,* clap) facing a partner (without clapping partner's hands).

Step 2: THESE GROUPS OF TWO WILL FIT NICELY WITH MARCH MUSIC. ON THE SIGNAL, YOU AND YOUR PARTNER BEGIN LAP, CLAP. After the eight-beat introduction in the recording, the teacher should indicate the downbeat (beat 1) in the music and say aloud "one, two." Observe and help students having difficulty. (You might want students to feel the twos with marching before trying the stick game in Step 3.)

Indicator of Success

Step 3: Try a stick game with the music. Choose two students to sit cross-legged on the floor, facing each other. Give each pair two rhythm sticks to hold vertically. The pattern for the game is

Beat 1: hit own sticks on floor
Beat 2: hit own sticks together

Indicator of Success

Try the motions without the music, and then with the music. Signal the downbeat as before. Have other pairs of students try the stick game.

SUMMARY

STICK GAMES ARE A GOOD WAY TO SHOW BEATS GROUPED IN TWOS. Elicit from students that the first beat in the grouping is called the downbeat.

ASSESSMENT

As students listen to a different composition (see "Other Music," next page), they perform beats in groups of two, after locating the downbeat.

Follow-Up

Cooperative Learning

1. In small groups, discover other ways to show groups of twos in body movements: for example, clap/pat-a-cake, step-clap. Transfer these body rhythms to classroom instruments or paper plates (hold like cymbals).
2. Sing familiar songs in twos, and use body rhythms or instruments to show twos. Or use barred instruments and cymbals to show the twos of "Kang Ding City," Section Four.

Cooperative Learning

3. In small groups, have students notate example 1 in Step 1 and then perform using body rhythms. Students could take turns pointing to quarter notes and performing lap, clap, lap, clap, and so on.
4. Conduct beats in twos with this march. (For conducting patterns, see p. 195.)

Social Studies

5. Look at and discuss pictures of a band, such as a marching band led by a drum major or a concert band led by a director/conductor. Identify family members who are in bands (or other musical groups) at school or church. How do these musical groups influence student's lives and make them better? What would our lives be like *without* music? Learn how a band is a *group,* with roles as in other groups (e.g., leaders, followers, innovators, isolates).

Projects for College Students

6. Locate and perform or conduct twos in music suggested by your instructor, from "Other Music," below, or in your personal music collection.

Poetry

7. Find children's poems that move in twos and learn to read them expressively.
8. Listen to Judith Lang Zaimont's "July" from *A Calendar Set* (*The Music Connection* 4) and discover quotations from "The Stars and Stripes Forever" as well as "Yankee Doodle" and "Columbia, the Gem of the Ocean."

> *Note*
>
> John Philip Sousa, known as "The March King," wrote almost 150 marches that are striking in their rhythmic and instrumental effects. "The Stars and Stripes Forever" (1897) is one of his most famous. Sousa led the United States Marine (Corps) Band for twelve years before forming his own band that toured worldwide.

Other Music (in twos)

"Colonel Bogey March," by Alford, *Bowmar Orchestral Library,* "Marches"; *The Music Connection* 7

"Hanami Odori" (Japan), in *Flower Dance: Japanese Folk Melodies,* Nonesuch recording

"Hoe-Down" (*Rodeo*), by Copland, *Bowmar's Adventures in Music Listening,* Level 2; *Bowmar Orchestral Library,* "Dances," Part 1; *The Music Connection* 3; *Share the Music* 4

"March Militaire," by Schubert, *Bowmar Orchestral Library,* "Marches"

"March of the Dwarfs," by Grieg, *Bowmar Orchestral Library,* "Nature and Make Believe"

Finale from *William Tell* Overture, by Rossini, *Bowmar Orchestral Library,* "Overtures"

"Semper Fidelis," by Sousa, *The Music Connection* 6

"Russian Dance" (*Nutcracker* Suite), by Tchaikovsky, *Bowmar Orchestral Library,* "Stories in Ballet and Opera"; *Share the Music* 2

"Washington Post March," by Sousa, *Share the Music* 5

MUSIC CONCEPT Phrases often end on a long tone (*Form*)

Music "My Father's House" (American song), p. 342

Objective To identify aurally longer ending tones and words at phrase endings and to demonstrate that recognition by singing and signing

Materials CD, track 28

Diagram of signing (p. 343)

A bag containing notecards with words or phrases that suggest voiceless communication, e.g., "be quiet," "yes," "no," "stop," happy, sad, cold, hot, sleepy, scared, "Come with me," "Yum!" "Yuck!" drinking, washing hands, combing hair, etc.

FOCUS

Step 1: Seat students in a semicircle and play a game by asking individuals to come to the front and pull a notecard out of the bag (eyes closed!). Ask each student to silently read what is on the card (or whisper it to him or her) and then to act out the message until the class guesses it. Note how they told each other something without words—they did it with signs!

Key Terms: ***long tone, beats, clear ending***

Step 2: Tell students that they are going to try signing while singing a song. Sing or play recording of "My Father's House" (verse 1) and have students LISTEN FOR IMPORTANT WORDS THAT WILL GIVE US PLENTY OF TIME TO USE SIGNS ALONG WITH WORDS. After hearing the music, write on board students' correct responses: *me, house,* and *peace.* EACH WORD IS A LONG TONE HELD THROUGH SEVERAL BEATS. Listen again, raising hands on long-duration words. Note that THIS LONG TONE GIVES EACH PHRASE A CLEAR ENDING.

Step 3: Introduce sign language for "me." Review words for first phrase adding (and holding) the motion on "me." Sing or play recording encouraging students to do the sign for "me" when it comes in the song.

Similarly introduce the sign for "house" and have students sing the first four phrases with signs for "me" and "house." Stress holding signs and tones to produce clear phrase endings.

Finally, introduce the sign for "peace." Practice the two movements for "peace." Learn how phrases 5 and 6 have words and melody identical to phrases 1 and 2. Discuss the need to use long, slow motions on "peace" to last four beats. (The "peace" sign has two gestures; each gesture lasts for two beats.)

Indicator of Success

Step 4: With recording, sing entire song signing the three words, until class is secure. Listen to and watch to be sure students HOLD THE LONG TONES AND SIGNS, SO EACH PHRASE HAS A CLEAR ENDING.

SUMMARY

me
| | | |

house
| | | |

peace
| | | |

Conclude by asking students to review the word that ended each phrase and how long each lasted. (*four beats*) THAT'S WHY IT WAS EASY TO SHOW THE CLEAR PHRASE ENDINGS WITH SIGNS. Put lines under long words (see margin). Have a final sing-through, while teacher points to beat lines under words. Congratulate students on their singing and signing and ask them to give themselves applause the "signing way" (shake both hands in the air overhead, with an excited, happy expression on face).

ASSESSMENT

As students review or become familiar with a different song, they sing and use gestures along with the long sounds/words at phrase endings.

Follow-Up

1. Learn signs for the entire song (see p. 343).
2. Learn about the whole note (𝅝): draw it, name it, and follow whole notes on a chart while singing the song.
3. Add a tambourine accompaniment. Tap the tambourine on the song's quarter notes and shake it on the whole notes.

Projects for College Students

Kodály Adaptation

4. Learn tonic *sol–fa* syllables and Curwen hand signs for pitches in the song. (Begin by discovering *mi–re–do* each time it occurs.) Identify and sing all syllables, adding Curwen hand signs.

Kodály Adaptation

5. Read "The Kodály Approach," pp. 70–74, and based on the reading, evaluate the Kodály adaptations in the elementary music series books (Grades 2 or 3). List each book examined, along with brief, evaluative annotations.

Other Music

"Down in the Valley," see Section Four
"My Hat" ("Mein Hut")
"Rocky Mountain," *The Music Connection* 3; *Share the Music* 2
"Sally, Go 'Round the Sun," see Section Four

MUSIC CONCEPT Each instrumental family has its own distinctive sound (*Timbre*)

Music

Canzona (Excerpt), by Giovanni Gabrieli ("Gah-bree-ELL-ee") (Italian, 1557–1612)
Trout Quintet, fourth movement (Excerpt), by Franz Schubert (Austrian, 1797–1828)
Serenade for Wind Instruments, Theme and Variations (K. 361) (Excerpt), by Wolfgang Mozart (Austrian, 1756–91)
Toccata, third movement (Excerpt), by Carlos Chávez ("SHAH-vehs") (Mexican, 1899–1978)

Objective

To identify aurally the instrumental families and to demonstrate that recognition by choosing words that subjectively describe the timbre, and by circling the appropriate word on a worksheet

Materials

CD, tracks 29, 30, 31, 32
Room-sized pictures of selected instruments (see photographs, p. 194)
Worksheet for each student (see p. 193)

FOCUS

Key Terms: ***woodwind, strings, brass, percussion***

Write key terms on board as they are introduced.

Step 1: I'M THINKING OF A SPECIAL WORD THAT DESCRIBES BROTHER, SISTER, MOTHER, AND OTHERS. WHAT IS IT? (*family/families*) Discuss.

Step 2: Mention that instruments come in families too, and display pictures of brass instruments. Point to familiar ones such as trumpet and trombone and ask students to name the instruments. Then decide WHAT DO THEY HAVE IN COMMON THAT MAKES THEM BRASS FAMILY MEMBERS? (*brass material, cup-shaped mouthpieces that are lip vibrated, long cylinders that are wound up and end in flaring bells*) Play an excerpt of Canzona and ask students to THINK OF A WORD THAT DESCRIBES HOW THE TRUMPET OR TROMBONE SOUNDS TO YOU. Encourage subjective terms such as *bright, strong, buzzy, brassy,* and *sparkling.*

Step 3: Play an excerpt of the *Trout* Quintet and ask students to identify the instruments. (*strings*) Ask WHAT SPECIAL WORD CAN YOU THINK OF TO DESCRIBE STRINGED INSTRUMENTS? (*"sweet," "warm," etc.*) Briefly discuss that strings and brass have very different sounds. Look at pictures of instruments such as violin or double bass and identify their similarities. (*strings that are bowed or plucked, wooden bodies of similar shape but different sizes*)

Step 4: Show photos of familiar woodwind instruments such as clarinet and flute. BECAUSE OF THE MATERIALS AND CONSTRUCTION, WOODWINDS WILL SOUND DIFFERENT FROM STRINGS. Discuss the similarities and differences of woodwind instruments. (*wood or metal bodies, single-reed or double-reed mouthpieces—except the flute's open hole the player blows across*) Play a brief excerpt of Serenade and ask for words to describe the woodwind family sound, such as *mellow, woody* or *nasal.*

Step 5: Play an excerpt of Toccata, and have students identify the orchestral family. (*percussion*) Discover some words to describe their difference from other families, for example, *sharp* or *hollow,* or the "snaps, crackles and pops" in the orchestra. Display pictures of percussion instruments and discuss how PERCUSSION ARE ALL PLAYED BY STRIKING OR SHAKING. Identify some that are struck (drums, cymbals), and some that are shaken (maracas, sleighbells).

Step 6: Distribute the worksheet (p. 193) to each student. Read the words aloud, and tell students that four selections will be heard. LISTEN TO NUMBER ONE, AND MARK WHAT YOU HEAR: WOODWIND, STRINGS, BRASS, OR PERCUSSION. Play excerpts from the four compositions; scramble the order. Correct answers immediately after hearing each composition and name the composer and title of each.

Indicator of Success

SUMMARY

Help students conclude that EACH ORCHESTRAL "FAMILY" HAS ITS OWN SPECIAL SOUND. Briefly elicit from them the special characteristics of each family.

ASSESSMENT

As students hear compositions featuring families of instruments (see "Other Music," below), they identify and describe the instruments.

Follow-Up

1. Use classroom instruments to discover that percussion instruments can have a *definite pitch* such as xylophone, timpani (kettledrum), chimes, or be of *indefinite pitch* such as tambourine, triangle, cymbals, bass drum.

Cooperative Learning

2. Have students work in small groups to complete an orchestra seating chart. Give each an enlarged copy of the diagram on p. 195, and have them put pictures of instruments in the appropriate sections. They could look for pictures in magazines or mail-order catalogues, make their own drawings, or draw the entire chart and instruments. Have groups post and explain their charts.
3. Have students discuss the different audience behaviors that are appropriate for different musical events: orchestral concert, parade, rock concert, and so on.

Projects for College Students

4. Prepare a class to attend a young people's concert. Review the orchestral families and seating plan, and the music to be heard.
5. Make a timeline patterned after the "Timeline of Music and History," Appendix E. Include the five style periods and five composers featured in this model experience and in the following model experience, "Jesu, Joy of Man's Desiring" (J. S. Bach). Review contemporary historical events, music elements, and types of compositions of the five style periods.

Related Literature and Media for Children (see p. 193)

Other Music

Prelude to Act III (*Lohengrin*), by Wagner, *Bowmar Orchestra Library,* "Music of the Drama: Wagner" (brass)

"Scherzo" (Excerpt), from String Quartet in B Minor, by Teresa Carreño, *Share the Music* 4 (strings)

"Suite for Wind Quintet," first movement, by Ruth Crawford Seeger, *Share the Music* 5 (woodwinds: bassoon, clarinet, flute, oboe)

Young Person's Guide to the Orchestra, by Britten (all instruments), *Bowmar Orchestral Library,* "Ensembles, Large and Small"

MUSIC CONCEPT Beats can be grouped in threes (*Rhythm*)

Music "Jesu, Joy of Man's Desiring," from Cantata No. 147 (Excerpt), by Johann Sebastian Bach (German, 1685–1750)

Objective To identify aurally beat groupings in three and to demonstrate that recognition using the conducting pattern for triple meter along with the music

Materials CD, track 33

FOCUS

Key Terms: ***beat, downbeat, threes***

Step 1: WATCH THESE MOVEMENTS AND SEE IF YOU CAN DISCOVER ANY KIND OF BEAT GROUPING. Do beats in twos and involve class in body movements (lap, clap).

Step 2: Demonstrate body movements that show groups of threes (e.g., lap, clap, clap). Draw three quarter notes on the board and have a student point to the notes as the class performs steady beats in threes. Speak "1, 2, 3" aloud and have students join you in saying "1, 2, 3" as they do the body movements.

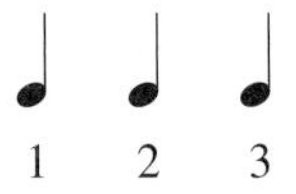

Special Learners
Encourage students to show beat groupings in any way they can.

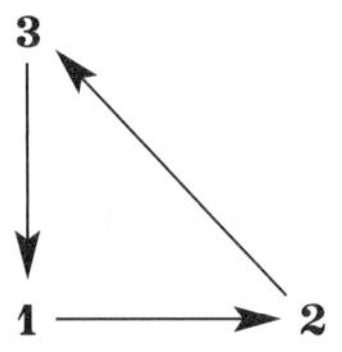

Each student should use the dominant hand and arm for conducting.

Step 3: Tell students that I KNOW A MUSICIAN WHO SHOWS STEADY BEATS TO OTHER MUSICIANS. Ask students if they can GUESS WHO I AM AND WHAT I'M DOING. (*a conductor, conducting*) (Teacher positions self at front of room, gives cue, begins conducting.) Briefly discuss conductor's location in front of the musical group and the use of arms to keep the steady beat. Tell students they are now going to learn the conductor's pattern for steady beats in threes. Draw the conducting diagram on the board (see margin), omitting numbers.

Demonstrate the pattern for the class, reversing your movements or standing with back to class. Ask them WHICH MOVEMENT IS THE FIRST (OR DOWNBEAT) IN THE PATTERN? (*the downward motion*) Label each movement in the pattern: "1, 2, 3."

Have students try the pattern until most seem secure, giving verbal cues such as "down, right, up" as needed. (Use a tempo similar to that of "Jesu, Joy of Man's Desiring.") Move throughout the class to help students.

Step 4: As soon as the class is secure, have students stand and conduct with the music. Be sure to indicate the downbeat.

Indicator of Success

SUMMARY Briefly discuss with students their experiences keeping a steady beat, locating the downbeat, and conducting music in beat groupings of three.

ASSESSMENT As students become familiar with similar compositions (see "Other Music," next page), they use the conducting pattern for triple meter along with the music, after locating the downbeat.

Follow-Up

Cooperative Learning

1. In small groups, have students create handgames in beat groupings of twos or threes. Perform, and have class decide whether example is in two or three.

2. Engage students in learning more about J. S. Bach by listening to the CD *Mr. Bach Comes to Call* (See "Related Literature," below). Challenge students to signal when they hear the excerpt of "Jesu, Joy of Man's Desiring" in the story.

Projects for College Students

3. In the *Music Educators Journal* (March 1992), read articles about conductor Catherine Comet, composer Ellen Taaffe Zwilich, and trombonist Rebecca Bower. How could you use this material in the classroom to help students understand what it means to be a classical musician?

Music Fundamentals
Technology

4. Study the meter or time signatures that identify beat groupings of twos, threes, and fours (see Appendix A or use a music software program such as *Music Ace* or *Essentials in Music Theory*). Learn conducting patterns for these meters (see p. 195). Locate six songs in Section Four with meter signatures illustrating two, three, and four beat groupings.

Related Literature and Media for Children

Ketcham, Sallie and Salley Ketcham. (1999). *Bach's Big Adventure.* Orchard Books; ISBN: 0531301400.

Mr. Bach Comes to Call, Classical Kids Series. Audiocassette or audio CD. Wea/Atlantic/Children's Group.

Portraits of Composers, Set 1. Bowmar. Posters and miniature-sized portraits.

The Bach Book Music History Coloring Book. Bandon, OR: Composer Comix. (P.O. Box 1758, Bandon, OR 97411)

Winter, Jeanette. (1999). *Sebastian: A Book about Bach.* Browndeer Press; ISBN: 015200629X.

Other Music (threes)

"Anitra's Dance" (*Peer Gynt* Suite no. 1), by Grieg, *Bowmar Orchestral Library,* "Legends in Music"; *Share the Music* 6

"Arabian Dance" (*Nutcracker* Suite), by Tchaikovsky, *Bowmar Orchestral Library,* "Stories in Ballet and Opera"; *The Music Connection* 3

"German Waltz—Paganini" (*Carnaval*), by Schumann, *Bowmar Orchestral Library,* "Pictures and Patterns"

"Minuet," by Mozart, *Bowmar Orchestral Library,* "Pictures and Patterns"

MUSIC CONCEPT Pitches in a melody can move by step (*Melody*)

Music "Ebeneezer Sneezer," by Lynn Freeman Olson, p. 294

Objective To identify aurally pitches stepping up or down and to demonstrate that recognition by singing and by playing resonator bars

Materials CD, track 34
Resonator bars C, D, E, F, G, A, B, C^1 and step frame (if available)
Two mallets

FOCUS

Key Terms: ***steps, stepping, pitches moving up, down***

Step 1: Hide the resonator bars (on step frame) from view and have students close their eyes; then play the sequence C–D–E–F–G–A–B–C^1. Ask YOU CAN'T SEE, BUT DID THE PITCHES MOVE UP OR DOWN? (*up*) DID THEY MOVE BY STEP OR BY SKIP? (*step*) Replay with bars in full view and discuss how the pitches move up in order, by steps.

Write the letter names on the board arranged from low to high, or use music notation, noting that the first and last pitches are the same. (*C*)

Indicator of Success

Repeat the playing, and have students SHOW WITH YOUR HANDS HOW THE PITCHES STEP UP. Then select pairs of students, one to play the step bars while the other points to letter names (or notation) on board. The class can use hand motions, too. Write the pitches on the board moving from high to low, and similarly have students play bars and point to notation for the descending pitches.

Step 2: Explain they are going to hear a silly song, using those pitches, and ask them to DISCOVER HOW THE PITCHES IN THE SONG MOVE: UP OR DOWN? (*up, until it goes quickly down at the end*) Introduce "Ebeneezer" while you play the bars: sing or play the recording. (Recording must be in tune with the bars.)

Write the name "Ebeneezer Sneezer" on the board and practice saying it. Sing/play the song again and ask students to tell what kind of a man Ebeneezer is (*topsy-turvy*) and how the notes suggest this (*they move down at the song's end*).

Step 3: Focus on learning the words by writing key words on the board or on cards. (Cards could be coordinated with the 8 pitches: C= Ebeneezer; D= topsy; E= elbows, and so on.) Repeat singing (with teacher playing bars) until students are secure.

Step 4: Review the descending pitches (last phrase) and select a bar player. Have class sing this "Oh, Ebeneezer, what a man" phrase with the bar player. Repeat with different student bar players on the descending pitches.

Indicator of Success

Sing the entire song, with singers using hand motions throughout, teacher playing bars on upward-moving phrases, and student bar players performing the last phrase. Change bar players and repeat as long as interest is high.

SUMMARY

Review the pitches moving up and down by steps, in order; review that the first and last pitches have the same name.

ASSESSMENT

As students sing songs that move by step (see "Other Music," below), they identify and play stepwise pitches on a step bar.

Follow-Up

1. Have students show pitch levels by touching hands to different parts of the body: C—knees, D—thighs, E—hips, F—waist, G—chest, A—shoulders, B—head, and C^1—hands above head.

Kodály Adaptation

2. Sing the song using Curwen hand signs (p. 72) for each pitch. Use notation on p. 294.

Science

3. Experiment filling eight bottles with water to create "Ebeneezer's" pitches. (Seal bottles against evaporation and spillage.) Emphasize it is the length of the air that determines the pitch, not the amount of water.

Cooperative Learning

4. In small groups, have students write the letter names C through C^1 arranged in order from low to high (or use music notation) and then sing "Ebeneezer," pointing to each letter name or note.

Projects for College Students

5. Distribute eight resonator bars (C through C^1) in random order to eight students and ask them to form a row, in mixed-up order. Beginning with the person on the left, have students play the bars in this "out-of-order" sequence.

   Challenge class to arrange the bar players in stepwise order, aurally. With class members' help, locate the lowest pitch and place player in far left position. Locate the highest pitch and place player to far right. Then locate the bar that should follow low C, and so forth.

Music Fundamentals
Technology

6. Study the whole- and half-step distances for the major scale (W W H W W W H) as in C–D–E–F–G–A–B–C (the C-Major scale). Notate other major scales following this sequence beginning on different pitches such as: G, D, F, B♭. (All should sound like *do, re, mi, fa, sol, la, ti, do.*) See Appendix A or use a music software program such as *Music Ace* or *Essentials of Music Theory.*

7. Study "St. Paul's Steeple," Section Four, and perform with resonator or chime bars. Transpose to different major scales such as D, F, or G. Notate in new scales or keys.

Other Music (in C Major) (see Section Four)

"Do–Re–Mi" (*Sound of Music*)
"Joy to the World"
"St. Paul's Steeple"

MUSIC CONCEPT The rhythm of a melody includes short and long sounds (*Rhythm*)

Music "Hanukkah" (Hebrew folk song), p. 306

Objective To identify the short and long sounds in the rhythm of the melody and to demonstrate that recognition in body movements and singing

Materials
CD, track 35
Barred melody instrument or resonator bars E, G
Four large drawings or pictures: (1) children smiling; (2) children dancing; (3) candles burning in a menorah; (4) children spinning a top

Step 1: Show pictures and establish what each shows. (*smiling, dancing, candles, and playing*) Ask DO THESE CHILDREN LOOK HAPPY? Briefly discuss how birthdays and some religious celebrations are happy occasions.

FOCUS

Step 2: Explain they are going to do hand movements with a song about Hanukkah, a happy Jewish celebration. Write *Hanukkah* (pronounced "HAH-nuh-kah") on the board. Sing or play a recording of the song and have them TELL HOW MANY TIMES YOU HEAR THE WORD "HANUKKAH." (*six times*)

Key Terms: ***short sounds, long sounds***

Sound the G and E bars, and sing the first two measures of the song, "Hanukkah, Hanukkah." Have students echo your singing.

Step 3: Demonstrate how hand movements fit with the "Hanukkah" words, stressing the two short sounds, followed by a longer one (short, short, long). Emphasize that WE USE A DIFFERENT MOVEMENT FOR EACH SHORT OR LONG SOUND. Reverse your movements so students can mirror them. Practice pattern with students until secure, and then add singing.

Ha - nu - kkah, *Ha - nu - kkah*

R L clap R L clap

R=patsch right thigh
L=patsch left thigh

Step 4: Learn the *first* phrase's melody, rhythm, and hand movements (see below). Explain THE LAST, LONG SOUND NEEDS A "PATTY-CAKE" MOVEMENT. You could use the word *hold* on the last sound. Practice until secure and then add singing (phrase 1 only).

Ha - nu - kkah, *Ha - nu - kkah,* *mer - ry hol - i - day!*

R L clap hands R L clap hands R L R L clap partner's hands (patty-cake)

Step 5: Play the entire song and have students listen and DECIDE IF YOU CAN USE THOSE SAME SHORT AND LONG MOVEMENTS ANYWHERE ELSE IN THE SONG. (*yes—the same pattern "fits" four times because each phrase has the same pattern of short and long sounds*) Without music, have them do the pattern four consecutive times, as in the song. Students should face a partner so they can "patty-cake" at the end of each phrase. When one phrase's pattern is secure, do movements as they sing the song.

Indicator of Success

SUMMARY Ask pairs of students to demonstrate their short and long movement patterns as the class sings the song. Elicit from students what they learned about the celebration of Hanukkah and the rhythm of the song.

ASSESSMENT

After students learn or review a different song (see "Other Music," below), they perform hand movements along with the song's repeated rhythms.

Follow-Up

Kodály Adaptation

1. Speak rhythm syllables for all the notes in "Hanukkah."

Special Learners

2. Using the picture cards to help students remember the word order, learn all the words and the melody of "Hanukkah."
3. Play a game in which students have to guess familiar songs from their rhythms alone (e.g., "This Old Man," "Jingle Bells," "Frère Jacques!"). Clap or play on rhythm instruments such as tone block or tambourine.

Social Studies

4. Learn more about Hanukkah, the menorah and the dreydl. Sing songs: "Hanukkah," "Hanukkah Song," and "My Dreydl," found in Section Four. See Note.

Note

Hanukkah commemorates the rededication of the Temple in Jerusalem in 165 B.C. During the Festival of Lights, the Menorah ("meh-NOH-rah") is used. The menorah is a candelabrum with holders for eight candles, plus the shamash ("SHAH-mahsh"), a larger candle from which the others are lighted. On the first night of Hanukkah, the candle on the far right is lighted from the shamash. On the second night, that candle and the one beside it are lighted. One more candle is lighted each night, until on the eighth night all are burning. These candles are lighted as a reminder of the miracle that occurred in the rededicated temple in 165 B.C.: When the holy lamp was lighted, there was enough oil for only one day, but the lamp kept burning for eight days. During the Hanukkah celebration, children often sing and play with the dreydl ("DRAY-dull"), a square-sided top.

Projects for College Students

5. Check the guidelines established by your city school district or by your state board of education pertaining to study of religious celebrations in public schools. How do these guidelines allow for cultural diversity and for the ways in which art, music, and dance can enrich individual and group life? Evaluate your own childhood experiences and those of classmates. Do current elementary music series provide teachers with appropriate materials about a variety of celebrations? If not, what other resources can be found?

Music Fundamentals

6. Notate and perform several eight-beat phrases that use combinations of eighth notes, quarter notes, and half notes.

Related Literature and Media for Children

Nayer, Judy. (1998). *The Eight Nights of Hanukkah.* Troll Assoc.; ISBN 0816745501.
Silverman, Maida. (1999). *Festival of Lights: The Story of Hanukkah.* Aladdin Paperbacks; ISBN 0689830831.

Other Music

"A Ram Sam Sam," *The Music Connection* 3
"Frère Jacques!" see Section Four
"This Old Man," see Section Four

MUSIC CONCEPT Drones and ostinatos can add harmony to a melody (*Harmony*)

Music "Chatter with the Angels" (African-American song), p. 285

Objective To identify a drone and an ostinato as repetitive accompaniment patterns and to demonstrate by playing a drone and ostinato to accompany a song

Materials

CD, track 36
Alto xylophone or resonator bars F and C (a fifth apart)
Metallophone or resonator bar F

FOCUS

Key Terms: ***drone, ostinato, accompaniment***

Special Learners Students can sign the key words such as land, band, and long.

Step 1: Sing or play recording of song, asking students to DISCOVER WHAT THE ANGELS ARE DOING. (*chattering*) Discuss and review all the words. Repeat, with students patsching in a slow, steady rhythm. (𝅗𝅥𝅗𝅥) Encourage students to join in singing as soon as possible.

Step 2: When words are secure, review what an accompaniment is. LET'S ADD AN ACCOMPANIMENT TO "CHATTER WITH THE ANGELS."

Hold up a set of resonator bars or place an alto xylophone in full view. Point to F and ask students to decide what pitch is five notes higher. *(C)* Ask a student to play those two pitches simultaneously in a slow steady rhythm. (𝅗𝅥𝅗𝅥) Write the letter names or the notation on the board.

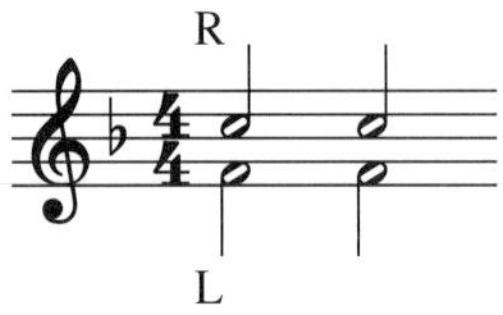

Step 3: THESE TWO PITCHES PLAYED TOGETHER ARE CALLED A DRONE. Write word on board next to pitch names. Have the drone player begin, and when the part is secure, the class should join in singing. Repeat with different drone players.

Step 4: Next, have students add an ostinato as an accompaniment to their singing. Using the F resonator bar or the F on a metallophone, have a student play the rhythm of the words "Chatter with the angels" over and over. Then, have the class join in singing while the student plays the ostinato accompaniment. WHEN A MELODY PATTERN LIKE THIS IS REPEATED OVER AND OVER AS AN ACCOMPANIMENT, IT IS CALLED AN OSTINATO. (Write word on board.) Repeat with different ostinato players.

Indicator of Success

Step 5: Finally, combine the drone and ostinato for an accompaniment. Have a drone player begin alone, followed by an ostinato player (this could serve as an introduction), then have the singers join the instruments, followed by the drone and ostinato performers extending their playing at the end for a coda.

SUMMARY

Review these accompaniment patterns by eliciting from students what was the same and what was different about the drone and ostinato. Conclude with one final performance with introduction and coda.

ASSESSMENT Students play as drone and/or ostinato accompaniment with similar songs (see "Other Music," next page).

Follow-Up

Orff Adaptation

1. Compose and arrange other ostinatos to accompany "Chatter with the Angels." Perform each in contrasting higher or lower registers on barred instruments of different timbres, or use different rhythm instruments such as wood block or drum.

Kodály Adaptation

2. Sing tonic *sol–fa* syllables for "all day long" (*mi–re–do*). Use Curwen hand signs too.
3. Sing and create additional verses: "March with the angels," "Skip with the angels."

Projects for College Students

Orff Adaptation

4. Play drone and ostinato accompaniments for other songs on barred instruments or Autoharp. One-chord songs and pentatonic melodies may be accompanied by drones and ostinatos. See "Other Music."
5. Read the Orff-*Schulwerk* section in Chapter V. Then examine elementary music series textbooks for second and third grades to see how they have incorporated the Orff ideas.

Music Fundamentals

6. Notate fifths above the pitches given:

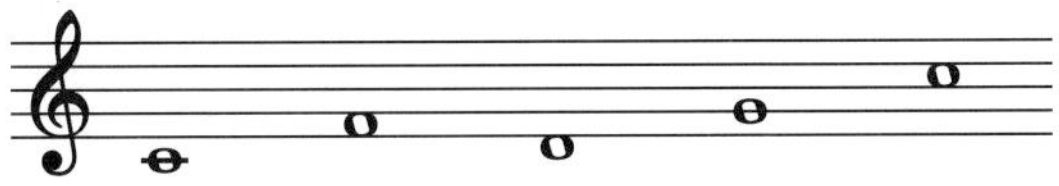

7. Accompany songs in Level II with Autoharp or some other instrument. Prepare an introduction for each song.

Other Music (see Section Four)

"Charlie over the Ocean"
"Circle Right"
"Long-Legged Sailor"
"Scotland's Burning"

MUSIC CONCEPT A song usually ends on the home tone (tonic) (*Melody*)

Music "Song of the Dragon" (Chinese folk melody), p. 386

Objective To identify visually and aurally the home tone and to demonstrate that recognition by identifying the home tone at the song's end and playing it as a song accompaniment

Materials
CD, track 37
Resonator bar (C) and one mallet
Dragon hand puppet depicting the Chinese New Year dragon
5 large poster-size strips of paper, each displaying the words for one of the 5 song phrases

---

FOCUS

Step 1: Introduce the Chinese New Year's celebration and the importance of the dragon (see Note, p. 196). Use the dragon puppet and/or a story such as the Vaughn book (see Related Literature, p. 185). Involve students in the discussion asking them to share what they know about the celebration.

Sing or play the recording of "Song of the Dragon" and invite students to listen and FIND OUT MORE ABOUT THE DRAGON AND THE NEW YEAR FESTIVAL. After listening, have students mention key words they heard (e.g., *100 legs, big head, drum, gong*).

Cooperative Learning

Special Learners Students can sign key words such as legs, fear, New Year, and here.

Step 2: Divide the class into five groups and assign each group one song phrase to learn. Distribute a phrase strip to each group. Ask them to review the meaning of their phrase and practice repeating the words together. Finally, ask each group to select a representative to bring their phrase strip to the front of class and, with the teacher's guidance and another listening to the song, arrange the phrases in song order on the board.

Step 3: As a class, have students determine which phrases have the same words. (*4 and 5*) Invite class to join in singing the last two phrases of the song. And then, help them learn the entire song using the phrase strips.

Key Term: ***home tone***

Step 4: After students are secure with the words, have them sing the entire song again, but to HOLD THE LAST NOTE ("HERE") AS LONG AS YOU CAN, AND WATCH FOR A SURPRISE. (On the last word, hold up the dragon puppet while students sustain the note.) Explain that THE LAST NOTE IS CALLED THE HOME TONE and that the dragon helps to point it out. Help students decide that this final, sustained tone makes the song sound finished.

Indicator of Success

Step 5: Give the resonator bar to one student, and the dragon puppet to a different one. Have them play and use the puppet on the home tone as the class sings. Emphasize that SONG OF THE DRAGON AND MANY SONGS HAVE A HOME TONE THAT HELPS IT SOUND FINISHED.

SUMMARY

Conclude by having students try a dragon dance with the song. Form a line, facing front, with hands on shoulders of students ahead of them. The leader (preferably, the teacher initially) holds the dragon puppet and leads the "dragon" SLOWLY on a winding path throughout the classroom. Encourage slowly bending up and down, side to side, and finally, dropping down on the final tone—the home tone.

ASSESSMENT

After students learn or review a different song (see "Other Music"), they identify the song's home tone and sing and play it.

Follow-Up

Orff Adaptation

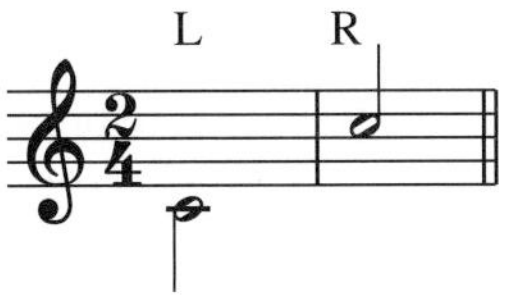

1. Play the home tone as an ostinato along with the song. Place the bars C and C^1 where all can see and play alternately, beginning on low C. (See margin.) Place the low bar on *your* right, and have students patsch (*mirror*) your right–left playing. (Use the song's tempo.) When movements are secure, perform with the song. (Bars must be in tune with recording.)
2. Learn and perform the drum and gong parts for the last phrase. Or, play the rhythm of the last phrase five consecutive times as a song accompaniment, suggesting a Chinese percussion ensemble. (See also the "Dragon Dance" notation on p. 196.)

Multicultural

3. Plan a Chinese New Year celebration. Invite members of your Chinese community to visit and describe their traditions, or see "Related Literature," below. Prepare and eat Chinese food, wear traditional clothing, play Chinese music, have a parade and dragon dance (with percussion accompaniment).

Projects for College Students

Music Fundamentals
Technology

4. Identify and circle the home tone (tonic) in songs from Levels I and II. Review key signatures in Appendix A or in a music software program such as *Music Ace* or *Essentials of Music Theory.*

Orff Adaptation

5. Accompany the song with the Dragon Dance for Percussion (p. 196).

Related Literature and Media for Children

China's Instrumental Heritage. Lyrichord LLST 7921.
Kuo-Hang, Han, and Patricia Shehan Campbell. (1996). *The Lion's Roar: Chinese Luogu Percussion Ensembles.* 2nd ed. Danbury, CT: World Music Press.
Vaughan, Marcia. (1996). *The Dancing Dragon.* Mondo Publishing.

Other Music (see Section Four)

"London Bridge"
"This Old Man"
"Wishy Washy Wee"

MUSIC CONCEPT Melodies can include skips of an octave (*Melody*)

Music "Hop Up, My Ladies" (American folk song), p. 317

Objective To identify aurally the interval of an octave and to demonstrate that recognition by moving, by singing, and by playing it on a barred melody instrument or resonator bars

Materials CD, track 38
Barred melody instrument or resonator bars C, D, E, F, G, A, B, C^1 and two mallets

---

FOCUS

Step 1: Sing the song or play the recording, alerting students to listen for the words "Hop up." BE READY TO TELL HOW THE SONG MOVES ON THE WORDS "HOP UP." (*up*)

Key Terms: ***skip, up, low, high, octave***

Step 2: LISTEN AGAIN AND SEE IF "HOP UP" SKIPS A LARGE DISTANCE OR A SMALL DISTANCE. (*large*) To "feel" the large skip, have students clap at waist, then above heads for the "Hop Up" part. Clap quickly, just as it happens in the song. Sing "Hop up" (C to C^1) as they clap; repeat until secure.

Step 3: As students listen to the words in the song's refrain, invite them to sing and clap on each "Hop up." After listening, review the words and repeat with students singing as much of the song as they can.

Step 4: Display the melody instrument. Ask students to count the white bars from C to C^1. (*eight*) Determine which bars are needed to play "Hop up." (*C and C^1*) Locate these two. WHEN TWO TONES WITH THE SAME NAME ARE EIGHT BARS APART, THEY ARE CALLED AN OCTAVE. Discover words sharing the same root as octave: *octopus, octagon,* and so forth. Write words and pattern in staff notation. Help students discover that the lower pitch is played on the longer bar, the higher pitch on the shorter bar.

Indicator of Success

Step 5: Several students should be able to play the C to C^1 octave. (The teacher can hold the instrument and move throughout the class.) Try singing "Hop up" as each student plays the octave.

SUMMARY

Complete the experience by singing the song, along with low-to-high clapping, playing the octave, and pointing to staff notation. Finally, ask WHAT IS THE NAME FOR THE 8-NOTE SKIP IN OUR SONG? Have them briefly share their understanding of octave.

ASSESSMENT After students learn or review a different song (see "Other Music," next page), they sing, play, and move to the octave.

Follow-Up

Dance/Movement

1. Create a dance corresponding to the two different sections of "Hop Up," or try the following ideas. During the verse, pairs "trot" in a circle with hands joined in "skater's position." For the refrain, dancers drop hands and face center. On each of the octave phrases they hop up, "reaching for the sky" while using low to high arm movements, and then clap three times. On the last phrase, each person "fast-steps" in a small circle of his or her own.

Kodály Adaptation

2. Use tonic *sol–fa* syllables and Curwen hand signals along with the octave skip. Write the octave in staff notation. Learn pitch names.
3. Locate and play other octaves on a melody instrument: D to D^1, and so forth.

Projects for College Students

5. Identify, then sing, *sol–fa* syllables for the notes in the refrain.

Music Fundamentals

6. Write octaves on the music staves below.

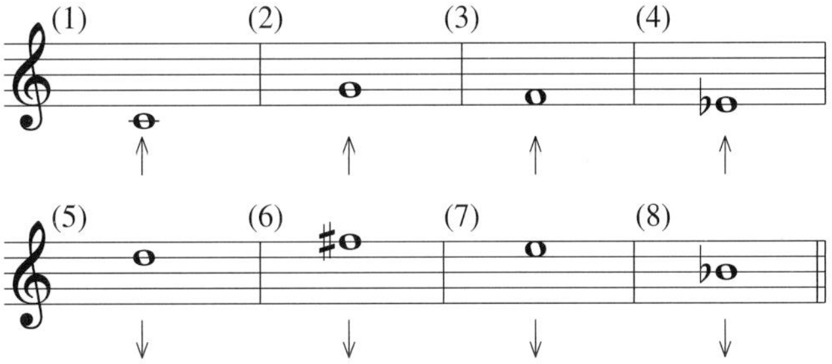

Other Music (C to C^1 octaves)

"Christmas Is Coming"
"Over the Rainbow," *The Music Connection* 4
"Sarasponda," see Section Four
"This Is Halloween," see Section Four
"This Is My Country," *Share the Music* 4

EVALUATION FOR COLLEGE STUDENTS

A. Identify those music concepts within melody, rhythm, form, harmony, and expressive qualities that children in grades 2 and 3 can perceive.
   1. melody concepts
   2. rhythm concepts
   3. form concepts
   4. harmony concepts
   5. expressive qualities concepts

B. Describe at least three developmental characteristics of children in grades 2 and 3. Refer to singing range, language development, and so on. How will these characteristics suggest appropriate musical experiences?

C. Define these musical terms:
   1. phrase
   2. beat groupings (meter) in twos and threes
   3. tonic or home tone
   4. drone
   5. timbre
   6. octave
   7. ostinato

D. Identify the four orchestral families, and name two instruments in each.

E. Identify the tonic or home tone for each of the following songs in Section Four.

   "Old Brass Wagon"

   "Sandy Land"

   "Skip to My Lou"

   "Puncinella"

F. Name the composer of
   1. *Nutcracker* Suite
   2. *Carnival of the Animals*
   3. "Jesu, Joy of Man's Desiring," from Cantata no. 147
   4. "The Stars and Stripes Forever"

G. In small groups, discuss and compare the important components, including the origins, of the Kodály method and the Orff-*Schulwerk* approach. Find two model experiences in Level II—one that illustrates application of the Orff approach and another that illustrates application of the Kodály method. Be prepared to justify your selections.

H. Review the information in the "World Music" section in Chapter IV and the "Integrating Music, the Arts, and Other Subjects" in Chapter VI. In small groups, discuss how the "Song of the Dragon" model experience, p. 184, meets music-learning goals for multicultural music. Similarly, discuss how the "Anaguta Drum" model experience, p. 140, meets learning goals in subjects other than music. Decide which of the nine National Standards for Music Education are addressed in these readings and two model experiences. How important is world music and curricular integration in elementary classroom music programs?

ORIGINAL MODEL EXPERIENCE ASSIGNMENT— LEVEL II

Plan one or two original model experiences for children in grades 2/3 (Level II). Base each experience on *one* of the two specified listening selections. (Refer to CD.) Each experience should be prepared in a step-by-step sequence using a similar format to the models in *The Musical Classroom* (see the sample outline that follows). Specific information about each component of the experience follows.

1. The *music concept and the musical selection* are specified. Plan how to present this concept and music to children.
2. State the *objective* for the experience, making sure that how and what students will do to demonstrate their understanding is included (see pp. 104–105).
3. *Model sequence.* Be sure to include key terms and age-appropriate music-making activities. Pay special attention to the opening ("Focus") and closing ("Summary") of the experience. Specify the exact part of the music that is the main focus of the experience. Identify by rhythm, pitches, or placement in music.

Plan two *follow-up activities.* One activity should be a follow-up to the music concept presented in the model experience. Another follow-up activity should focus on a different subject area such as science or social studies.

	1.		2.
MUSIC CONCEPT	Beats can be grouped in threes (*Rhythm*)	*or*	Pitches can be high or low (*Melody*)
Music	"Elephant," from *Carnival of the Animals* (Saint-Saëns), CD, track 8		"Kangaroos," from *Carnival of the Animals* (Saint-Saëns), CD, track 23
Objective			
Materials			

FOCUS
Key Terms

Step 1:

Step 2:

Step 3:

Step 4:

Indicators of Success
SUMMARY

ASSESSMENT ______________________________

Follow-Up (One activity to reinforce music concept and one related to another curricular area)

Music 1.

______________________ 2.

(other curricular area)

ORIGINAL MODEL EXPERIENCE ASSIGNMENT—LEVEL II

Plan one to three original model experiences for children in grades 2/3 (Level II). Base each experience on *one* of the three specified songs. (See Section Four.) Each experience should be prepared in a step-by-step sequence using a similar format to the models in *The Musical Classroom* (see the sample outline that follows). Specific information about each component of the experience follows.

1. The *music concept* is not specified, but the *musical selection* is. After reviewing your chosen musical selection, decide which Level II concept would be a good focus for your experience. Plan how to present this concept and music to children.
2. State the *objective* for the experience, making sure that how and what students will do to demonstrate their understanding is included (see pp. 104–105).
3. *Model sequence.* Be sure to include key terms and age-appropriate music-making activities. Pay special attention to the opening ("Focus") and closing ("Summary") of the experience. Specify the exact part of the music that is the main focus of the experience. Identify the lyrics, rhythm, pitches, or placement in music.

Plan two *follow-up activities.* One activity should be a follow-up to the music concept presented in the model experience. Another follow-up activity should focus on a different subject area such as the visual arts or language arts.

MUSIC CONCEPT

Music	1. "My Dreydl," p. 340	*or*	2. "Matarile" p. 338, CD, track 16	*or*	3. "Long-Legged Sailor," p. 333

Objective

Materials

FOCUS
Key Terms

Step 1:

Step 2:

Step 3:

Step 4:

Indicators of Success
SUMMARY

ASSESSMENT

(One activity to reinforce music concept and one related to another curricular area)

Follow-Up

Music 1.

______________ 2.

(other curricular area)

EVALUATING AN ELEMENTARY MUSIC SERIES TEXTBOOK ASSIGNMENT—LEVEL II

Evaluate the teacher's edition of an elementary music series textbook for grade two or grade three. (See descriptions of the three series in Appendix C and select one.) Prepare an evaluation of no more than three pages. The written report should demonstrate knowledge of music concepts and vocabulary.

Describe how well and to what extent the textbook and resources represent a comprehensive music curriculum. Refer to the chapter categories described in Section One of *The Musical Classroom.* Briefly describe the textbook's organization, visual presentation, directions for teachers, ease of use, and various resources (e.g., recordings, handbooks). Include discussion and supporting data on the following topics.

1. Elements of music and music concepts
2. Music-making activities
3. The world of music
4. Approaches to curriculum
5. Curricular developments
6. Planning and assessing music learning

Conclude by indicating if you can imagine yourself using this music textbook. Why or why not?

RESOURCE FILE—LEVEL II

Note ("Cielito Lindo" Model Experience, p. 168)

Note

Singing and dancing are more common in Mexican and other Latin American groups than in the general American population. In fact, music and culture are almost synonymous in these Latino communities. Music is an important part of family life and social events, such as weddings, baptisms, dances, and funerals. Latinos in the United States all enjoy popular musical styles from the Caribbean (Afro-Caribbean and *salsa*), and each community also has its own distinctive music. Mariachi is important to Mexican Americans, who are concentrated mainly in Los Angeles, the West, the Southwest, and Texas. (Based on information by Patricia Shehan Campbell in "Steven Loza on Latino Music," *Music Educators Journal,* September 1995, pp. 45–52.)

Mariachi ("Cielito Lindo" Model Experience, p. 168)

The number of instruments in a mariachi varies. Big mariachi groups may include several of each instrument shown in illustration on next page, guitars, and a Mexican folk harp. The bass of the small group shown is the large guitarrón ("ghee-tah-rone"), a low-pitched Mexican version of the guitar, which has a rounded back. The *vihuela* ("vee-WEH-lah") is a smaller, high-pitched version of the guitarrón.

Left to right: Trompeta, trompeta, violin, guitarrón, vihuela.

Illustration based on drawings from *Music and You: Songs in Spanish for Intermediate Grades,* Barbara and Merrill Staton, Senior Authors. Marilyn Davidson, Ann Davis, Nancy Ferguson, Phyllis Kaplan, Susan Snyder, Authors. Macmillan/McGraw-Hill. Used by permission. © 1989.

Instruments ("Cielito Lindo" Model Experience, p. 168)

Guitarra

Guitarrón

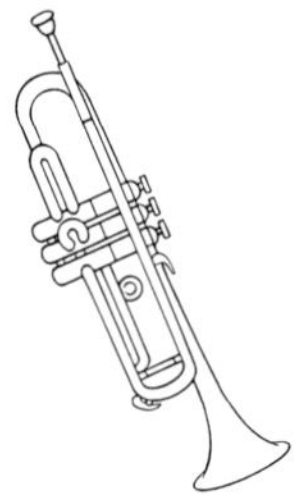

Trompeta

Vihuela

Violin

Illustrations are from *Music and You: Songs in Spanish for Intermediate Grades,* Barbara and Merrill Staton, Senior Authors. Marilyn Davidson, Ann Davis, Nancy Ferguson, Phyllis Kaplan, Susan Snyder, Authors. Macmillan/McGraw-Hill. Used by permission. © 1989.

Related Literature and Media for Children ("Cielito Lindo" Model Experience, p. 168)

ANCONA, GEORGE. (1998). *Barrio: El Barrio De Jose.* Harcourt Brace; ISBN 015201188085.

AVALOS, CECILIA. (1989). *A Mariachi I'll Be!* Modern Curriculum Press; ISBN 0813644194.

BERGER, MELVIN. (1989). *The Science of Music.* New York: Harper. Intermediate grades.

BROWN, TRICIA. (1986). *Hello Amigos.* New York: Holt.

MACMILLAN, DIANNE, and DOROTHY FREEMAN. (1986). *Martha Rodrigues: Meeting a Mexican-American Family.* New York: Messner.

The Many Faces of Mexico. (1976). Films, Inc., 1744 Wilmette, Wilmette, IL 60091. Dance, music, fiestas.

PERL, LILA. (1983). *Piñatas and Paper Flowers: Holidays of the Americas in English and Spanish.* Houghton Mifflin Co.; ISBN 089919155X.

Worksheet ("Canzona" Model Experience, p. 174)

1	2	3	4
Woodwind	Woodwind	Woodwind	Woodwind
Strings	Strings	Strings	Strings
Brass	Brass	Brass	Brass
Percussion	Percussion	Percussion	Percussion

Related Literature and Media for Children ("Canzona" Model Experience, p. 174)

BLACKWOOD, ALAN. (1987). *Musical Instruments.* New York: Watts.

HAUSCHERR, ROSEMARIE. (1992). *What Instrument Is This?* Chicago: Scholastic.

HAYES, ANN. (1991). *Meet the Orchestra.* Harcourt Brace; ISBN 015200269.

HUSKIN, KARLA. (1986). *The Philharmonic Gets Dressed.* HarperTrophy; ISBN 006443124X.

LILLEGARD, DEE. (1987, 1988). *Brass.* New York: Children's Press. Lillegard's books include *Percussion, Strings,* and *Woodwinds.*

Meet the Instruments. Bowmar. Orchestral instruments on large posters, miniature study prints, and video.

MOSS, LLOYD. (1995). *Zin! Zin! Zin! A Violin.* Simon & Schuster; ISBN 0671882392 (Caldecott Honor Book).

PAKER, JOSEPHINE. (1995). *I Wonder Why Flutes Have Holes: And Other Questions About Music.* Kingfisher Books; ISBN 1856975835.

PRELUTSKY, JACK, ed., and MEILO SO, illus. (1999). *The 20th Century Children's Poetry Treasury.* New York: Alfred A. Knopf; ISBN 0679893148. Outstanding collection of 211 poems and illustrations with an emphasis on the sound of the language. See poems "Tuning Up," "My Violin," "Music Class," and "The Girl Who Made the Cymbals Bang."

Instruments of the Orchestra
("Canzona" Model Experience, p. 174)

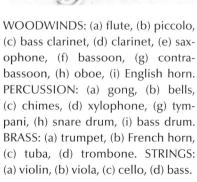

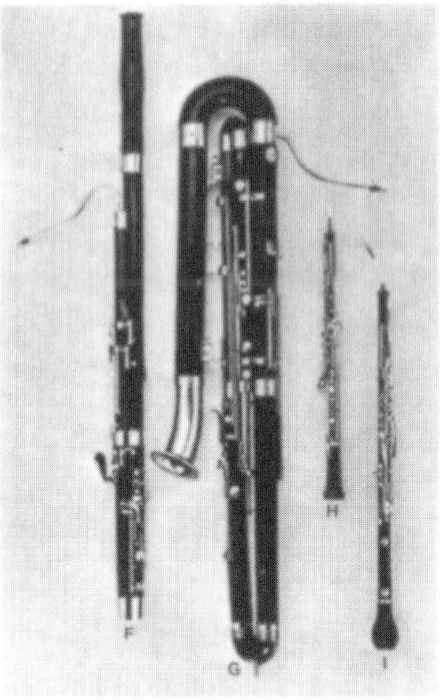

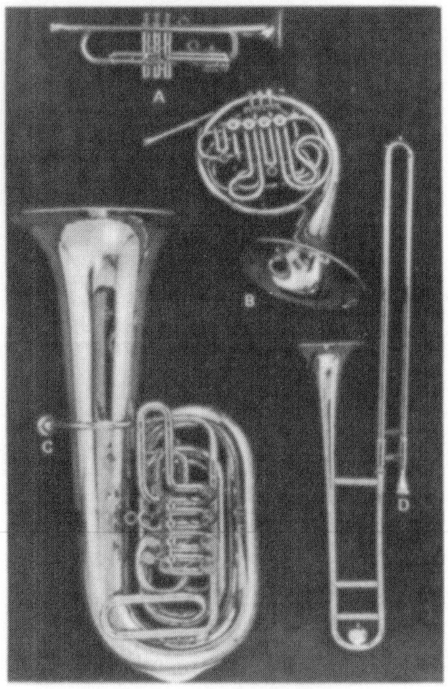

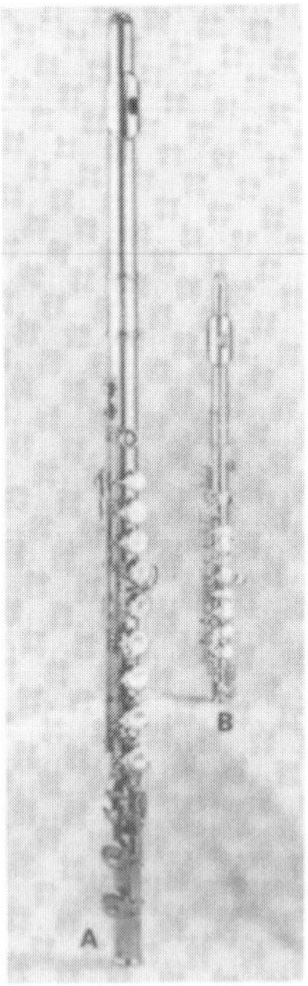

WOODWINDS: (a) flute, (b) piccolo, (c) bass clarinet, (d) clarinet, (e) saxophone, (f) bassoon, (g) contrabassoon, (h) oboe, (i) English horn. PERCUSSION: (a) gong, (b) bells, (c) chimes, (d) xylophone, (g) tympani, (h) snare drum, (i) bass drum. BRASS: (a) trumpet, (b) French horn, (c) tuba, (d) trombone. STRINGS: (a) violin, (b) viola, (c) cello, (d) bass.

Orchestra Seating Chart ("Canzona" Model Experience, p. 174)

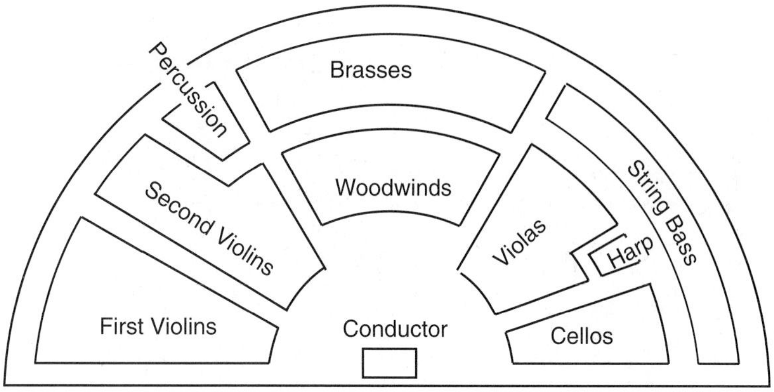

Conducting Patterns ("Jesu, Joy of Man's Desiring" Model Experience, p. 176)

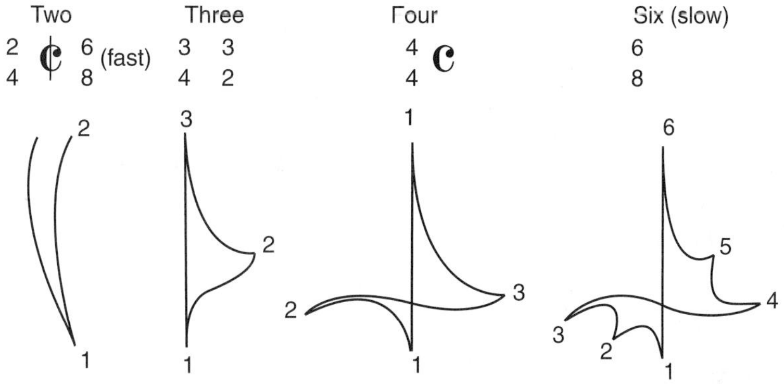

Dragon Dance for Percussion
("Song of the Dragon" Model Experience, p. 184)

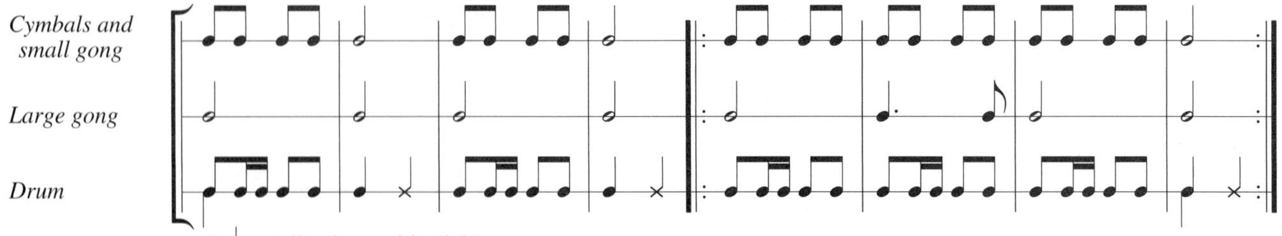

(×♩ = strike drum with stick)

(𝅘𝅥 = strike drum with both sticks)

(♩ = alternate sticks for drum roll)

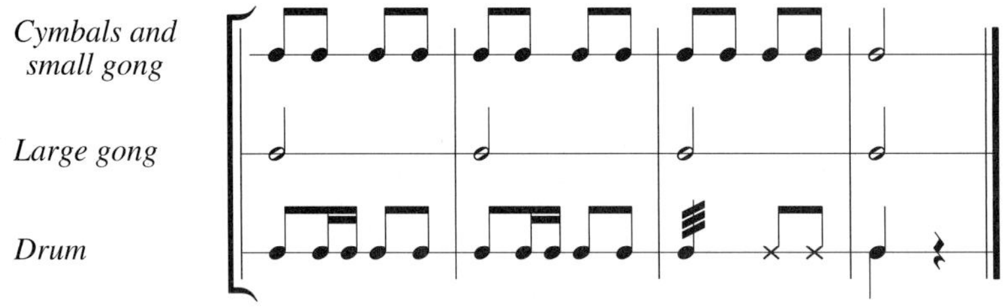

Note ("Song of the Dragon" Model Experience, p. 184)

To the Chinese, the dragon represents good luck, strength, change, and even life itself, because it symbolizes a natural force in the Taoist religion. It was the imperial emblem, suggesting dignity and power. (In contrast, the Western dragon is evil and destructive.) The large, colorful dragon head in Chinese New Year parades has lots of red—a lucky color. Its long body (usually of cloth) hides all but the legs of the dragon dancers; the number of dancers depends on the length of the body.

Note ("Song of the Dragon" Model Experience, p. 184)

Chinese New Year is celebrated according to the lunar calendar, between January 21 and February 20. Customs vary in different Chinese communities, but many have theatricals or parades with a dragon, dancing, and firecrackers to frighten away last year's evil. The New Year celebration lasts from one to two weeks and is a time to settle debts, gather with the family, honor ancestors, wear new clothes, and exchange gifts with friends and relatives—including red envelopes with "lucky money" tucked inside.

Level III: Model Experiences for Fourth and Fifth Grades

Photo by Patricia Hackett

SEQUENCE OF SONGS/LISTENING SELECTIONS—LEVEL III (GRADES 4–5)

SEQUENCE OF MUSIC CONCEPTS—LEVEL III (GRADES 4–5)

Elements of Music	*Music Concepts*
MELODY	Pitches can move by stepping up or down ("Pianists")
FORM	Phrases in a melody can be the same or different ("Hawaiian Rainbows")
TIMBRE	Each instrument has a characteristic timbre that when combined with others can create a sound piece (Haiku sound piece)
FORM	Sections of a composition can contrast with one another and sections can be repeated (ABA) ("Carillon")
FORM	The initial section of a composition alternates with contrasting sections in rondo form ("Viennese Musical Clock")
HARMONY	Chords consist of three or four pitches stacked in thirds ("Hey, Lidee")
FORM	In call-and-response form, responses can be identical to the call, or contrasting ("Stomp Dance," "Mai Wakaringano," "Ho Jamalo")
MELODY	A melody can exhibit a distinctive contour as it moves up or down or repeats ("Corn Grinding Song")
TIMBRE	Instruments can be identified and grouped by their timbres and materials ("Haoli Dance," "Rippling Water," "Barong Dance")
TIMBRE	Sounds are produced by vibrations and amplified on both acoustic and electronic instruments ("Wabash Cannon Ball")
FORM	Each of the three phrases in "twelve-bar" blues consists of four "bars" ("Joe Turner Blues")

FORM	Sections of a composition can contrast with one another and sections can be repeated (AABBACCA) ("Piffle Rag")
MELODY	Music can be based on major or minor tonality ("When the Saints Go Marching In" and "Diga Diga Doo")
RHYTHM	Beat groupings of twos and threes can be combined to create asymmetric meter ("Take Five")
HARMONY	Chord tones can be played one after another as a song accompaniment ("Jamaica Farewell")
ELEMENTS	The elements of music can be identified and compared in music of different historical periods ("Four on the Floor" and *Archduke* Trio)

DEVELOPMENTAL CHARACTERISTICS OF FOURTH- AND FIFTH-GRADE CHILDREN

In order to plan meaningful music learning and appropriate musical experiences, teachers need to understand the developmental characteristics of children at each stage of their growth. The following are important developmental characteristics of fourth- and fifth-grade students. These address their physical, mental, cognitive, and musical growth as well as their development in terms of relationships with people and their surroundings. While many students exhibit these developmental characteristics, some may function at a younger level or even an older level. The needs of special learners are described on pp. 90–95.

CONCRETE EXPERIENCES	Students continue to learn best through hands-on, concrete experiences even though they can cognitively internalize their understandings.
IMPROVED READING SKILLS	Their language-reading skills are steadily improving and their music reading and notating skills are developing.
GIRLS MATURING FASTER	Physical growth is slow and steady. Girls mature faster than boys.
PLAYING INSTRUMENTS	Students have reached a higher level of small muscle development. They can play a wide variety of tuned and untuned classroom instruments and can coordinate two skills, such as singing while playing an Autoharp. Therefore, students are ready to start instruction on orchestral instruments, such as clarinet, trumpet, violin, and percussion.
IMPROVED SINGING VOICES	Singing voices improve in quality and become more dependable. Because the vocal cords and lungs are more developed, students have greater control of their voices and breathing. Boys' voices are more resonant and girls' voices are clear and light. Students' singing ranges are wider—the typical range is larger than an octave and may be as much as twelve or more pitches.
SING IN HARMONY	Students are able to sing a part while another is sung simultaneously. They can sing in harmony by performing descants, partner songs, rounds and songs in two parts.
GROUP WORK	Students need to "belong," and peer group approval takes on new importance. They enjoy working in both small and large groups. Cooperative learning groups work particularly well with this age level.
INDEPENDENT WORK	Students are able to work independently.
INTERESTS BROADEN	Students are more interested in and aware of their larger world. Popular music becomes especially important and multicultural music can fascinate them.
NEED PRAISE	Children continuously need positive reinforcement for their achievements (both academic and social).

MUSIC CONCEPT Pitches can move by stepping up or down (*Melody*)

Music "Pianists," from *Carnival of the Animals,* by Camille Saint-Saëns ("sa[h] saw[n]s") (French, 1835–1921)

Objective To identify aurally and visually melodies that step up and down and to demonstrate that recognition by playing a barred instrument and by raising colored cards as the music is heard

Materials

CD, track 39
Barred melody instrument and three mallets
Pegboard, about two feet square
Twenty-four golf tees: seven yellow
nine blue
eight white
Construction-paper squares, enough for each student to use *one* color:
yellow for one-third of the class
blue for one-third of the class
white for one-third of the class

FOCUS

Key Terms: *up, down, step*

Step 1: TODAY WE'RE GOING TO LISTEN TO SOME MELODIES THAT MOVE UP AND DOWN. Set up the tees on the pegboard as shown below. (This can be done prior to the lesson.)

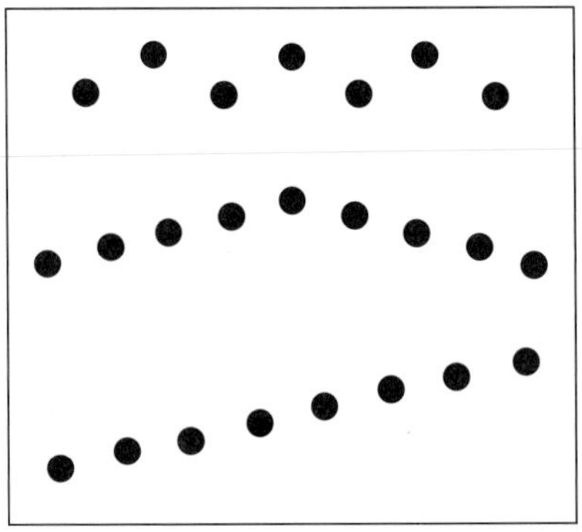

yellow (1 2 1 2 1 2 1)

blue (1 2 3 4 5 4 3 2 1)

white (1 2 3 4 5 6 7 8)

Special Learners Students who are visually impaired can point to/touch each peg on the board.

Call the students' attention to each row of tees and elicit from them that:
the yellow row moves back and forth, by step;
the blue row moves up by step, then down by step;
the white row moves up, by step.

Step 2: Select a student to play the "white melody" on the barred instrument. Help the player to decide whether to begin on low C or high C. (Low C, because the melody moves up.) Have class name each pitch that the player will perform. Distribute white cards to one-third of the class. Instruct students to lay cards on their desks until asked to use them.

Continue the process above with two additional players, one for the "yellow melody" and one for the "blue melody." Hand out yellow and blue cards.

Indicator of Success

Play a listening game: The three players should move to a part of the room where they cannot be seen. Ask them to take turns playing their melodies. Have the class raise their colored cards when they hear "their" melody. Verify each correct answer before going on to the next melody.

Indicator of Success

Step 3: Tell the class THESE SAME MELODIES ARE IN A PIECE ABOUT PIANISTS. THEY MOVE VERY QUICKLY, BUT SEE IF YOU CAN HEAR THEM. Melodies occur in this order: yellow, blue, white. They are repeated four times. Play at least two times with class raising cards to identify their melodies. (no cards on coda) Finally, repeat with students moving their cards in the direction of their melody.

SUMMARY

Ask the class to summarize what they have learned about the direction of the three melodies. (*how they move up and down by step*)

ASSESSMENT

Standards 2b (p. 30), 6e (p. 20)*

As students become familiar with different music (see "Other Music," below), they play and identify pitches stepping up or down.

Follow-Up

Cooperative Learning

Standard 5b (p. 48)

1. In small groups, have students write the pitches of one of the three melodies in staff notation and then play. Learn syllables, pitch names, numbers, or all three.

a.

b.

c.

2. Discover that "Pianists" does not end on the home tone.

Projects for College Students

Music Fundamentals Technology

Standard 5b (p. 48)

3. Practice notating major scales using *Music Ace* or *Essentials of Music Theory* software.

Other Music (Section Four unless indicated)

"Choral Theme"
"Frère Jacques!"
"Lovely Evening"
"We Shall Overcome"
"Barcarolle" (*Tales of Hoffmann*), by Offenbach, CD, track 18
"Chopin" (*Carnaval*), by Schumann, *Bowmar Orchestral Library,* "Pictures and Patterns"
"Danca Brasileira," by Guarnieri, *Bowmar Orchestral Library* , "Dances," Part 1

*See p. 111 for an explanation of how the National Standards for Music Education are identified within Level III model experiences.

MUSIC CONCEPT Phrases in a melody can be the same or different (abab) (*Form*)

Music "Hawaiian Rainbows" (song from Hawaii), p. 308

Objective To identify same and different phrases in a song and to demonstrate that recognition by movements, singing, and connecting pitches and labeling phrases

Materials
CD, track 40
Song notation with movement directions for teacher, p. 308
Two colored markers, one red, one green
Chart (see p. 236)

FOCUS
Key Terms: ***phrase, pitches, same, different***

Step 1: As students listen to the song, have them determine what state is being sung about. (*Hawaii*) Ask what song words they remember and briefly have them share and discuss what they know about Hawaii.

Explain that in ancient Hawaii singers performed hand movements for their songs. Demonstrate traditional movements with the music (see p. 308). Stand and face the class, but reverse your movements. Emphasize *slow* and *graceful* movements.

Step 2: Display the chart and review the words. Teach movements for phrase 1 ("rainbow," "clouds"). Call students' attention to the pitches, and have a student DRAW A LINE TO CONNECT THE PITCH NAMES, using the red marker. Discuss how the line leaps high (octave jump) and then descends. Sing phrase 1, clarifying and repeating as needed. Sing with movements.

Indicator of Success

Step 3: Teach phrase 2 movements ("colors," "sky"). Have a different student DRAW A LINE CONNECTING PHRASE 2 PITCHES, using the green marker. Discuss how the line moves high and low. Sing phrase 2 with movements. Ask ARE THE PITCHES IN PHRASE 1 AND 2 THE SAME? (*no*) Sing phrases 1 and 2 with movements.

Indicator of Success

Step 4: Teach movements for phrase 3 ("rainbow," "me"); have a student connect the pitches using the red marker. Ask ARE THESE PITCHES THE SAME AS ANY OTHER PHRASE? (*yes—phrase* 1) Help students understand that the two red phrases have the same melody pitches. ARE THE WORDS THE SAME? (*only at the beginning*) Sing phrase 3 with movements.

Indicator of Success

Step 5: Teach phrase 4 movements ("mountains," "sea"), then have a student connect its pitches, using the green marker. Sing phrase 4. Ask students WHY DID WE USE THE GREEN MARKER FOR BOTH PHRASES 2 AND 4? (*the pitches are the same*) Help them understand that identical melodies can have different words. Sing phrases 3 (begins on F) and 4 with movements. Sing the entire song with movements.

SUMMARY

Briefly review the same and different phrases shown by the red and green lines, noting same and different pitches. Label each phrase as follows: 1—a; 2—b; 3—a; 4—b. Have a final sing-through with movements.

ASSESSMENT

Standard 1b (p. 39)

After students become familiar with a different song (see "Other Music," below), they identify same and different phrases.

Follow-Up

Cooperative Learning

Standard 2b (p. 30)

1. Give one barred melody instrument with two mallets to each of four pairs of students and have them practice one assigned phrase of the song. (Each could play half a phrase.) Perform with singers.

Social Studies

Cooperative Learning

2. Have class discover Hawaii's natural beauty through slides or photographs such as those in *Hawaii Is a Rainbow* (see p. 236). List on the board features students notice: beaches, palm trees, volcanoes, rainbows, and so on. Divide the class into randomly assigned groups of three or four; have them list features of their *own* community's natural beauty and then report to the entire class. On the board make a list of their own region's features, alongside Hawaii's. Decide which features are the *same* and which are *different.*

Science

3. Help students learn that rainbows develop when falling water droplets are illuminated by a strong light source (the sun), and help them learn the order of rainbow colors (ROYGBV= red, orange, yellow, green, blue, violet). Or project sunlight through a triangular prism onto a white wall and have students discover that white light can be separated into colors (same colors and order as in the rainbow).

Multicultural

4. Construct Hawaiian instruments to play with "Hawaiian Rainbows." Make *uli-uli* (feathered gourd rattle) by putting rice or popcorn inside an empty beverage can, close the top, then decorate the sides and add feathers. A gourd drum (*ipu*) substitute could be a large plastic bottle. Split bamboo sticks (*puili*) are cut so one end is frayed; a usable substitute for *puili* is a tightly rolled (and tied) newspaper cut in the same way. For *ili ili* (pebble castanets) find two flat, smooth pebbles (1″ in diameter) and click them together. Try a rhythm pattern such as ♩♩♫♩.

Projects for College Students

Standard 9b (p. 62)

5. Compare "Hawaiian Rainbows," a song influenced by Western music, and a chant in traditional style, "Pele E," p. 350. Associate each following element with the appropriate song, and decide which of the elements is Western and which Hawaiian: Hawaiian language/English language; harmony/no harmony; limited-range melody/wide-ranging melody; abab form/paired phrases (couplet).

Related Literature and Media for Children (see p. 236)

Other Music (Section Four unless indicated)

"The Battle Hymn of the Republic" (abac twice)
"Choral Theme" (aaba)
"Hey, Ho! Nobody Home" (abca)
"The Yellow Rose of Texas" (abac), *The Music Connection* 7; *Share the Music* 5
"We Gather Together" (abcd)

MUSIC CONCEPT Each instrument has a characteristic timbre that when combined with others can create a sound piece (*Timbre*)

Music Haiku sound piece

Objective To create an original accompaniment to a haiku poem by choosing and playing classroom instruments in combination with a haiku poem and evaluating the resulting composition

Materials Assorted classroom instruments including sticks, claves, wood blocks, drums, castanets, sand blocks, maracas, Autoharp(s), several rubber and wooden mallets. (For total, see step 4 below.) Haiku poem on board (see margin below)

FOCUS

These barnacled rocks,
just uncovered by the tide . . .
how busy they sound!
Haiku poem by James W. Hackett

Key Terms: ***special sound, timbre***

A barnacle strains plankton from water during high tide; during low tide the plates at the top of the shell close to trap water and prevent dessication. The closing of the barnacle's shell produces a barely audible popping.

Step 1: Briefly mention the origin of the haiku poem on the board (see Note). Read expressively the haiku for the class, asking students to LISTEN AND EXPLAIN WHAT IS CAUSING THE POEM'S BUSY SOUNDS. (*barnacles*) Discuss barnacles (see margin note) and the phrase "barnacled rocks." Have the class read the poem aloud, slowly, with expression. Repeat several times. Explain they are going to form small groups to create an accompaniment for the poem.

Step 2: Have class as a whole decide WHAT SOUNDS ARE SUGGESTED BY THE POEM? (*tide, barnacles, water splashing against rocks*) Display assorted classroom instruments and ask for ideas about how to suggest each of the sounds. (A sound for a barnacle might be rapidly alternating rubber mallets on a wood block.) Discuss briefly how each instrument has a unique timbre. For example, some are "dry," some "mellow," and some "ringing."

Without the poem, have several students try out their ideas using different instruments. Each sound should last for several seconds. Evaluate. DID YOUR INSTRUMENT PRODUCE THE SPECIAL SOUND YOU WANTED? (Remember, the sound can be only suggestive, not literal.)

Step 3: Select successful players for three contrasting sounds and have them simultaneously play while the class reads the poem. Remind them that their sounds need to be continuous, not just a single one. Mention THE INSTRUMENTS WILL OVERLAP THIS TIME, PRODUCING YET ANOTHER SPECIAL SOUND.

Evaluate the performances. Did they play loudly (or softly) enough? Balance in dynamics? Last long enough? Play at an appropriate moment? Repeat the playing, reading, and evaluating. Consider having an instrument perform an introduction and a coda.

Cooperative Learning

Step 4: Divide the class into groups of five students. Give them one or two minutes to designate members as follows: one poem reader; three instrumentalists; one secretary. Explain that the secretary will write down the reasons for their choice/combination of instrumental sounds. Have the instrumentalists in each group select an instrument from the assortment in the classroom. (In addition to instrument sounds, students could tap a chair or table, or "scrub" feet on the floor.)

Have groups follow the whole-class procedure: select and try instruments, add the poem, and evaluate as they go along. Be sure they understand that each group will later perform their sound piece for the class and explain their choices. Establish a ten-minute time allotment and move between the groups to assist as needed. Give a signal one minute before the deadline. After a final run-through, begin the group performances/explanations.

Indicator of Success SUMMARY

As students perform for each other, listen to the group's justifications and NOTICE THE SPECIAL SOUND OF EACH INSTRUMENT AND COMBINATION.

ASSESSMENT

Standard 3d, 4a (p. 46)

As students become familiar with different poems (see other haiku poems in Appendix D), they use instruments expressively to create a sound piece and justify their choices.

Follow-Up

Standard 4b (p. 46)

1. Have the class choose ideas from the various group compositions to combine into a class composition. Videotape the class composition.
2. Read the text of "Sakura" (p. 356) and a haiku poem about cherry blossoms (see p. 356), and identify words about nature. Learn the song and hand gestures, deciding how the focus on nature might affect the performance.

Language Arts

3. Have each student compose a haiku poem. Because a haiku focuses on nature, the writing experience should include visiting a natural setting. Information about writing haiku is available from Japan Air Lines International Service (1450 Broadway, Suite 3900, New York, NY 10018), which sponsors worldwide children's haiku events. Also see Appendix D.

Science

4. Include barnacles in the study of how animals are grouped according to their structure as invertebrate (barnacle) or vertebrate animals.

Projects for College Students

Multicultural Social Studies

Standard 8b (p. 88–89)

5. Enlist the help of parents and community to create a traditional Japanese environment in the classroom. Read about the daily life of a Tokyo boy (see London, "Related Literature," p. 236). Have students research, locate, and arrange items such as tatami (matting) for the floor, low tables, and cushions for seating, and devise a tokonoma (large display niche) with scroll painting and/or flower arrangements. Remove shoes, wear kimonos; have a meal of rice and tea. Listen to recordings of and view a film about Japanese music (see "Related Literature," p. 236).

Note

In its traditional three-line form, the Japanese haiku is a nature poem consisting of seventeen syllables, ideally composed in a five–seven–five arrangement. With masters such as Basho, the haiku became an art of Zen Buddhism and was highly valued by the Japanese. Today, haiku poems are written in many languages and are popular throughout the world. Although haiku's traditional form is occasionally modified, haiku poetry retains its focus on nature and its characteristic spirit of naturalness, simplicity, and directness.

Related Literature and Media for Children (see p. 236)

Other Haiku Poems (see Appendix D)

MUSIC CONCEPT Sections of a composition can contrast with one another and sections can be repeated (ABA) (*Form*)

Music "Carillon," from *L'Arlésienne* Suite no. 1, by Georges Bizet ("bee-ZAY") (French, 1838–1875)

Objective To identify the pattern heard in the A section and to demonstrate that recognition by playing the pattern and by raising hands when it is heard in the recording

Materials
CD, track 41
Resonator bars E, F♯, G♯
Notation (see below)

FOCUS

Key Terms: ***pattern, ostinato, repeat, contrast, sections, ABA***

Step 1: Hold up the E, F♯, and G♯ bars. Discuss which bar sounds the lowest (*E*) and which the highest (*G♯*); F♯ is right in between. Have a student PLAY E, F♯, G♯ BARS OVER AND OVER AGAIN in a steady rhythm without pauses.

Step 2: Have other students find the six different combinations of the three bars, such as E, G♯, F♯ and F♯, G♯, E. Then ask them to focus on the G♯, E, F♯ pattern and notate it on the board:

Kodály Adaptation *Sol–fa* syllables and Curwen hand signs may be used.

G♯ E F♯
3 1 2

Have several students play the pattern shown above; stress keeping a steady beat without pauses.

A carillon consists of bells hung in a tower, played manually or mechanically.

Step 3: THIS PATTERN, HEARD OVER AND OVER IN A COMPOSITION, IS CALLED AN "OSTINATO." Write term on board and review their previous ostinato experiences. Select one player to perform the ostinato with the recording. (Play only the first third or the A section of "Carillon.")

Indicator of Success

Step 4: After students discover that this ostinato pattern is heard throughout the A section, explain that the composition is much longer. Challenge them to discover if section A is repeated and if there is a section different from A. Find another student to play the pattern and indicate that the player should perform whenever the ostinato pattern or A section is heard. Ask the class to help the performer by raising their hands if they hear another A section. (Play entire composition. The form is ABA.)

SUMMARY Determine that the ostinato is heard in the first and last sections and that it is not heard in the contrasting middle section. Discuss the different melodies, rhythms, instruments, and tempos of the two sections. Write the letters ABA on the board to label the form.

ASSESSMENT

Standards 6a (p. 20), 5b (p. 48), 2a (p. 30)

Students demonstrate the difference between sections in similar compositions in ABA form (see "Other Music," next page.)

Follow-Up

Movement

Standard 6e (p. 20)

1. Create a movement experience for "Carillon" that expresses the repeated and contrasting sections. Explore movements in space (sliding) and in place (swaying). Long scarves may be used to feel the *flow* in the "B" section.

Language Arts

2. Discuss different types of bells (carillons, sleigh bells, etc.). Create a story about how a bell made a difference in the life of a boy or a girl.

Orff Adaptation

Standard 4b (p. 46)

3. Using metallophones, glockenspiels, and xylophones, compose a piece in ABA form. Set up a pentatonic scale, such as G–A–B–D^1–E^1. Use the rhythm of a familiar song or poem for the A section and improvise a contrasting B section.

Projects for College Students

Visual Art

Standard 8a (p. 88–89)

4. Study the facades of French cathedrals for balance and contrast, using photographs of Notre-Dame (Paris), Sacre-Coeur (Paris), and the Rheims cathedral. Examine features such as doors, windows, spires, and domes. Note similarities and differences in the use of balance and contrast in the visual arts and music.

Cooperative Learning

5. In small groups, label the ABA sections in "Shoo, Fly," "Hey, Lidee," and "Music Touches Children Most of All" in Section Four. Share and compare your decisions.

Other Music (in ABA Form)

"Circus Music" (*Red Pony* Suite), by Copland, *The Music Connection* 2 & 3

"Cortege," by Lili Boulanger, *Share the Music* 3

"Dance of the Sugar Plum Fairy" (*Nutcracker* Suite), by Tchaikovsky, *Bowmar Orchestral Library,* "Stories in Ballet and Opera"; *Share the Music* 2; *Bowmar'sAdventures in Music Listening,* Level 1

"Gavotte" (*Classical Symphony*) by Prokofiev, *Bowmar Orchestral Library,* "Symphonic Styles"; *The Music Connection* 4; *Share the Music* 3

"Laideronette, Empress of the Pagodas" (*Mother Goose Suite*), by Ravel, *Bowmar Orchestral Library,* "Fairy Tales in Music"

"Run, Run" (*Memories of Childhood*), by Octavio Pinto, *Bowmar Orchestral Library,* "Classroom Concert"

"Hey, Lidee," see Section Four

"Shoo, Fly," see Section Four

MUSIC CONCEPT

The initial section of a composition alternates with contrasting sections in rondo form (*Form*)

Music

"Viennese Musical Clock," from *Háry János Suite,* by Zoltán Kodály ("KOH-dye") (Hungarian, 1882–1967)

Objective

To identify aurally the recurrence of the first section, A, as it alternates with contrasting sections B, C, and D and to demonstrate that recognition by placing like and differing objects in the correct order

Materials

CD, track 42
Objects: four apples and three different fruits (or kitchen utensils, flowers, toys, etc., similarly selected)

FOCUS

Key Terms: ***section, same, different, rondo***

Step 1: Place the fruit in the following order, where all can see.

Introduction	A	B	A	C	A	D	A	Coda
	apple	banana	apple	cantalope	apple	date	apple	

Ask students to describe the arrangement. (*four apples, alternating with different fruit*) THESE PIECES OF FRUIT SHOULD HELP YOU REMEMBER WHAT YOU HEAR AS WE LISTEN TO A RECORDING. The teacher should break up the arrangement, setting out each piece one at a time as the music plays. (Notice the brief introduction and coda.)

Special Learners Students who are visually impaired can set out the objects.

Step 2: Students should be able to explain why there are four apples. (*four similar sections of music*) Help them realize that each different fruit represents a different section of the music. WHEN ONE SECTION RETURNS OFTEN AND ALTERNATES WITH DIFFERENT SECTIONS, THE DESIGN IS CALLED *RONDO.*

Indicator of Success

Step 3: Have a student set out the fruit as the music plays. (Or choose two students: one to set out the A section apples, the other student the B, C, and D section fruit.) Lay them in order (not scrambled) for students to lift into full view as needed. Repeat with a student for each section.

SUMMARY

Kodály's rondo depicts the moving and changing figures of a large mechanical clock in Vienna.

The musical design in which one section keeps returning and alternating with different sections IS CALLED A ____________? (*rondo*) Write on chalkboard. Then write the following letter pattern and ask how it is the same as rondo form: "A B A C A D A." (*each letter represents a different section; A alternates with different letters*)

ASSESSMENT

Standard 6a (p. 20)

Students demonstrate the difference between sections in similar compositions in rondo form (see "Other Music," next page).

Follow-Up

Cooperative Learning

1. In small groups, have students look at pictures of different clocks (grandfather, cuckoo, etc.) and decide what is the same and different about each, then share their observations with the class. As a class, decide which clock could represent A, B, and so on, and place pictures in order while listening again to "Viennese Musical Clock."

Creative Movement
Cooperative Learning
Standard 6d (p. 20)

2. Form four groups and have students create appropriate movements for each type of clock in 1, above. For example, group A might portray a grandfather clock, and group B, a cuckoo clock. Members of the group should integrate their movements so that each person depicts one part of a clock. For example, one person might serve as the pendulum, another as the face of a grandfather clock. Have groups do their movements individually and then with the music.

3. Sing the "Bingo" melody with rondo words: "There is a form that we all know, And rondo is its name-o," and so on.

Projects for College Students

Orff Adaptation
Standard 3d (p. 46)

4. Chant and/or clap an eight-beat phrase, the rhythm of a familiar melody, a short rhyme, or a proverb. Use as the A theme of a rondo, and improvise contrasting B, C, and D sections of the same length. Transfer your rhythms to four different barred instruments.

5. Review and summarize one of the books listed in the Orff-*Schulwerk* section of Chapter V.

> *Note*
>
> Rondo form can be in five parts (ABACA) or more; the A section always recurs in the tonic (home) key. Rondo form developed from *rondeau,* a French poetic form, and was first used by French keyboard composers. Rondo is found in much instrumental music of the Viennese classical period. Sonatas and symphonies often include a rondo movement, sometimes as the *finale.*

Other Music

Electronic Rondo, by Kingsley (ABACA), *The Music Connection* 4

"Knightsbridge March," by Coates (ABACABACA), *Bowmar Orchestral Library,* "Under Many Flags"

"The March of the Siamese Children" (*The King and I*), by Rodgers (ABACABA), *Bowmar Orchestral Library,* "Marches"

"Romanze" (*Eine kleine Nachtmusik*), by Mozart (ABACA), *Bowmar Orchestral Library,* "Fashions in Music;" *Bowmar's Adventures in Music Listening,* Level 2; *The Music Connection* 4

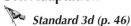

MUSIC CONCEPT Chords consist of three or four pitches stacked in thirds (*Harmony*)

Music "Hey, Lidee" (American song), p. 313

Objective To identify pitches in two chords (C, G7) and to demonstrate that recognition by playing C–E–G (I) and G–B–D–F (V7) as a song accompaniment

Materials
CD, track 43
Song notation for each student, with a chord symbol above each measure
Resonator bars C, E, G, B, D[1], F[1] and seven mallets
Autoharp (in tune with recording and resonator bars)

FOCUS

Key Terms: ***chord, chord root, pitch, chord tone, skipping***

Step 1: Sing or play a recording of the song's *refrain,* with teacher playing Autoharp chords in a one-strum-per-measure rhythm. Ask students to LISTEN TO THE REPEATING WORDS AND SING ALONG AS SOON AS YOU CAN. Review words and repeat singing as needed. Finally, call attention to your Autoharp accompaniment and tell students WE'RE GOING TO LEARN AN ACCOMPANIMENT FOR "HEY, LIDEE" ("LIE-dee").

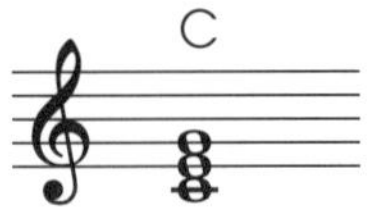

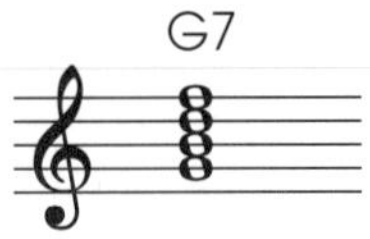

Step 2: Distribute the song notation and have students locate the *refrain:* its words, two staves, eight measures, and the eight C and G7 chord symbols. As students identify the chord symbols, write the order on the board:

C	C	C	G7
G7	G7	G7	C

POINT TO EACH CHORD SYMBOL IN YOUR MUSIC AS YOU SING while teacher points to symbols on the board, using the one-chord-per-measure rhythm. (Play first chord just before "Hey" on the rest/downbeat.)

Indicator of Success

Step 3: Select one student to play the C bar for the C chord, another student to play the G bar for the G chord. Practice bar playing with teacher pointing to symbols on the board. (Use the song's tempo.) Repeat with singing, pointing, and bar players. Note that ALTHOUGH C AND G ARE THE MOST IMPORTANT PITCHES (AND ARE THE CHORD ROOTS) IN EACH CHORD, CHORDS ALWAYS INCLUDE MORE THAN ONE PITCH.

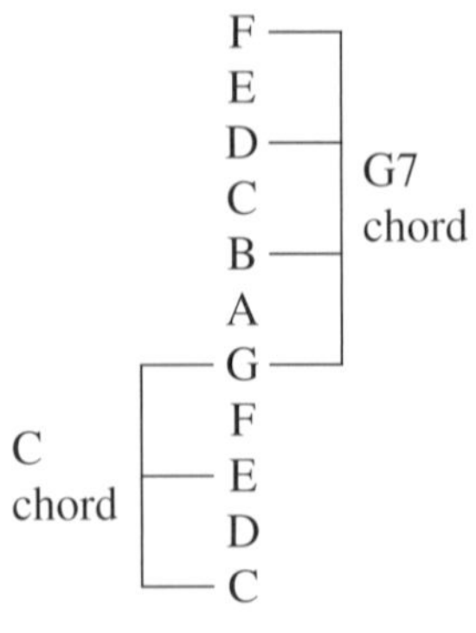

Step 4: Slowly strum a C chord on the Autoharp, and ask DOES THE AUTOHARP SOUND ONE PITCH (STRING) OR SEVERAL PITCHES? (*several*) Explain this is because three different pitches are needed, not only the C. Write (C, D, E, F, and G) on board, as shown in the margin. Notice WHICH PITCHES ARE SKIPPED? (*D and F*) Have a student place the C, E, and G resonator bars on a table, and then play them simultaneously.

Explain THIS IS A SPECIFIC KIND OF HARMONY CALLED A CHORD. Write "chord" on the board, and review the every-other-pitch idea. Play the C chord on the bars and Autoharp several times.

Step 5: Challenge the students to determine FOR THE G CHORD, WHAT THREE PITCHES ARE NEEDED? (G, B, D[1], skipping A and C[1])

Write pitch names on board, as in the margin. Call attention to the 7 in the G7 symbol, which indicates a four-note chord. Challenge students to name the needed fourth pitch. (F^1, skipping E) Select *two* players for the G7 chord (each plays two notes in the four-note chord), and practice the chord with Autoharp.

Indicator of Success

Step 6: Bar players should perform with teacher pointing to chord symbols. (Use the song's tempo.) When secure, repeat with teacher playing Autoharp, some students playing bars, and the rest of the class singing and pointing to song notation. Change bar players and repeat as long as interest remains high.

SUMMARY

Conclude by reviewing how CHORDS INCLUDE THREE OR FOUR PITCHES. Elicit from students what pitches are in the C chord and G7 chord and how the chords are formed by using every other pitch.

ASSESSMENT

Standards 2b (p. 30), 1a (p. 39)

As students become familiar with different songs (see "Other Music," below), they identify pitches in the I and V7 chords and play them as a song accompaniment.

Follow-Up

1. Learn the song's verses. (The chord pattern is the same for both verse and refrain.)
2. Locate C (first pitch) and G (fifth pitch) in the C major scale. Sing "Hey, Lidee," and raise one finger on the C (I) chord and five fingers on the G7 (V7) chord.

Special Learners

3. When playing I and V7 chords on instruments, color-code the chords in two different colors, in the song notation and on the instruments.

Projects for College Students

Cooperative Learning

Standard 5b (p. 48)

4. In small groups, review the chart of chords in Appendix A and notate the pitches for the I and V7 chords in several major keys. Begin with F and G major.
5. Prepare accompaniments for songs from "Other Music."
6. Determine how harmony/chords are introduced in the elementary music series, in the Kodály approach, or in Orff-*Schulwerk*.

Other Music (Section Four unless indicated)

One-Chord Songs

"Frère Jacques!" (D major)
"Zum Gali Gali" (D minor)

Two-Chord Songs (I and V7)

"Down by the Riverside" (F major), *The Music Connection* 5; (G major), *Share the Music* 4
"Down in the Valley" (G major)
"Hey, Ho! Nobody Home" (D minor)
"Pay Me My Money Down" (C major), *Share the Music* 4
"Three Sailors" (G major)

MUSIC CONCEPT

In call-and-response form, responses can be identical to the call, or contrasting (*Form*)

Music

"Stomp Dance" (Cherokee Indian) (Excerpt)
"Mai Wakaringano (Africa) (Excerpt)
"Ho Jamalo" (India–Pakistan) (Excerpt)

Objective

To identify aurally and visually the responses that are identical to or contrast with the call and to demonstrate that awareness through body movements and by visually identifying shapes on a chart.

Materials

CD, tracks 44, 45, 46
Chart (see below)

Multicultural Unit

This model experience can be part of a multicultural unit. See next two models that follow.

FOCUS

Key Terms: ***call, response, same, different***

Step 1: IF I ASK YOU TO ANSWER MY CLAPPING, WHAT WILL YOU DO? (Teacher claps: | | ⊓ | and class probably claps an identical response.) Tell students to clap a clear echo to a series of calls (at least 8) that you will clap. Establish an underlying framework of four beats. LISTEN, AND THEN CLAP AN EXACT RESPONSE TO MY CALL.

Special Learners
Encourage students to show responses in any way they can.

Step 2: Have students look at the two sets of shapes on the chart. Ask WHICH ONE LOOKS LIKE THE CLAPPING WE JUST DID. (*"A"*) Discuss why.

A		B	
○	●	□	●
△	▲	X	●
□	■	△	●
X	**X**	◇	●

Step 3: Explain that we will hear a "Stomp Dance" song of the Cherokee Indians. Invite students to share what they know about Native Americans, the Cherokee (and their relocation from the Carolinas to Oklahoma), and to guess what movements might be used in a "stomp" dance. (*stomping*) Explain that the "Stomp Dance" is part of an old ceremony that praises the Creator and that dancers stomp in a circle around a nighttime fire.

Play the recording of "Stomp Dance" and note that THE SINGERS ECHO THE LEADER EXACTLY. WATCH "A" AS YOU LISTEN. After listening, discuss the identical call/response. Replay, pointing to the shapes. (The words are syllables with no exact meaning.)

Mai Wakaringano
(*my wah-kah-ring-gone-oh*)

Step 4: Mention that music from around the world can use call-and-response form. See Note, p. 237. Introduce "Mai Wakaringano" as a call-and-response from the southern part of Africa (Zimbabwe). Review what students know about this area and its people. (Zimbabwe is the former British colony of Rhodesia that gained independence in 1965.) Explain that the story is about a mother who keeps her beautfiul daughter (Karingano) safely in a cave until she is ready to be married.

Indicator of Success

Focus attention on "B" and ask how it is different from "A." (*the responses are different from the calls*) Invite students to LISTEN FOR THE RESPONSE THAT REPEATS. (*mai wakaringano*) Practice pronouncing "Mai wakaringano" (*means "mother of Karingano"*), and repeat singing the responses. Review that the response was always the same but the calls were different.

Ho Jamalo
(*ho jah-mah-low*)

Step 5: Challenge students, as they hear "Ho Jamalo" from India, to LISTEN TO THE CALL AND DECIDE IF THE RESPONSES ARE THE

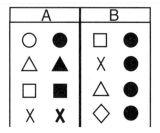

Indicator of Success

SAME AS THE CALL, OR DIFFERENT. IS IT DESIGN "A" OR "B"? *(responses are different from the call; sometimes a call is repeated)* Have them write either "A" or "B" on a paper. (Answer is "B.") Move quickly throughout the class to check answers. Announce the correct answer. Explain that "Ho Jamalo"means "let us be together again." Villagers sing this to welcome loved ones returning from fishing or trading. Replay the music while pointing to the chart, and invite students to sing the "Ho Jamalo" response.

SUMMARY

Conclude by reviewing the two kinds of call-and-response form. *(identical call and response, or response remains the same and the call changes)* Briefly elicit from students what they learned about the three songs and the cultures that created them. (Cherokee, Africa, India)

ASSESSMENT

Standards 6a, b (p. 20), 9b (p. 62)

As students sing a familiar call-and-response song (see "Other Music," below), they correctly identify calls and responses that are identical and those that are contrasting.

Follow-Up

Standard 3a (p. 46)

1. Play a clapping game in which students clap the same response—for example, ♩♩♫♩—to contrasting four-beat calls by the teacher.

Orff Adaptation

Standard 5a (p. 48)

2. Notate the teacher's clapped patterns that use only quarter and eighth notes. Students should first draw the stems and later add the note heads. Try patterns such as ♩♩♫♩, ♫♩♫♩, and ♫♫♩♩.

Cooperative Learning

3. In small groups, students should share one new fact they learned about each of the three songs. Encourage discussion about their discoveries.

Projects for College Students

Cooperative Learning

4. Clap eight-beat calls and responses in small groups. Use identical responses and contrasting responses. Notate several sets of calls and responses.

Visual Art
Multicultural

Standard 8a (p. 88–89)

5. Develop a follow-up for this model experience that presents visual art from each of the three cultures: Native American, African, and Indian. Prepare to help a group of students identify and compare the elements found in your chosen examples, focusing on aspects such as repetition, contrast, balance, color, form, line, and texture. Review the similarities and differences in the meaning of these common terms (e.g., repetition, contrast) in the visual arts and music.

Other Music

Identical call and response
"Che Che Koolay," see Section Four
"Sing about Martin," see Section Four
Contrasting response
"All Night, All Day," *The Music Connection* 1, 3, & 4; *Share the Music* 1
"Happy Go Lucky Local (Part I)," *Duke Ellington Orchestra,* LaserLight CD 15753
"Going Down to Cairo," *The Music Connection* K
"Michael, Row the Boat Ashore," see Section Four
"Sing Hallelu," see Section Four
"Sinoc mi je lane moje dolazio Mile," in *Village Music of Yugoslavia* (1995), Wea/Atlantic/Nonesuch

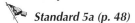

MUSIC CONCEPT

A melody can exhibit a distinctive contour as it moves up or down or repeats (*Melody*)

Music

"Corn Grinding Song" (Navajo Indian)

Objective

To identify aurally the repeated pitches and the pitches that move up and down in a melody and to demonstrate that recognition by tracing the contour of the melody as it is heard

Materials

CD, track 47
Worksheet for each student, showing a line drawing of the melodic contour (see p. 237)
Optional: Poster-sized version of contour chart (see p. 237)
Map of Native American areas, see *Music Educators Journal* (July 1994), vol. 82, no. 1, p. 19
Picture of Navajo woman grinding corn; see *Encylopedia Americana,* vol. 20, p. 3 (1992 edition)
Draw "practice contour" on board (see step 3, below)

Multicultural Unit

This model experience can be part of a multicultural unit. See model that precedes and follows.

Step 1: Discuss with class how important corn is to Native Americans, and that they grind corn (meal) to use in cooking. Show a photo of a Navajo woman kneeling on the ground in front of a stone with corn on it and rubbing a smaller stone back and forth over the corn to crush it. Have students share ideas about how easy or difficult the task of grinding corn might be, and ask them if Navajos still grind corn using stones. Learn the location of the Navajo reservation and that Navajos also live throughout the United States. (Use picture of corn grinding, map, and Note, p. 237, to introduce Native Americans, Navajos, and Navajo corn-grinding songs.)

FOCUS

Key Terms: ***up, down, repeated pitches***

Step 2: Invite students to listen to a Navajo woman singing a corn-grinding song and to be ready to tell how the song's melody moves—DOES IT MOVE UP AND DOWN? DOES IT REPEAT AT ALL BY STAYING ON THE SAME PITCH? Play recording, and after listening and discussing the up/down/repeating pitches, note how the singer sometimes moved quickly from low to high.

Step 3: Have students look at the practice contour on the board and decide how the line resembles the corn-grinding music. (*it moves up and down, as well as staying level*) Call attention to the dotted line that represents the singer's quick vocal jump from low to high. Have students move their arms from low to high, to show the ups, downs, and jump of the line while you trace the contour.

Special Learners
For students who are visually impaired, glue yarn to an enlarged version of the line drawing and have students feel and trace the contour as they listen.

("Practice contour")

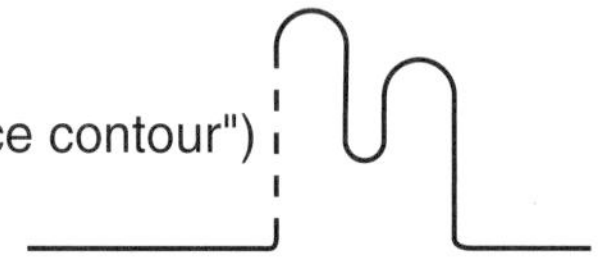

Indicator of Success

Step 4: Play the first twenty-two beats of the song and ask the class to MOVE YOUR ARMS FROM LOW TO HIGH ALONG WITH THE SINGER'S VOICE. Practice until students demonstrate that they understand.

Indicator of Success

Step 5: Distribute the worksheet (see p. 237) and have the students trace the up, down, and repeated pitches as they hear them. Play the entire piece. Teachers *must* move throughout the class to observe the degree of student success.

If some students finished too soon, discover why. (Perhaps they drew too quickly, not really listening for the high and low tones.) Play and trace the melody several times, perhaps using a different color crayon for each hearing. Encourage students to hum or sing the melody as they trace it.

SUMMARY

Look at the contour of the entire melody and discover how often it leaps to its highest point. (*four times*) The rest of the time, the melody stays on the same repeated tone. Some students will notice the two sections where the contour leaps to a "midpoint." Conclude by briefly eliciting information about Native Americans, Navajos, corn, and corn-grinding songs discussed in step 1.

ASSESSMENT

Standards 6e (p. 20), 9b (p. 62)

Students trace the melodic contour of a familiar song as they sing (see "Other Music," below) and identify when the melody goes up or down, or repeats.

Follow-Up

Standard 1a (p. 39)

1. Keep time with the singer's voice by singing "Hay, yea, yea, yea, yea" on a repeated pitch for four beats. Push the breath on each "yea."

Projects for College Students

Dramatization
Multicultural

2. Read one of the listed books for young people (see "Related Literature," p. 238) and suggest how it might be dramatized in a grade 4 or 5 classroom. Identify the characters and scenes needed, briefly mentioning costumes and scenery.

Multicultural

3. In your chosen story (from project 2), list scenes for possible sound effects and music. Locate a song or recording to use in your dramatization. Review "Other Music," the Native American songs in Section Four of this text, or those in *The Melody Book,* 3d ed. (Hackett, 1998). Be sure your song or recording is from the same culture as your story.

Standard 9c (p. 62)

Multicultural

4. Read "David P. McAllester on Navajo Music," in *Music Educators Journal* (July 1994), vol. 82, no. 1, pp. 17–23. Report on some of the following: Who are the Navajo people? Where and how do they live? What kinds of music are used, and for what purposes? What role does music play in religion? How do children take part in tribal music activities? How are the music and the culture changing?

Cooperative Learning

5. Review and discuss one of the following books in a small group. Decide how each might be used in the classroom: *Keepers of the Earth* and *Moving within the Circle* (see p. 238). Share your findings with the class.

Related Literature and Media for Children (see p. 238)

Other Music (see p. 238)

MUSIC CONCEPT Instruments can be identified and grouped by their timbres and materials (*Timbre*)

Music "Haoli Dance" (Tunisia) (Excerpt)
"Rippling Water" (Vietnam) (Excerpt)
"Barong Dance" (Bali) (Excerpt)

Objective To identify aurally four contrasting instrumental groups and to demonstrate that recognition by circling the appropriate word on a worksheet and locating the country of origin on a map

Materials CD, tracks 48, 49, 50
Drum or drumhead with drumstick or mallet
Several grains of rice or popcorn
Worksheet for each student (see p. 239)
An instrument from each classification, or see photos on p. 239.

Multicultural Unit This model experience can be part of a multicultural unit. See two preceding models.

FOCUS

Step 1: Position the drum or drumhead at the front of the room where all can see, and put several grains of rice on the head of the drum. Discuss WHAT WILL HAPPEN WHEN THE DRUMHEAD IS STRUCK. (*the rice will move*) Have a student play the drum to demonstrate. Challenge the class to EXPLAIN WHY THE RICE MOVES. (*the drumhead is vibrating*) Help the class decide that the vibration of the skin or membrane creates the drum's special timbre.

Step 2: Challenge the students to name some other materials that can produce a musical sound, such as wood, metal, strings (of gut or wire), seeds, and fiber. Explain that instruments of the world are classified and grouped by anthropologists according to their material and sound, and there are special terms for these groupings.

Key Terms: ***timbre, membranophone, chordophone, aerophone, idiophone***
("mehm-BRAN-uh-fone
KORD-uh-fone
AIR-uh-fone
IH-dee-uh-fone")

Review WHAT VIBRATES IN A DRUM? (the skin head or membrane) This is why the drum can be called a *membranophone.* Write the word on the board and discuss the stem *-phone* (Greek *phonos,* "sound"). Have students think of other words using the *phonos* stem, such as phonograph and microphone.

Using instruments and photos, discuss the other classifications: *chordophone* (Greek, *chordos,* string)—guitars, zithers, violins, harps; *aerophone* (a cylinder of air)—flutes, oboes; *idiophone*—solid instruments that produce sound when struck, shaken, or scraped, such as sticks, xylophones, bells, and gongs. Write names on board.

Cooperative Learning

Indicator of Success

Step 3: Divide the class into groups of two to six. Distribute a worksheet (p. 239) to each student and explain that students should circle the appropriate instrument category as they hear each selection. Listen to the first piece, and then give groups one or two minutes to make a choice. Have each group state and give reasons for their choice. Identify the correct instrument classification. Have students locate the country of origin and draw a line from the country to the instrument illustration(s). Replay the selection. Continue similarly for each piece. Answers are found on p. 238.

SUMMARY

Ask students WHAT DETERMINES THE TIMBRES OF EACH INSTRUMENT? (*the material that vibrates*) Elicit from them the various groupings and instrument examples in each category.

ASSESSMENT

Standard 6d (p. 20)

As students hear different world music (see "Other Music," below), they group instruments according to the classifications above.

Follow-Up

Standard 9b (p. 62)

Multicultural

1. Have a World Music Week featuring cultures in the local community. Each grade level in a school could contribute a song or dance from a different culture. Begin with music from this text or from *The Melody Book,* 3d ed. (Hackett, 1998). Learn how the particular song or dance fits into the culture and also about the culture's families, work, food, and so forth (see "Related Literature," p. 240).
2. Continue with instrumental timbre and classifications study by exploring the next model experience "Wabash Cannon Ball." This focuses on electrophones—instruments that produce their sound electronically.

Projects for College Students

Cooperative Learning

3. In teams, decide how you would categorize the instruments with which you are familiar. Use five minutes to list and group the instruments into categories. (Electronic instruments are classified as electrophones.)

Cooperative Learning

Standard 9b (p. 62)

4. In small groups, select a song or dance from a particular culture to present to a class; provide background on its cultural setting. Sources for cultural information are found in "Related Literature and Media for Children," p. 240, and world music "Resources," p. 58.

Related Literature and Media for Children (see p. 240)

Other Music

"Anaguta Drums," CD, track 13

Cycles, Vol. 2: Native American Flute Music (1992), by R. Carlos Nakai. Audio CD, Canyon. Contemporary compositions

"Muno Muno," CD, track 14

Chinese Music of the Pipa, performed by Wu Man (1993). Audio CD, Nimbus 5368 (Chinese lute)

See also "Other Music," pp. 141 and 169.

MUSIC CONCEPT Sounds are produced by vibrations and amplified on both acoustic and electronic instruments (*Timbre*)

Music "Wabash Cannon Ball" (traditional American song), p. 383

Objective To compare the source of vibrations and amplification on an acoustic and an electronic instrument and to demonstrate that recognition aurally and through class discussion

Materials

CD, track 51
Piece of string about two feet long
Barred instrument with removable bars (preferably a metallophone) and a mallet
Autoharp
Omnichord, electronic keyboard, QChord, or any available electronic instrument

---

FOCUS

Key Terms: ***acoustic, electronic, vibrations, amplification***

Step 1: LET'S TRY SOME SOUND EXPERIMENTS! Remove a bar from the metallophone and ask a student to thread the string through one of the holes, suspending the bar on the string. Ask another student to hit the bar with the mallet. Discuss the vibrations, the soft sound, and the term *acoustic vibration.*

Step 2: Place the bar back on the metallophone and ask another student to hit the bar with the mallet. Discover the louder sound (caused by the resonating chamber of the metallophone serving as an amplifier) and introduce the term *acoustic amplification.* Summarize that all acoustic instruments have something that physically vibrates and physically amplifies the sound.

Electrophones are instruments that produce their sounds electronically.

Step 3: Display an Omnichord (an electronic Autoharp), an electronic keyboard, a QChord, or any available electronic instrument. Plug in the instrument and ask students to speculate about what vibrates in an electronic instrument. Summarize that *electrical vibrations* are caused by a series of electrical impulses (like turning a light on and off). Review that the metallophone made a sound even when it was not attached to its amplifier. Unplug the electronic instrument and discover what happens to its sound—electronic instruments produce no sound when there is no amplifier. Plug in again and experiment with the various sounds on the electronic instrument.

Cooperative Learning

Step 4: Create an accompaniment for the song "Wabash Cannon Ball" on both an acoustic and an electronic instrument. Use the metallophone or the Autoharp (identify the sound source and amplifier) and whatever electronic instrument is available. The G, C, and D7 chords can be played on the Autoharp, Omnichord, and metallophone, and just the chord roots might be played on the metallophone and electronic keyboard. Students should work in pairs and take turns performing while the class sings the lyrics. An introduction should be prepared for each performance. (The "country" drum pattern on the Omnichord would work well for the accompaniment.)

Indicator of Success As a group, have students make two lists of familiar acoustic and electronic instruments. Have the class develop a definition for acoustic and electronic instruments as they compare and contrast the two categories.

SUMMARY

Finally, ask the class to tell, without looking, whether they hear an acoustic or an electronic instrument as sounds are performed on each by the teacher or a student.

ASSESSMENT

Standards 3d (p. 46), 2b (p. 30)

After listening to several musical selections (see "Other Music," below), students identify the sound source as either electronic or acoustic.

Follow-Up

Technology

1. Students should share electronic instruments they have at home, including electronic games that produce musical sounds. Ask them to be prepared to demonstrate and discuss the different effects possible.

Cooperative Learning

Standard 2b (p. 30)

2. Working in groups of four, students should learn to play Autoharp or QChord accompaniments for the songs listed in "Other Music." In addition to singing and playing, group members might be assigned special tasks such as one checking to see that correct chords are played while another helps when mistakes are made.

Projects for College Students

3. Locate several listening examples (see "Other Music"), some using electronic instruments and some using standard acoustic instruments. Prepare a chart or worksheet for students to use as they listen and identify the timbres. Encourage students to explain how they made their choices.

Other Music

"Allegro," from *Brandenberg Concerto No. 3,* by Bach, *Share the Music* 5 (electronic version)
"Carillon," from *L'Arlésienne* Suite no. 1, by Bizet, CD, track 41; *The Music Connection* 4 (acoustic)
Electronic Rondo, by Kingsley, *The Music Connection* 4 (electronic)
"Jesu, Joy of Man's Desiring," by Bach, CD, track 33 (acoustic)
"Viennese Musical Clock," from *Háry János Suite,* by Kodály, CD, track 42; *Share the Music* 2 (acoustic)
"It's a Small World," see Section Four
"John B. Sails," *The Music Connection* 5, 8
"Michael, Row the Boat Ashore," see Section Four
"This Land Is Your Land," see Section Four

This model experience is based on suggestions presented in Jackie Wiggins, *Synthesizers in the Elementary Music Classroom: An Integrated Approach* (Reston, Va.: Music Educators National Conference, 1991).

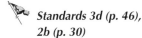

MUSIC CONCEPT Each of the three phrases in "twelve-bar" blues consists of four "bars" (measures) (*Form*)

Music "Joe Turner Blues" (African American blues), p. 325

Objective To identify aurally and visually the song phrases and to demonstrate this recognition through singing and body movements

Materials
CD, track 52
Wood block
Tambourine
Chart 1 (see p. 240)

Jazz Unit This model experience can be part of a jazz unit. See the next three models that follow.

FOCUS

Step 1: Write the term *blues* on the board and help students to decide that it refers to a sad type of music. Briefly discuss the origin of the blues (see Note, next page) and how sadness is universal—all kinds of people of any age can have "the blues." Play the recording and ask students to LISTEN AND TELL THE STORY OF THE "JOE TURNER" SONG. Have them retell the story in their own words.

Key Terms: ***phrase, beat, "twelve-bar" blues***

bar = measure

Step 2: Have students listen to verse 1 and tell WHICH LINE OF WORDS IS THE SAME, AND WHICH LINE IS DIFFERENT? (*phrases 1 and 2 are the same; phrase 3 is different—but related)* Have class sing verse 1. Clarify mistakes and repeat as needed.

Refer to the phrase chart and notice that VERSE ONE HAS THREE LINES OF WORDS, AND IT ALSO HAS THREE LINES OF BEATS. Each vertical mark, straight or wavy, represents one steady beat. Ask students to COUNT THE NUMBER OF STEADY BEATS IN EACH PHRASE. (*sixteen*) Each half, as indicated by straight and wavy lines, consists of eight beats.

Indicator of Success

Step 3: Have students tap steady beats with pencils as they sing verse 1. Start tapping after the introduction, on the word *tell.* The teacher should point to steady beats on the chart during the singing.

Step 4: Divide class into three groups: one group for tapping the beats (as in step 3), a second group to clap the first eight beats, and a third group to snap fingers on the last eight beats of each phrase. Rehearse the three groups without singing.

Indicator of Success

As soon as the class is able, sing with body rhythms and add instruments (verse 1). Group 2 can include one wood-block player, and group 3 a tambourine player.

SUMMARY

Discuss how the performance of the class showed their understanding that (1) the words of phrases 1 and 2 are repeated in "twelve-bar" blues; (2) each phrase is four measures (bars) long; (3) three phrases multiplied by four bars equals "twelve-bar" blues; (4) the two halves of each phrase balance one another; and (5) the second half of each phrase includes instrumental improvisation that "answers" the singing. Conclude by singing verse 1 again, with body movements and instruments.

ASSESSMENT

Standards 1a (p. 39), 6a (p. 20)

As students become familiar with other blues songs (see "Other Music," below), they perform body movements along with phrases and describe the form and text of twelve-bar blues.

Follow-Up

Special Learners

Standards 2a, b (p. 30)

1. See Chart 2, p. 240. Play chord roots or chords on a barred instrument, resonator bars, Autoharp, or a keyboard/synthesizer. Perform in a steady-beat rhythm with the song. Color-code each chord name, such as C chord, red. Color-code the instrument too.

Language Arts
Cooperative Learning

2. In small groups, create new lyrics for "Joe Turner Blues." Consider topics such as the environment, historical or legendary figures, or school activities. Follow the three-line format and use body movements. Share with the entire class.

Projects for College Students

Standards 2b (p. 30), 5b (p. 48)

3. Explore the blues scale. Compare with the C major scale and identify the differences. Play on resonator bars, xylophone, or keyboard. Notate the scales.

Blues scale:	C	D	E♭	E♮	F	G♭	G♮	A	B♭	B♮	C
C major scale:	C	D	E	F	G	A	B	C			

Cooperative Learning

Standard 3d (p. 46)

4. In groups of four, improvise a blues melody. Use the blues scale above and play on a barred or keyboard instrument. Use the three-phrase format. One person could do body rhythms while the others improvise melodic phrases. Exchange roles.

Related Literature and Media for Children (see "Jazz," p. 59)

Note

Often melancholy and slow in tempo, blues is music of African Americans and was developed in the early twentieth century. There were several types of blues (field, rural, and urban), with the urban blues most widely known. It has a specific harmonic pattern and a definite (but flexible) form of phrases and text. Blues had a profound influence on the development of jazz through musicians such as Louis Armstrong and Edward "Duke" Ellington.

Other Music

"Lost Your Head Blues," by Bessie Smith, *Share the Music* 7 (song)
"Rock Around the Clock," *Share the Music* 6 (song)
"Parker's Mood," by Charlie Parker, *Share the Music* 5 (instrumental)
"West End Blues" (Louis Armstrong) (instrumental), *Great Original Performances: 1923–1931,* Audio CD, *Lousiana Red Hot Records,* B000003428

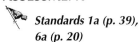

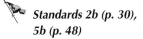

MUSIC CONCEPT

Sections of a composition can contrast with one another and sections can be repeated (AABBACCA) (*Form*)

Music

"Piffle Rag," by Gladys Yelvington (American, 1891–1957)

Objective

To identify aurally the repeating and contrasting sections in a composition and to demonstrate that recognition by raising hands for the A sections and completing a listening worksheet

Materials

CD, track 53
Listening worksheet for each student (p. 241)

Jazz Unit

This model experience can be part of a jazz unit. See model that precedes and two that follow.

FOCUS

Key Terms: ***sections, repeating/contrasting, ragtime***

Step 1: LISTEN TO THIS MUSIC AND NAME THE INSTRUMENT AND THE STYLE OF MUSIC HEARD. (*piano, ragtime*) Play the opening of "Piffle Rag." After the listening, briefly discuss with students a bit about when ragtime was popular and some of its special characteristics.

Step 2: Tell the class that they are going to determine the form of this piece. Write "A" on the board and ask students to begin tapping the steady beats (after the introduction) and through the initial A section. (Teacher should stop the recording after the first forty beats.)

Step 3: Distribute the listening worksheet and discuss that "Piffle Rag" has an introduction, eight sections, and "A" is heard more than once. LISTEN FOR THE "A" SECTION AND RAISE YOUR HAND EACH TIME IT BEGINS. Play the recording, identifying the sections by number and encouraging students to write an "A" in the appropriate box. (Form is Intro. A A B B A C C A.)
1 2 3 4 5 6 7 8

Step 4: Challenge the students to fill in the rest of the worksheet as they listen to the entire piece again. Note that contrasting sections should be labeled "B" and "C" and that contrasting sections might repeat as "A" did. (Again, the teacher should identify the sections by number as students listen.)

Indicator of Success

Step 5: Discuss their answers and discuss the contrasting and repeating sections as characteristic of a "rag" format. Repeat the listening to confirm the form. Students could clap or tap for "A," snap fingers from side to side for "B," and sway for "C."

SUMMARY

Ask questions about what made each section distinctive and how they could recognize each. Review the meaning of form and the specific form of this piece.

ASSESSMENT

Standard 6a (p. 20)

After listening to several musical selections (see "Other Music," next page), students identify the sectional form for each.

Follow-Up

Cooperative Learning

Standard 6c (p. 20)

1. Using the listening worksheet, pairs of students should listen to "Piffle Rag" and jot down the distinctive musical characteristics that they can identify in each section. Encourage students to use musical terms such as *tempo, steady beat, accent,* and *dynamics* in their analyses. Pairs should listen independently, then discuss with their partner, and finally, as a team, share their answers with the class.

2. Create a hand jive with clapping, patsching, tapping, etc., for the 32 beats of the "A" section and make up different hand motions for "B" and "C."

Visual Art

Standard 8b (p. 88–89)

3. Study the painting *Composition on the Word "Vie"* by Herbin. Discover how the forms and colors repeat and contrast. Note similarities and differences in the use of contrast and repetition in the visual arts and music.

Projects for College Students

Standard 9d (p. 62)

4. Review the background of ragtime and the rag composers.

Standard 6c (p. 20)

5. Create a call chart (similar to the listening worksheet used in this lesson) to use with this rag or one of the selections in "Other Music." First, decide on the form and where in the music each number will be called. Second, write a brief description of the rhythm, melody, timbre, dynamics, and so on, that is heard after each number. Third, use the call chart with a group of peers and evaluate its effectiveness.

Other Music

"Chicken Chowder," by Irene Giblin (American, 1888–1974), *The Music Connection* 8

"The Entertainer," by Scott Joplin, *Share the Music* 7

"Red Rambler Rag," by Julia Lee Niebergall (American, 1886–1968), *The Music Connection* 1

Note

American ragtime in its golden age spanned a period of roughly twenty-five years, from the late 1890s to the early 1920s. The music originated with African Americans. Piano "rags" featured a syncopated melody against a steady oompah bass and were divided into three or four sections, each symmetrical in length. Although Scott Joplin is the undisputed "King of Ragtime," many other men and women composed fine rags. In fact, over 150 women are known to have composed and published piano rags at the beginning of this century. The women ragtime composers were mainly white, whereas ragtime in general was a black, male-dominated field. Most of the women composed in their twenties and thirties and then, once they married, apparently gave up their composing. Gladys Yelvington, who hailed from Indianapolis, wrote "Piffle Rag" at the age of twenty. Yelvington also played the piano for silent movies.

MUSIC CONCEPT Music can be based on major or minor tonality (*Melody*)

Music "When the Saints Go Marching In" (African American spiritual), p. 388
"Diga Diga Doo" (Fields and McHugh, Americans) (Excerpt)

Objective To identify aurally the difference between major and minor tonality and to demonstrate that recognition by singing songs and circling the appropriate word on a worksheet

Materials CD, tracks 54, 55
Resonator bars C, D, E♭, E, F, G

Jazz Unit This model experience can be part of a jazz unit. See models that precede and follow.

FOCUS

Key Terms: ***tonic, major, minor***

Step 1: Display the resonator bars C, D, E, F, and G. Play "When the Saints Go Marching In," asking students CAN YOU IDENTIFY THIS FAMILIAR SONG? After they have identified the song, have students sing with you. On a repeat of the singing, have students raise their hands when they hear the final note of the song. Identify the home tone or tonic C, review its meaning, and write "C D E F G" on the board either in letters or, if the class has the background, in staff notation.

Step 2: Exchange the E resonator bar with the E♭ bar and play the song again, asking the class to see if "Saints" still has a tonic of C and if it sounds the same. Discuss how the tonic was the same but that the change to E♭ (lowering the third pitch) gave the song a different sound. Write "C D E♭ F G" on the board so students can visually compare this version with the original. Explain that the original was in *C major* and the altered version was in *C minor.* Sing the song twice: once in the original major and once in minor. (If students have studied major and minor scales, they should be reminded that the song contains the first five pitches in each.)

Step 3: SOME SONGS ARE IN MAJOR AND SOME ARE IN MINOR. Challenge students to decide if the previously learned song "Hey, Lidee" is in major or minor. First, using the resonator bars, have class sing the C major five-note pattern and then the C minor five-note pattern. Finally, have them listen to "Hey, Lidee" played on the resonator bars or on a recording to make their decision. (*major*) Conclude by singing the song accompanied by the resonator bars.

Cooperative Learning

Step 4: Ask students (in pairs) to listen to "Diga Diga Doo" to determine whether it is in major or minor. (*minor*) After one listening, partners should confer and then listen once again before deciding on their answer.

Indicator of Success

SUMMARY

Step 5: Have pairs share their answers and explain their choices. Provide brief information about "Diga Diga Doo." Finally, elicit from students how they would describe the differences in major and minor. Refer to both ("Diga Diga Doo" and the two song versions).

> *Note*
>
> "Diga Diga Doo" (1927) is a song made famous by the Duke Ellington Orchestra. Duke Ellington (American, 1899–1974) was a leader of one of the most popular big bands of the jazz era.

ASSESSMENT

Standards 1a (p. 34), 6c (p. 20)

Students review familiar songs and determine whether each is based in major or minor (see "Other Music," below).

Follow-Up

1. Help students determine the whole- and half-step distances between pitches in the C major pattern (C–D–E–F–G) and in the C minor pattern (C–D–E♭–F–G). Duplicate keyboard charts such as the following (without answers) and have students mark the whole steps and the half steps.

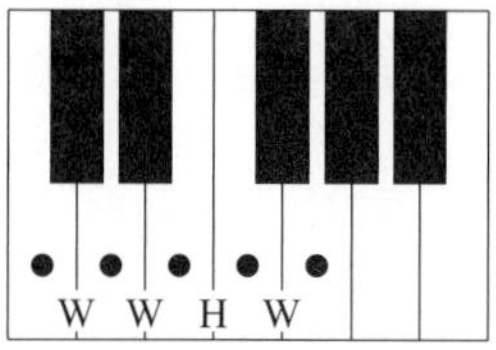

C major

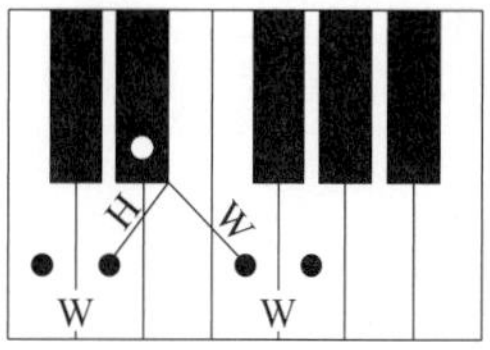

C minor

Cooperative Learning

2. Working in pairs or small groups, play an identification game with major and minor chords on the Autoharp, Chromaharp, Omnichord, or QChord. One student can play the chords while others identify.

Projects for College Students

Standard 5b (p. 48)

Music Fundamentals

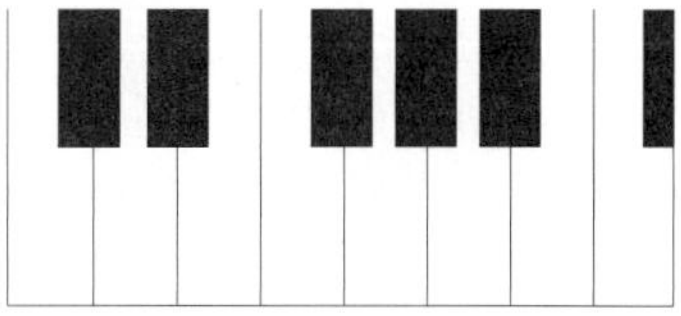

3. Study the whole–half-step arrangement of the major and the harmonic minor scale. Notate the C major scale and the C harmonic minor scale on the following staffs. Check your answers with the scale chart in Appendix A.

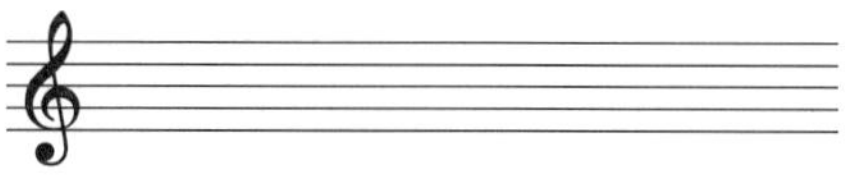

C major scale

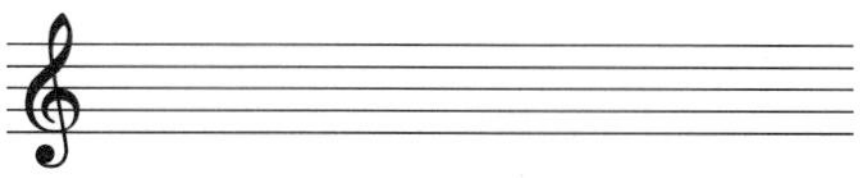

C harmonic minor scale

Other Music

"Danse Macabre," by Saint-Saëns (minor), *Bowmar Orchestral Library,* "Legends in Music"; *The Music Connection* 5

"In the Hall of the Mountain King," from *Peer Gynt* Suite no. 1, by Grieg (minor), *Bowmar Orchestral Library,* "Legends in Music"; *Bowmar's Adventures in Music Listening,* Level 2; *The Music Connection* K & 2; *Share the Music* 2

"Musette," from *Armide* Ballet Suite, by Gluck (major)

Rondeau (Suite no. 2 in B Minor), by Bach (minor)

Romanza Appassionata, op. 31, by Cecile Chaminade (major); *The Music Connection* 8

"Kum Ba Yah," see Section Four (major)

"Erie Canal," see Section Four (verse—minor, refrain—major)

"It's a Small World," see Section Four (major)

"Zum Gali Gali," see Section Four (minor)

MUSIC CONCEPT Beat groupings of twos and threes can be combined to create asymmetric meter (*Rhythm*)

Music "Take Five," (Excerpt) by Paul Desmond (American, b. 1924)

Objective To identify aurally the alternation of groups of two and three steady beats and to demonstrate that recognition in body movements

Materials CD, track 56
Paper for each student

Jazz Unit This model experience can be part of a jazz unit. See models that precede.

FOCUS

Key Terms: ***beats, accent, downbeat, asymmetric meter***

> = accent

Cooperative Learning

Step 1: LET'S REVIEW BEAT GROUPINGS OF THREES AND TWOS. Have students patsch in threes with left hand on left thigh for 1 and right hand on right thigh for 2 and 3 (1—left, 2—right, 3—right). When students are secure with the threes, change to beat groupings of twos (1—left, 2—right). Stress with both groupings the accent on the downbeat.

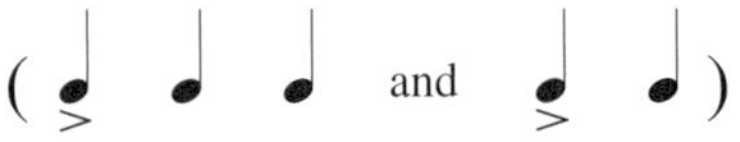

Step 2: Write $\frac{3}{4}$ on the board and ask a student to notate the correct number of quarter notes per measure in threes. .

Do the same with twos .

Ask HOW MANY BEATS WOULD WE HAVE IF WE COMBINED A GROUP OF THREES AND A GROUP OF TWOS? (*five*) Write  and have class perform this combination, accenting the 1 and the 4 (1—left, 2—right, 3—right, 4—left, 5—right). Ask if the threes and twos could be combined in a different order within the five-beat grouping. (*yes*) Write this new combination on the board: . Perform this combination accenting the 1 and the 3 (1—left, 2—right, 3—left, 4—right, 5—right).

Step 3: In pairs, have students notate the two versions of $\frac{5}{4}$ on a single piece of paper.

1. 

2. 

Challenge the class to listen to the jazz piece "Take Five" and decide which combination of five they hear: 2 + 3 or 3 + 2. (*3 + 2*) All students should patsch the steady beat with the music and focus attention on the accents. After listening once, ask pairs to consult about their answers and then invite everyone to listen again. Finally, have several pairs share answers and give reasons why.

Indicator of Success

> *Note*
>
> "Take Five" is an example of "cool jazz" developed in the 1950s by groups such as the Dave Brubeck Quartet.

SUMMARY

Invite class to patsch the beat grouping "1 2 3 4 5" with the music. (accents > under beats 1 and 4)

Ask questions about the beat groupings of twos and threes that equal five. Note that this five-beat grouping is referred to as asymmetric meter.

ASSESSMENT

Standards 6e (p. 20), 5a (p. 48)

Students demonstrate alternation of steady beats grouped in twos and threes in "Other Music," below.

Follow-Up

Cooperative Learning

1. In pairs, students should create other body rhythms to show the $\frac{5}{4}$ grouping. For example, partners could strike hands together (patty-cake style) on beats 1 and 4 and clap the other beats.

Cooperative Learning

Standard 3c (p. 46)

2. Have each student decide the number of syllables in his or her first name. Then form groups so there are five syllables total for the group's members' names. Have each group practice chanting their name pattern of five beats until they are secure. Then have each group chant its pattern twice. Finally, connect the chanting by having each group take its turn *without dropping a beat* between groups.

Projects for College Students

Standard 5a (p. 48)

Music Fundamentals

3. Create and notate four measures in $\frac{5}{4}$ meter. Use a variety of notes and rests (𝅗𝅥. 𝄽 𝄾 𝅘𝅥𝅮 etc.).

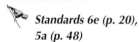

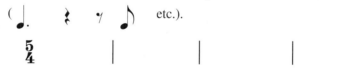

Visual Art

Standard 8b (p. 88–89)

4. Study these paintings: Frank Stella's *Brooklyn Bridge: Variations on an Old Theme* and Van Gogh's *Landscape with Cypresses.* Compare their symmetry, focal point(s), shapes, colors, and textures. Compare how symmetry/asymmetry is achieved in these paintings and in the Desmond music.

Other Music

"America" (*West Side Story*), by Bernstein, *The Music Connection* 6
"Mars, the Bringer of War" (*The Planets*), by Holst
Symphony no. 6, by Tchaikovsky, second movement
"Tanz" (*Carmina Burana*), by Orff, *The Music Connection* 5 & 6

MUSIC CONCEPT Chord tones can be played one after another as a song accompaniment (*Harmony*)

Music "Jamaica Farewell" (traditional calypso song from the West Indies), p. 323

Objective To identify aurally and visually chord roots and rearranged chord tones and to demonstrate that recognition by playing these chord tones as an improvised accompaniment to a song

Materials

CD, track 57
Song notation for each student
Resonator bar set and six mallets
Sketch of steel drum (see below) on board and another on chart board about twenty-four inches in diameter
Photo of steel-drum players, p. 53; steel-drum Note, p. 242
Autoharp

FOCUS

Key Terms: ***chord root, chord tones, broken-chord accompaniment***

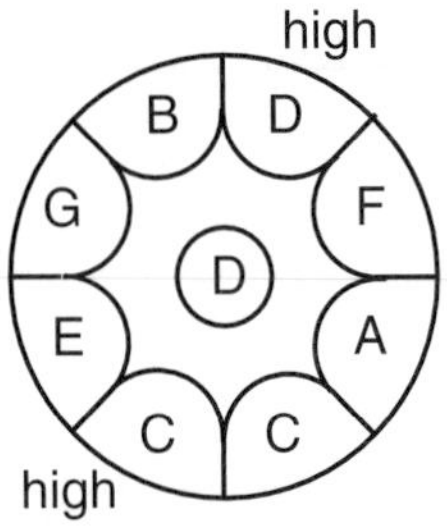

Guitar "pan" or drum (approximately 24" in diameter).

Step 1: Display photo of steel-drum players and ask students to name the instrument and where it is from. (*Caribbean, Trinidad*) Sing the song (with Autoharp) or play the recording and have students listen for WHO IS SINGING THIS CALYPSO SONG? (*a traveler who sails to Jamaica*) and WHAT IS THAT PERSON SINGING ABOUT? (*finding a girlfriend and being sad to leave her*) Review unfamiliar expressions such as "me heart." Using Autoharp accompaniment, teach the song one or two phrases at a time, joining phrases as learned. Work on precise enunciation, an important part of the style.

Step 2: Call attention to your Autoharp accompaniment and tell students WE'RE GOING TO LEARN A STEEL-DRUM-STYLE ACCOMPANIMENT FOR "JAMAICA FAREWELL." Refer to the photo of steel-drum players and then to the sketch of the pan on the board. Explain that TO MAKE A STEEL DRUM, WEST INDIANS CUT OFF THE BOTTOM OF A FIFTY-FIVE-GALLON OIL DRUM AND DIVIDE THE TOP INTO SECTIONS RESEMBLING A TURTLE'S SHELL. Notice that each section corresponds to one key on a piano or one resonator bar.

Step 3: Place the chart board on a table. One or two students should set resonator bars on top of the chart. Place the D bar diagonally in the center and put the others in sections around it, following the design in the margin.

Step 4: Give a mallet to each of three students and ask them to locate one bar each: C, F, and G. THESE ARE THE ROOTS OF THE THREE CHORDS WE NEED TO ACCOMPANY "JAMAICA FAREWELL." Write on board:

Chord numerals can also be used: I IV V_7

```
   C           F           G7          C
‖: | | | |     | | | |     | | | |     | | | | :‖
```

Each player will perform four steady beats per chord symbol. The teacher should play the three chords on Autoharp along with the bar players. Repeat the sixteen-beat phrase over and over.

Indicator of Success

Step 5: Add singers. Begin the chord roots first and play sixteen beats as an introduction, then continue throughout the song. Repeat as needed to refine performance.

		f	
g	c	d	g
e	a	b	e
C	F	G7	C

Each player uses different bars, except the F bar, which must be shared by the G7-chord and F-chord players.

Step 6: Briefly review chord tones, then add other pitches to each chord root on the board (see margin). Give each player a second mallet, and explain they will now be responsible for playing three or four pitches/bars. (For example, the F-chord player uses F, A, and C.) Rehearse, having players move freely and quickly among the pitches in their chord. Remind them IT DOESN'T MATTER IN WHAT ORDER YOU PLAY THE BARS IN YOUR BROKEN CHORD. Help them *keep within the four-beat span.*

Indicator of Success

Step 7: Combine bar players and singers. Again the teacher and players should perform a sixteen-beat introduction before the singers enter. Repeat with different players. (New players can stand behind those they will replace so that they can learn the broken-chord accompaniment.)

SUMMARY

Help students realize that CHORD TONES CAN BE REARRANGED AND USED IN MANY WAYS TO MAKE ACCOMPANIMENTS INTERESTING. Review the pitches of chords used by players.

ASSESSMENT

Standards 1a (p. 39), 2b (p. 30)

As students become familiar with different songs using a repeating harmony (see "Other Music," below), they identify pitches in the I, IV, and V7 chords and play them as a broken-chord accompaniment to a song.

Follow-Up

Standard 3b (p. 46)

1. Compose and arrange rhythm patterns for a polyrhythmic accompaniment to "Jamaica Farewell" using Latin rhythm instruments or good homemade substitutes.

Language Arts
Cooperative Learning

2. In small groups, create a new set of words for "Jamaica Farewell." (Calypso lyrics were often improvised. See Note, p. 242.) Share with the class.

Project for College Students

Standard 5b (p. 48)

3. Review the chart of chords in Appendix A and notate on a staff the pitches for the I, IV, and V7 chords in several major keys. Begin with F and G major.

Related Literature and Media for Children (see p. 242)

Other Music (with repeating harmony)

"I Love the Mountains" (F, Dmin, Gmin, G7), see Section Four
"Oh, How Lovely Is the Evening" (F, C7), see Section Four
"Pay Me My Money Down," *Share the Music* 4 (C, G7)
"Tzena, Tzena" (D, G, A7), *The Music Connection* 5 or *Share the Music* 5
"El Merecumbe" (steel-band recording), *The Music Connection* 4 & 7
"Highlife," in *Steel Band/Trinidad: The Sound of the Sun,* Nonesuch recording

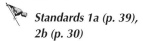

MUSIC CONCEPT

The elements of music can be identified and compared in music of different historical periods (*Elements of Music*)

Music

"Four on the Floor," (Excerpt) by Libby Larsen (American, b. 1950)
Archduke Trio, second movement, (Excerpt) by Ludwig van Beethoven (German, 1770–1827)

Objective

To identify aurally music from earlier times and music from the twentieth century and through a comparison of the musical elements, describe the similarities and differences between the two compositions.

Materials

CD, tracks 58, 59
Large blank sheets of paper—1 for each team
Musical Clues List on large paper—1 for each team (see p. 242)
Two similar objects (or photos) that represent different time periods (1 contemporary and 1 older), such as a digital watch and a pocket watch or a 78 rpm record and a compact disc

---

Step 1: Show students the two similar objects (or photos). Have students brainstorm what is the same, what is different, and how they knew which is contemporary and which is older. List answers on board.

FOCUS

Key Terms: ***timbre, tempo, dynamics, beat, texture, repetition***

Step 2: Challenge students to now listen to excerpts from the two musical examples. Without revealing the titles or the composers' names, ask students to DECIDE WHICH PIECE SOUNDS LIKE IT WAS WRITTEN JUST A FEW YEARS AGO AND WHICH OVER 150 YEARS AGO. ("Four on the Floor," 1983; *Archduke* Trio, 1811) After the class has shared their "educated guesses," discuss briefly when and where Beethoven lived in comparison with Larsen, an active contemporary composer. Note that music from different time periods may sound different but still have much in common.

Cooperative Learning

Step 3: Challenge students to figure out what was the same and what was different musically in the two pieces. In groups of four, give teams two large pieces of paper and ask them to write Larsen in the middle of one and Beethoven in the middle of the other. Give each team a second paper that includes a list of "musical clues." Review the clues and what they mean. As the students listen to the Larsen piece, encourage them to consult the clues list and jot down their ideas on their corner of the "Larsen" paper. Follow the same procedure for the Beethoven piece. (Students may need several opportunities to listen to the two pieces.)

Indicator of Success

Step 4: After listening to both excerpts, the teams should read each other's clues and discuss their answers. Then, each team should be given a large blank paper and be asked to divide their paper in two columns—labeling one the *same* and the other *different.* As a team, group members should decide which musical clues were the same for the two pieces and which were different and then write those on their team paper. Each team should share its conclusion with the class.

SUMMARY

Step 5: Listen to each example once again noticing those prominent similarities and differences that the teams have identified. Involve students in summarizing that music of different historical periods uses the elements of music in similar and contrasting ways.

ASSESSMENT

Standards 9a (p. 62), 6c (p. 20)

Students should be able to find similarities and differences in other music of contrasting historical periods. (See "Other Music," below.)

Follow-Up

1. Listen to "Four on the Floor" and follow the call chart in *The Music Connection* 5.

Cooperative Learning

Standard 6c (p. 20)

2. Distribute copies of the Venn Diagram (p. 242). Ask students, in small groups, to label one circle Larsen and the other Beethoven. Using the information they discovered about the two pieces, write the special musical characteristics of each in the proper circle, but the characteristics common to both in the overlapping area.

Standard 9d (p. 62)

3. Learn about Beethoven's life through the book, CD-ROM, or video *Beethoven Lives Upstairs.* See Appendix F, "Western Art Music."

Projects for College Students

Visual Art

Standard 8a (p. 88–89)

4. Discover similarities and differences in two paintings, e.g., "Bonaparte Crossing the Alps" (1800, David) and "Summer Days" (1936, O'Keeffe). Compare subject matter, realism/abstraction, color, line, use of space, shape/form, and repetition. Note how both the visual arts and music use same and different elements (e.g., instruments/color) in different historical periods.

Other Music

"Jesu, Joy of Man's Desiring" (Bach, 1685–1750), CD, track 33
Serenade for Wind Instruments (Mozart, 1756–91), CD, track 31
Toccata, third movement (Chávez, 1899–1978), CD, track 32
"Devil's Dance" (Stravinsky, 1882–1971), CD, track 19

Note

Libby Larsen is one of America's most active contemporary composers. Her compositions, which include works for theatre, opera, orchestra, ballet, and chamber groups, are performed throughout the world. "Four on the Floor" (1983) celebrates American music and was inspired by boogie-woogie. The title refers to speed—gunning a car in high (or fourth) gear and putting the gas pedal down to the floorboards. In fact, Larsen says that "breakneck is the theme of the piece—an America that is speeding up faster and faster, jazzing into eternity."

Note

Ludwig van Beethoven is one of the outstanding composers of all times. He composed nine symphonies, numerous piano sonatas and concertos, string quartets and trios. This trio was dedicated to Beethoven's friend and piano student Archduke Rudolph of Austria. Beethoven was a contemporary of Napoleon I, and his music has an intensity and power that symbolizes this dynamic historical period. He continued to compose throughout his life even though he began to lose his hearing in the early 1800s. Imagine not being able to hear the wild applause when his famous Ninth Symphony premiered in 1824! (The familiar "Choral Theme" from this symphony is in Section Four.)

EVALUATION FOR COLLEGE STUDENTS

A. Identify those music concepts within melody, rhythm, form, harmony, and expressive qualities that children in grades 4 and 5 can perceive.

1. melody concepts
2. rhythm concepts
3. form concepts
4. harmony concepts
5. expressive qualities concepts

B. Describe at least three developmental characteristics of children in grades 4 and 5. How will these characteristics suggest appropriate musical experiences?

C. Describe these terms and give a musical example of each:

1. jazz
2. blues
3. rondo
4. ABA form
5. "call-and-response" form

D. Name one music instrument in each category:

1. aerophone
2. chordophone
3. idiophone
4. membranophone
5. electrophone

E. Analyze the phrases of the following songs. Circle the correct analysis. (Songs are found in Section Four.)

"Clap Your Hands"	abab	aabb	aaba
"Hawaiian Rainbows"	abab	aabb	aaba
"Choral Theme"	abab	aabb	aaba

F. Notate the C, G, and F major scales.

G. What pitches are in the following chords?

C ____ ____ ____

F ____ ____ ____

G ____ ____ ____

D ____ ____ ____

G7 ____ ____ ____ ____

F7 ____ ____ ____ ____

H. In small groups, consider what you have learned about the K–4 National Standards for Music Education by: (1) naming the nine content standards; (2) recalling what skills and understandings fourth-grade students are expected to have developed in each of the nine content areas; and (3) reflecting on how you as teachers can best help students meet these standards.

I. In small groups, discuss the musical and nonmusical reasons why music of a wide variety of cultures should be included in the elementary classroom music curriculum. Prioritize your list of reasons and share the Top 5 with the class.

ORIGINAL MODEL EXPERIENCE ASSIGNMENT—LEVEL III

Plan one or two original model experiences for students in grades 4/5 (Level III). Base each experience on *one* of the two specified listening selections (refer to CD). This example should be prepared in a step-by-step sequence using a similar format to the models in *The Musical Classroom* (see the sample outline that follows). Specific information about each component of the experience follows.

1. The *music concept* and the *musical selection* are specified. Plan how to present this concept and music to fourth- and fifth-grade children.
2. State the *objective* for the experience, making sure that how and what students will do to demonstrate their understanding is included (see pp. 104–105).
3. *Model sequence.* Be sure to include key terms and age-appropriate music-making activities. Pay special attention to the opening ("Focus") and closing ("Summary") of the experience. Specify the exact part of the music that is the main focus of the experience. Identify by rhythm, pitches, or placement in music.
4. *Standards.* Identify by number and letter the particular content and achievement standard(s) that are addressed in the model experience.

Plan two *follow-up activities.* One activity should be a follow-up to the music concept presented in the model experience. Another follow-up activity should focus on a different subject area such as language arts, dance, or the visual arts.

	1.		2.
MUSIC CONCEPT	Sections of a composition can contrast with one another and sections can be repeated (ABA) *(Form)*	*or*	Phrases in a melody can be the same or different *(Form)*
Music	"Hungarian Dance, no. 5" (Brahms), CD, track 4		"Chinese Dance" from *Nutcracker* (Tchaikovsky), CD, track 21

Objective

Materials

FOCUS
Key Terms

Step 1:

Step 2:

Standards:

Step 3:

Step 4:

Indicators of Success
SUMMARY

Assessment

Follow-Up

One activity to reinforce music concept and one related to another curricular area

Music

1.

2.

____
(other curricular area)

ORIGINAL MODEL EXPERIENCE ASSIGNMENT—LEVEL III

Plan one or two original model experiences for students in grades 4/5 (Level III). Base each experience on *one* of the two specified songs (see Section Four). Each experience should be prepared in a step-by-step sequence using a similar format to the models in *The Musical Classroom* (see the sample outline that follows). Specific information about each component of the experience follows.

1. The *music concept* is not specified, but the *musical selection* is. After reviewing your chosen musical selection, decide which Level III concept would be a good focus for your experience. Plan how to present this concept and music to children.
2. State the *objective* for the experiencing, making sure that how and what students will do to demonstrate their understanding is included (see pp. 104–105).
3. *Model sequence.* Be sure to include key terms and age-appropriate music-making activities. Pay special attention to the opening ("Focus") and closing ("Summary") of the experience. Specify the exact part of music that is the main focus of the experience. Identify by lyrics, rhythm, pitches, or placement in music.
4. *Standards.* Identify by number and letter the particular content and achievement standard(s) that are addressed in the model experience.

Plan two *follow-up activities.* One activity should be a follow-up to the music concept presented in the model experience. Another follow-up activity should focus on a different subject area such as social studies or visual arts.

MUSIC CONCEPT

Music	"Hawaiian Rainbows," p. 308, CD, track 40	*or*	"Wabash Cannon Ball," p. 383, CD, track 51
Objective			
Materials			
FOCUS **Key Terms**	**Step 1:**		
	Step 2:		
Standards:	**Step 3:**		
	Step 4:		
Indicators of Success **SUMMARY**			
ASSESSMENT			
Follow-Up	One activity to reinforce music concept and one related to another curricular area		
Music	1.		
______________________ **(other curricular area)**	2.		

EVALUATING AN ELEMENTARY MUSIC SERIES TEXTBOOK ASSIGNMENT—LEVEL III

Compare the teacher's editions of *two different* elementary music series books for either grade 4 or grade 5. (See descriptions of the three series in Appendix C and select one.) Prepare an evaluation of no more than five pages. The written report should demonstrate knowledge of music concepts and vocabulary.

Concisely describe the similarities and differences between the textbooks in organization, visual presentation, directions for teachers, ease of use, and resources (e.g., recordings, handbooks). Include discussion and supporting data on the following topics.

1. Elements of music and music concepts
2. Music-making activities
3. The world of music
4. Approaches to curriculum
5. Curricular developments
6. Planning and assessing music learning

Conclude by indicating which music textbook you would choose to use. Justify your choice.

RESOURCE FILE—LEVEL III

Related Literature and Media for Children ("Hawaiian Rainbows" Model Experience, p. 202)

Beamer, Nona. (2000). *Na Mele Hula: A Collection of Hawaiian Hula Chants.* Honolulu: University of Hawaii Press; ISBN 0939154579.

Feeney, Stephanie. (1985). *Hawaii is a Rainbow.* Honolulu: University of Hawaii Press.

Hawaiians: The Story of an Island People. Two videocassettes; documentary features Hawaiian musicians. Available from Hawaiian Music Island, www.mele.com.

Kane, Herb Kawainu. (1996). *Pele: Goddess of Hawaii's Volcanoes.* Honolulu: The Kawainui Press; ISBN 0943357012. Author is illustrator.

Kane, Herb Kawainu. (1998). *Ancient Hawaii.* Honolulu: The Kawainui Press; ISBN 9043357020. Author is illustrator.

Muggs, Robert, and Vicky Holt Takamine. (1989). *Kumu Hula: Keepers of a Culture.* Video. Features twenty male and female hula masters. Available from Hawaiian Music Island, www.mele.com.

Te Rangi Hiroa (Peter H. Buck). (1964). Arts and Crafts of Hawaii IX: Musical Instruments. Book by former director of Bishop Museum. Available from Hawaiian Music Island, www.mele.com.

Phrase Chart ("Hawaiian Rainbows") Model Experience, p. 202)

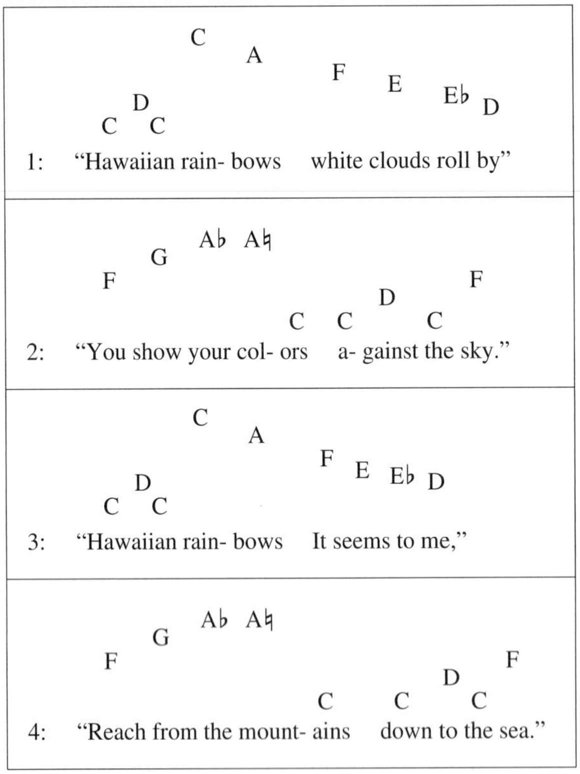

Related Literature and Media for Children ("Haiku Sound Piece" Model Experience, p. 204)

Discovering the Music of Japan. (1967). Video, color, 20 min. Introduction to three Japanese instruments (shakuhachi, koto, and shamisen). Available from West Music Company; (800)397-9378; www.swest@westmusic.com

Hamanaka, Sheila. (1990). *The Journey.* New York: Orchard. Illustrated story of Hamanaka's Japanese American family.

Japan: Semi-Classical and Folk Music. Baker & Taylor. Video; ISBN 630209247

London, Jonathan. (1998). *Moshi Moshi.* Millbrook Press; ISBN 0761301100. Yoshi Miyake, Illustr. Modern Japan through the eyes of visiting American boys.

Soh Daiko: Taiko Drum Ensemble (1991). Lyrichord LLCT 7410; ASIN B000002245.

Yokokura, Nikki. (1995). *Exotic Japan: Guide to Japanese Culture and Language.* CD-ROM. The Voyager Company. Intermediate grades. (1351 Pacific Coast Highway, Santa Monica, CA 90401)

Uchida, Yoshiko. (1993). *The Bracelet.* New York: Philomel; ISBN 039922503X. A Japanese American girl's family moves to an internment camp during World War II.

Note ("Stomp Dance" Model Experience, p. 212

Call-and-response form is found in many styles, as illustrated in these three examples from Native America, Africa, and India–Pakistan. Call and response is well developed in the music of Africa and has been retained in the African cultures of the New World. The form is used in both vocal and instrumental music, and the caller is often a soloist, who is then answered by a group. The soloist frequently embellishes and improvises on the call. Call-and-response forms are highly developed in jazz. They are also found in African American children's games and street songs and in popular music, gospel music, spirituals, and blues.

Contour Worksheet ("Corn Grinding Song" Model Experience, p. 214)

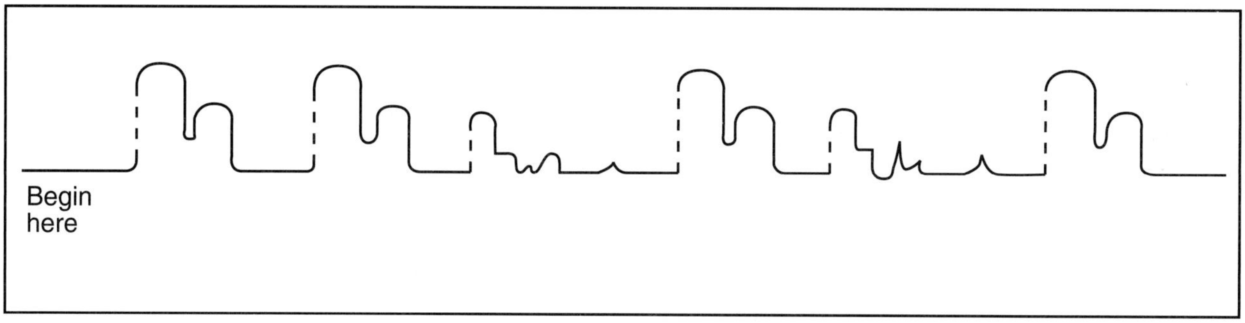

Note ("Corn Grinding Song" Model Experience, p. 214)

The Navajo "Corn Grinding Song" is sung by a woman, accompanied by a steady drum beat. It was not unusual, however, for a Navajo man to sing grinding songs *for* the women as they worked. Navajo melodies often display a high-to-low "pendulumlike" movement as exhibited in this corn-grinding song. Navajo vocal style is strongly nasal, with pulsation on held tones. In the "Corn Grinding Song," there are both words and vocables. The meaning of the words is not known, and the vocables are syllables without exact meaning.

Related Literature and Media ("Corn Grinding Song" Model Experience, p. 214)

ALIKI. (1986). *Corn Is Maize: The Gift of the Indians.* Harper Trophy; ISBN 0064450260

BRUCHAC, JOSEPH, and MICHAEL J. CADUTO. (1999). *Keepers of the Earth: Native American Stories, Cooperative Learning, and Environmental Activities for Children.* Golden, CO: Fulcrum; ISBN 1555913857

BURTON, BRYAN. *Moving within the Circle: Contemporary Native American Music and Dance.* Danbury, CT: World Music Press. Songs, dances, and listening lessons (including Navajo music) in this book-tape-slide set. All ages

CAMERON, ANNE. (1997). *How Raven Freed the Moon.* Canada: Harbour Publishing; ISBN 0920080677. Northwest Indian legend recounts raven's magic tricks.

MCDERMOTT, GERALD. (1977). *Arrow to the Sun.* New York: Viking Press; ISBN 0130402114. A Pueblo Indian boy, created by an unexplained spark of life, searches for his father (the sun).

MILES, MISKA. (1972). *Annie and the Old One.* Boston: Little, Brown & Co.; ISBN 0316571172. Navajo girl attempts to delay her beloved grandmother's death. Caldecott Honor book.

ODELL, SCOTT. (1990). *Island of the Blue Dolphins.* Boston: Houghton Mifflin; ISBN 0395536804. Based on the true story of a California Indian who refused relocation from her tribal island. Caldecott Medal book.

ODELL, SCOTT. (1999). *Sing Down the Moon.* Econo-Clad Books; ISBN 0395536804

Other Music ("Corn Grinding Song" Model Experience, p. 214)

Four Corners Singers. Yei Be Chai Songs. Canyon Records CR 7152, audio CD.

"Navajo Riding Song," *Share the Music* K

See also Appendix F, "World Music Recordings"

Answers for Worksheet ("Haoli Dance" Model Experience, p. 216)

1. "Haoli Dance" from Tunisia is a popular song.

   Answers:

   aerophones (oboes)

   membranophone (small drum with one head)

2. "Rippling Water" is a modern Vietnamese composition that suggests moving water.

   Answers:

   chordophone (16-stringed zither)

   chordophone (moon-shaped lute)

   chordophone (two-stringed fiddle)

3. "Barong Dance" is from Bali, a small Indonesian island east of Java. The dance is accompanied by the *gamelan,* a Balinese orchestra composed primarily of bronze instruments played with mallets. This dance drama depicts the triumph of good over evil and features the *Barong,* a mythological figure with a fantastic dragon–lion head and a body covered with feathers. Three dancers are needed for the Barong's head and body.

   Answers:

   membranophone (a barrel-shaped drum with two heads)

   idiophones (several xylophone-like bronze instruments in several sizes, played with mallets)

   idiophones (tuned gongs)

   aerophone (bamboo flute)

Worksheet ("Haoli Dance" Model Experience, p. 216)

1.	2.	3.
membranophones idiophones chordophones aerophones	membranophones idiophones chordophones aerophones	membranophones idiophones chordophones aerophones

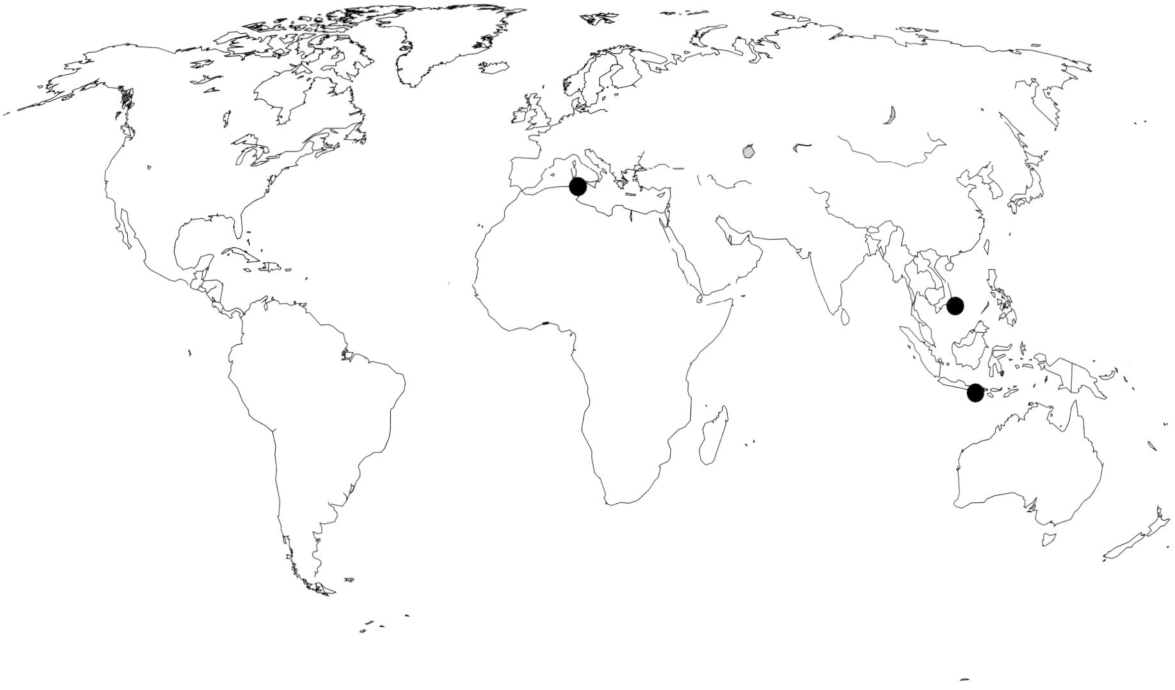

Two-stringed fiddle

Balinese boys playing *saron*

Zither

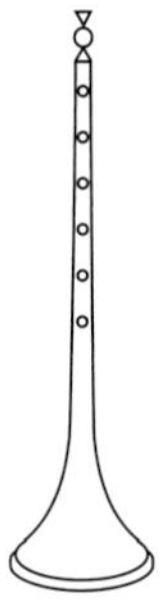

Oboe (about 18″ in length)

Related Literature and Media for Children ("Haoli Dance" Model Experience, p. 216)

BISHOP, CLAIRE. (1999). *Five Chinese Brothers.* Econo-Clad Books; ISBN 0833519986. A story of love and teamwork.

COHEN, BARBARA. (1987). *The Carp in the Bathtub.* New York: Kar-Ben; ISBN 0930493679. Humor in New York City Jewish life.

KILBORNE, SARAH S., and MELISSA SWEET, illustr. (1999). *Leaving Vietnam: The Journey of Tuan Ngo, a Boat Boy.* Simon & Schuster. ISBN 068980797X.

KRASNO, RENA, and ILIANA C. LEE, illust. (1997). *Kneeling Carabao and Dancing Giants: Celebrating Filipino Festivals.* Pacific View Press. ISBN 18811896153

LEVINSON, RIKI. (1985). *Watch the Stars Come Out.* Puffin. ISBN 0140555064. Turn-of-the-century immigration.

MASTERS, ELAINE, and SHARON ALSHAMS, illustr. (1998). *The Thief in Chinatown* (Adventures in Hawaii Series). ISBN 0896103013

Phrase Charts ("Joe Turner Blues") Model Experience, p. 220)

Chart 1

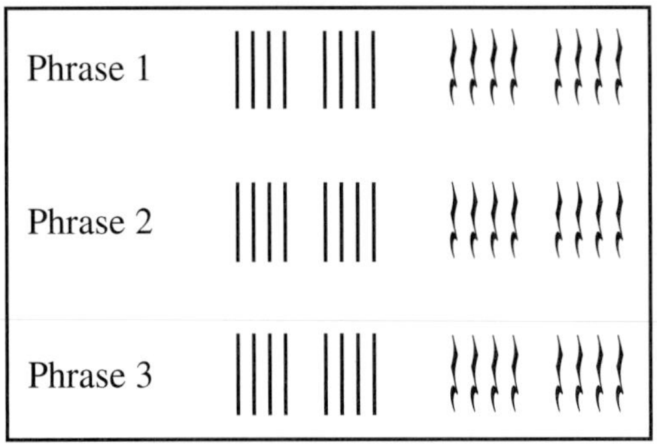

Each phrase has 4 bars (16 beats). The first half (8 beats) is vocally active and the second half is sometimes filled in by instrumental improvisation.

Chart 2

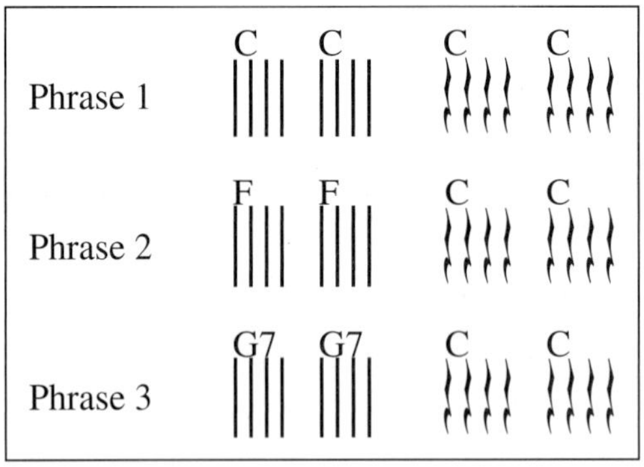

Listening Worksheet ("Piffle Rag" Model Experience, p. 222)

	Form	Musical Characteristics
	INTRODUCTION	
1	A	
2		
3		
4		
5		
6		
7		
8		

Note ("Jamaica Farewell" Model Experience, p. 228)

Steel drums ("pans") were invented in Trinidad after World War II, using discarded fifty-five gallon oil drums left behind by the military. They were used for calypso music—originally a satirical, highly political song genre. Pans are played, manufactured, and tuned in sets that may include (from highest to lowest) the "lead," "tenor," "guitar," and "bass" pans. Each drum has a number of pitches outlined on its top, ranging from about thirty on a lead pan to three on a bass pan. The guitar pan shown on page 228 is an early type used in the 1950s. Since then, new tuning systems provide a greater number of pitches and allow many styles of music to be performed, including classical music. In today's large band, one type of pan is often doubled (or trebled), allowing for even more pitches. For example, a set of three guitar pans (all played by one person) is built with slightly different pitches on each drum, so their combined range is three times that of a single pan. Although calypso has been succeeded in popularity by reggae and rap, it remains in the repertoire of many steel bands. Calypso is often performed during Jamaica's annual Carnival, when texts may be improvised during song contests.

Related Literature and Media for Children ("Jamaica Farewell" Model Experience, p. 228)

BARTHOLOMEW, JOHN. (1986). *The Steel Band.* London: Oxford University Press. Maps, history, photos, descriptions, music, music projects, and resources.

BURNETT, MICHAEL. (1985). *Jamaican Music.* London: Oxford University Press. Maps, history, photos, descriptions, music, music projects, and resources.

CHANG, KEVIN O'BRIEN, and WAYNE CHEN. (1998). *Reggae Routes: The Story of Jamaican Music.* Temple University Press; ISBN 1566396298

Musical Clues List ("Four on the Floor" Model Experience, p. 230)

Big changes in louds and softs
Little change in louds and softs
Mainly fast tempo
Mainly slow tempo
Moderate tempo
Big changes in tempo
Little changes in tempo
Steady beat
No steady beat
Clashing sounds
Singable melody
Instruments entering at different times
Instruments playing together
Played by: piano
violin
cello
double bass
Thick texture
Thin texture
Repetition
Accents

Venn Diagram ("Four on the Floor" Model Experience, p. 230)

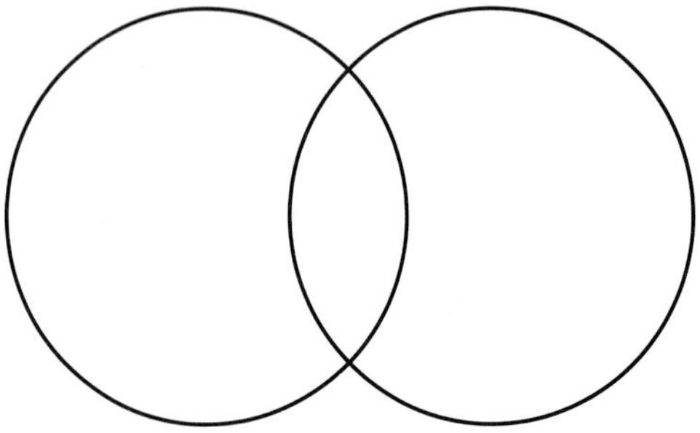

Section Three
Instruments

THE AUTOHARP AND THE CHROMAHARP

THE GUITAR AND THE UKULELE

THE KEYBOARD

THE RECORDER

THE VOICE

The Autoharp and the Chromaharp

Autoharp and Chromaharp are trade names for the chorded zither—an instrument that can be used to accompany singing. Chorded zither is the generic name for any instrument that has strings suspended across a flat, wooden soundbox and bars that are pressed to produce chords.

There are several models of chorded zithers. The twelve-chord and the fifteen-chord models are the ones generally used in elementary classrooms. Five-, twenty-one-, and twenty-seven-bar models are also available, as is an electric model that includes a microphone pickup for use with an amplifier. A diagram of the bar arrangements of the twelve-chord and fifteen-chord instruments follows:

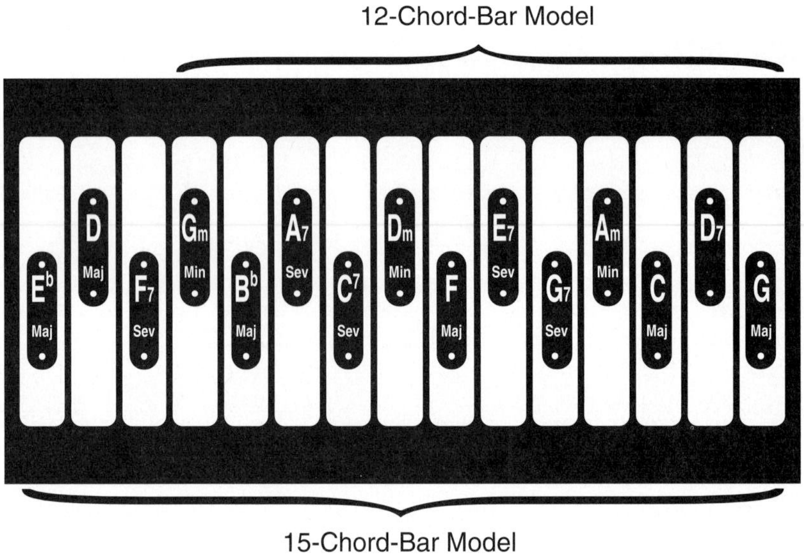

PLAYING POSITION

- Place the instrument on your lap or on a table in front of you, with the longest side near you.
- Rest your *left hand* on the chord buttons. By pressing a button on a chord bar, you damp (silence) certain strings. Those strings that sound are the pitches of the chord indicated on the chord bar.
- Use your right hand to strum across the strings with the fingernail of your index finger. (Or use a plastic or felt pick.) Strumming is usually done to the left of the chord bars in a crossover fashion, but beginners may more comfortably strum to the right of the chord bars.
- Strum from near your body, and swing your hand outward across the strings.

Playing position Photo by Patricia Hackett

ACCOMPANIMENTS

An accompaniment should enhance the character and mood of the song and also match the song's rhythm.

Basic Strum

The basic strum is steady and continuous and is produced by starting near the body and swinging the hand outward across the strings (bass to treble).

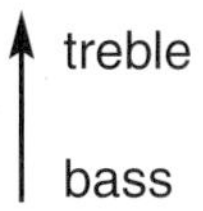

Often the basic strum is varied to include strumming in specific places on the strings: bass, middle, or treble.

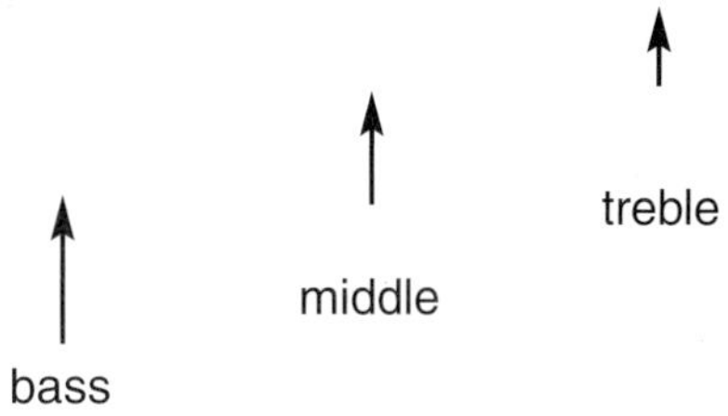

Accents

Accents are created by strumming on the bass strings. Various patterns with accents may be used to complement songs in the following meter signatures:

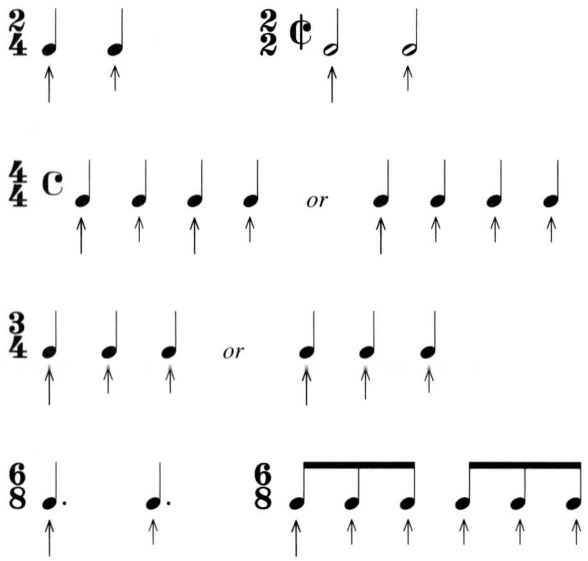

Special Effects

- *Drone or bagpipe.* Press two chord buttons with the same letter names simultaneously, such as G major and G minor.
- *Banjo.* Strum to the right of the chord bars, and strum in a rhythm that is faster than the beat. Use a flat pick for best banjolike results.
- *Harp.* Strum by starting away from your body (treble to bass) and vary the length of the strums.
- *Slavic.* Press and hold a chord button down while scrubbing or lightly bouncing two or more mallets (rubber or wood) on the strings.

SONGS FOR AUTOHARP OR CHROMAHARP ACCOMPANIMENT

The following list includes songs that use one, two, and three chords.
Songs are found in Section Four unless indicated.

One-Chord Songs	*Chord*
"Down Came a Lady"	C
"Counting Chant"	C
"Eena Deena"	C
"It's Raining!"	C
"Pease Porridge Hot"	C
"Sally, Go 'Round the Sun"	C
"Frère Jacques!"	D
"Chatter with the Angels"	F
"God Bless All"	F
"Wake Me!"	F
"Dulce"	Dmin
"Shalom, Chaverim"	Dmin

Two-Chord Songs	*Chords*
"Do as I'm Doing"	C, G7
"Hello, There!"	C, G7
"Hey, Lidee"	C, G7
"Jim-Along, Josie"	C, G7
"Looby Loo"	C, G7
"Love Somebody"	C, G7
"Wishy Washy Wee"	C, G7
"Bow, Belinda"	D, A7
"Matarile"	D, A7
"Long-Legged Sailor"	F, C7
"Lovely Evening"	C, F
"Sandy Land"	F, C7
"Circle Right"	G, D7
"Hot Cross Buns"	G, D7, p. 271
"Mary Had a Little Lamb"	G, D7, p. 272
"Three Sailors"	G, D7
"Trampin' "	G, D7, p. 271
"This Is Halloween"	Gmin, D7

Three-Chord Songs	*Chords*
"Ebeneezer Sneezer"	C, F, G7
"Hickory, Dickory, Dock"	C, F, G7
"Kum Ba Yah"	C, F, G7
"This Old Man"	C, F, G7
"When the Saints Go Marching In"	C, F, G7
"America"	C, F, G7
"Old Brass Wagon"	D, G, A7
"Oh, Susanna"	F, B♭, C7
"Thank You for the Chris'mus"	G, C, D7
"Wabash Cannon Ball"	G, C, D7

TUNING AN AUTOHARP OR A CHROMAHARP

An Autoharp or a Chromaharp must be kept in tune. Since frequency of use and the weather affect the instrument, occasional tunings are necessary. The instrument can be tuned quickly and accurately with an electronic chromatic tuner. If an electronic chromatic tuner is not available, follow the tuning procedures suggested in the elementary music series.

The Guitar and the Ukulele

THE GUITAR

The modern guitar is the most widely used instrument in folk and popular music throughout the world. The classical (acoustic) guitar has a mellow tone and is a good choice for beginning players because of its nylon strings and wide neck.

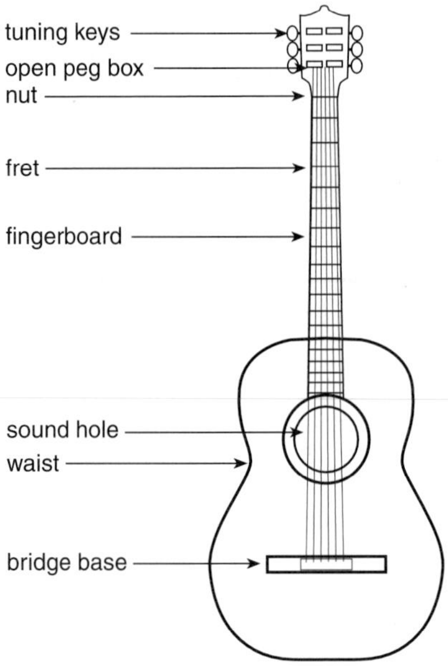

Classical guitar

PLAYING POSITION

- Hold the guitar with the neck at a slight upward angle, and keep the face of the instrument in an almost vertical position in relation to your body. The guitar's body can rest on your thigh (see photo).
- Position your right-hand thumb and fingers near the sound hole (see photo).
- Support the guitar's neck using the thumb of the left hand (rather than the palm of the hand). This position allows the fingers to move freely on the strings.
- Arch the left-hand fingers in a nearly vertical position while playing.

Left-handers can finger chords as described, or restring their guitars, reversing the order of the strings. Chords are then fingered with the right hand and strummed with the left hand.

Folk-style playing position
Courtesy of MENC: The National Association for Music Education

A guitar strap (crossing over and around the shoulder) allows the player to stand while playing the guitar. The advantages of a standing position are increased mobility and good posture while singing. (A music store that sells a guitar strap will also attach it.)

FINGERING FOR THE GUITAR

Finger designations are shown below. The left-hand fingerings are shown in guitar chord diagrams.

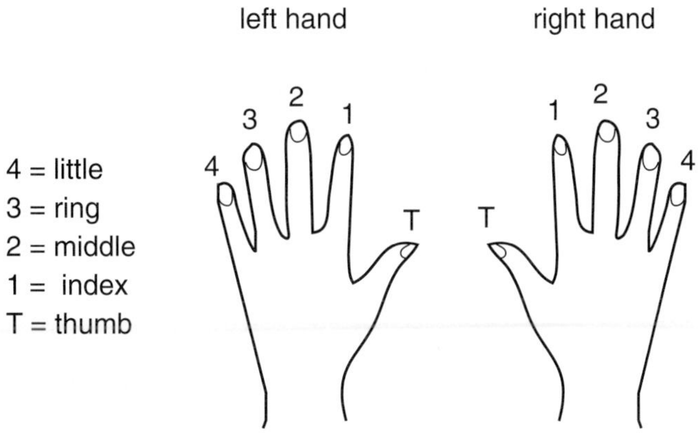

Chord diagrams for guitar playing look like the fingerboard of the guitar. They show the strings and the frets; numbers (sometimes circled) show where to put the fingers to play chords.

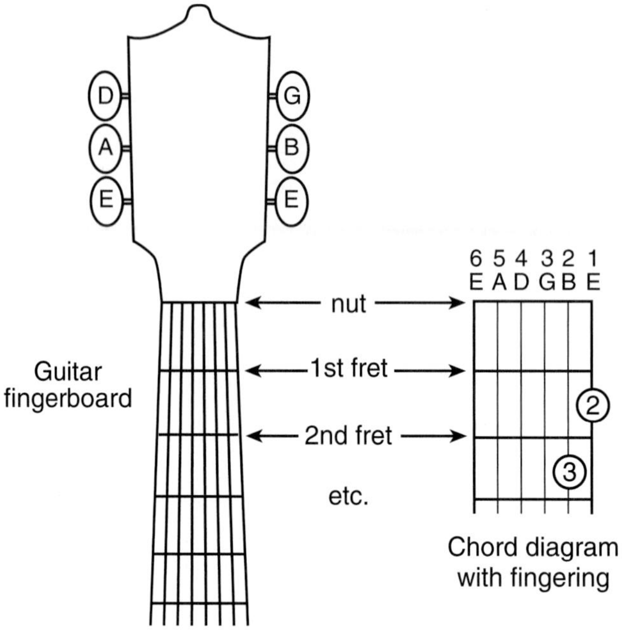

A chord chart for guitar is presented on p. 254.

TUNING THE GUITAR

The six strings of the guitar are tuned to the pitches shown on the following page. The relative tuning method is the one most commonly used by guitarists. Twist the tuning key while continuously plucking the string to check its pitch.

Strings

E Tune the bass E string to low E on the piano or guitar pitch pipe.

A With the second finger of the left hand, press down the bass E string at the *fifth* fret. Pluck the A string, and match it to the sound of the bass E string that is being pressed down.

D Press down the A string at the *fifth* fret. Pluck the D string, and match it to the pitch of the A string.

G Press down the D string at the *fifth* fret. Pluck the G string, and match it to the sound of the D string.

B Press down the G string at the *fourth* fret. Pluck the B string, and match it to the sound of the G string.

E Press down the B string at the *fifth* fret. Pluck the treble E string, and match it to the sound of the B string.

Strum an E minor or an E major chord to check your tuning.

LOCATION OF PITCHES ON THE GUITAR

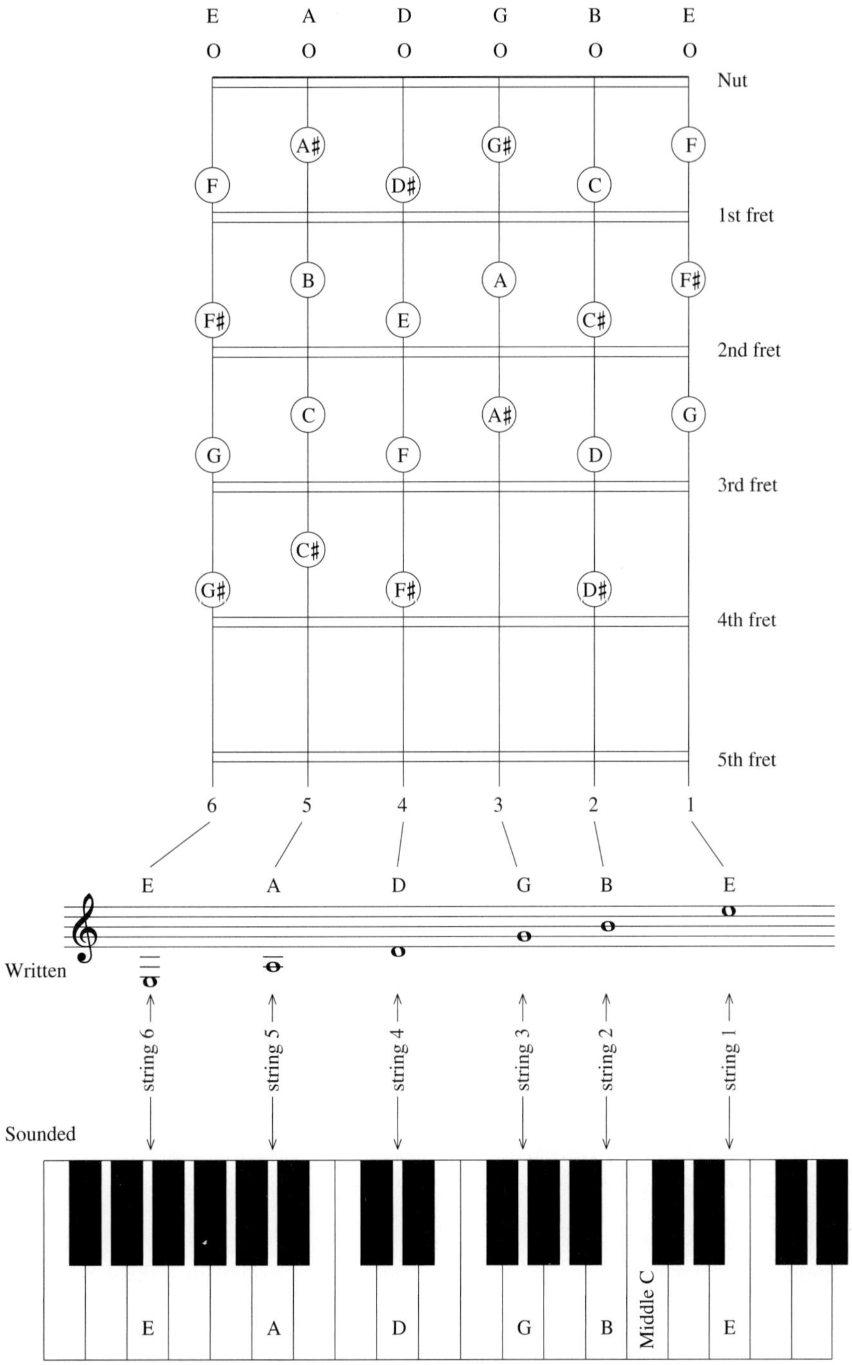

Additional Tips for Tuning

- Sing the desired pitch while tuning.
- Reverse the foregoing steps.
- If a string is difficult to tune, lower it well below the desired pitch and gradually bring it up to pitch.

GUITAR STRUMS

The six strokes and strums illustrated and described here are presented in order of difficulty.

The Brush Stroke

↓

The right-hand thumb sweeps downward across all strings in a brush stroke. Keep a steady beat as you strum.

The Thumb ("Rest") Stroke

The right-hand thumb plucks and then rests on the next string—for just a moment. The thumb usually plucks the root of each chord (sometimes labeled *R* in chord diagrams). The player can alternate between plucking the root and the fifth of a chord (sometimes labeled *5* in chord diagrams).

The Thumb-Brush Stroke

T ↓

This strum is a combination of the brush and the thumb strokes. The thumb of the right hand plucks the string, rests momentarily, and then sweeps downward across the remaining strings.

The Arpeggio Strum

T 1 2 3

Plucking strings one at a time (arpeggio) adds expression to an accompaniment. While fretting a chord with the left hand, place the right-hand fingers as follows:

1. Index finger just under the G string.
2. Middle finger just under the B string.
3. Ring finger just under the treble E string.

Then one at a time, snap each finger into the palm of the hand: index (1), middle (2), and ring (3). (Do this without moving your arm.) Keep each finger on its string until time to play. The thumb begins the arpeggio strum by plucking the chord root (sometimes labeled *R* in the chord diagram): T 1 2 3.

The Thumb-Pluck Strum

T 1/2/3

Place fingers as described for the arpeggio strum. The thumb plucks the string and rests, and then the index, middle, and ring fingers simultaneously pluck the G, B, and E strings.

The Syncopated Strum

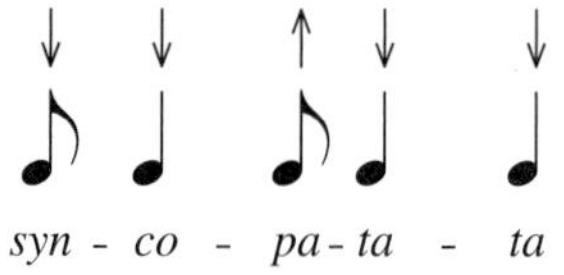

In this syncopated strum, all movements are downward, except the strum on "pa." The index finger should lead each moment.

SONGS FOR GUITAR ACCOMPANIMENT

The following list includes songs that use one, two, three, and four chords, with a recommended guitar strum for each. Songs are found in Section Four unless indicated.

D Major	*Chords*	*Strum*
"Frère Jacques!"	D	Thumb-brush
"Grizzely Bear"	D	Brush
"Bow, Belinda"	D, A7	Brush
"London Bridge"	D, A7	Brush
"Matarile"	D, A7	Thumb-brush
"Shoo, Fly"	D, A7	Brush
"Skip to My Lou"	D, A7	Brush
"Over My Head"	D, A	Thumb-brush
"Tinga Layo"	D, G, A7	Syncopated
"Up on the Housetop"	D, G, A7	Thumb-brush

D Minor

"Shalom, Chaverim"	Dmin	Thumb-brush
"Zum Gali Gali"	Dmin	Thumb-pluck

E Major

"He's Got the Whole World in His Hands"	E, B7	Thumb-pluck
"Old Texas"	E, B7	Arpeggio
"This Land Is Your Land"	E, B7, A	Thumb-pluck
"Bingo"	E, A, B7	Brush

E Minor

"Ghost of Tom"	Emin, D	Thumb-pluck
"Green Gravel"	Emin, D	Arpeggio

G Major

"Charlie over the Ocean"	G	Thumb-brush
"Who's That Yonder"	G	Brush
"Circle Right"	G, D (play D for D7)	Brush
"Down in the Valley"	G, D (play D for D7)	Arpeggio
"The Hokey Pokey"	G, D (play D for D7)	Thumb-brush
"Hot Cross Buns"	G, D (play D for D7)	Brush p. 270
"Mary Had a Little Lamb"	G, D (play D for D7)	Brush p. 272
"Old Brass Wagon"	G, C, D7	Thumb-pluck
"Thank You for the Chris'mus"	G, C, D7	Syncopated
"Wabash Cannon Ball"	G, C, D7	Thumb-pluck
"Mango Tree"	G, D7, E, Amin	Brush
"I'd Like to Teach the World to Sing"	G, D, A7, A, C	Thumb-brush

A Major

"Silent Night"	A, D, E7	Arpeggio
"America, the Beautiful"	A, D, E7, B7	Thumb-brush

THE UKULELE

The ukulele is an instrument from Hawaii that comes in soprano and baritone sizes. The baritone ukulele is larger and lower pitched than the soprano. Both instruments have four strings, making them easier to play than a six-stringed guitar. These four strings are shown in chord diagrams with only four lines (instead of the guitar's six). The baritone's strings are tuned D-G-B-E, the same as the four highest guitar strings. This means that the chord diagrams are similar, and most songs for guitar can be played on baritone ukulele. (Playing the baritone can lead smoothly to guitar playing because of these similarities.)

Strums, Songs, and Chords for Baritone Ukulele

Strums on the preceding "Guitar Strums" chart can be used with the baritone ukulele, as can the preceding "Songs for Guitar Accompaniment." Frequently used chords for baritone ukulele are shown in chord diagram charts that follow (on the right-hand side of the page).

Frequently Used Chords for Guitar

When strumming the thumb stroke, play the string labeled *R* (chord root), or alternate between playing *R* and *5* (chord fifth). The third finger of the left hand sometimes changes strings to play the chord fifth; this is indicated by a circled 3 on the chord diagram.

Major Keys I IV V

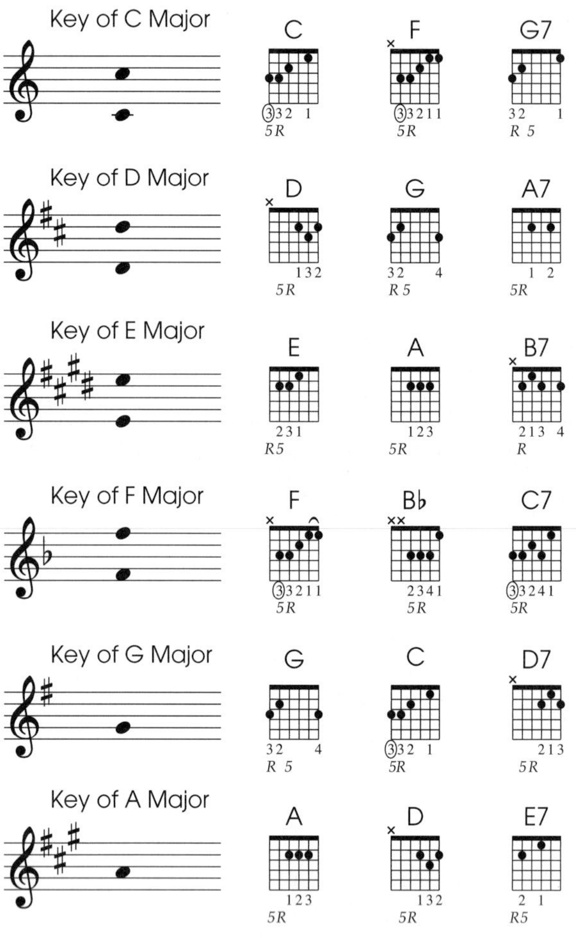

Selected additional chords:

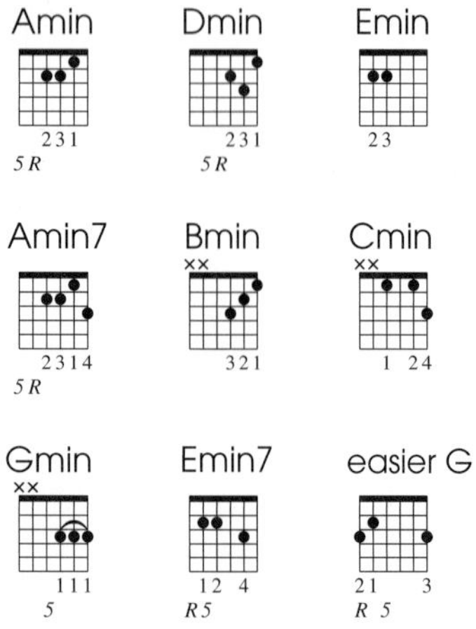

Frequently Used Chords for Baritone Ukulele

Major Keys I IV V

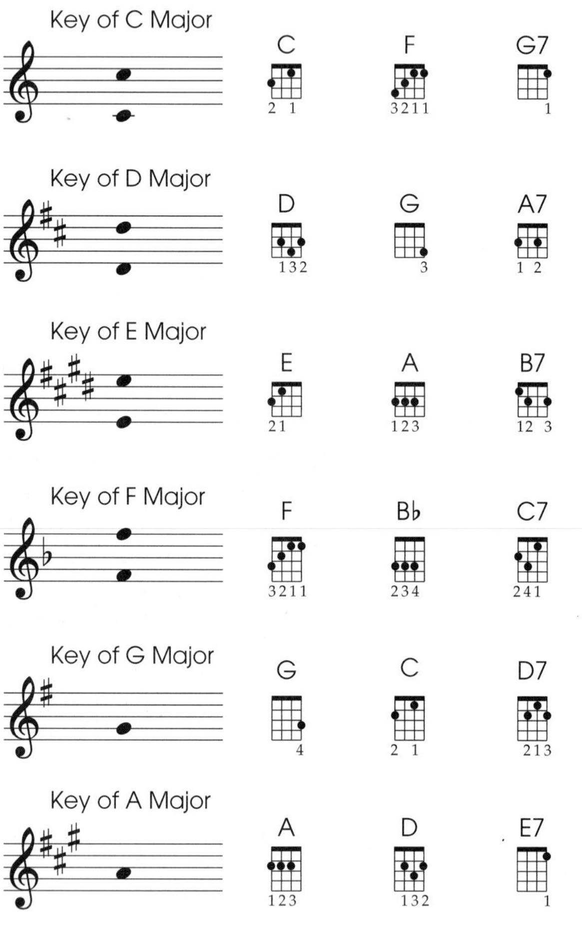

Selected additional chords:

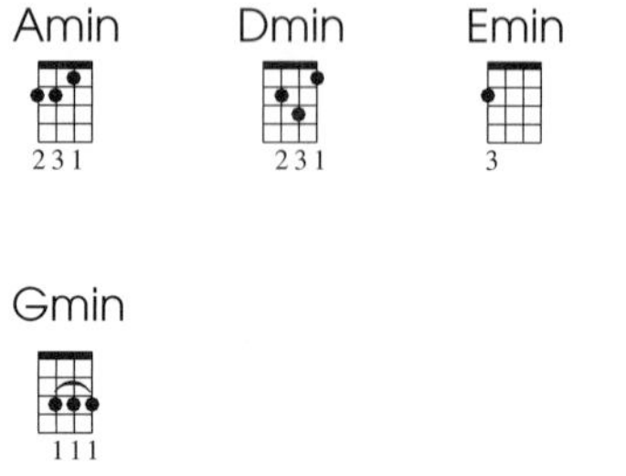

The Keyboard

A variety of keyboard instruments enjoy popularity today, including the piano, electronic keyboards, synthesizers, and barred instruments played with mallets. All of these instruments have in common a specific pattern of black and white keys (or bars), and all are excellent tools for visualizing and performing music. The following information pertains to the piano.

PLAYING POSITION

- Sit directly in front of the middle of the keyboard, far enough back so that your arms and elbows can move freely.
- Lean a bit forward at the waist, keeping your torso straight.
- Keep your hands, wrists, and forearms level with the keyboard.
- Curve fingers gently and slightly arch your hand.
- Strike the keys (don't press!) with the fleshy part of the fingers and keep fingers close to the keys.

Hand position

FINGERING

The numbers 1 through 5 are assigned to specific fingers of both hands. The thumbs are 1; the index fingers, 2; the middle fingers, 3; the ring fingers, 4; and the little fingers, 5. These same arabic numbers (usually written very small) appear above or below the notes in piano music to indicate the preferred fingering.

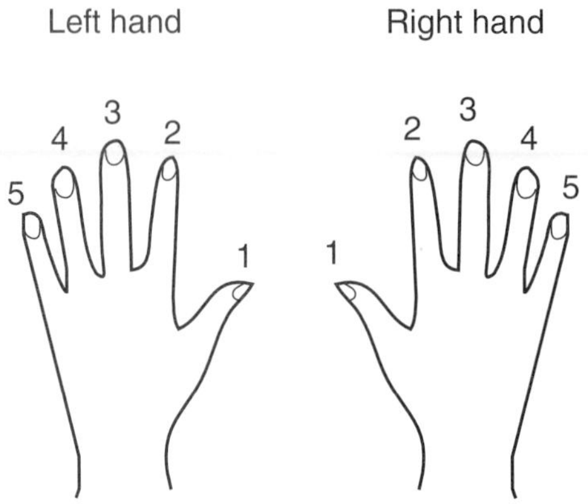

NAMES OF THE KEYS

The first seven letters of the alphabet—A, B, C, D, E, F, and G—are used to name the eighty-eight keys of the piano. The black keys use the same letter names as the white keys but with the addition of a ♯ (sharp) or a ♭ (flat). Notice that each black key has two names.

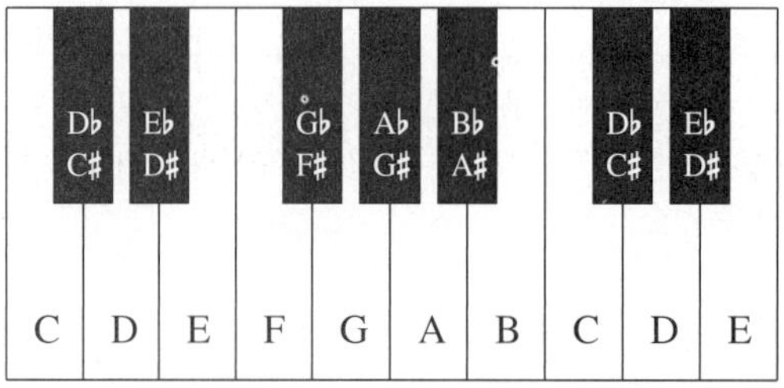

STAFF NOTATION

The *grand* or *great staff*—actually two staves—is used to notate piano music. The upper staff identifies the higher notes, usually played by the right hand (RH), and the lower staff specifies the lower notes, usually played by the left hand (LH). The *treble clef,* or *G clef,* encircles the second line (G) of the higher staff. The *bass clef,* or *F clef,* has dots above and below the fourth line (F) of the lower staff. Ledger lines (short lines) can be added above and below the staves to extend the pitch range. Notice that stems point up on notes below the middle line of the staff and point down on notes on and above the middle line.

Grand Staff

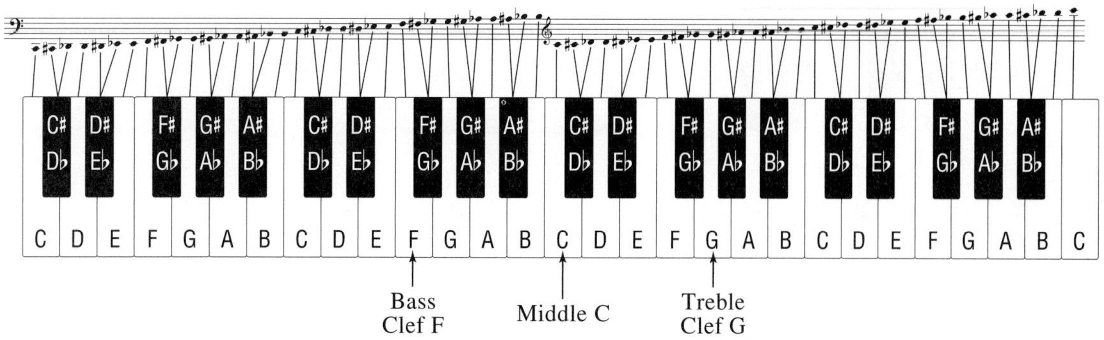

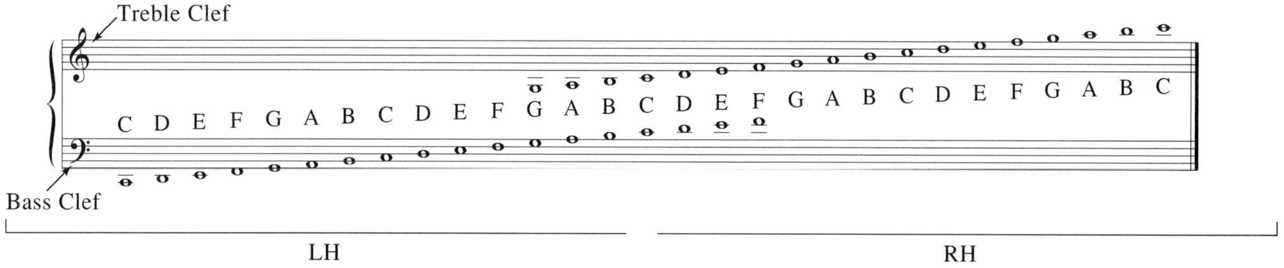

PLAYING MELODIES WITH THE RIGHT HAND

The right hand often plays the melody line. For simple melodies that include the first five pitches of a scale, the thumb and fingers touch consecutive keys in what is known as the *five-finger pattern.*

Major Five-Finger Pattern

The major five-finger pattern includes five pitches with the following whole- and half-step distances between keys:

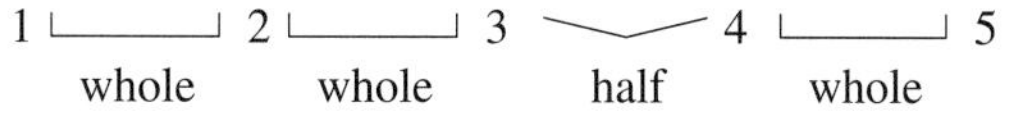

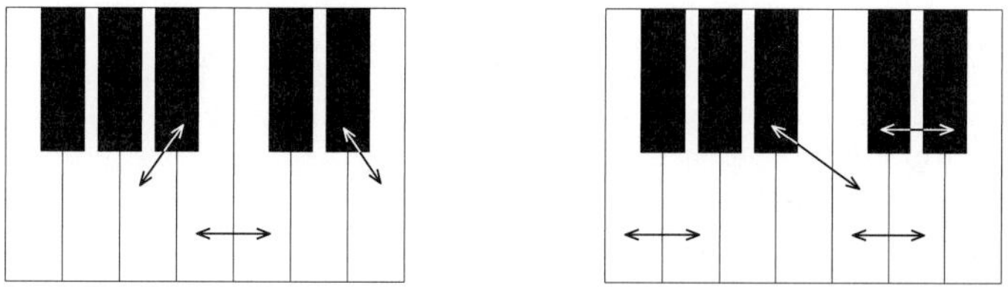

half steps whole steps

All five notes in the pattern are identified by different letter names. Any key or pitch can be used as the first pitch (*tonic*).

The following major five-finger patterns are sometimes used in simple melodies:

C Major Five- Finger Pattern

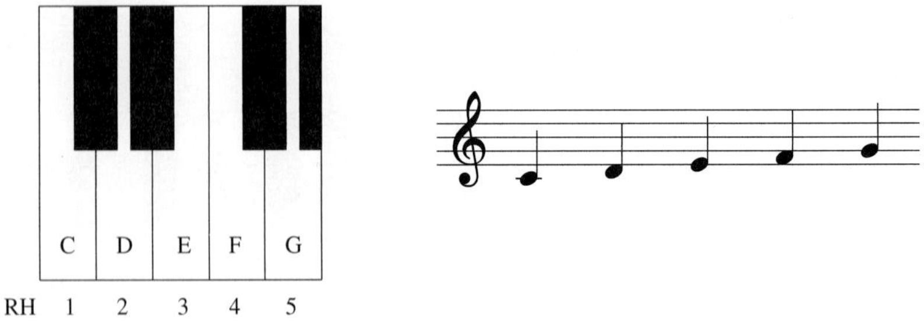

D Major Five- Finger Pattern

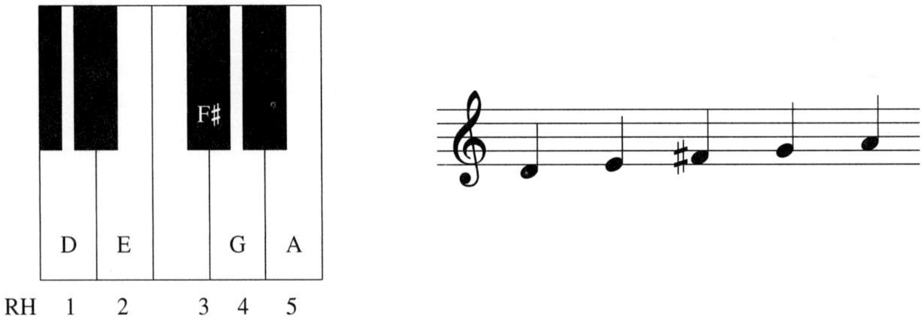

F Major Five- Finger Pattern

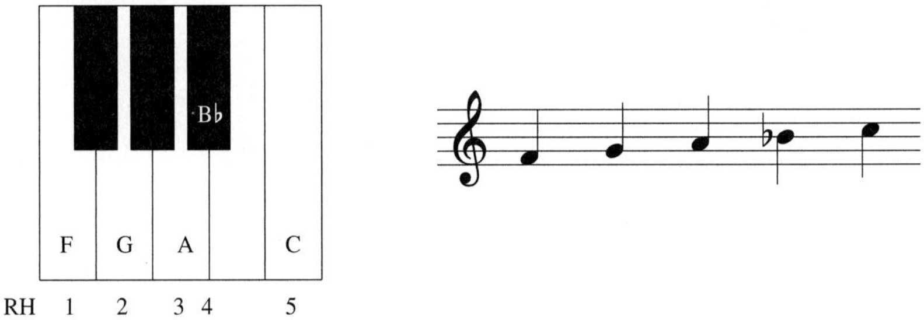

G Major Five- Finger Pattern

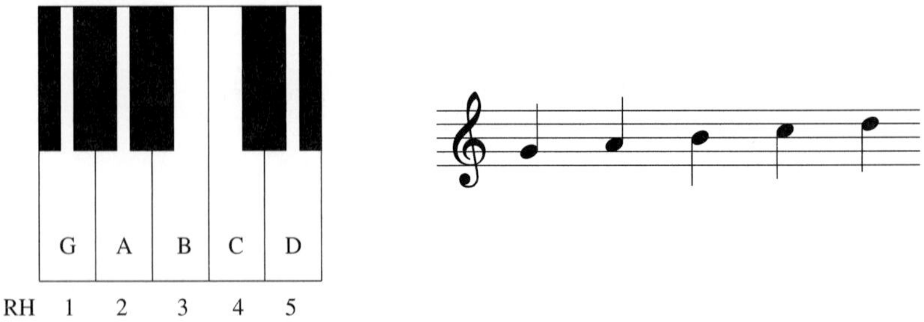

Minor Five-Finger Patterns

The minor five-finger pattern includes five pitches with the following whole- and half-step distances between keys:

1 — 2 — 3 — 4 — 5

Whole Half Whole Whole

The following minor five-finger patterns are sometimes used in simple melodies:

A Minor Five- Finger Pattern

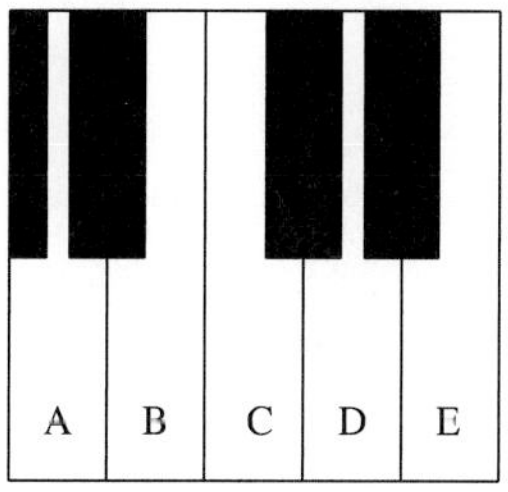

RH 1 2 3 4 5

D Minor Five- Finger Pattern

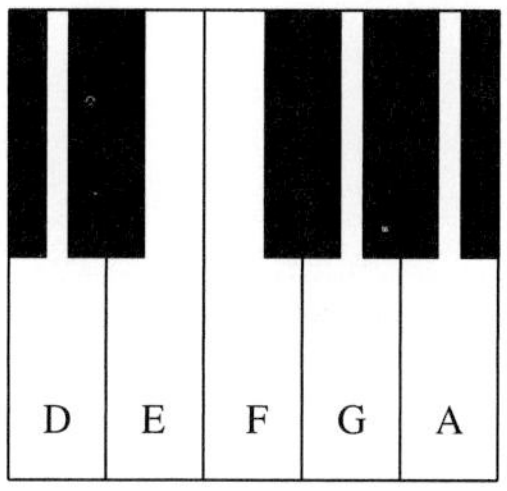

RH 1 2 3 4 5

E Minor Five- Finger Pattern

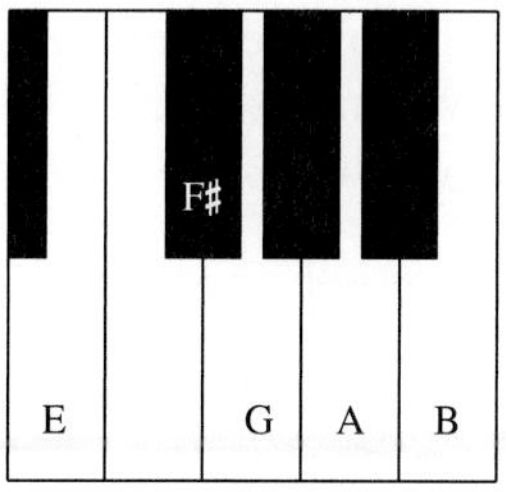

RH 1 2 3 4 5

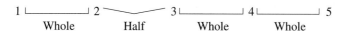

MELODIES USING THE FIVE-FINGER PATTERNS

A list of melodies that can be performed in the five-finger patterns follows. (For specific five-finger patterns refer to the preceding charts. Songs are found in Section Four unless indicated.)

C Major Five-Finger Pattern	*Chords*
"Down Came a Lady"	C
"Pease Porridge Hot"	C
"Swing a Lady"	C
"Go Tell Aunt Rhody"	C, G7
"Love Somebody"	C, G7
"Jim-Along, Josie"	C, G7
"Hey, Lidee"	C, G7
"My Dreydl"	C, G7
"When the Saints Go Marching In"	C, F, G7
"Wishy Washy Wee"	C, G7
D Major Five-Finger Pattern	
"Hop, Old Squirrel"	D, A7
"Matarile"	D, A7
D Minor Five-Finger Pattern	
"Dulce"	Dmin
F Major Five-Finger Pattern	
"Lady, Come"	F
"Fais Do Do"	F, C7
"Long-Legged Sailor"	F, C7
G Major Five-Finger Pattern	
"Who's That Yonder?"	G
"Hot Cross Buns"	G, D7, p. 270
"Mary Had a Little Lamb"	G, D7, p. 272

PLAYING MELODIES BEYOND THE FIVE-FINGER POSITION

Many melodies extend above and below the five-finger position. Some require expanding the hand to cover the additional pitches. For example, "Five Angels" (see Section Four) spans six pitches (C to A), requiring the expanded hand position.

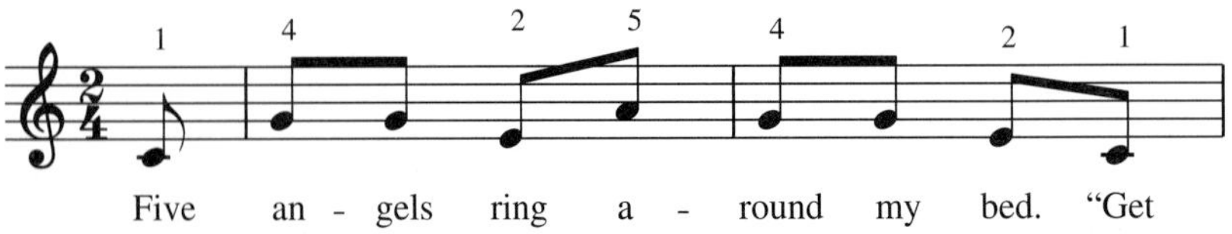
1 4 2 5 4 2 1
Five an - gels ring a - round my bed. "Get

Other melodies require crossover or crossunder fingering or both. The first part of "Joy to the World" (see Section Four) descends eight pitches and needs crossover fingering.

JOY TO THE WORLD

Fingering for melodies must fit the shape and scope of the melody. Choose a fingering that requires as little motion as possible and is consistent. Avoid placing the same thumb or finger on two consecutive notes, and try not to use the thumb on a black key. For most piano playing, unless otherwise indicated, move from one pitch to another in a smooth, connected style (legato) by lifting one finger just as the next finger strikes.

PLAYING CHORDS WITH THE LEFT HAND

The left hand often plays three or more pitches simultaneously (a *chord*) to accompany the melody. The names of the needed chords are indicated by letter names written above the melody (called "lead sheet" notation).

Triads

A *triad* is a chord with three pitches with the interval of a third between each pitch. Combining the first, third, and fifth pitches of the major five-finger pattern forms a *major triad.* For example, a C major triad includes the pitches C, E, and G. C is the *root* (strongest note) of the chord and gives the chord its name.

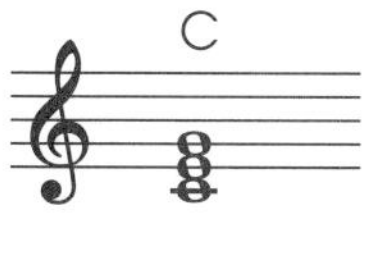

Seventh Chords

A *seventh chord* consists of four pitches again with the interval of a third between each. It is identified with a "7" following the letter name (e.g., G7).

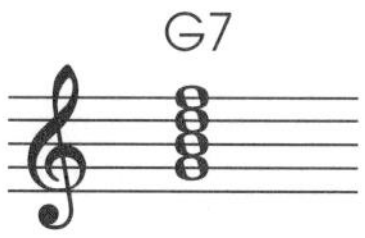

Chord Inversions

Many melodies are accompanied by more than one chord. The physical movement of changing from one chord to another needs to be as smooth and easy as possible. Therefore, pitches in a chord are often rearranged for ease in playing, as shown on the chart "Piano Position Chords in Selected Major Keys," starting on the next page.

Pitches in a specific triad can be played in any arrangement, *inversion,* as long as the original pitches are retained. For example, the C major chord can be played C–E–G or E–G–C or G–C–E. Similarly, the F major chord can be rearranged as follows: F–A–C, A–C–F, or C–F–A.

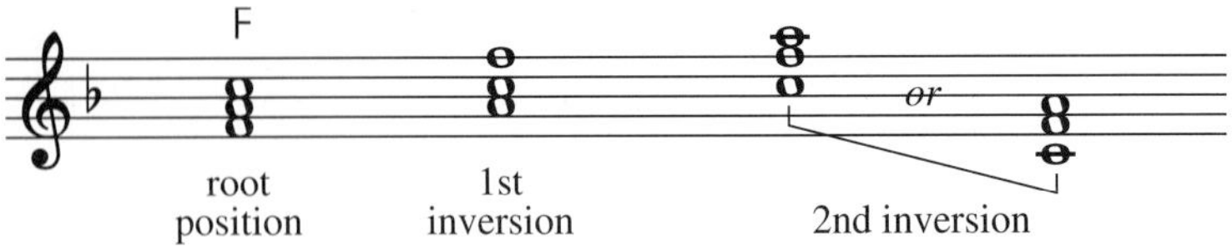

To make the seventh chord easier to play, when the chord is inverted, a note is omitted. For example, the G7 chord (G–B–D–F) is frequently played B–D–F–G, with the D omitted:

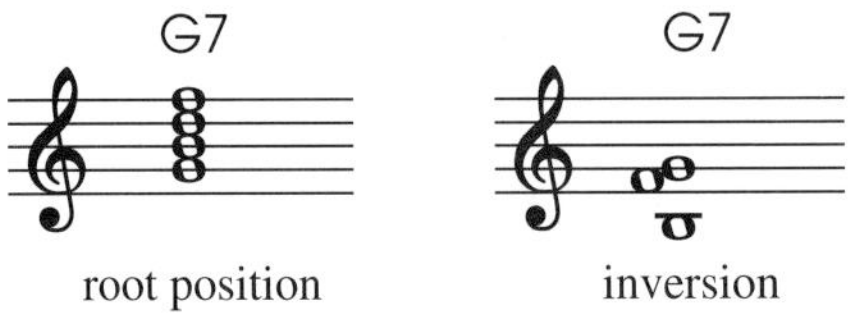

Chord Accompaniments

When all three chord tones are played simultaneously, the result is a block chord. Block chords can serve as an accompaniment to a melody, although other versions of chords are possible. The chords presented in the preceding notated examples are all written as block chords.

To determine which chords to play, locate the uppercase letters above the melody line. These letters specify the chord name (or *root*) of the different chords used in a melody, its quality (i.e., major, minor, seventh), and when each chord occurs. The player should continue playing (rhythmically) the chord until a different chord is indicated. For example, when a single chord name is shown only once at the beginning of a one-chord melody, the player should repeat the chord throughout—probably on the first beat of each measure.

PIANO POSITION CHORDS IN SELECTED MAJOR KEYS

Key of C Major

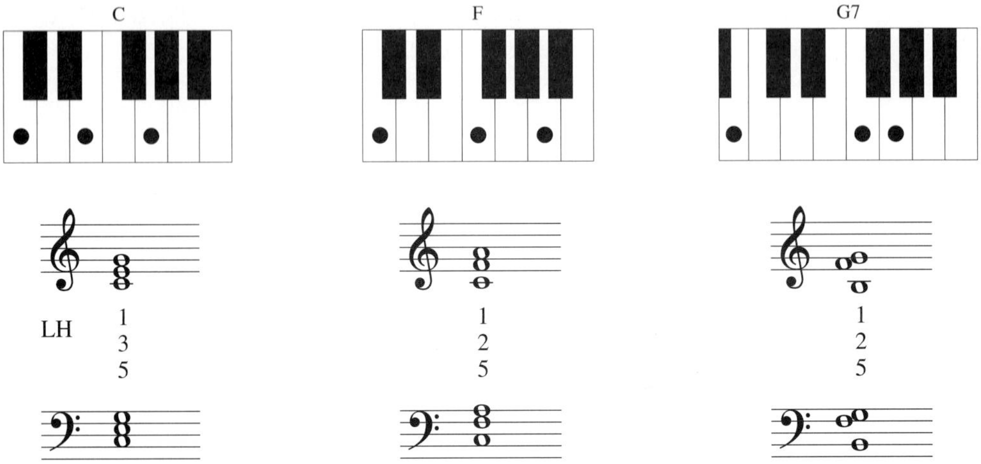

Key of G Major

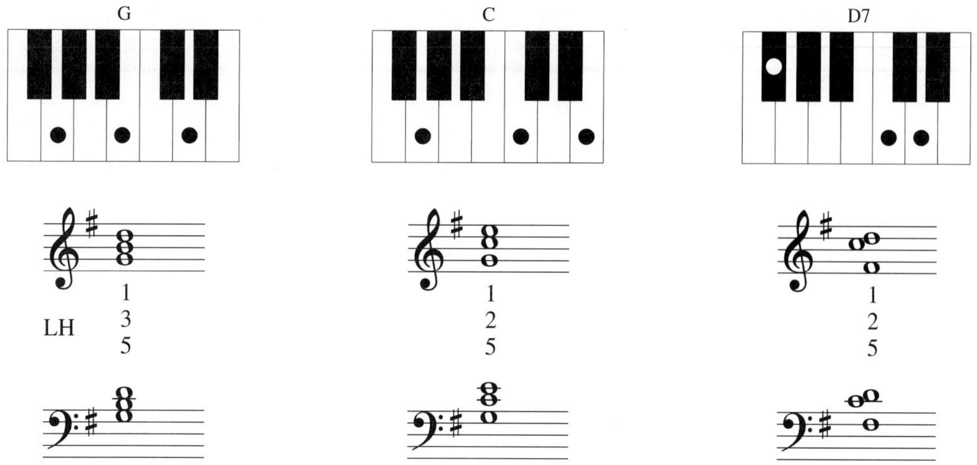

Key of D Major

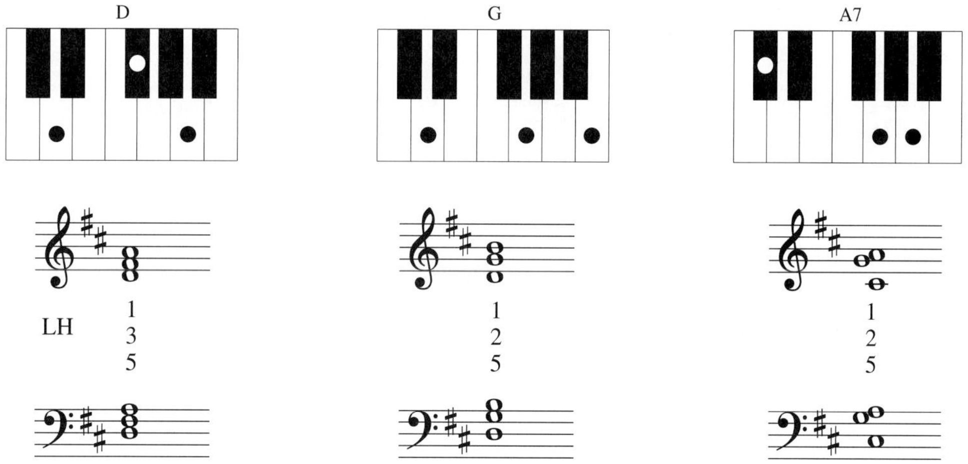

Key of A Major

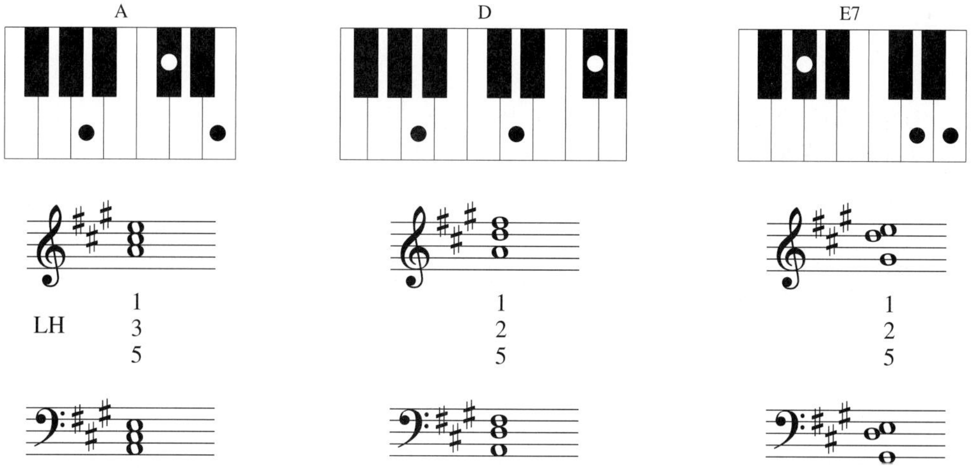

Key of F Major

F

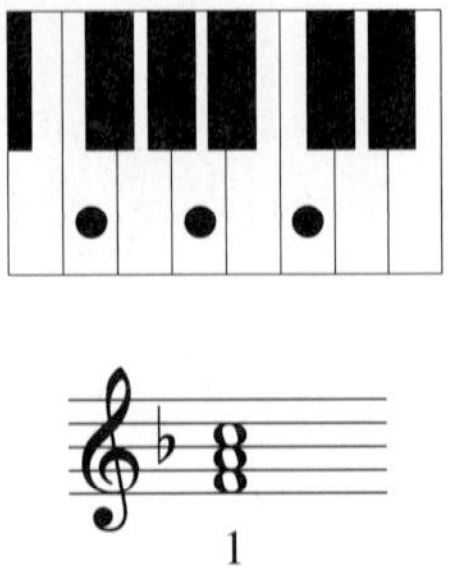

LH 1 3 5

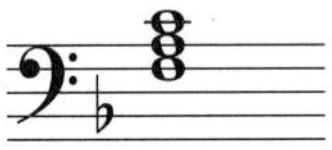

B♭

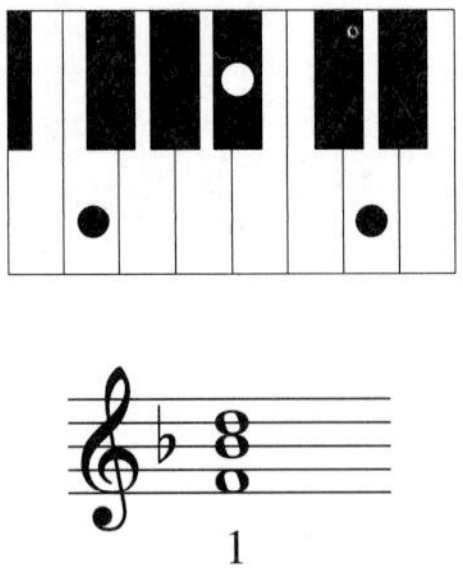

1 2 5

C7

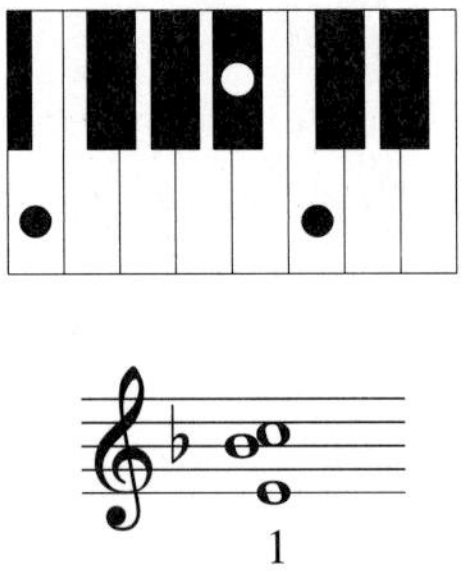

1 2 5

Key of B♭ Major

B♭

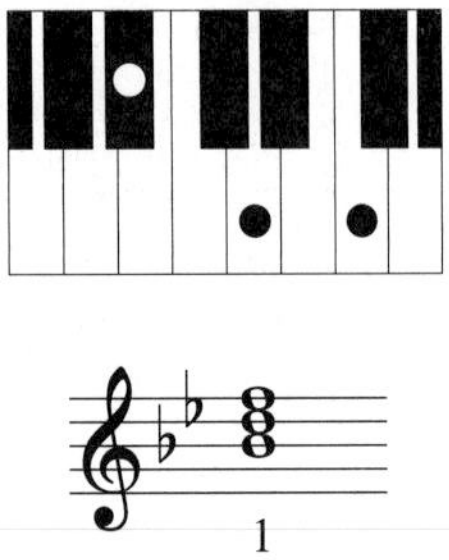

LH 1 3 5

E♭

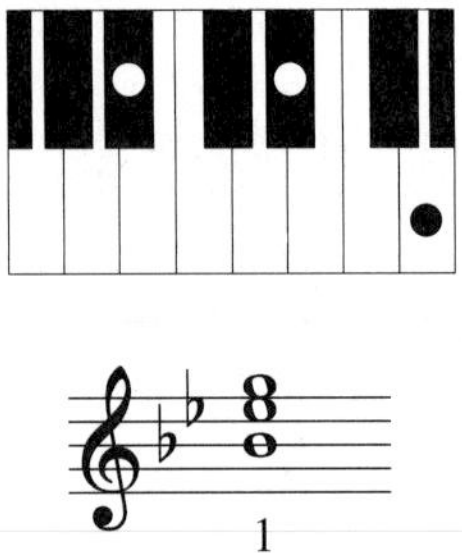

1 2 5

F7

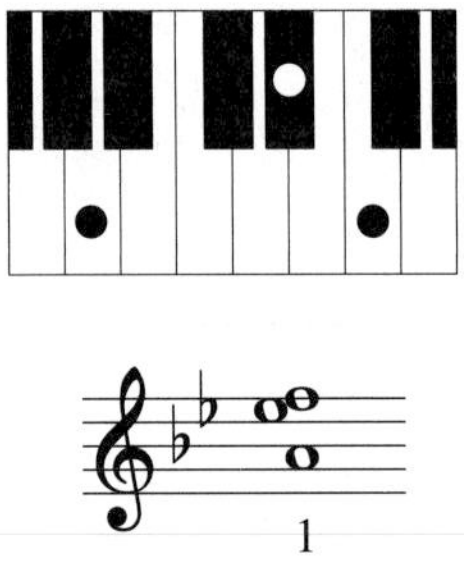

1 2 5

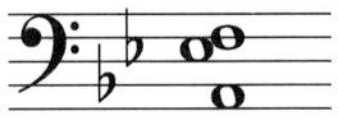

Key of E♭ Major

E♭

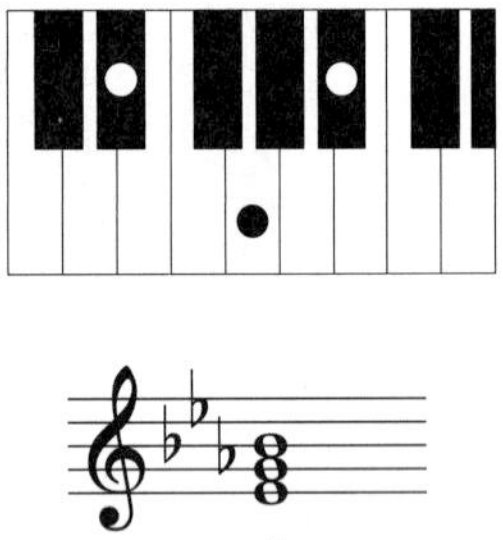

LH 1 3 5

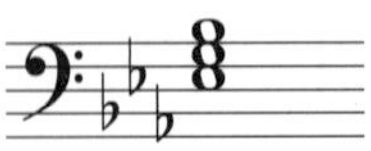

A♭

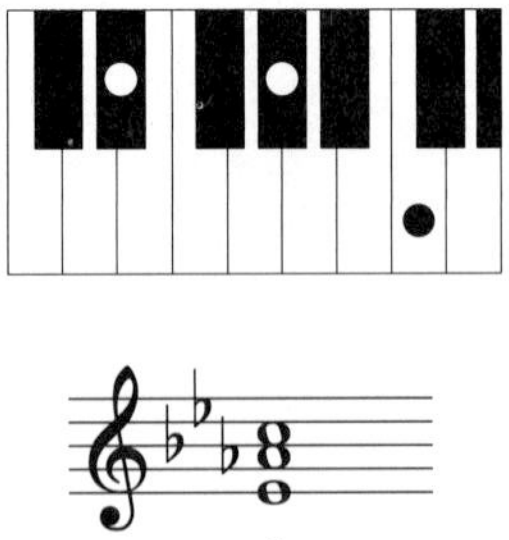

1 2 5

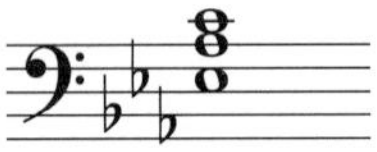

B♭7

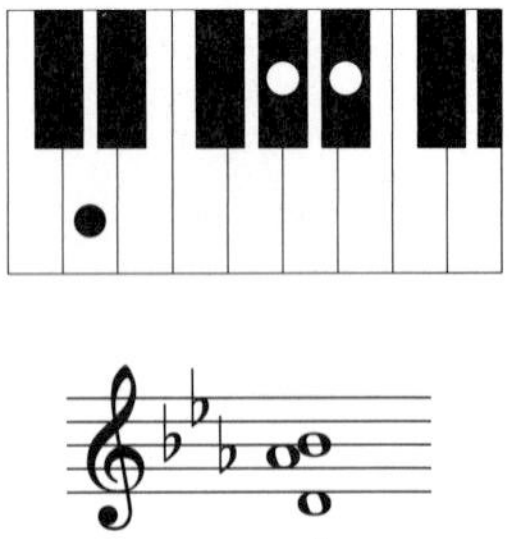

1 2 5

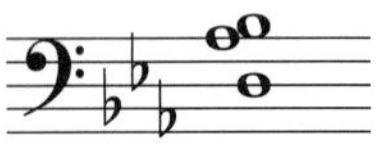

PIANO POSITION CHORDS IN SELECTED MINOR KEYS

Key of A Minor

Amin

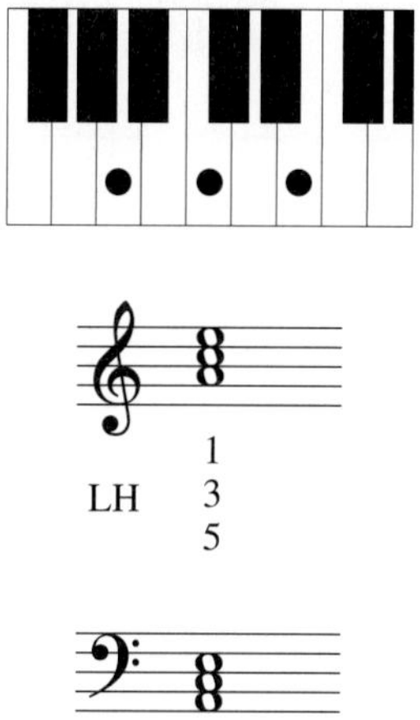

Dmin

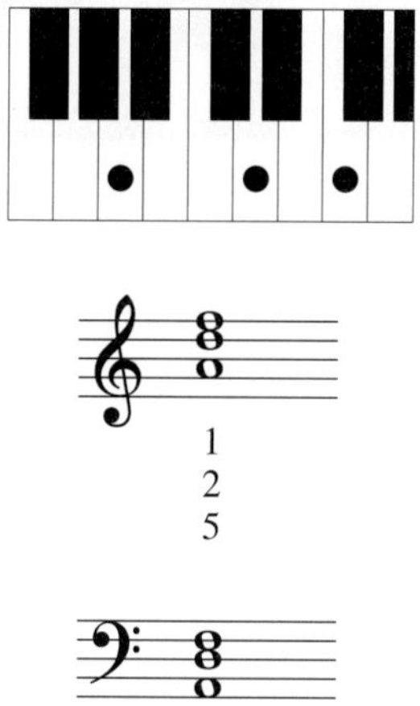

E7
LH
1
3
5
1
2
5
1
2
5

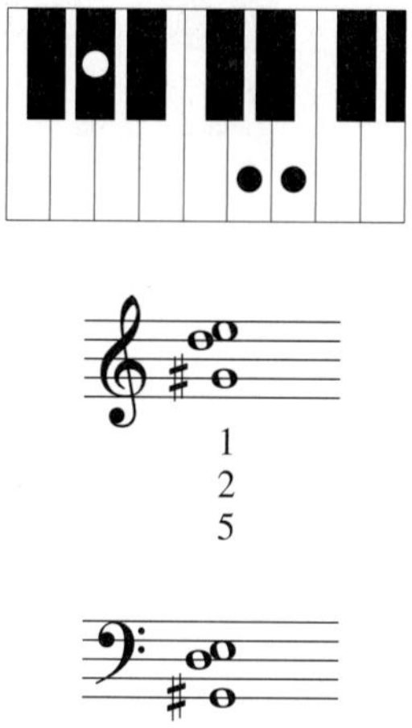

Key of E Minor

Emin

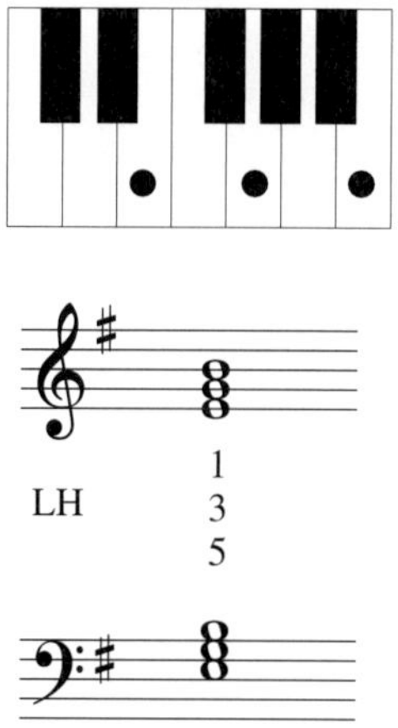

Amin

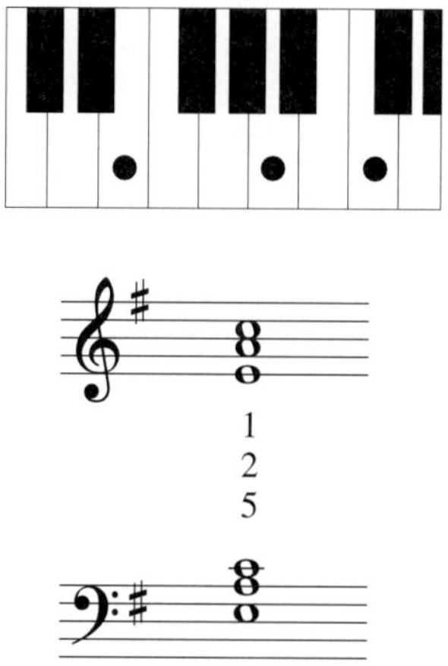

B7
LH
1
3
5
1
2
5
1
2
5

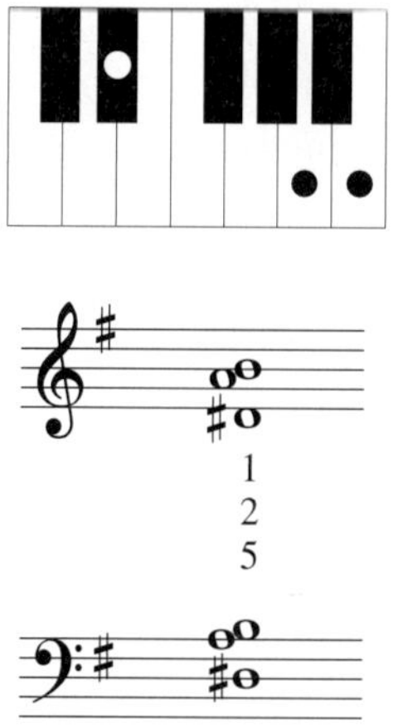

Key of G Minor

Gmin

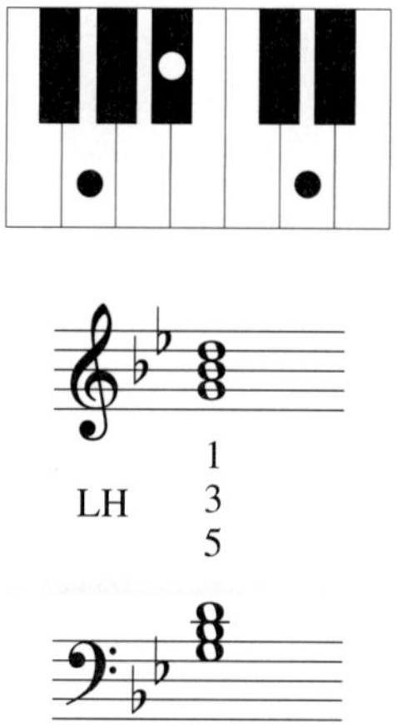

Cmin

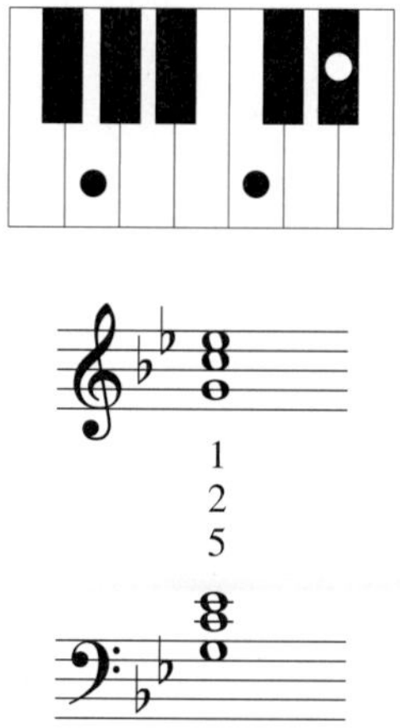

D7
LH
1
3
5
1
2
5
1
2
5

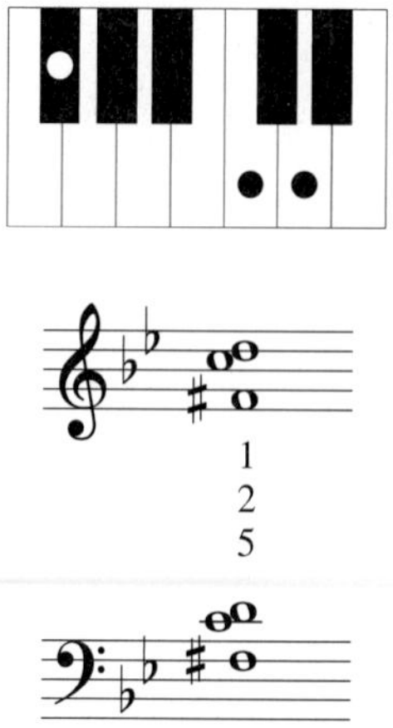

Key of D Minor

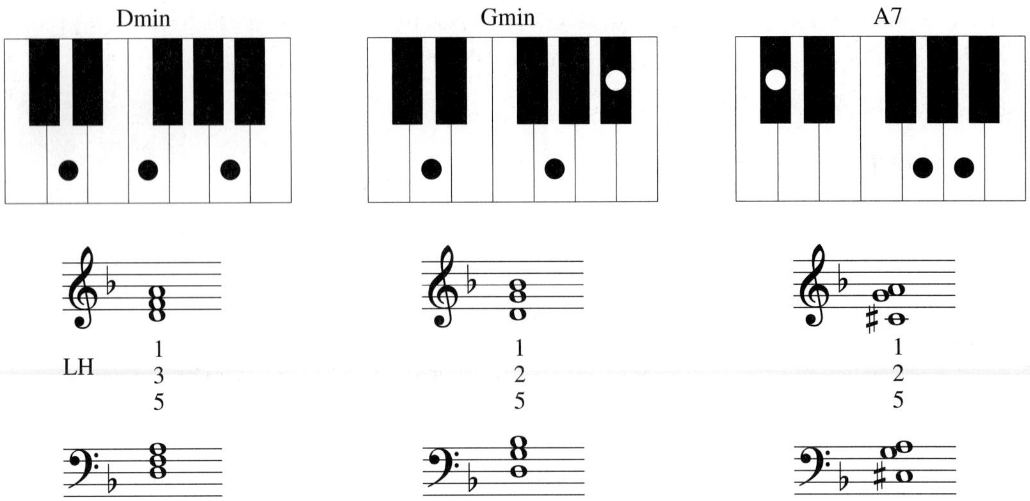

MELODIES REQUIRING KEYBOARD EXPERIENCE

The following melodies are challenging. Players with some keyboard experience might try these songs in the sequence given here. (Songs are found in Section Four.)

	Chords
"Kum Ba Yah"	C, F, G7
"Wishy Washy Wee"	C, G7
"Oh, Susanna"	F, B♭, C7
"Fais Do Do"	F, C7
"America"	C, F, G7
"This Is Halloween"	Gmin, D7
"Song for the Sabbath"	Dmin, Gmin, A7
"He's Got the Whole World in His Hands"	E, B7
"Dayenu"	C, G7
"We Three Kings"	Emin, Amin, B7, G, C, D7

The Recorder

The recorder is a flute originally made of wood and played in a vertical position. Widely used during the Renaissance, recorders are again popular after an early-twentieth-century revival. They are relatively easy to play for both teachers and students.

PLAYING POSITION

- Place the left hand (LH) at the top and right hand (RH) at the bottom. LH thumb covers hole on back and RH thumb is behind the fifth hole.
- Hold the recorder at a 45-degree angle away from your body, with arms relaxed and positioned close to the body and fingers curved.
- Place the mouthpiece between your lips and slightly in front of your teeth (between the teeth but not touching them).
- Close your lips around the mouthpiece, opening them slightly to take a breath.

BREATHING

- Try to produce a light, steady stream of breath—the control of the breath is important for playing "in tune."
- Blow more gently on low pitches and increase breath pressure on high pitches.
- Ration each breath to last through all the notes in a phrase, unless other directions are given. Blow gently on the first note of a phrase to help ration the breath.

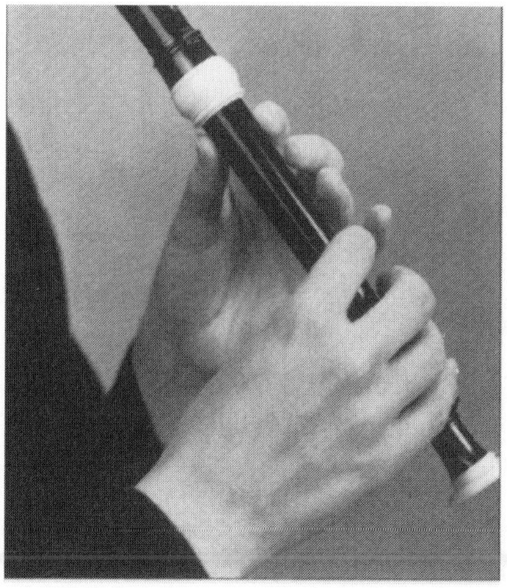

Picture 1. Correct hand position
Courtesy of Sweet Pipes, Inc., Forth Worth, Texas

Picture 1. Correct mouth placement
Courtesy of Sweet Pipes, Inc., Forth Worth, Texas

TONGUING

- Form the syllable "doo" with your tongue against the back of the upper front teeth (or the gums just above the teeth).
- Articulate each note separately—but keep in mind the goal of a steady stream of tone, *briefly* interrupted by the consonant *d* in "doo."
- End the syllable "doo" with the first half of the consonant *t*, as in "doot," for short notes (staccato, or detached).
- Play the group of notes on a single "doo," when two or more notes are slurred together (legato or connected) as shown by a curved line above or below the notes.

THE RECORDER FAMILY

Recorders come in several pitch ranges. The small soprano recorder has a brilliant tone and is high in pitch, whereas the alto recorder produces a softer tone and has a slightly lower range. The tenor recorder is lower in range than the alto and more mellow in tone. The bass recorder sounds the lowest pitches and produces a resonant tone. Because the soprano recorder is used mostly for melody playing and is commonly used in the schools, the following information pertains only to this recorder.

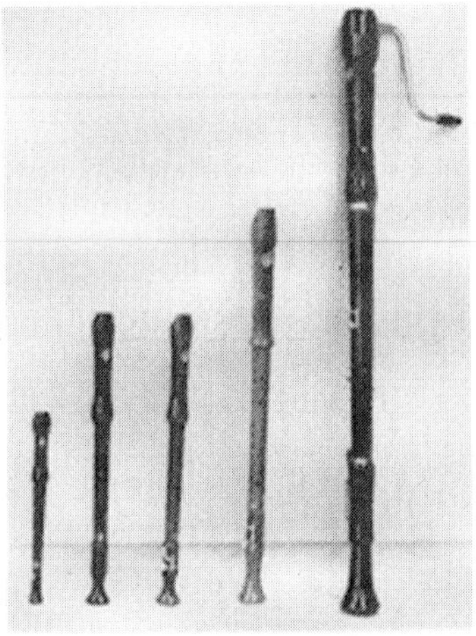

The recorder family (left to right): Soprano recorder, alto recorder without key, alto recorder with key, tenor recorder with key, bass recorder

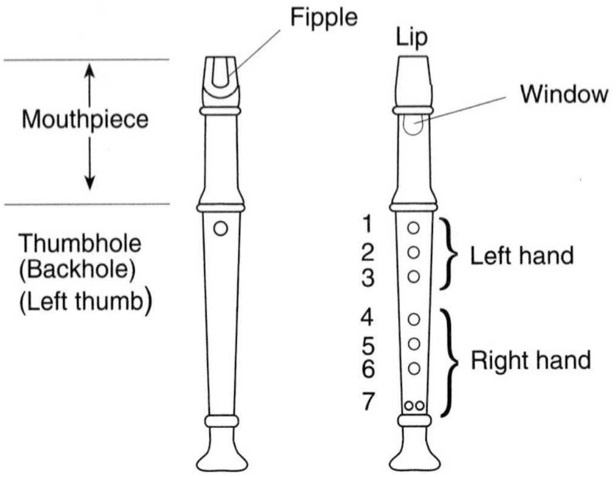

Soprano recorder (back and front views)

FINGERING CHART FOR SOPRANO RECORDER
Baroque (English) Fingering

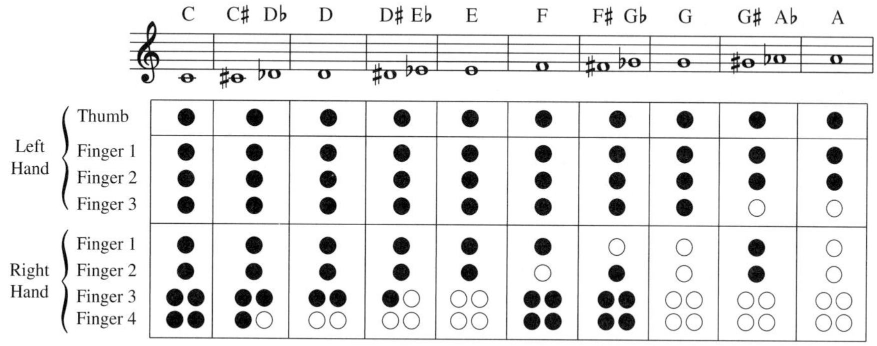

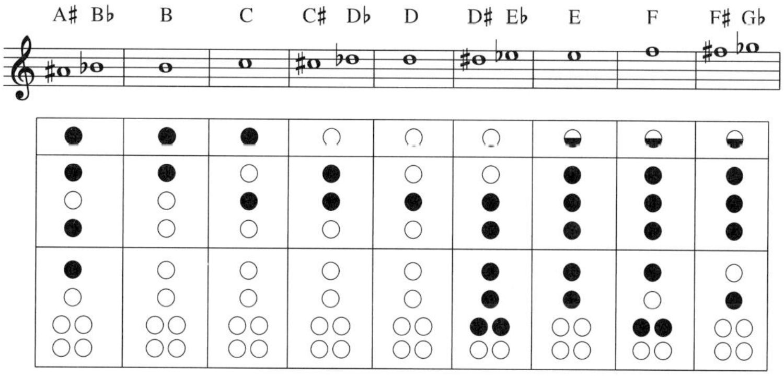

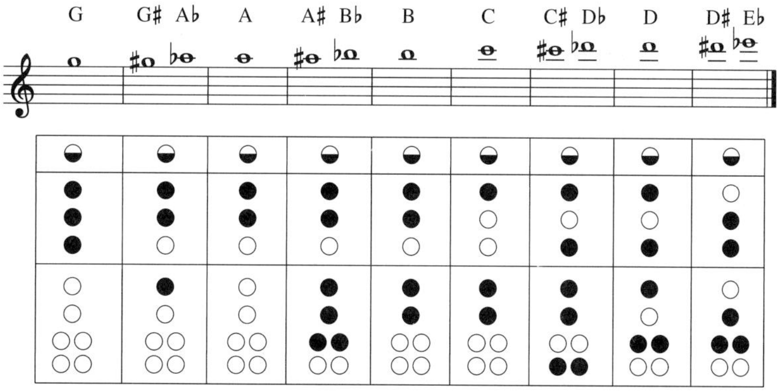

○ open hole   ● closed hole   ◒ slightly opened thumb hole

NOTE: The soprano recorder sounds one octave higher than written.

SONGS FOR SOPRANO RECORDER

Songs are presented according to a sequence of specific pitches as shown. (Songs are found in Section Four unless indicated.)

New Pitch	*Song*	*Pitches*
G, A, B	"Hot Cross Buns"	G, A, B p. 270
	"Trampin' "	G, A, B p. 271
	"Who's That Yonder?"	G, A, B
	"Counting Chant"	E, G
E	"Eena, Deena"	E, G
	"Yokuts Grinding Song"	E, G
	"Bobby Shaftoe"	E, G, A p. 271
	"Bye, Baby Bunting"	E, G, A
	"Rain, Rain"	E, G, A
	"Starlight, Starbright"	E, G, A

New Pitch	*Song*	*Pitches*
D (low)	"Charlie over the Ocean"	D, G, A, B
	"Circle Right"	D, E, G, A, B
	"Wake Me!"	D, E, G, A, B p. 272
F	"Bounce High, Bounce Low"	D, F, G
	"Pele E"	D, F, G
	"Dulce"	D, F, G, A
C (low)	"It's Raining!"	C, E, G, A
	"Ring Around the Rosy"	C, E, G, A
	"Twinkle, Twinkle Little Star"	C, D, E, F, G, A
	"Michael, Row the Boat Ashore"	C, D, E, F, G, A
	"My Father's House"	C, D, E, F, G, A
C (high)	"Ebeneezer Sneezer"	C, D, E, F, G, A, B, C
F♯	"Hop, Old Squirrel"	D, E, F♯
	"Hot Cross Buns"	D, E, F♯ p. 271
	"Over My Head"	D, E, F♯
	"Green Gravel"	D, E, F♯, G, B
D (high)	"Down in the Valley"	D, F♯, G, A, B, C, D
	"Mary Had a Little Lamb"	D, E, G, A, B p. 272
	"We Three Kings"	D, E, F♯, G, A, B, C, D
	"Choral Theme"	D, G, A, B, C, D
	"Scarborough Fair"	C, D, E, F, G, A, B, C, D
B♭	"Lady, Come"	F, G, A, B♭, C
	"Fais Do Do"	F, G, A, B♭, C
	"Hanukkah Song"	D, E, F, G, A, B♭, D
C♯	"I'd Like to Teach the World to Sing"	D, E, F♯, G, A, B, C, D
G♯	"Do–Re–Mi"	C, D, E, F, F♯, G, G♯, A, B, B♭, C
	"Yankee Doodle Boy"	D, E, F♯, G, G♯, A, B, C, D

HOT CROSS BUNS

English Song

TRAMPIN'

African American Spiritual

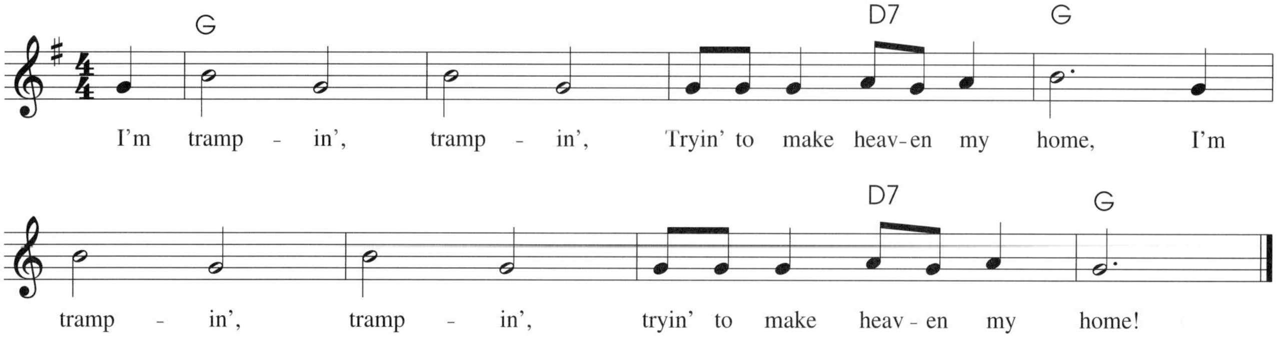

I'm tramp - in', tramp - in', Tryin' to make heav-en my home, I'm

tramp - in', tramp - in', tryin' to make heav - en my home!

HOT CROSS BUNS

English Song

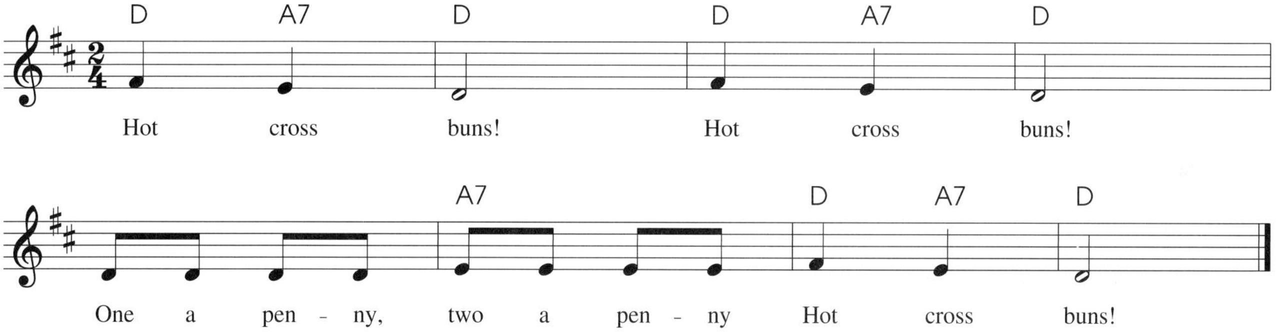

One a pen - ny, two a pen - ny Hot cross buns!

BOBBY SHAFTOE

Traditional

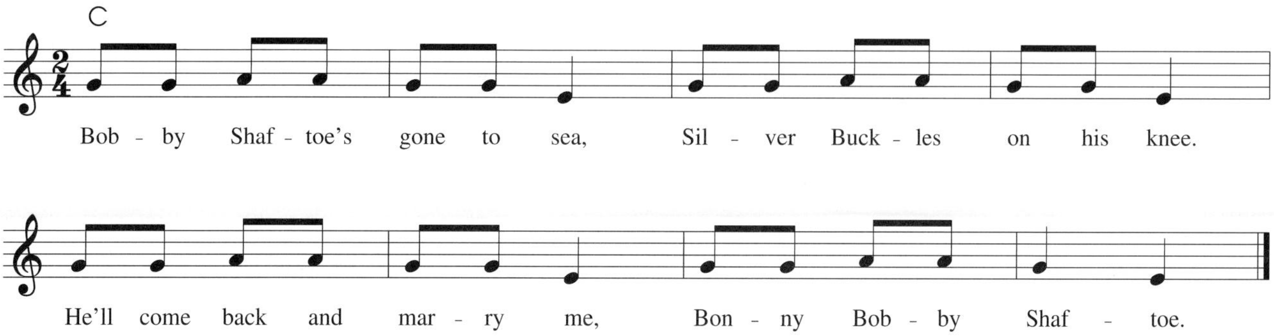

C
Bob - by Shaf - toe's gone to sea, Sil - ver Buck - les on his knee.
He'll come back and mar - ry me, Bon - ny Bob - by Shaf - toe.

See also "Eena, Deena" and "Counting Chant" in Section Four.

WAKE ME!

African American Song

G
Wake me! Shake me! Don't let me sleep too late. Gon-na
get up bright and ear-ly in the morn-in', Gon-na swing on the Gold-en Gate.

DOWN CAME A LADY

Traditional

G
Down came a la - dy, Down came two,
Down came old Dan - iel's wife and she was dressed in blue.

SWING A LADY

Traditional

G
Swing a la - dy um tum, Swing a la - dy 'round.
D7
G
Swing a la - dy um tum, Prom - e - nade a - round.

MARY HAD A LITTLE LAMB

Traditional

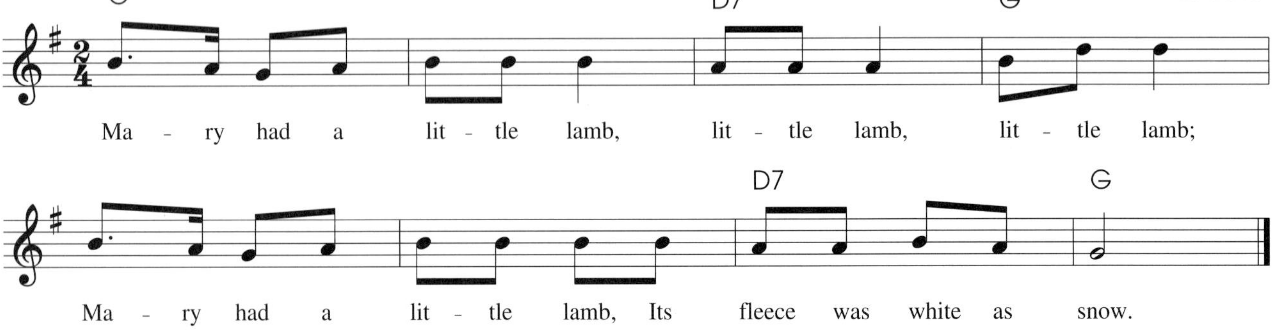

The Voice

The voice is an incredible instrument for expressing emotion through speech and song. In singing, as in speech, sound originates in an impulse that starts deep in the body and moves upward through the abdomen, the respiratory system, the vocal cords, and the resonating cavities in the head.

The many parts of the voice include a vibrator, an activator, resonators, articulators, and the breathing mechanism. The larynx ("LARE-inks"), located in the throat at the top of the trachea, or windpipe, is the voicebox. Inside the larynx are the vocal cords (narrow, elastic folds). The vocal cords are the *vibrator*—they vibrate when a column of air (breath pressure from the respiratory system) pushes through them. This breath pressure *activates* the voice. The inner surfaces of the larynx, throat, mouth, and nose are the *resonators,* which give the sound intensity and quality. The *articulators* (the lips, teeth, tongue, jaw, and palate) help modify vowels and form consonants.

BODY POSITION FOR SINGING

Correct body posture is essential for good singing.

- Posture lineup: ears over shoulders over hips over ankles. Balance weight on both feet with knees slightly flexed (not locked).
- Keep shoulders down, chest elevated, neck relaxed, and jaw loose.
- Position arms and hands at the side unless holding music. Hold music with raised arms, out in front of the chest.

BREATHING

Correct body position and posture place the lungs and rib cage in the proper position for breathing. Controlled use of the breath governs the steadiness and volume of sound.

- Breathe deeply (think of a deep, centered column of air) and try not to make a sound as you inhale. As the lungs fill with air and expand, the rib cage will expand in the front, side, and back, and the diaphragm (located just below the rib cage) will descend.
- Release the breath gradually and economically, and consciously control the release using the muscles of the abdominal walls and chest. As the air is released, the vocal cords (located at the Adam's apple) begin vibrating and creating pitch.

The pitch of a tone is determined by the vocal cords' thickness and length, and by the rapidity of their vibration. For example, to produce a high pitch, the vocal cords stretch, become thinner, and vibrate rapidly.

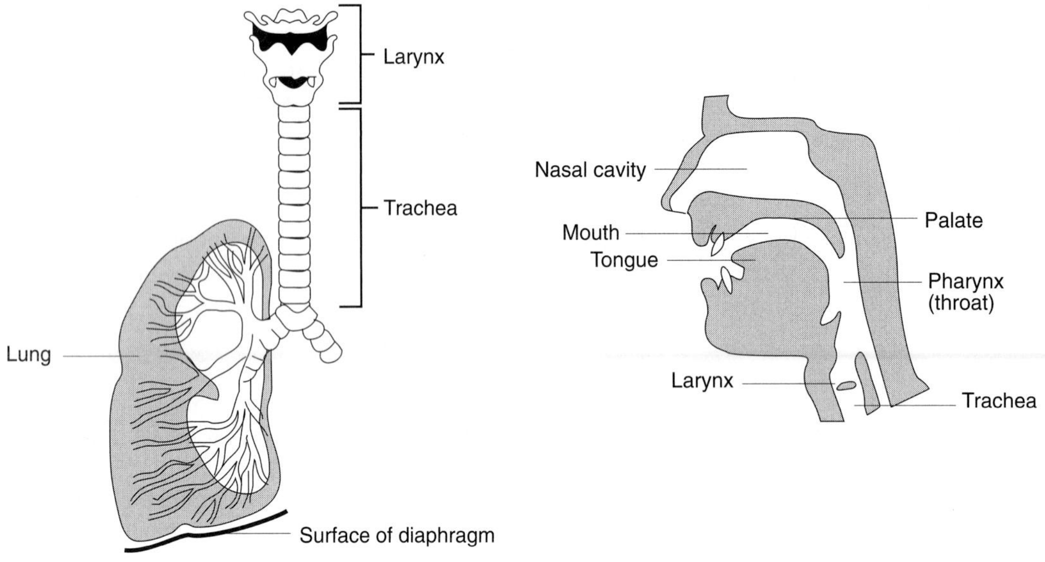

The Vocal Instrument

RESONATORS

The inner surfaces of the larynx, throat, mouth, and nose (resonators) give an individual voice its distinctive timbre. The tone is also affected by how vowels are produced.

- On a vowel, open the mouth at least one inch. The tongue lies forward in the mouth with the tongue tip touching the gums at the back of the front teeth.
- Sing and sustain (on a single pitch) each vowel: a, e, i, o, u. Evaluate the degree to which you produce a resonant tone, with accurate pitch and desired volume.
- Listen carefully and decide where you feel resonance in your larynx, throat, mouth, and nose.

ARTICULATORS

The lips, teeth, tongue, and jaw (articulators) all contribute to enunciation, which in singing is exaggerated beyond that of normal speech. (This is particularly true of Western art song and choral music.)

The articulation vocalise below combines vowels and consonants.

- Sing the vocalise, and punctuate the vowel sounds with short, precisely articulated consonants.
- Listen intently, to sing each pitch accurately and with the desired timbre. (Sing each scale tone, up to high C.)

ARTICULATION VOCALISE

RANGE

Range refers to the set of pitches extending from the highest to the lowest pitch that an individual can sing. The range (also the pitch and the timbre) of each voice depends upon the sex, age, and physical maturity of the singer. The following staff notation and keyboard diagram shows typical adult vocal ranges. Determine the highest and lowest pitches you can sing comfortably, then use the diagram to identify the vocal classification that is closest to your own range. (Information about children's voices is found in the section "Singing," in Chapter III.)

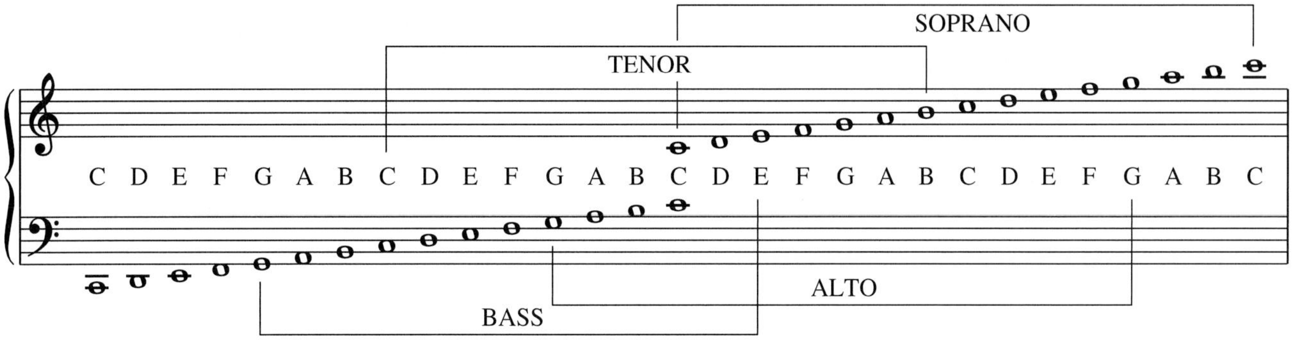

Section Four
Songs

ALL AROUND THE KITCHEN

African American Play Song

Call
Gmin
Response
G
All a - round the kit - chen, Cock - a - doo - dle, doo - dle, doo.
Call
Gmin
Response
G
All a - round the kit - chen, Cock - a - doo - dle, doo - dle, doo.
Call
G
Response
Now ___ stop right still, Cock - a - doo - dle, doo - dle, doo.
Call
Response
Put your hand on your hip, Cock - a - doo - dle, doo - dle, doo.
Call
Response
Let your right foot slip, Cock - a - doo - dle, doo - dle, doo.
Call
Response
Then ___ do it like this, Cock - a - doo - dle, doo - dle, doo.
Call
Gmin
Response
G
All a - round the kit - chen, Cock - a - doo - dle, doo - dle, doo.
Call
Response
G
All a - round the kit - chen, Cock - a - doo - dle, doo - dle, doo.

From Library of Congress Archives of Folksong, *tape 88*

AMERICA

Samuel F. Smith
(American, 1808–1895)

Arr. Henry Carey
(English, c. 1690–1743)

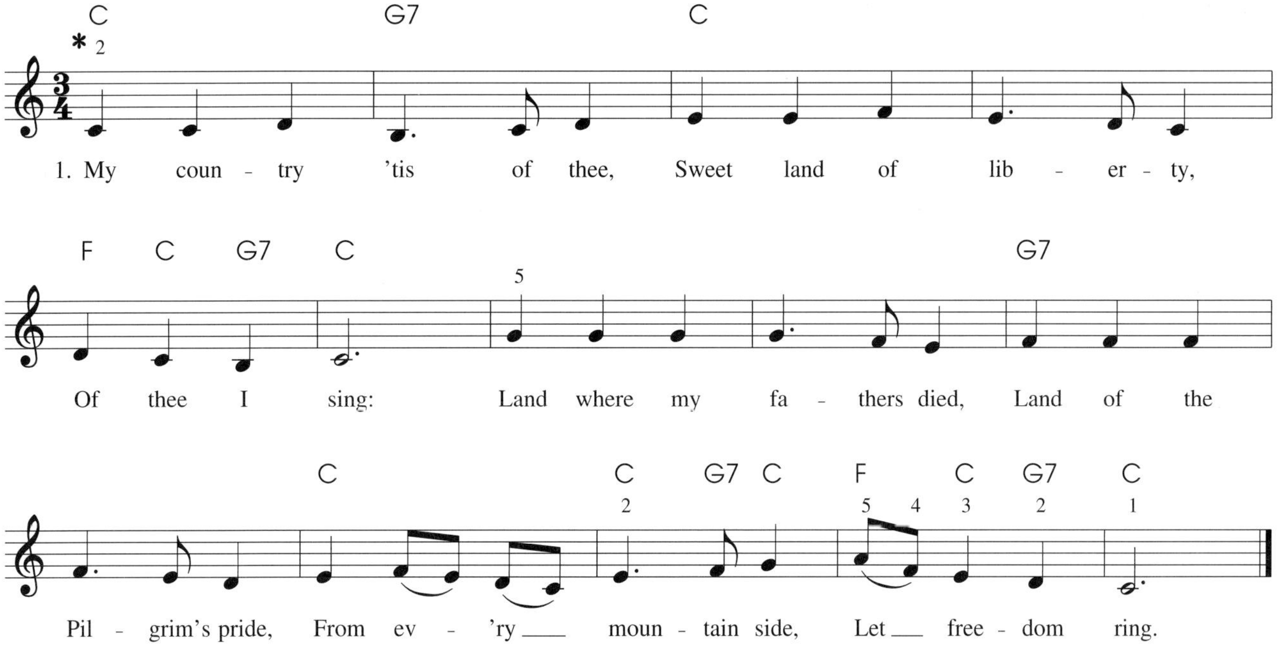
C G7 C
1. My coun - try 'tis of thee, Sweet land of lib - er - ty,
F C G7 C G7
Of thee I sing: Land where my fa - thers died, Land of the
C C G7 C F C G7 C
Pil - grim's pride, From ev - 'ry mount - tain side, Let free - dom ring.

* Small numbers indicate fingering for the keyboard.

2. My native country, thee, Land of the noble free, Thy name I love;
   I love thy rocks and rills, Thy woods and templed hills,
   My heart with rapture thrills, Like that above.

3. Let music swell the breeze, And ring from all the trees, Sweet freedom's song;
   Let mortal tongues awake, Let all that breathe partake,
   Let rocks their silence break, The sound prolong.

4. Our father's God, to thee, Author of liberty, To thee we sing:
   Long may our land be bright, With freedom's holy light,
   Protect us by thy might, Great God, our King!

On July 4, 1832, a choir trained by Lowell Mason gave the first public performance of what was then called "My Country 'Tis of Thee." Mason, who successfully introduced music into public school education, had lent a German songbook to Samuel Smith. Smith, a young divinity student, wrote a new patriotic American text for one of the hymns, apparently unaware of "God Save the Queen," its British counterpart.

AMERICA, THE BEAUTIFUL

Katherine Lee Bates
(American, 1859–1929)

Samuel Augustus Ward
(American, 1847–1903)

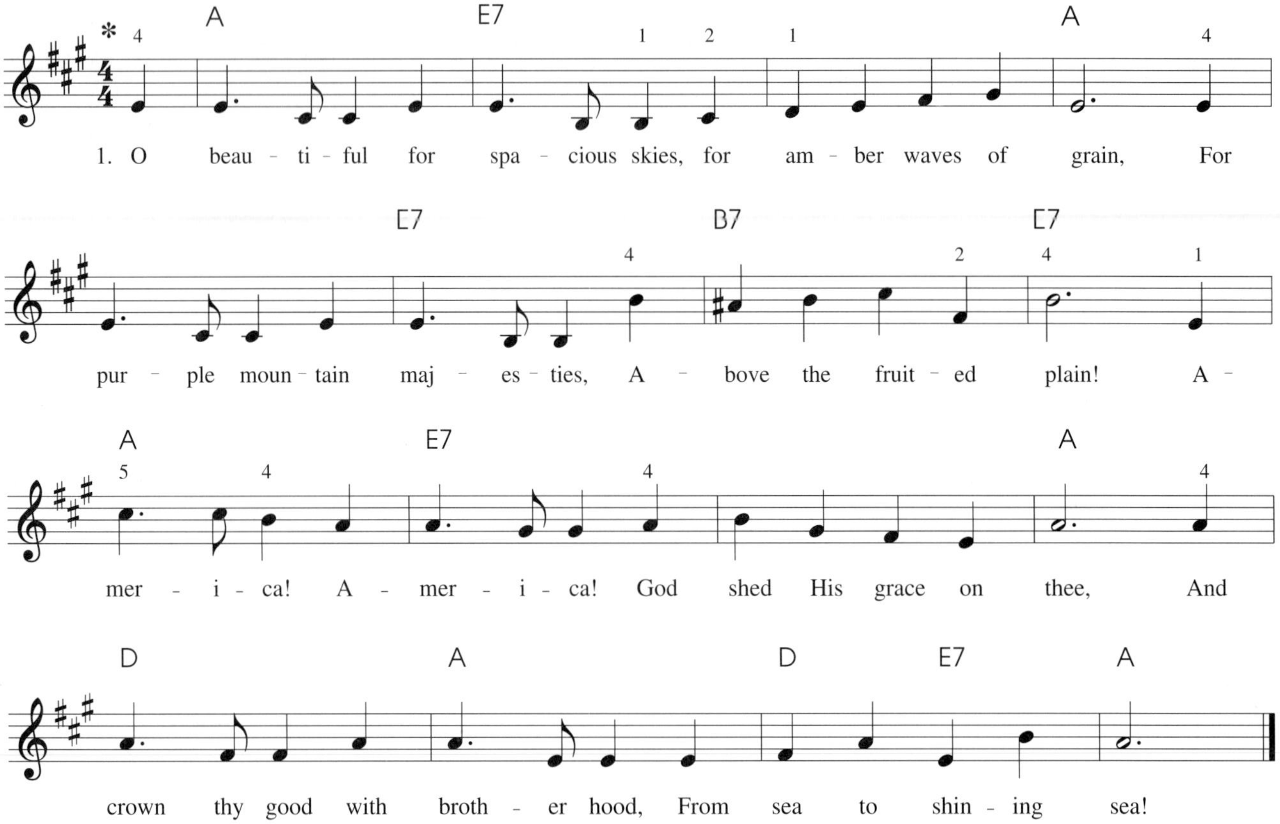
A E7 A
1. O beau - ti - ful for spa - cious skies, for am - ber waves of grain, For
E7 B7 E7
pur - ple moun - tain maj - es - ties, A - bove the fruit - ed plain! A -
A E7 A
mer - i - ca! A - mer - i - ca! God shed His grace on thee, And
D A D E7 A
crown thy good with broth - er hood, From sea to shin - ing sea!

* Small numbers indicate fingering for the keyboard.

2. O beautiful for pilgrim feet, Whose stern impassioned stress,
   A thoroughfare of freedom beat, Across the wilderness.
   America! America! God mend thine ev'ry flaw,
   Confirm thy soul with self control, Thy liberty in law.

3. O beautiful for heroes prov'd in liberating strife,
   Who more than self their country lov'd and mercy more than life.
   America! America! May God thy gold refine,
   Till all success be nobleness, and ev'ry gain divine.

4. O beautiful for patriot dream, That sees beyond the years,
   Thine alabaster cities gleam, Undimmed by human tears.
   America! America! God shed His grace on thee,
   And crown thy good with brotherhood, From sea to shining sea!

Inspired by a visit to the big sky country of the American West, a Wellesley professor of English wrote the poem she would later couple with the tune of an existing hymn. "America, the Beautiful" invites us to share the awe of Katherine Lee Bates more than eighty years after her journey to the summit of Pike's Peak

THE BATTLE HYMN OF THE REPUBLIC

Julia Ward Howe
(American, 1819–1910)

William Steffe
(American, 1830–c. 1890)

(See next page.)

Julia Ward Howe visited wartime Washington, D.C., a frenzied and frightening place. After inadvertently witnessing a battle at a nearby army camp, Howe returned to her hotel. There she penned—in just a few hours—the now-famous verses set to an existing hymn tune of William Steffe. Published in 1862, "The Battle Hymn of the Republic" quickly became a favorite with the Union army.

THE BATTLE HYMN OF THE REPUBLIC

(countermelody for refrain)

2. I have seen Him in the watchfires of a hundred circling camps,
They have builded Him an altar in the evening dews and damps;
I can read His righteous sentence by the dim and flaring lamps,
His day is marching on. *Refrain*

3. He has sounded forth the trumpet that shall never call retreat,
He is sifting out the hearts of men before His judgment seat,
Oh, be swift, my soul, to answer Him, be jubilant, my feet,
Our God is marching on. *Refrain*

BINGO

Model Experience and Game, p. 166

American Folk Song

BOUNCE HIGH

Traditional

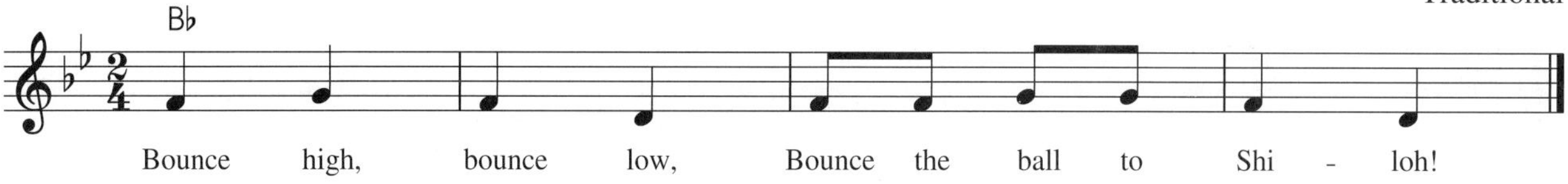

B♭
Bounce high, bounce low, Bounce the ball to Shi - loh!

BOW, BELINDA

American Folk Song

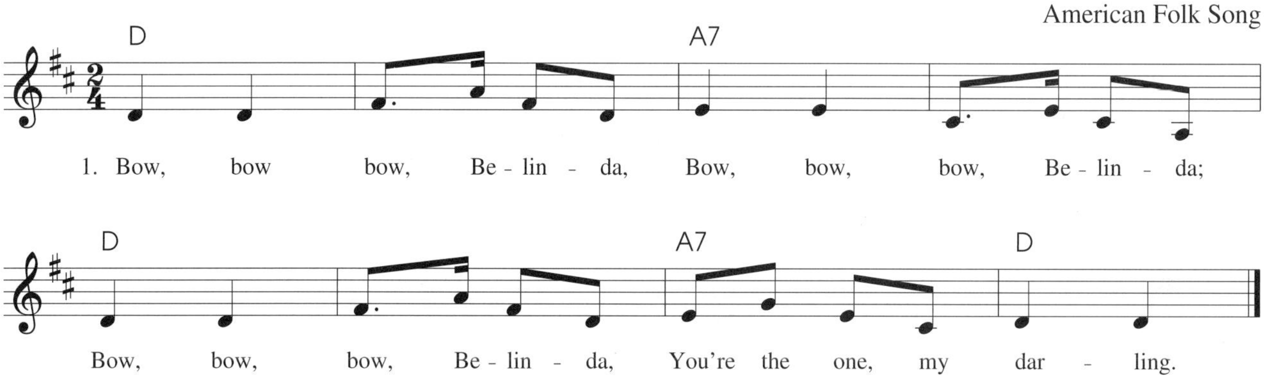

1. Bow, bow bow, Be - lin - da, Bow, bow, bow, Be - lin - da;

Bow, bow, bow, Be - lin - da, You're the one, my dar - ling.

2. Right hand 'round, O, Belinda
3. Left hand 'round, O, Belinda
4. Both hands 'round, O, Belinda
5. Back to back, O, Belinda
6. Skip, O skip, O, Belinda

BYE, BABY BUNTING

Traditional

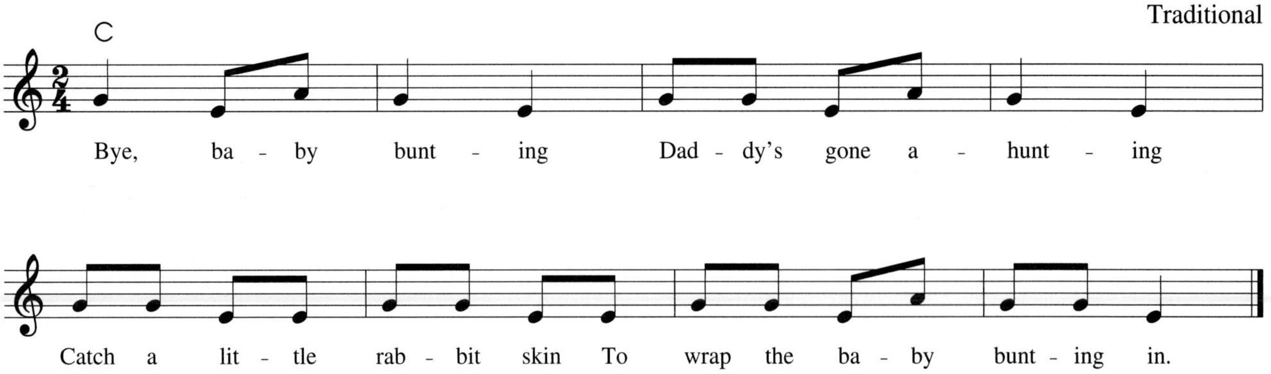

Catch a lit - tle rab - bit skin To wrap the ba - by bunt - ing in.

CANDLES OF HANUKKAH

Hebrew Folk Song

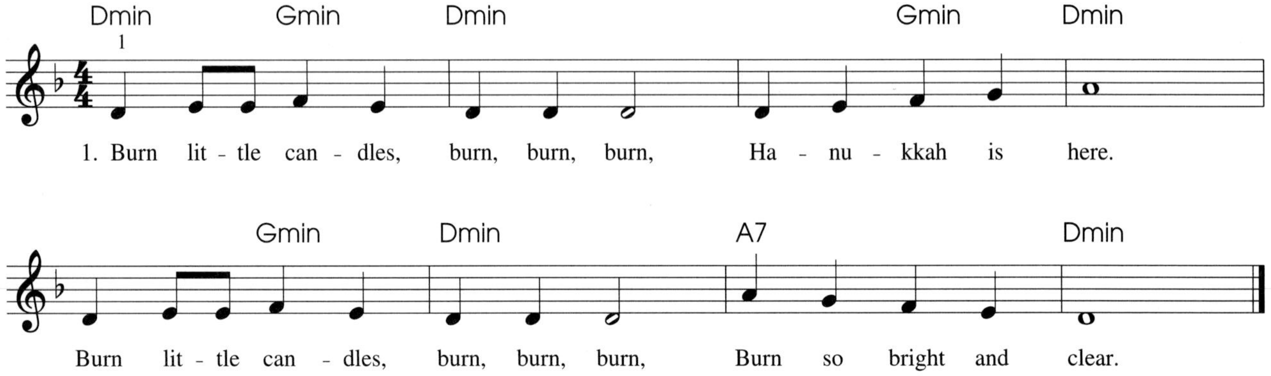

2. Eight little candles in a row, Hanukkah is here.
   Eight little candles in a row, Burn so bright and clear.

3. Dance, little candles, dance, dance, dance, Hanukkah is here.
   Dance, little candles, dance, dance, dance, Hanukkah is here.

CHARLIE OVER THE OCEAN

Traditional

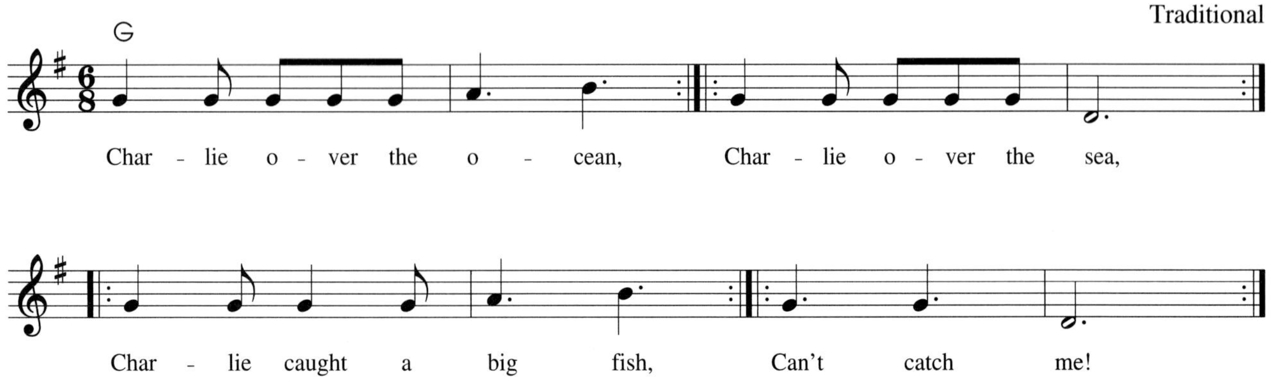

G
Char - lie o - ver the o - cean, Char - lie o - ver the sea,
Char - lie caught a big fish, Can't catch me!

CHATTER WITH THE ANGELS

Model Experience, p. 182

African American Song

Verse
F
1. Chat-ter with the an - gels soon in the morn-ing, Chat-ter with the an - gels, In that land.
Chat-ter with the an - gels soon in the morn-ing, Chat-ter with the an - gels, Join that band.
Refrain
I hope to join that band, And chat-ter with the an - gels all day long.

2. March with the angels
3. Walk with the angels
4. Dance with the angels
5. Skip with the angels
6. Spin with the angels
7. Shake with the angels
8. Drum with the angels

CHE CHE KOOLAY

Singing Game from Ghana

Call
Response
Call
Che che kool - ay.
Che che kool - ay.
Che che kof - ee - sah.
Response
Call
Response
Che che kof - ee - sah.
Kah - fee sah - lang - ah.
Kah - fee sah - lang - ah.
Call
Response
Call
Response
Ta - ta - shee lang - ah.
Ta - ta - shee lang - ah.
Coom - a - dye - day.
Coom - a - dye - day.

Game

Children form a circle around a leader. The leader sings the calls and makes the motions described below. The players in the circle respond by singing and imitating the caller. Players move constantly during the singing, twisting their bodies or bouncing up and down.

Che che koolay: Hands on head; all twist their bodies along with the beat as they sing.
Che che kofeesah: Hands on shoulders; twisting continues.
Kahfee sahlangah: Hands on waist; twisting continues.
Tatashee langah: Hands on knees; all change to an up-and-down movement, bending the knees along with the beat.
Coomadyeday: Hands on ankles; up-and-down movement continues. Following the last word of the song, players jump as they shout "hey!"

CHORAL THEME

("Ode to Joy" from Symphony No. 9)

Friedrich Schiller
(German, 1759–1805)

Ludwig van Beethoven
(German, 1770–1827)

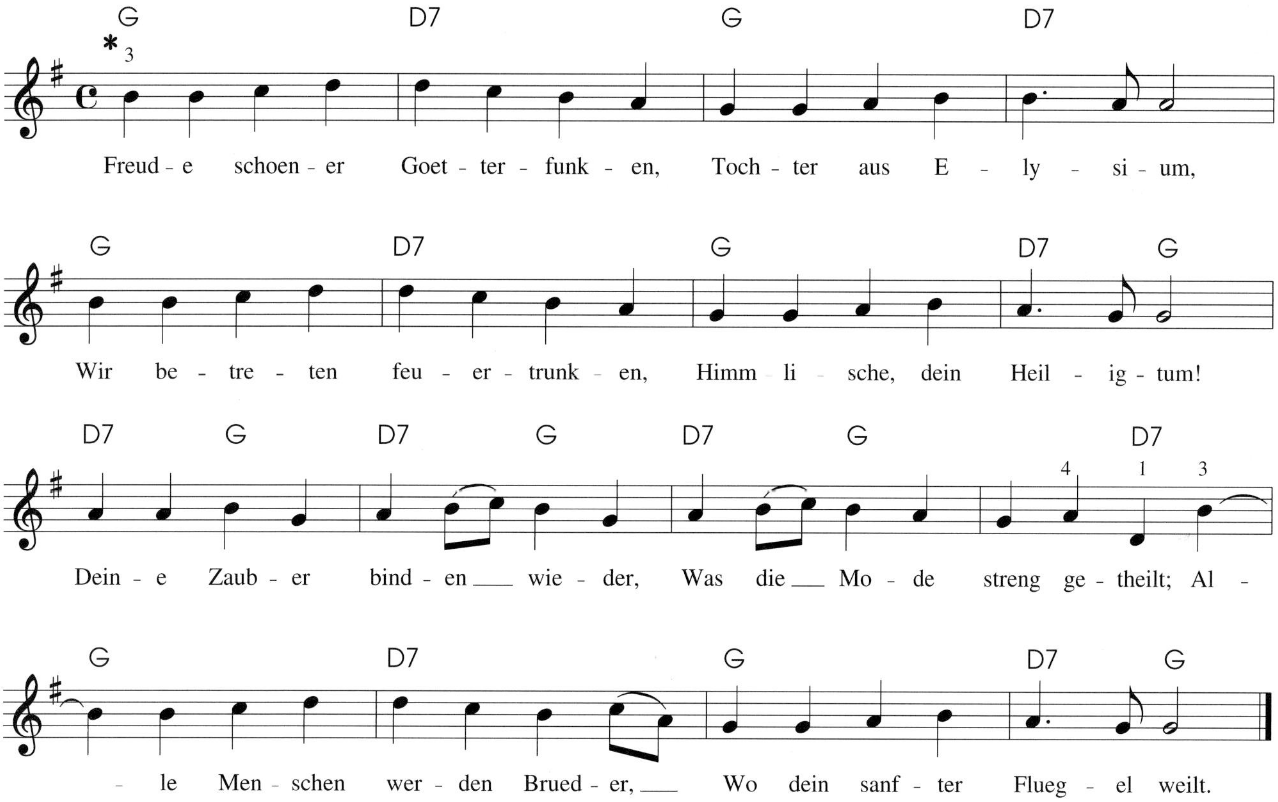

* Small numbers indicate fingering for keyboard.

1. Some ideas come and go, But true ideas will remain,
   Love's the source of all creation, Love is that which unifies.
   All one family, Yes, one family. Come let us live hand in hand.
   Man and nature are related - All is one and one is all.

2. When we learn and live this oneness, All will live in harmony;
   We are free when love is selfless, Love is for eternity.
   All one family, Yes, one family. Come let us live hand in hand.
   Man and nature are related - All is one and one is all.

Two ideas from Schiller's Ode are expressed in this Choral Theme and in Beethoven's choral finale of his Ninth Symphony—that joy unites all humankind and that the basis of joy is the love of God.

The English text shown above was created by students and teachers of The Wilhelm Schôle in Houston, Texas.

CIRCLE RIGHT

American Play-Party Song

G D7
1. Cir - cle right, do, oh do, oh! Cir - cle right, do, oh do, oh!
G D7 G
Cir - cle right, do, oh do, oh! Shake them 'sim - mons down.

2. Circle left, do, oh, do, oh! *(Sing 3 times)* Shake them 'simmons down.
3. Boys to the center, do, oh, do, oh! *(Sing 3 times)* Shake them 'simmons down.
4. Girls to the center, do, oh, do, oh! *(Sing 3 times)* Shake them 'simmons down.
5. 'Round your partner, do, oh, do, oh! *(Sing 3 times)* Shake them 'simmons down.
6. Promenade your corner, do, oh, do, oh! *(Sing 3 times)* Shake them 'simmons down.

CLAP YOUR HANDS

American Folk Song

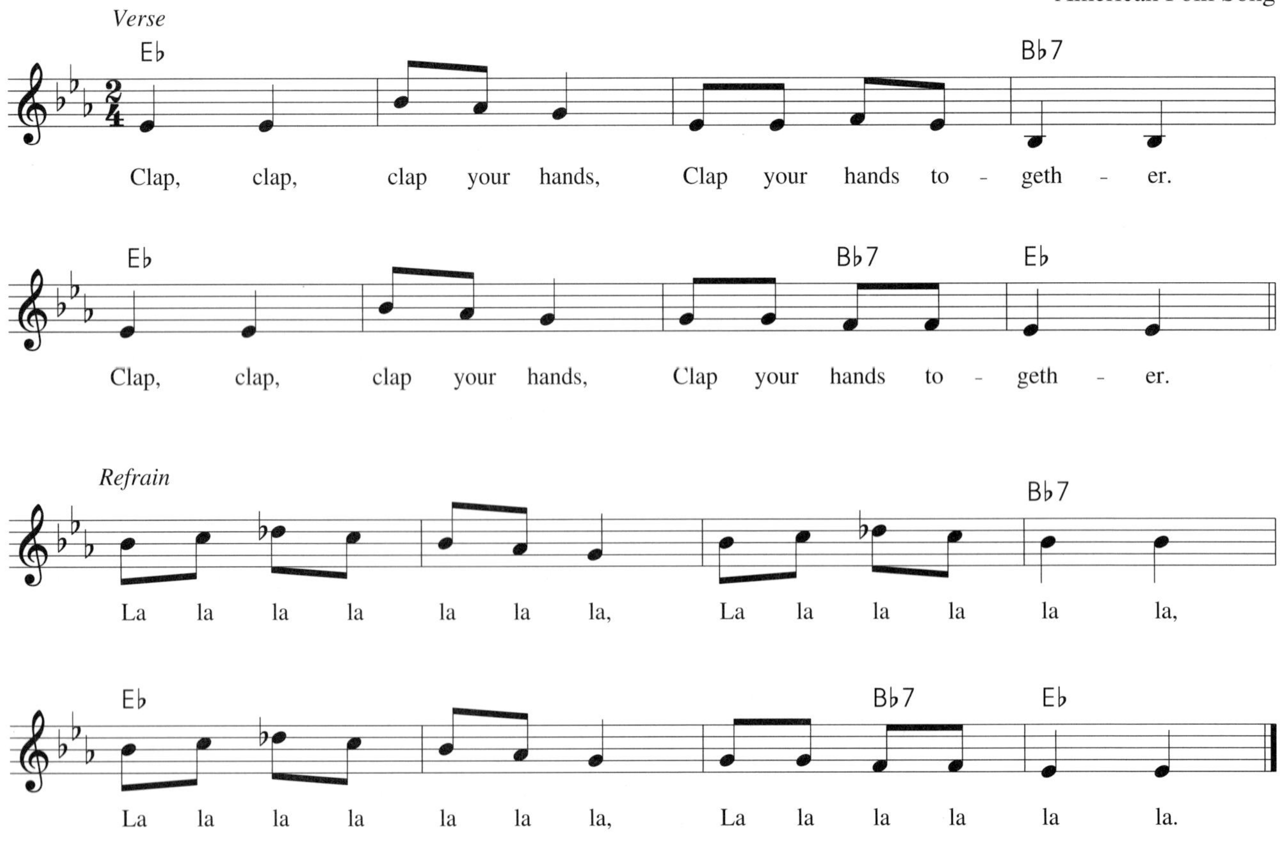
Verse
E♭ B♭7
Clap, clap, clap your hands, Clap your hands to - geth - er.
E♭ B♭7 E♭
Clap, clap, clap your hands, Clap your hands to - geth - er.
Refrain
B♭7
La la la la la la la, La la la la la la,
E♭ B♭7 E♭
La la la la la la la, La la la la la la.

COUNTING CHANT

Traditional Chant

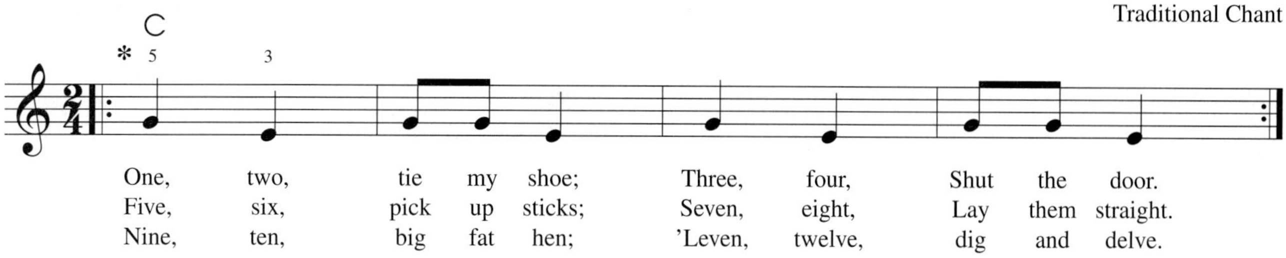
C
✻ 5 3
One, two, tie my shoe; Three, four, Shut the door.
Five, six, pick up sticks; Seven, eight, Lay them straight.
Nine, ten, big fat hen; 'Leven, twelve, dig and delve.

✻ Small numbers indicate fingering for keyboard.

THE CUCKOO

Austrian Folk Melody

Verse
F C7
1. Oh, I went down to the wood-land brook, Where the wa - ter's so
F C7
good: And I heard there the cuck - oo, As she called from the
F
wood.
Refrain
C7 F C7
Ho - le - ah ho - le-ra - hi - hi - ah, Ho - le-rah, cuck-oo,
F
Ho - le-ra - hi - hi - ah, Ho - le-rah, cuck - oo, ho - le-rah - hi - hi - ah,
C7 F
Ho - le - rah cuck - oo, Ho - le - rah - hi - hi - ah - ho.

2. After Easter come sunny days, That will melt all the snow;
Then I'll marry my maiden fair, We'll be happy I know. *Refrain*

3. When I've married my maiden fair, What then can I desire;
Oh, a home for her tending, And some wood for the fire. *Refrain*

DAYENU*

Hebrew Passover Song

Verse
C G7 C G7 C G7 C G7
1. He has led us out of E - gypt, led His peo- ple out of E - gypt, He has led us out of E - gypt,
Refrain (gradually getting faster)
C G7 C C G7 C
da - ye - nu. Da - da - ye - nu, da - da - ye - nu,
G7 C G7
Da - da - ye - nu, da - ye - nu da - ye - nu da - ye - nu, Da - da - ye - nu,
C G7 C
da - da - ye - nu, Da - da - ye - nu, da - ye - nu da - ye - nu.

* *Dayenu* ("dye-AY-noo") means "It would have been enough."

2. He has given us the Sabbath, given us the holy Sabbath,
   He has given us the Sabbath, dayenu. *Refrain*

3. He has given us the Torah, given us the blessed Torah,
   He has given us the Torah, dayenu. *Refrain*

DO AS I'M DOING

Traditional

C
Do as I'm do - ing, Fol - low, fol - low me.
G7 C
Do as I'm do - ing, Fol - low, fol - low me.

DON GATO*

Margaret Marks

Mexican Folk Song (adapted)

Dmin C Dmin
1. Oh, Se - ñor Don Ga - to was a cat, ______ On a
2. "I a - dore you!" wrote the la - dy cat, ______ Who was
C Dmin
high red roof Don Ga - to sat. ______ He went
fluff - - y white and nice and fat. ______ There was
D7 Gmin
there to read a let - ter, meow, meow, meow, Where the
not a sweet - er kit - ty, meow, meow, meow, In the
A7 Dmin
read - ing light was bet - ter, meow, meow, meow, 'Twas a
coun - try or the cit - y, meow, meow, meow, And she
A7 Dmin
love note for Don Ga - to! ______
said she'd wed Don Ga - to! ______

* Don Gato ("DOHN GAH-toe") means "Mister Cat."

3. Oh, Don Gato jumped so happily
   He fell off the roof and broke his knee,
   Broke his ribs and all his whiskers, meow, meow, meow.
   And his little solar plexus, meow, meow, meow.
   "¡Ay carramba!" cried Don Gato!

4. Then the doctors all came on the run
   Just to see if something could be done,
   And they held a consultation, meow, meow, meow.
   About how to save their patient, meow, meow, meow.
   How to save Señor Don Gato!

5. But in spite of ev'rything they tried
   Poor Señor Gato up and died,
   Oh, it wasn't very merry, meow, meow, meow.
   Going to the cemetery, meow, meow, meow.
   For the ending of Don Gato!

Sing verse 6 slowly

6. When the funeral passed the market square
   Such a smell of fish was in the air,
   Though his burial was slated, meow, meow, meow.
   He became reanimated! meow, meow, meow.
   He came back to life, Don Gato!

DO–RE–MI

Oscar Hammerstein II
(American, 1895–1960)

Richard Rodgers
(American, 1902–1979)

* One group of singers can sing the small notes on "loo."

DOWN CAME A LADY

Traditional

C
* 1
Down came a la - dy, Down came two.
Down came old Dan - iel's wife and she was dressed in blue.

* Small numbers indicate fingering for keyboard.

DOWN IN THE VALLEY

American Folk Song

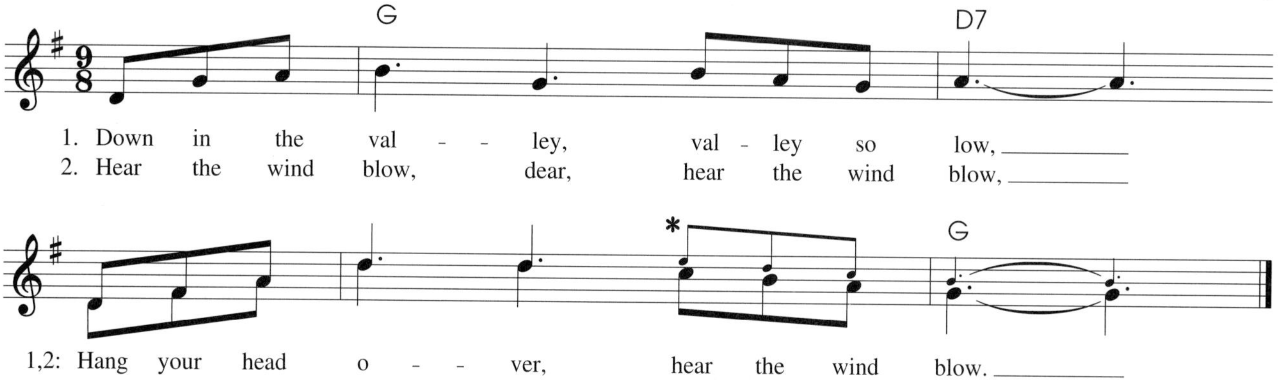

2. Hear the wind blow, dear, hear the wind blow, ______

1,2: Hang your head o - - - ver, hear the wind blow. ______

* One group of singers can sing the smaller notes.

3. Roses love sunshine, violets love dew,
   Angels in heaven, know I love you.

4. Know I love you, dear, know I love you,
   Angels in heaven, know I love you.

5. If you don't love me, love whom you please,
   Throw your arms 'round me, give my heart ease.

6. Give my heart ease, dear, give my heart ease,
   Throw your arms 'round me, give my heart ease.

7. Build me a castle forty feet high,
   So I can see her, as she goes by.

8. As she rides by, love, as she rides by,
   So I can see her, as she goes by.

DULCE*

Hispanic Children's Song

* *Dulce* ("DOOL-say") means "sweet."

** Small numbers indicate fingering for keyboard.

EBENEEZER SNEEZER

Model Experience, p. 178

Lynn Freeman Olson
(1938–1987)

* Small numbers indicate fingering for keyboard.

EENA, DEENA

English Chant

C
* 5 3
Ee - na, dee - na, di - na, duss. Kat - la, wee - na, wi - na, wuss.
Spit, spot, must be done, Twid - lum, twad - lum, Twen - ty one.

* Small numbers indicate fingering for keyboard.

ERIE CANAL

American Song

E - rie Ca - nal! She's a good old work - er and a good old pal,

in our day, Filled with lum - ber, coal, and hay, And we know ev - ery

(See next page.)

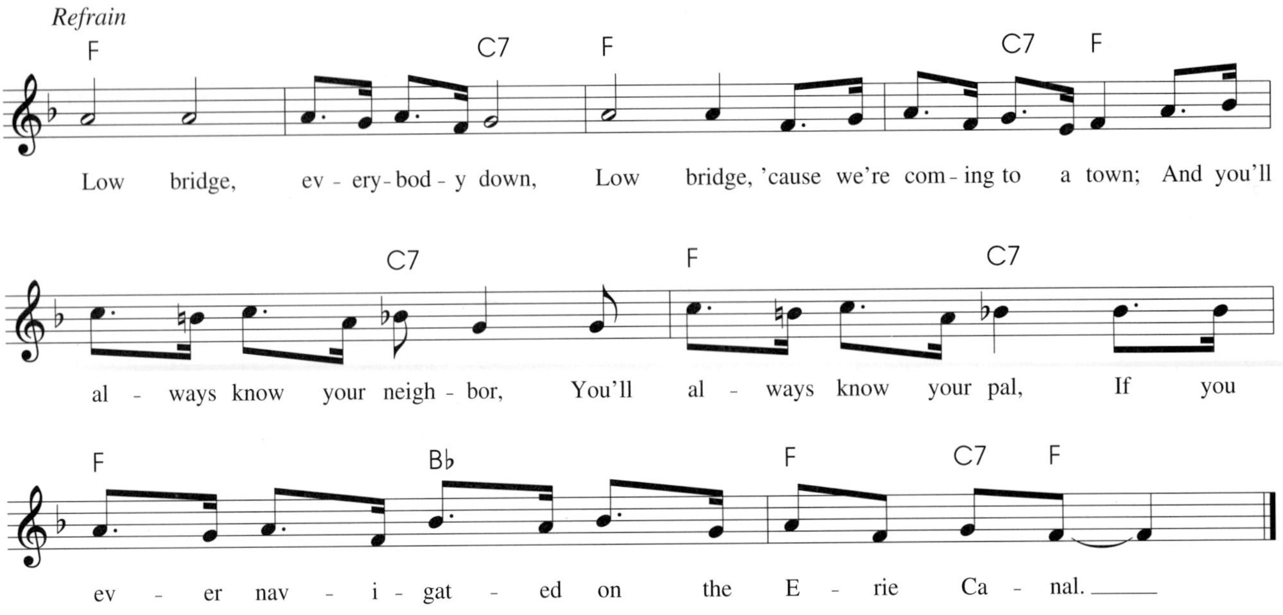
Refrain
F C7 F C7 F
Low bridge, ev - ery - bod - y down, Low bridge, 'cause we're com - ing to a town; And you'll
C7 F C7
al - ways know your neigh - bor, You'll al - ways know your pal, If you
F B♭ F C7 F
ev - er nav - i - gat - ed on the E - rie Ca - nal.

2. Git up there, Sal, we passed that lock, Fifteen miles on the Erie Canal!
And we'll make Rome by six o'clock, Fifteen miles on the Erie Canal!
Just one more trip and back we'll go, Through the rain and sleet and snow,
'Cause we know every inch of the way, From Albany to Buffalo. *Refrain*

The Erie Canal connects Lake Erie to the Atlantic Ocean via New York State's Hudson River. It was a main route for transporting goods during the period of westward expansion. Completed in 1825, the Erie Canal is 363 miles long, 150 feet wide, and 12 feet deep. Flat-bottomed barges used on the canal were hauled by canalers—men who drove mules on the towpaths along the banks. "Erie Canal" is the most famous of many canalers' songs. Children can read about the Erie Canal in the following books: Peter Spier, The Erie Canal *(New York: Doubleday, 1970), and R. Conrad Stein,* The Erie Canal *(Chicago: Children's Press [Grolier], 1985).*

FAIS DO DO

French Folk Melody

*Small numbers indicate fingering for keyboard.

French text

Fais do do, colas mon p'tite frère,
Fais do do, t'auras du lo lo.
Maman est en haut, Qui fait du gateau.
Papa est en bas, qui fait du chocolate,
Fais do do, colas mon p'tite frère,
Fais do do, t'auras du lo lo.

FIVE ANGELS

Model Experience, p. 134

German Folk Song

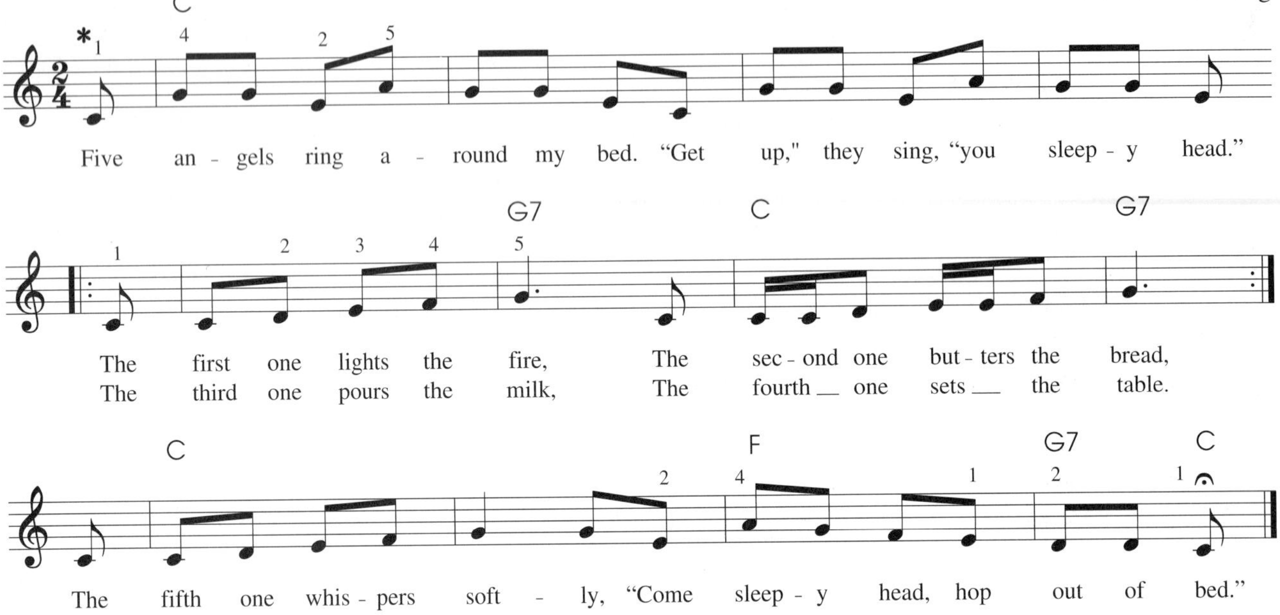
C G7 C G7 C F G7 C
Five an - gels ring a - round my bed. "Get up," they sing, "you sleep - y head."
The first one lights the fire, The sec - ond one but - ters the bread,
The third one pours the milk, The fourth one sets the table.
The fifth one whis - pers soft - ly, "Come sleep - y head, hop out of bed."

* Small numbers indicate fingering for keyboard.

FIVE FAT TURKEYS

Traditional

F C7 F C7 F C7 F B♭ C7 F
Five fat tur - keys are we, We
slept all night in a tree. When the cook came a - round we
could - n't be found, So that's why we're here, you see!

FRÈRE JACQUES!

French Round

D
Frè - re Jac - ques! Frè - re Jac - ques! Dor - mez vous? Dor - mez vous?
("freh - reh jhah - keh freh - reh jhah - keh dor - may voo dor - may voo
Son - nez les ma - ti - nes, Son - nez les ma - ti - nes, Din, din, don! Din, din, don!
soh - nay lay mah - tee - neh soh - nay lay mah - tee - neh dihn dihn dawn dihn dihn dawn")

English version

Are you sleeping? Are you sleeping?
Brother John? Brother John?
Morning bells are ringing, morning bells are ringing,
Ding, ding, dong! Ding, ding, dong!

Christmas text

1. Like a choir of angels singing
   O'er the dells, o'er the dells,
   Comes the sound of ringing, comes the sound of ringing,
   Christmas bells, Christmas bells.

2. "Christ is born!" their message bringing,
   Sound the bells, sound the bells!
   Hear them gaily ringing, hear them gaily ringing,
   Christmas bells, Christmas bells.

GET ON BOARD

African American Spiritual

Verse
F
C7
1. The gos - pel train's a - com - in', I hear it close at hand. I
F
B♭
F
C7
F
hear the wheels a - rumb - lin', And rol - lin' through the land.
Refrain
B♭
F
Get on board, lit - tle child - ren, Get on board, lit - tle child - ren, Get on
B♭
F
C7
F
board, lit - tle child - ren, There's room for man - y - a more.

2. I hear the train a-comin', She's comin' 'round the curve,
She's loosened all her steambrakes, And strain' ev'ry nerve. *Refrain*

GHOST OF TOM

Traditional Halloween Round

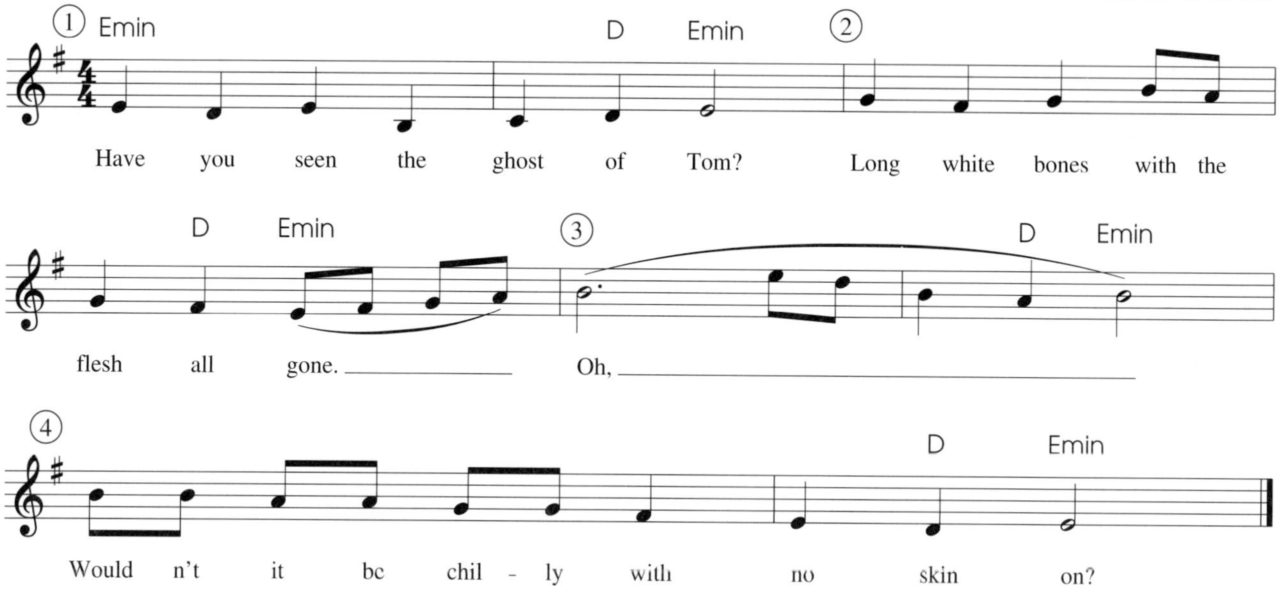

GLOCKENJODLER

Austrian Folk Song

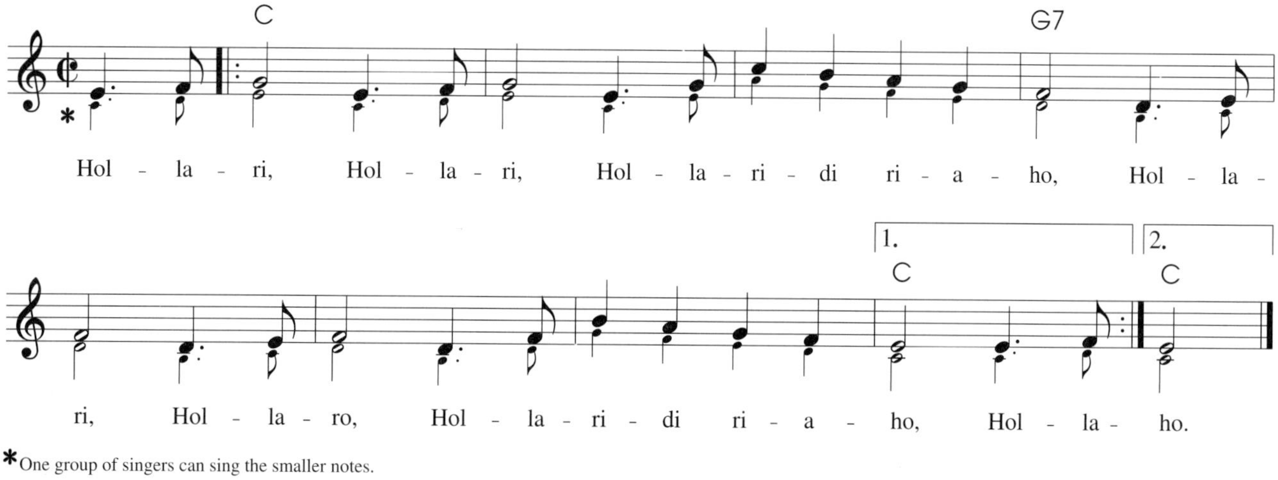

*One group of singers can sing the smaller notes.

GOGO

English words by Margaret Marks

Song from Kenya
As sung by Mary Okari

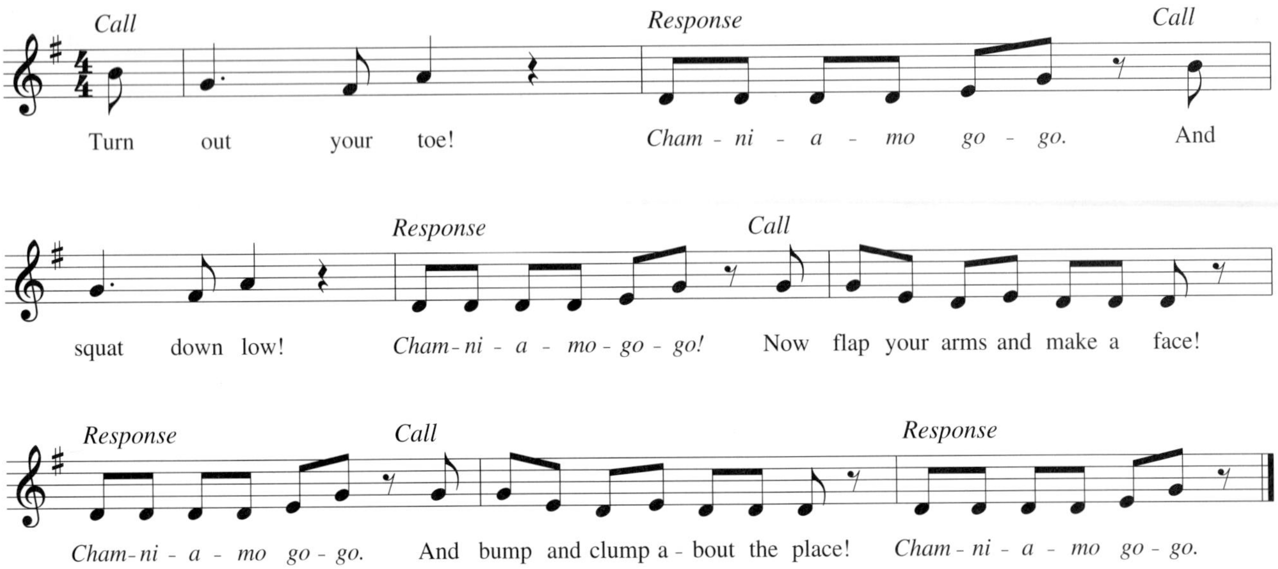

Call
Turn out your toe!
Response
Cham - ni - a - mo go - go.
Call
And squat down low!
Response
Cham- ni - a - mo - go - go!
Call
Now flap your arms and make a face!
Response
Cham- ni - a - mo go - go.
Call
And bump and clump a - bout the place!
Response
Cham - ni - a - mo go - go.

GO TELL AUNT RHODY

American Folk Song

* Small number indicates fingering for keyboard.

2. The one she's been savin', *(Sing 3 times)*
   To make a feather bed.

3. She died in the mill pond, *(Sing 3 times)*
   A-standin' on her head.

4. The goslings are weeping, *(Sing 3 times)*
   Because their mother's dead.

GOD BLESS ALL

Traditional Round

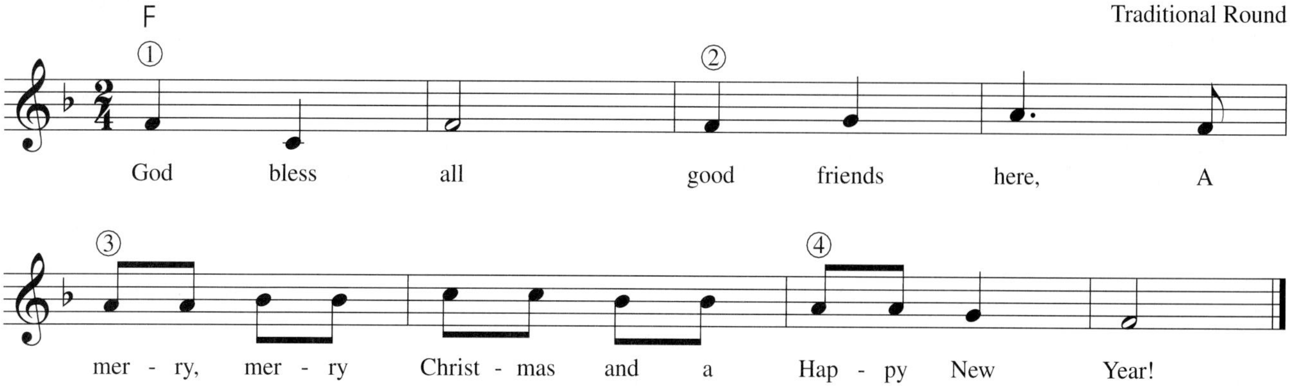
F
①
②
God bless all good friends here, A
③
④
mer - ry, mer - ry Christ - mas and a Hap - py New Year!

GREEN GRAVEL

American Folk Song

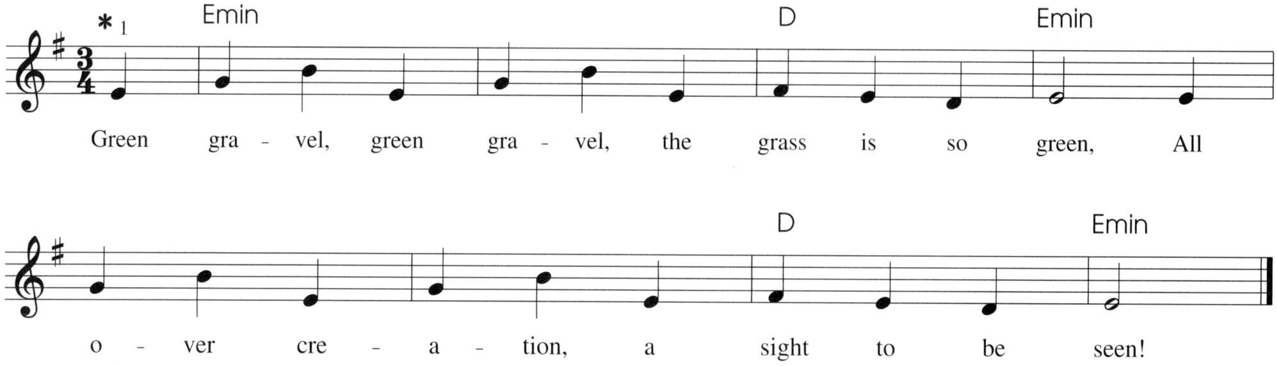
* 1
Emin
D
Emin
Green gra - vel, green gra - vel, the grass is so green, All
D
Emin
o - ver cre - a - tion, a sight to be seen!

* Small number indicates fingering for keyboard.

GRIZZELY BEAR

Andrew B. Crane

Call
D
Response 1
Call
Tell ___ me who was the griz - ze - ly, Griz - ze - ly bear. Tell ___ me
Response 2
Call
who was the griz - ze - ly, Griz - ze - ly bear. Jack - o - Dia - monds was the griz - ze - ly,
Response 1
Call
Response 2
Call
Griz - ze - ly bear. Jack - o - Dia - monds was the griz - ze - ly, Griz - ze - ly bear. He made a
Response 1
Call
noise in the bot - tom like a Griz - ze - ly bear. He made a noise in the bot - tom like a
Response 2
Call
Griz - ze - ly bear. Well ___ my ma - ma was scared of that
Well ___ my pa - pa went a hunt - ing for the
Response 1
Call
Response 2
Griz - ze - ly bear. Well ___ my ma - ma was scared of that Griz - ze - ly bear.
Well ___ my pa - pa went a hunt - ing for the

HA, HA, THIS-A-WAY

American Folk Song

2. I went to a little school, Little school, little school.
I went to a little school, I've been told. *Refrain*

HANUKKAH

Model Experience, p. 180

Hebrew Folk Song

C
F
Ha - nu - kkah, Ha - nu - kkah, mer - ry hol - i - day!
G7
C
Ha - nu - kkah, Ha - nu - kkah, time to dance and play.
F
Ha - nu - kkah, Ha - nu - kkah, bright the can - dles burn.
G7
C
Round and round, round and round, watch the drey - dl turn!

HANUKKAH SONG

Yiddish Folk Song

Dmin A7 Dmin
O Ha - nu - kkah, O Ha - nu - kkah, come light the me - no - rah,
A7 Dmin
Let's have a par - ty, we'll all dance the ho - ra. Gath - er round the ta - ble, we'll
A7 Dmin A7 Dmin
give you a treat, Shin - ing tops to play with and pan - cakes to eat; And
Dmin Gmin Dmin
while we are play - ing the can - dles are burn - ing ___ low.
Gmin Dmin Gmin
One for each night, they ___ shed a sweet light. To re -
1.
Dmin A7 Dmin
mind us of days long a - go.
2.
Dmin A7 Dmin
mind us of days long a - go.

* One group of singers can sing the smaller notes.

HAWAIIAN RAINBOWS

Model Experience, p. 202

Modern Hawaiian Song

Ha - wai - ian rain - bows, White clouds roll by,

Slowly swing arms over the head from left to right to show the shape of a rainbow.

Swing arms back from right to left. At the same time, hold one hand over the other to show clouds.

You show your col - ors A - gainst the sky.

Swing arms from left to right. At the same time, make a rippling motion with the fingers as if pointing to all the colors of the rainbow.

Raise both hands high to the right (palms up). Move the left hand "across the sky" to the left side.

Ha - wai - ian rain - bows. It seems to me,

Slowly swing arms over the head from left to right to show the shape of a rainbow.

Place the right hand under the left elbow and point the index finger of the left hand toward the chest ("It seems to me").

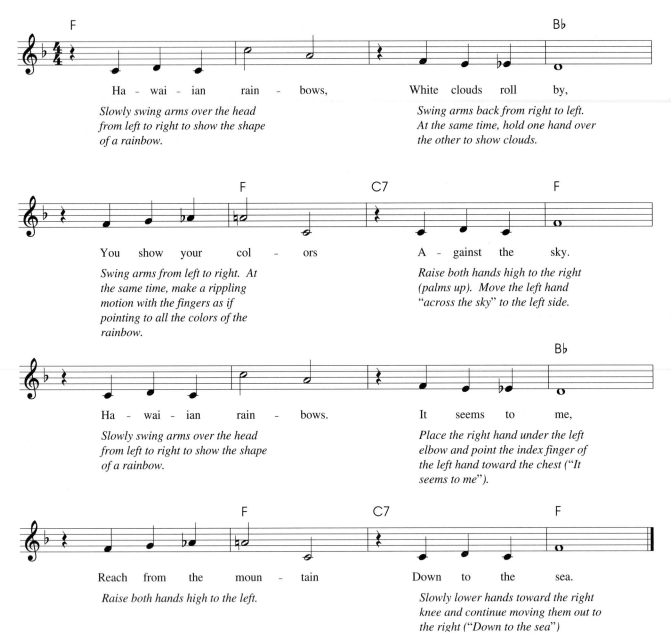

Reach from the moun - tain Down to the sea.

Raise both hands high to the left.

Slowly lower hands toward the right knee and continue moving them out to the right ("Down to the sea")

Formation

Dancers kneel and sit low on their heels. To begin, they stretch both arms high to the left, with fingers pointing up and palm facing out. Each motion is smooth and flowing and is performed slowly, so it extends through two measures.

HEAD–SHOULDERS, BABY

Model Experience, p. 138

African American Game Song

1. Head - shoul - ders, Ba - by, one, two, three; Head - shoul - ders, Ba - by, one, two, three; Head - shoul - ders, head - shoul - ders, Head - shoul - ders, Ba - by, one, two, three.

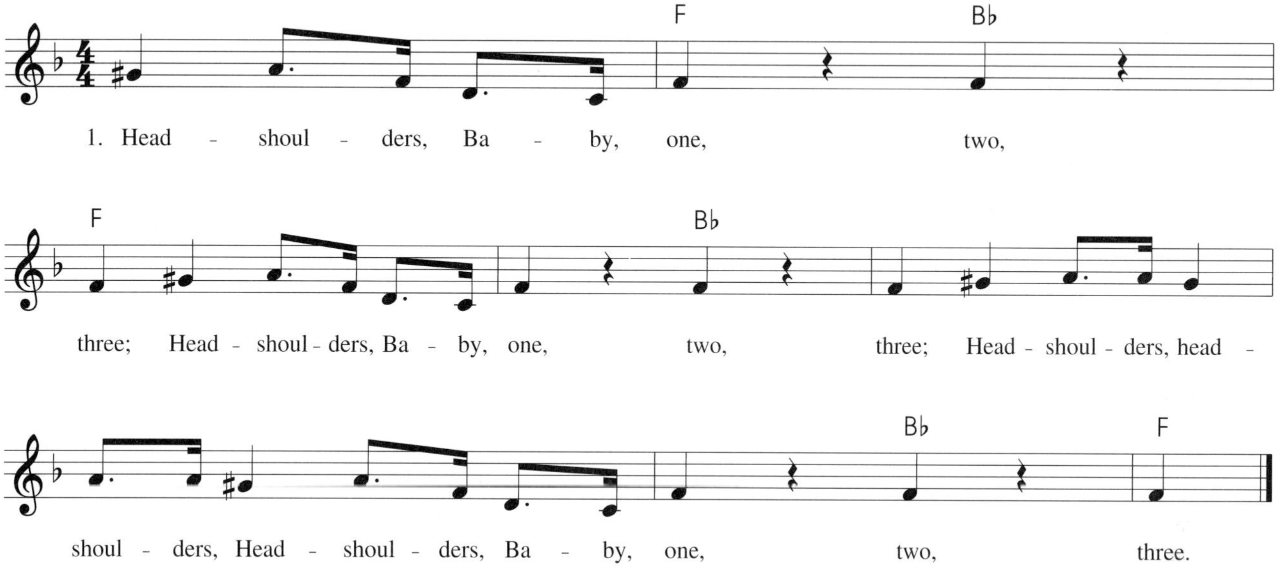

2. Shoulders–chest, Baby, one, two, three; Shoulders–chest, Baby, one, two, three; Shoulders–chest, shoulders–chest, Shoulders–chest, Baby, one, two, three.

3. Chest–knees, Baby, one, two, three; Chest–knees, Baby, one, two, three; Chest–knees, chest–knees, Chest–knees, Baby, one, two, three.

4. Knees–ankles, Baby, one, two, three; Knees–ankles, Baby, one, two, three. Knees–ankles, knees–ankles, Knees–ankles, Baby, one, two, three.

5. Ankles–knees, Baby, one, two, three; Ankles–knees, Baby, one, two, three; Ankles–knees, ankles–knees, Ankles–knees, Baby, one, two, three.

6. Knees–chest, Baby, one, two, three; Knees–chest, Baby, one, two, three; Knees–chest, knees–chest, Knees–chest, Baby, one, two, three.

7. Chest–shoulders, Baby, one, two, three; Chest–shoulders, Baby, one, two, three; Chest–shoulders, chest–shoulders, Chest–shoulders, Baby, one, two, three.

8. Shoulders–head, Baby, one, two, three; Shoulders–head, Baby, one, two, three; Shoulders–head, shoulders–head, Shoulders–head, Baby, one, two, three.

9. That's all, Baby, one, two, three, That's all, Baby, one, two, three; That's all, that's all. That's all, Baby, one, two, three. *Coda* (following verse 9)

(See next page.)

Coda
F
I ain't been to 'Fris - co, And I ain't been to school, I
ain't been to col - lege, but I ain't no fool. To the front, to the
Bb F Bb F
back, To the front, to the back, to the si - si - side.

Movements for Coda

On sung measures:	create movements.
On spoken measures:	put hands on hips, elbows out. Jump on both feet in the direction of the words "front," "back," and "side."

HELLO, THERE!

Traditional

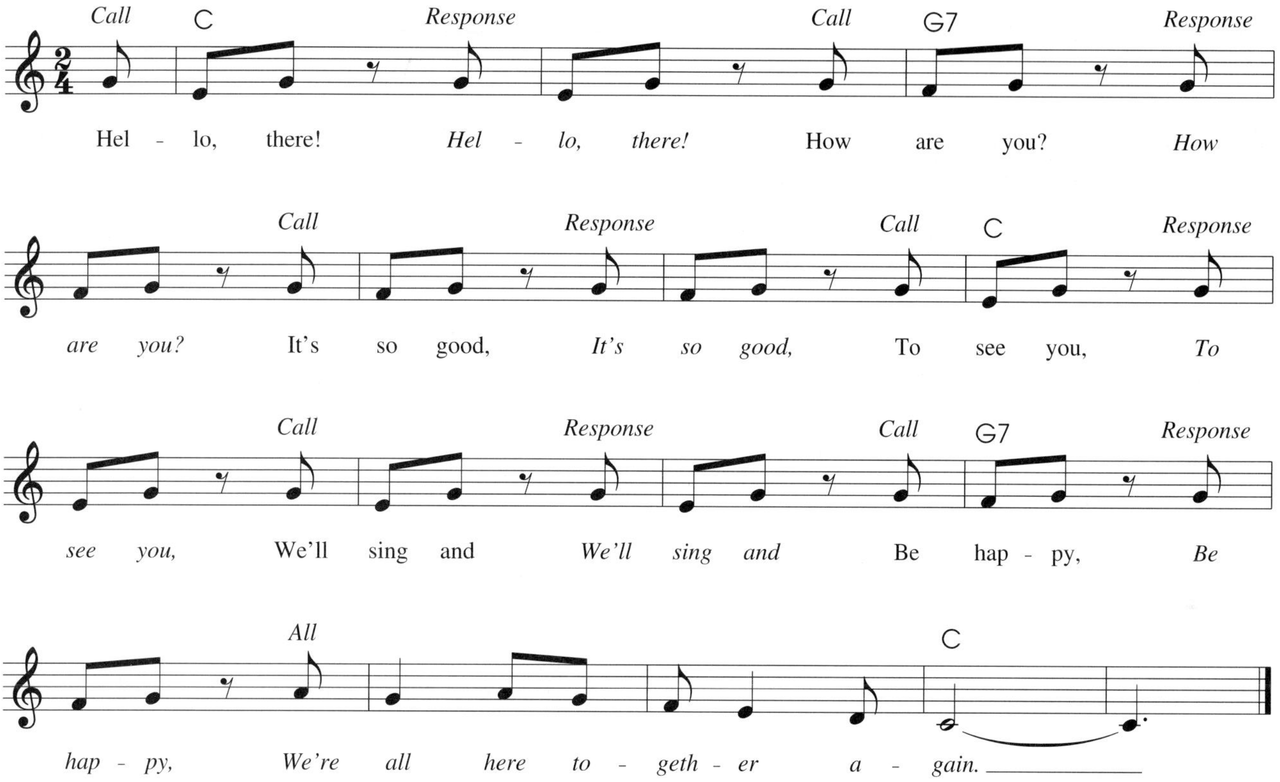
Call C Response Call G7 Response
Hel - lo, there! Hel - lo, there! How are you? How
Call Response Call C Response
are you? It's so good, It's so good, To see you, To
Call Response Call G7 Response
see you, We'll sing and We'll sing and Be hap - py, Be
All C
hap - py, We're all here to - geth - er a - gain.

HE'S GOT THE WHOLE WORLD

African American Spiritual

2. He's got the wind and rain in His hands, *(Sing 3 times)*
He's got the whole world in His hands.

3. He's got both you and me in His hands, *(Sing 3 times)*
He's got the whole world in His hands.

HEY, HO! NOBODY HOME

English Round

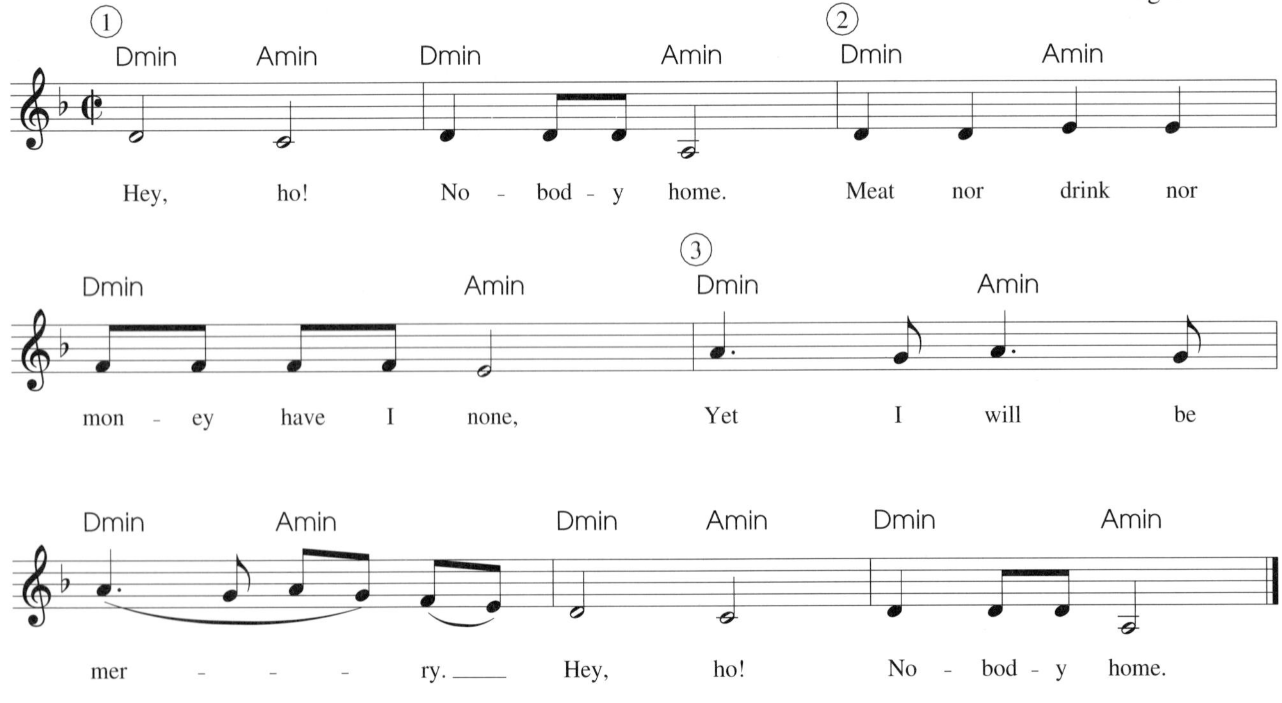

HEY, LIDEE

Model Experience, p. 210

American Song

Refrain
C
*5
G7
Hey, li - dee, li - dee, li - dee, Hey, li - dee, li - dee - lo.
C
Fine
Hey, li - dee, li - dee, li - dee, Hey, li - dee, li - dee - lo.
Verse
G7
1. This is a sil - ly kind of song, Hey, li - dee, li - dee - lo, You
C
D. C. al Fine
make it up as you go a - long, Hey, li - dee, li - dee - lo.

* Small number indicates fingering for keyboard.

2. I have a girl she's ten feet tall, Hey, li - dee, li - dee - lo,
   She sleeps in the kitchen with her feet in the hall. Hey, li - dee, li - dee - lo.

3. Ev'ry - body sing the chorus, Hey li - dee, li - dee - lo,
   Either you're against us or you're for us, Hey - li - dee, li - dee - lo.

HICKORY, DICKORY, DOCK

Words from Mother Goose

J. W. Eliot

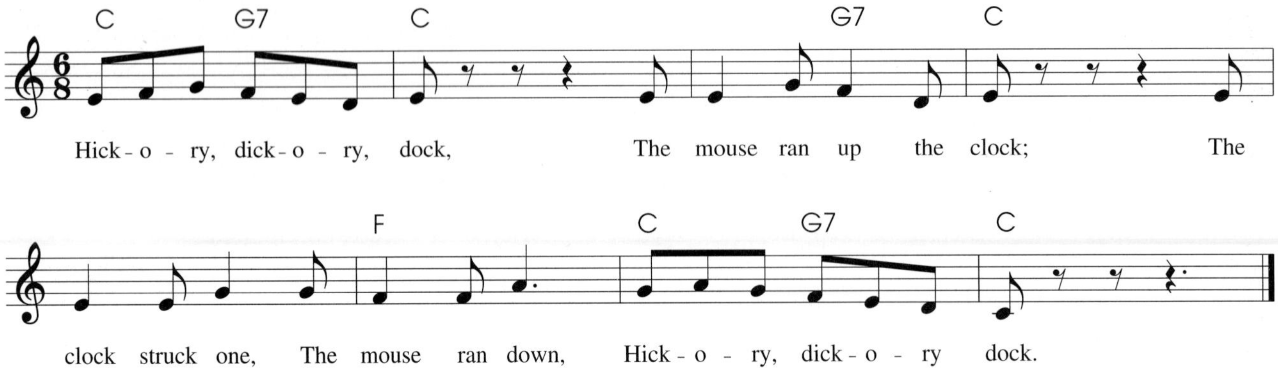
C G7 C G7 C
Hick - o - ry, dick - o - ry, dock, The mouse ran up the clock; The
F C G7 C
clock struck one, The mouse ran down, Hick - o - ry, dick - o - ry dock.

THE HOKEY POKEY

American Folk Song

G
1. You put your right foot in, You take your
2. You put your left foot in, You take your
right foot out, You put your right foot in, And you
left foot out, You put your left foot in, And you
D7
shake it all a - bout, And then you do the ho - key po - key, And you
shake it all a - bout, And then you do the ho - key po - key, And you
G
turn your-self a - bout, And that's what it's all a - bout!
turn your-self a - bout, And that's what it's all a - bout!

3. right hand in, right hand out
4. left hand in, left hand out
5. right shoulder in, right shoulder out
6. left shoulder in, left shoulder out
7. right hip in, right hip out
8. left hip in, left hip out
9. whole self in, whole self out.

HOP, OLD SQUIRREL

American Folk Song

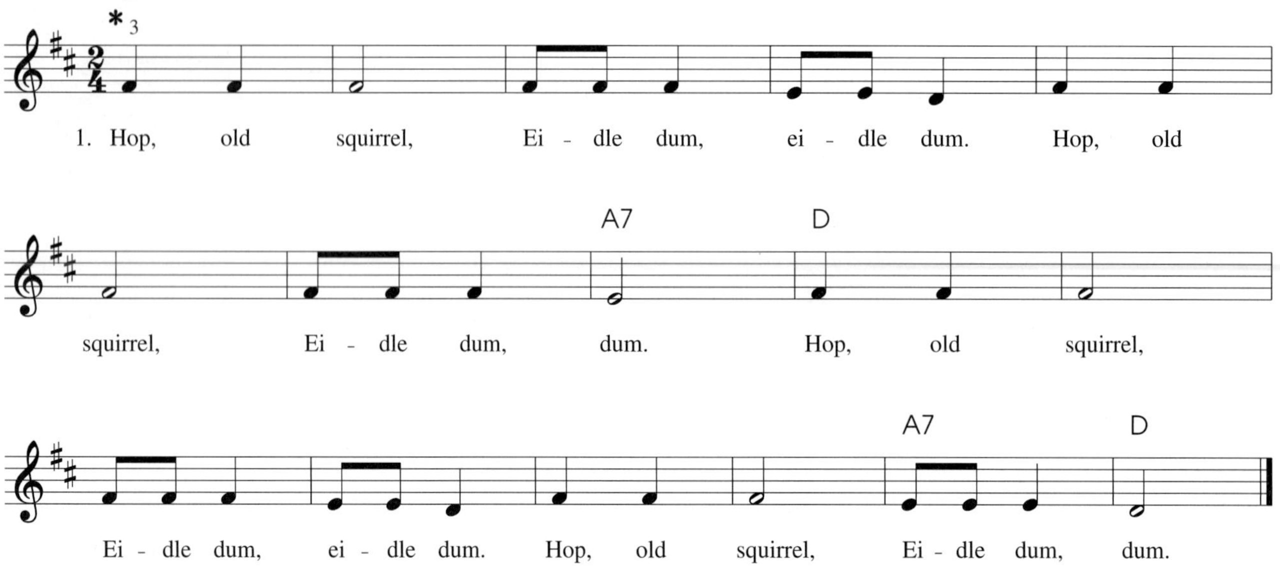
D
*3
1. Hop, old squirrel, Ei - dle dum, ei - dle dum. Hop, old
A7 D
squirrel, Ei - dle dum, dum. Hop, old squirrel,
A7 D
Ei - dle dum, ei - dle dum. Hop, old squirrel, Ei - dle dum, dum.

* Small number indicates fingering for keyboard.

2. Jump, old squirrel, Eidle dum, eidle dum. Jump old squirrel, Eidle dum, dum. *(Sing 2 times)*
3. Run, old squirrel, Eidle dum, eidle dum. Run old squirrel, Eidle dum, dum. *(Sing 2 times)*
4. Hide, old squirrel, Eidle dum, eidle dum. Hide old squirrel, Eidle dum, dum. *(Sing 2 times)*

HOP UP, MY LADIES

Model Experience, p. 186

Verse American Folk Song

1. Did you ev - er go to meet - ing, Un - cle Joe, Un - cle Joe?, Did you ev - er go to meet - ing, Un - cle Joe? _____ Did you ev - er go to meet - ing, Un - cle Joe, Un - cle Joe? Don't mind the weath - er, if the wind don't blow.

Refrain

Hop up, my la - dies, three in a row, Hop up, my la - dies, three in a row, row, up, my la - dies, three in a row, Don't mind the weath - er if the wind don't blow.

2. Does your horse carry double, Uncle Joe, Uncle Joe?
 Does your horse carry double, Uncle Joe?
 Does your horse carry double, Uncle Joe, Uncle Joe?
 Don't mind the weather if the wind don't blow. *Refrain.*

3. Is your horse a single-footer, Uncle Joe, Uncle Joe?
 Is your horse a single-footer, Uncle Joe?
 Is your horse a single-footer, Uncle Joe, Uncle Joe?
 Don't mind the weather if the wind don't blow. *Refrain.*

HUSH LITTLE BABY

Traditional American Lullaby

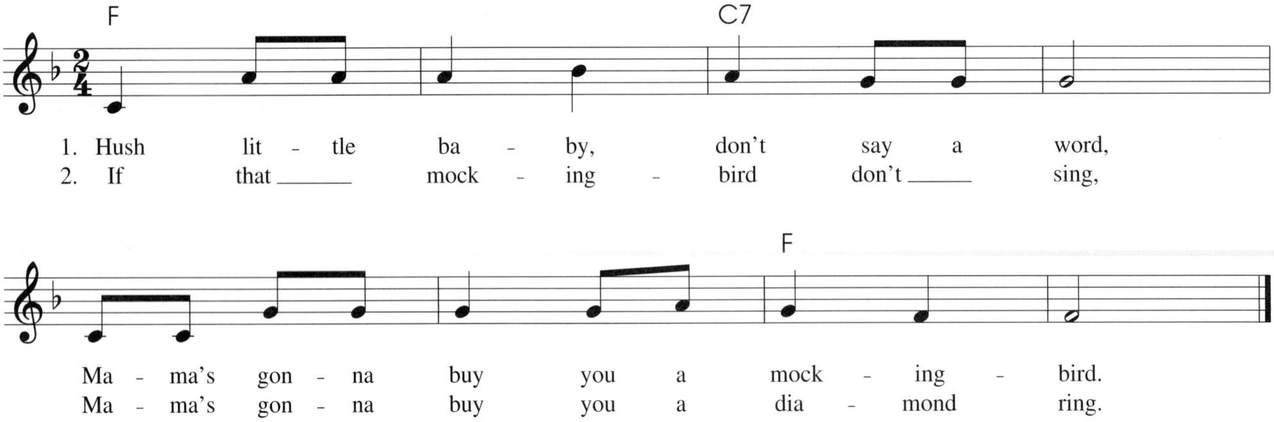
F
C7
1. Hush lit - tle ba - by, don't say a word,
2. If that ___ mock - ing - bird don't ___ sing,
F
Ma - ma's gon - na buy you a mock - ing - bird.
Ma - ma's gon - na buy you a dia - mond ring.

3. If that diamond ring turns brass,
   Mama's gonna buy you a looking glass.

4. If that looking glass gets broke,
   Mama's gonna buy you a billy goat.

5. If that billy goat don't pull,
   Mama's gonna buy you a cart and bull.

6. If that cart and bull turn over,
   Mama's gonna buy you a dog named Rover.

7. If that dog named Rover don't bark,
   Mama's gonna buy you a pony cart.

8. If that pony cart falls down,
   You'll be the saddest little (boy/ girl) in town.

I'D LIKE TO TEACH THE WORLD TO SING

Words and music by Bill Backer, Billy Davis,
Roger Cook, and Roger Greenway (Americans)

* One group of singers can sing the smaller notes on "*loo*."

I LOVE THE MOUNTAINS

Composer Unknown

1
F Dmin Gmin C7
I love the moun - tains, I love the rol - ling hills,
2
F Dmin Gmin C7
I love the flow - ers, I love the daf - fo - dils,
3
F Dmin Gmin C7
I love the fire - side, When all the lights are low;
4
F Dmin Gmin C7 F
Boom - de - ah - da, boom - de - ah - da. Boom - de - ah - da, boom - de - ah - da - boom!
Coda (sing in unison)
C7 F
Boom did - dle - dee dum - dum Boom, boom.

IT'S A SMALL WORLD

Words and music by
Richard M. Sherman and
Robert B. Sherman (Americans)

Verse
G D7
1. It's a world of laugh - ter, a world of tears; It's a
G
world of hopes and a world of fears. There's so
G7 C
much that we share that it's time we're a - ware, It's a
D7 G
small world af - - ter all!
Refrain
D7
It's a small world af - ter all, It's a
G G7
small world af - ter all. It's a small world
C D7 G
af - ter - all. It's a small, small world.

(See next page)

2. There is just one moon and one golden sun.
   And a smile means friendship to ev'ryone.
   Though the mountains divide and the oceans are wide,
   It's a small world after all! *Refrain*

To create harmony, perform the verse and refrain simultaneously.

Refrain as sung in

Germany:	Es ist eine kleine Welt . . .
Spain:	Es un mundo pequeño . . .
Philippines:	Maliit na daigdig . . .
Nigeria:	Ona kpo otete . . .
Malaysia:	Bumi kita tidak besar . . .

IT'S RAINING!
(¡Qué llueva!)

Mexican Children's Song

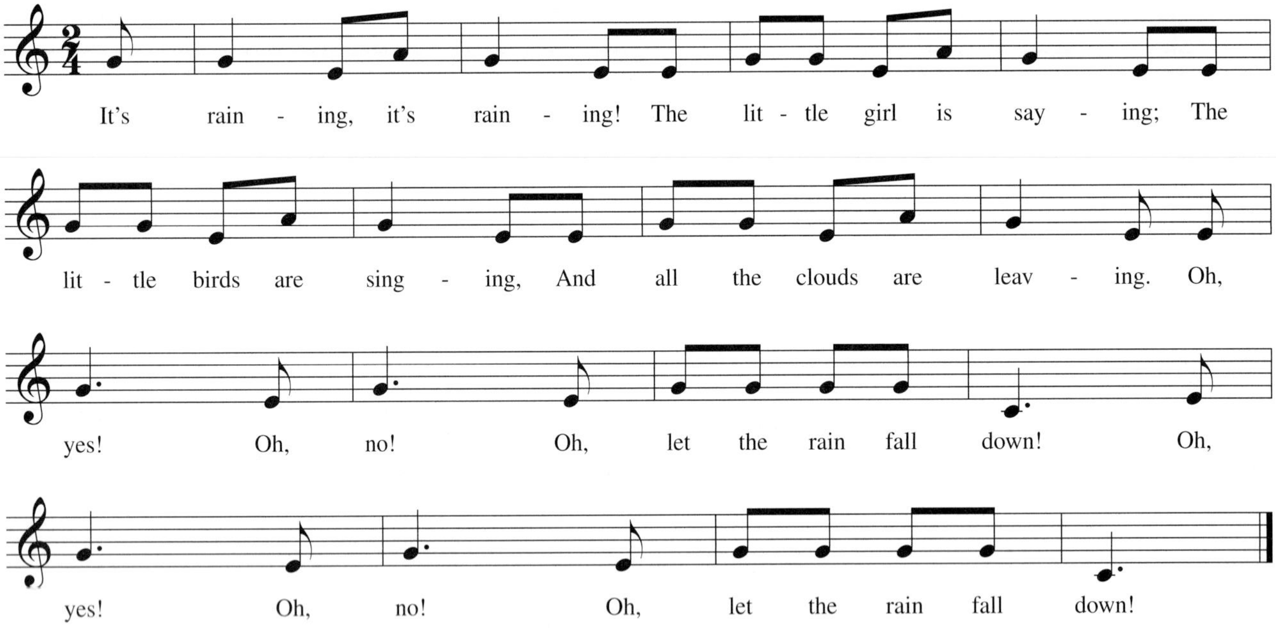

It's rain - ing, it's rain - ing! The lit - tle girl is say - ing; The
lit - tle birds are sing - ing, And all the clouds are leav - ing. Oh,
yes! Oh, no! Oh, let the rain fall down! Oh,
yes! Oh, no! Oh, let the rain fall down!

Spanish text and pronunciation

¡Qué llueva, qué llueva! La chiquita diciendo;
kay yway-vah kay yway-vah lah chee-kee-tah dee-keeaye-doh

Los pajaritos cantan, Las nubes se levantan.
lohss pah-hah-ree-toess kahn-tahn lahss noo-behss say lay-vahn-tahn

¡Qué si! ¡Qué no! ¡Qué caiga el chaparrón!
kay see kay noe kay kahee-gah ehl chah-pah-rrohn

¡Qué si! ¡Qué no! ¡Qué caiga el chaparrón!
kay see kay noe kay kahee-gah ehl chah-pah-rrohn

JAMAICA FAREWELL

Model Experience, p. 228

Traditional Calypso
from the West Indies

Verse
C F
1. Down a - way where the folks all play and the
G7 C
sun shines dai - ly on the moun - tain top, I took a trip on a
F G7 C
sail - in' ship and when I reached Ja - mai - ca I made a stop,
Refrain
F
But I'm sad to say, I'm on my way,
G7 C
won't be back for man - y a day. Me heart is down, me head is
F G7 C
turn - in' a - round, I had to leave a lit - tle girl in Kings - ton town.

2. Sounds of laughter ev'rywhere and the dancing girls sway to and fro.
I must declare that my heart is there though I've been from Maine to Mexico. *Refrain*

JIM-ALONG, JOSIE

American Folk Song

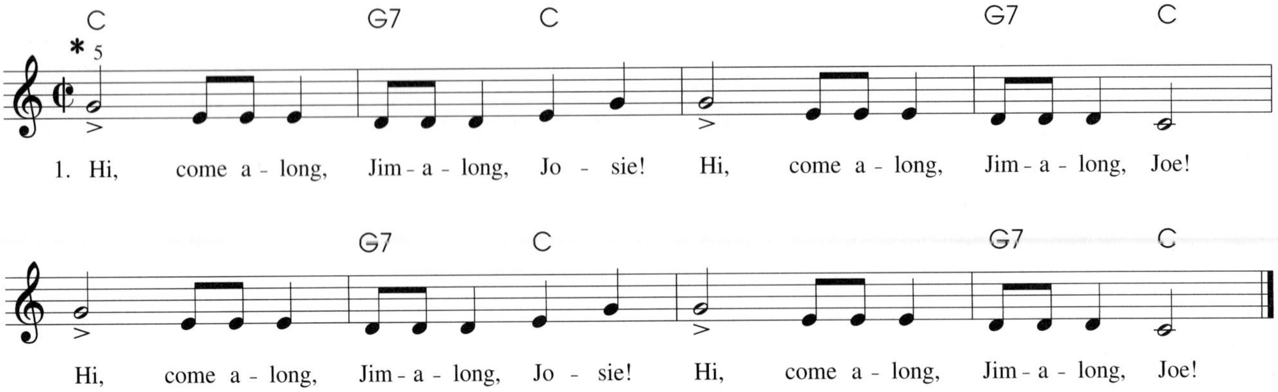
C G7 C G7 C
*5
1. Hi, come a - long, Jim - a - long, Jo - sie! Hi, come a - long, Jim - a - long, Joe!
G7 C G7 C
Hi, come a - long, Jim - a - long, Jo - sie! Hi, come a - long, Jim - a - long, Joe!

* Small number indicates fingering for keyboard.

2. Hi, walk along, walk along, Josie! Hi, walk along, walk along, Joe!
   Hi, walk along, walk along, Josie! Hi, walk along, walk along, Joe!

3. Hi, hop along, hop along, Josie! Hi, hop along, hop along, Joe!
   Hi, hop along, hop along, Josie! Hi, hop along, hop along, Joe!

JOE TURNER BLUES

Model Experience, p. 220

American Blues

C
1. They tell me___ Joe Turn - er's___ come and gone,___
F
C
They tell me___ Joe Turn - er's___ come and gone,___
G7
C
He left me___ here to sing_______ this_______ song.

2. He came here with forty links of chain,
He came here with forty links of chain,
He left me here to sing this song.

3. Joe Turner, he took my man away,
Joe Turner, he took my man away,
He left me here to sing this song.

JOHN THE RABBIT

Model Experience, p. 130

American Folk Song
Collected by John Work

Call
Dmin
Response
Call
Old John the rab - bit, Oh, yes! Old John the rab - bit,
Response
Call
Response
Call
Oh, yes! Got a might-y bad hab - it, Oh, yes! Of go-ing to my gar - den,
Response
Call
Response
Call
Oh, yes! And eat - ing up my peas, Oh, yes! And cut - ting down my cab - bage,
Response
Call
Response
Call
Oh, yes! He ate to - ma - toes, Oh, yes! And sweet po - ta - toes,
Dmaj
Response
Call
Response
Call
Oh, yes! And if I live, Oh, yes! To see next fall,
Dmaj
Response
Call
Response
Call
Oh, yes! I won't plant Oh, yes! A gar - den at all!

* Small numbers indicate fingering for keyboard.

JOY TO THE WORLD

Isaac Watts
(1674–1748)

George F. Handel
(German, 1685–1759)

C G7 C F C G7 C
1. Joy to the world, the Lord is come; Let
F G7 C
earth re - ceive her King, Let
ev - 'ry heart pre - pare Him room, And
G7
heav'n and na - ture sing, And heav'n and na - ture sing, And
C F C F C G7 C
heav'n and heav'n and na - ture sing.

* Small numbers indicate fingering for keyboard.
** One group of singers can sing the smaller notes.

2. Joy to the world, the Savior reigns;
Let men their songs employ,
While fields and floods, rocks, hills and plains,
Repeat the sounding joy, Repeat the sounding joy,
Repeat, repeat, the sounding joy.

KANG DING CITY

English text by P. Hackett

Chinese Folk Song

Cres - cent moon hang - ing in the sky, Sil - ver clouds on the
* "Pow mah leeoh leeoh duh shang, shang Yee dwoh leeoh leeoh duh
moun - tain, Bright, bright, stars in a night of calm,
yuhn, Ah! Dwahn, dwahn, leeoh, leeoh, duh jah oo dsigh,
Kang Ding, cit - y of the moon, Ah! Kang Ding! Kang Ding!
Kahng dihng leeoh leeoh, duh chung, Ah! Yooeh leeahng, wahn
shin - ing home! Kang Ding, cit - y of the moon, Ah!
wahn Kahng ding leeoh leeoh duh chung, Ah!"

* *Chinese version (phonetic pronunciation)*

KUM BA YAH

African American Song

* Small numbers indicate fingering for keyboard.

2. Someone's praying, Lord, Kum ba yah. *(Sing 3 times)*
   Oh, Lord Kum ba yah.

3. Someone's singing, Lord, Kum ba yah. *(Sing 3 times)*
   Oh, Lord Kum ba yah.

4. Someone's shouting, Lord, Kum ba yah. *(Sing 3 times)*
   Oh, Lord Kum ba yah.

LADY, COME

English Round

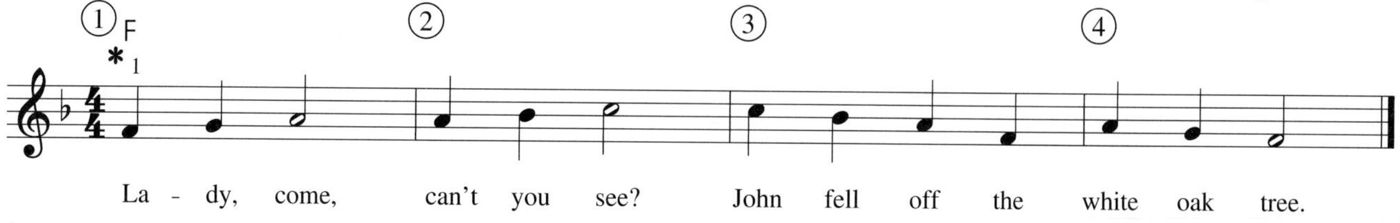

F
La - dy, come, can't you see? John fell off the white oak tree.

* Smaller number indicates fingering for keyboard.

LET THERE BE PEACE ON EARTH

Jill Jackson (American)

Sy Miller (American)

* One group of singers can sing the smaller notes.

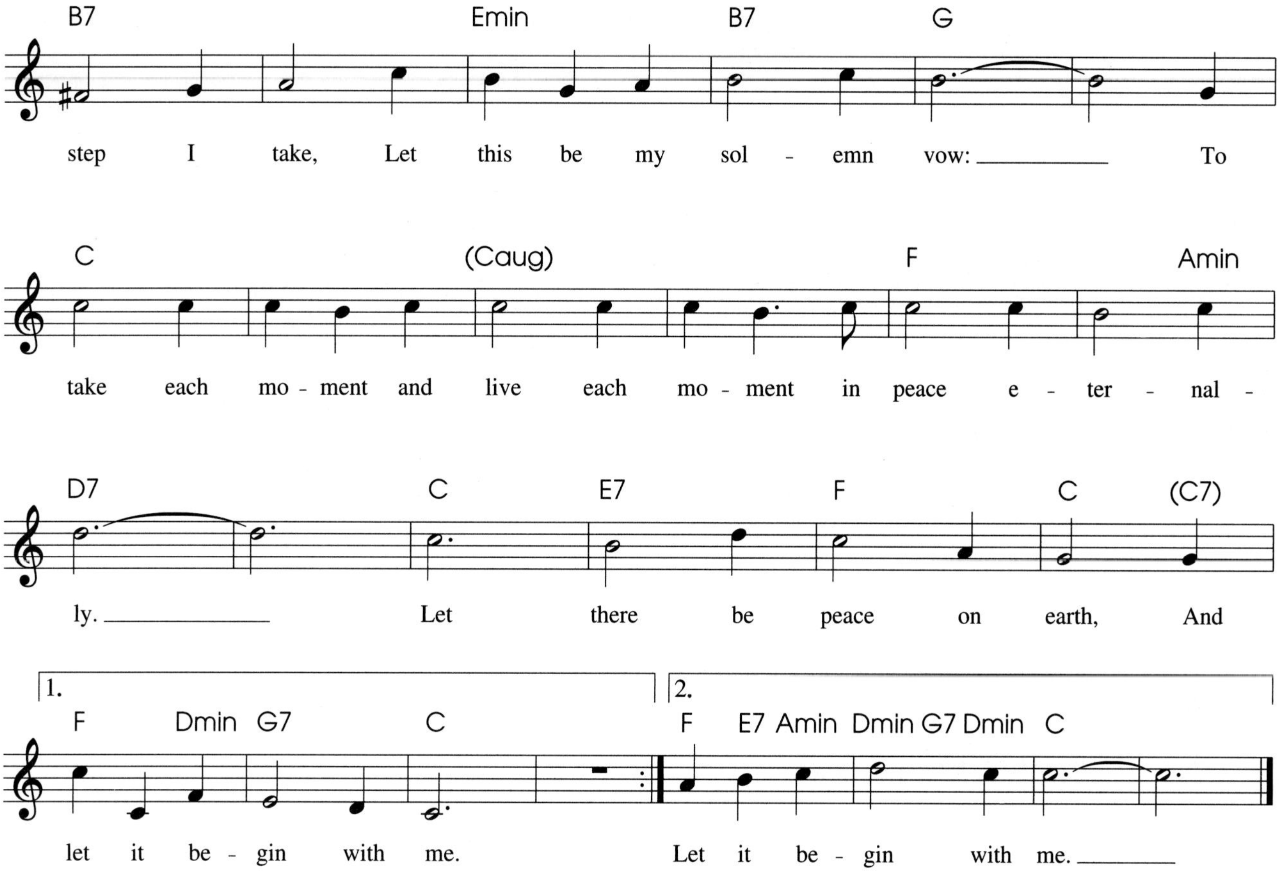
B7 Emin B7 G
step I take, Let this be my sol - emn vow: To
C (Caug) F Amin
take each mo - ment and live each mo - ment in peace e - ter - nal -
D7 C E7 F C (C7)
ly. Let there be peace on earth, And
1.
F Dmin G7 C
let it be - gin with me.
2.
F E7 Amin Dmin G7 Dmin C
Let it be - gin with me.

LONDON BRIDGE

Children's Game Song

D
* 4
A7
D
1. Lon - don bridge is fall - ing down, fall - ing down, fall - ing down.
A7
D
3 1
Lon - don bridge is fall - ing down, My fair la - dy - O.

* Small numbers indicate fingering for keyboard.

2. Take the key and lock her up, lock her up, lock her up,
   Take the key and lock her up, My fair lady-O.

3. Build it up with silver and gold, silver and gold, silver and gold,
   Build it up with silver and gold, My fair lady-O.

LONG-LEGGED SAILOR

Traditional

F 1 C7 F
1. Did you ev - er, ev - er, ev er in your long - leg - ged
C7
life Meet a long - leg - ged sail - or with a long - leg - ged
F C7 F
wife? No I nev - er, nev - er, nev - er in my long leg ged
C7 F
life, Met a long - leg - ged sail - or with a long - leg - ged wife.

* Small number indicates fingering for keyboard.

2. short-legged
3. knock-kneed
4. bow-legged
5. cross-legged

LOOBY LOO

Model Experience, p. 126

American Folk Song

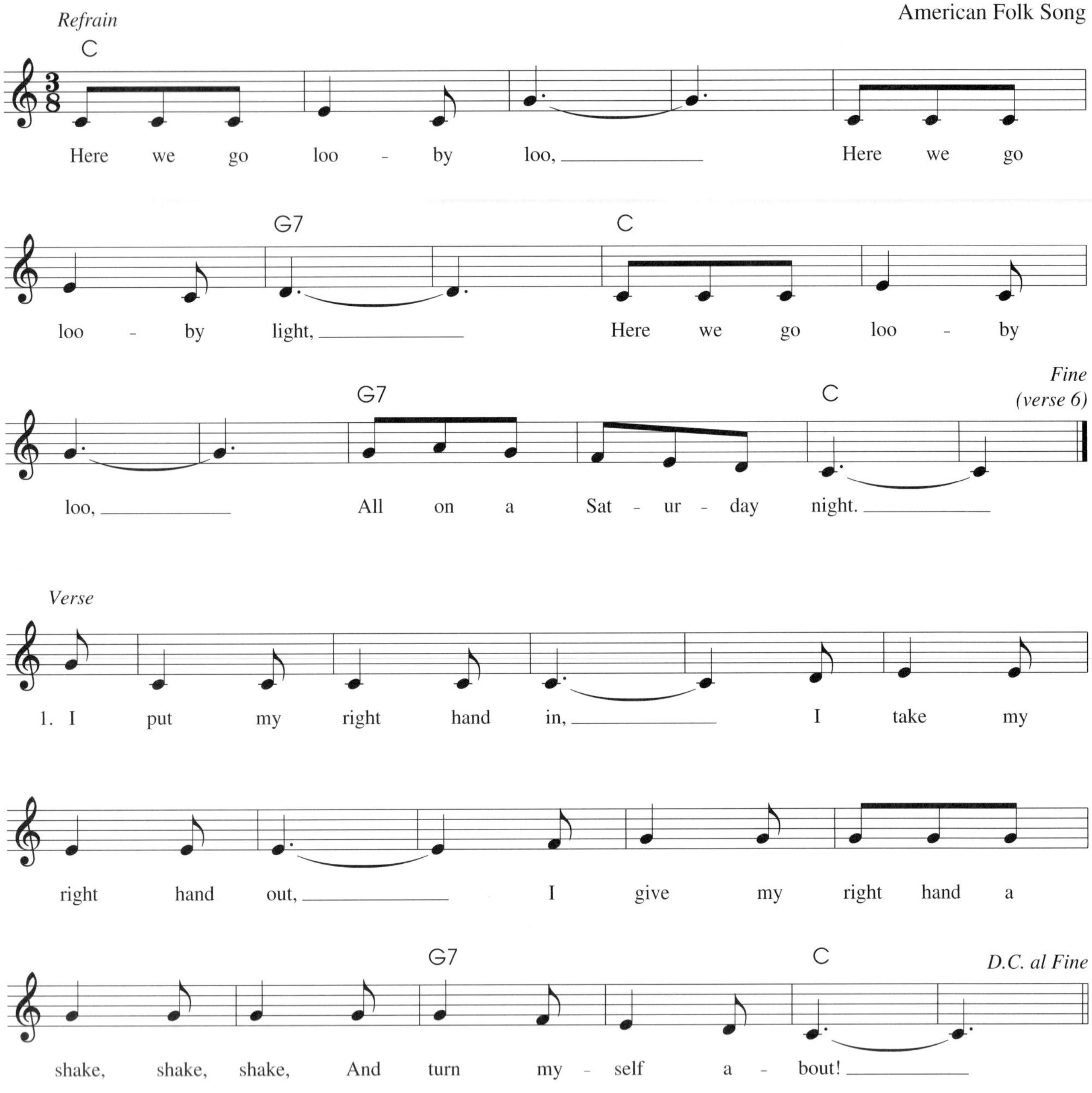
Refrain
C
Here we go loo - by loo,
Here we go loo - by light,
G7
C
Here we go loo - by loo,
G7
C
All on a Sat - ur - day night.
Fine (verse 6)
Verse
1. I put my right hand in,
I take my right hand out,
I give my right hand a shake, shake, shake,
G7
C
And turn my - self a - bout!
D.C. al Fine

2. Left hand in, left hand out
3. Right foot in, right foot out
4. Left foot in, left foot out
5. Big head in, big head out
6. Whole self in, whole self out

A hot bath was a luxury in 19th-century America—and even into the 20th century! Water heated over a fire (or in a coal stove's water tank) was transferred bucket-by-bucket into a wood or metal bathing tub. To test the temperature of the water, the bather first put in one hand (or foot). "Looby loo" tells about this, and the "shake, shake, shake" is shaking the hand dry! It's easy to imagine why bathing was a weekly event.

LOVELY EVENING

German Round

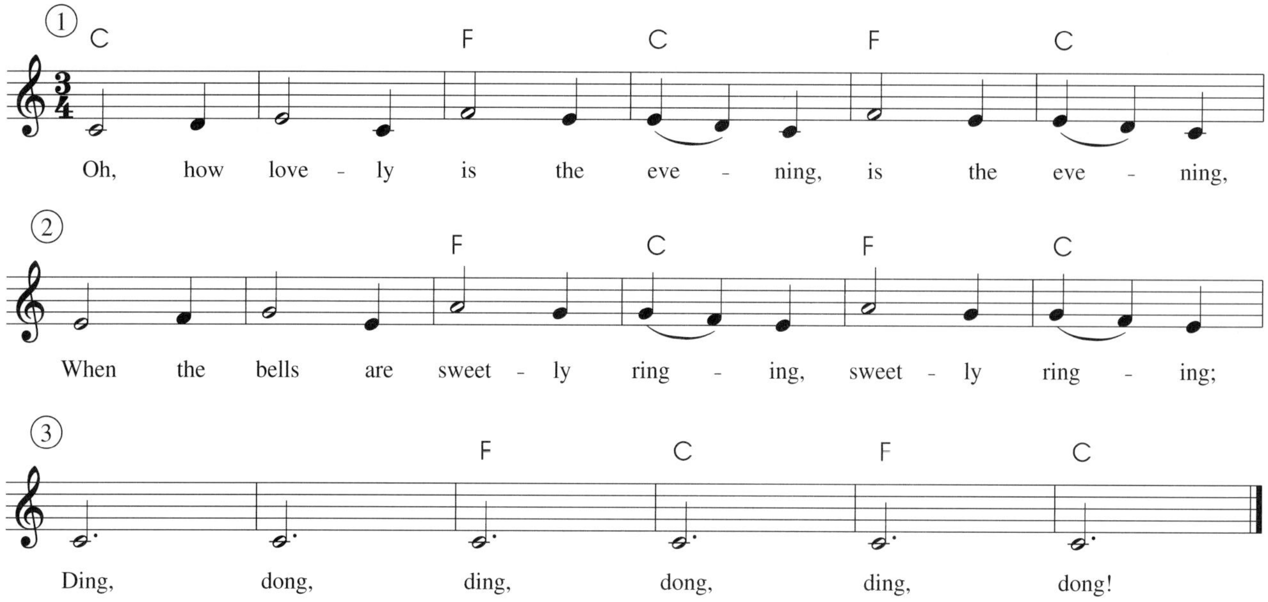
1
C F C F C
Oh, how love - ly is the eve - ning, is the eve - ning,
2
F C F C
When the bells are sweet - ly ring - ing, sweet - ly ring - ing;
3
F C F C
Ding, dong, ding, dong, ding, dong!

German version

O wie wohl ist mir am Abend, mir am Abend,
("oh vee vohl ist meer ahm ah-bend meer ahm ah-bend

Wenn zur Ruh die Glocken läuten, Glocken läuten;
venn tsoor roo dee gloh-kehn loy-ten gloh-kehn loy-ten")

Bim, bam, bim, bam, bim, bam!

Spanish version

Fray Martin al campanario, campanario,
("fray mahr-teen ahl cahm-pah-nah-ree-oh cahm-pah-nah-ree-oh

Subey toca, la campana, la campana,
soo-beh-ee toh-cah lah-cahm-pan-nah lah-cahm-pah-nah

Tan, tan, tan, tan, tan, tan!
tahn tahn tahn tahn tahn tahn")

LOVE SOMEBODY

American Folk Song

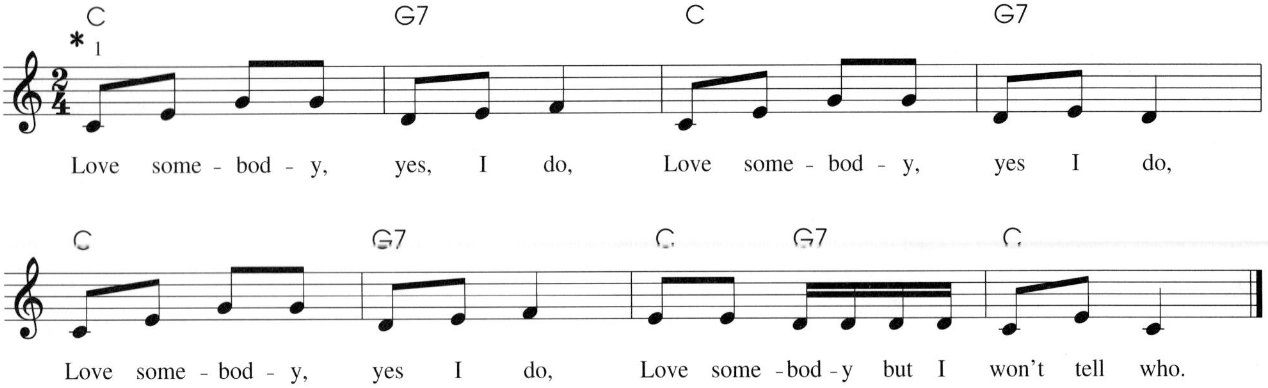
C G7 C G7
*
1
Love some - bod - y, yes, I do, Love some - bod - y, yes I do,
C G7 C G7 C
Love some - bod - y, yes I do, Love some - bod - y but I won't tell who.

* Small number indicates fingering for keyboard.

THE MANGO (ISANG BUTONG MANGGA)

English text by
P. Hackett

Tagalog Song
Collected and transcribed by Miriam B. Factora

G
I found a man - go seed, And want - ed fruit to
* I - sang bu - tong man - ga a - king i - ti - na -
D7
grow, I put it in the ground, Be - side my bun - ga -
nim, Ta - nim na nang ta - nim, ta - nim na nang ta -
G E
low. It grew and bore some fruit, That was - n't what I
nim, Ngu - nit i - sang a - raw, ang man - ga'y na - mu -
Amin G D7 G
thought, And when I tried to eat it A man - go it was not!
nga, Na - mu - nga nang na - mu - nga, na - mu - nga ng i - ba!

* *Pronunciation guide for Tagalog text*

a as in "saw"
i as in "field"
o as in "song"
ng as in "long"
u as in "suit"

The mango is the national fruit of the Philippines.

MATARILE

Model Experience, p. 144

Mexican Folk Song

D A7 D
1.–3. What do you want? Ma - ta - ri - le, ri - le, ri - le,
A7 D
What do you want? Ma - ta - ri - le, ri - le, ron.
A7 D
I want to jump, march, run, Ma - ta - ri - le, ri - le, ri - le.
A7 D
I want to jump, march, run, Ma - ta - ri - le, ri - le, ron.

2. What do you want? Matarile, rile, rile,
What do you want? Matarile, rile, ron.
I want to march, Matarile, rile, rile,
I want to march, Matarile, rile, ron.

3. What do you want? Matarile, rile, rile,
What do you want? Matarile, rile, ron.
I want to run, Matarile, rile, rile,
I want to run, Matarile, rile, ron.

Spanish verses with pronunciation

1. ¿Qué quiere usted? Matarile, rile, rile.
"Kay kyay- ray oo- sted mah- tah- ree- leh, ree- leh ree- leh

¿Qué quiere usted? Matarile, rile, ron.
Kay kyay- ray oo- sted mah- tah- ree- leh, ree- leh rone.

Quiero saltar, Matarile, rile, rile.
Kyay- roh sahl- tar, mah- tah- ree- leh, ree- leh, ree- leh

Quiero saltar, Matarile, rile, ron.
Kyay- roh sahl- tar, mah- tah- ree- leh, ree- leh rone."

2. ¿Qué quiere usted? Matarile, rile, rile.
"Kay kyay- ray oo- sted mah- tah- ree- leh, ree- leh ree- leh

¿Qué quiere usted? Matarile, rile, ron.
Kay kyay- ray oo- sted mah- tah- ree- leh, ree- leh rone.

Quero marchar, Matarile, rile, rile.
Kyay- roh sahl- tar, mah- tah- ree- leh, ree- leh, ree- leh

Quero marchar, Matarile, rile, ron.
Kyay- roh sahl- tar, mah- tah- ree- leh, ree- leh rone."

3. ¿Qué quiere usted? Matarile, rile, rile.
"Kay kyay- ray oo- sted mah- tah- ree- leh, ree- leh ree- leh

¿Qué quiere usted? Matarile, rile, ron.
Kay kyay- ray oo- sted mah- tah- ree- leh, ree- leh rone.

Quiero correr, Matarile, rile, rile.
Kyay- roh koh- rare, mah- tah- ree- leh, ree- leh, ree- leh

Quiero correr, Matarile, rile, ron.
Kyay- roh koh- rare, mah- tah- ree- leh, ree- leh rone."

MICHAEL, ROW THE BOAT ASHORE

African American Spiritual

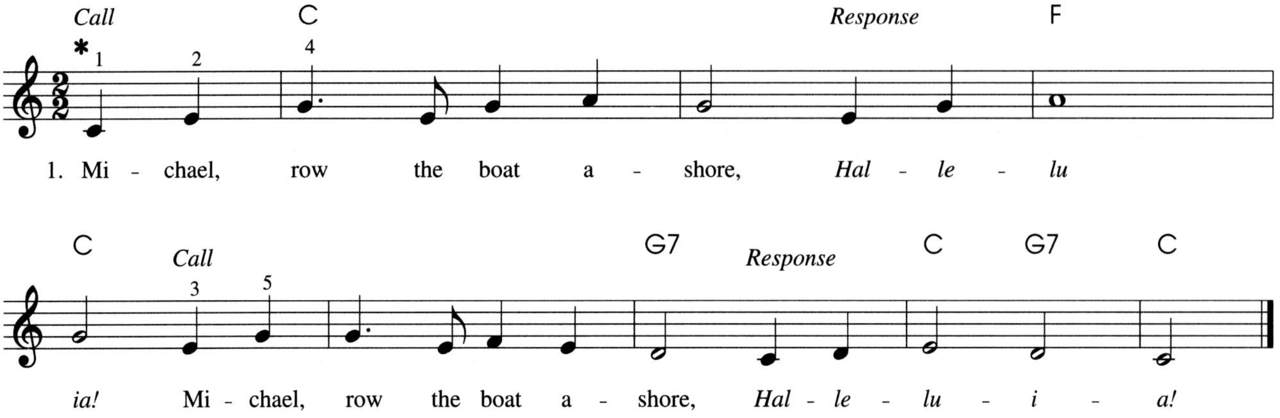

* Small numbers indicate fingering for keyboard.

2. Jordan River is deep and wide, *Halleluia!*
   Jordan River is deep and wide, *Halleluia!*

3. Gabriel, blow the trumpet horn, *Halleluia!*
   Gabriel, blow the trumpet horn, *Halleluia!*

4. Trumpet sounds the world around, *Halleluia!*
   Trumpet sounds the world around, *Halleluia!*

5. Michael, haul the boat ashore, *Halleluia!*
   Michael, haul the boat ashore, *Halleluia!*

MISS MARY MACK

African-American Play Song

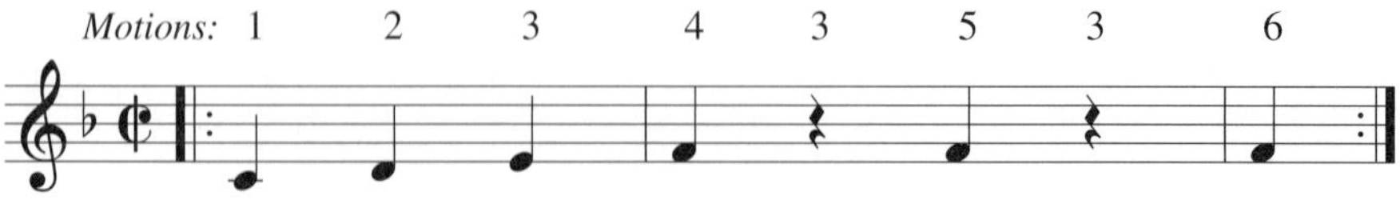

1.	Miss	Mar -	y	Mack,	Mack,	Mack,
2.	All	dressed	in	black,	black,	black
3.	With	sil -	ver	buttons,	buttons,	buttons,
4.	All	down	her	back,	back,	back,
5.	She	asked	her	mother,	mother,	mother,
6.	For	fif -	teen	cents,	cents,	cents,
7.	To	see	the	elephants,	elephants,	elephants,
8.	Jump	over	the	fence,	fence,	fence,
9.	They	jumped	so	high,	high,	high,
10.	They	reached	the	sky,	sky,	sky,
11.	And	never	came	down,	down,	down,
12.	'Til the	fourth of	Ju -	ly,	Ju - -	ly,
13.	And	that's	the	story,	story,	story,
14.	Of	Mar -	y	Mack,	Mack,	Mack,

Game: motions for each number

1: cross hands, hit on shoulders
2: patschen (slap thighs)
3: clap own hands
4: clap partner's right hand
5: clap partner's left hand
6: clap both partner's hands

MY DREYDL

S. S. Grossman E. S. Goldfarb

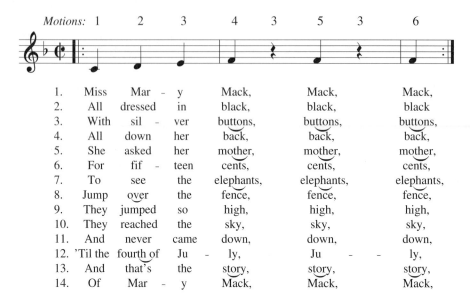

* Small numbers indicate fingering for keyboard.

MUSIC TOUCHES CHILDREN MOST OF ALL

Teresa Jennings
(American)

MY FATHER'S HOUSE

Model Experience, p. 172

Traditional American Song

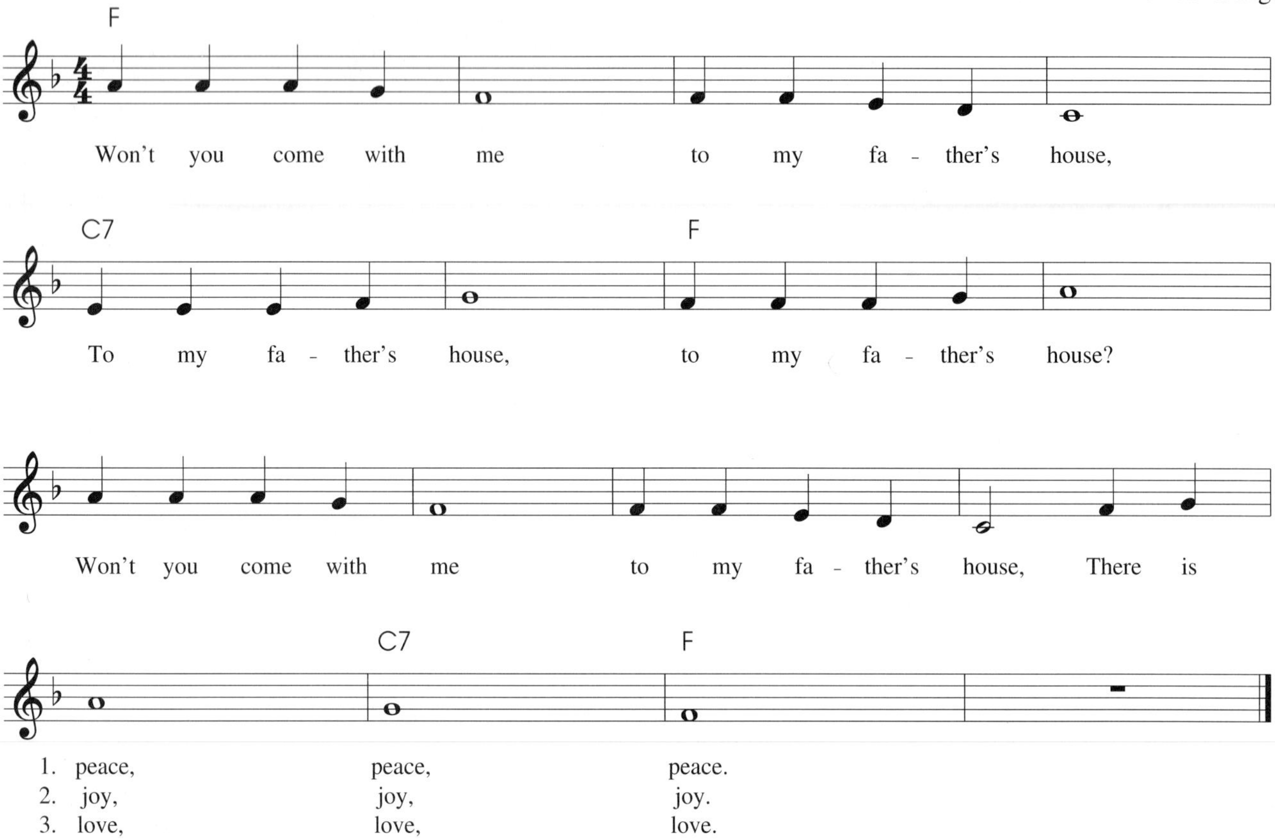
F
Won't you come with me to my fa - ther's house,
C7
F
To my fa - ther's house, to my fa - ther's house?
Won't you come with me to my fa - ther's house, There is
C7
F
1. peace, peace, peace.
2. joy, joy, joy.
3. love, love, love.

SIGNING FOR "MY FATHER'S HOUSE"

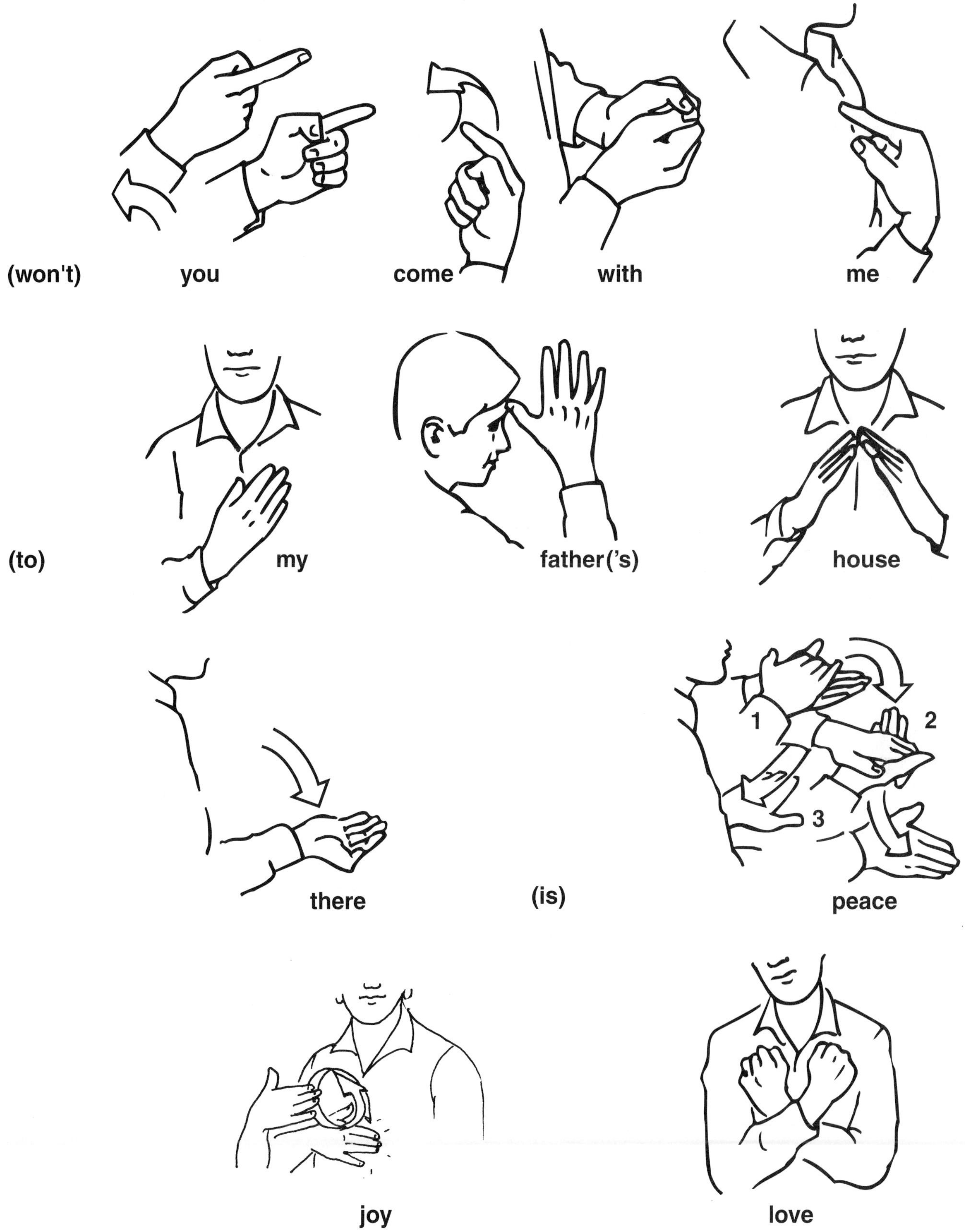

OH, SUSANNA

Stephen Foster
(American, 1826–1864)

Verse
F
C7
1. I came from Al - a - ba - ma, With my ban - jo on my knee, I'm
F
C7
F
going to Loui - si - an - a, My true love for to see; It
C7
rained all night the day I left, The weath - er it was dry; The
F
C7
F
sun so hot I froze to death; Su - san - na, don't you cry.
Refrain
B♭
F
C7
Oh Su - san - na, Oh, don't you cry for me, I've
F
C7
F
come from Al - a - ba - ma, With my ban - jo on my knee.

2. I had a dream the other night, When ev'ry thing was still;
I thought I saw Susanna, A'comin' down the hill.
The buckwheat cake was in her mouth, The tear was in her eye;
Says I, I'm comin' from the south, Susanna, don't you cry! *Refrain*

OLD BRASS WAGON

American Dance Song

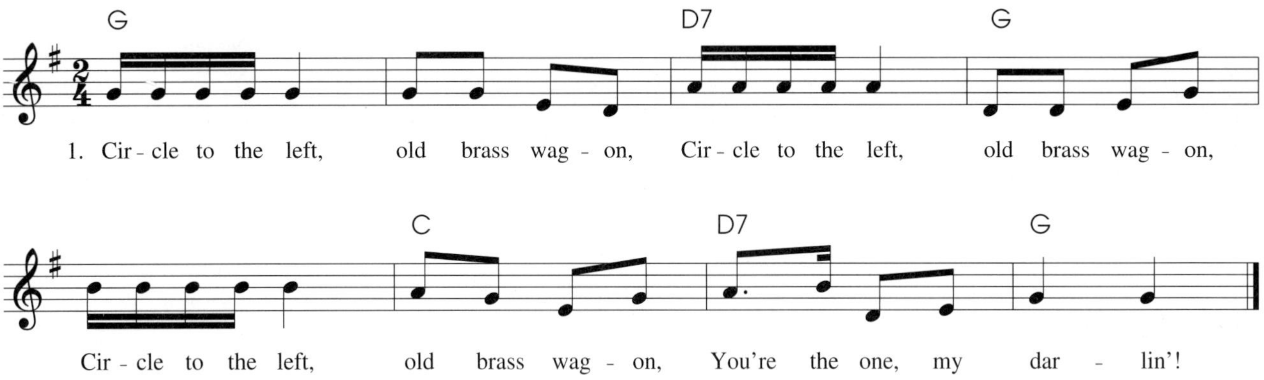
G
D7
G
1. Cir - cle to the left, old brass wag - on, Cir - cle to the left, old brass wag - on,
C
D7
G
Cir - cle to the left, old brass wag - on, You're the one, my dar - lin'!

2. Circle to the right, old brass wagon, Circle to the right, old brass wagon,
   Circle to the right, old brass wagon, You're the one, my darlin'!

3. Swing, oh, swing, old brass wagon, Swing, oh, swing, old brass wagon,
   Swing, oh, swing, old brass wagon, You're the one, my darlin'!

4. Skipping all around, old brass wagon, Skipping all around, old brass wagon,
   Skipping all around, old brass wagon, You're the one, my darlin'!

Formation

Form a single circle of partners, girls on boys' right.

Dance

Verse 1: All circle left.
Verse 2: All circle right.
Verse 3: Partners face each other, join hands, and swing once around.
Verse 4: Girls stand on boys' right, forming an inner circle; partners link arms and skip clockwise around the circle.

OLD HOUSE

African American Work Song

* Small numbers indicate fingering for keyboard.

2. New house. *Build it up!*
   Who's going to help me? *Build it up!*
   Bring me a hammer. *Build it up!*
   Next thing you bring me, *Build it up!*
   Is a carpenter man. *Build it up!*

OLD TEXAS

Cowboy Song

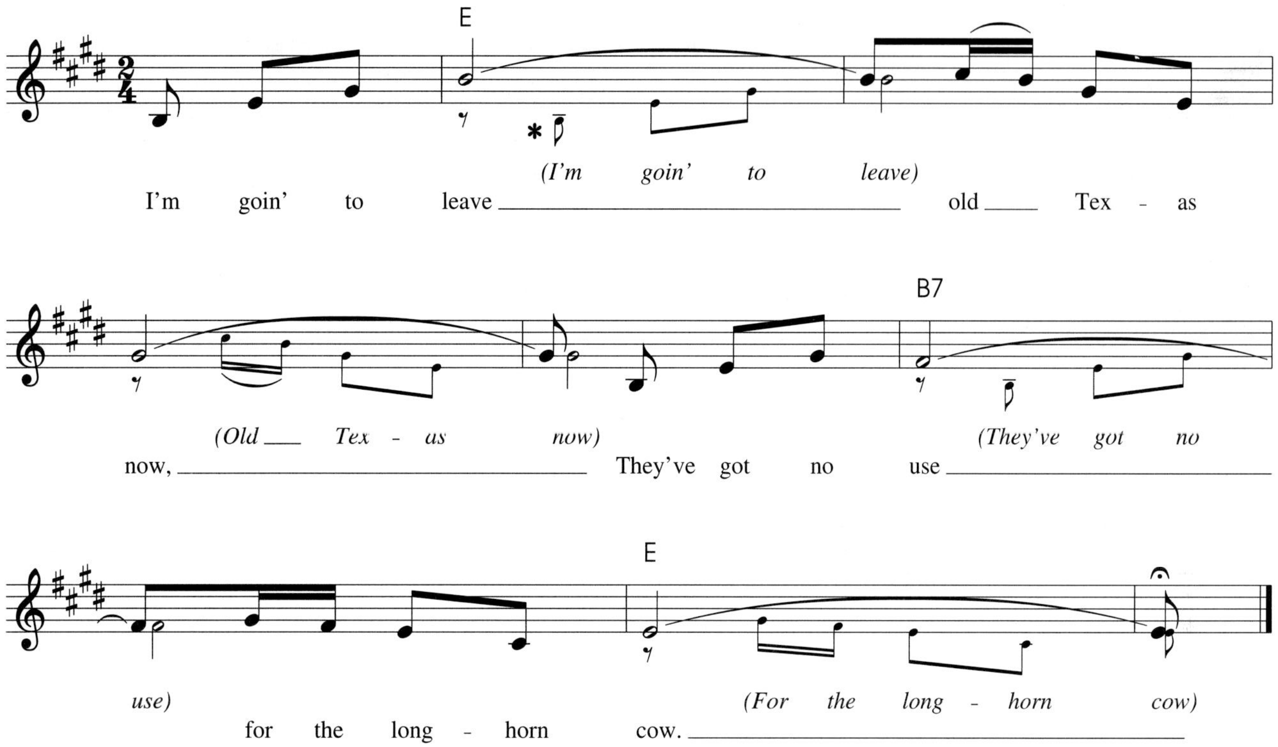
E
(I'm goin' to leave)
I'm goin' to leave ___ old ___ Tex - as
(Old ___ Tex - as now)
B7
(They've got no
now, ___ They've got no use ___
use)
E
(For the long - horn cow)
for the long - horn cow. ___

* One group of singers can sing the smaller notes.

2. They've plowed and fenced my cattle range,
   And the people there are all so strange.

3. I'll take my horse, I'll take my rope,
   And hit the trail upon a lope.

4. Say adios to the Alamo,
   And turn my head toward Mexico.

5. I'll make my home on the wide, wide range,
   For the people there are not so strange.

6. For the hard, hard ground shall be my bed,
   And my saddle seat shall hold my head.

No one is certain just how cowboy songs originated or whether the tunes were composed by the men themselves. Most likely they were based on existing melodies, borrowed from popular ballads, railroad songs, or mountain songs of the late nineteenth century. After the cowboys' evening meal, the most musical of the group might strike up a solo as the men sat around the fire or chuck wagon. Hardly any one singer remembered all the verses, so other men might add stanzas to keep things going. Fortunately, a few collectors relished these songs that eased the loneliness of life on the trail, and preserved them for later generations.

OVER MY HEAD

African American Spiritual

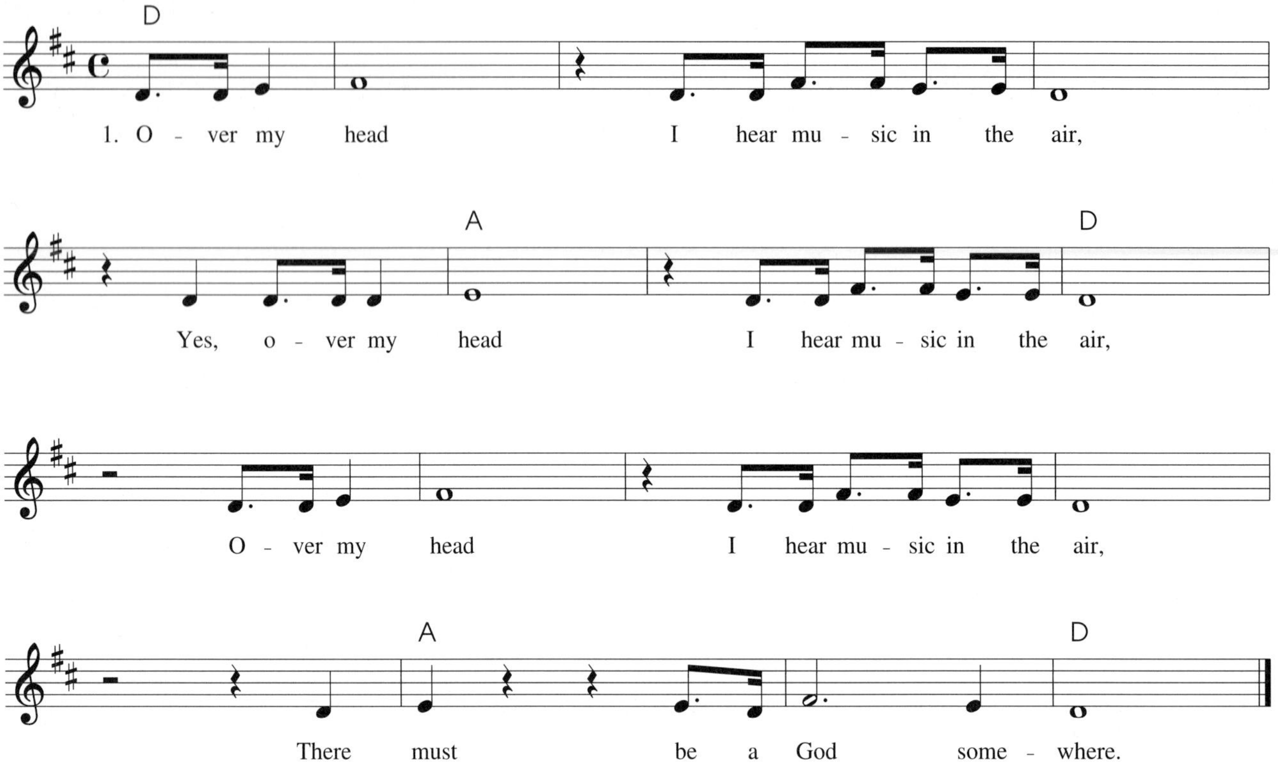
D
1. O - ver my head I hear mu - sic in the air,
A
D
Yes, o - ver my head I hear mu - sic in the air,
O - ver my head I hear mu - sic in the air,
A
D
There must be a God some - where.

Have a group echo back each phrase, sing in harmony, or improvise upon the three-note melody.

2. In my feet there is dancing in the street, *(Sing 3 times)*
   There must be joy somewhere.

3. In my heart there's a play about to start, *(Sing 3 times)*
   There must be joy somewhere.

4. In my eyes there's a rainbow of surprise, *(Sing 3 times)*
   There must be joy somewhere.

Each verse of "Over My Head" is about a different art and is sometimes called "The National Standards Song."

OVER THE RIVER

Lydia M. Child
(American, 1802–1880)

American Song

C F
1. O - ver the riv - er and through the wood, To grand - fa - ther's house we
C G7 C
go; The horse knows the way to car - ry the sleigh through the
G7 C
white and drift - ed snow. O - ver the riv - er and
F C
through the wood, Oh, how the wind does blow! It
F C G7 C
stings the toes and bites the nose, As o - ver the ground we go.

2. Over the river and through the wood, And straight to the barnyard gate;
We seem to go so very slow, And it's so hard to wait.
Over the river and through the wood, Now grandmother's cap I spy.
Hurrah for the fun, the pudding's done, Hurrah for the pumpkin pie!

3. Over the river and through the wood, Now soon we'll be on our way;
There's feasting and fun for ev'ryone, For this is Thanksgiving day.
Over the river and through the wood, Get on, my dapple grey,
The woods will ring with the songs we sing, For this is Thanksgiving day.

PEASE PORRIDGE HOT

Traditional

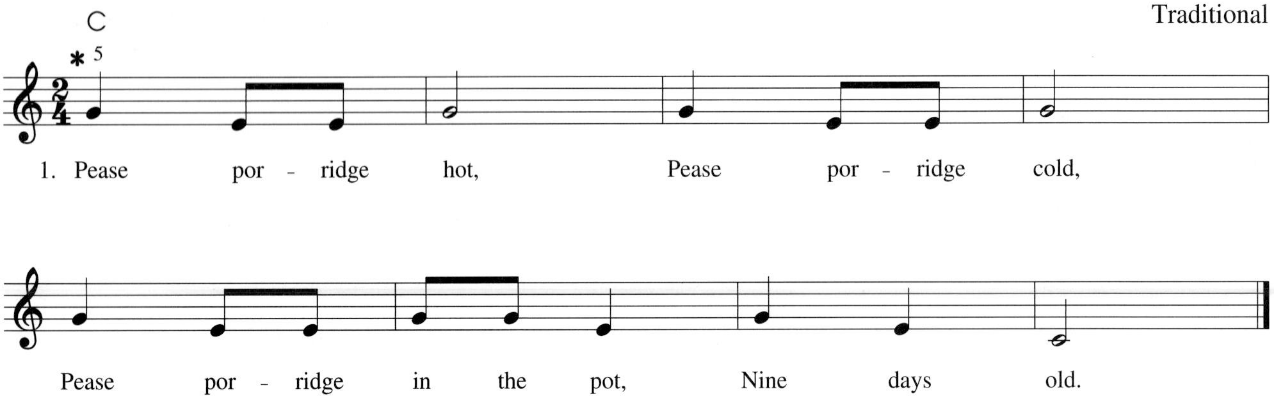
C
* 5
1. Pease por - ridge hot, Pease por - ridge cold,
Pease por - ridge in the pot, Nine days old.

* Small number indicates fingering for keyboard.

2. Some like it hot,
Some like it cold,
Some like it in the pot,
Nine days old.

PELE E

Pele is the Hawaiian fire goddess

Traditional Hawaiian

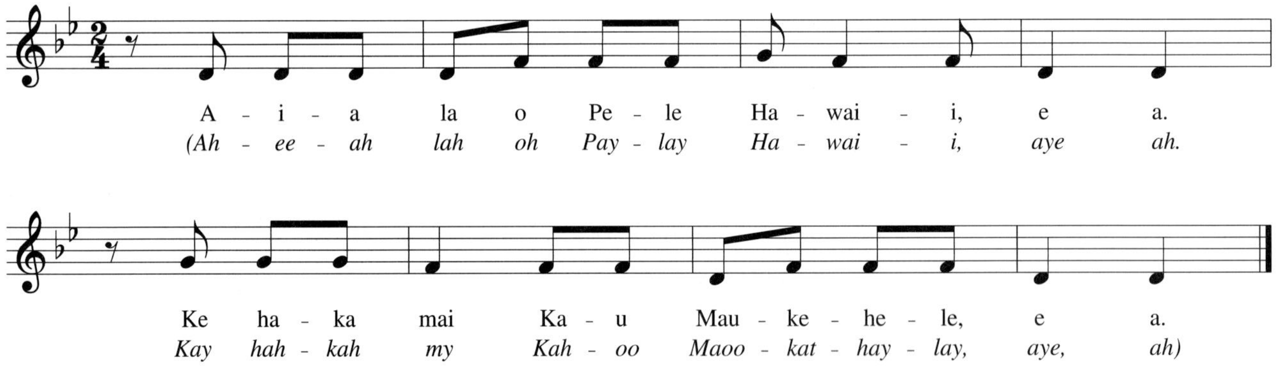
A - i - a la o Pe - le Ha - wai - i, e a.
(Ah - ee - ah lah oh Pay - lay Ha - wai - i, aye ah.
Ke ha - ka mai Ka - u Mau - ke - he - le, e a.
Kay hah - kah my Kah - oo Maoo - kat - hay - lay, aye, ah)

Translation

"O, she is here - Pele - in Hawaii, e a.
O, see her dancing in Maukehele, e a."

Throughout
= high drum
= low drum

PIPE DANCE SONG

Sauk- Fox Indian Song
As sung by Don Patterson,
Ponca Singers, Ponca, Oklahoma

Transcribed by P. Hackett

Begin in a moderate tempo ♩ = 104
Sing three times, gradually accelerating throughout to ♩ = 200

Nee - kah - na - way, twee - ah - way - ha,
Drum
Nee - kah - na - way, twee - ah - way - ha, Nee - kah - na - way, twee -
ah - way - ha, Hay, yea, Nee - kah - na - way, twee -
ah - way - ha, Nee - kah - na - way, twee - ah - way - hah,

Translation

'Twee- ah- way- ha (My friend)
Nee- kah- na- way (Take care of horses' feet)

Dance

A large group of spectators forms a circle around two dancers. On the drum roll, the two dancers quiver, standing in place and swaying the torso.

On ♩♩♩♩ the two dancers do traditional toe-heel dance steps. As they dance, they hold the calumet (pipe) in one hand and offer it - as a symbolic gesture of peace and solidarity - to the various spectators who form the circle.

PUNCINELLA

French Song

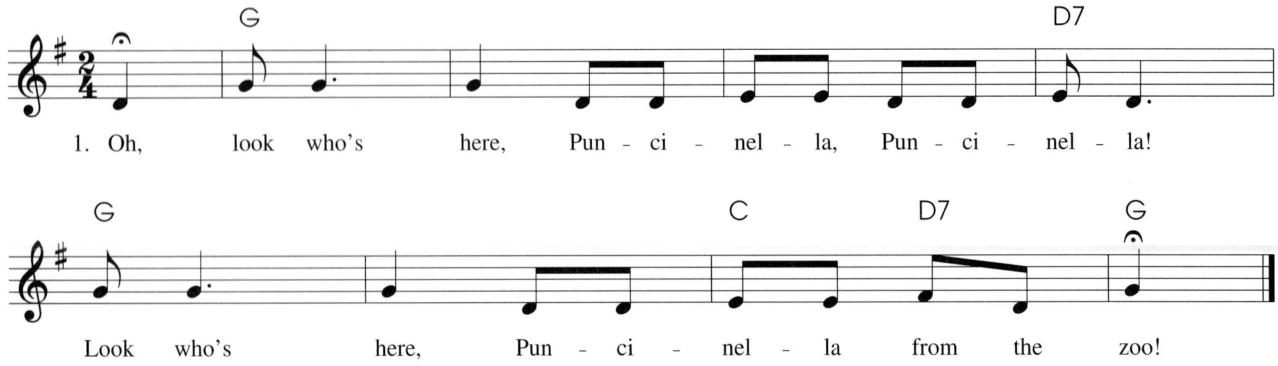

G
D7
1. Oh, look who's here, Pun - ci - nel - la, Pun - ci - nel - la!
G
C
D7
G
Look who's here, Pun - ci - nel - la from the zoo!

2. Oh, what can you do, Puncinella, Puncinella!
   Oh, what can you do, Puncinella from the zoo!

3. Oh, we can do it too, Puncinella, Puncinella!
   We can do it, too, Puncinella from the zoo!

4. Oh, who do you choose, Puncinella, Puncinella!
   Oh, who do you choose, Puncinella from the zoo!

Singing Game

Class forms a circle.

Verse 1: "Puncinella" is selected to walk in a circle while class claps and sings.

Verse 2: "Puncinella" creates and performs a motion while class sings.

Verse 3: Class copies "Puncinella" motion and sings.

Verse 4: "Puncinella" closes eyes, spins and points to the next "Puncinella" on last word "zoo."

PUT YOUR HAND IN MY HAND

Teresa Jennings
(American)

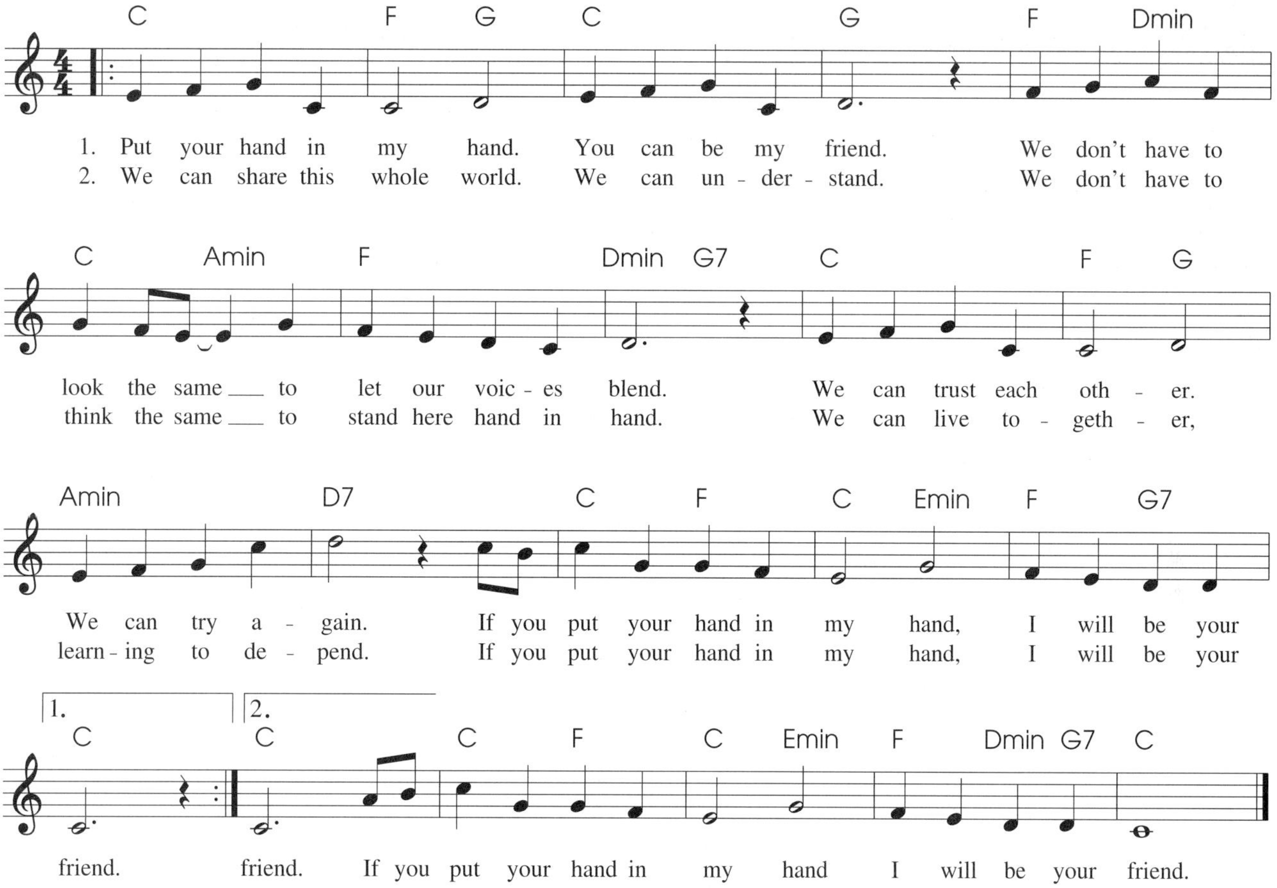

C F G C G F Dmin
1. Put your hand in my hand. You can be my friend. We don't have to
2. We can share this whole world. We can un - der - stand. We don't have to
C Amin F Dmin G7 C F G
look the same ___ to let our voic - es blend. We can trust each oth - er.
think the same ___ to stand here hand in hand. We can live to - geth - er,
Amin D7 C F C Emin F G7
We can try a - gain. If you put your hand in my hand, I will be your
learn - ing to de - pend. If you put your hand in my hand, I will be your
1. 2.
C C C F C Emin F Dmin G7 C
friend. friend. If you put your hand in my hand I will be your friend.

RAIN, RAIN

Traditional

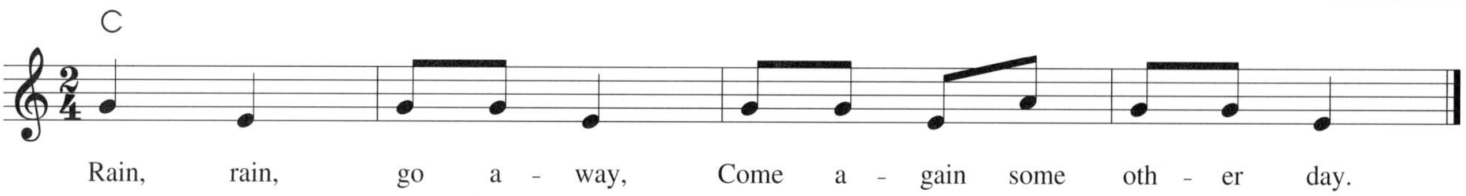

C
Rain, rain, go a - way, Come a - gain some oth - er day.

RIDING IN THE BUGGY

Model Experience, p. 118

American Folk Song

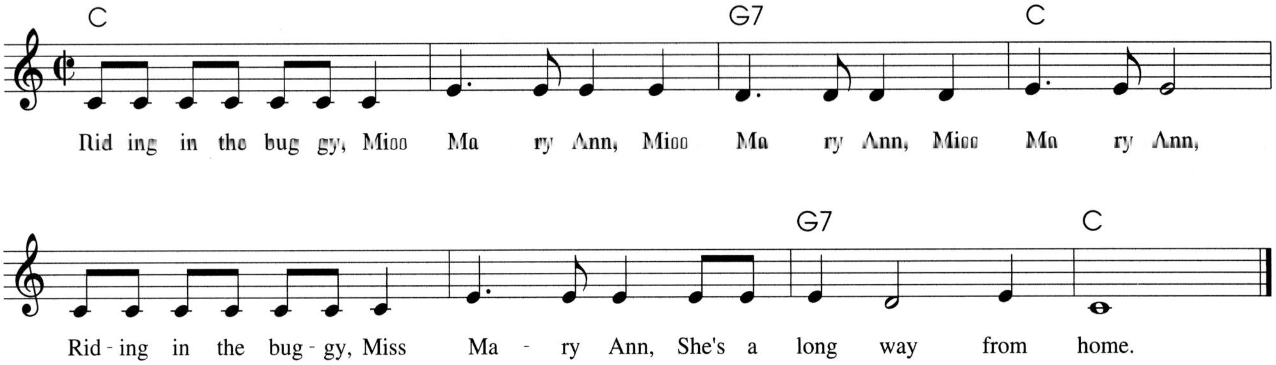
C G7 C
Rid ing in the bug gy, Miss Ma ry Ann, Miss Ma ry Ann, Miss Ma ry Ann,
G7 C
Rid - ing in the bug - gy, Miss Ma - ry Ann, She's a long way from home.

RIG–A–JIG–JIG

American Folk Song

Verse
C G7 C
As I was walk - ing down the street, Down the street, down the street, A
G7 C
nice young girl / nice young boy I chanced to meet, Heigh - o, heigh - o, heigh - o.
Refrain
G7 C
Rig - a - jig - jig, and a - way we go, A - way we go, a - way we go;
G7 C
Rig - a - jig - jig, and a - way we go, Heigh - o, heigh - o, heigh - o.

RING AROUND THE ROSY

Traditional

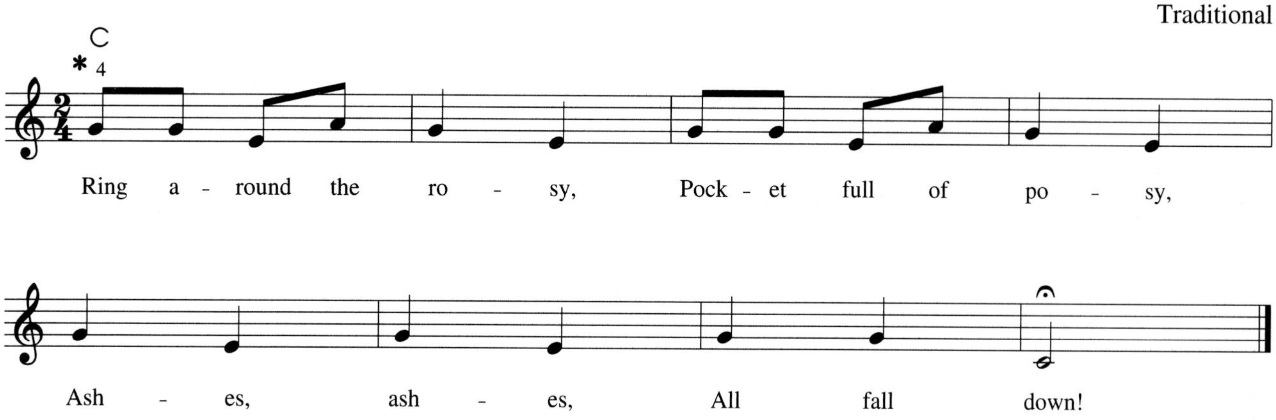

C
* 4
Ring a - round the ro - sy, Pock - et full of po - sy,
Ash - es, ash - es, All fall down!

* Small number indicates fingering for keyboard.

ROCK-PASSING SONG

(Obwisana)

African Play Song
(West Africa: Ghana)

Ob - wi - sa - na sa na - na, Ob - wi - sa - na sa,
ohb wih sah nah sah nah nah
Ob - wi - sa - na sa na - na. Ob - wi - sa - na sa.

Translation

Oh, Gramma, I just hurt my finger on a rock.

Game

Players sit in a tight circle, each holding a pebble in the right hand. Players pass (and pick up) a pebble while singing and keeping steady beats. At the song's end, they must have one pebble in front of them. On beat 1 of each measure, they place the pebble in front of the player on their right. On beat 2, they pick up the "new" pebble in front of them. On the last beat of the song, any player who has no pebble (or several) must leave the circle.

SAKURA
(Cherry Bloom)

Japanese Folk Song

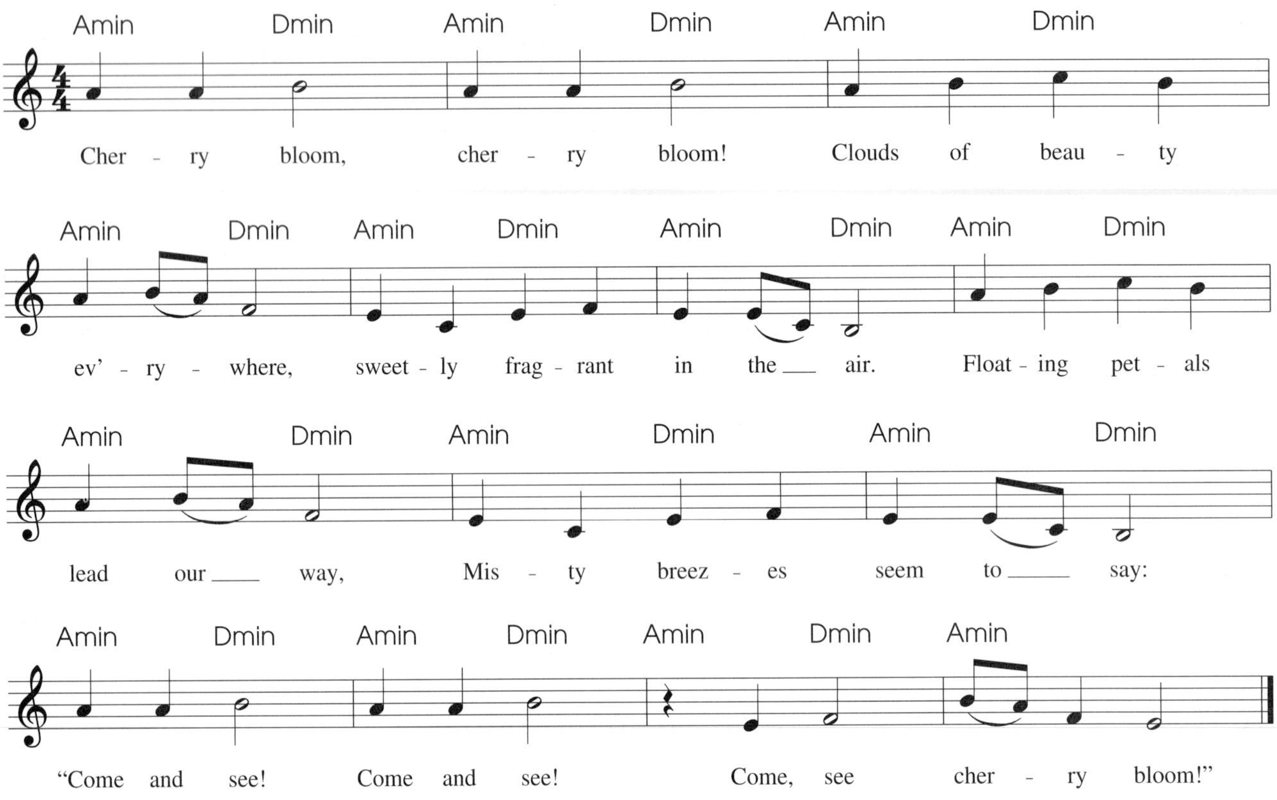

Japanese text

Sa - ku - ra, Sa - ku - ra, Yo - yo - i - no
"sah - koo - rah sah - koo - rah yoh - yoh - ee - noe

so - ra - wa, Mi - wa - ta - su ka - gi - ri. Ka - su - mi - ka
soh - rah - wah mee - wah - tah - soo kah - gee - ree kah - soo - mee - kah

ku - mo - ka, Ni - o - i - zo i - zu - ru
koo - moh - kah nee - oh - ee - zoh ee - zoo - roo

I - za - ya, i - za - ya, Mi - ni yu - ka - n.
ee - zah - yah ee - zah - yah mee - nee yoo - kah - n"

A haiku poem about cherry blossoms

The waterbird swims
parting with her breast
the cherry petals. (by Rôka; Japan, 1672–1703)

Pronunciation of the haiku poem in Japanese

"Mee- zoo- to- ree no
moonuh nee wahkuhyookoo
sahkoorah kahnah." (by Rôka; Japan, 1672–1703)

SALLY, GO 'ROUND THE SUN

Model Experience, p. 122

American Folk Song

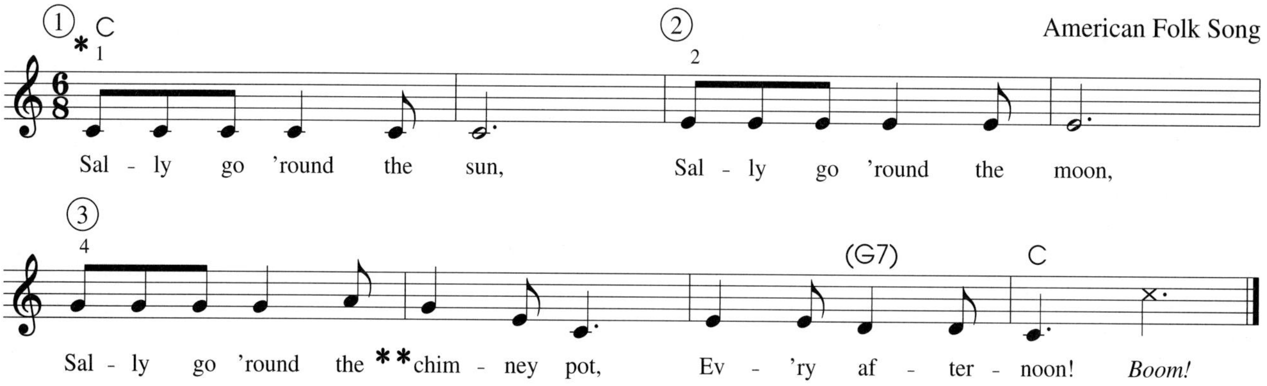
C
(G7)
C
Sal - ly go 'round the sun,
Sal - ly go 'round the moon,
Sal - ly go 'round the **chim - ney pot,
Ev - 'ry af - ter - noon! *Boom!*

* Small numbers indicate fingering for keyboard.
** A chimney pot is a pipe at the top of a chimney (to increase the draft).

SANDY LAND

American Play-Party Song

F
C7
1. Make my liv - in' in sand - y land, Make my liv - in' in sand - y land.
F
C7
F
Make my liv - in' in sand - y land, La - dies, fare you well.

2. Raise my 'taters in sandy land, *(Sing 3 times)*
   Ladies, fare you well.

3. Swing, oh swing in sandy land, *(Sing 3 times)*
   Ladies, fare you well.

4. Right and left in sandy land, *(Sing 3 times)*
   Ladies, fare you well.

5. Promenade in sandy land, *(Sing 3 times)*
   Ladies, fare you well.

Formation

Players choose a partner and form a single circle. Girls are on the right so that players alternate boy, girl, boy, girl, and so forth. All join hands.

Dance

Verse 1: All walk to the left.
Verse 2: All walk to the right.
Verse 3: Partners swing, linking right arms, and skip in a small clockwise circle.
Verse 4: Partners face each other and begin grand right and left. (In grand right and left, players clasp right hands and quickly pass their partner on the right. Then they clasp left hands with the next dancer and pass on the left, alternating right and left hands throughout.) Repeat verse 4 until original partners meet again.
Verse 5: The boy promenades around the circle with the girl on his left.

SARASPONDA

Composer Unknown

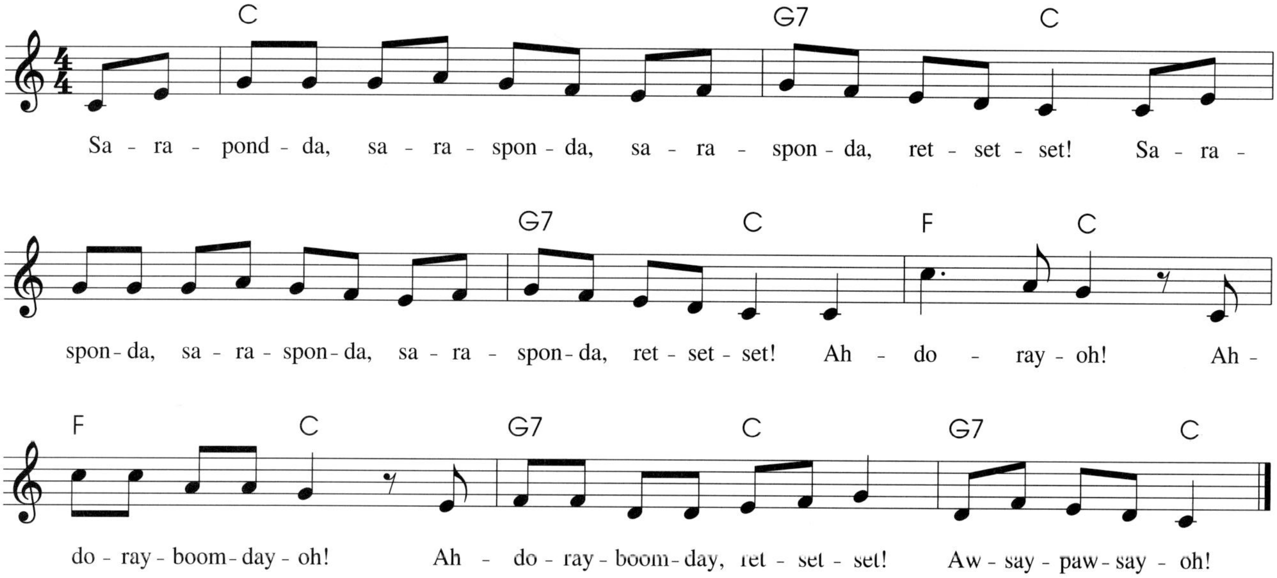
C G7 C
Sa - ra - pond - da, sa - ra - spon - da, sa - ra - spon - da, ret - set - set! Sa - ra -
G7 C F C
spon - da, sa - ra - spon - da, sa - ra - spon - da, ret - set - set! Ah - do - ray - oh! Ah -
F C G7 C G7 C
do - ray - boom - day - oh! Ah - do - ray - boom - day, ret - set - set! Aw - say - paw - say - oh!

Sing as an introduction and as harmony during measures 1–4:

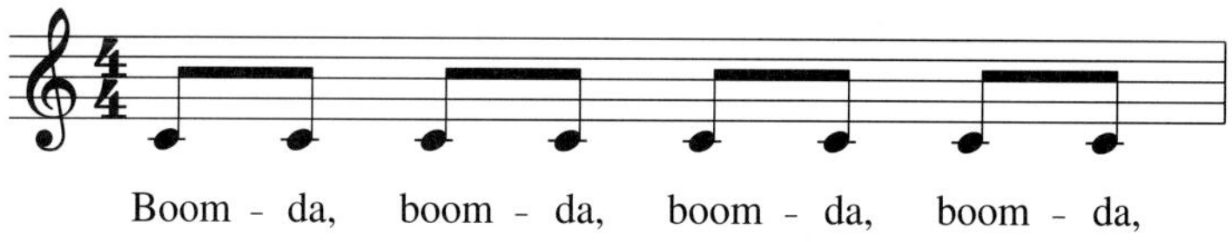
Boom - da, boom - da, boom - da, boom - da,

SCARBOROUGH FAIR

Old English Song

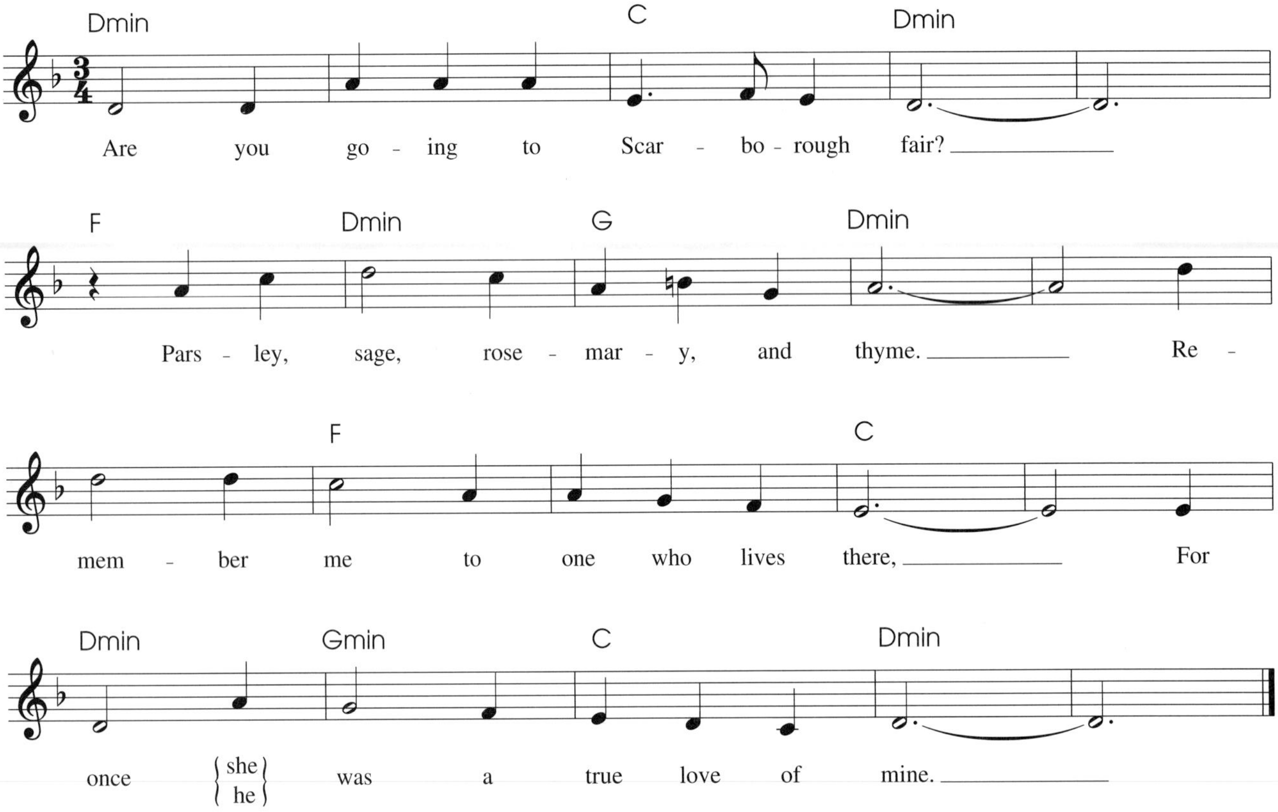
Dmin C Dmin
Are you go - ing to Scar - bo - rough fair?
F Dmin G Dmin
Pars - ley, sage, rose - mar - y, and thyme. Re -
F C
mem - ber me to one who lives there, For
Dmin Gmin C Dmin
once she/he was a true love of mine.

SCOTLAND'S BURNING

Traditional Round

1 F
Scot - land's burn - ing, Scot - land's burn - ing,
2
Look out! Look out!
3
Fire! Fire! Fire! Fire! Pour on wa - ter, pour on wa - ter!

SHALOM, CHAVERIM

Israeli Round

English text

Farewell, good friends, Farewell, good friends,
Farewell, farewell!
Till we meet again, till we meet again,
Farewell, farewell!

SHOO, FLY

Model Experience and Dance, p. 158

Billy Reeves

Frank Campbell

Refrain
D
A7
D
Shoo, fly, don't both - er me, Shoo, fly, don't both - er me.
Fine
A7
D
Shoo, fly, don't both - er me, For I be - long to some - bod - y.
Verse
A7
I feel, I feel, I feel, I feel like a morn - ing star. I
D.C. al Fine
D
A7
feel, I feel, I feel, I feel, I feel like a morn - ing star. So

SILENT NIGHT

Josef Mohr
(Austrian, 1792–1848)

Frranz Grüber
(German, 1787–1863)

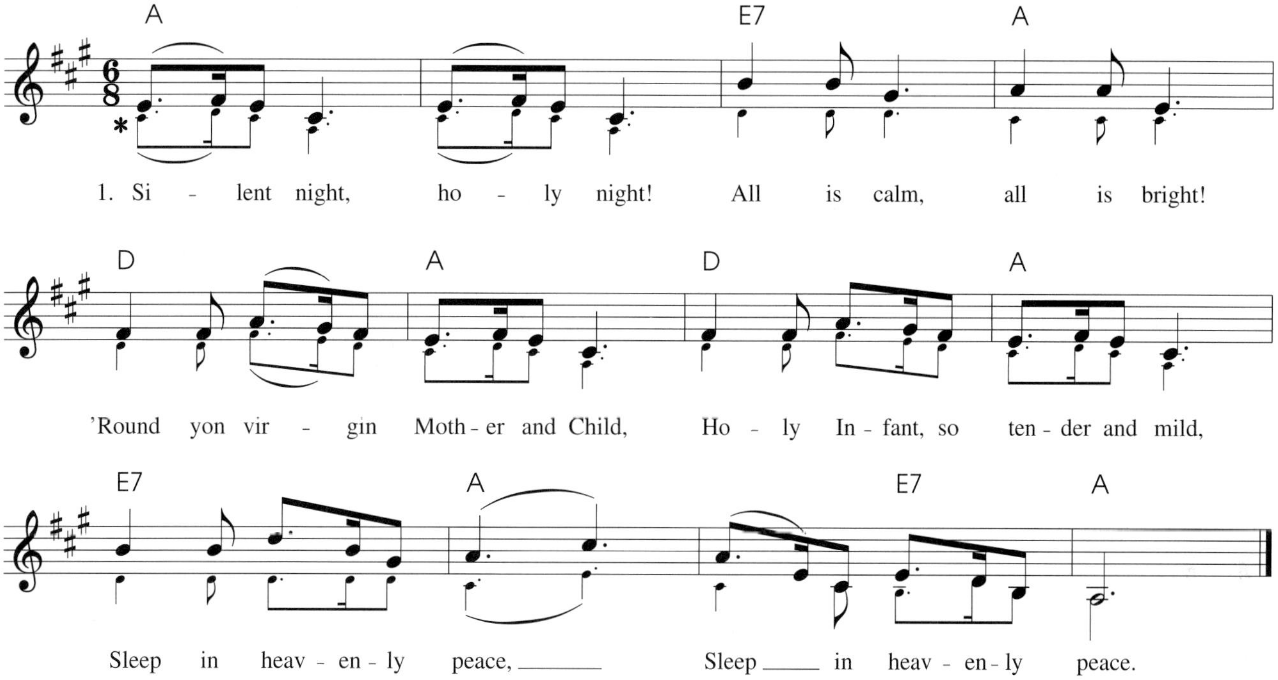
A E7 A
1. Si - lent night, ho - ly night! All is calm, all is bright!
D A D A
'Round yon vir - gin Moth - er and Child, Ho - ly In - fant, so ten - der and mild,
E7 A E7 A
Sleep in heav - en - ly peace, Sleep in heav - en - ly peace.

* One group of singers can sing the smaller notes.

2. Silent night, holy night! Shepherds quake at the sight!
Glories stream from heaven afar, Heavenly hosts sing "Alleluia!"
Christ the Savior, is born, Christ, the Savior is born.

3. Silent night, holy night! Son of God, love's pure light!
Radiant beams from Thy holy face, With the dawn of redeeming grace,
Jesus, Lord, at Thy birth, Jesus, Lord, at Thy birth.

German version, verse 1

Stille Nacht, Heilige Nacht!
"shtee- leh nockt hie- lih- geh nockt
Alles schläft, einsam wacht
ah- lehs shlayft ine-sahm vahkt
Nur das traute hochheilige Paar
noor dahs trou- tuh hoke- hie- lih- guh pahr
Holder Knabe im lockigen Haar,
hohld- ehr knah- beh eem lock- ih- gehn hahr
Schlaf in himmlischer Ruh!
shlaf een heem- lih- sher roo
Schlaf in himmlischer Ruh.
shlaf een heem- lih- sher roo."

"Silent Night" was composed on the day before Christmas, 1818, at Oberndorf, Austria. The organ at St. Nicholas Church had broken down, and could not be repaired before the Christmas Eve services. So Franz Grüber, the church organist, composed "Silent Night" and presented it on Christmas Eve, with guitar accompaniment. The poem was provided by Josef Mohr, the church pastor and local schoolmaster. "Silent Night" was popularized by a touring troupe of singers from the Tyrol.

SING ABOUT MARTIN!

Model Experience, p. 146

Words and Music by
"Miss Jackie" Weissman

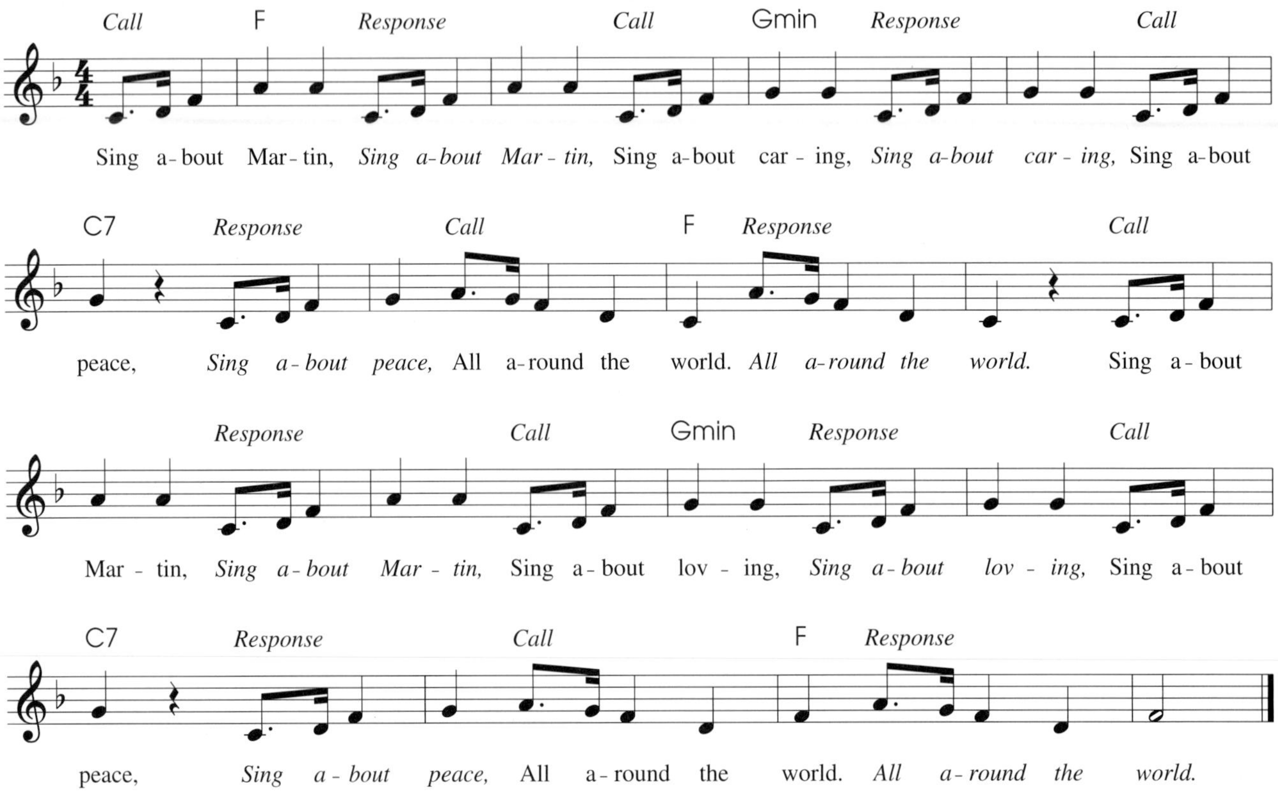
Call F Response Call Gmin Response Call
Sing a-bout Mar-tin, *Sing a-bout Mar-tin,* Sing a-bout car-ing, *Sing a-bout car-ing,* Sing a-bout
C7 Response Call F Response Call
peace, *Sing a-bout peace,* All a-round the world. *All a-round the world.* Sing a-bout
Response Call Gmin Response Call
Mar-tin, *Sing a-bout Mar-tin,* Sing a-bout lov-ing, *Sing a-bout lov-ing,* Sing a-bout
C7 Response Call F Response
peace, *Sing a-bout peace,* All a-round the world. *All a-round the world.*

SING HALLELU

African American Spiritual

3. Where was He born? *Sing hallelu. (Sing 4 times)*
4. Born in a stable, *Sing hallelu. (Sing 4 times)*
5. Where did she lay Him? *Sing hallelu. (Sing 4 times)*
6. Laid Him in a manager, *Sing hallelu. (Sing 4 times)*
7. What did she name Him? *Sing hallelu. (Sing 4 times)*
8. Named Him King Jesus, *Sing hallelu. (Sing 4 times)*

SKIP TO MY LOU

American Folk Song

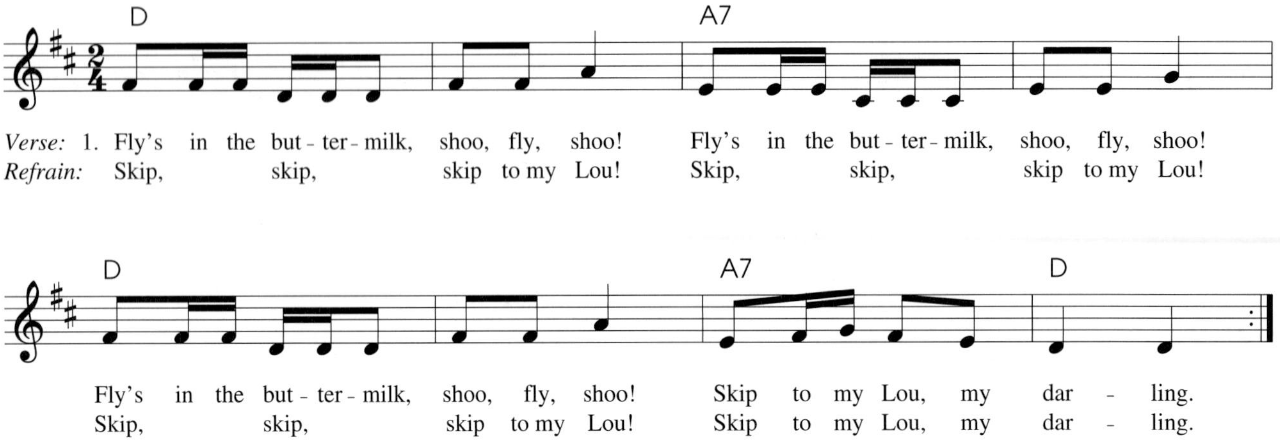
D
A7
Verse: 1. Fly's in the but - ter - milk, shoo, fly, shoo! Fly's in the but - ter - milk, shoo, fly, shoo!
Refrain: Skip, skip, skip to my Lou! Skip, skip, skip to my Lou!
D
A7
D
Fly's in the but - ter - milk, shoo, fly, shoo! Skip to my Lou, my dar - ling.
Skip, skip, skip to my Lou! Skip to my Lou, my dar - ling.

2. Little red wagon, painted blue, *(Sing 3 times)* Skip to my Lou, my darling. *Refrain*
3. Lost my partner, what'll I do? *(Sing 3 times)* Skip to my Lou, my darling. *Refrain*
4. I'll get another one, better than you! *(Sing 3 times)* Skip to my Lou, my darling. *Refrain*

SONG FOR THE SABBATH

Hebrew Song

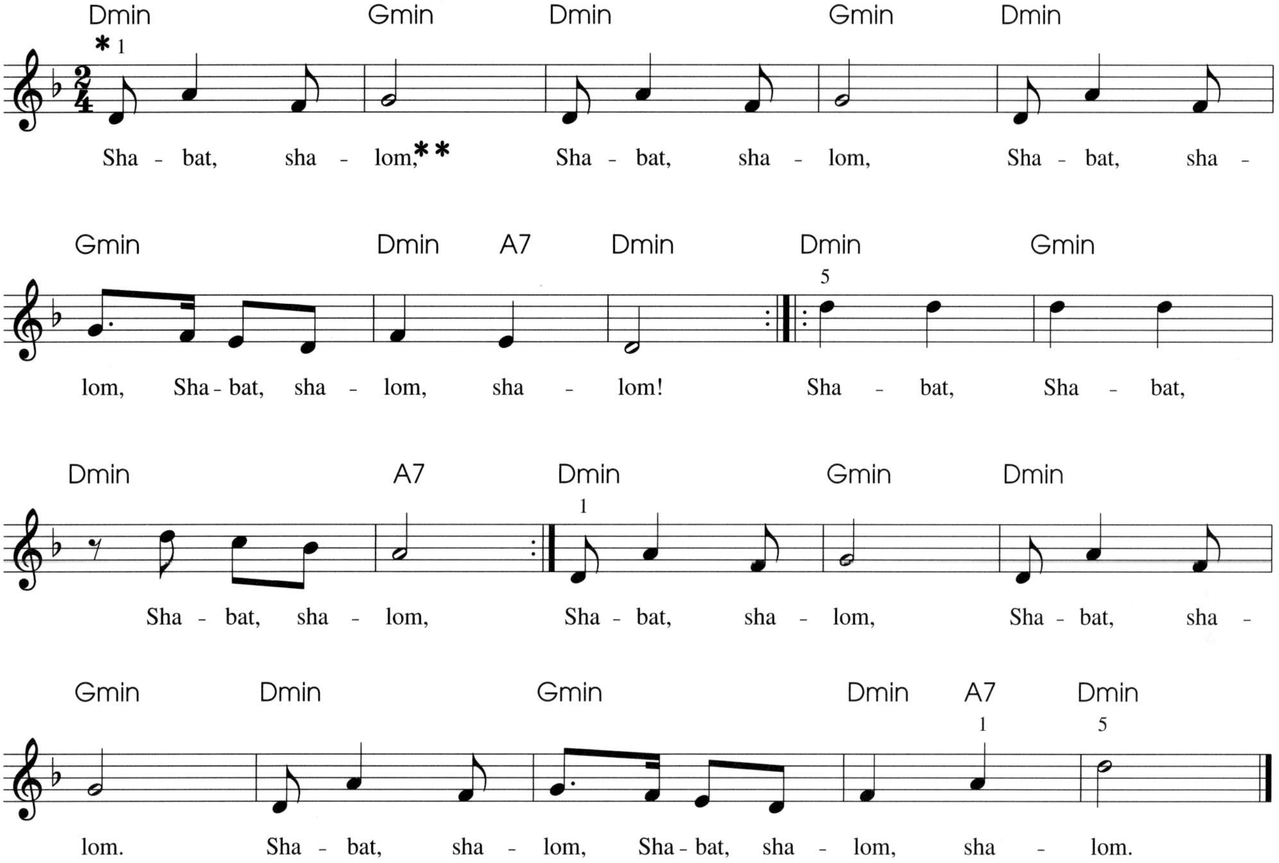

* *Small numbers indicate fingering for keyboard.*

** *Shabat shalom* ("sha- BAHT shah- LOME") means "welcome the Sabbath."

SONG OF THE DRAGON

Model Experience, p. 184

Adapted by P. Hackett

Chinese Folk Melody

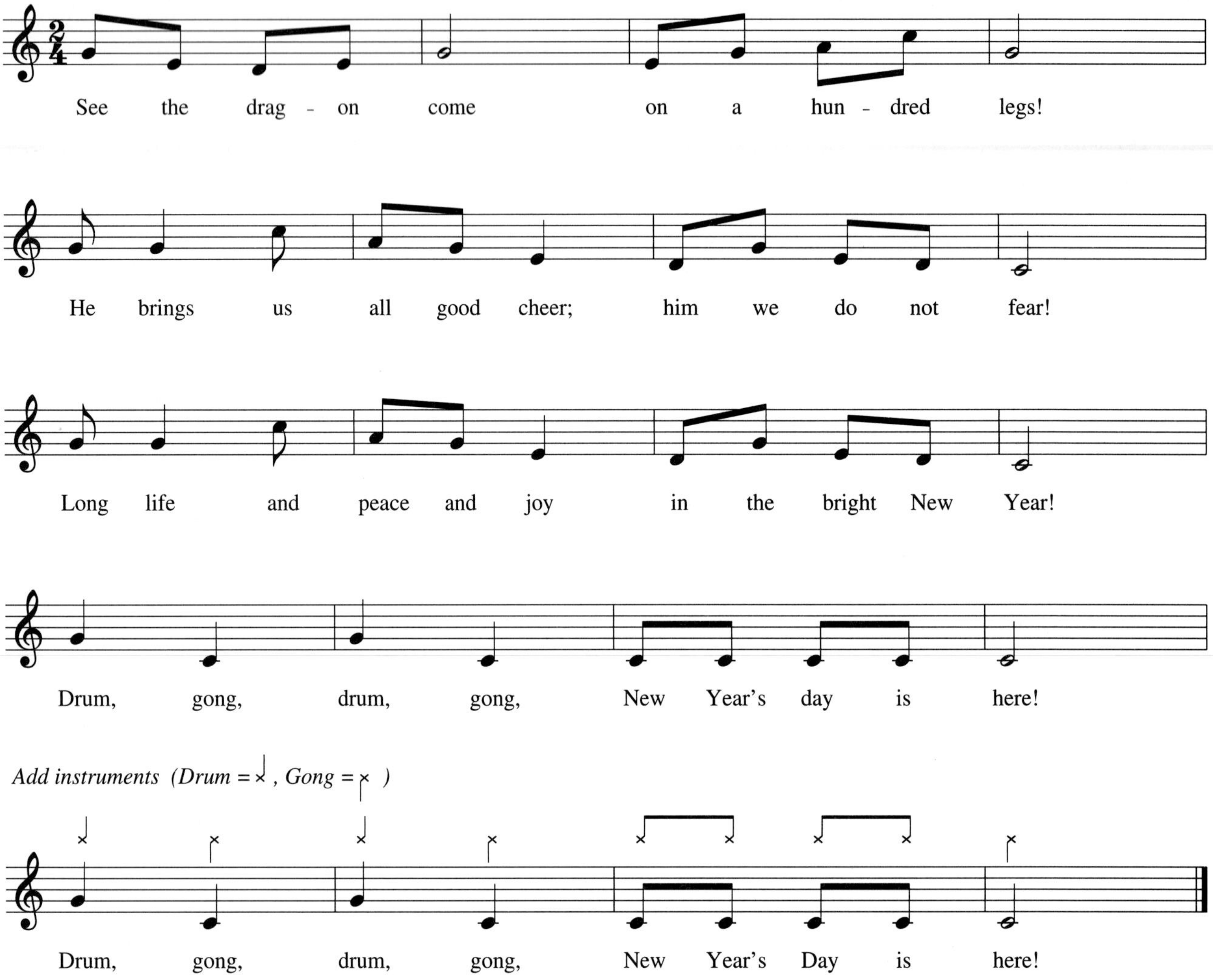

See the drag - on come on a hun - dred legs!
He brings us all good cheer; him we do not fear!
Long life and peace and joy in the bright New Year!
Drum, gong, drum, gong, New Year's day is here!
Add instruments (Drum = , Gong =)
Drum, gong, drum, gong, New Year's Day is here!

STARLIGHT, STARBRIGHT

Traditional

C
Star - light, star - bright, First star I see to - night,
Wish I may, wish I might, Have the wish I wish to - night.

THE STAR-SPANGLED BANNER

Francis Scott Key
(American, 1779–1843)

Music attributed to J. S. Smith
(English, 1750–1836)

Ab Fmin Bb7 Eb
Oh, say! can you see, by the dawn's ear - ly light, What so
Ab Eb Ab
proud - ly we hailed at the twi - light's last gleam - ing? Whose broad
Fmin Bb7 Eb
stripes and bright stars, through the per - il - ous fight, O'er the
Ab Eb Ab
ram - parts we watched were so gal - lant - ly stream - ing? And the
Eb
roc - kets' red glare, the bombs burst - ing in air, Gave
Ab Eb Ab Bb7 Eb
proof through the night that our flag was still there. Oh,
Ab Db Bbmin Ab Eb7
say, does that star - span - gled ban - ner yet wave O'er the
Ab Eb7 Ab
land of the free and the home of the brave?

An American flag waves both day and night over Ft. McHenry in Baltimore and over a grave at Frederick in northwestern Maryland. These commemorate the attorney Francis Scott Key and the incident in 1814 that inspired him to write "The Defense of Ft. McHenry," later entitled "The Star-Spangled Banner." Key and a friend undertook a mission to secure the release of an American physician held prisoner on a British flagship. The venture was successful, but their boat was detained in Chesapeake Bay by the British, who began a bombardment of nearby Ft. McHenry. The shelling stopped during the night, but only after the morning fog lifted could the Americans see their flag still flying over the fort. On that very day—September 14—Key set down his verses. The text was immediately associated with a well-known hymn tune, already familiar to Key. Since 1931, "The Star-Spangled Banner" has been the national anthem of the United States. Elementary students will enjoy Steven Kroll's illustrated By the Dawn's Early Light: The Story of the Star-Spangled Banner *(New York: Scholastic, 1994).*

ST. PAUL'S STEEPLE

English Folk Song

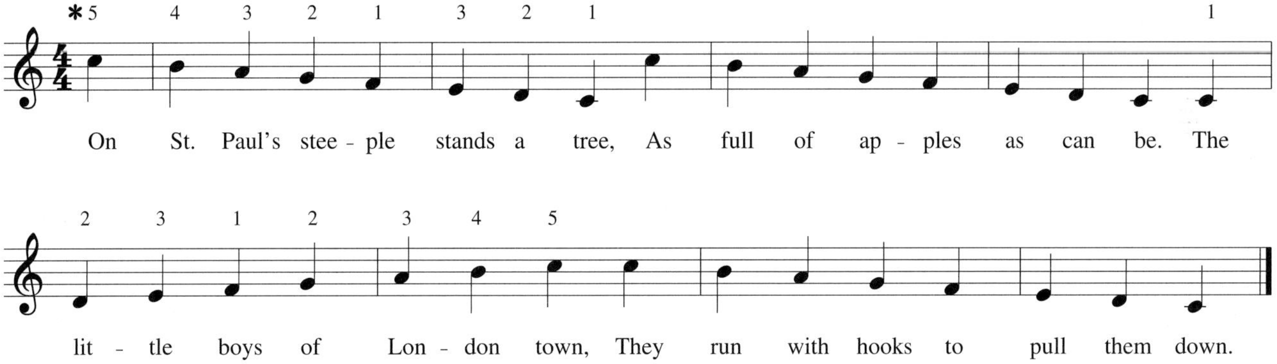

On St. Paul's stee - ple stands a tree, As full of ap - ples as can be. The

lit - tle boys of Lon - don town, They run with hooks to pull them down.

* Small numbers indicate fingering for keyboard.

SWING A LADY

Traditional

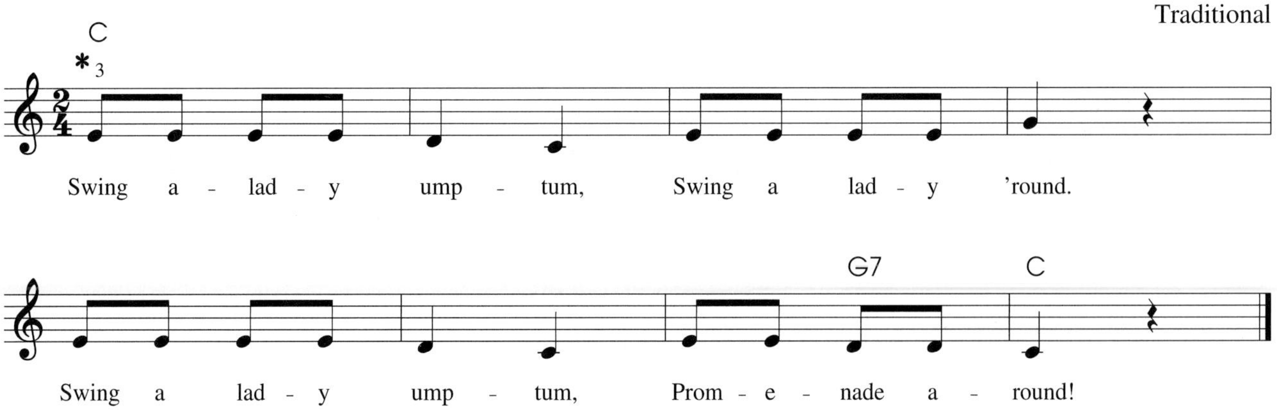

C
*3
Swing a - lad - y ump - tum, Swing a lad - y 'round.
G7 C
Swing a lad - y ump - tum, Prom - e - nade a - round!

* Small number indicates fingering for keyboard.

THANK YOU FOR THE CHRIS'MUS

Folk Song from Jamaica
Collected by Olive Lewin

G
Thank you for the Chris' - mus, Thank you for the
D7 G C
New Year, And thank you for the chance to live to
G D7 G C D7
see an - oth - er Chris' - mus. La la la la, Do - in' the
G C D7 G
bam - boo walk La la la la, Do - in' the bam - boo walk.

THIS IS HALLOWEEN

Lucille Wood

Gmin
D7
1. One lit - tle skel - e - ton hop - ping up and down,
Gmin
Hop - ping up and down, hop - ing up and down; One lit - tle skel - e - ton
D7
Gmin
hop - ping up and down, For this is Hal - low - een.

2. Two little witches, flying through the air, *(Sing 3 times)*
   For this is Halloween.

3. Three little pumpkins, walking in a row, *(Sing 3 times)*
   For this is Halloween.

4. Four little goblins, stepping down the street, *(Sing 3 times)*
   For this is Halloween.

5. Five little children, playing trick or treat, *(Sing 3 times)*
   For this is Halloween.

THIS LAND IS YOUR LAND

Woody Guthrie

Woody Guthrie
(American, 1912–1967)

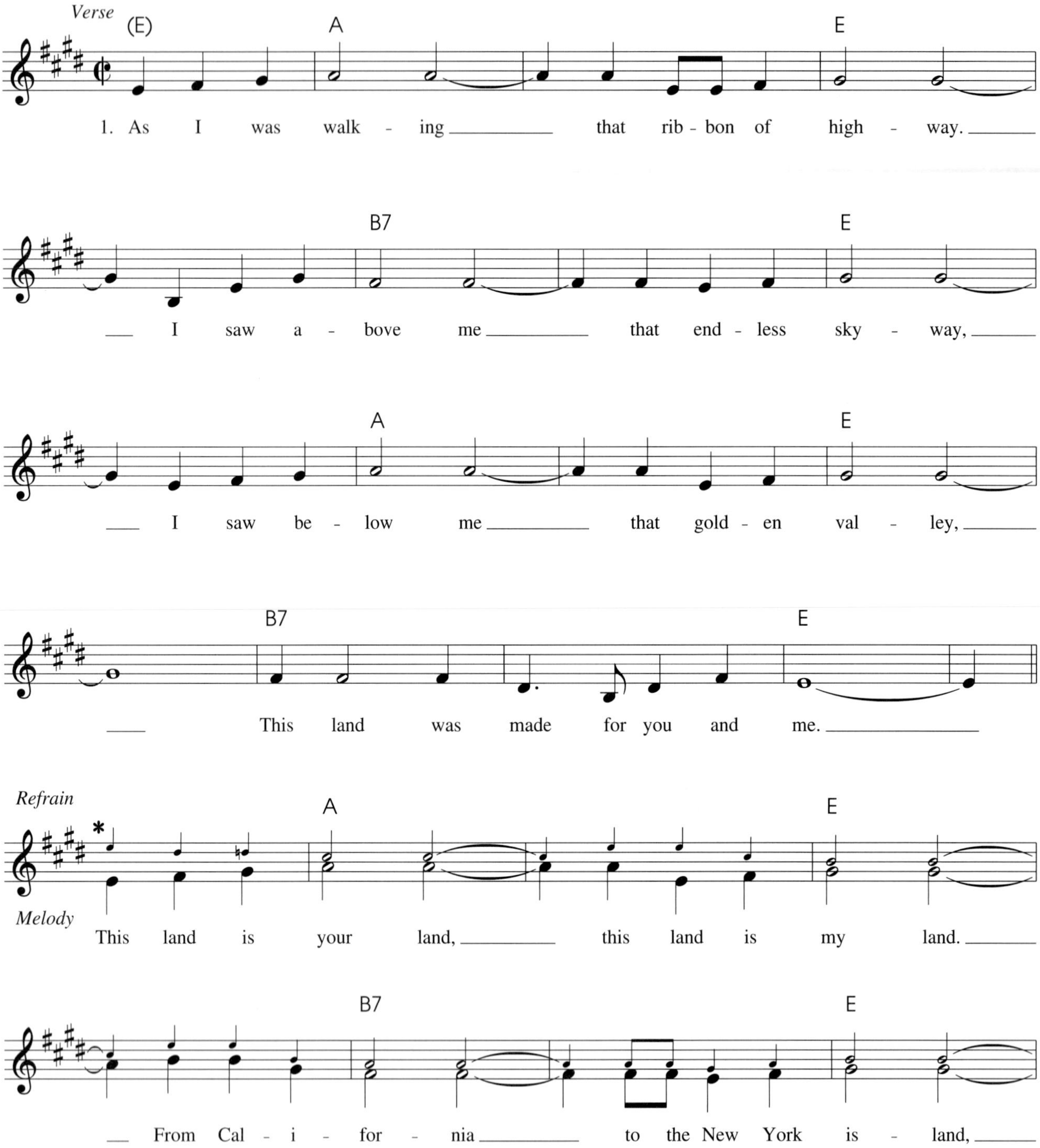
Verse
(E) A E
1. As I was walk - ing ___ that rib - bon of high - way. ___
B7 E
___ I saw a - bove me ___ that end - less sky - way, ___
A E
___ I saw be - low me ___ that gold - en val - ley, ___
B7 E
___ This land was made for you and me. ___
Refrain
*
Melody
A E
This land is your land, ___ this land is my land. ___
B7 E
___ From Cal - i - for - nia ___ to the New York is - land, ___

* One group of singers can sing the smaller notes.

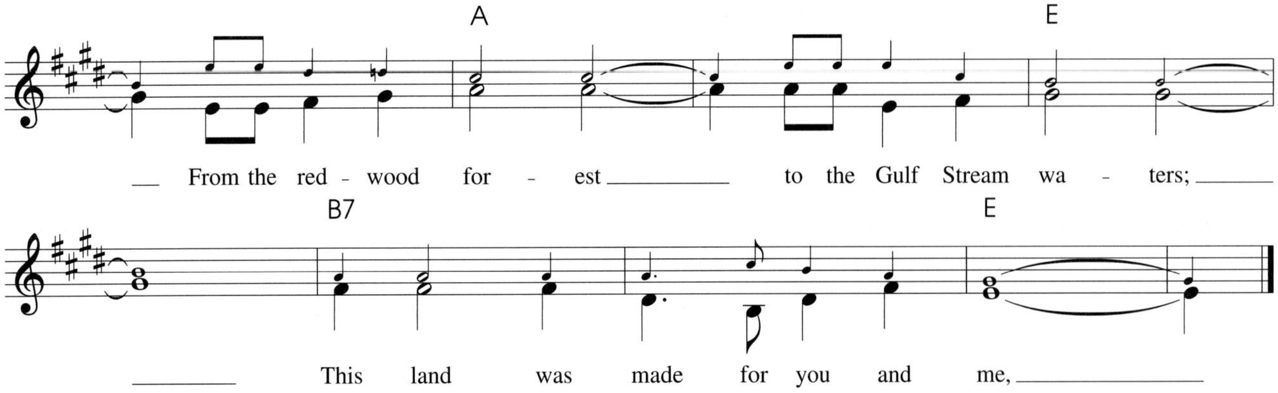
A
E
From the red - wood for - est to the Gulf Stream wa - ters;
B7
E
This land was made for you and me,

2. I've roamed and rambled, and I followed my footsteps,
   To the sparkling sands of her diamond deserts,
   And all around me a voice was sounding,
   This land was made for you and me. *Refrain*

3. When the sun came shining, and I was strolling,
   And the wheat-fields waving and the dust clouds rolling,
   As the fog was lifting, a voice was chanting,
   This land was made for you and me. *Refrain*

Woodrow Wilson Guthrie, American folk singer, guitarist, and composer of ballads, was born in Okemah, Oklahoma, on July 14, 1912. By the age of thirteen, he was earning his living as a wandering singer, performing in saloons, migrant labor camps, and hobo jungles. Later he composed ballads, performed on radio, and wrote a newspaper column. His songs are filled with stories of how ordinary people became victims of the 1930s depression. He also celebrates the beauty of the American landscape in songs such as "This Land Is Your Land," one of his nearly one thousand songs. Woody's son Arlo Guthrie (born 1947) is also a folk-song writer, composing "Alice's Restaurant" and starring in the 1969 film version. Woody influenced many singers and songwriters, including Bob Dylan. After a long battle with Huntington's disease, Woody died in 1967 in New York City.

THIS OLD MAN

Traditional

C
F
G7
1. This old man, he played one, He played knick - knack on my drum,
C
G7
C
Knick - knack pad - dy - whack give a dog a bone, This old man came rol - ling home.

2. two, shoe
3. three, knee
4. four, door
5. five, hive
6. six, sticks
7. seven, heaven
8. eight, gate
9. nine, time
10. ten, again

THREE SAILORS

Folk Song

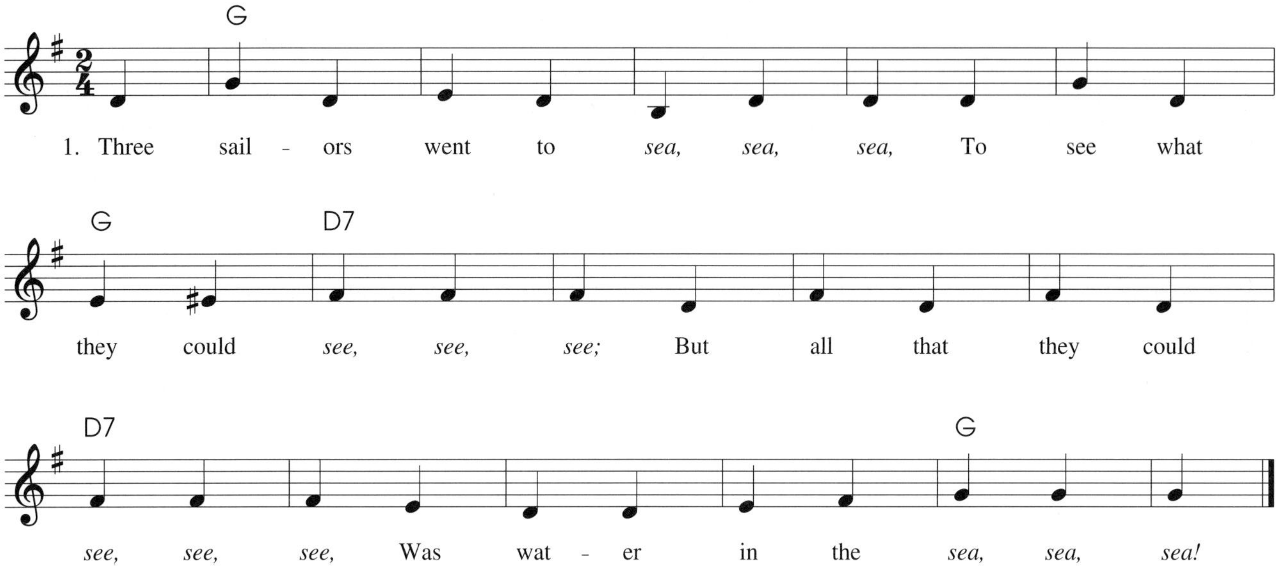
G
1. Three sail - ors went to *sea, sea, sea,* To see what
G D7
they could *see, see, see;* But all that they could
D7 G
see, see, see, Was wat - er in the *sea, sea, sea!*

2. *chop, chop, chop.*
3. *me, me, me.*
4. *see, chop, me.*

(On "chop," bring your left hand in front and "chop" it with your right hand.)

(On "me," slap your chest.)

(On "see," place your right hand above your eyes, as in a salute.)

TINGA LAYO

Calypso Song
from the West Indies

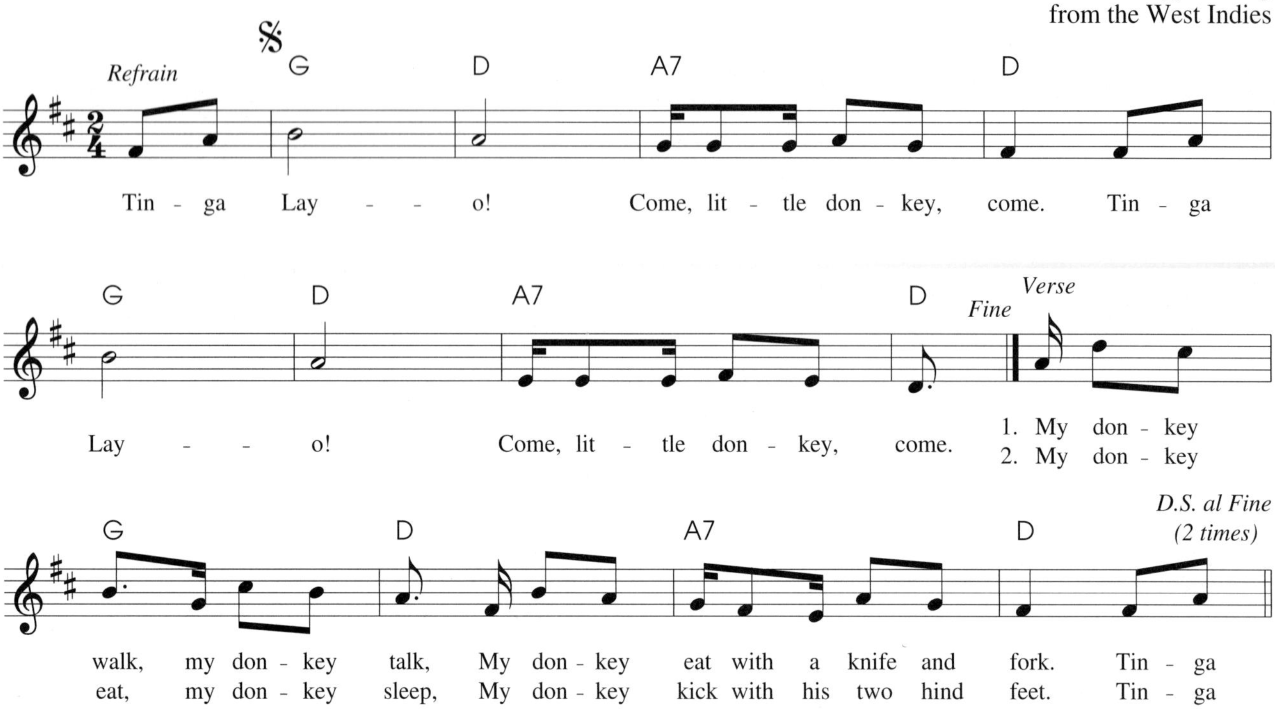
Refrain
G D A7 D
Tin - ga Lay - - o! Come, lit - tle don - key, come. Tin - ga
G D A7 D
Fine
Verse
Lay - - o! Come, lit - tle don - key, come.
1. My don - key
2. My don - key
D.S. al Fine
(2 times)
G D A7 D
walk, my don - key talk, My don - key eat with a knife and fork. Tin - ga
eat, my don - key sleep, My don - key kick with his two hind feet. Tin - ga

Spanish text (refrain)

¡Tinga Layo! ¡Ven, mi burrito, ven!
Tinga layo, vehn, mee boor- eet- to, vehn
¡Tinga Layo! ¡Ven, mi burrito, ven!
Tinga layo, vehn, mee boor- eet- to, vehn

TWELVE DAYS OF CHRISTMAS

English Folk Song

F C7 F Bb F C7 F
1. On the first day of Christ-mas my true love sent to me A par - tridge _ in a pear tree.
C7 F
2. On the sec - ond day of Christ - mas my true love sent to me
3. On the third ___ day of Christ - mas my true love sent to me
4. On the fourth ___ day of Christ - mas my true love sent to me
C7 F Bb F C7 F
Two tur - tle doves, And a par - tridge ___ in a pear tree.
Three French ___ hens, And a par - tridge ___ in a pear tree.
Four col - ly birds, And a par - tridge ___ in a pear tree.
C7 F
5. On the fifth day of Christ - mas my true love sent to me
G7 C F Bb
Five gold - en rings; Four ___ col - ly birds, three French hens,
G7 C F Bb F C7 F
Two ___ tur - tle - doves and a par - tridge ___ in a pear tree.
C7 F
6. On the sixth day of Christ - mas my true love sent to me
7. On the seventh day of Christ - mas my true love sent to me
8.–12.

(See next page)

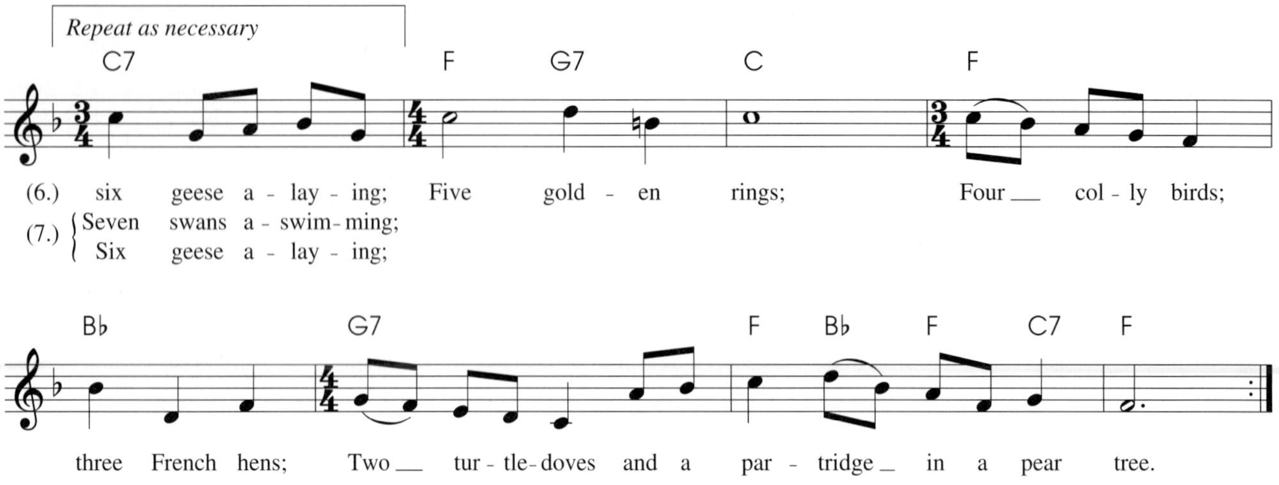
Repeat as necessary
C7 F G7 C F
(6.) six geese a - lay - ing; Five gold - en rings; Four col - ly birds;
(7.) Seven swans a - swim - ming;
Six geese a - lay - ing;
B♭ G7 F B♭ F C7 F
three French hens; Two tur - tle - doves and a par - tridge in a pear tree.

8. On the eighth day
   Eight maids a-milking . . .

9. On the ninth day
   Nine ladies dancing . . .

10. On the tenth day
    Ten lords a-leaping . . .

11. On the eleventh day
    Eleven pipers piping . . .

12. On the twelfth day of Christmas
    My true love sent to me,
    Twelve drummers drumming; Eleven pipers piping;
    Ten lords a-leaping; Nine ladies dancing;
    Eight maids a-milking; Seven swans a-swimming;
    Six geese a-laying; Five golden rings;
    Four colly birds; Three French hens;
    Two turtle doves and a partridge in a pear tree.

TWINKLE, TWINKLE, LITTLE STAR

Jane Taylor
(English, 1783–1824)

French Folk Melody

C F C G7 C G7 C
* 1 4 5 4
Twin - kle, twin - kle, lit - tle star, How I won - der what you are.
A, B, C, D, E, F, G, H, I, J, K, L, M, N, O, P.
F C G7 C F C G7
5
Up a - bove the world so high, like a dia - mond in the sky,
Q, R, S, T, U and V, W ___ and X, Y, Z,
C F C G7 C G7 C
1 4 5 4
Twin - kle, twin - kle, lit - tle star, How I won - der what you are.
Tell me what you think of me, I can say my "A, B, C's"!

* Small numbers indicate fingering for keyboard.

UP ON THE HOUSETOP

Benjamin R. Hanby
(American, 1833–1867)

Verse
D
1. Up on the house - top the rein - deer pause,
G D A7 D
Out jumps good old San - ta Claus; Down through the chim - ney with
G D A7 D
lots of toys, All for the lit - tle ones' Christ - mas joys.
Refrain
G D A7 D
Ho, ho, ho! Who would-n't go! Ho, ho, ho! Who would-n't go,
G D A7 D
Up on the house-top, click, click, click, Down through the chim-ney with good Saint Nick!

2. First comes the stocking of little Nell, Oh, dear Santa fill it well;
   Give her a dolly that laughs and cries, One that can open and shut its eyes. *Refrain*

3. Next comes the stocking of little Will, Oh, just see what a glorious fill;
   Here is a hammer and lots of tacks, Also a ball and a whip that cracks. *Refrain*

WABASH CANNON BALL

Model Experience, p. 218

Traditional

Verse
G
1. From the coast of the At - lan - tic to the wide Pa - ci - fic
C D7
shore, From the warm and sun - ny South - land to the
D7 G
isle of Lab - ra - dor, There's a name of great im -
G C
por - tance that is known by one and all, It's the
D7 G
West - ern com - bi - na - tion called the Wa - bash Can - non Ball.
Refrain
G C
Just lis - ten to the jin - gle, the rum - ble and the roar Of the
D7 G
might - y lo - co - mo - tive as she steams a - long the shore, Hear the

(See next page)

G
C
thun - der of the en - gine, hear the lone - some whis - tle call, It's the
D7
G
West - ern com - bi - na - tion called the Wa - bash Can - non Ball.

2. There are cities of importance that are reached along the way,
 Chicago and St.Louis and Rock Island, Sante Fe,
 And Springfield and Decatur and Peoria, Montreal,
 On the Western combination called the Wabash Cannon Ball. *Refrain*

WAKE ME!

Model Experience, p. 142

African American Song

F
1. Wake me! Shake me! Don't let me sleep too late. Gon - na
F
get up bright and ear - ly in the morn - in', Gon - na swing on the Gold - en Gate.

2. Wake me! Shake me!
 Don't let me sleep too late.
 Gonna comb my hair so early in the mornin',
 Gonna swing on the Golden Gate.

3. Wake me! Shake me!
 Don't let me sleep too late.
 Gonna wash my face so early in the mornin',
 Gonna swing on the Golden Gate.

WE GATHER TOGETHER

English text by Theodore Baker

Netherlands Folk Song

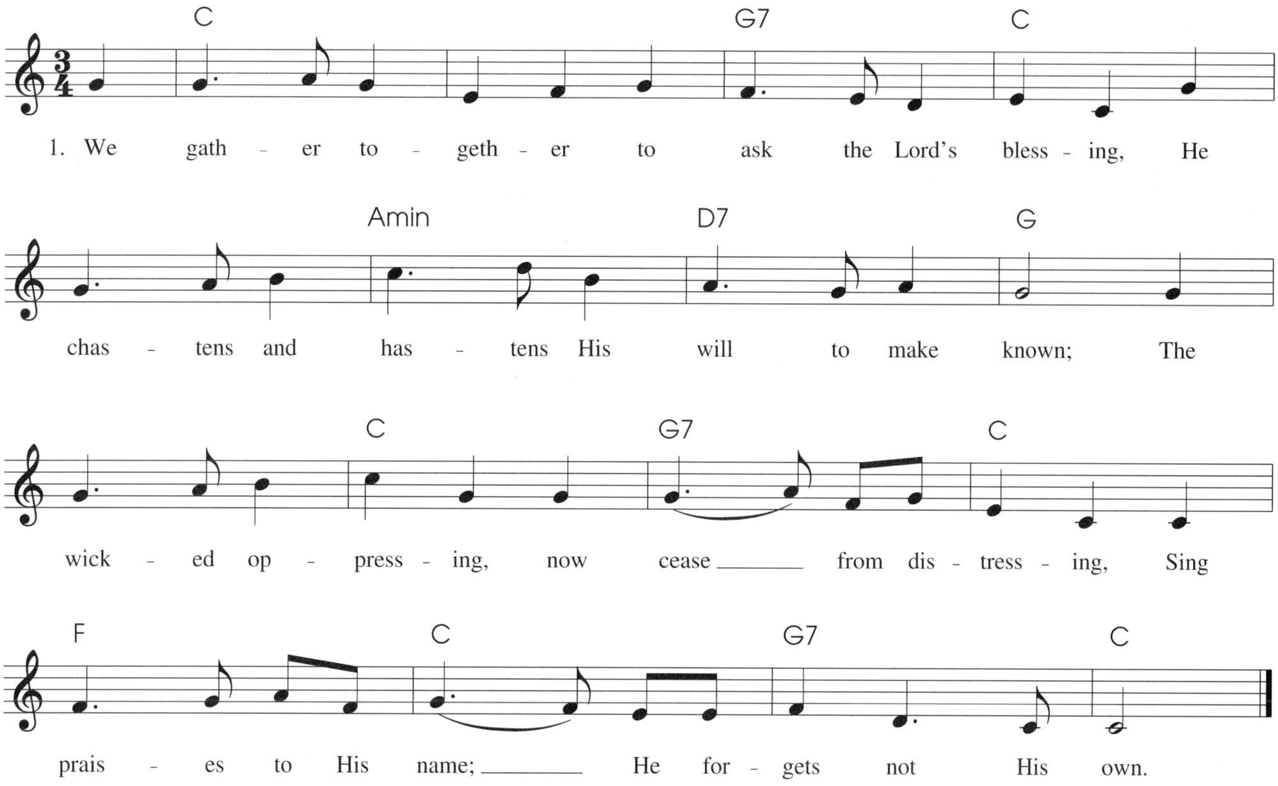

2. Beside us to guide us, our God with us joining,
   Ordaining, maintaining His kingdom divine,
   So from the beginning the fight we were winning;
   Thou, Lord, was at our side, all glory be Thine.

3. We do all extol Thee, Thou leader triumphant,
   And pray that Thou still our defender will be.
   Let thy congregation escape tribulation,
   Thy name be ever praised! O Lord make us free!

WE SHALL OVERCOME

Civil Rights Song

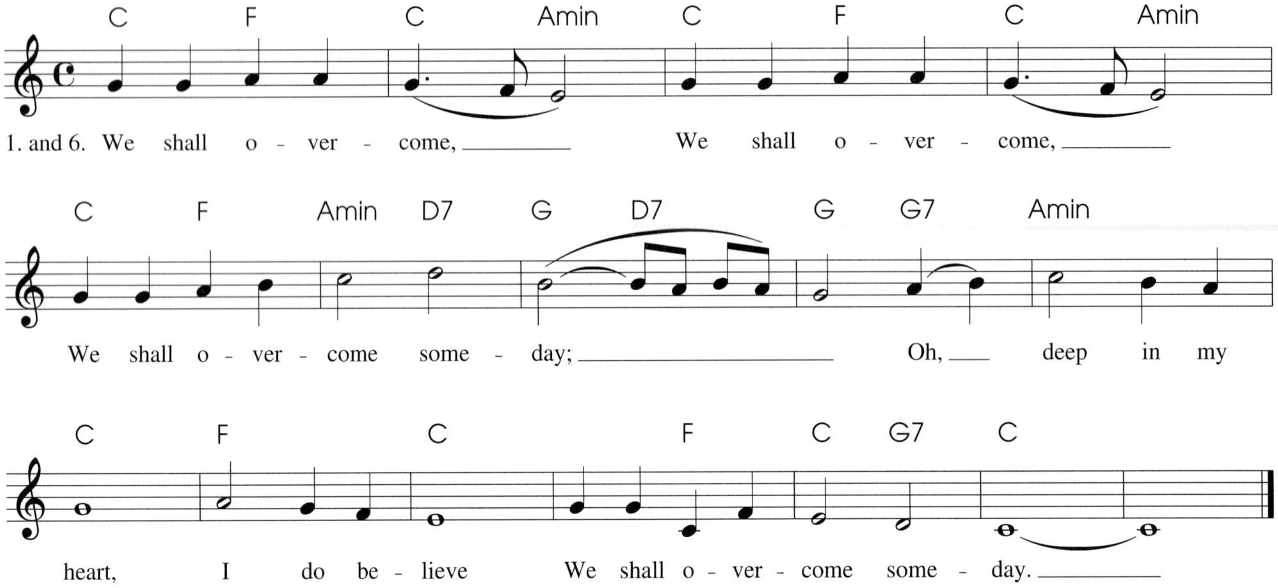
C F C Amin C F C Amin
1. and 6. We shall o - ver - come, We shall o - ver - come,
C F Amin D7 G D7 G G7 Amin
We shall o - ver - come some - day; Oh, deep in my
C F C F C G7 C
heart, I do be - lieve We shall o - ver - come some - day.

2. We'll walk hand in hand
3. The truth will make us free
4. We are not afraid
5. We shall live in peace

WE THREE KINGS

John H. Hopkins
(American, mid 19th century)

Melchior

2. Born a King on Bethlehem's plain,
Gold I bring, to crown Him again,
King forever, ceasing never,
Over us all to reign. *Refrain*

Caspar

3. Frankincense to offer have I,
Incense owns a Deity nigh,
Pray'r and praising, all men raising,
Worship Him, God most high. *Refrain*

Balthazar

4. Myrrh is mine, its bitter perfume
Breathes a life of gathering gloom,
Sorrowing, sighing, bleeding, dying,
Seal'd in the stone- cold tomb.
Refrain

All

5. Glorious now behold Him arise,
King and God and sacrifice,
"Alleluia! Alleluia!"
Earth to the heav'n replies.
Refrain

WHEN THE SAINTS GO MARCHING IN

Model Experience, p. 224

African American Spiritual

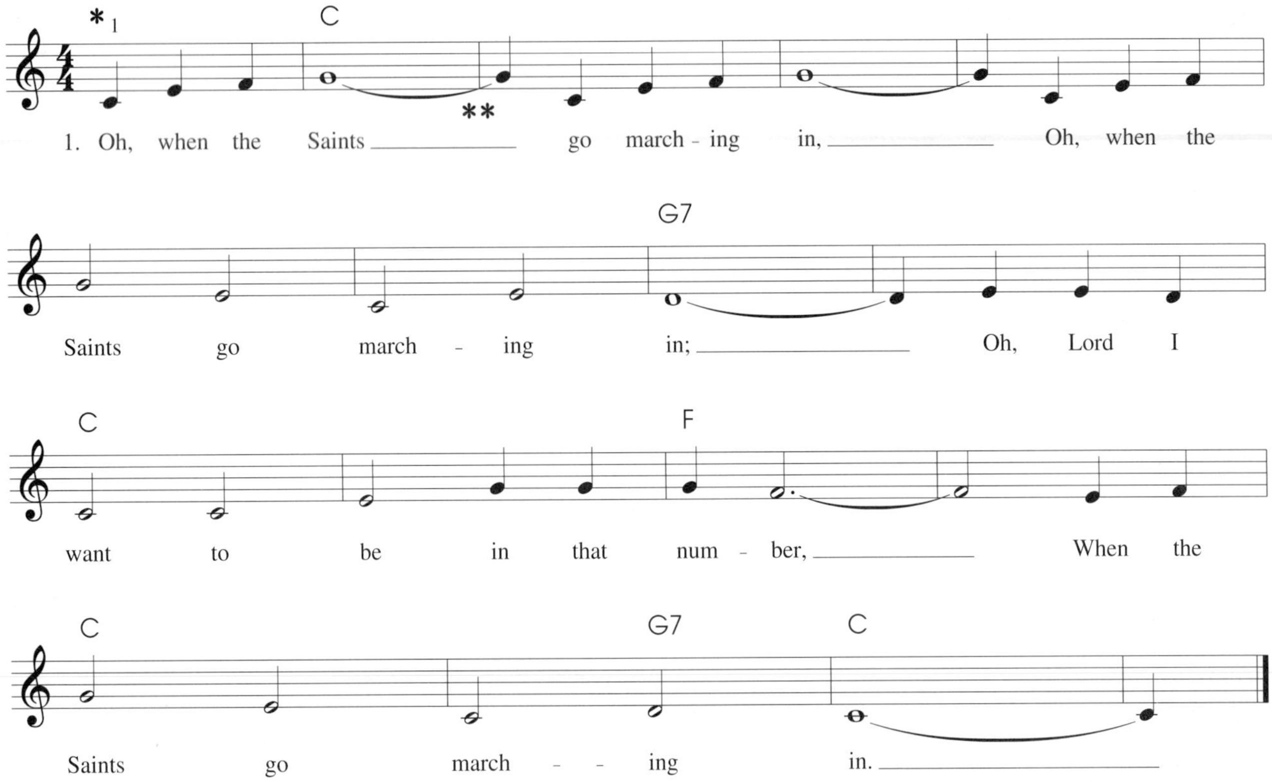

* Small number indicates fingering for keyboard.

** A tie (◌‿◌) connects two identical notes. Sing/play the first note only, and hold it through the time value of the second note. A tie is often used to connect notes across a bar line.

2. Oh, when the sun refuse to shine, Oh, when the sun refuse to shine;
   Oh, Lord I want to be in that number, When the sun refuse to shine.

3. Oh, when I hear that trumpet blow, Oh, when I hear that trumpet blow;
   Oh, Lord I want to be in that number, When I hear that trumpet blow.

4. Oh, when the stars have disappeared, Oh, when the stars have disappeared;
   Oh, Lord I want to be in that number, When the stars have disappeared.

5. Oh, when the day of judgment comes, Oh, when the day of judgment comes;
   Oh, Lord I want to be in that number, When the day of judgment comes.

WHO CHOPPED THE CHERRY TREE DOWN?

Aralaine W. Anderson
(American, 1908–1970)

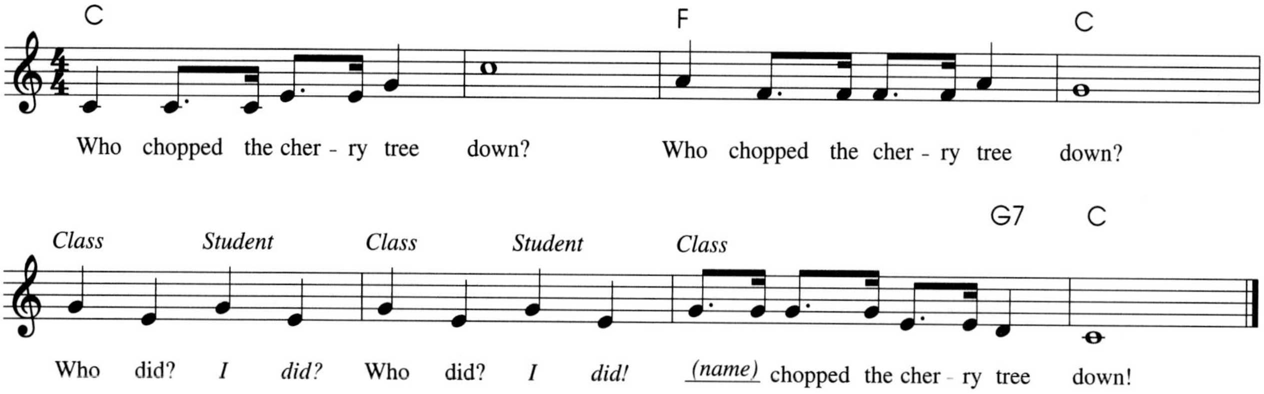

C
F
C
Who chopped the cher - ry tree down? Who chopped the cher - ry tree down?
G7
C
Class
Student
Class
Student
Class
Who did? I did? Who did? I did! (name) chopped the cher - ry tree down!

WHO'S THAT YONDER

African American Song

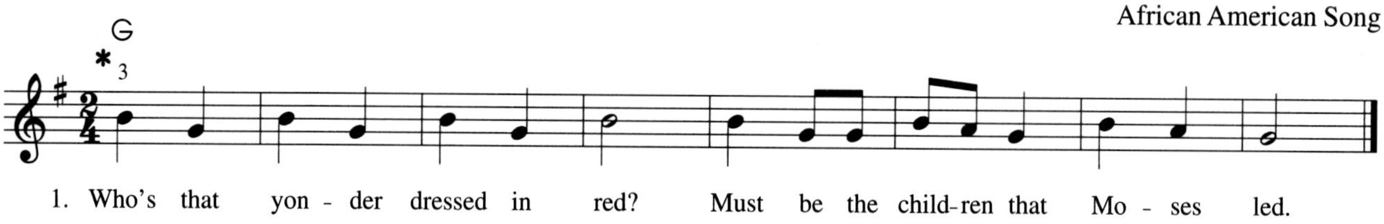

G
* 3
1. Who's that yon - der dressed in red? Must be the child-ren that Mo - ses led.

* Small number indicates fingering for keyboard.

2. Who's that yonder dressed in white?
Must be the children of the Israelite.

3. Who's that yonder dressed in blue?
Must be the children comin' through.

4. Who's that yonder dressed in black?
Must be the hypocrites turning back.

WILLOWBEE

Model Experience, p. 162

American Game Song

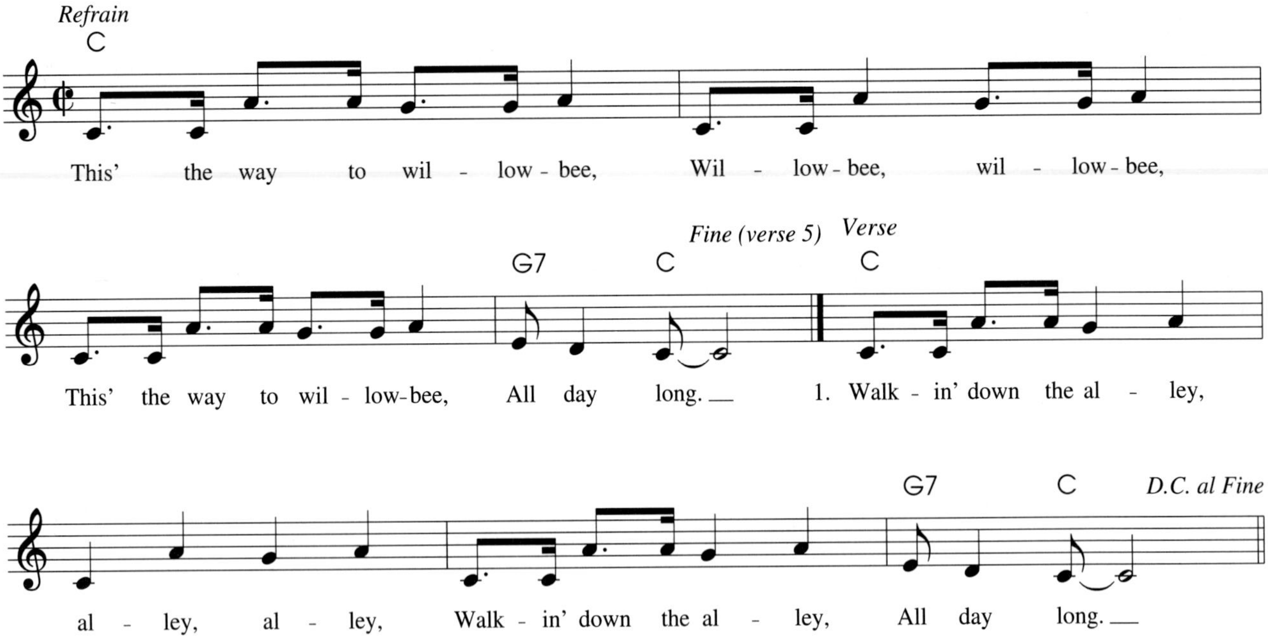
Refrain
C
This' the way to wil - low - bee, Wil - low - bee, wil - low - bee,
Fine (verse 5)
Verse
G7 C C
This' the way to wil - low-bee, All day long. 1. Walk - in' down the al - ley,
G7 C
D.C. al Fine
al - ley, al - ley, Walk - in' down the al - ley, All day long.

2. Dancin' down the alley
3. Skatin' down the alley
4. Skippin' down the alley
5. Hoppin' down the alley

WISHY WASHY WEE

Model Experience, p. 136

American Folk Song

* Small number indicates fingering for keyboard.

Formation

Players stand in a large circle with two sailors in the center.

Dance

During the verse, all stand in place while the two sailors link elbows and swing in the center. At the end of the verse on "come along with me" each of the two sailors stops in front of a person standing in the circle. During the refrain, these two join hands. They dance by hopping on the left foot, at the same time sliding the right heel forward, and then hopping on the right foot while sliding the left heel forward. This alternating footwork continues. At the same time, the right hand pushes straight ahead along with the right heel, and then the left hand pushes straight ahead with the left heel, and so forth. (Hands remain joined.)

On "come along with me," at the end of the refrain, the four dancers change places. The two players from the circle move to the center and become the new sailors for a repetition of the song. The dance continues until every player in the circle has an opportunity to dance as a sailor.

YANKEE DOODLE

American Revolutionary War Song

Verse
F C7 F C7
1. Fath'r and I went down to camp A - long with Cap - tain Good - win. And
F B♭ C7 F
there we saw the men and boys As thick as hast - y pud - din'.
Refrain
B♭ F
Yan - kee Doo - dle keep it up, Yan - kee Doo - dle dan - dy;
B♭ F C7 F
Mind the mu - sic and the step, And with the girls be hand - y.

2. And there was Captain Washington, Upon a slapping stallion,
A- giving orders to his men, I gues there was a million. *Refrain*

The song "Yankee Doodle" is over two hundred years old. During the French and Indian War, a British army doctor created verses poking fun at the ragtag attire of the Colonial fighters. No one knows the origin of the tune or of the term "Yankee doodle." But the scruffy "Yankees" were as amused by the satire as the British, and the song was adopted by the Colonials—to become almost their battle march during the Revolutionary War. Intermediate grade students can read about our patriotic songs (including "Yankee Doodle") in Robert Kroske, America the Beautiful *(New York: Garrard, 1972).*

YANKEE DOODLE BOY

George M. Cohan
(American, 1878–1942)

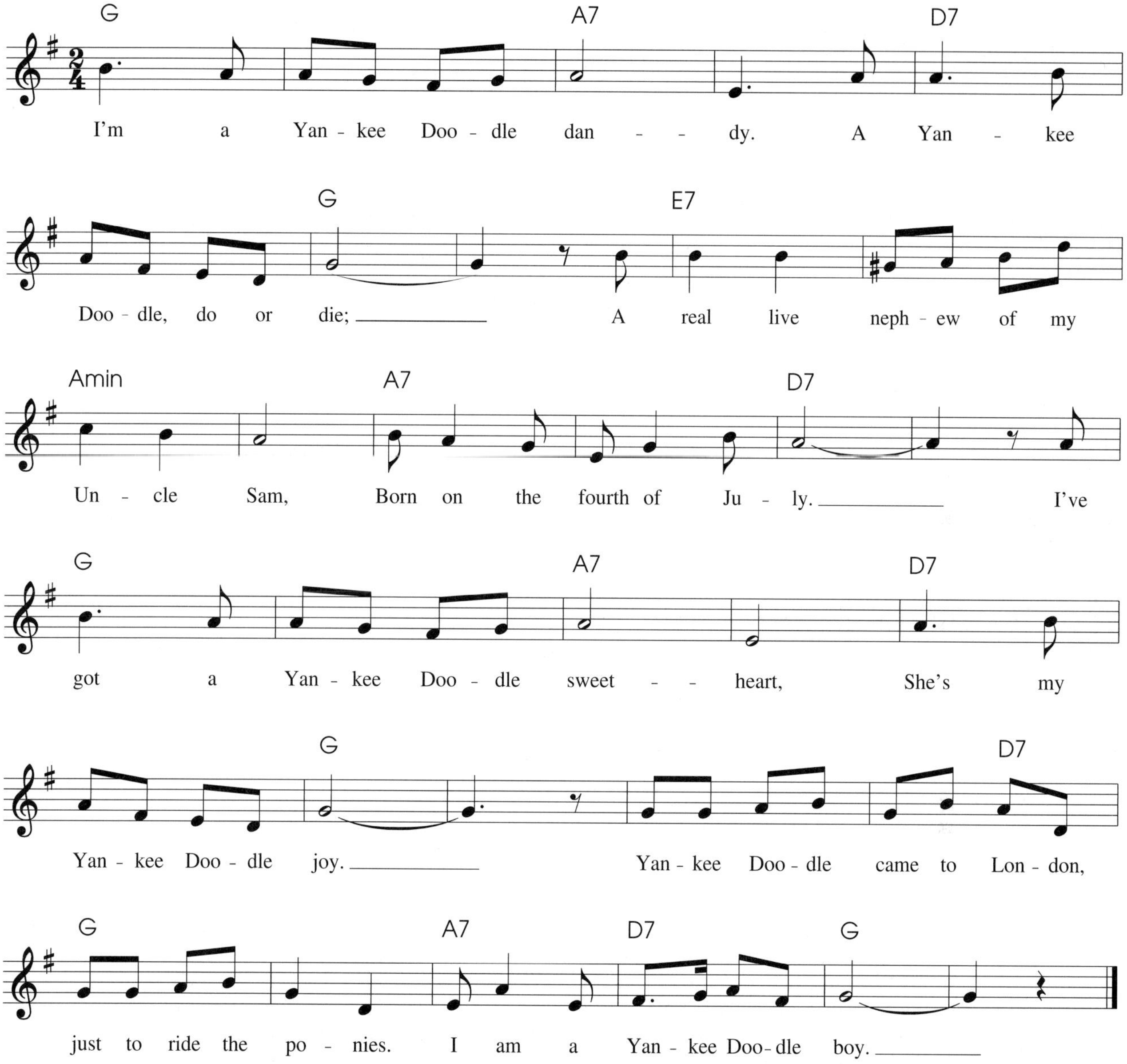
G A7 D7
I'm a Yan - kee Doo - dle dan - - dy. A Yan - kee
G E7
Doo - dle, do or die; A real live neph - ew of my
Amin A7 D7
Un - cle Sam, Born on the fourth of Ju - ly. I've
G A7 D7
got a Yan - kee Doo - dle sweet - - heart, She's my
G D7
Yan - kee Doo - dle joy. Yan - kee Doo - dle came to Lon - don,
G A7 D7 G
just to ride the po - nies. I am a Yan - kee Doo- dle boy.

YOKUTS GRINDING SONG

Transcribed and adapted by P. Hackett

California Indian Song

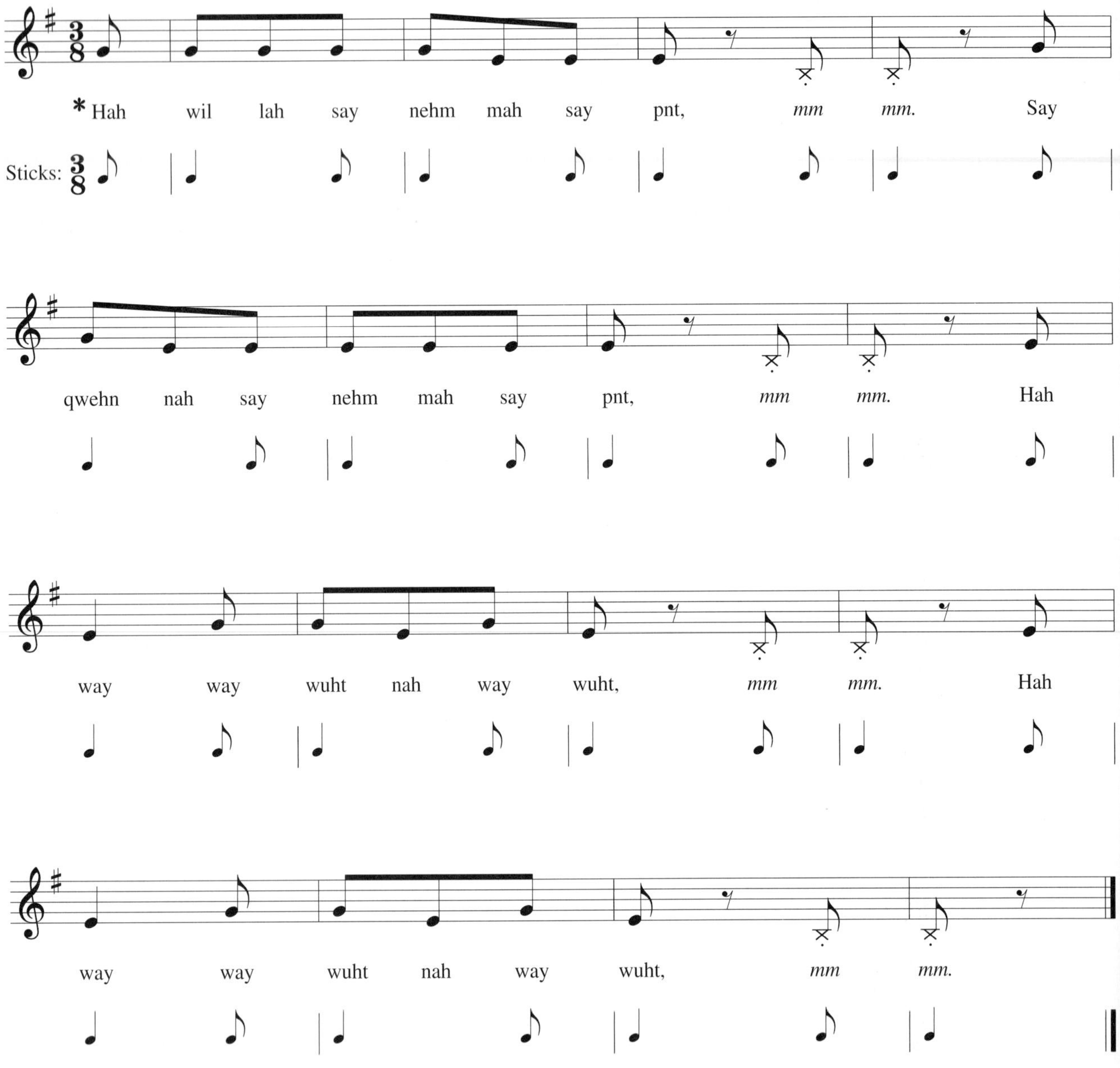
* Hah wil lah say nehm mah say pnt, *mm* *mm.* Say
Sticks:
qwehn nah say nehm mah say pnt, *mm* *mm.* Hah
way way wuht nah way wuht, *mm* *mm.* Hah
way way wuht nah way wuht, *mm* *mm.*

* Yokuts use slurred enunciation in this acorn grinding song about the magical properties of acorns. There is no precise translation for the song's text.

More than one hundred different Native American groups lived amicably in the central two-thirds of California. No groups practiced agriculture, perhaps because food was usually plentiful. Acorns were a staple and were varied by game, shellfish, berries, seeds, and roots. Many California Indian songs are similar to the "Yokuts Grinding Song" because they include only a few different pitches and are expressed in one to three short musical phrases. The "song" above is a short version of the original, which was much longer, with the three phrases alternating and repeating in no regular order.

ZUM GALI GALI

Israeli Folk Melody

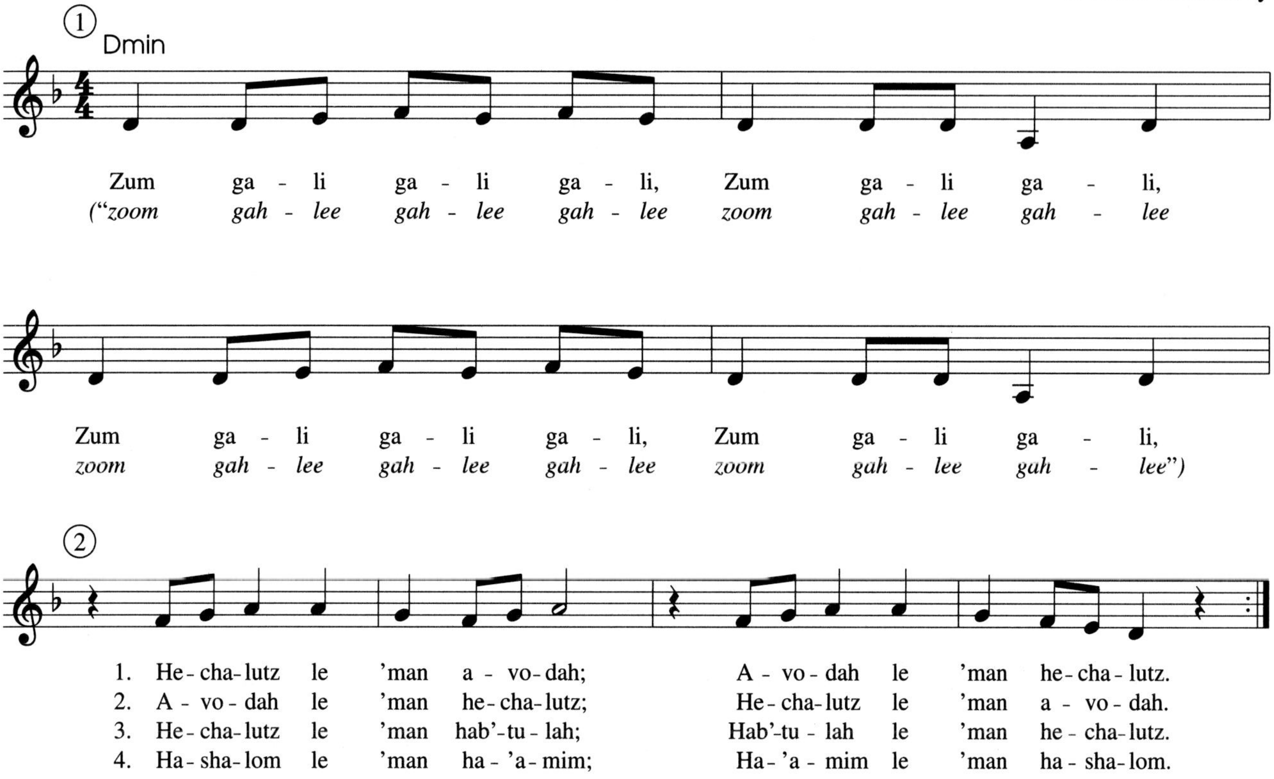
①
Dmin
Zum ga - li ga - li ga - li, Zum ga - li ga - li,
("zoom gah - lee gah - lee gah - lee zoom gah - lee gah - lee
Zum ga - li ga - li ga - li, Zum ga - li ga - li,
zoom gah - lee gah - lee gah - lee zoom gah - lee gah - lee")
②
1. He-cha-lutz le 'man a - vo-dah; A - vo - dah le 'man he-cha - lutz.
2. A - vo - dah le 'man he-cha-lutz; He - cha-lutz le 'man a - vo - dah.
3. He-cha-lutz le 'man hab'-tu - lah; Hab'-tu - lah le 'man he - cha-lutz.
4. Ha-sha-lom le 'man ha - 'a - mim; Ha-'a - mim le 'man ha - sha-lom.

Section Five
Appendixes

Appendix A
Reference Material for Music Fundamentals

RHYTHM NOTATION

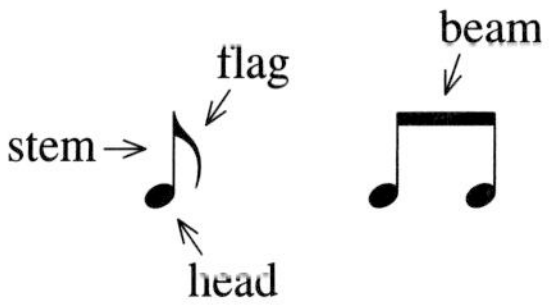

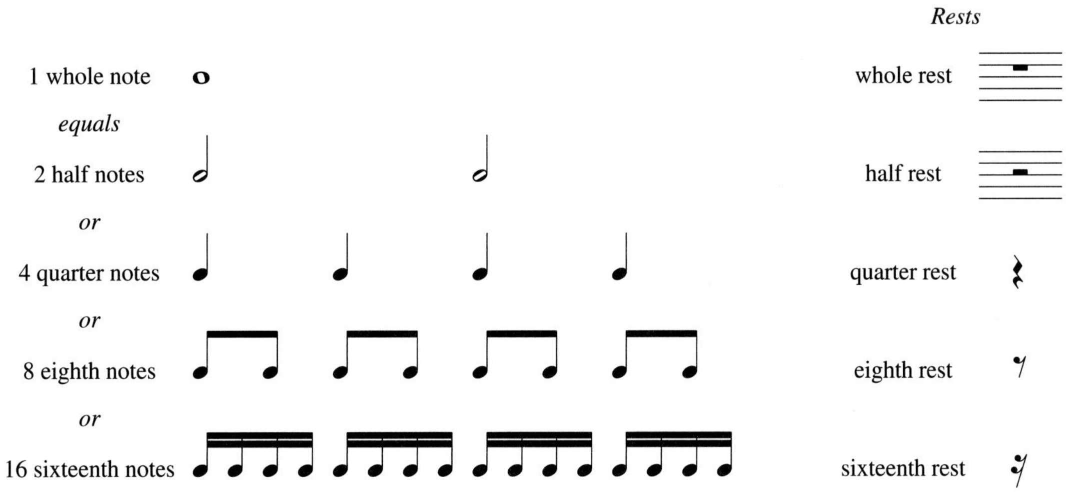

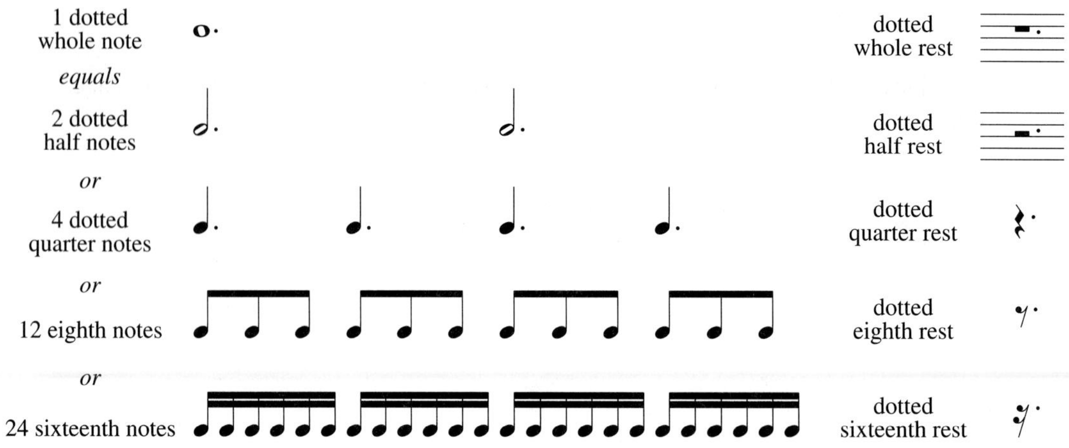

METER SIGNATURES

Meter signatures are the two numbers, one above the other, that appear at the beginning of a piece of music. The top number specifies the beat grouping or meter, and the bottom number indicates the note that receives the beat.

2 = two beats in a measure
4 = the quarter note (♩) receives the beat

C *and* **4** = four beats in a measure
4 = the quarter note (♩) receives the beat

3 = three beats in a measure
4 = the quarter note (♩) receives the beat

6 = six beats in a measure
8 = the eighth note (♪) receives the beat

¢ *and* **2** = two beats in a measure
2 = the half note (𝅗𝅥) receives the beat

PITCH NOTATION

The Staff

The staff is a series of five horizontal lines on or between which musical notes are written. The lines and spaces of the staff are numbered from the bottom up.

The staff

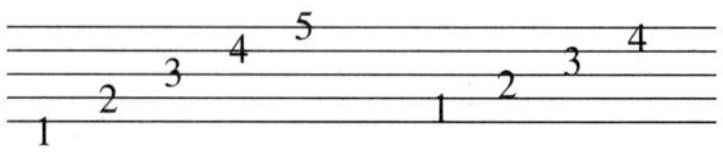

Ledger Lines

Short lines called ledger lines can be added above or below the staff to extend the range of pitches.

Ledger lines

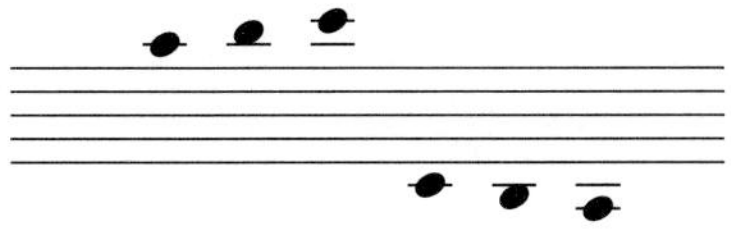

Treble or G Clef

This clef sign establishes G above middle C on the second line.

Treble or G clef

Bass or F Clef

This clef establishes F below middle C on the fourth line.

Bass or F clef

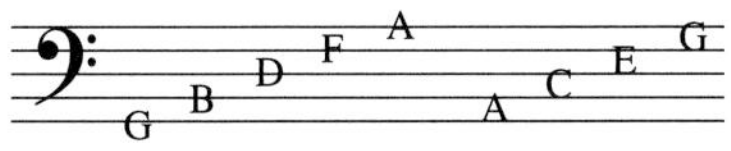

Placement of Stems

When notes are on or above the middle line of the staff, stems go down and are placed on the left side. When notes are below the middle line, stems go up on the right side of the note head.

Placement of stems

Accidentals

Accidentals are signs introduced before a note to change the pitch for one measure only. They are placed in the same space or on the same line as the note head:

♯ (sharp): raises the pitch one half step
♭ (flat): lowers the pitch one half step
♮ (natural): cancels a preceding sharp or flat
𝄪 (double sharp: raises the pitch of a sharped note an additional half step
𝄫 (double flat): lowers the pitch of a flatted note an additional half step

TREBLE AND BASS CLEF NOTATION

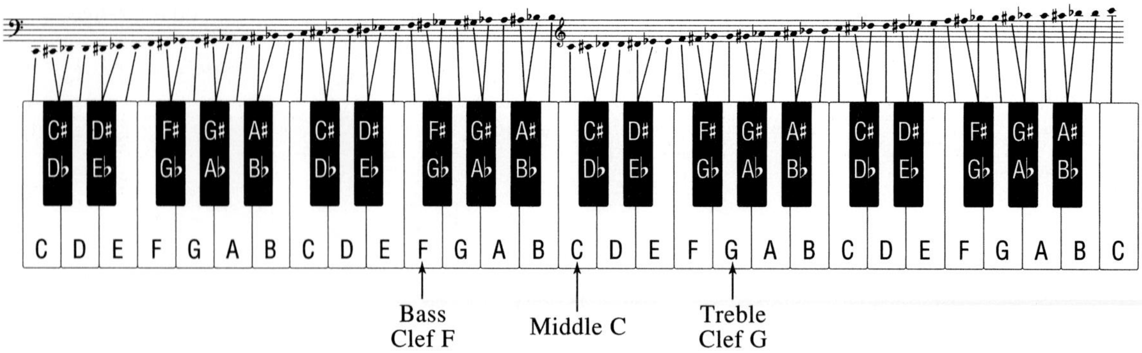

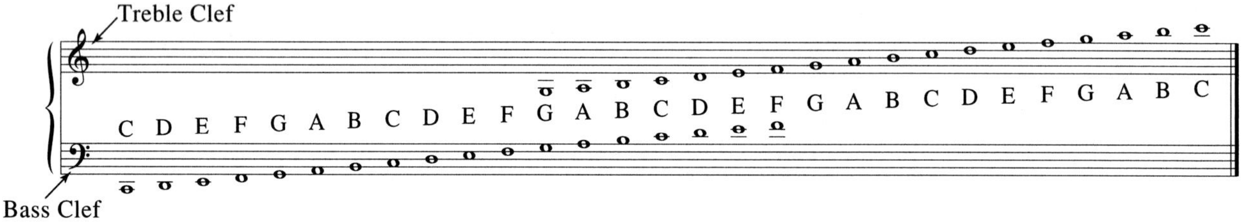

SCALES

The chromatic scale is a twelve-tone scale consisting entirely of half steps.

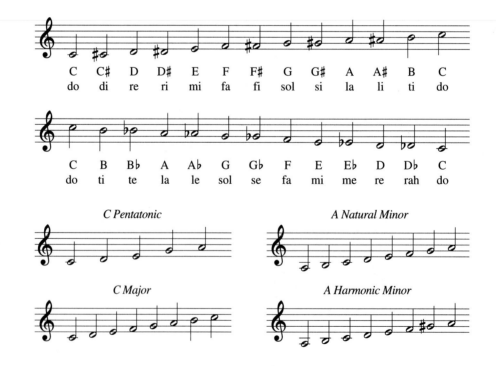

C C# D D# E F F# G G# A A# B C
do di re ri mi fa fi sol si la li ti do

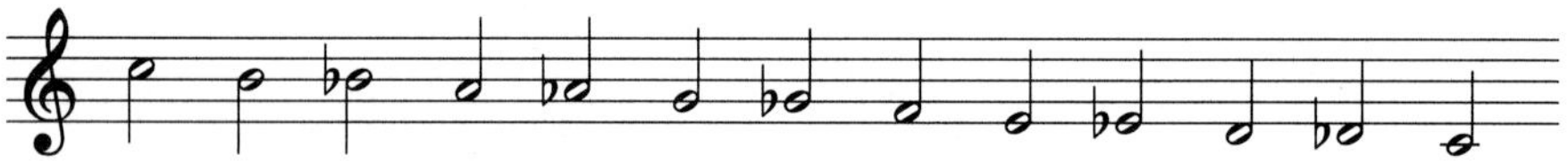

C B Bb A Ab G Gb F E Eb D Db C
do ti te la le sol se fa mi me re rah do

C Pentatonic

A Natural Minor

C Major

A Harmonic Minor

Frequently Used Major Scales (with Piano Fingerings)

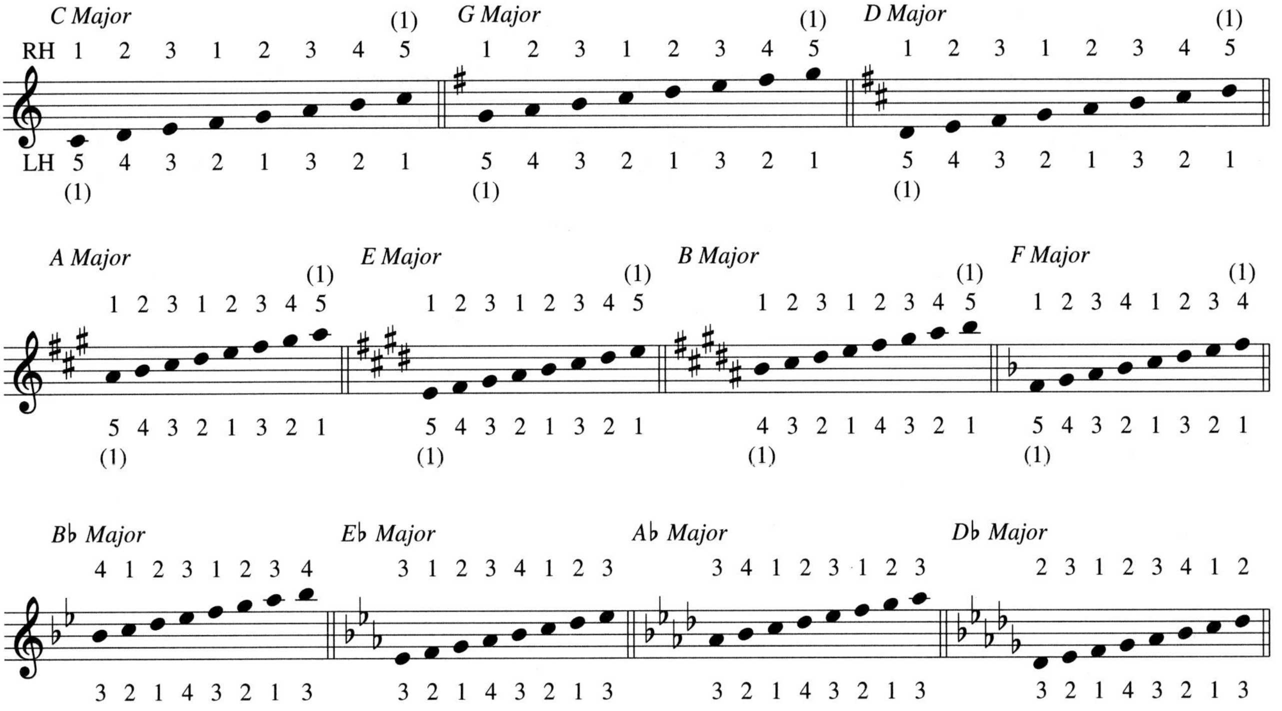

Frequently Used Minor Scales (with Piano Fingerings)

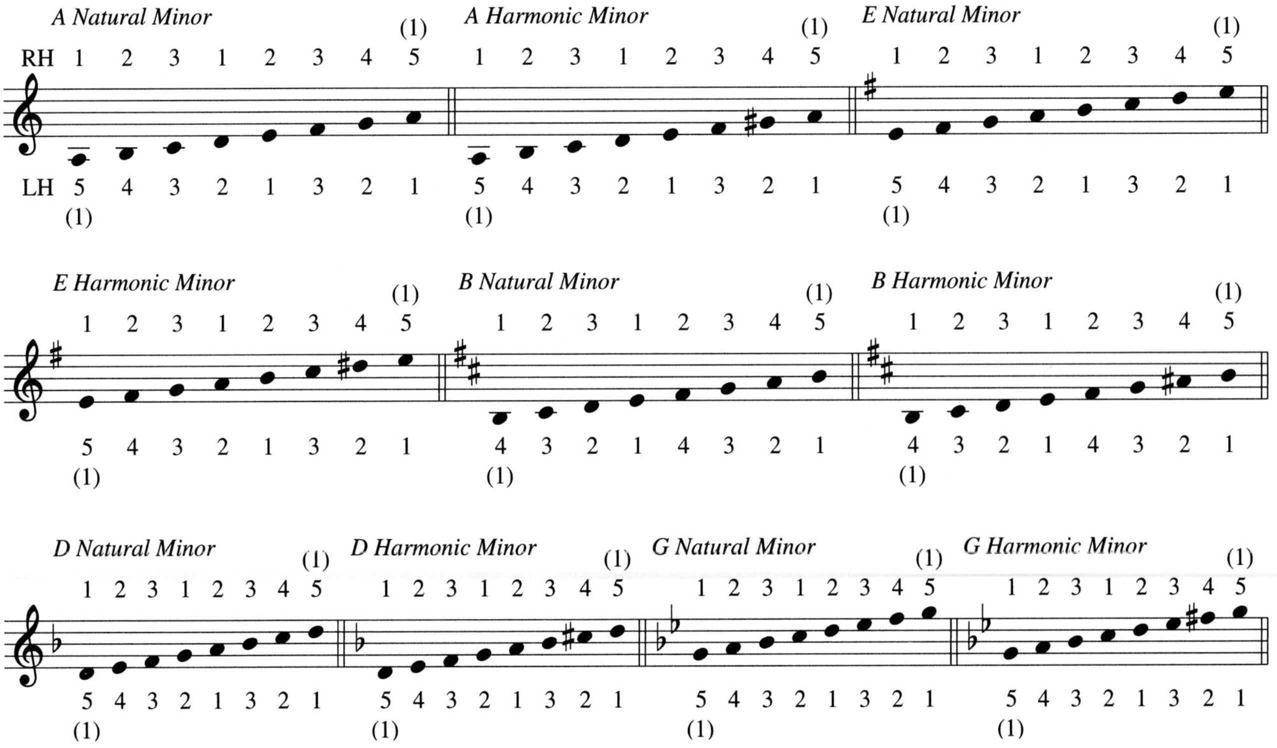

Circle of Fifths (Major and Minor Keys)

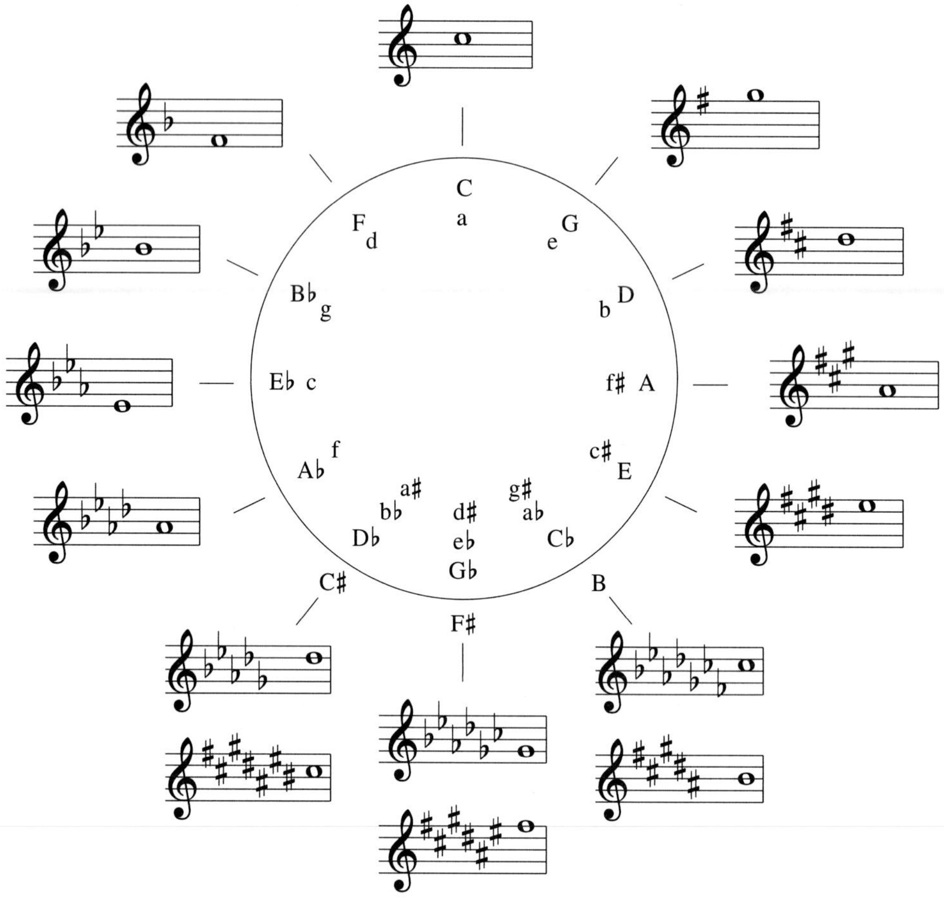

KEY SIGNATURES FOR MAJOR AND MINOR SCALES

Identifying Major and Minor from Key Signatures

- In a key signature of sharps, the sharp farthest right is 7 (*ti*). The next line or space above (one half step above) is 1 or 8 (*do*), the tonic for *major.* 6 (*la*) is the tonic for *minor.*
- In a key signature of flats, the next-to-the-last flat is 1 or 8 (*do*), the tonic for *major.* (You have to *memorize* that the key of F has one flat.) 6 (*la*) is the tonic for *minor.*
- The major and minor keys paired inside the circle share the same key signature, so they are *relative* keys.

Intervals

An interval is the distance between two notes. Intervals are identified by *number* and *quality.* To determine the number identification, count the number of steps covered by the two notes (including steps on which both notes appear). To determine the quality of each interval, count the exact number of half steps between the two notes.

Intervals of the C Major Scale

Intervals of seconds, thirds, sixths, and sevenths are always major; unisons, fourths, fifths, and octaves are always perfect.

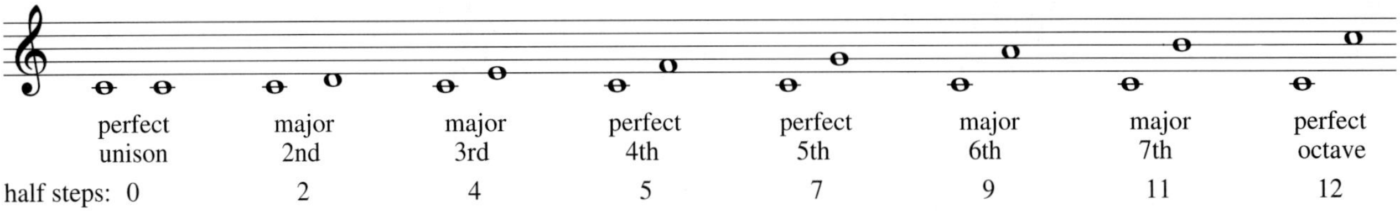

Interval Quality

A *minor* interval is a half step smaller than a major interval.
A *diminished* interval is a half step smaller than a perfect interval.
An *augmented* interval is a half step larger than a perfect interval.

CHORDS

Triad: Three-note chord built in thirds.

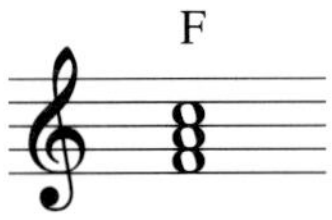

Seventh chord: Four-note chord built in thirds.

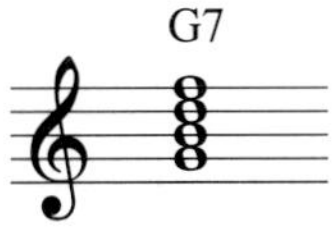

Major triads include a major third (four half steps) and a minor third (three half steps).
Minor triads include a minor third and a major third.

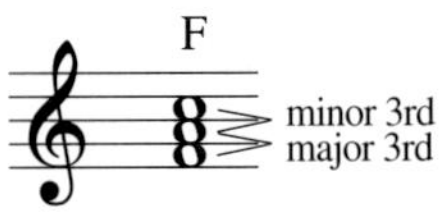

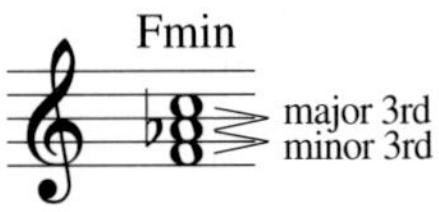

Chords in Major Keys

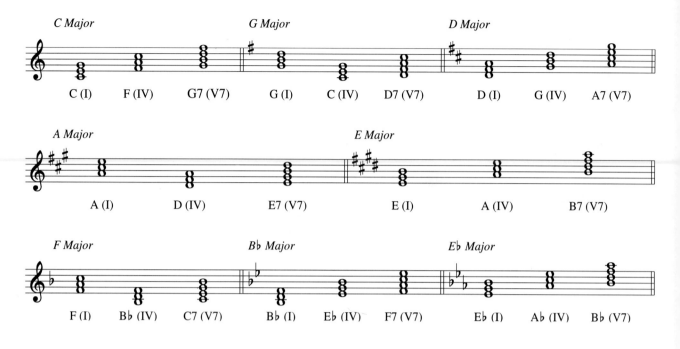

C Major *G Major* *D Major*

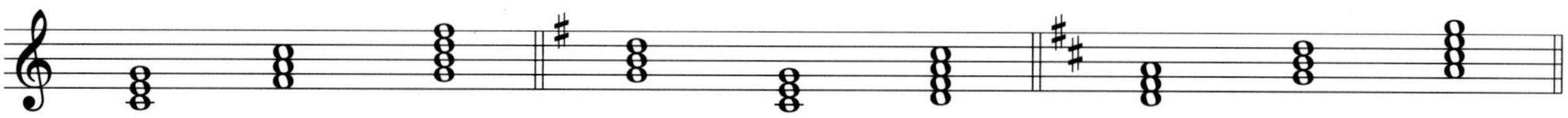

C (I) F (IV) G7 (V7) G (I) C (IV) D7 (V7) D (I) G (IV) A7 (V7)

A Major *E Major*

A (I) D (IV) E7 (V7) E (I) A (IV) B7 (V7)

F Major *B♭ Major* *E♭ Major*

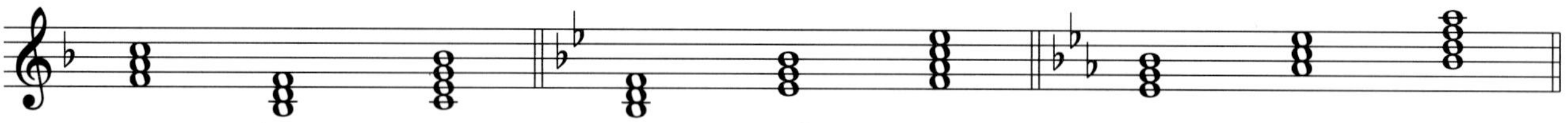

F (I) B♭ (IV) C7 (V7) B♭ (I) E♭ (IV) F7 (V7) E♭ (I) A♭ (IV) B♭ (V7)

Chords in Minor Keys

A Harmonic Minor *E Harmonic Minor* *B Harmonic Minor*

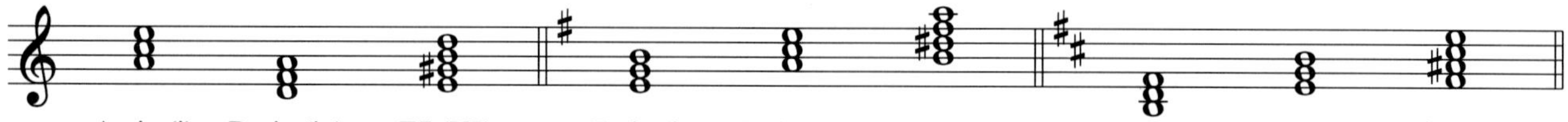

Amin (i) Dmin (iv) E7 (V7) Emin (i) Amin (iv) B7 (V7) Bmin (i) Emin (iv) F♯7 (V7)

D Harmonic Minor *G Harmonic Minor*

Dmin (i) Gmin (iv) A7 (V7) Gmin (i) Cmin (iv) D7 (V7)

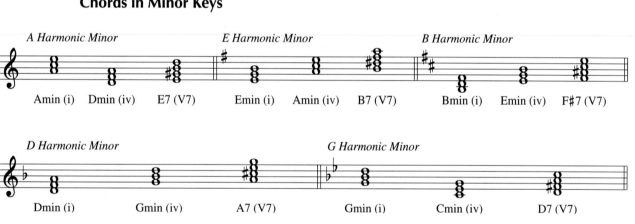

MUSICAL TERMS AND SIGNS

Dynamic Terms and Signs

pp	*Pianissimo,* very soft
p	*Piano,* soft
mp	*Mezzo piano,* medium soft
mf	*Mezzo forte,* medium loud
f	*Forte,* loud
ff	*Fortissimo,* very loud

<	Crescendo (*cresc.*), gradually louder
>	Decrescendo (*decresc.*), gradually softer
>	Diminuendo (*dim., dimin.*), gradually softer

Common Tempo Terms

Accelerando (*accel.*), gradually increasing tempo
Adagio, slowly, leisurely
Allegretto, moderately fast
Allegro, fast, lively
Andante, moderately
Andantino, slightly faster than andante
a tempo, return to original tempo
Largo, very slow
Lento, slow
Moderato, moderately
Presto, very rapidly
Ritardando (*rit.*), gradually slower and slower
Vivace, animated, lively

Additional Signs and Symbols

Da capo (D.C.), from the start
D.C. al Fine, from the start, ending at *Fine*
Dal segno (D.S.), from the sign 𝄋
D.S. al Fine, from the sign, ending at *Fine*
Fermata (𝄐), hold
Fine, the end

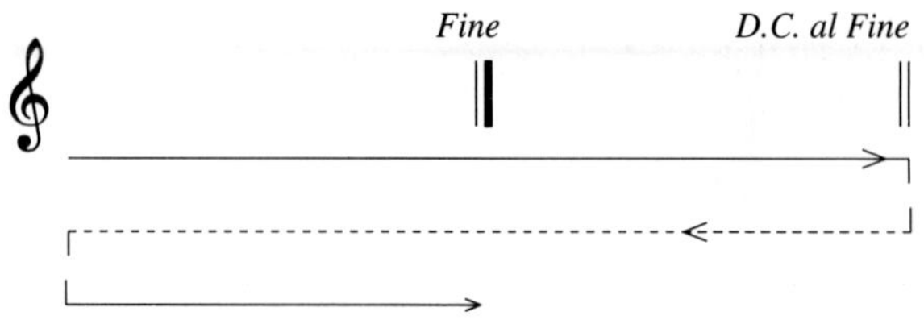

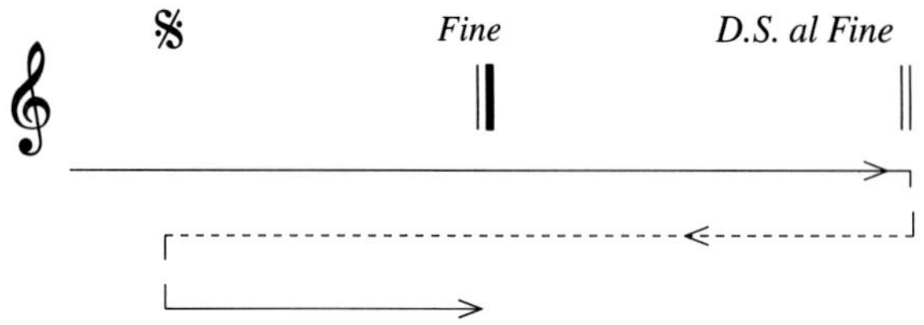

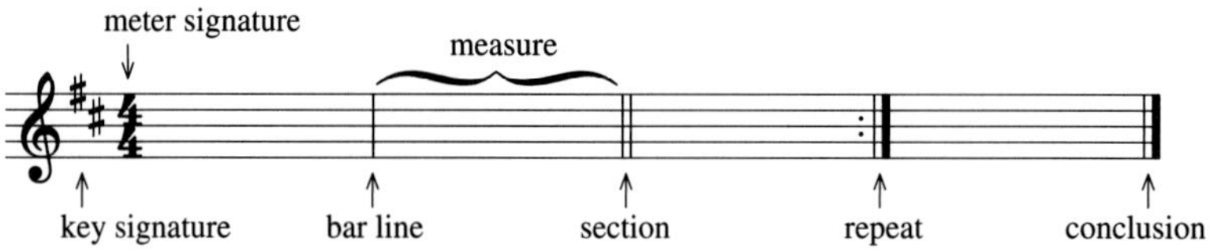

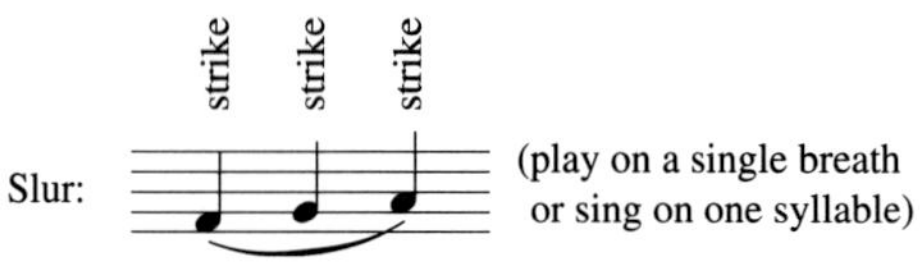

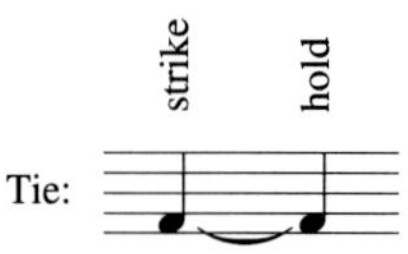

Appendix B
Evaluation Forms

SELF-EVALUATION FORM
FOR MODEL EXPERIENCE PRESENTATION

Presenter ____

Date ____

Model Experience ___________________________________

1. What was the most effective part of your presentation?

2. What was the most challenging part?

3. What revisions would you make in order for the presentation to be more effective?

4. Rate yourself on how well you handled the following teaching aspects of the model experience presentation:

Excellent	Very good	Satisfactory	Needs improvement	
				Grabbed students' attention to open the lesson
				Actively involved learners throughout
				Interacted with learners throughout
				Maintained eye contact with the students
				Asked clear, direct questions
				Gave clear directions
				Reinforced the music concept and key musical terms
				Used procedures and equipment so they enhanced learning and did not distract from it
				Used accurate pitches for songs
				Used correct rhythms
				Closed lesson effectively

EVALUATION FORM
FOR MODEL EXPERIENCE PARTICIPANTS

Presenter ____________________

Date ____________________

Model Experience ____________________

1. What did you learn about music as a result of this model experience presentation?

2. List three good things that the presenter did.

3. Suggest one area for improvement.

EVALUATION FORM FOR MUSIC SOFTWARE

Reviewer ____________________

Program Title ____________________

Publisher ____________________

Price ____________________ Grade Level ____________________

Computer Macintosh ____ Windows ____

Format Floppies ____ CD Rom ____

Rate each of the following on a scale of 1 to 7 and offer additional comments:

	(excellent)					*(poor)*	
1. Adequate Documentation (written materials informative?)	**1**	**2**	**3**	**4**	**5**	**6**	**7**

Comments: ____________________

2. Presentation Techniques (accurate, engaging, user-friendly format, clear instructions?)	**1**	**2**	**3**	**4**	**5**	**6**	**7**

Comments: ____________________

3. Visual/Audio Effects (graphics and audio effective?)	**1**	**2**	**3**	**4**	**5**	**6**	**7**

Comments: ____________________

4. Music Content (appropriate and accurate?)	**1**	**2**	**3**	**4**	**5**	**6**	**7**

Comments: ____________________

5. Instructional Strategies (effective and creative?)	**1**	**2**	**3**	**4**	**5**	**6**	**7**

Comments: ____________________

6. Technical Considerations (crashproof, easy to use?)	**1**	**2**	**3**	**4**	**5**	**6**	**7**

Comments: ____________________

Program Strengths/ Weaknesses ____________________

____

Appendix C
Elementary Music Series

THE MUSIC CONNECTION

(2000) Jane Beethoven, Dulce Bohn, Patricia Shehan Campbell, Carmen E. Culp, Jennifer Davidson, Lawrence Eisman, Sandra Longoria Glover, Charlotte Hayes, Martha Hilley, Mary E. Hoffman, Sanna Longden, Hunter March, Bill McCloud, Janet Montgomery, Marvelene Moore, Catherine Nadon-Gabrion, Mary Palmer, Carmino Ravosa, Mary Louise Reilly, Will Schmid, Carol Scott-Kassner, Jean Sinor, Sandra Stauffer, Judith Thomas. Glenview, IL: Silver Burdett Ginn/Scott Foresman (Scott Foresman, 1900 East Lake Avenue, Glenview, IL 60025; phone 800-848-9500; www.sbgmusic.com). Kindergarten–Grade 8.

Program Philosophy The authors and editors of THE MUSIC CONNECTION set out to create a music series that would reflect the philosophies of the National Standards for Arts Education—in essence, "[since] music is a basic expression of human culture, every student should have access to a balanced, comprehensive, and sequential program of study in music."

Program Organization Section I, Concepts, presents lessons arranged in a spiral sequence of units based on music elements. A carefully chosen selection of material—songs, related listening selections, movement activities, and instrumental parts—forms the core of each unit. Optional assessments are part of every lesson, including What Do You Hear? assessments, which allow students to make active choices about the qualities of music they are learning to perceive.

Section II, Themes, develops understanding of the music of other cultures and music's social and historical connections as well as reinforcing music concepts. Here one can find units devoted to such items as story songs, holidays, travel, American and world heritage, and multicultural awareness.

Section III, Reading, is a sequenced arrangement of materials for teaching sight-singing with the Kodály pedagogical approach.

Many teaching and learning aids are found throughout the program. Section organizers contain a breakdown of all the elements involved in each lesson—focus and objectives, songs, instruments used, skills involved, curriculum connections, Orff activities and lessons, movement activities, and so on. Each lesson provides one or more skills activities (Skills strands) involving movement, listening, singing, playing instruments, thinking, reading, and others. Two scope and sequence charts—one devoted to concepts, the other to skills—help with curriculum planning. The charts map out the content of the entire program over all nine grades. The Meeting Individual Needs section of the Teacher Edition provides insights and suggestions on handling challenges of mainstreaming, classroom management, cooperative learning, thinking skills, and meeting the needs of the gifted and talented. Throughout the Teacher Editions, features called "Spotlight On. . ." highlight pertinent information concerning parts of the lesson—a composer biography, discussion of certain kinds of ethnic music, celebrations, and so on. Teacher Editions are filled with on-page teaching suggestions for integrating the curriculum. These include children's literature, language arts, science, mathematics, art, and social studies. Lesson-relevant discussions of multicultural interest are offered in Cultural Connections in each Teacher Edition. These short paragraphs are written by scholars in the field of multiculturalism, and provide insight into the various cultural groups that make up today's United States.

Program Components THE MUSIC CONNECTION provides several components, including pupil's and teacher's books, a Big Book for kindergarten and grade 1, and CD packages for each grade. Teacher Resource Books offer assessments and graphic organizers, activities, Orff, keyboard, and signing for all grades K–8, as well as reading music worksheets and calendar planners (grades K–6), music reading transparency masters (grades 1–6), and recorder selections (grades 3–8). Additional materials include Listening Guide Transparencies (grades 1–8), Keyboard Accompaniments (grades K–8), Orff Orchestrations (grades 1–6), Emergent Literacy Through Music folders (grades K–2), Activities for the Substitute Teacher, and two booklets featuring multicultural songs with lesson plans—*¡Cantaremos!* and *Bridges to Asia* (grades 1–8).

THE MUSIC CONNECTION technology products capture students' interest and supplement teaching needs. They include Music Magic Video Library, Teacher-to-Teacher Video, The MIDI Connection, Rock Rap 'n Roll, Visual MT, Master Tracks Pro, Rhapsody, Making Music, and Making More Music. Compact disc recordings for every grade level contain all songs, listening selections, recorded interviews, the Sound Bank, Call Charts, and What Do You Hear? assessments. These are stereo recordings with a Teach-A-Part and Pick-A-Track format.

(Description provided by the Music Department, Silver Burdett Ginn/Scott Foresman)

SHARE THE MUSIC

(2000) Coordinating Authors: Judy Bond, Marilyn Copeland Davidson, Mary Goetze, Vincent P. Lawrence, Susan Snyder. Authors: René Boyer-Alexander, Margaret Campbelle-Holman, Robert de Frece, Doug Goodkin, Betsy M. Henderson, Michael Jothen, Carol King, Nancy L. T. Miller, Ivy Rawlins. New York: McGraw-Hill School Division (Two Penn Plaza, New York, NY 10121; customer service phone: 800–442–9685; www.mmhschool.com). (Kindergarten through Grade 8)

Share the Music teaches basic music concepts and skills through a proven learning sequence—*experience, imitate and explore, describe, identify and label, practice, reinforce, read or interpret visual representation, create,* and *maintain.* Students build music literacy and understanding through singing, playing instruments, listening, moving, creating, music reading, critical thinking, and both creative and cognitive assessment experiences. The Kodály, Orff, Dalcroze, and traditional music approaches are integrated into the lesson plans and reflected in the sequence of song and listening materials in the pupil books.

Special features of the series:

1. "Time for Singing," a section of familiar folk and popular songs, opens each grade level, K–6.
2. Themes for each unit are supported by an opening theme song and poem and by extensive suggestions for thematic instruction in the Teacher's Editions K–6.
3. A reading and reinforcement section entitled "More Songs to Read" in Grade 1–6 supports the music literacy and concept development strands that are woven throughout the units.
4. Culturally authentic and age-appropriate song and listening selections are supported by comprehensive helps for the teacher, including recorded pronunciation guides by native speakers for non-English songs and cultural background information.

5. An illustration program that combines artwork, photographs, maps, and artifacts from around the world provides visual support for the lessons and supports interdisciplinary learning.
6. Music concepts and skills are fostered through a careful choice of song materials. Lesson plans include clear behavioral objectives, frequent informal assessment, and alternative teaching strategies. A sequenced movement curriculum is included as a part of music learning.
7. Integrated curriculum materials and a wide range of related arts activities help the classroom teacher connect music learning to the total classroom experience.
8. Books are organized to meet the needs of music specialists and classroom teachers in both 9-month and 12-month schools.
9. Compact discs include recorded lessons, interviews, and unit assessments as well as all song and listening materials. The recordings highlight the natural sound of children's voices with artistic and captivating accompaniments.
10. A sequenced choral development strand begins in Grade 4 and culminates in Grades 7 and 8.

Components include pupil editions for grades 1–8, Big Books for grades K–2, teacher's editions with piano accompaniments and compact discs for all grade levels. In addition, Teacher's Resource Packages contain teacher's resource masters and listening map transparencies for grades K–8; playing the recorder for grades 3–6; playing the guitar for grade 6; orchestrations for Orff instruments for grades 1–6; signing for primary grades (one volume for grades K–2); signing for intermediate grades (one volume for grades 3–6); songs to sing and read (one volume for all grades); Share World Music (one volume for all grades with compact discs); *Musica para todos* (K–3 and 4–6, with compact discs); and a master index.

Integrated technology products available with the series include *Share the Music MiDisaurus* (for grades 1–3); *Share the Music Interactive Recorder* (Grades 3 up); *Music with MIDI* teacher's manual and disks (grades 1–8); *Share the Music* Videos (grades K–8); *Music Ace*™ and *Music Ace 2*™ software and user's manual (grades 1–6); *Music Time*™ notational software and teacher's manual (grades 3–8).

(Description by Alice Trimmer, Executive Editor, Music, McGraw-Hill School Division.)

JUMP RIGHT IN: THE MUSIC CURRICULUM

(2000), Edwin E. Gordon, Beth M. Bolton, Cynthia C. Taggart, Alison M. Reynolds, Wendy H. Valerio. Chicago: GIA Publications, Inc. (7404 S. Mason Ave., Chicago, IL 60638. Phone: 708-496-3800 or 800-442-1358; fax 708-496-3828; www.giamusic.com). Kindergarten through grade 8; grades 1 and 2 released in 2000; other grades in preparation. Hardcover student book, teacher's guide, piano accompaniment book, and CD recording set for each grade.

In writing *Jump Right In: The Music Curriculum*, we have tried to achieve several goals. First, we believe that music is learned in the same way that a language is learned. Children interact with language first by listening and experimenting with it with no expectation for correctness. Eventually, children develop solid listening and, eventually, speaking vocabularies. Only after they can already understand spoken language and speak themselves do they learn to read and write.

We have sequenced the instruction of *Jump Right In: The Music Curriculum* to parallel this learning process. Students first develop an extensive aural and oral music vocabulary. Only then do we introduce music reading and writing. Because music is learned aurally and orally, teachers must serve as models of excellent musicianship. As a result, we have written our Teaching Plans so that teachers must sing, chant, move, play, and create in order to teach them successfully. Teachers should provide the musical models to which their students aspire, for unless students have excellent aural models, they will be unable to learn music efficiently.

Second, we have tried to achieve a balance of tonalities and meters when choosing repertoire to include in the series. Most of the music heard in the United States is in Major tonality and Duple meter. However, our understandings of Major tonality and Duple meter are limited because we have nothing with which to compare them.

By involving our students in making music in less frequently heard tonalities and meters, they will not only develop an understanding of the unusual tonalities and meters but they will also have a better and richer understanding of Major and Duple. In other words, they will learn what Major and Duple are by learning what they are not.

Third, we have tried to involve students in music of other cultures. When choosing repertoire, we included many songs from other countries and cultures and presented those songs in as authentic a form as possible. We have also encouraged teachers to go beyond what is written in the main Teaching Plans and explore the cultural context of the songs with students.

Fourth, we believe that students should be given opportunities to perform alone as well as in a group. Only by performing alone can students gain a full understanding of their own performances. Also, by hearing students perform alone, teachers will be able to assess the progress of individuals rather than the overall progress of a group. In this way, the teacher will be better able to address the needs of individual students.

Finally, we have written all books so that they conform to the new National Standards for Music Education. By teaching the plans as they are presented within *Jump Right In: The Music Curriculum,* students will have the opportunity to achieve all of the goals as defined for each of the levels within the Standards document.

(Description by Alec Harris, Education Director for G.I.A. Publications.)

Appendix D
A Collection of Chants, Proverbs, and Poems

CHANTS

Engine, Engine

Engine, engine, number nine,
Going down the Chicago line,
If the train comes off the track,
Do you want your money back?

Pease, Porridge Hot

Pease porridge hot,
Pease porridge cold,
Pease porridge in the pot
Nine days old.

Some like it hot,
Some like it cold,
Some like it in the pot
Nine days old.

Old Mother Witch

Old mother witch,
Fell in a ditch,
Picked up a penny,
Thought she was rich.

Teddy Bear

Teddy bear, Teddy bear,
Turn around.
Teddy bear, Teddy bear,
Touch the ground.
Teddy bear, Teddy bear,
Show your shoe.
Teddy bear, Teddy bear,
That will do.

Solomon Grundy

Solomon Grundy,
Born on a Monday,
Christened on Tuesday,
Married on Wednesday,
Took ill on Thursday,
Worse on Friday,
Died on Saturday,
Buried on Sunday,
This is the end,
Of Solomon Grundy.

Oliver Twist

Oliver Twist can't do this,
Touch his knees, touch his toes,
Clap his hands and over he goes.

Eena, Deena

Eena, deena, dina, duss.
Katla, weena, wina, wuss.
Spit, spot, must be done.
Twiddlum, twaddlum, twenty-one.

Raindrops

Pitter, patter, raindrops,
Splitter, splatter, raindrops,
Windshield wipers, windshield wipers,
Swish, swish, swish.

Five Little Monkeys

Five little monkeys, jumping on the bed,
One fell off and bumped his head.
Mama called the doctor and the doctor said:
"No more monkeys jumping on the bed!"
(Traditional)

Doctor Foster

Doctor Foster went to Glouster
In a shower of rain.
He stepped in a puddle right up to his middle,
And he never went there again.
(Traditional)

Five Little Pumpkins

Five little pumpkins sitting on a gate.
The first one said, "Oh, my, it's getting late!"
The second one said, "There are witches in the air!"
The third one said, "But I don't care!"
The fourth one said, "Let's go and have some fun!"
The fifth one said, "Let's run, run, run, run, run!"
Then "Oooo" went the wind, and out went the light,
And the five little pumpkins rolled out of sight.
(Traditional)

Wee Willie Winkie

Wee Willie Winkie runs through the town,
Upstairs and downstairs, in his nightgown;
Rapping at the window, crying through the lock,
"Are the children in their beds?
Now it's eight o'clock."
(Mother Goose)

Ice Cream Soda

Ice cream soda,
Delaware punch.
Tell me the name of your
Honeybunch.

Acka Backa

Acka backa soda cracker,
Acka backa boo.
Acka backa soda cracker,
Out goes you.

Jack and Jill

Jack and Jill went up the hill
To fetch a pail of water.
Jack fell down and broke his crown
And Jill came tumbling after.
Up Jack got and home he did trot
As fast as he could caper.
He went to bed to mend his head
In vinegar and brown paper.
(Mother Goose)

Bumblebee

Bee, bee, bumblebee,
Stung a man upon his knee,
Stung a pig upon his snout,
Goodness gracious, you are out!

Rima de Chocolate

Uno, dos, tres, CHO-
(Cuente con los dedos de la mano.)
Uno, dos, tres, -CO-
Uno, dos, tres, -LA-
Uno, dos, tres, -TE
Bate, bate chocolate.
(Frote las manos como usa un molinillo en una chocolatera.)

Chocolate Rhyme

One, two, three, CHO-
(Count with fingers.)
One, two, three, -CO-
One, two, three, -LA-
One, two, three, -TE
Stir, stir the chocolate.
(Rub hands together as if using a chocolate beater.)

PROVERBS

A bird in the hand is worth two in the bush.
A penny saved is a penny earned.
A rolling stone gathers no moss.
A quiet tongue makes a wise head.
Busy as a bee.
Great oaks from little acorns grow.
Haste makes waste.
Honesty is the best policy.
Hungry bellies have no ears.
Liars should have good memories.
Little strokes fell great oaks.
Many hands make light work.
Many things are lost for want of asking.
No pain, no gain.

HAIKU POEMS*

Searching on the wind,
the hawk's cry . . .
is the shape of its beak.
(James W. Hackett)

A leaf on the stream
sinks slowly through the current
to the deepest pool.
(James W. Hackett)

Crow pecks into the sand,
swallows what he finds, then
shudders all over.
(James W. Hackett)

With every gust of sun,
a halo of golden down
surrounds the hawk.
(James W. Hackett)

Wind sounds through the trees . . .
while here, gnats play in the calm
of wooded sunlight.
(James W. Hackett)

On this silent snow,
each crunching step echoes dryly
into my teeth.
(James W. Hackett)

A cloud of bugs
busy going nowhere
in a ray of sun.
(James W. Hackett)

POEMS

Rain

The rain is raining all around,
It falls on field and tree,
It rains on the umbrellas here,
And on the ships at sea.
(Robert Louis Stevenson)

The Grasshopper and the Elephant

Way down south where bananas grow,
A grasshopper stepped on an elephant's toe.
The elephant said, with tears in his eyes,
"Pick on somebody your own size."

(Anonymous)

Maggie

There was a small maiden named Maggie,
Whose dog was enormous and shaggy;
The front end of him
Looked vicious and grim—
But the tail end was friendly and waggy.

(Anonymous)

The Clam

You may leave the clam on the ocean floor, It's all the same to the clam,
For a hundred thousand years or more, It's all the same to the clam;
You may carry him home in a gunny sack
And pour Tabasco on his back.
And use him for a midnight snack, It's all the same to the clam.

You may carry him 'round to bring you luck, It's all the same to the clam,
Or use him for a hockey puck, It's all the same to the clam.
You may dress him in the latest style,
Or pry him open with a file,
The clam will neither frown nor smile, It's all the same to the clam.

You may call him Bob, or Fran, or Nell, It's all the same to the clam;
Or make an ashtray from his shell, It's all the same to the clam;
You may take him riding on the train,
Or leave him sitting in the rain,
You'll never hear the clam complain, It's all the same to the clam.

So the world may stop, or the world may spin, It's all the same to the clam;
Or the sky may come a-falling in, It's all the same to the clam,
And man may sing his endless song
Of wronging rights and righting wrongs,
The clam just sets and gets along, It's all the same to the clam.
(Shel Silverstein)

*© 1983 by James W. Hackett from *The Zen Haiku and Other Zen Poems of J. W. Hackett,* published by Japan Publications, Tokyo, Japan. (Available from used book dealers.) Includes suggestions for writing haiku in English.

My Shadow

I have a little shadow that goes in and out with me,
And what can be the use of him is more than I can see.
He is very, very like me from the heels up to the head;
And I see him jump before me, when I jump into my bed.

The funniest thing about him is the way he likes to grow—
Not at all like proper children, which is always very slow;
For he sometimes shoots up taller like an India-rubber ball,
And he sometimes gets so little that there's none of him at all.

He hasn't got a notion of how children ought to play,
And can only make a fool of me in every sort of way.
He stays so close beside me, he's a coward you can see;
I'd think shame to stick to nursie as that shadow sticks to me!
One morning, very early, before the sun was up,
I rose and found the shining dew on every buttercup;
But my lazy little shadow, like an arrant sleepyhead.
Had stayed at home behind me and was fast asleep in bed.

(Robert Louis Stevenson)

Appendix E
Timeline of Music and History

	Medieval c. 500–c. 1420	Renaissance c. 1420–c. 1600
	500, 900, 1100, 1200, 1300, 1400	1500, 1550, 1600
MUSICAL STYLE PERIODS AND COMPOSERS	Pope Gregory the Great (c. 540–604) Leonin (12th century) Hildegard (1098–1179) Vitry (1290–1361) Machaut (1300–1377) Landini (1325–1397)	Isaac (c. 1450–1517) Josquin (1450–c. 1521) Palestrina (c. 1524–1594) Luther (1483–1546) G. Gabrieli (c. 1557–1612) Gesualdo (1560–1613) Monteverdi (1567–1643) Ockeghem (c. 1430–1495) Morley (1557–1602) Dufay (c. 1400–1474) Tallis (c. 1505–1585)
SIGNIFICANT HISTORICAL FIGURES AND EVENTS	China's Song dynasty (420–476) Dante (1265–1321) Crusades begin (1096) Chartres Cathedral rebuilt (1194–1260) Kublai Khan (1215–1294) Marco Polo travels to China (1271) Alhambra Palace (1238–1358) Chaucer (c. 1340–1400) Gutenberg (c. 1398–1468) Peru's Machu Picchu (15th century)	Aztec King Montezuma I (1440–1469) Da Vinci (1452–1519) Michelangelo (1475–1564) Shakespeare (1564–1616) Dürer (1471–1528) Columbus journeys to America (1492) Henry VIII (1491–1547) Luther's Reformation (1517)
MUSIC ELEMENTS	**Melody:** moves mostly in steps; limited vocal range; uses church modes **Harmony:** monophonic; polyphonic for 2 to 4 voices; use of imitation in 14th century **Rhythm:** moves in free chant rhythm; beat groupings of 3s in 13th century; beat groupings of 2s in 14th century **Form:** free vocal chant forms; songs with verses, hymns; free and fixed poetic forms for secular music **Timbre:** small choirs (monophonic chants); soloists (polyphonic music); instrumental music (generally improvised)	**Melody:** moves mostly in steps; expanded vocal range **Harmony:** 4 parts; use of imitation, dissonance (cadence points); text painting **Rhythm:** beat groupings of 2s; syncopation; more complex rhythms **Form:** fixed poetic forms are replaced by imitation; songs with verses; hymns **Timbre:** polyphonic; 5 or more voices in 16th century; homophony; music for specific instruments; secular: soloists, small ensembles; sacred: small choirs, polyphony
TYPES OF COMPOSITIONS	Mass; plainchant setting of parts of the mass; motet (mostly secular); secular songs; instrumental dances	Polyphonic settings of parts of mass; motet; secular songs; instrumental dances; instrumental pieces

	Baroque c. 1600–c. 1750	Classic c. 1750–c. 1820
	1600 · 1650 · 1700 · 1750	1760 · 1780 · 1800 · 1820
MUSICAL STYLE PERIODS AND COMPOSERS	Schültz (1585–1672) Frescobaldi (1583–1643) Lully (1632–1687) Buxtehude (1637–1707) Corelli (1653–1713) Purcell (1649–1695) Couperin (1668–1733) Vivaldi (1675–1741) Rameau (1683–1764) J. S. Bach (1685–1750) Handel (1685–1759) D. Scarlatti (1685–1757)	Gluck (1714–1787) C. P. E. Bach (1714–1788) Haydn (1732–1809) Billings (1746–1800) Mozart (1756–1791) Beethoven (1770–1827)
SIGNIFICANT HISTORICAL FIGURES AND EVENTS	Harvard University 1636 Reign of Peter the Great (1689–1725) Taj Mahal in India (1632–1635) Louix XIV builds Versailles Palace (1661–1708) First black slaves to America (1619) Bashō (poet, 1644–1694) Isaac Newton (1642–1727)	Goethe (1749–1832) G. Washington (1732–1799) Franklin (1706–1790) Jefferson (1743–1826) French Revolution (1789) American Revolution (1775–1781) Simon Bolivar (1783–1830) Napoleon (1769–1821) Jacques-Louis David (1748–1825)
MUSIC ELEMENTS	**Melody:** moves in steps and skips; sequential; use of ornamentation **Harmony:** major–minor scales; polyphonic; homophonic; chord progressions I IV V **Rhythm:** free (recitative); steady, clear meters **Form:** AB ABA; fugue; development of multimovement compositions **Timbre:** small choral groups; small orchestras—strings, wings, continuo; soloists	**Melody:** motivic; short phrases; 8-bar phrases **Harmony:** major–minor scales; use of modulation; change of key within a movement; homophony **Rhythm:** free (recitative); clear meters; rhythmic variety **Form**: sonata; rondo; theme and variations; AB ABA; multimovement compositions **Timbre:** instruments more prominent than voice; larger orchestra—without use of continuo
TYPES OF COMPOSITIONS	Mass and motet with instrumental accompaniment; opera; cantata; oratorio; sonata; concerto; fugue; suite	Mass; oratorio; opera; solo concerto; unaccompanied sonata; instrumental works: symphony, concerto, sonata, string quartet

	Romantic c. 1820–1900	Contemporary c. 1900–
MUSICAL STYLE PERIODS AND COMPOSERS	Brahms (1833–1897); Berlioz (1803–1869); Liszt (1811–1886); Mendelssohn (1809–1847); Mussorgsky (1839–1881); Rimsky-Korsakov (1844–1908); Tchaikovsky (1840–1893); Schubert (1797–1828); Wagner (1813–1883); Verdi (1813–1901); C. Schumann (1819–1896); Bizet (1838–1875); Chopin (1810–1849); Saint-Saëns (1809–1847); R. Schumann (1810–1856); Offenbach (1819–1880); Sousa (1854–1932); J. Strauss (1825–1899); Schoenberg (1874–1951); Ives (1874–1954); Debussy (1862–1901); Bartók (1881–1945); Stravinsky (1881–1971); Ibert (1890–1962); Joplin (1868–1917); Mahler (1860–1911); Kodály (1882–1967); Berg (1885–1935); Boulanger (1887–1979); Ponce (1882–1948)	Libby Larsen (b. 1950); Paul Desmond (b. 1924); Copland (b. 1900); Thos. "Fats" Waller (1904–1943); Edward "Duke" Ellington (1899–1974); Bernstein (1918–1990); Yelvington (1891–1957); Glass (b. 1937); Gershwin (1898–1937); Chávez (1899–1978)
SIGNIFICANT HISTORICAL FIGURES AND EVENTS	Freud (1856–1939); Darwin (1809–1882); Dickens (1812–1870); Marx (1818–1883); Victoria (1819–1901); Millet (1814–1875); Degas (1834–1917); Cassatt (1844–1926); H. Rousseau (1844–1910); Van Gogh (1853–1890); Mondrian (1872–1944); F. Remington (1861–1909); F. T. Johnson (1874–1939); Picasso (1881–1973); Einstein (1879–1955); Georgia O'Keefe (1887–1986); Hitler (1889–1945)	Martin Luther King Jr. (1929–1968); Airplane invented (1903); World War I (1914–1918); Russian Revolution (1917); Television (1929); World War II (1939–1945); Lawrence (b. 1917); F. Stella (1880–1946); W. Thiebaud (b. 1920); Moon walk (1969); Berlin Wall falls (1989)
MUSIC ELEMENTS	**Melody:** lyrical; phrases less regular; longer phrases **Harmony:** major–minor scales; expanded use of modulation and chromaticism; harmony; counterpoint **Rhythm:** variety of meters; varied rhythmic patterns; meter change within movements **Form:** multimovement works; classical forms are expanded **Timbre:** growth of orchestra; large chorus; large bands; small ensembles	**Melody:** 12-tone row **Harmony:** major–minor scales; atonal; new methods of tonal harmony; homophony; counterpoint; polytonality **Rhythm:** variety of meters; varied rhythmic patterns; shifting meter, asymmetric meter **Form**: forms of all previous periods are used, with extensive changes; freer forms developed **Timbre:** same as previous; large bands; emphasis on percussive sound
TYPES OF COMPOSITIONS	Classical forms are expanded; symphonic poem; solo song cycle; piano piece	Forms from all previous periods are used and expanded; impressionism; expressionism; electronic music; minimalism

Appendix F
Resources

Topics are found in the following arrangement:
Addresses and Web sites
Advocacy, see Chapter I, p. 7
Dalcroze Eurhythmics, see Chapter V, pp. 74-76
General Music Retailers
Integrating Music
Jazz
Kodály Approach
Movement
Multicultural, see "World Music," below
Orff-*Schulwerk*
Prekindergarten
Recorder Books
Selected Music Software
Singing
Western Art Music
World Music
Women in Music

ADDRESSES AND WEB SITES

American Music Conference (AMC), (760) 438-8001. www.amc-music.com.

ArtsEdge: Linking the Arts and Education Through Technology. Cooperative Web site of the John F. Kennedy Center for the Performing Arts and the National Endowment for the Arts: artsedge.kennedy-center.org. Integrative arts education and related links; African music/arts link (Africa music.org); suitable for children's independent use.

American Guild of English Handbell Ringers, Inc. 1055 East Centerville Station Road, Dayton, OH 45459-5503; (800) 878-5459; www.agehr.org.

American Orff-*Schulwerk* Association (AOSA), P.O. Box 291089, Clevelend, OH 44139; www.aosa.org. Membership and AOSA video library information; Web site includes many arts education links (folk and classical music, libraries, folk tales and literature, dance, visual arts).

The Association for Childhood Education International (ACEI), (800) 423-3563; www.udel.edu.

Classical

Dalcroze Society of America, www.dalcrozeusa.org. Web site includes extensive Dalcroze bibliography.

Dalcroze Society of America, President, Dr. Stephen Moore, E-Mail: stephenmoore@oberlin.edu.

Dalcroze School of Music, 129 W. 67th Street, New York, NY 10023; (212) 501-3308; www.dalcroze.com.

Early Childhood Music Association (ECMA), www.ecma.org.

Early Childhood News (The Journal of Professional Development). www.earlychildhoodnews.com/.

Early Childhood Special Research Interest Group (SRIG) of MENC: 1806 Robert Fulton Dr., Reston, VA 22091-4348; (800) 828-0229; www.menc.org.

ERIC Clearinghouse on Elementary and Early Childhood Education; www.ericeece.org.

The Getty Center, 1200 Getty Center Drive, Los Angeles, CA 900490-1679; (310) 440-7300.

Getty Center's ArtsEdNet Web site for educators: www.artsednet.getty.edu. Site offers the Multicultural Art Print Series for classrooms K–12; extensive links to arts-related Web sites.

The J. Paul Getty Museum web site displays many art works: www.getty.edu/museum.

Indiana University School of Music Worldwide Internet Music Resources, www.music.indiana.edu/music_resources.

International Society for Music Education (ISME); www.isme.org.

Kodály Center of America, Box 9521, Fall River, MA 02720; (508) 672-3048.

MENC: The National Association for Music Education,1806 Fulton Drive, Reston, VA 20191-4348; (800) 336-3768; www.menc.org.

MuSICA Research Notes (Electronic Newsletter of MuSICA: The Music & Science Information Computer Archive of the Center for the Neurobiology of Learning and Memory, University of California Irvine, Irvine CA 92697-3800; (714) 824-5512; www.musica.vci.edu.

National Association for the Education of Young Children (NAEYC), 1509 Sixteenth St., Washington, DC 20009-5786; (202) 232-8777; www.naeyc.org.

National Institute on Early Childhood Development and Education (U.S. Department of Education); www.ed.gov/offices/OERI/ECI.

Organization of American Kodály Educators(OAKE);www.oake.org.

Membership information; the journal *Kodály Envoy;* video rental library.

Smithsonian Folkways Recordings; 955 L'Enfant Plaza, Suite 7300, Washington, DC 20560-0953; (202) 287-3262; www.si.edu/folkways. Extensive catalog of folk and jazz recordings; many music links.

Society for Music Teacher Education (SMTE); bibliographic compendium of professional literature. Organized by categories (i.e., general music, elementary classroom teacher education) and by author and index. See MENC at www.menc.org "on-line resources."

GENERAL MUSIC: RETAILERS, DISTRIBUTORS, MANUFACTURERS

All companies offer general music and professional books, song books, recordings, classroom, rhythm, and Orff-Schulwerk instruments, small winds, and audiovisual materials. Only specialty items are noted in listings below.

ABA Music for Children, 217 Madrona SE, Salem, OR 97302-5138; (503) 399-0345.

Alfred Music Corporation, Inc., P. O. Box 10003, 16320 Roscoe Blvd.; Van Nuys, CA 91410-0003; (818) 821-6083; www.alfredpub.com. Music publishing (only).

Friendship House, 29313 Clemens Rd., Suite 2-G, Westlake, OH 44145-0623; (800) 791-9876; www.friendshiphouse.com. Includes musical gifts and awards.

Gamble Music Company, 312 South Wabash Avenue, Chicago, IL 60604; (800) 621-4290; www.gamblemusic.com.

General Music Store, 19880 State Line Rd., South Bend IN 46637; (800) 348-5003.

Global Connection, 4201 N-2 South Noland Road, Independence, MO 64055; (800) 386-2441. Handmade ethnic instruments and other multicultural supplies.

HSS, a division of Hohner, Inc. P.O. Box 9167, Richmond, VA 23227-0167; (804) 550-2700. Distributor for Sonor Orff-Schulwerk instruments.

John's Music Center, 4501 Interlake Ave. N., no. 9, Seattle, WA 98103; (800) 473-5194; www.johnsmusic.com. Includes multicultural instruments and drums.

Lentine's Music Inc., 844 North Main St., Akron, Ohio 44310; (800) 822-6752; www.lentine.com. Features music software, computer hardware, MIDI keyboards, etc.

LMI: Music Products for Education, 1776 Armitage Ct., Addison, IL, 60101-4225; (800) 456-2334. Includes software, MIDI keyboards, steel drums.

Malecki Music Inc., 621 North Argonne, P. O. Box 143088, Spokane, WA 99214-3088; (800) 541-2001; maleckimusic.com. Music publications only.

Malmark, Inc.-Bellcraftsmen; P.O. Box 1200, Bell Crest Park, Plumsteadville, PA 18949; (800) HANDBEL; www.malmark.com. Handbells, choir chimes, and ringing accessories.

MMB Music, Inc. (Magnamusic Baton), 3526 Washington Ave., St. Louis, MO 63103-1019; (800) 543-3771; www.mmbmusic.com. (Web site has excellent links to music and arts sites).

Music for Little People, P.O. Box 1460, Redway, CA 95560; (800) 727-2233. Audio-related products and prekindergarten materials (only).

Music Is Elementary, P.O. Box 24263, Cleveland, OH 44124; (800) 888-7502.

Musik Innovations, 9600 Perry Highway, Pittsburgh, PA 19237; (800) 677-8863; www.musikinn.com. Includes handbells, choir chimes, and ToneChimes.

Oscar Schmidt International, 230 Lexington Dr., Buffalo Grove, IL 60089; (800) 877-6863; Manufactures Autoharps and other instruments.

Peripole-Bergerault, Inc., 2041 State Street, Salem, OR 97301-4349; (800) 443-3592. Manufactures handbells, Bergerault Orff-Schulwerk instruments, prekindergarten instruments (including MusicPlay toys by Barbara Andress), and other instruments.

Rhythm Band, Inc., P.O. Box 126, Fort Worth, TX 76101-0126; (800) 424-4724; www.rhythmband.com. Classroom instruments (only).

Schulmerich Carillons, Carillon Hill, P.O. Box 903, Sellerville, PA 18960-0903; (800) 772-3557; www.schulmerichbells.com. English handbells (only).

Suzuki Corporation Musical Instrument Corporation, P.O. Box 261030, San Diego, CA 92196-1030; (800) 854-1594; www.suzukimusic.com. Manufactures QChords, ToneChimes, rhythm instruments, barred and other instruments.

Sweet Pipes, 6722 Brentwood Stair, Fort Worth, TX 76112; sweetpipes.com. Baroque recorders and related products.

West Music Company, Inc.; P.O. Box 5521, Coralville, IA 52241; (800) 373-0479; www.westmusic.com. Includes multicultural materials and instruments; Orff-*Schulwerk* instruments; electronic instruments and software; music therapy resources.

Yamaha Corporation of America, 6600 Orangethorpe Ave., Buena Park, CA 90620; (800) 253-8490; www.yamaha.com. Manufactures electronic keyboards and other instruments.

INTEGRATING MUSIC, ARTS, AND OTHER SUBJECTS

Ardley, Neil. (1991). *Science Book of Sound.* New York: Harcourt Brace. Grades 2–5.

Bates, Katherine Lee, Neil Waldman, illustr. (1993). *America the Beautiful.* Atheneum; ISBN 0689318618.

Cole, Joanna, ed. (1999). *Best Loved Folktales of the World.* Econo-Clad Books. ISBN 0833512269. 154 stories.

Drew, Helen. (1993). *My First Music Book.* Dorling Kindersley; ISBN 156458259. Ages 6–10. Homemade instruments.

Fox, Dan, and P. Fox. (1987). *Go In and Out the Window: An Illustrated Songbook for Young People.* Henry Holt & Company, Inc.; ISBN 0805006281. Illustr. from the Metropolitan Museum of Art.

Goodkin, Doug. (1997) *A Rhyme in Time: Rhythm, Speech Activities and Improvisation for the Classroom.* Miami, FL: Warner Brothers Publications; ISBN 0769215122. Grades preK–8.

Hamilton, Virginia, with Leo and Diane Dillon, illustr. (1995). *Her Stories: African American Folktales, Fairy Tales, and True Tales.* Scholastic Trade: ISBN 0590473700. 17 stories; author is winner of Newbery Medal and MacArthur Foundation grant.

Hart, Tony, and Susan Hellard, illustr. (1994). *Picasso* (Famous Children Series). Barrons Juveniles; ISBN 0812018265.

Perry, Sarah. (1995). *If* . . . Oxford University Press; ISBN 0892363215. (Getty Trust Publications: J. Paul Getty Museum) Ages 4-8. Watercolors offer a surrealistic view of the natural world; brief text. (Version with Spanish text, *Y Si;* ISBN 0892365420.) Art to elicit integrative experiences.

Pinkney, Andrea Davis, and Brian Pinkney, illustr. (1995). *Alvin Ailey.* Hyperion Press; ISBN 0786810777. African American dancer.

Prelutsky, Jack, and Meilo So, illustr. (1997). *The Beauty of the Beast: Poems from the Animal Kingdom.* New York: Alfred A. Knopf; ISBN 067987058. 200 poems to inspire integrative experiences.

Rosen, Michael, ed., and Whoopi Goldberg, illustr. (1992). *South and North, East and West: An Oxfam Book of World Tales.* Cambridge, MA: Candlewick Press; ISBN 1564021173. Ages 4–8.

Spier, Peter, illustr. and Francis Scott Key. (1992). *The Star-Spangled Banner.* New York: Doubleday. Ages 4–8. Book.

Venezia, Mike. (1991). *Paul Klee.* Children's Press. "Musical feeling" of painter's work may encourage creative efforts.

Waring, Dennis. (1999). *Great Folk Instruments to Make and Play.* Sterling Publications; ISBN 1895569435. How to make 50 instruments using non-traditional materials. Age 8 up.

JAZZ BOOKS AND RECORDINGS

Claverie, Jean. (1997). *Little Lou.* New York: Children's Educational Paperbacks; ISBN 0395880742. Ragtime in Chicago, early twentieth century.

Collins, David R. (1998). *Bix Beiderbecke: Jazz Age Genius.* Morgan Reynolds; ISBN 1883846366. Book; intermediate grades.

Diller, Harriet. (1996). *The Big Band Sound.* Honesdale, PA: Caroline House/Boyds Mill Press. ISBN 0876143109. Story book.

Hacker, Carlotta. (1999). *Great African Americans in Jazz.* Econo-Clad Books: ISBN 0613050908. Book.

Hill, Willie L., Jr. (1997). *The Instrumental History of Jazz.* MENC/International Association of Jazz Educators. Two audio CD boxed set with multimedia features (Mac, PC); 56-page book.

Mitchell, Barbara. (1987). *Raggin': A Story about Scott Joplin.* Minneapolis, MN: Carolrhoda Books; ISBN 0876143109.

Orgill, Roxanne. (1997). *If I Only Had a Horn: Young Louis Armstrong.* Leonard Jenkins, illustr. New York: Houghton Mifflin Co.; ISBN 0395759196. Book.

Pinkney, Andrea Davis. (1998). *Duke Ellington: The Piano Prince and His Orchestra.* Brian Pinkney, illustr. Disney Productions; ISBN 0786801786. Caldecott Honor Book.

Pinkney, J. Brian, and Brian Pinkney. (1997). *Max Found Two Sticks.* Aladdin Paperbacks; ISBN 068981593X. Storybook.

Raschka, Chris. (1992). *Charlie Parker Played BeBop.* Orchard Books; ISBN 05310599.

Raschka, Chris. (1997). *Mysterious Thelonious.* Orchard Books.

Rich, Anna, and Arthur Flowers. (1996). *Cleveland Lee's Beale Street Band.* Bridgewater Books; ISBN 0816736529. Storybook.

Shaik, Fatima, E. B. Lewis, illustr. (1998). *The Jazz of Our Street.* Dial Books: ISBN 0803718853. Storybook set in New Orleans.

Smithsonian Folkways Recordings. Extensive catalog of jazz masters. See "Addresses," above.

Weiss, George David, and Bob Thiele, Ashley Bryan, illustr. (1995). *What a Wonderful World.* New York: Atheneum. Book about Louis Armstrong.

KODÁLY APPROACH

Daniel, Katinka. (1982). *The Kodály Approach.* Method books for levels 1–3; Method Book 2 contains the Song Collection. Champaign, IL: Mark Foster Music.

Daniel, Katinka. (1981). *Kodály in Kindergarten: 50 Lesson Plans, Curriculum, Song Collection.* Champaign, IL: Mark Foster Music.

Eisen, Ann, and Lamar Robertson. *An American Methodology: An Inclusive Approach to Music Literacy.* K–6 curriculum.

Erdei, Peter. (1974). *150 American Folk Songs to Sing, Read, and Play.* Boosey & Hawkes.

Forrai, Katalin. *Music in Preschool,* revised ed. Boosey & Hawkes. Curriculum for ages 3-5.

Let the Fun Begin. (1993). Video, 20 min. Contact the Kodály Center of America (see "Addresses," above). Shows children and their games, and how games can be used in school and day-care settings. Accompanying booklet with words, rhythms, and actions.

Szonyi, Erzebet. (1974). *Musical Reading and Writing.* Boosey & Hawkes. 8 vols. plus three teacher's manuals.

Music Is for Everyone: The Pedagogical Legacy of Zoltán Kodály. Four English-language videos demonstrating Kodály's music-learning theories with students ages 3 through 14. Film available from Qualiton Imports, Ltd., 2402 40th Ave., Long Island City, NY 11101; phone: (718) 937-8515; fax: (718) 729-3239.

Music Lessons. Film available from OAKE; see "Addresses," above.

MOVEMENT RESOURCES

Bennett, Peggy D., and Douglas R. Bartholomew. (1997). "Folk-Song Games" in *Song Works I.* Belmont, CA: Wadsworth Publishing Company; ISBN 0534513271. Includes 37 song-games with musical and integrative activities.

Burton, Leon H., and Takeo Kudo. (2000). *SoundPlay: Understanding Music through Creative Movement.* Reston, VA: MENC: National Association for Music Education; ISBN 1565451309. Book with audio CD; lessons with specially composed music; correlated to National Standards.

Choksy, Lois, and David Brummitt. (1987). *120 Singing Games and Dances.* Englewood Cliffs, NJ: Prentice Hall.

Hackett, Patricia. (1998). *The Melody Book: 300 Selections from the World of Music for Piano, Guitar, Autoharp, Recorder, and Voice, 3d ed.* Upper Saddle River, NJ: Prentice Hall. Includes singing games and dances.

Weikart, Phyllis. (1988). *Movement Plus Rhymes, Songs, and Singing Games.* Ypsilanti, MI: The High/Scope Press (600 North River St., Ypsilanti, MI 48198). Ages 3–7 activities.

Weikart, Phyllis. (1996). *Rhythmically Moving.* The High/Scope Press. Traditional and contemporary folk dances (128) on nine audio recordings, or video.

Weikart, Phyllis S. (1982). *Teaching Movement and Dance: A Sequential Approach to Rhythmic Movement,* 3d ed. Ypsilanti, MI: The High/Scope Press. Instructions for teaching 110 beginning-level folk dances. Can be used with Weikart's *Rhythmically Moving.*

ORFF-*SCHULWERK*

American Orff-*Schulwerk* Association. *Orff-Schulwerk: A Simple Gift to Education.* Video; color, 30 min. Teacher demonstrates Orff-*Schulwerk* with grade 4 students; brief discussion of benefits of Orff approach to school and community. See West Music, "General Music Retailers," above.

American Odyssey. Video. Available from AOSA. See "Addresses," above.

Boshoff, Ruth. (1984). *All Around the Buttercup: Early Experiences with Orff-Schulwerk.* New York: Schott.

Frazee, Jane, with Kent Kreuter. (1987). *Discovering Orff: A Curriculum for Music Teachers.* New York: Schott. Grades 1–5.

Goodkin, Doug. *Name Games.* Grades K–8. Rhythmic speech activities.

Goodkin, Doug. (1997). *A Rhyme in Time: Rhythm, Speech Activities and Improvisation for the Classroom.* Miami, FL: Warner Brothers Publications. Grades preK–8. Movement, language, speech activities.

Hampton, Walt. *Hot Marimba! Zimbabwean-Style Music for Orff Instruments.* World Music Press. Book with audio recording. Graded pieces with copy-permissible scores; teaching suggestions; cultural information.

Kriske, Jeff, and Randy DeLelles. *As American as Apple Pie.* Grades K–6. 21 American folk songs with Orff-*Schulwerk* arrangements.

Keetman, Gunild. (1974). *Elementaria: First Acquaintance with Orff-Schulwerk,* translated by Margaret Murray. London: Schott & Co.

Music for Children: Orff-Schulwerk American Edition, coordinated by Hermann Regner. Vol. 1: Preschool (1982), vol. 2: Primary (1977), vol. 3: Upper Elementary (1980). New York: Schott.

Nash, Grace, and Janice Rapley. (1990). *Music in the Making.* Van Nuys, CA: Alfred Music Corporation, Inc.; www.alfredpub.com.

Orff, Carl, and Gunild Keetman. (1973). *Music for Children.* English adaptation by Doreen Hall and Arnold Walter. Vol. 1: Pentatonic, vol. 2: Major: Bordun, vol. 3: Major: Triads, vol. 4: Minor: Bordun, vol. 5: Minor: Triads. Mainz: B. Schotts Söhne.

Saliba, Connie. (1994). *One World, Many Voices: Folk Songs of Planet Earth.* Memphis Musicraft Publications; ISBN 0934017212. Songs (60) with Orff-*Schulwerk* arrangements; movement, games and poems; prekindergarten through grade 2.

Steen, Arvida. (1992). *Exploring Orff.* New York: Schott. Grades K–5 curriculum.

PREKINDERGARTEN: CURRICULUM

Burton, Leon H. and Takeo Kudo. (2000). *SoundPlay: Understanding Music through Creative Movement.* Reston, VA: MENC: National Association for Music Education; ISBN 1565451309. Book with audio CD; lessons with specially composed music; correlated to National Standards.

Reilly, Mary Louise, and Lynn Freeman Olson. (1985). *It's Time for Music: Songs and Lesson Outlines for Early Childhood Music.* Van Nuys, CA: Alfred Music Corporation, Inc. (See "General Music Retailers," above.) Ages 3–7; teacher's book, songbook with lesson plans, audio CD or cassette with children singing.

Valerio, W. H., A. M. Reynolds, B. M. Bolton, C. Taggart, and E. E. Gordon. (1998). *Music Play.* Chicago, IL: G.I.A. Publications; ISBN 1579990274. Early childhood; curriculum with audio CD (see publisher's address, Appendix C).

PREKINDERGARTEN: LISTENING

African Lullaby. (1999). Ellipsis Arts. Recording. (African musicians)

Bach, J.S. *Sonatas for Flute and Harpsichord.* Recording.

Celtic Lullaby. (1998). Ellipsis Arts. Recording.

Grieg, Edvard. *Peer Gynt Suite.* Recording.

Mussorgsky, Modeste. *Pictures at an Exhibition.* Recording.

Partch, Harry. (1997). *The Harry Partch Collection, Vol. 1.* Composers Recordings Inc., No. 751; ASIN: B000002616. Audio CD.

Prokofiev, Sergei. *Peter and the Wolf.* Recording. Several book versions available.

Rubin, Marc, and Alan Daniel. (1992). *The Orchestra.* Buffalo, NY: Firefly Books.

Sound and Spirit: Welcoming Children Into the World. (1999). Ryko; ASIN: B00000JRMO. Recording.

Tubby the Tuba. Book with video. Teaches instrument families. Available from Friendship House (see "General Music Retailers," above).

Van Kampen, Vlasta, and Irene C. Eugen. (1989). *Orchestranimals.* New York: Scholastic; ISBN 0590731637. Book.

Vivaldi, Antonio. *The Four Seasons* by Antonio Vivaldi. Recording.

See also "Western Art Music Recordings," below.

PREKINDERGARTEN: MOVING AND PLAYING INSTRUMENTS (BOOKS, RECORDINGS)

Bach, J.S. "Allegro" from *Brandenburg Concerto No. 3.* Recording.

"Baris" from *Music from the Morning of the World: The Balinese Gamelan and Ketjak, the Ramayana Monkey Chant.* Audio CD. WEA/Atlantic/Nonesuch.

Burton, Leon, and Takeo Kudo. (2000). *SoundPlay: Understanding Music through Creative Movement.* Reston, VA: MENC: National Association for Music Education; ISBN 1565451309. Book with audio CD.

Feierabend, John M. (1989). *Music for Very Little People.* Boosey & Hawkes. Fifty songs with rhythmic activities; book with audiocassette. Additional materials by Dr. Feierabend available from general music retailers (see above).

Glass, Philip. (1987). "Lightning" from *Glass: Songs from Liquid Days.* Sony Classics No. 39564. Audio CD.

Kleiner, Lynn. *Babies Make Music.* Video; Orff-*Schulwerk* for caregivers.

Kleiner, Lynn, Cecilia Riddell, and Debbie Cavalier. (1984). *Kids Make Music.* Video; toddlers to age 5; singing, dancing, rhyming, percussion activities taught by teacher and puppet.

Kleiner, Lynn. *Kids Make Music Too!* Video, ages 3–8; based on Orff-*Schulwerk* philosophy.

Kleiner, Lynn. *Kids Make Music, Babies Make Music Too!* (1998). Book, video, or audio CD (songs, rhymes, dances orchestrated for Orff barred and percussion instruments).

Pinkney, Andrea, and Brian Pinkney, illustr. (1997). *Shake Shake Shake.* Book. Harcourt Brace; ISBN 015200632X. Storybook. (African *shekere*)

Pinkney, Andrea, and Brian Pinkney, illustr. (1997). *Watch Me Dance.* Harcourt Brace; ISBN 0152006311. Storybook.

Saliba, Connie. (1994). *One World, Many Voices: Folk Songs of Planet Earth.* Memphis Musicraft Publications; ISBN 0934017212. Songs with Orff-*Schulwerk* arrangements; 60 songs, movement, games and poems; prekindergarten through grade 2.

Turner, Barrie Carson, Sue Williams, illustr. (1999). *Carnival of the Animals* (by Camille Saint-Saëns). Henry Holt & Company, Inc.; ISBN 0805061800. Book with audio CD.

Voices of Forgotten Worlds: Traditional Music of Indigenous People. (1996). Illustrated book with 2 audio CDs; includes Australian aboriginal music.

Wirth, Marian, et al. *Musical Games, Fingerplays and Rhythmic Activities for Early Childhood.* Parker Publications; ISBN 013607085X. Book.

PREKINDERGARTEN: SINGING

Fox, Dan, and P. Fox. (1987). *Go In and Out the Window: An Illustrated Songbook for Young People.* Henry Holt & Company, Inc.; ISBN 0805006281. Illustrations from The Metropolitan Museum of Art.

Hart, Jane, ed. (1982). *Singing Bee! A Collection of Favorite Children's Songs.* Lothrop Lee & Shepard; ISBN 0688419755.

Jenkins, Ella. *Early Childhood Songs.* Additional Jenkins albums available at Smithsonian Folkways.

Palmer, Hap. *Babysong.* Additional Palmer recordings available at LMI Music; (800) 456-2334.

Raffi. *Baby Beluga.* (1997) See also *Down By the Bay* and *Five Little Ducks.* New York: Crown Books.

Seeger Family. (1992). *Animal Folk Songs for Children and Other People.* Book and recording.

Sharon, Lois, and Bram. *One Elephant, Deux Elephants, Mainly Mother Goose,* and *Smorgasbord.* Recordings. Drive Entertainment.

Sweet Honey in the Rock. (1989). *All for Freedom.* WEA/Warner Brothers. Recording.

Taback, Simms. (1997) *There Was an Old Lady Who Swallowed a Fly.* New York: Viking; ISBN 0670869392. Storybook of song. Caldecott Honor Book.

Taj Mahal. (1992). *Shake Sugaree: Taj Mahal Sings and Plays for Children.* WEA/Warner Brothers. Recording.

See also "Singing," below.

RECORDER BOOKS (SOPRANO)

Burakoff, Gerald, and Sonya Burakoff. *Recorder Time, Book I.* Soprano recorder; available audio CD has accompaniments. Sweet Pipes, 6722 Brentwood Stair, Fort Worth, TX 76112; (817) 446-3299; sweetpipes.com.

Burakoff, Gerald, and Sonya Burakoff. *Hands On Recorder.* Soprano recorder; grades 3 and 4; available audio CD has accompaniments. Sweet Pipes.

Crook, Beth, and Gerald Burakoff. *Recorder and More.* Soprano recorder. Sweet Pipes.

Froseth, James O. *Do It! Play Recorder,* Book 1. Soprano recorder. CD and teacher's edition available. GIA Publications Inc. 7404 S. Mason Ave., Chicago, IL 60638; (800) 442-1358; giamusic.com.

King, Carol. *Recorder Routes: A Guide to Introducing Soprano Recorder. 2nd ed.* Memphis, TN: Memphis Musicraft. May be used with Orff-*Schulwerk* approach.

The Ed Sueta Recorder Curriculum. Book one. Soprano Recorder; CD and audio tapes available. Macie Publishing Co., 10 Astro Place, Suite 100, Rockaway, NJ; (888) 697-1333

SINGING: BOOKS AND VIDEOS

Campbell, Patricia Shehan, Sue Williamson, and Paul Perron. *Traditional Songs of Singing Cultures: A World Sampler.* Book with audio CD.

East, H. (1989) *The Singing Sack: 28 Song-stories from Around the World.* London: A & C Black. Book.

Erdei, Peter, and Katalin Komlos. (1974). *150 American Folk Songs for Children to Sing and Play.* New York: Boosey & Hawkes.

Finckel, E. A. (1993). *Now We'll Make the Rafters Ring: 100 Traditional and Contemporary Rounds for Everyone.* Pennington, NJ: A Cappella Books.

Hackett, Patricia. (1998). *The Melody Book: 300 Selections from the World of Music for Piano, Guitar, Autoharp, Recorder, and Voice. 3d ed.* Upper Saddle River, NJ: Prentice Hall; ISBN 0132819171.

Phillips, Kenneth H. *Teaching Kids to Sing.* Six-part video series. Available from West Music Co.

Phillips, Kenneth H. (1994). *Teaching Kids to Sing.* Exercise and Vocalise cards to accompany the video series, above.

Society for General Music. (1994). *Singing in General Music.* Reston, VA: Music Educators National Conference. Video, color, 26 min.

Swears, Linda. *Teaching the Elementary School Chorus.* Video, 63 min., with conductor Henry Leck, a countertenor, and a children's choir. Available from West Music Co. See "General Music Retailers," above.

For more singing resources, see also "World Music," below.

SELECTED MUSIC SOFTWARE FOR THE ELEMENTARY CLASSROOM

The following selected software is currently available and appropriate for use in the elementary music classroom. The programs, arranged alphabetically by title, are briefly described, and pertinent information on platform requirements and format is listed. While most programs are distributed by a variety of venders, either the publisher or the main distributor is given for each.

Adventures in Musicland—Electronic Courseware Systems, (800) 832-4965, www.ecsmedia.com

Macintosh/Windows

Four different games in the setting of Alice in Wonderland: Melody Mixup (reproduces a growing melody), Music Match (tests memory matching pairs of musical symbols on cards), Picture Perfect (names various musical instruments), and Sound Concentration (challenges aural memory by matching pairs of sounds displayed on top hats). Ages 3+

Beethoven Lives Upstairs—Music in Motion, (800) 445-0649, www.musicmotion.com

Windows, CD-ROM

Based on the Susan Hammond's Classical Kids Series video, this interactive program invites students to travel back to nineteenth-century Vienna. Students will travel through young Christoph's house (The Main Room, Christoph's Room) and down the streets of Vienna (The Bell Tower, Town Square, Art Studio) with Beethoven as their guide. They will get to play a variety of interactive games, paint pictures, create a journal, "play" Beethoven's piano, and even view scenes from the video *Beethoven Lives Upstairs*! Ages 8+

Big Kidmusic—Ars Nova Software, (800) 445-4866, www.ars.nova.com

Macintosh, CD-ROM

A colorful and comprehensive program, not a game, that allows children to become familiar with music notation while being entertained with favorite songs. The program offers the unique feature of seeing and hearing solfeg syllables sung in real time. On same CD-ROM as *A Little Kidmusic.* Ages 8+

Clef Notes—Electronic Courseware Systems, (800) 832-4965, www.ecsmedia.com

Macintosh/Windows

A program to help students improve the speed with which they identify music notes as they are placed on the staff. Scores are stored in a Hall of Fame at the end of each session. Ages 6+

Early Music Skills—Electronic Courseware Systems, (800) 832-4965, www.ecsmedia.com

Macintosh/Windows

A tutorial and drill program focusing on four basic music-reading skills: recognition of lines and spaces, comprehension of the numbering sequence for the staff, visual and aural identification of notes moving up and down, and recognition of notes stepping and skipping up and down. Ages 5–9

Essentials of Music Theory—Alfred Publishing Co., Inc., (800) 292-6122; www.alfredpub.com

Macintosh/Windows, CD-ROM

A three-volume series introducing music fundamentals through concise lessons, followed by short exercises for immediate reinforcement. Integrates ear training and uses audio and visual examples to reinforce music fundamentals. A complete scorekeeping and recordkeeping track can follow up to 200 students. Adults

Hyperstudio—Roger Wagner Publishing, (800) 545-7677, www.hyperstudio.com

Macintosh/Windows

Multimedia writing tool that allows students to communicate and deliver ideas on disc, CD-ROM, or over the Internet. It offers the possibility to bring together text, sound, graphics, and video. Ages 9+

Juilliard Music Adventure—Theatrix Interactive. (800) 795-8749, www.theatrix.com

Macintosh/Windows, CD-ROM

Story-based program (a magical castle with a mischievous gnome, a fire-breathing dragon, and a "wise" queen) with an interactive structure and music games that offer opportunities to compose, arrange, and listen for instrumental timbres. Ages 9+

Kids—Electronic Courseware Systems, (800) 832-4965, www.ecsmedia.com

Macintosh (MIDI required) Windows (MIDI optional)

A four-disc game series that includes Zoo Puppet Theater (uses animals to introduce finger numbers for the keyboard), Race Car Keys (teaches keyboard geography), Dinosaur's Lunch (teaches treble-clef notation), and Follow Me (asks the student to play notes that have been presented aurally). Ages 5-9

A Little Kidmusic—Ars Nova Software, (800) 445-4866, www.ars.nova.com

Macintosh, CD-ROM

A colorful and comprehensive program, not a game, that allows children to become familiar with music notation while being entertained with favorite songs. The program offers the unique feature of seeing and hearing solfeg syllables sung in real time. On same CD-ROM as *Big Kidmusic.* Ages 3–7

Making Music—Silver Burdett Ginn/Scott Foresman, (800) 848-9500, www.sbgmusic.com

Macintosh/Windows, CD-ROM

A program that allows students the opportunity to compose (using a musical sketch pad and movable music construction blocks), to learn the components of music visually and aurally, and to experience this through a creative atmosphere that encourages them to let their imaginations go wild, create a structure as they go, and make music right from the beginning. Ages 3–12

Making More Music—Silver Burdett Ginn/Scott Foresman, (800) 848-9500, www.sbgmusic.com

Macintosh/Windows, CD-ROM

Making More Music, an advanced version of *Making Music,* is intended for grades 3 and up, and presents more sophisticated composition tools and music fundamentals instruction.

The MIDI Connection—Silver Burdett Ginn/Scott Foresman, (800) 848-9500, www.sbgmusic.com

Macintosh/Windows

A package for each grade, 2–8, that includes a teaching guide, three MIDI discs, and student workbooks. *The MIDI Connection* gives teachers and students music files that they can customize to suit their creative and educational purposes. For example, students can mute a track to make a simpler accompaniment or record new harmonies or rhythms to accompany the arrangement.

MiDisaurus, Vols. 1–8—Musicware, (800) 997-4266, www.musicwareinc.com

Macintosh/Windows, CD-ROM

MiDisaurus, an 8-volume software series, "uses an edutainment approach" to teach keyboard-based music fundamentals. MiDisaurus, the musical dinosaur, introduces students to the world of music through colorful animation, fun-filled games, and tunes to play and sing. Includes units on composers, forms, instrument families, world music, rhythm, notation, articulations, and notation. Ages 4-10

Music Ace—Harmonic Vision, (303) 455-5223, www.harmonicvision.com

Macintosh/Windows, CD-ROM

This music education software program contains 24 comprehensive lessons, games, and a Music Doodle Pad. Unique features include: tracking of student progress, extensive teacher and student paper–based materials, and the Music Doodle Pad that allows students to compose and record their own music using a variety of instrument sounds, or listen to and modify popular music selections from the "jukebox" section of the Music Doodle Pad. Ages 8+

Music Ace 2—Harmonic Vision, (303) 455-5223, www.harmonicvision.com

Macintosh/Windows, CD-ROM

This music education software program is a continuation and more advanced version of *Music Ace.* It too offers 24 comprehensive lessons covering music fundamentals, plus 24 games to practice music skills and reinforce lesson concepts. Unique features include: tracking of student progress, extensive teacher and student paper–based materials, and the Music Doodle Pad that allows students to compose and record their own music using a variety of instrumental sounds, or listen to and modify popular music selections from the "jukebox" section of the Music Doodle Pad. Ages 10+

Musical Stairs—Electronic Courseware Systems, (800) 832–4965, www.ecsmedia.com

Macintosh/Windows

An aural–visual drill-and-practice game that introduces intervals in treble and bass clef and relates the intervals to the piano keyboard. Ages 5–9

Musicus—Electronic Courseware Systems, (800) 832–4965, www.ecsmedia.com

Macintosh/ Windows

A game program based on the popular computer game called "Tetris." This game is designed to help students gain a better perspective of the relative lengths of notes and combinations of tied notes. Ages 8+

Rock Rap 'n Roll—Silver Burdett Ginn/Scott Foresman, (800) 848-9500, www.sbgmusic.com

Macintosh/Windows

A music-making "machine" that invites students to "jam" like pros using pre-composed original music. Also, allows students the option to modify and manipulate sounds and record their own vocals or sound effects. Ages 7+

SimTunes—Maxis, www.maxis.com

Windows, CD-ROM

Creative software that allows children to make their own musical pictures. Similar to the presentation format of *Music Ace* and *Making Music.* Children may already be familiar with other nonmusic software from Maxis such as *SimTown, SimPark, SimFarm, SimCity,* etc. Ages 8+

Symbol Simon—Electronic Courseware Systems, (800) 832–4965, www.ecsmedia.com

Windows

Two colorful games—Invention Island and Hatch Match—designed to help players identify music symbols and match with definitions while developing reasoning and memory skills. Ages 7+

Thinkin' Things Collection 2—Edmark, (800) 691-2986, www.edmark.com

Macintosh/Windows, CD-ROM

A set of tools and toys that develop spatial awareness, improve memory, foster creativity, etc. Kids explore rhythm notation on their own high-tech jammin' machine, match band members to rhythm lines they play, and learn tunes with "toony" on four wacky xylophones. Ages 6+

Zap!—Edmark, (800) 691-2986, www.edmark.com

Macintosh/Windows

This program covers the physics of sound, light, and electricity. The "setting" is a rock concert, for which the student must do hands-on tinkering to fix broken electric amps, guitar, lighting, etc. Ages 8-12

WESTERN ART MUSIC: BOOKS

Ammon, Richard. (Fall 1992). "Stories from Opera and Ballet." *General Music Today* 6 (1):36-37. List of books for young readers.

Cowan, Catherine, and Kevin Hawkes, illustr. (1998). *My Friend the Piano.* Lothrop Lee & Shepard; ISBN 0688132391. Ages 5–8. A young student hates to practice, and her piano falls silent (by going out of tune).

Englander, Roger. (1994). *Opera: What's All the Screaming About?* New York: Walker and Co.; ISBN 0802774431. Book with audio CD includes introduction to opera, plus the story of "Carmen" with musical highlights. Ages 10 up. Author is five-time Emmy Award winner.

Guy, Suzanne, and Donna Lacy. (1998). *The Music Box: The Story of Christofori.* Brunswick Publishing Co.; ISBN 1556181736.

Huskin, Karla. (1986). *The Philharmonic Gets Dressed.* New York: HarperTrophy; ISBN 006443124X. Ages 4–8.

Isadora, Rachel. (1997). *Young Mozart.* New York: Viking. Ages 4-8.

Ketcham, Sallie, Salley Ketcham, and Timothy Bush, illustr. (1999). *Bach's Big Adventure.* New York: Orchard Books; ISBN 0531301400. Storybook; ages 4-8.

Nichol, Barbara, and Scott Cameron, illustr. (1999). *Beethoven Lives Upstairs.* New York: Orchard Books. Book; ages 7-12.

Meet the Instruments. Bowmar. Color photos of instrument "families" on 14″ × 22″ art board.

Portraits of Composers. Set 1: Classical Composers (Bach to Mahler). Set 2: Modern Composers (Debussy to Hanson). Bowmar. Large posters.

Price, Leontyne. (1990). *Aida,* illustrated by Leo and Diane Dillon. New York: Gulliver/Harcourt Brace Jovanovich.

Rachin, Ann. (1992). *Bach* (Famous Children Series). (1992). Barrons Juveniles; ISBN 0812049918. Also in the series are Beethoven, Chopin, Mozart, and Tchaikovsky.

Weil, Lisl. (1991). *Wolferl: The First Six Years in the Life of Wolfgang Amadeus Mozart, 1756–1762.* New York: Holiday House; ISBN 0812308760.

Winter, Jeanette. (1999) *Sebastian: A Book About Bach.* Browndeer Press; ISBN 015200629X. Book; ages 4–8.

WESTERN ART MUSIC: RECORDINGS, VIDEOS, NEWSLETTER

Beethoven Lives Upstairs. (1992). Video, color, 52 min. Book; audio CD available. Eros Financial Investment Inc., in association with Classical Productions for Children. Intermediate grades.

Beethoven Lives Upstairs. (1996). Interactive media. (Based on book and video of the same name.) See "Selected Music Software for the Elementary Classroom" (above) for a full description.

Bowmar Orchestral Library. (1994, 1967). Compiled and edited by Lucille Wood. Warner Brothers Publications Inc. Collection of orchestral and chamber music (325 compositions) packaged by levels in three series, each including 12 audio CDs. Each CD is accompanied by lesson guides for teacher use.

Bowmar's Adventures in Music Listening. (1996–97). Compiled by Leon Burton, Charles Hoffer, William O. Hughes, and contributing editor June Hinckley. Warner Brothers Publications Inc. Collection of orchestral works and music from around the world (90 compositions) organized on three levels: Level 1 (K–2nd), Level 2 (3rd–5th), and Level 3 (6th–8th); 3 audio CDs. An audiocassette is available for Level 1, as well as a Big Book containing illustrations depicting the style, period, and story behind each of the listening selections. A teacher's guide and a student workbook accompany each CD.

Hammond, Susan. *Classical Kids Series.* 30-min. audio CDs and cassettes about Beethoven, Handel, J. S. Bach, Mozart, Tchaikovsky, Vivaldi, in the style of old-time radio; ages 8–12.

Pautz, Mary. *Invitation to Listen.* M & R Newsletters, P. O. Box 51064, New Berlin, WI 53151. (8 issues a year)

A Prokofiev Fantasy with Peter and the Wolf. (1993). Video; ASIN 6302992990. Orchestral instruments introduced through the characters' melodies. Age 5 and up.

See also Prekindergarten: "Listening" and "Moving."

See also elementary music series *The Music Connection* and *Share the Music* that include numerous song recordings and listening selections (incl. multicultural recordings). See Appendix C for full descriptions.

WOMEN IN MUSIC RESOURCES

Great Women Biographical Card Games. Game IV: Composers. Ten great women composers are introduced in a rummy or "Go Fish" type game. Available from the Women's History Resource Center, 7738 Bell Rd., Windsor, CA 95492.

Kamen, Gloria. *Hidden Music.* (1996). New York: Atheneum. Biography of Fanny Mendelssohn. Concludes with biographical sketches of other women classical musicians.

Monceaux, Morgan. (1994). *Jazz: My Music, My People.* New York: Knopf. Stories about 19 women jazz musicians. Caldecott Medal Book.

National Women's History Month School Celebration Starter Kit. A kit that contains multiple items to help celebrate March as Women's History Month. Available from the Women's History Resource Center, 7738 Bell Rd., Windsor, CA 95492.

"Notable Women Composers." A poster by artist Paulette Jellinek featuring an abstract watercolor as background to basic facts about almost 400 women composers from the ninth through the twentieth century. Available from Hildegard Publishing Co., Box 332, Bryn Mawr, PA 19010.

"Notable Women" Kit: Photo Displays Set I and Set II. Twenty-four photographs and biographies, including singer Marian Anderson, violinist Kyung-Wha Chung, and singer/songwriter Buffy Sainte-Marie. Available from the Women's History Resource Center, 7738 Bell Rd., Windsor, CA 95492.

Plantamura, Carol. *Women Composers.* A coloring book complete with short bibliographies of 28 women musicians from earliest times to the present day. Available from Friendship House. (see Appendix F)

WORLD MUSIC SONG BOOKS (SOME WITH RECORDINGS)

Adzinyah, Abraham Kobena, Dumisani Maraire, and Judith Cook Tucker. (1997). *Let Your Voice Be Heard!* Danbury, CT: World Music Press. Book and audio CD or cassette; stick, stone, hand and name game songs.

Amaoku, W. Komla. (1971). *African Songs and Rhythms for Children; Orff-Schulwerk in the African Tradition.* New York: Schott. Songbook with audiocassette. Folkways Smithsonian C-SF 45011.

Boshkoff, Ruth, and Kathy Sorenson. (1995). *Multicultural Songs, Games, and Dances.* Fargo, ND: Organization of American Kodály Educators. 24 songs. Available from OAKE and MENC (see "Addresses," above).

Burton, J. Bryan. (1993). *Moving within the Circle: Contemporary Native American Music and Dance.* Danbury, CT: World Music Press. 24 dances and songs; cultural information; grades K–12. Book with audio CD or cassette featuring Native American musicians; slide set available.

Campbell, Patricia Shehan, Ellen Brabson-McCullough, and Judith Cook Tucker. (1994). *Roots and Branches: A Legacy of Multicultural Music for Children.* Danbury, CT: World Music Press. Songs, games, photos in book with audio CD or cassette.

Campbell, Patricia Shehan, Sue Williamson, and Peter Perron. (1996). *Traditional Songs of Singing Cultures: A World Music Sampler.* Miami, FL: Warner Brothers Publications/International Society for Music Education: ISBN 1576238598. Songbook and audio CD or cassette. Fifty songs and singing games from 23 cultures; ages 3–10. Large format with cultural information, photos, maps.

East, Helen, comp., and Mary Currie, illustr. (1998). *The Singing Sack: 28 Song-Stories from Around the World.* A & C Black; ISBN 0713631155. Book and audiocassette with multicultural instruments and musicians.

Fulton, Eleanor, and Pat Smith. (1998/1978). *Let's Slice the Ice,* rev. ed. St. Louis, MO: MMB Music. Songbook of multicultural ring games and chants.

Hackett, Patricia. (1998). *The Melody Book: 300 Selections from the World of Music for Piano, Guitar, Autoharp, Recorder, and Voice.* 3d ed. Upper Saddle River, NJ: Prentice Hall; ISBN 0132819171.

Imoto, Yoko, illustr. (1997). *Best-Loved Children's Songs from Japan.* Tokyo: Heian International Publishing Company; ISBN 0893468371. English and Japanese lyrics; ages 4–8.

Jones, Bessie, and Bess Lomax Hawes. (1987). *Step It Down: Games, Plays, Songs and Stories from the Afro-American Heritage.* Athens: University of Georgia Press. Book; audiocassette by Rounder Records, no. 8004. Age 5 up.

Nguyen, Phong Thuyet, and Patricia Shehan Campbell. (1990). *From Rice Paddies and Temple Yards: Traditional Music of Vietnam.* Danbury, CT: World Music Press. Book and audio CD or cassette with Vietnamese musicians.

Orozco, Jose-Luis, and Elisa Kleven, illustr. (1999). *De Colores and Other Latin-American Songs.* New York: Puffin; ISBN 1400565485. Ages 4–8; in Spanish and English.

Sam, Sam-Ang, and Patricia Shehan Campbell. (1991). *Silent Temples, Songful Hearts: Traditional Music of Cambodia.* Danbury, CT: World Music Press. Book with audio CD or cassette with Cambodian singers.

Serwadda, W. Moses, Leo and Diane Dillon, illustr. (1987). *Songs and Stories from Uganda.* Danbury, CT: World Music Press. Book and audio CD or cassette with Ugandan singers.

See also "Singing," and "Prekindergarten: Singing," above.

WORLD MUSIC RECORDINGS, VIDEOS, PUBLISHER

Ballard, Louis. (1973/new edition forthcoming). *American Indian Music for the Classroom.* Phoenix, AZ: Canyon Records. Audio recordings; slides; pronunciation guides, cultural information.

Bringing Multicultural Music to Children. (1992). Reston, VA: Music Educators National Conference. Video, color, 27 min.

Discovering the Music of . . . (series). BFA. Old but useful videos include Native American, Japanese, Latin American music. Available from Friendship House (see "General Music Retailers," above).

Hawaiian Rainbows. Rounder Records no. 6018. Audio CD.

Japan: Semi-Classical and Folk Music. (1991). Baker & Taylor, audio CD or video.

JVC/Smithsonian Folkways Video Anthology of World Music and Dance, The. (1989). Video sets for each of three cultures: The Americas, Africa, and Europe. Available from Smithsonian Folkways (see "Addresses and Web Sites," above).

Rounder Records, www.com/rounder. Folk/world music company.

Schmid, Will. *World Music Drumming.* Milwaukee, WI: Hal Leonard Corporation. Cross-cultural drumming curriculum with 30 lesson plans. Teacher's book, enrichment book, video available. Grades 6–8 with elementary grade applications.

Smithsonian Folkways World Music Collection. (1997). Smithsonian Folkways; ASIN B000001DLX. Audio CD; 28 selections.

Sounds of the World. (1986-1989). Reston, VA: Music Educators National Conference. Three audiocassettes with guides.

Teaching Music with a Multicultural Approach. (1991). Four videos, 25–37 min. each. Music of four cultures presented by experts. Reston, VA: Music Educators National Conference. World Music Press, P.O. Box 2565, Danbury, CT 06813-2565; (800) 810-2040. Publisher. www.worldmusicpress.com. Web site offers an excellent "Checklist for Evaluating Multicultural Materials."

Glossary

AB A musical form consisting of two sections, A and B, that contrast with each other (binary form).

ABA A musical form consisting of three sections, A, B, and A. Two are the same, and the middle one is different (ternary form).

accent A stress or emphasis given to certain tones. An accent sign is >.

accidental A sign introduced before a note of a composition that changes the pitch for one measure only: ♯ (sharp), ♭ (flat), ♮ (natural), 𝄪 (double sharp), 𝄫 (double flat).

accompaniment Music that goes with or provides harmonic or rhythmic support for another musical part (usually a melody).

acoustic A term often used to distinguish instruments from their electronic counterparts, e.g., piano.

aerophone ("AIR-uh-fone") From the Greek, *aeros,* wind, and *phonos,* sound. An instrument in which the sound-producing agent is a column of air, such as flute and oboe.

anacrusis ("ana-CREW-sis") See **upbeat.**

arrangement The adaptation of a composition for performance in a medium for which it was not conceived.

asymmetric meter Meter in which the beat groupings are irregular, such as $\frac{5}{4}$ or $\frac{7}{4}$. Often created by combining two meters: $\frac{2}{4}$ and $\frac{3}{4} = \frac{5}{4}$.

atonal 20th-century music in which no tonic, or home tone is apparent.

avant-garde A French term meaning "advance guard" or "vanguard"; refers to modern and innovative music of the period covering approximately the 1930s through the 1970s.

bar or bar line A vertical line through the staff to indicate a boundary for a measure of music.

bass clef The symbol 𝄢, which determines that the fourth line of the staff is F below middle C.

beam A line connecting stems of notes in rhythmic groups; flags are used for single notes.

beat The underlying pulse present in most music; the rhythmic unit to which one responds in marching or dancing.

beat groupings See **meter** and **downbeat.**

blues "Sorrow songs" created by African Americans that influenced the development of jazz. Special characteristics include flatted 3rd and 6th scale tones, the use of groups of 12 measures or "bars"; 7th chords; syncopation; and improvisation.

brass instruments Instruments made of brass in which a column of air is the sound-producing agent, including trumpets, horns, trombones, and tubas. (Also see **wind instruments.**) A characteristic shared feature is their cup-shaped mouthpiece.

cadence A point of arrival that punctuates a musical phrase and section; the ending.

call-and-response form A responsorial form in which there is alternating (and sometimes overlapping) of solo and chorus.

calypso A kind of music developed in the West Indies, characterized by its rhythms and commentary on contemporary events and personalities.

canon A composition in which all parts have the same melody throughout but start at different times. A round is a type of canon.

cantata An extended vocal composition in several movements based on a continuous narrative text.

chant A term with several meanings. The rhythmic recitation of rhymes or poems without a sung melody is the definition used in this text.

chorale German hymn tune.

chord A combination of three or more pitches a third apart, sounded simultaneously.

chordophone ("KORD-u-fone") From the Greek, *chordos,* string, and *phonos,* sound. An instrument in which the sound-producing agent is the stretched string, such as zither, lute, and harp.

chord progression A series of chords sounding in succession.

chord root The pitch on which a chord is constructed; the most important pitch in the chord.

chord tones The individual pitches within a chord.

chromatic scale A 12-tone scale consisting entirely of half steps.

classical music A term for art music of Western European civilization, usually created by a trained composer.

clef A symbol placed on a staff to designate a precise pitch that identifies the other pitches in the score.

coda A short passage added to the end of a composition; a musical way of saying "the end."

compound meter A grouping of beats (meter) in which the beat is divided into 3 equal parts.

concept An understanding that remains in the mind following a learning experience.

concerto An extended composition for solo instrument or instruments and orchestra, usually in three movements.

conjunct Stepwise pitch movement, such as C to D to E.

consonance A relative term used to describe the pleasant, agreeable effect of certain tones sounded simultaneously. Intervals of 3rds, 6ths, and octaves are generally considered to be consonant.

countermelody A melody that sounds simultaneously with another melody.

crescendo Gradually becoming louder.

Curwen hand signs Hand positions for each degree of the scale: *do, re, mi,* etc.

decrescendo Gradually becoming softer.

descant A second melody less important than and usually sung above the principal melody.

diatonic A 7-tone scale, consisting of 5 whole steps and 2 half steps, utilizing every pitch name. Major and minor scales are diatonic scales.

disjunct Pitch movement by intervals larger than a 2nd, such as C to F to A.

dissonance A relative term used to describe the disagreeable effect of certain tones sounded simultaneously. Intervals of 2nds and 7ths are considered to be dissonant.

dominant The fifth degree of the scale; a chord constructed on the fifth degree of the scale.

downbeat The first beat of a measure (beat grouping), usually accented.

drone An accompaniment created by sounding one or more tones (usually 2 tones, 5 notes apart) simultaneously and continuously throughout a composition; a special type of harmony.

duple meter A grouping of beats into two ($^{2}_{4}$, $^{2}_{2}$).

dynamics The degree and range of loudness of musical sounds.

electronic music Music made by creating, altering, and imitating sounds electronically.

electrophone ("Ee-LEC-truh-fone") An instrument in which the acoustical vibrations are produced, amplified, or modified (or all three) by electric devices, as in the electric guitar.

enharmonic tones Tones sounding the same pitch but written differently, as E♭ and D♯.

ethnomusicology The study of all the music of people in a specified area, frequently in a cultural context.

expressive qualities Those qualities (dynamics, tempo, timbre) that, combined with other musical elements, give a composition its unique musical identity.

falsetto A method of singing used by male singers, particularly tenors, to reach tones above the normal range of their voices.

fine ("fee-nay") Italian term meaning "the end."

flat A symbol that indicates that the written pitch is to be lowered a half step: ♭.

folk song A song having no known composer, usually transmitted orally, and reflecting the musical consensus of a cultural group.

form The overall structural organization of a musical composition and the interrelationships of musical events within the overall structure.

fugue A composition in which voices or parts follow or "chase" each other; a theme is presented and then is imitated by two or more parts.

glissando A very rapid sliding passage up or down the white or black keys.

haiku A form of nature poetry that originated in Japan, ideally consisting of 17 syllables composed in a 5–7–5 arrangement.

half step An interval comprising 2 adjacent pitches, as D to D♯.

harmonic minor scale A minor scale in which the pattern of whole steps and half steps is whole–half–whole–whole–half–whole *plus* half–half.

harmony The simultaneous sounding of 2 or more pitches.

heterophonic A musical texture in which slightly different versions of the same melody are sounded together.

home tone See **tonic.**

homophonic A musical texture in which all parts move in the same rhythm but use different pitches, as in hymns; also, a melody supported by chords.

idiophone ("IH-dee-uh-fone") From the Greek, *idios,* self, and *phonos,* sound. An instrument in which the sound-producing agent is a solid (but elastic) material capable of producing sound, such as wood or metal. The many idiophones include gongs, chimes, xylophones, and sticks.

imitation The restatement of a theme in different voices (parts).

impressionism A musical style of the late 19th and early 20th centuries, in which musical textures and timbres were used to convey impressions—to hint—rather than to make precise "statements."

improvisation Music extemporaneously performed, often within a framework determined by the musical style.

interlude A brief section of music inserted between stanzas of a song or sections of a larger work.

interval The distance between 2 tones, named by counting all pitch names involved:

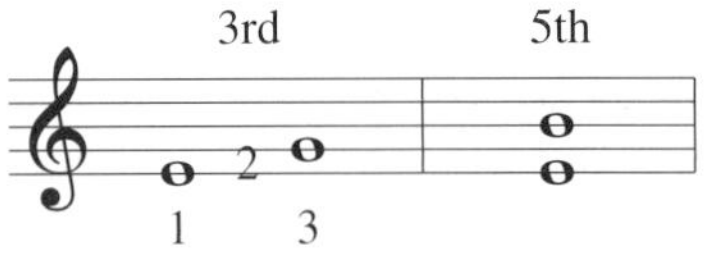

introduction A brief section of music that precedes the main body of a composition.

inversions Rearrangement of the pitches of a chord; e.g., CEG becomes GCE.

jazz A style that originated with African Americans in the early 20th century, characterized by improvisation and syncopated rhythms.

key The scale and tonality of a composition.

key signature The sharps or flats at the beginning of the staff after the clef sign, indicating in which key or on what scale the composition is written.

legato ("leh-GAH-toe") Tones moving in a connected, smooth manner (opposite of **staccato**).

ledger lines ("LEH-jer") Short lines above or below the 5-line staff, on which higher or lower pitches may be indicated.

lyrics The words of a song.

major interval An interval a half step larger than the corresponding minor interval.

major scale A scale in which the pattern of whole steps and half steps is whole–whole–half–whole–whole–whole–half.

major triad A 3-note chord with a major 3rd (4 half steps) and a minor 3rd (3 half steps).

measure A group of beats delineated by bar lines; informally called a "bar."

melodic rhythm Durations of pitches used in a melody.

melodic sequence See **sequence.**

melody A linear succession of sounds (pitches) and silences moving through time.

membranophone ("Mehm-BRAN-uh-fone") From the Latin, *membranum,* skin, and the Greek *pho-nos,* sound. An instrument in which the sound-producing agent is a stretched skin; mainly drums.

meter The grouping of beats in music.

meter signature Two numerals that show the number of beats grouped in a measure and the basic beat:

4 = four beats in a measure
4 = quarter note (♩) is basic beat

Occasionally written $\frac{4}{♩}$.

middle C The C midway between the treble and bass clefs; approximately midway on the piano keyboard.

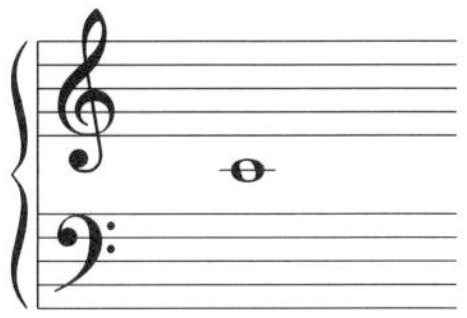

minor interval An interval a half step smaller than the corresponding major interval.

minor scale A scale in which one characteristic feature is a half step between the second and third tones. There are 3 forms of minor scales: natural, harmonic, and melodic.

minor triad A 3-note chord that includes a minor 3rd (3 half steps) and a major 3rd (4 half steps).

monophonic music A musical texture created when a single melody is heard without harmony.

motive A brief rhythmic/melodic figure or pattern that recurs throughout a composition as a unifying element.

natural A sign that cancels a sharp or flat: ♮. A note that is neither sharp nor flat, such as C, D, E, F, G, A, or B on the piano keyboard.

octave Two pitches that are 8 notes apart and share the same letter name (C–C).

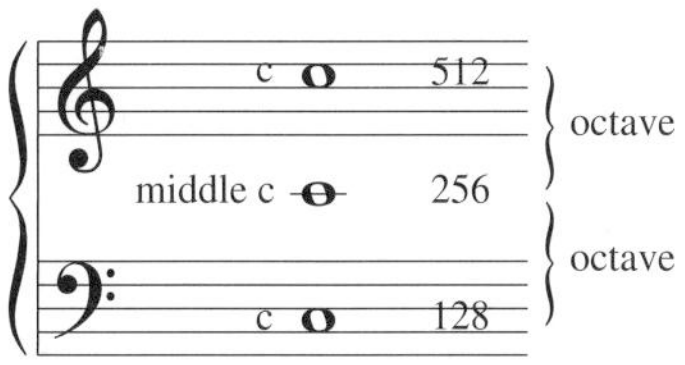

ostinato ("ah-stih-NAH-toe") A continuous repetition of a melodic or rhythmic pattern.

partner songs Two or more different melodies that share a similar meter and chord sequence and can be sung simultaneously when they are in the same key and tempo.

patschen or **patsch** ("PAH-chn") A thigh slap.

pattern See **motive.**

pentatonic scale A 5-tone scale often identified with the pattern of the black keys of the piano. Many other 5-tone arrangements are possible.

percussion instruments Generic term for instruments that are sounded by shaking or striking one object with another. Percussion instruments include those of definite pitch (kettledrum, glockenspiel, xylophone, chimes) and those of indefinite pitch (drums, triangle, cymbals). In classifying world-music instruments, percussion is commonly divided into two types, **membranophones** and **idiophones** (see separate entries).

phrase A musical segment with a clear beginning and ending, comparable to a simple sentence or a clause in speech.

pitch The vibrations per second of a musical tone; the "highness" or "lowness" of a tone.

polyphonic A musical texture created when 2 or more melodies sound simultaneously.

polyrhythms Two or more contrasting rhythmic patterns that occur simultaneously.

polytonal Music that employs 2 or more tonalities (or keys) simultaneously.

quadruple meter A grouping of beats into four ($\frac{4}{4}$, $\frac{4}{8}$, $\frac{4}{2}$).

range The highest and lowest pitches of a melody, or of an instrument or voice.

ragtime A type of early-20th-century American popular music, usually for piano, that features a syncopated ("ragged") melody against an oompah bass.

refrain Phrases recurring at the end of each verse of a song; sometimes called the "chorus."

resonance The intensification and enriching of a musical tone by supplementary vibration of, e.g., the inner surfaces of the larynx, throat, mouth, and nose.

resonator bars Individually pitched metal bars fastened to hollow resonator blocks.

rest The notation for silence.

rhythm All the durations of sounds and silences that occur in music.

rhythm of the melody See **melodic rhythm.**

rhythm pattern Any grouping, generally brief, of long and short sounds and silences.

rondo A musical form consisting of a recurring section with 2 or more contrasting sections, as ABACA.

root The tone on which a chord is built. A chord using C as its root is labeled a C chord.

round A melody performed by 2 or more groups entering at stated and different times.

scale A pattern of consecutive pitches arranged in ascending or descending order. Scales are identified by their specific arrangement of whole steps and half steps. See **chromatic scale, major scale, minor scale, pentatonic scale,** and **whole-tone scale.**

score A composite of all the written notational parts of a composition.

section A distinct portion of a composition; one of a number of parts that together make a composition. A section consists of several phrases.

sequence The repetition of a melodic pattern on a higher or lower degree of the scale.

seventh chord A 4-note chord built in 3rds.

sharp A symbol (♯) that raises the pitch a half step.

shifting meter The changing of beat groupings in music, as from groups of twos to groups of threes.

skip A melodic interval exceeding a 2nd or whole step.

sonata An extended composition in several movements for 1 to 2 instruments.

staccato ("stuh-CAH-toe") Detached, short sounds often indicated by a dot over or under a note (opposite of **legato**).

staff Five parallel lines used in traditional music notation.

steady beat See **beat.**

steel drums Instruments that originated in the West Indies and are constructed from oil drums. The drums, or "pans," come in four basic sizes, each differing in the number of pitches: the "ping-pong" (soprano), alto pan, guitar pan (tenor), and bass pan.

step An interval of a 2nd, such as A to B.

stringed instruments Instruments in which the stretched string is the sound-producing agent. (The sound is initiated by a bow, fingers, or sticks.) Instruments in this large group include violin and harp. (Also see **chordophone,** the scientific name for stringed instruments.)

subdominant The fourth degree of the scale; a chord constructed on the fourth degree of the scale.

suite A group of musical pieces related to one idea.

symphony An extended composition for orchestra in several movements.

syncopation ("sin-co-PAY-shun") Placement of accents on normally weak beats or weak parts of beats; this shifting of accents creates the effect of the rhythm of the melody not coinciding with the beat.

tempo The rate of speed of the music.

tessitura The range of the majority of pitches in a voice part, not including an occasional high or low note.

texture The distinguishing character of the music resulting from the ways in which the vertical (harmonic) and horizontal (melodic) elements are combined.

theme and variations A composition in which each section is a modified version of the original musical theme.

timbre ("TAM-br") The tone color or tone quality of sound that distinguishes one sound source from another.

time Commonly used in place of more precise terms, namely, *meter, rhythm, tempo, duration.*

time signature See **meter signature.**

tonal center See **tonic.**

tonality The relationship of tones in a scale to the tonic.

tonal music Music that is centered on a particular tonal center or tonic.

tone A sound of definite pitch. Tones also have duration, intensity, and timbre.

tone row An ordering of the 12 tones of the chromatic scale as the tonal and structural basis of a composition.

tonic The central tone of the key and the first note of the scale; usually the last note of a composition.

tonic *sol–fa* Syllables using a movable *do,* in which *do* is the tonic in a major key and *la* is the tonic in a minor key.

transposition Changing a piece of music from one key (scale/tonality) to another.

treble clef The symbol 𝄞, which determines that the second line of the staff is G above middle C.

triad A 3-note chord with pitches a 3rd apart.

triple meter A grouping of beats into threes ($\frac{3}{4}$, $\frac{3}{8}$, $\frac{3}{2}$).

twelve-tone row See **tone row.**

unison Sung or played on the same pitch.

upbeat An unaccented beat, often the last beat of a beat grouping or measure. In conducting, the upbeat is indicated by an upward motion of the hand. An upbeat before the first downbeat of a musical phrase is called an anacrusis.

verse A group of lines, often 4 in number; also called a stanza.

vibrato A scarcely noticeable wavering of the pitch.

vocal register The different parts of the range of a voice that are characterized by their place of production and sound quality, e.g., head register, chest register.

whole step An interval made up of 2 consecutive half steps; as C to D.

whole-tone scale A scale of 6 different tones, each a whole step apart.

wind instruments Generic name for instruments in which an enclosed column of air is the sound-producing agent. Includes **brass instruments** and **woodwind instruments** (see separate entries). Also see **aerophone,** the scientific name for this category.

woodwind instruments Instruments in which a column of air is the sound-producing agent, such as clarinets, oboes, and flutes. (Also see **wind instruments.**) Commonly called the "woodwind family," though not all modern instruments are made of wood. Their timbre depends mainly on the shape of the bore (cylinder), and the mouthpiece: mouth-hole (flute), single reed (clarinet), or double reed (oboe).

Contents of CD

LEVEL I

CD Track

LEVEL II

CD Track

LEVEL III

Music Index

Subject Index